COMPUTER NETWORKS

(The Complete Text Book for MCA, M. Sc. (IT), B.E., B.Sc.(IT), BCA, PGDCA and other IT Related Examinations for leading Indian Universities)

ACKNOWLEDGEMENTS

We gratefully acknowledge the contribution made by the following persons in bringing out this book in this form:

- Mr. D. S. Sastry
  M. Sc.
  Scientist-Editor (Retd.),
  National Institute of Science Communication (CSIR),
  New Delhi

- Mr. D. S. R. Murty
  M. Sc.
  Scientist-Editor (Retd.),
  National Institute of Science Communication (CSIR),
  New Delhi

- Ms. Geetha Iyer

- Ms. Vineeta Pillai

COMPUTER NETWORKS

(The Complete Text Book for MCA, M. Sc. (IT), B.E., B.Sc.(IT), BCA, PGDCA and other IT Related Examinations for leading Indian Universities)

by

Dr. Madhulika Jain

Vineeta Pillai

Satish Jain

B.Sc. B.E.(Electronics), M.Tech. (I.I.T Kanpur)

BPB PUBLICATIONS

B-14, CONNAUGHT PLACE, NEW DELHI-110001

FIRST INDIAN EDITION 2002

Reprinted 2013

Distributors:

MICRO BOOK CENTRE
2, City Centre, CG Road,
Near Swastic Char Rasta,
AHMEDABAD-380009 Phone: 26421611

COMPUTER BOOK CENTRE
12, Shrungar Shopping Centre, M.G. Road,
BANGALORE-560001 Phone: 5587923, 5584641

MICRO BOOKS
Shanti Niketan Building, 8, Camac Street,
KOLKATTA-700017 Phone: 22826518, 22826519

BUSINESS PROMOTION BUREAU
8/1, Ritchie Street, Mount Road,
CHENNAI-600002 Phone: 28410796, 28550491

DECCAN AGENCIES
4-3-329, Bank Street,
HYDERABAD-500195 Phone: 24756400, 24756967

MICRO MEDIA
Shop No. 5, Mahendra Chambers, 150 D.N. Road,
Next to Capital Cinema V.T. (C.S.T.) Station,
MUMBAI-400001 Ph.: 22078296, 22078297

BPB PUBLICATIONS
B-14, Connaught Place, **NEW DELHI-110001**
Phone: 23325760, 23723393, 23737742

INFO TECH
G-2, Sidhartha Building, 96 Nehru Place,
NEW DELHI-110019
Phone: 26438245, 26415092, 26234208

INFO TECH
Shop No. 2, F-38, South Extension Part-1
NEW DELHI-110049
Phone: 24691288, 24641941

BPB BOOK CENTRE
376, Old Lajpat Rai Market,
DELHI-110006 PHONE: 23861747

ISBN 81-7656-609-8

Published by Manish Jain for BPB Publications, B-14, Connaught Place, New Delhi-110 001 and Printed by him at Akash Press, New Delhi.

Dedicated to

Sri Raja Rajeshwari

Godess who blesses Immense Power of Knowledge

PREFACE

This book covers the syllabus for Computer Networks paper of MCA, M.Sc. (IT), BE, BCA, B.Sc. (IT) and PGDCA courses of most of the Indian universities and engineering colleges. Our objective is to explain to students this highly technical subject in easy-to-understand and simple language. It is felt that most of the books available in the market do not cover the entire syllabus for these courses to meet the needs of the students. As the subject of Networking requires a thorough understanding of the basics, we have pressed into service all our practical experience in networking as well as in academics by bringing out this book to meet the needs of students, of all streams namely, science, commerce and arts.

Changes in the field of computer science as well as in communication engineering are taking place at a very rapid pace and many new technologies/concepts are emerging. This has led us to insert latest topics and concepts. These topics include Satellite Communication, Fiber Optics, ISDN, High Speed Modems and Data Link Protocols. Two additional appendices are added, one on the network design and the other on Broadcast Networks. These topics, it is hoped, will be useful for practical engineers to use the concepts to implement networks.

A very comprehensive glossary of technical terms as well as index given at the end makes this book user friendly. These would be very handy for ready reference of key concepts as well as locating page numbers of major topics discussed in this book.

A special feature of this book is that the important information has been shown with a (☞) mark to draw attention of the reader, thus providing a digest of concept(s) presented on those pages.

The book covers the syllabus for BCA, B.Sc. (IT) courses of Guru Nanak Dev University, Amristar. It also covers the syllabus of Guru Gobind Singh Indraprastha University, New Delhi for MCA and B.Sc. (IT) courses. In addition, the book covers the syllabus for similar courses and B.E, B.Tech courses of engineeering colleges and universities.

We shall feel highly obliged to the readers if they send us their critical opinion of the presentation, readability and coverage in this book as well as suggestions for improvement.

26th May, 2002 — Authors

end of each chapter to help readers respond to the problems appearing in the examination. A comprehensive index and set of question papers appeared in the past examinations are added for easy access and thorough understanding of the subject matter.

➢ **Computer Organization and System Software** (As per the DOEACC syllabus for A3 paper effective from January, 2000 Examination) *Pages 400 Price Rs. 180.00*

This book describes building blocks of computer, register transfer language and architecture of a simple processor in easy to understand language with ample number of illustrations. CPU Organization, Assembly language programs and various Arithmetic algorithms are all explained in such a manner, that students of commerce and art streams can understand these technical topics very easily. Input/Output Organization, Memory Organization are some of the hardware features of a computer which are evolving every day. Concepts behind these systems are covered with maximum number of diagrams and easy to understand examples. A special characteristic of this book is that large number of objective questions and solved sample papers are included at the end of each Chapter. Readers can evaluate their progress easily by solving these papers and comparing answers.

➢ **Data Communication and Networking** (As per DOEACC syllabus for A9 Paper effective from January, 2000 Examination) *Pages 425 Price Rs. 180.00*

The book is designed to cover A9 paper of the 'A' Level examination prescribed by DOEACC in a clear and simple language. It describes asynchronous, synchronous data, multiplexers, and data transmission modes in a very simple manner. It also deals with introduction of radio, VHF, microwave, VSAT and satellite communication links. Data modem, multichannel data communication and pulse code modulation are dealt in detail. Data networks and topology are described with large number of illustrations and examples for ease of understanding. Fiber optic communication and data communication systems are explained in a way that even a novice can easily grasp the functioning of the complex technology. Each chapter ends with review questions and test paper including answers.

➢ **Computer Organization and Architecture** (As per the syllabus for MCA, BE, BCA, B.Sc. (IT) and PGDCA courses of most of the Indian Universities and Engineering colleges) *Pages 324 Price Rs. 135.00*

This book describes, in easy language, building blocks for computer, register transfer language and architecture of a simple processor. CPU Organization, Assembly language programs and Arithmetic algorithms are all explained in such a manner, that students of all streams can understand technical subjects very easily. An introduction is given to parallel and vector processing which are advanced methods used in super computers. System programming is introduced for better understanding of computer architecture. A special characteristic of this book is that large number of solved sample answers are included at the end of each Chapter.

➢ **The Principles of Electronics** (As per the syllabus for MCA, M. Sc. (IT), BE, BCA, B.Sc. (IT) and PGDCA courses of most of the Indian Universities and Engineering colleges) *Pages 378 Price Rs.*

In this book, concepts like band theory, transistors, voltage, current sources and elecronics related theorems, are explained in easy-to-understand language. An appendix on Number Systems is added in order to widen the perspective of the readers. The book covers the syllabus for BCA and B.Sc. (IT) courses of Guru Nanak Dev University, Amristar and syllabus of Guru Gobind Singh Indraprastha University, New Delhi for MCA and M.Sc.(IT) courses. In addition, the book covers the syllabus for similar courses and B.E, B.Tech. courses of engineeering colleges and Indian and foreign universities.

USEFUL TIPS FOR THE EXAMINEE

Dear Reader,

Every examination has its peculiarities and the best results are often obtained by identifying that particular feature and working with the help of right strategies, which in turn can be adopted by correctly analysing the question paper.

The authors have tried to present an aid to guide you to analyse the question paper and consequently help to chalk out your own effective plan of action.

The instructions given on the first page of the question paper should always be read *very* carefully.

How to avoid mistakes?

After having given an initial reading to all the questions, first attempt only those questions about which you are very ***sure*** regarding the correct answer. It is while taking a second go at the questions, that you answer the remaining ones, always making sure that you spend only a *limited* amount of time on each one of them.

While answering descriptive questions the time limit should be strictly kept in mind and every effort must be made to attempt all the questions, by keeping the answers brief and to the point. Remember you can also resort to making a sketch/diagram in your answer wherever possible, instead of describing it in words, because "a thousand words can be effectively expressed by a small diagram." As the number of questions are normally more for an average student, this precious time saved enables you to have a wider coverage of the paper.

☞ While attempting the descriptive type of questions, keep a check on the length of your answers and keep in mind the time frame available for answering the remaining questions.

The last stage, being the revision stage, you should save at least 10 minutes to revise all your answers. Try to find the gross errors, like units of measurement, or wrong question number for a specific answer, etc., which do happen because of the inherent tension of the examination.

How to prepare for the examination?

Having familiarised with the format of the "Computer Networks" paper, let us turn our attention to the strategy for preparing for the examination.

This book has covered the complete syllabus in an easy-to-understand manner. But it is advised that in addition to this book, you may refer to other books on Computer Networking available in a library. This will enable you to broaden the horizon of your knowledge.

Make your own notes, by reading each topic from this book and referring to some other standard books. Once you are quite sure about the comprehension of the topic, try to answer the Test Paper given at the end of each chapter in this book.

After you have answered them, compare your response with the answers available in the text of this book. Wherever you find your answers differ, re-study that part again.

Last, but not the least, you should simulate examination conditions by conducting a demo examination, taking any of the Test Papers given at the end of each chapter of this book or any of the Sample Papers given at the end of the book. Attempt these papers completing the answers within the assigned time. After a day or two, evaluate your answers and if any doubts still persist, clarify them from a good text book available in the library or a subject specialist immediately. This way, you will be sure about the subject and will have confidence while answering the actual question paper.

WISH YOU A GRAND SUCCESS in the examination, and a very bright future.

Authors

CONTENTS

Chapter 2. OSI and TCP/IP Models 26

Chapter 3. Digital Transmission Interfaces and Modems 70

CHAPTER 1

Basic Concepts

1.1 COMPONENTS OF DATA COMMUNICATION

Communication, in the layman language, means to convey a message, an idea, a picture or speech that is received and understood clearly and correctly by the person for whom it is intended. There could be several methods of conveying the message. If the sender and the receiver are close by, you may send it by speaking loudly. If the distance is not very far, you may convey it by writing it on a piece of paper and sending it through a messenger. If the distance is large, you may send it by post. If the message is not very long, and sender as well as the person for whom the message is being conveyed are having telephones with them, you may pass it on telephone. But all these methods are characterised by an inherent factor, that is, the speed of conveying the message. That is how soon it reaches and the cost of sending the message. Postal method is probably the cheapest but there is an inherent delay of few days if the letter is sent from one city to other city. There is no surety that it will reach at the door step of the receiver. So there is every chance that the receiver may reply that he never got the letter.

Telephonic message is more reliable because the person on the other side of the phone can immediately confirm that he got the message and understood it. However, he/she may forget after a little while unless reminded. Telephonic communication is popular because it is cheap and instantaneous. You can talk to a person and convey a lot of message on telephone. But pictures cannot be sent on telephone. Large amount of data or messages cannot be remembered if conveyed on telephone. It is in this context, that data communication containing messages, pictures and voice assumes importance. Basic factors that need to be considered in the data communications are:

(a) The cost of conveying message, picture, or voice over a large distance should be small.

(b) The transmission should take place without an iota of doubt/confusion in the mind of the receiver. It means, there should be no interference like noise, etc.

(c) The message should reach within a reasonable time before it becomes obsolete. For example, the varying rates of shares/equity in the stock exchange need to be conveyed immediately so that buyers/sellers of shares can decide the action to be taken by them. If the results of an entrance examination are declared today, it must reach to all the schools the same day.

(d) The message should be safe and secured. It should only reach to the person for whom it is meant. Postal method of conveying a message is not secured at all. Telephonic conversation can be heard if some one taps the telephone line.

We shall therefore try to study Data Communications keeping in mind the above mentioned four very important factors.

In the case of sending and receiving messages or data from one place to other place, we have many elements working together. All these elements put together to work efficiently is known as a system. The communication system has the sole purpose of passing data or information in the most effective manner. Block diagram of a communication system is shown in Figure 1.1.

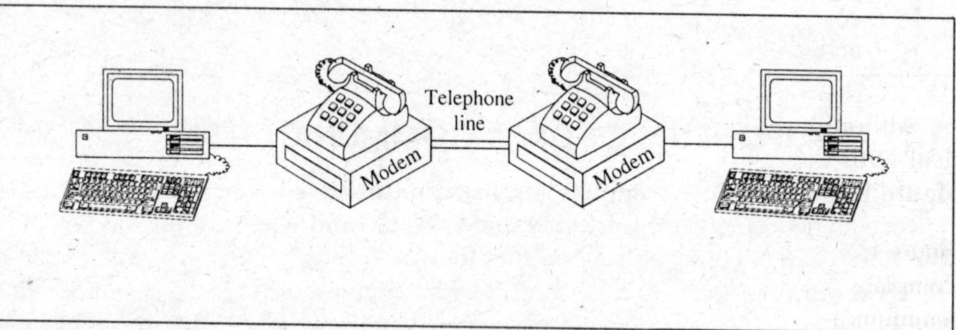

Figure 1.1 A communication system (link) using PCs and modems

☞ Communication system is the combination of hardware, software and data transfer links that make up a communication facility for transferring data in a cost effective manner.

A communication system itself can be either analog or digital (or a combination of the two). That is, the information can be transmitted in either analog or digital form within the communication networks. For example, computer generated data is digital whereas the telephone lines are convenient to carry analog signals. When digital data are to be sent over analog telephone lines, the digital signals must be converted to analog form. The technique by which a digital signal is converted to its analog form is known as *modulation*. The reverse process that is the conversion of analog signal to digital form at the destination device is called *demodulation*. The process of modulation and demodulation, that is, the conversion of digital data to analog from and vice versa is carried out by a special device called *modem* (short form for modulation/demodulation).

☞ As the PCs work on digital principle and the telephone lines carry analog signal most efficiently, we convert the digital pulses to analog form using a modem.

The analog form of message is sent via telephone line and then it reaches the destination, where it is again transformed into digital pulses by the other modem connected with the receiver PC (See Figure 1.1). Thus, the messages (or data) are transmitted and received by the two PCs.

As the analog signal passes through the telephone lines, its strength starts decreasing with the distance. So amplifiers are used to boost the strength of the signal. These amplifiers add noise to the signal which sometimes cause disruption of the message. But good quality modems, at the receiving end as well as at the sending end, are able to cut down the effect of noise.

☞ In a data communications network, the task of network designers is to select and co-ordinate the network components so that the necessary data are moved to the right place, at the right time, with a minimum of errors, and at the lowest possible cost. A number of communications processors are used by network designers to achieve their goals.

Although digital communications offer many advantages over analog, one may have to deal with many analog components and systems in a total communication system design. Figure 1.2 shows how a complete communication system looks from signal perspective.

Figure 1.2 Complete communication system from a signal perspective

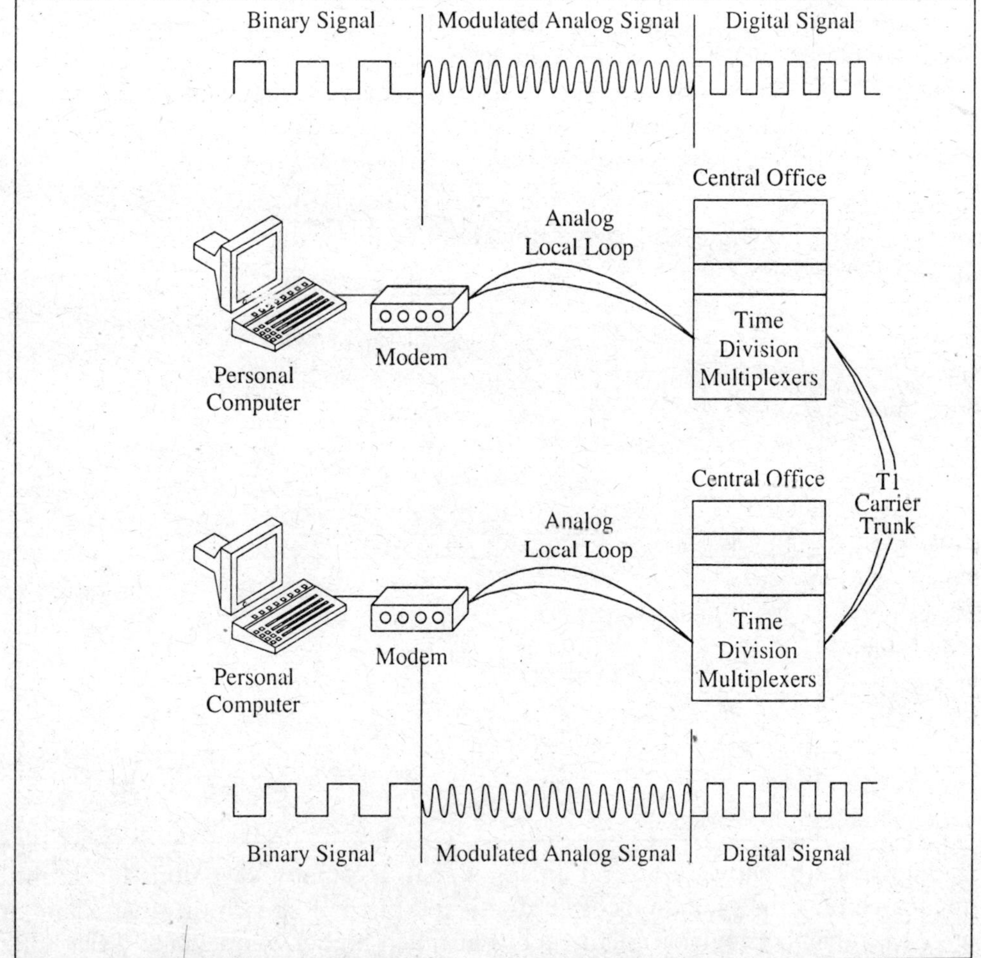

A good understanding of the differences between these digital and analog signals and how to bring the two together is the key to connectivity. The communications channels provide the link for data communications.

You will note in Figure 1.2 that the link between the PC to the central office or telephone exchange is by modulated analog signal created by the modem. The communication between exchange or central office to another trunk exchange or central office is by digital signal using time division multiplexers (codecs). The final communication between the trunk exchange and the PC is again by using modulated analog signal. Modem at the other end converts this analog signal to digital signal to be detected by the PC.

1.1.1 Difference between Analog and Digital Communication

The difference between the two basic forms of electronic communication, namely, analog and digital is like the difference between water streaming from a hose and bullets firing from a machine gun. An analog signal is a continuous electromagnetic wave, whose pattern varies to represent the message being transmitted. A digital signal, by contrast is a series of discrete electronic bursts and the bursts indicate the message.

Figure 1.3(a) shows analog signal. The key characteristics of an analog signal include strength, or amplitude (vertical distance between a wave trough and crest) and frequency (the number of times per second the wave cycle repeats).

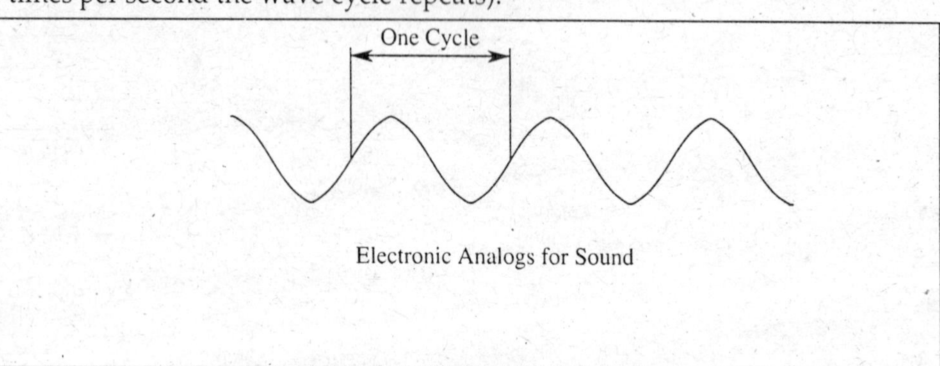

Figure 1.3(a) Analog signal showing a sine wave, representative of a pure tone

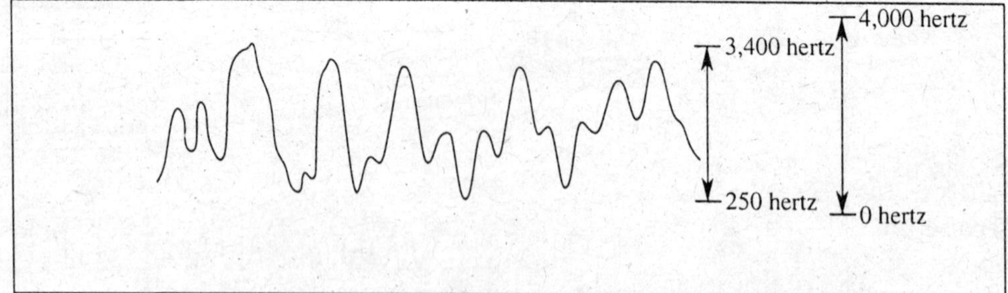

Figure 1.3(b) Typical sound signal in Analog form

Figure 1.3(b) shows a typical analog signal, the many variations in amplitude and frequency convey the gradations of loudness and pitch in speech or music. Similar signals are used to transmit television pictures, but at much higher frequencies. Telephone equipment allows the voice a band width of 4,000 hertz, which includes a guard band at top and bottom to prevent interference. T.V. Signals use band width of four million hertz (4 Mhz).

Figure 1.3(c) shows the binary digital form of electronic signal. Computer messages are composed of bytes, or groups of binary digits (group of eight bits) conveys the presence or absence of voltage in an electronic signal. For the byte shown in Figure 1.3(c), the voltage goes successively off, on, off, off, off, off, off, on.

Figure 1.3(c) Electronic pulses for binary digits

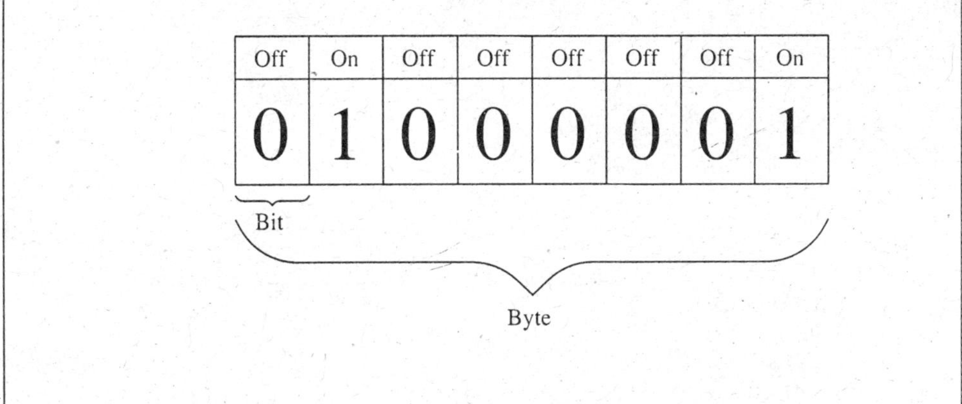

Figure 1.3(d) Two digital signals with different bits per second rate

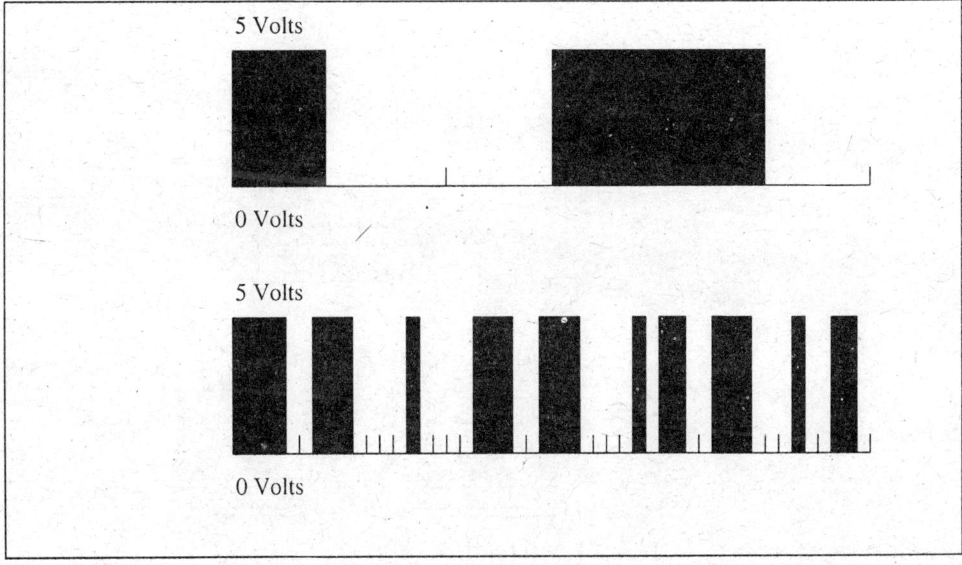

Figure 1.3(d) shows two digital signals, each made up of 0s (zero volts, white space) and 1s (five-volt pulses). These pulses are depicted as transmitted at different rates over a 1/50-second interval. The top signal carries 300 bits per second (bps) while the bottom one 2,400 bps.

1.2 DISTRIBUTED PROCESSING

Distributed processing is the decentralization of a computer system through the use of multiple computers interconnected by a communications network. It facilitates data processing capabilities at the location of the end-user. (See Figure 1.4)

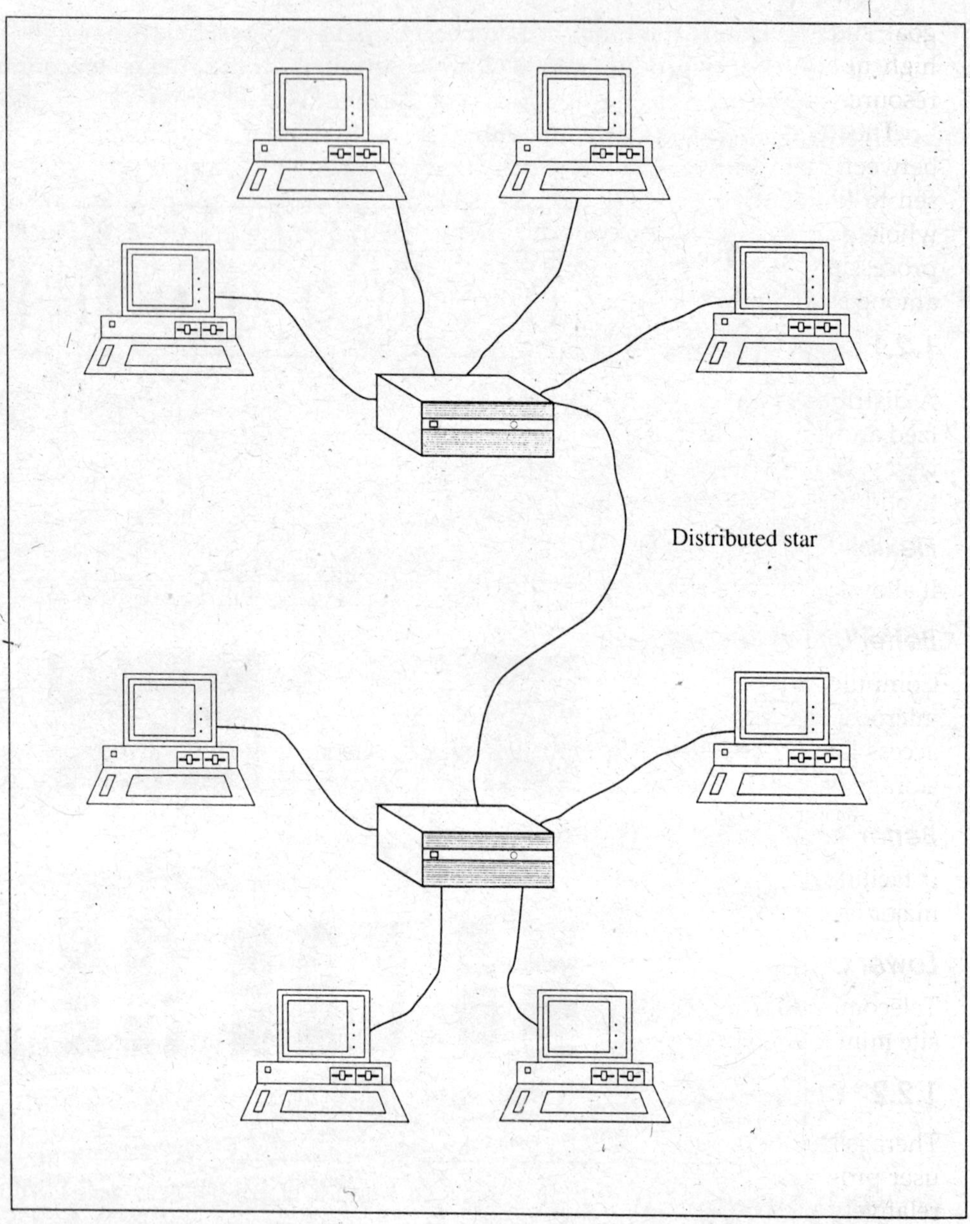

Figure 1.4 Distributed data network using star network

Distributed Processing is a form of information processing in which work is performed by separate computers that are linked through a communications network. Distributed processing is usually categorized as either plain distributed processing or true distributed processing. Plain distributed processing shares the workload among computers that can communicate with one another. True distributed processing has separate computers to perform different tasks in such a way that their combined work can contribute to a larger goal, such as the transfer of funds from one bank to another. This type of processing requires high quality of environment that allows hardware and software to communicate, share resources, and exchange information freely.

The term is loosely used to refer to any system of computers with communications between them. However, in a true distributed data processing system, each computer is chosen to handle its local workload, and the network is designed to support the system as a whole. A typical distributed star topology (network) is shown in Figure 1.4. Distributed data processing system enable sharing of several hardware and significant software resources among several users who may be located far away from each other.

1.2.1 Advantages of a Distributed Data Processing System

A distributed data processing system attempts to capture the advantages of both a centralized and a decentralized system. Each computer can be used to process data like a decentralized system. In addition, a computer at one location can also transfer data and processing jobs to and from computers at other locations.

Flexibility

It allows greater flexibility in placing true computer power at the location where it is needed.

Better Utilization of Resources

Computer resources are easily available to the end users. For example, users can use mini or microcomputer systems for processing small jobs. However, for complex jobs they can easily access large sophisticated computer systems. The same is true for other resources like mass storage devices, plotters, database and even a growing library of application programs.

Better Accessibility

It facilitates quick and better access to data and information especially where distance is a major factor.

Lower Cost for Communication

Telecommunication costs can be lower when much of the local processing is handled by on-site mini and microcomputers rather than by distant central mainframe computers.

1.2.2 Disadvantages of a Distributed Data Processing System

There is lack of proper security controls for protecting the confidentiality and integrity of the user programs and data that are stored online and transmitted over network channels. It is relatively easy to tap a data communication line. One technique used to protect security and privacy over data communications lines is encryption. Basically, encryption is a coding device placed at either end of a data communications line, putting a very complex code on the data. This code is extremely difficult to break. At the receiving end of the data communications line, a decryption device is used to decode the signal into a meaningful message.

Linking of Different Systems

Due to lack of adequate computing/communications standards, it is not possible to link different items of equipments produced by different vendors into a smoothly functioning network. Thus, several good resources may not be available to the users of a network.

Maintenance Difficulty

Due to decentralization of resources at remote sites, management from a central control point becomes very difficult. This normally results in increased complexity, poor documentation, and non-availability of skilled computer/communications specialists at the various sites for proper maintenance of the system.

1.3 STANDARDS AND ORGANIZATIONS

The organization for evolving standards in the field of Networking is IEEE of USA, the details of which are given in the subsequent subsection. Project 802 is one of the major standards IEEE has evolved and the same is described below.

1.3.1 Institute of Electrical and Electronics Engineers (IEEE)

IEEE is a worldwide nonprofit association of technical professionals that promotes the development of standards and acts as a catalyst for new technology in all aspects of the engineering industry including computer networking, telecommunications, etc. This institute has more than 3,30,000 individual members in 150 countries. Its activities include standard committees, technical publishing and conferences.

A major contribution of the IEEE in the field of computer networking is Project 802, a collection of standards for local area network (LAN) architectures, protocols and technologies. These standards continue to evolve under the auspices of various IEEE working groups and committees.

1.3.2 Project 802

This is an ongoing project of the IEEE for defining local area network (LAN) and wide area network (WAN) standards and technologies. The 802 specifications define the operation of the physical network components such as cabling, network adapters and connectivity devices such as hubs and switches. Project 802 has a number of subsections. These are described in Chapter 9.

1.4 LINE CONFIGURATION

Configuration means the process by which a computer component (hardware or software) is modified so as to make it work with another component. Two characteristics that distinguish various data line configurations are topology and whether the link is simplex, half duplex or full duplex.

1.5 TOPOLOGY AND TYPES OF TOPOLOGY

Topology is the way networks are physically connected together. Topology determines the complexity and therefore the cost of network cable installation. Cable installation can often be a major cost factor for network system. Topology also determines the strategy for physically expanding the network.

Different ways in which computers may be connected together are described in the following subsections.

1.5.1 Linear Bus Topology

In this layout, a single main cable connects each node, in what amounts to a single line of computers accessing it from end to end. Each node is connected to two others except the machines at either end of the cable, which are connected only to one other node. The network operating system keeps track of a unique electronic address for each node, and manages the flow of data based on this addressing scheme. This topology has the advantage of not requiring that every computer be up and running in order for the network to function. But because a single cable is dedicated to all the information traffic, performance can be slow at times. This topology is often found in client/server systems, where one of the machines on the network is designated as a file server meaning that it is dedicated solely to the distribution of data files, and is not usually used for information processing. (See Figure 1.5)

☞ In linear bus topology, all computers are connected by a single length of cabling with a terminator at each end. The bus topology is the simplest and most widely used network design. It is a passive topology. Only one computer at a time can send a message. Hence, the number of computers attached to a bus network can significantly affect the speed of the network. A computer must wait until the bus is free before it can transmit. Ethernet 10Base2 (also known as thinnet) is an inexpensive network based on the bus topology.

When a particular computer wants to send a message to another computer, it would send an addressing message to it and wait for a response. The response would indicate whether that computer is ready to receive the previous computer's message. After this communication is finished, it goes to the next one and establishes a link with it.

Advantages of the Bus Topology

(a) The bus is simple, reliable in very small networks, easy to use, and easy to understand.

(b) The bus requires the least amount of cable to connect the computers together and is therefore less expensive than other cabling arrangements.

(c) It is easy to extend a bus. Two cables can be joined into one longer cable with a connector, making a longer cable and allowing more computers to join the network.

Disadvantages of the Bus Topology

(a) Heavy network traffic can slow down a bus considerably. Because any computer can transmit at any time, and computers on most bus networks do not coordinate with each other to reserve times to transmit, a bus network with a lot of computers can spend a lot to its bandwidth (capacity for transmitting information) with the computers interrupting each other instead of communicating. The problem only gets worse as more computers are added to the network.

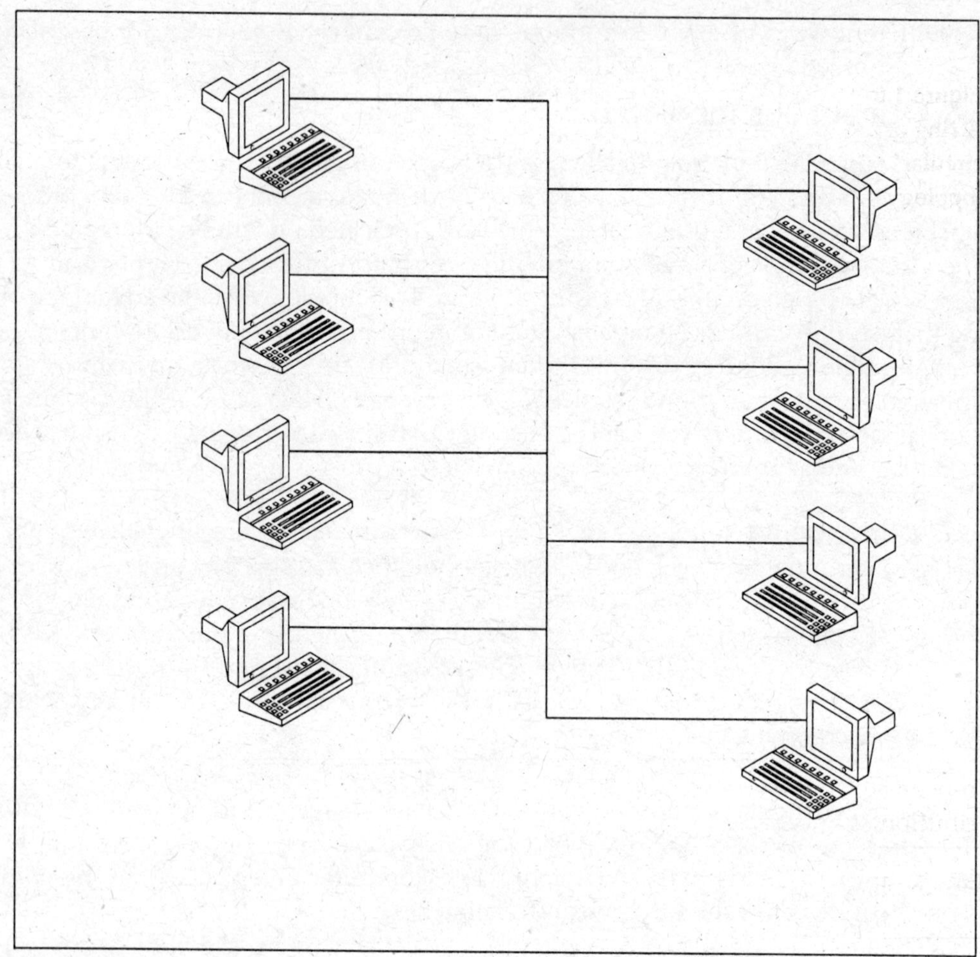

Figure 1.5
A linear bus topology

(b) It is difficult to troubleshoot a bus. A cable break or malfunctioning computer anywhere between two computers can cause them not to be able to communicate with each other. Cable break or loose connector will also cause reflections and bring down the whole network, causing all network activity to stop.

1.5.2 Circular or Ring Topology

This layout is similar to the linear bus, except that the nodes are connected in a circle using cable segments (See Figure 1.6). In this layout, each node is physically connected to only two others. Each node passes information along to the next, until it arrives at its intended destination. Since each computer re-transmits what it receives, a ring is an active network and is not subject to the signal loss problems which a bus topology experiences. There is no termination because there is no end to the ring.

Performance is faster on this system because each portion of the cabling system is handling only the data flow between two machines. This type of topology can be found in peer-

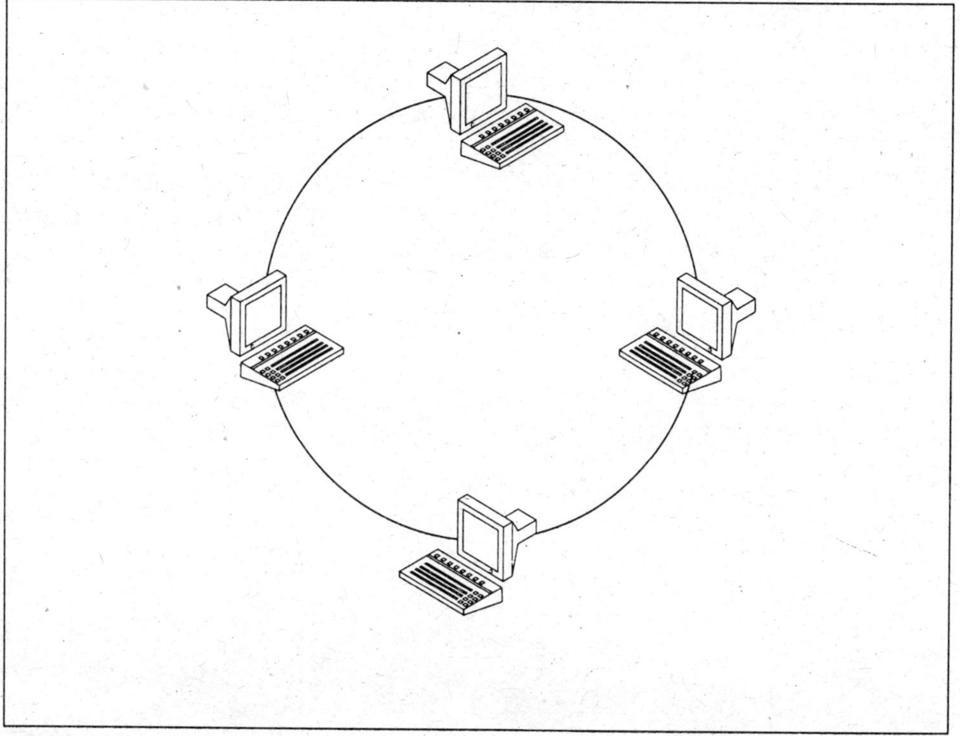

Figure 1.6
A ring or circular topology

to-peer networks, in which each machine manages both information processing and the distribution of data files.

☞ Fiber Distributed Data Interface (FDDI) is a fast fiber-optic network based on the ring topology.

Some ring networks do token passing. A short message called a token is passed around the ring until a computer wishes to send information to another computer. That computer modifies the token, adds an electronic address and data, and sends it around the ring. Each computer in sequence receives the token and the information and passes them to the next computer until either the electronic address matches the address of a computer or the token returns to its originator. The receiving computer returns a message to the originator indicating that the message has been received. The sending computer then creates another token and places it on the network, allowing another station to capture the token and begin transmitting. The token circulates until a station is ready to send and captures the token.

Advantages of Ring Topology

(a) Because every computer is given equal access to the token, no one computer can use the network solely.

(b) The fair sharing of the network allows the network to degrade gracefully (continue to function in a useful, if slower, manner rather than fail once capacity is exceeded) as more users are added.

Disadvantages of Ring Topology

(a) Failure of one computer on the ring can affect the whole network.
(b) It is difficult to troubleshoot a ring network.
(c) Adding or removing computers disrupts the network.

☞ In Ring topology computers are arranged in a circle. Data travels around the ring in one direction, with each device on the ring acting as a repeater. Ring networks typically use a token passing protocol.

1.5.3 Star Topology

Each computer on a star network communicates with a central hub that re-sends the message either to all the computers (in a broadcast star network) or only to the destination computer (in a switched star network). The hub in a broadcast star network can be active or passive. (See Figure 1.7)

Figure 1.7 A star topology

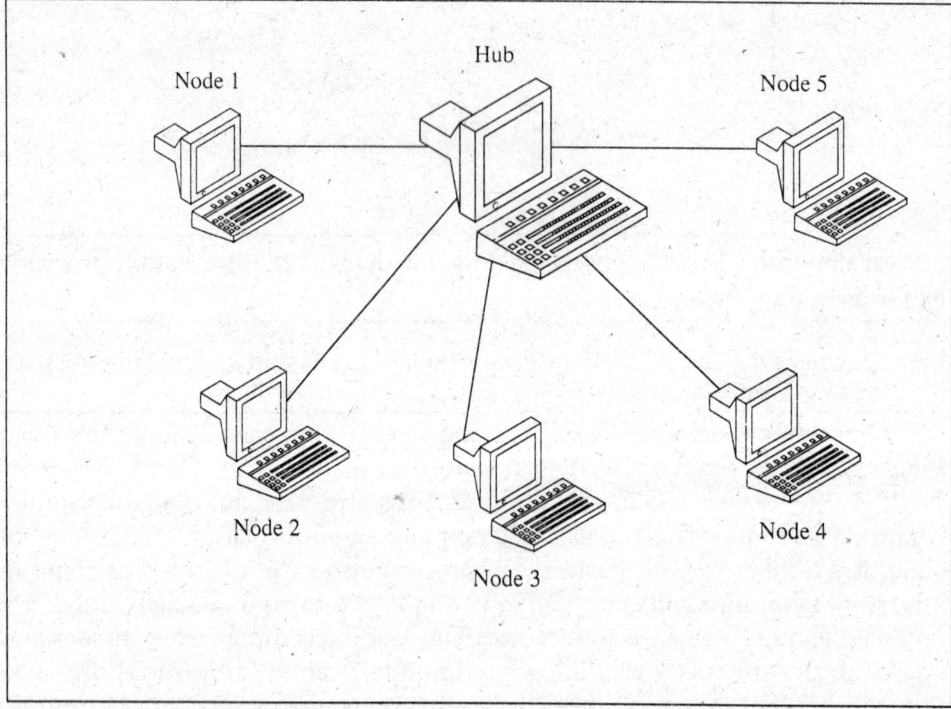

An active hub regenerates the electrical signal and sends it to all the computers connected to it. This type of hub is often called a multiport repeater. Active hubs and switches require electrical power to run. A passive hub merely acts as a connector point and does not amplify or regenerate the signal. Passive hubs do not require electrical power to run.

☞ Ethernet 10BaseT is a popular network based on the star topology.

You can use several types of cable to implement a star network. Hybrid hub can accommodate several types of cable in the same star network. You can expand a star network by placing another star hub where a computer might otherwise go, allowing several more computers or hubs to be connected to that hub. This creates a hybrid star network.

Advantages of Star Topology

(a) It is easy to modify and add new computers to a star network without disturbing the rest of the network. You simply run a new line from the computer to the central location and plug it into the hub. When the capacity of the central hub is exceeded, you can replace it with one that has a larger number of ports to plug lines into.

(b) The center of a star network is a good place to diagnose network faults. Intelligent hubs (hubs with microprocessors that implement features in addition to repeating network signals) also provide for centralized monitoring and management of the network.

(c) Single computer failures do not necessarily bring down the whole star network. The hub can detect a network fault and isolate the offending computer or network cable and allow the rest of the network to continue operating.

(d) You can use several cable types in the same network with a hub that can accommodate multiple cable types.

☞ Out of all the topologies, the Star topology is the most flexible and the easiest to diagnose when there is a network fault.

Disadvantages of Star Topology

(a) If the central hub fails, the whole network fails to operate.

(b) Many star networks require a device at the central point to rebroadcast or switch network traffic.

(c) It costs more to cable a star network because all network cables must be pulled to one central point, requiring more cable than other networking topologies.

1.5.4 Tree Topology

Tree is a network topology containing zero or more nodes that are linked together in a hierarchical fashion. The topmost node is called the root. The root may have zero or more child nodes, connected by edges (links); the root is the parent node to its children. Each child node can in turn have zero or more children of its own. Nodes sharing the same parents are called siblings. Every node in a tree has exactly one parent node (except for the root, which has none), and all nodes in the tree are descendants of the root node. These relationships ensure that there is always one and only one path from one node to any other node in the tree. (See Figure 1.8)

1.5.5 Graph

In this method of connection, zero or more nodes are linked together in an arbitrary fashion. Any two nodes in a graph may (or may not) be connected by a link. Not all the nodes in a

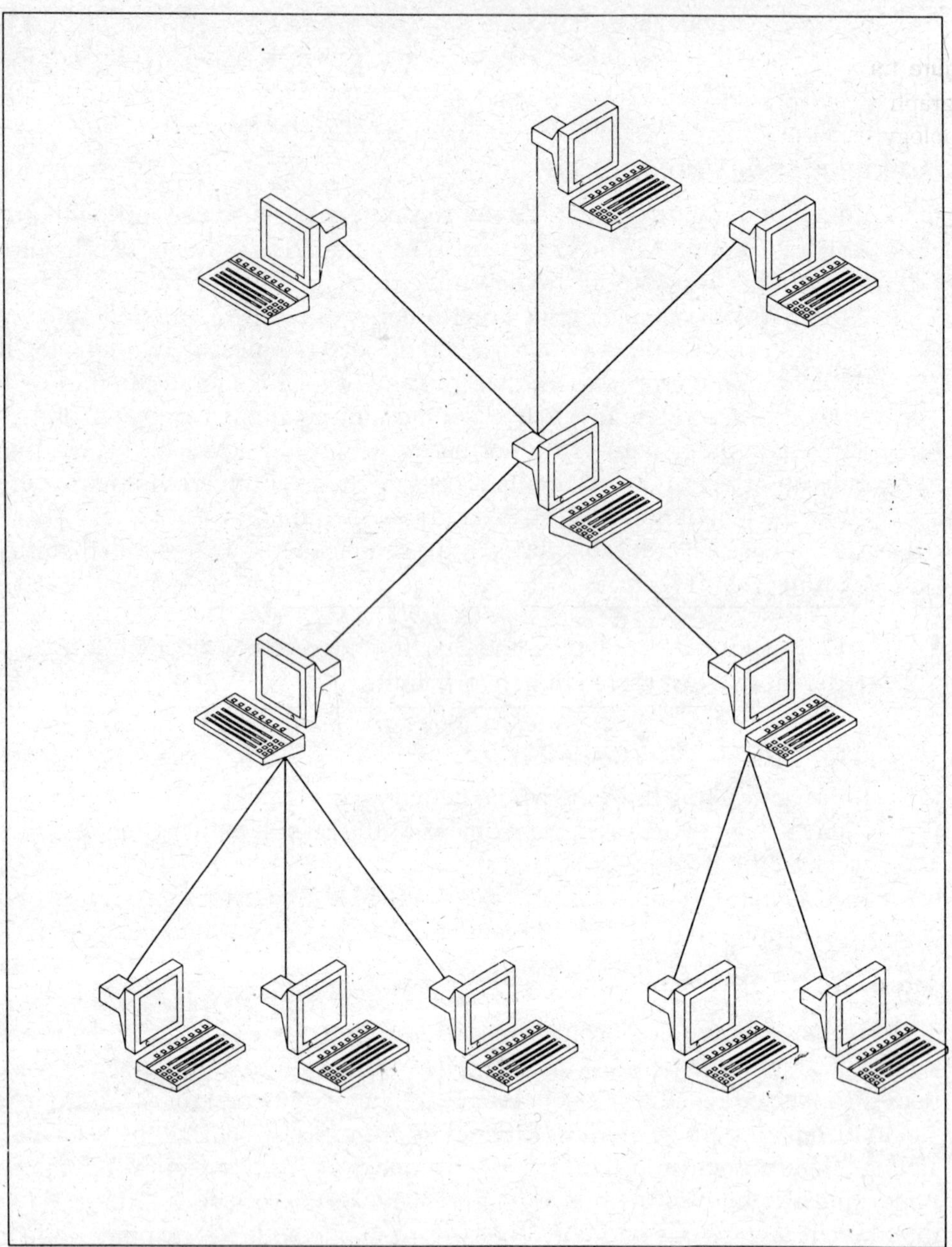

Figure 1.8
A tree topology

graph need to be connected, but if a path can be traced between any two nodes, the graph is a connected one (See Figure 1.9).

1.5.6 Star Bus and Star Ring Topology

Figure 1:10 shows the two most common combination networks.

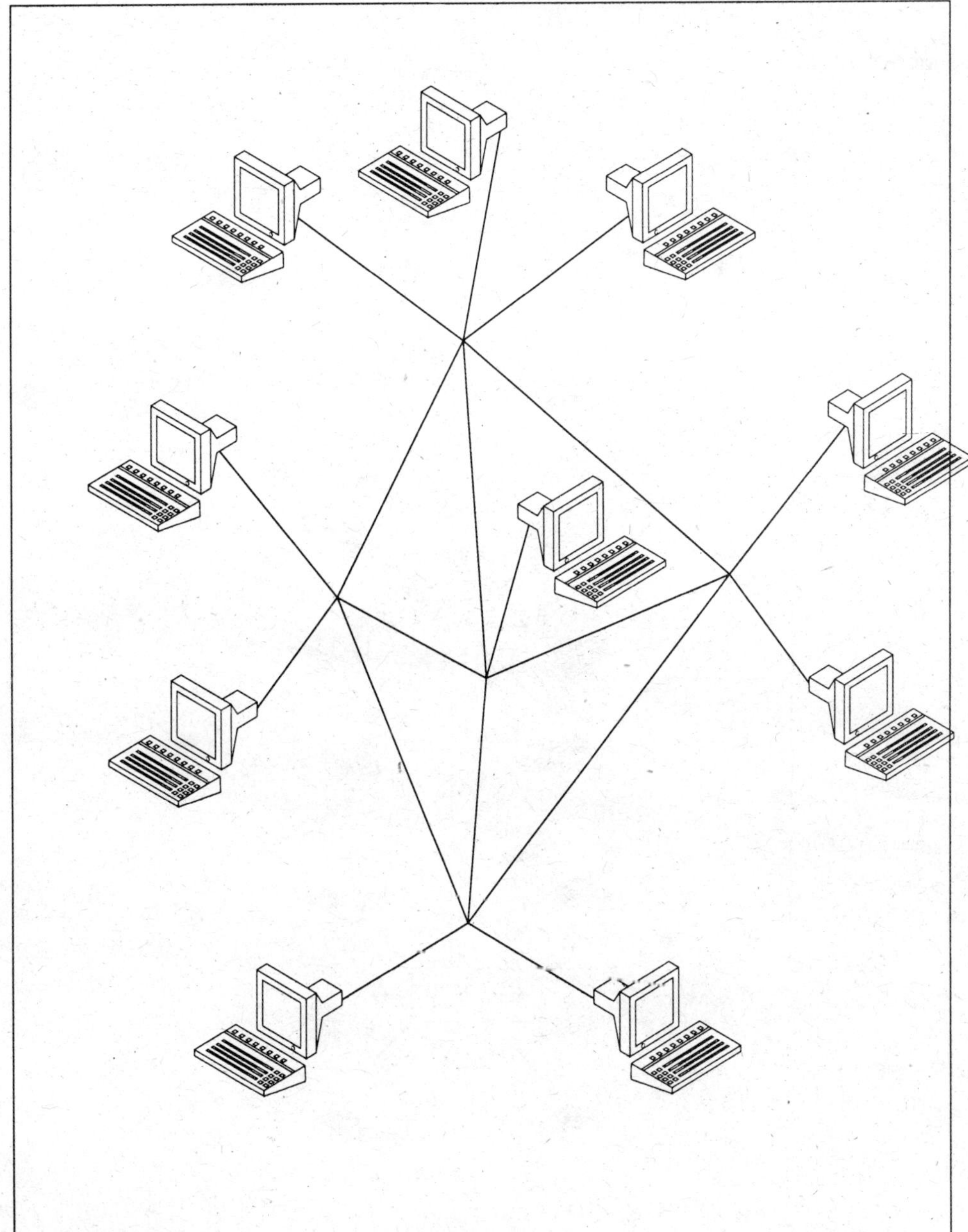

Figure 1.9
A graph topology

Star Bus Network

The star bus topology combines the bus and the star, linking several star hubs together with bus trunks. If one computer fails, the hub can detect the fault and isolate the computer. If the hub fails, computers connected to it will not be able to communicate, and the bus network will be broken into two segments that cannot reach each other.

Figure 1.10
Star Bus and Star Ring Topology

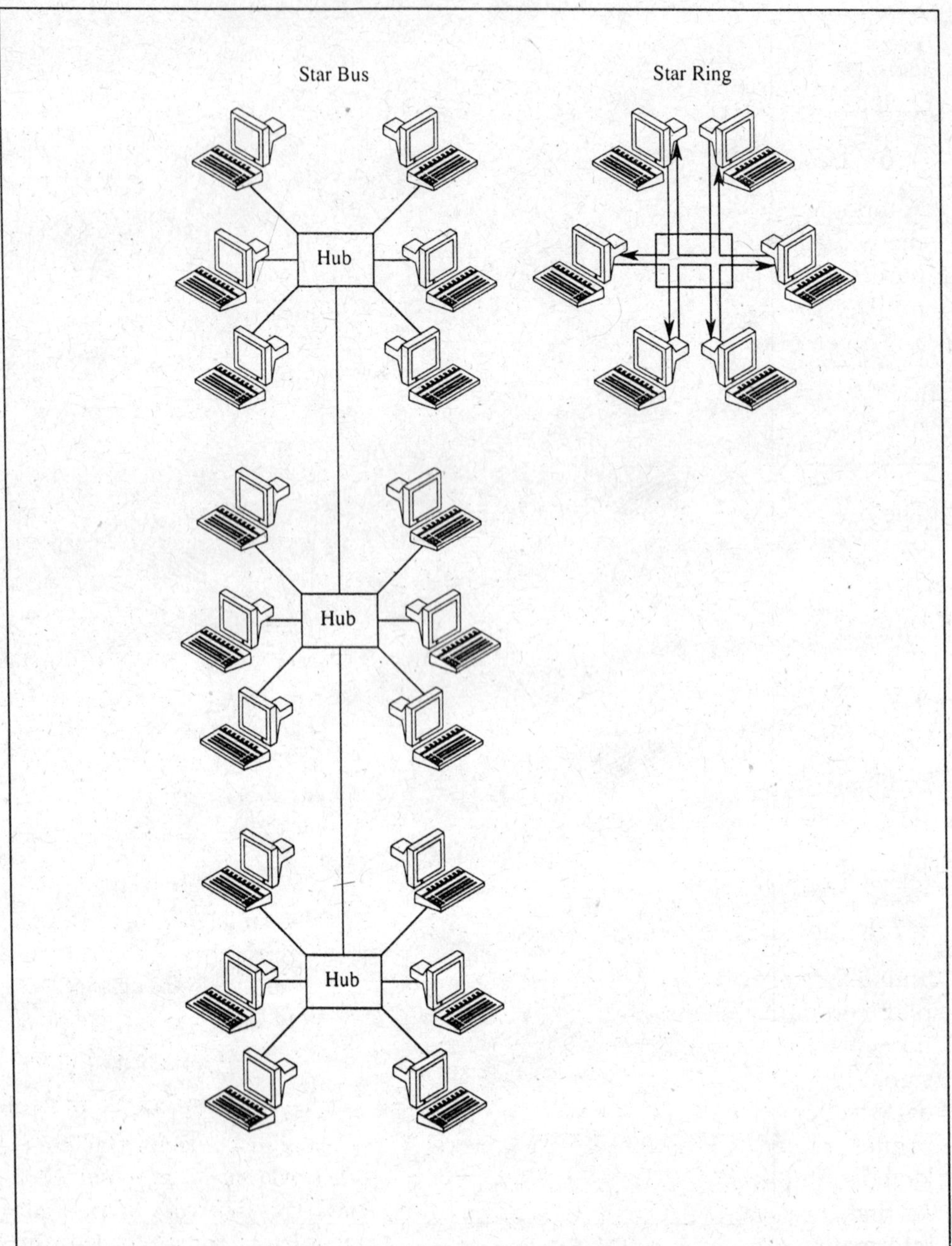

Star Ring Network

In the star ring, also called the star wired ring, the network cables are laid out much like a star network, but a ring is implemented in the central hub. Outlying hubs can be connected to the inner hub, effectively extending a loop of the inner ring.

☞ Token Ring is considered a star ring. Although its topology is physically a star, it functions logically in a ring.

1.6 LOGICAL TYPES OF TOPOLOGY

A topology is the arrangement of a network. The topology can refer to the physical layout of the network (which is where 10BASE2, 10BASE-T, and fiber come into the arrangement) or the logical layout of the network. Logical topology lays out the rules of the road for data transmission. In data networking, only one computer can transmit on one wire segment at any given time.

☞ In contrast to physical topology, logical topologies are largely abstract. Logical networks are essentially rules of the road.

The common logical topologies are the following. These are described in detail in Chapter 9.

(a) Ethernet
(b) Token Ring
(c) Fiber Distributed Data Interface (FDDI)
(d) Asynchronous Transmission Mode (ATM)

1.7 TRANSMISSION MODE

There are three modes of data transmission that correspond to the three types of circuits available. (See Figure 1.11). These are:

(a) Simplex
(b) Half-duplex
(c) Full-duplex

1.7.1 Simplex

Simplex communications imply a simple method of communicating, which they are. In simplex communications mode, there is a one-way communication transmission. Television transmission is a good example of simplex communications. The main transmitter sends out a signal (broadcast), but it does not expect a reply as the receiving units cannot issue a reply back to the transmitter. A data collection terminal on a factory floor (send only) or a line printer (receive only) are other examples. Another example of simplex communication is a keyboard attached to a computer because the keyboard can only send data to the computer. At first thought it might appear adequate for many types of application in which flow of information is unidirectional. However, in almost all data processing applications, communication in both directions is required. Even for a "one-way" flow of information from a terminal to a computer, the system will be designed to allow the computer to signal the terminal that data has been received. Without this capability, the remote user might enter data and never know that it was not received by the other terminal. Hence, simplex circuits are seldom used because a return path is generally needed to send acknowledgement, control or error signals.

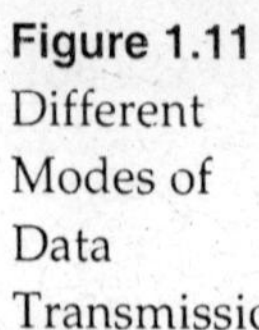

Figure 1.11 Different Modes of Data Transmission

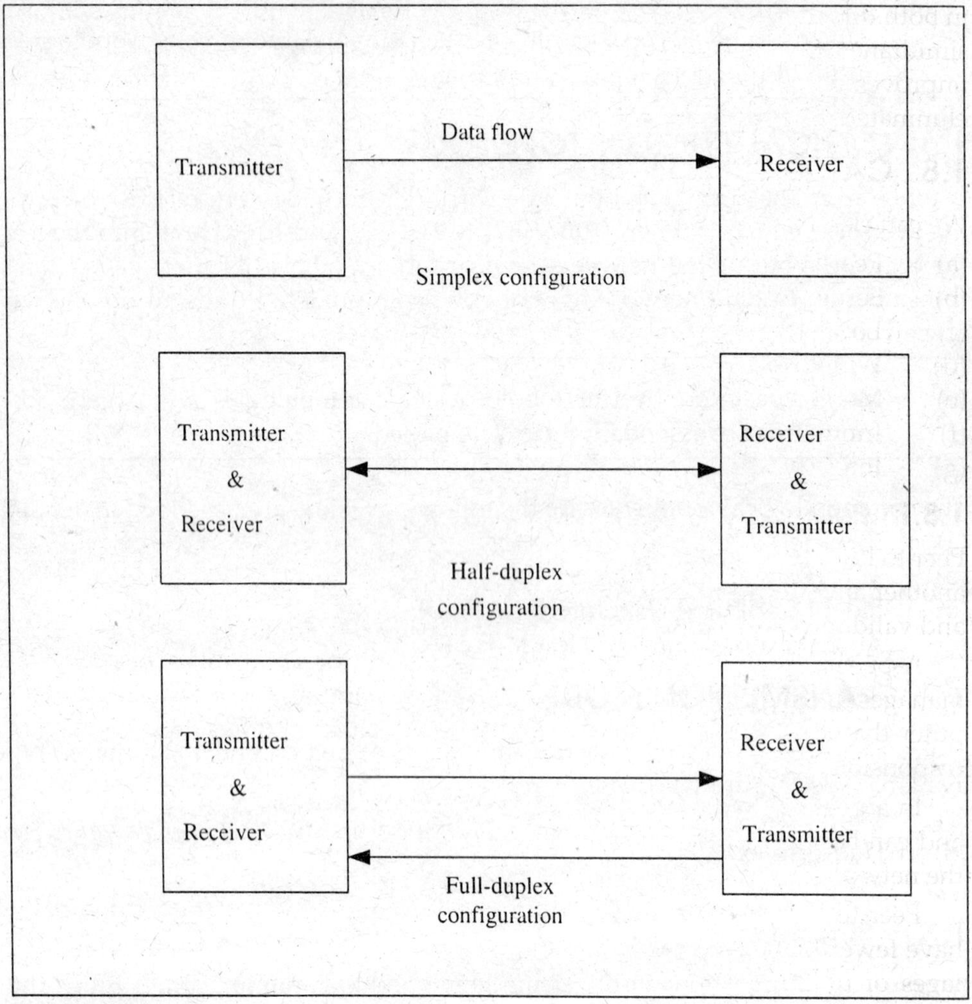

1.7.2 Half-duplex

In half-duplex mode, both units communicate over the same medium, but only one unit can send at a time. While one is in send mode, the other unit is in receive mode. It is like two polite people talking to each other—one talks, the other listens, but not both talk at the same time. Thus, a half duplex line can alternately send and receive data. It requires two wires. This is the most common type of transmission for voice communications because only one person is supposed to speak at a time. It is also used to connect a terminal with a computer. The terminal might transmit data and then the computer responds with an acknowledgement. The transmission of data to and from a hard disk is also done in half duplex mode.

1.7.3 Full-duplex

In a half-duplex system, the line must be *"turned around"* each time the direction is reversed. This involves a special switching circuit and requires a small amount of time (approximately 150 milliseconds). With high speed capabilities of the computer, this turn-around time is unacceptable in many instances. Also, some applications require simultaneous transmission in both directions. In such cases, a full-duplex system is used that allows information to flow simultaneously in both directions on the transmission path. Use of a full-duplex line improves efficiency as the line turn-around time required in a half-duplex arrangement is eliminated. It requires four wires.

1.8 CATEGORIES OF NETWORKS

We can classify the networks as follows:

(a) Peer-to-Peer networks
(b) Server based network
(c) Local Area network (LAN)
(d) Wide Area network (WAN)
(e) Metropolitan Area network (MAN)
(f) Intranet and Extranet Networks
(g) Internet

1.8.1 Peer to Peer Network

Peer to Peer network is a network in which the computers are managed independently of one another and have equal right of initiating communication with each other, sharing resources, and validating users. (See Figure 1.12)

A peer-to-peer network has no special server for aunthenticating users. Each computer manages its own security, so a separate user account might need to be created for each computer that a user needs to access. User usually stores files on their own computers and are responsible for ensuring that those files are appropriately backed up.

In a peer-to-peer network, each computer typically runs both client and server software and can be used to make resources available to other users or to access shared resources on the network.

Peer-to-peer networks are simple to set up and are often ideal for small businesses that have fewer than 10 computers and that cannot afford a server-based solution. The disadvantages of peer-to-peer networks are poor security and lack of centralized file storage and backup facilities.

1.8.2 Server Based Network

In a server based network security and storage are managed centrally by one or more servers.

In a server based network, special computers called servers handle network tasks such as authenticating users, storing files, managing printers, and running applications such as database and e-mail programs.

Security is generally centralised in a security provider, which allows users to have one user account for logging on to any computer in the network. Because files are stored centrally, they can be easily secured and backed up.

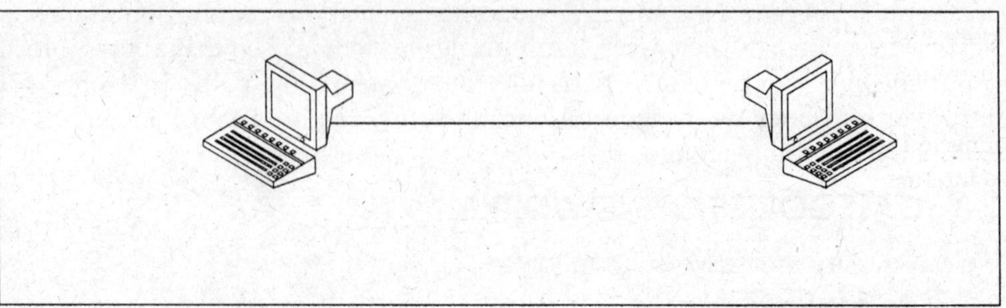

Figure 1.12 Peer-to-peer network connection

Server based networks are more costly and more complex to set up and administer than peer-to-peer networks, and they often require the services of a full-time network administrator. They are ideal for business that are concerned about security and file integrity and have more than 10 computers.

Microsoft Windows NT and Windows 2000 are ideal operating systems for server-based networks. They offer centralized network administration, networking that is easy to set up and configure, file and print sharing, user profiles that allow multiple users to share one computer or allow one user to log on to many computers.

The LANs, WANs and MANs are described in Chapter 9.

1.8.3 Intranet and Extranet

Intranet

Intranet is an internal company version of the Internet. Intranets allowed workers with PCs to access information from company computers via the same user-friendly browsing software IE5, etc. used on the Internet. Corporations that adopted this approach feel Intranets simplified employees' work and thus led to higher worker productivity

Extranet

An extranet is the part of a corporate intranet that allows companies to communicate with the intranets of their customers and suppliers, facilitating electronic transactions.

1.8.4 The Internet

The Internet is a computer-based global information system. The Internet is composed of many interconnected computer networks. Each network may link tens, hundreds, or even thousands of computers, enabling them to share information with one another and to share computational resources such as powerful supercomputers and databases of information.

The Internet has made it possible for people all over the world to effectively and inexpensively communicate with one another. Unlike traditional broadcasting media, such as radio and television, the Internet does not have a centralized distribution system. Instead, an individual who has Internet access can communicate directly with anyone else on the Internet, make information available to others, find information provided by others, or sell products with a minimum overhead cost. (See Figure 1.13)

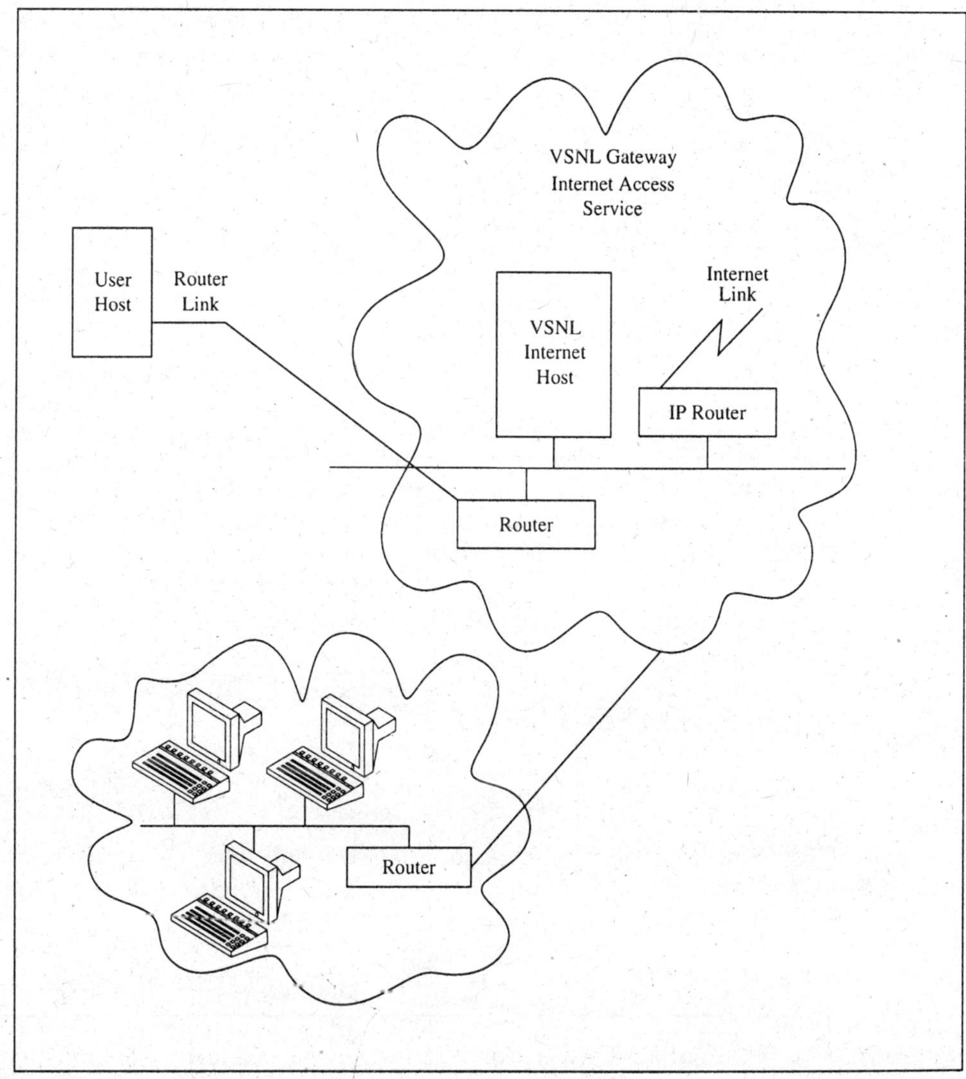

Figure 1.13 Illustrating PCs connected to the Internet

☞ The Internet's success arises from its flexibility. Instead of restricting component networks to a particular manufacturer or particular type, Internet technology allows interconnection of any kind of computer network.

No network is too large or too small, too fast or too slow to be interconnected. Thus, the Internet includes inexpensive networks that can only connect a few computers within a single room as well as expensive networks that can span a continent and connect thousands of computers.

Internet service providers (ISPs) allow Internet access to customers for a monthly fee. A customer who subscribes to an ISP's service uses the ISP's network to access the Internet.

Because ISPs offer their services to the general public, the networks they operate are known as public access networks. In the United States, as in many countries, ISPs are private companies; in countries where telephone service is a government-regulated monopoly, the government often controls ISPs.

REVIEW QUESTIONS WITH ANSWERS

Question Number 1. Compare and contrast the three modes of data communications namely, simplex, half-duplex and full-duplex.

Answer The three modes of data communications are compared in the following table.

Item	Simplex	Half Duplex	Full Duplex
Direction of Transmission of Message	Communication in one direction only	Both ways but transmission of communication in one direction at a time	Communication in both directions simultaneously
Confirmation of the communicated message	Not possible	Possible but slow	Possible
Number of wires required	Two	Two	Four
Cost of transmission	Cheapest	Average	Costliest
Example of user	T.V. And Radio transmission and broadcasting	Transmission of data from hard disk to memory in a PC	Telephonic communications
Efficiency	Low	Medium	High

Question Number 2. Differentiate between analog transmission and digital transmission of data. Give their relative advantages and disadvantages.

Answer The relative advantages and disadvantages of analog and digital transmission are as follows.

Item	Analog	Digital Transmission
Shape of the signal	It is in the form of continuous variable of physical quantities such as electric current.	It is in the form of discrete quantities and has binary digits.
Cost of transmission	Low	High

(Contd...)

Item	Analog	Digital Transmission
Efficiency	Low	High
Maintenance cost of Equipment	High	Low
Effect of noise	High	Low
Attenuation	High	Low
Security and privacy	Not very much	Coding of text can be readily applied to digital data and to analog data if it is converted into digital form.
Integration	Not possible	By treating both analog and digital data digitally, all signals have the same form and can be treated similarly. Thus, economies of scale and convenience can be achieved by integrating voice, video and digital data.
Example	Radio transmission from radio station.	Data transmission from hard disk to memory of a PC.

Question Number 3. What are modems? What purpose do they serve in data communication systems?

Answer Modems are the devices used to convert digital signals (to be communicated over an analog channel such as a telephone line) to sine wave at the sending end and back to digital signals at the receiving end. They are used as a mean to connect two distant located PCs so that PCs can communicate with each other using telephone lines. (See Figure 1.1).

Question Number 5. Write short notes on the following:

(a) Distributed processing

(b) Components of data communication system

Answer (a) *[Refer to Section 1.2]*

Answer (b) *[Refer to Section 1.1]*

Question Number 6. A computer network provides a number of applications. List down all the applications where computer networks can be used.

Answer Data communication networks have to day become an integral part of business, industry, and entertainment. Some of the network applications in different fields are as given below:

(a) **Sales and marketing:** Computer networks are used by marketing professionals to collect, exchange and analyse data relating to customers needs and product development cycles. Sales applications include teleshopping and on-line reservation services for hotels, airlines, etc.

(b) **Financial Services:** Financial services are now more and more dependent on computer networks. Applications include foreign exchange and investment services and electronic fund transfer (EFT)

(c) **Manufacturing:** Computer networks are used in many aspects of manufacturing, including computer aided design and manufacturing.

(d) **Electronic messaging:** E-mail is one of the most widely used application of networking because, the cost of sending messages is very low and the speed is very high.

(e) **Directory Services:** Directory services allow list of files to be stored in a central location to speed up world wide operation.

(f) **Information Services:** Network information services include bulletin boards and data banks.

(g) **Electronic Data Interchange (EDI):** EDI helps in exchanging business information (including documents such as purchase orders, and invoices processing without using paper.

(h) **Tele-conferencing:** This service allows conferences to occur without the participants being in the same place yet they can see and talk face to face on the computer screens.

(i) **Cellular Telephone:** Cellular networks make it possible to maintain wireless phone connections even while travelling.

TEST PAPER

Time: 2 Hrs. Marks: 50

Note: Answer all questions.

1. With the help of a diagram, explain the difference between analog and digital signals. What are the advantages and disadvantages of digital signal over analog signal?
2. What do you understand by the term topology as related to computer networking? Name the various types of topologies used for connecting PCs. With the help of diagrams, describe any two types of topologies. Compare the advantages and disadvantages of these two topologies.
3. Name the three types of transmission modes. Explain with a suitable example each mode of transmission.
4. Write short notes on:
   (a) Star bus and star ring topology
   (b) Internet
   (c) Advantages of distributed data processing system

CHAPTER 2

OSI and TCP/IP Models

2.1 INTRODUCTION

The problem of getting a computer of one brand to accept data created by another manufacturer's machine has confronted users of these devices since their earlier days. At one time the only practical way around this barrier was to retype the data from the computer into the second. This is a very time consuming procedure and has the chances of lot of errors.

As the computers proliferated, interfaces or adapters were invented that translated one machine's code into a form that others could understand, allowing a variety of computers to be hooked together in networks. But these interfaces were expensive, both in the aggregate, because a substantial number of them were needed to establish a large network, and singly, because each type of computer needed an interface of its own. Consequently, there was little opportunity to spread the cost of developing given interfaces by selling many copies of it.

Networking would be facilitated and the expense much reduced if computer manufacturers could agree on how to construct their products, so that each could communicate with the other. Towards this end, in 1977, the Geneva-based International Organization for Standardization set forth the Open Systems Inter connection (OSI) model. A master plan for computer-to-computer dialogue, the OSI model divides the communications process into *seven* layers. The model sets standards that permit a wide variety in the design of computer hardware and software. The model demands only that communication tasks remain in their assigned layers and that the output of each layer precisely matches the format established for it. Employing software created with the model's requirements in mind, users of computers built to conform to the plan are able to send data to and from one another's machines almost effortlessly.

2.1.1 What is Protocol?

By the term protocol, we mean the set of rules or standards designed to enable computers to connect with one another and to exchange information with as little error as possible. Protocol can describe low-level details of machine-to-machine interfaces (e.g. the order in which bits and bytes are sent across a wire) or high-level exchange between allocation programs (e.g. the way in which two programs transfer a file across the Internet).

An example will make the idea clear. Suppose there are two people one speaking Hindi and the other French. Since they have no common language, they each engage a translator whose common language is English.

The person in Location A and knows Hindi wants to send a message "*Mai Khargosh pasand karta hoon*" that is "I like rabbits" in English. The translator uses a common language say English. So the same is translated in English. He hands over the translated version to the secretary for *faxing* it to the other side. The secretary sends the message on Fax and the same is received in location B as a Fax message. The translator at location B reads the English translated message and converts it into French language so that the Person in Location B can understand the message. In the above example, each protocol is totally independent of the other one as long as the interfaces are not changed. The translators can switch from English to Dutch or for that matter to any other language say Russian but both must agree for this. Similarly, the secretaries can send the message by e-mail instead of FAX. This is the basic philosophy of using multilayer protocol.

☞ The protocol generally accepted for standardizing overall computer communications is a seven-layer set of hardware and software guidelines known as the OSI (Open System Inter-connection) model.

The word *protocol* thus, is used in reference to a multitude of standards affecting different aspects of communication. Some, such as the RS-232-C standard, affect hardware connections. Other standards govern data transmission, among these are the parameters and handshaking signals used in modem communications. Other protocols, such as the widely used XMODEM, govern file transfer and yet others such as CSMA/CD, define the methods by which messages are passed around the stations on a LAN. Thus taken as a whole, these various protocols represent attempts to ease the complex process of enabling computers of different makes to communicate with each other.

2.1.2 OSI MODEL (Open System Interconnection)

The OSI model was developed to standardize the procedures for exchange of information between processing systems. The OSI is a communications reference model that has been defined by the International Standards Organization (ISO). It is a seven-layer communications protocol intended as a standard for the development of communications systems worldwide.

Most vendors and suppliers of computer communications equipment have agreed to support OSI in one form or another. However, adherence to this standard is vital in order to achieve smooth universal communications. This model conceptually organizes the process of communications between computers in terms of seven layers called *Protocol Stacks*. The seven layers of the OSI model provide a way for you to understand how communications across various protocols take place.

Protocol Stacks

A protocol stack is a group of protocols arranged on top of each other as part of a communication process. Each layer of the OSI model has different protocols associated with it. When more than one protocol is needed to complete a communication process, the protocols are grouped together in a stack. A popular protocol stack is TCP/IP, which is widely used for UNIX and the Internet. Each layer in the protocol stack receives services from the layer below it and provides services to the layer above it. That means, layer N uses the services of the layer below it (layer N-1) and provides services to the layer above it (layer N+1). For two computers to communicate, the same protocol stacks must be running on each computer. Each layer of the protocol stack on one computer communicates with its equivalent, or peer, on the other computer. The computers can have different operating systems and still be able to communicate if they are running the same protocol stacks. For example, a WINDOWS NT machine running TCP/IP protocol stack can communicate with a IBM AS400 machine running TCP/IP. (See Figure 2.1)

☞ The entities comprising the corresponding layers on different machines are called peers.

Figure 2.1 Peer to peer communication between two computers

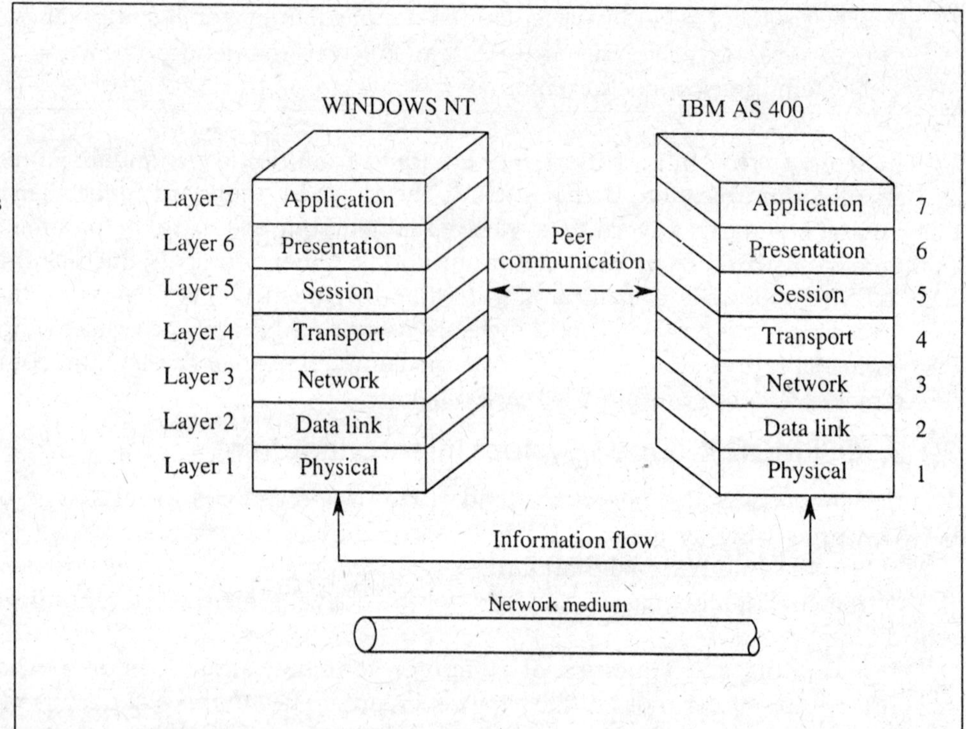

2.2 LAYERS AND THEIR FUNCTIONS

When a message is sent from one machine to another, it travels down the layers on one machine and then up the layers on the other machine. This route is illustrated in Figure 2.2.

As the message travels down the first stack, each layer it passes through (except the physical layer) adds a header. These headers contain pieces of control information that are read and processed by the corresponding layer on the receiving stack. As the message travels up the stack of the other machine, each layer strips the header added by its peer layer. (See Figure 2.3)

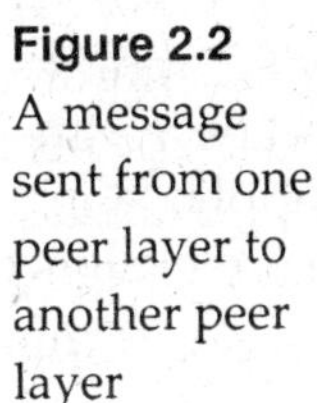

Figure 2.2
A message sent from one peer layer to another peer layer

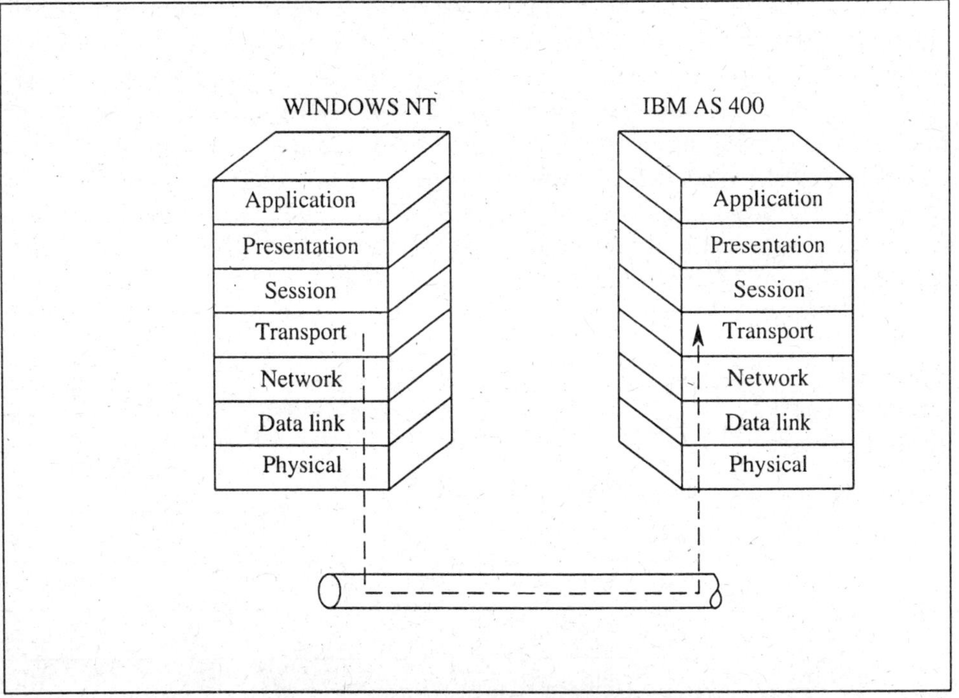

For example, suppose we are using two networked applications based on the WINDOWS NT, a popular network operating system from Microsoft Corporation and IBM AS400 operating systems. At layer 7, the WINDOWS NT application requests something from the IBM AS400 application. This request is sent to the WINDOWS NT application's layer 6. The layer receives the request as a data packet, adds its own header, and passes the packet down to

Figure 2.3
Headers attached with original data as it passes through layers

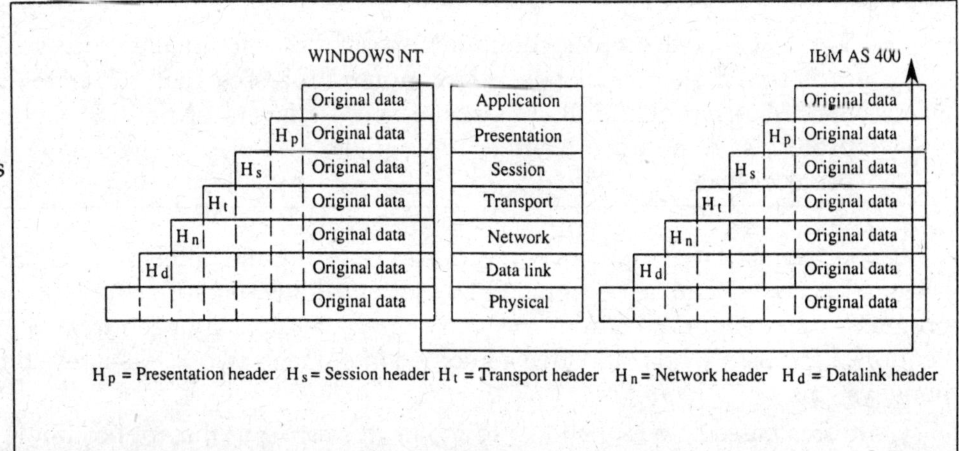

layer 5, where the process is repeated. As the request travels down the layers, headers are added until the request reaches the physical layer (which does not add a header).(See Figure 2.3).

Next, this requested packet travels across the network transmission media and begins its journey up the layers on the IBM AS400. The header that was put on at the data link layer of the WINDOWS NT application is stripped at the data link layer of the IBM AS400 application. The IBM AS400 data link layer performs the tasks requested in the header and passes the requests to the next higher layer. This process is repeated until the IBM AS400 application's layer 7 receives the packet and interprets the request inside. At each layer, the data packages, called service data units, are made up of data and headers from the layers above. For this reason they are commonly referred to by different names when they are at different layers, as shown in Figure 2.4. The term packet is applicable to a service data unit at any layer.

Figure 2.4
Common data package names

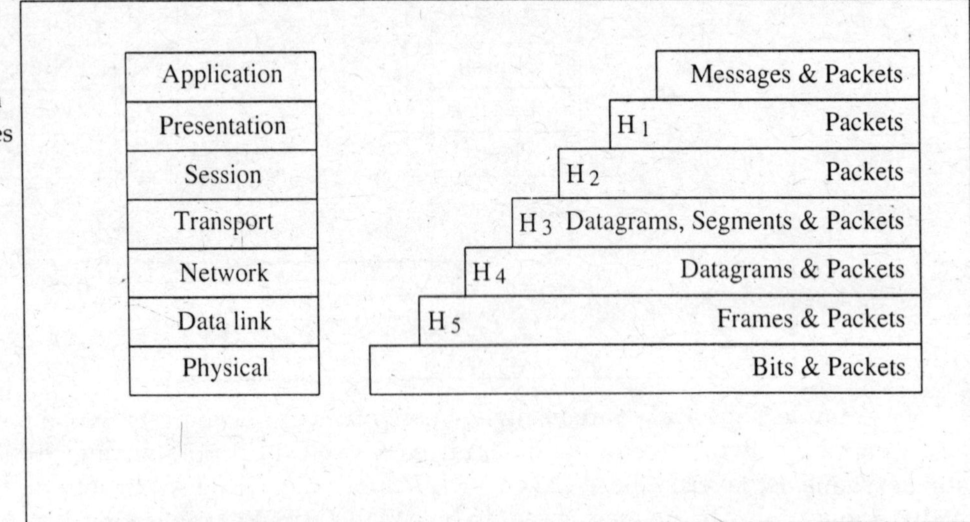

☞ The OSI model divides communication tasks into smaller pieces called subtasks. Protocol implementations are computer processes that relate to these subtasks. Specific protocols fulfill subtasks at specific layers of the OSI model. When these protocols are grouped together to complete a whole task, you have what is called a protocol stack.

Layers 1 and 2 are mandatory in order to transmit and receive in any communications system. Layers 3, 4 and 5 are provided by the controlling network software (network control programs and network operating systems) and have typically been treated as one layer by vendors. Layers 4, 5 and 6 are often combined into one or two layers in existing communications systems.

Control is passed from one layer to the next, starting at the application layer in one station, proceeding to the bottom layer, over the communications channel to the next station and back up the hierarchy.

From top to bottom, the layers of the OSI model are shown in Figure 2.5. These layers are further described in the following section.

Figure 2.5 The International Standards Organization's (ISO) seven layers of control for open systems

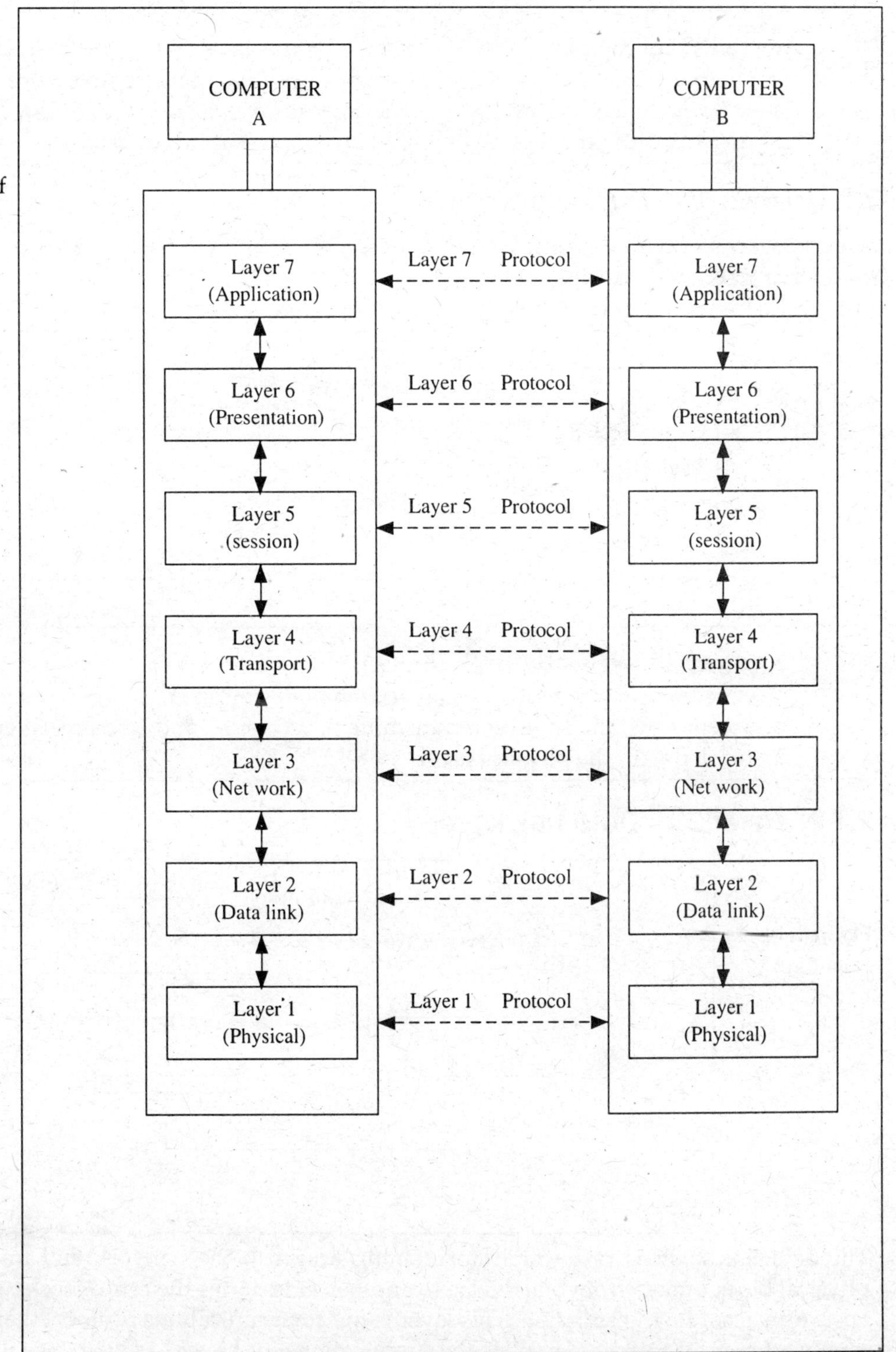

☞ In reality, no data is directly transferred from layer *n* on one machine to layer *n* on another machine. instead, each layer passes data and control information to the layer immediately below it, until the lowest layer is reached. Below layer 1 is the physical medium through which actual communication occurs.

2.2.1 Layer 1 — Physical Layer

The physical layer defines the actual set of wires, plugs and electrical signals that connect the sending and receiving devices to the network. The RS-422 interface is a common standard in this layer. However, RS-232 interface is a common standard for PCs. [See Figure 2.6]

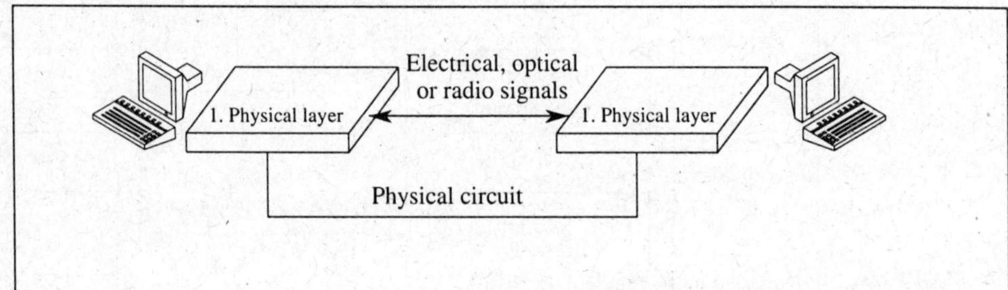

Figure 2.6 Physical Layer

☞ A physical layer makes a physical circuit with electrical, optical or radio signals. Passive hubs, simple active hubs, terminators, couplers, cables and cabling, connectors, repeaters, multiplexers, transmitters, receivers, and trans-receivers are devices associated with the physical layer.

2.2.2 Layer 2 — Data Link Layer

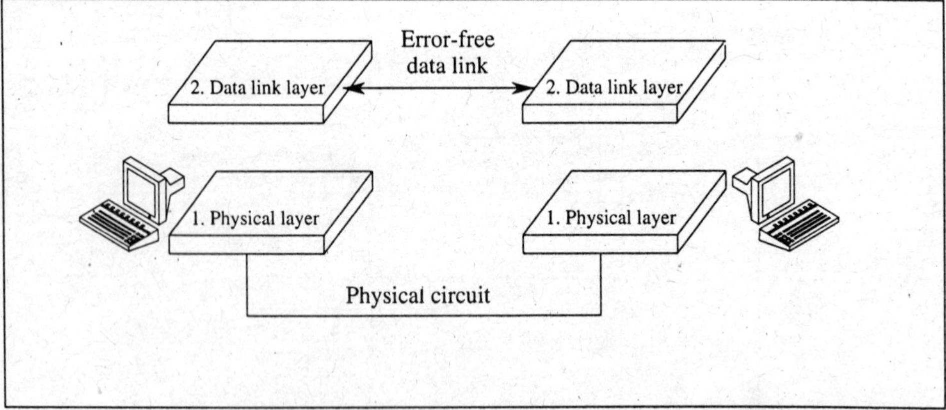

Figure 2.7 Data Link Layer

The data link layer is responsible for gaining access to the network and transmitting the physical block of data from one device to another. It includes the error checking necessary to ensure an accurate transmission. This layer is the communications protocol that is most commonly referenced and often implies the specifications for Layer I as well. (See Figure 2.7)

2.2.3 Layer 3 — Network Layer

The network layer makes *routing decisions* and forwards packets for devices that are farther away than a single link. A link connects two network devices and is implemented by the data link layer. Two devices connected by a link communicate directly with each other and not through a third device. In larger networks there may be intermediate systems between any two end systems, and the network layer makes it possible for the transport layer and layers above it to send packets without being concerned about whether the end system is immediately adjacent or several hops away.

The network layer translates *logical network addresses* into physical machine addresses. This layer also determines the quality of service (namely, priority of the message) and the route a message will take if there are several ways a message can get to its destination.

The network layer also may break large packets into smaller chunks if the packet is larger than the largest data frame the data link layer will accept. The network reassembles the chunks into packets at the receiving end. Figure 2.8 shows how the network layer moves packets across multiple links in a network.

The network layer performs several important functions that enable data to arrive at its destination. The protocols at this layer may choose a specific route through an internetwork to avoid the excess traffic caused by sending data over networks and segments that do not need access to it.

☞ Routers and gateways operate in the network layer.

Figure 2.8
The Network Layer

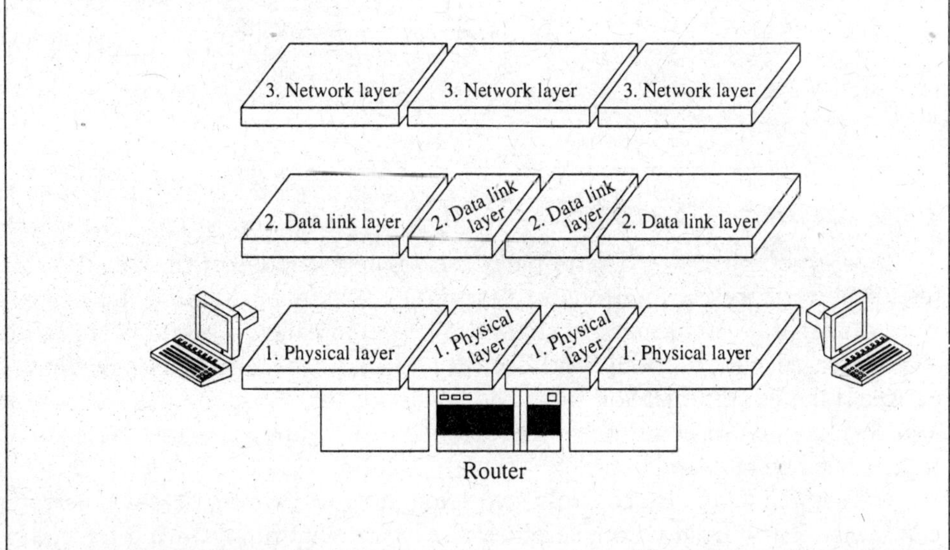

2.2.4 Layer 4 — Transport Layer

Layer 4 is responsible for converting messages into the structures required for transmission over the network. A high level of error recovery is also provided in this layer. This layer ensures that packets are delivered error free, in sequence, and with no losses or duplications.

The transport layer breaks large messages from the session layer into packets to be sent to the destination computer and reassembles packets into messages to be presented to the session layer. The transport layer typically sends an acknowledgment to the originator for messages received. Figure 2.9 shows how the transport layer operates.

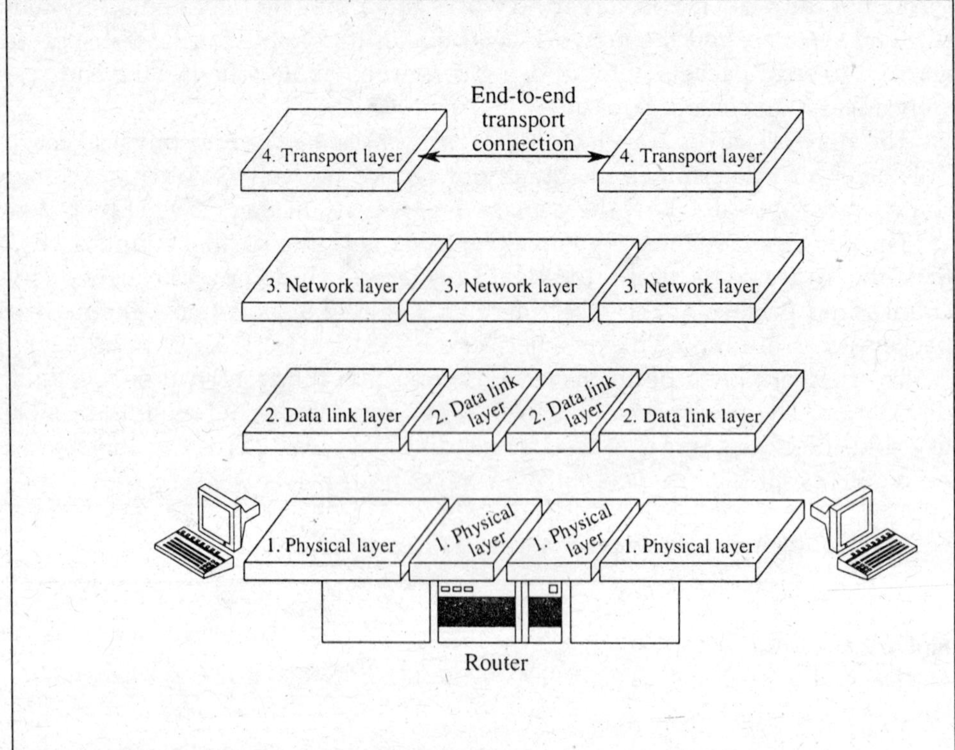

Figure 2.9
The Transport Layer.

2.2.5 Layer 5 — Session Layer

Layer 5 establishes and terminates the session, queues of the incoming messages and is responsible for recovering from an abnormally terminated session. This layer allows applications on separate computers to share a connection called a session. This layer provides services such as name lookup and security to allow two programs to find each other and establish the communication link. The session layer also provides for data synchronization and check points so that in the event of a network failure, only the data sent after the point of failure need be re-sent.

The session layer also controls the dialog between two processes determining whom they can transmit and from whom can they receive at what point during the communication. Figure 2.10 shows how the session layer operates.

☞ The session layer provides for dialog between application programs.

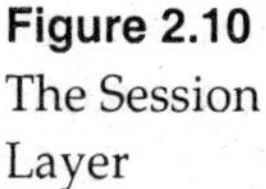

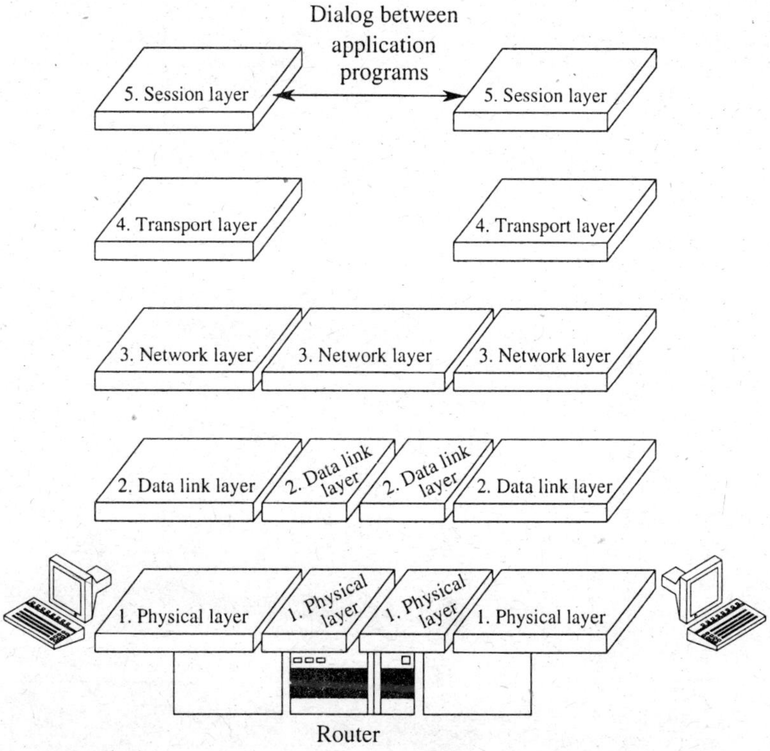

Figure 2.10
The Session Layer

2.2.6 Layer 6 — Presentation Layer

The presentation layer translates data between the formats the network requires and the formats the computer expects. The presentation layer does protocol conversion, data translation, compression and encryption, character set conversion, and the interpretation of graphics commands. A network redirector is what makes the files on a file server visible to the client computer. The network redirector also makes remote printers act as though they are attached to the local computer. The network redirector operates at presentation layer. Figure 2.11 shows how the presentation layer operates.

☞ The presentation layer adapts information to the local environment.

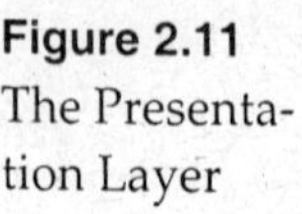

Figure 2.11 The Presentation Layer

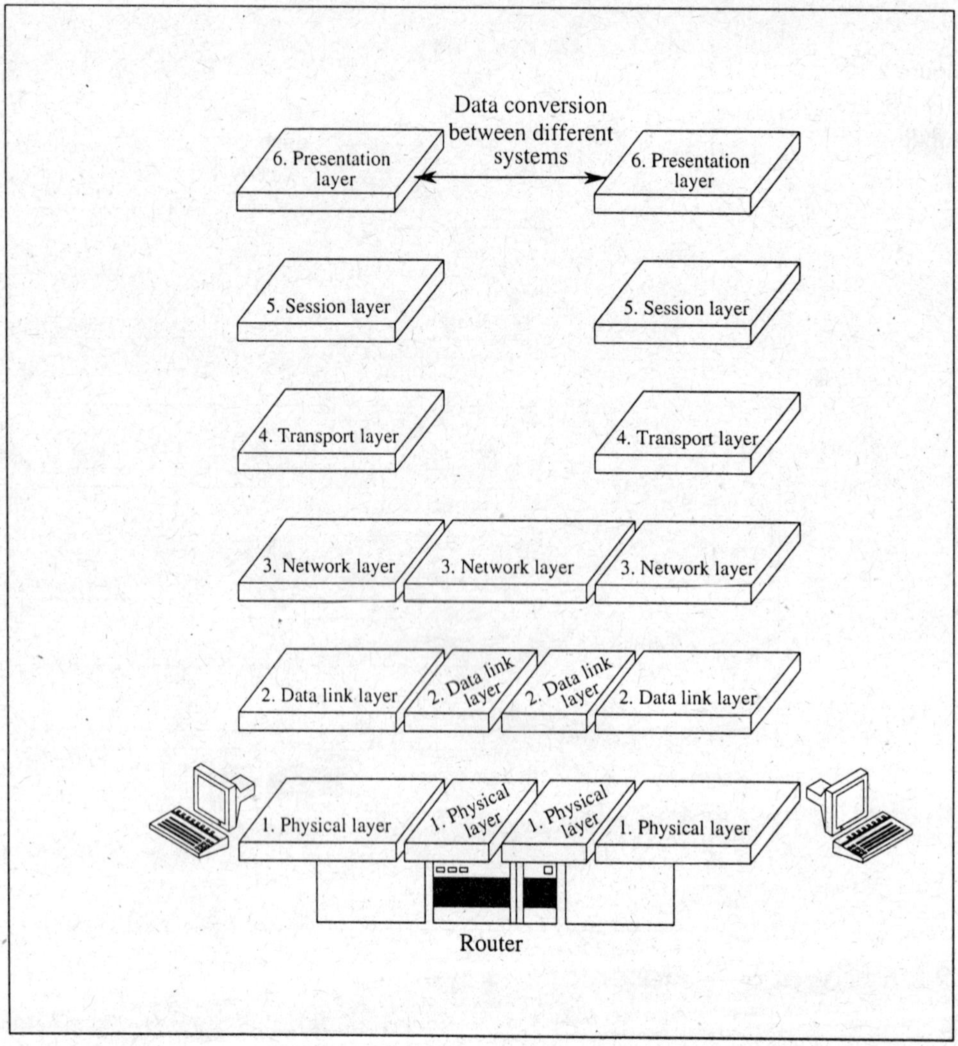

2.2.7 Layer 7 — Application Layer

The application layer is the topmost layer of the OSI model, and it provides services that directly support user applications, such as database access, e-mail, and file transfers. It also allows applications to communicate with applications on other computers as though they were on the same computer. When a programmer writes an application program that uses network services, this is the layer the application program will access. Figure 2.12 shows how the presentation layer operates. Electronic mail and query languages are examples of this layer.

☞ The Application layer provides for the connection of application programs on separate machines.

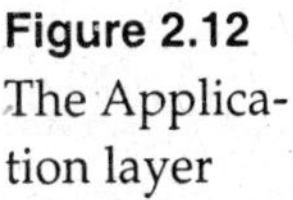

Figure 2.12 The Application layer

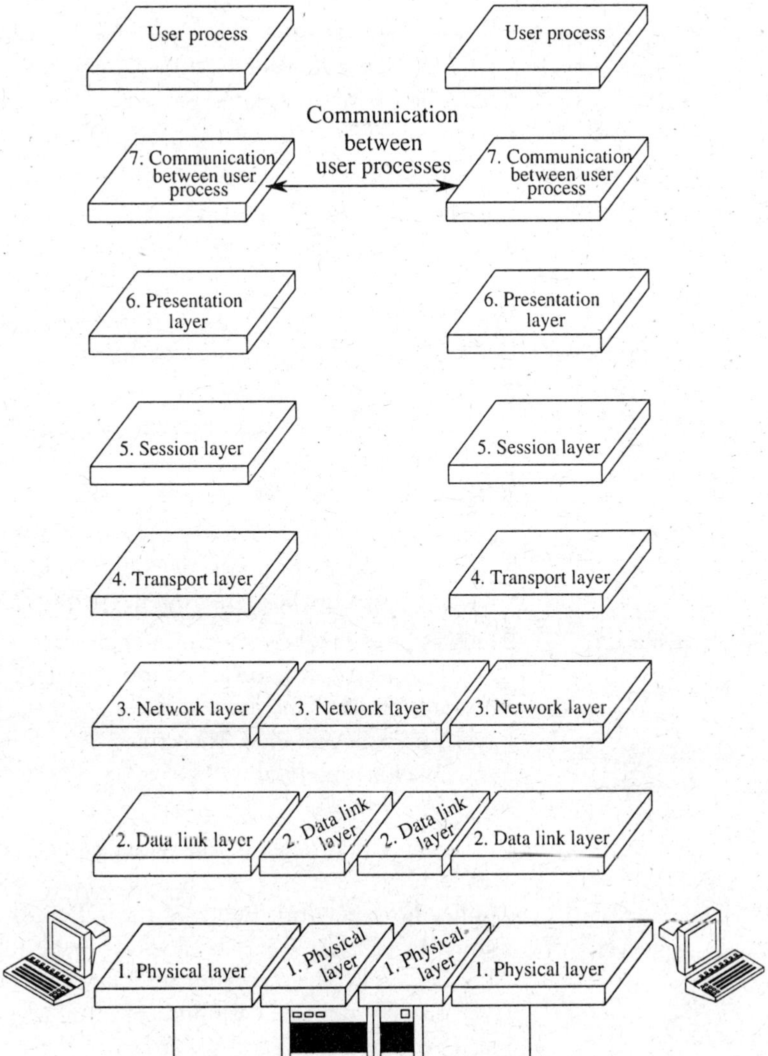

2.2.8 Functions performed by different layers

A summary of function performed by different layers in the OSI model is given in Table 2.1.

Table 2.1 Function performed by different layers in the OSI model

Layer Number	Layer Name	Description
7	Application layer	Interfaces user applications with network functionality, controls how applications access the network, and generates error messages. Protocols at this level include HTTP, FTP, SMTP, and NFS.
6	Presentation layer	Translates data to be transmitted by applications into a format suitable for transport over the network. Redirector software, such as the Workstation service for Microsoft Windows NT, is located at this level. Network shells are also defined at this layer.
5	Session layer	Defines how connections can be established, maintained, and terminated. Also performs name resolution functions.
4	Transport layer	Sequences packets so that they can be reassembled at the destination in the proper order. Generates acknowledgments and retransmits packets. Assembles packets after they are received.
3	Network layer	Defines logical host addresses such as IP addresses, creates packet headers, and routes packets across an internetwork using routers and Layer 3 switches. Strips the headers from the packets at the receiving end.
2	Data-link layer	Specifies how data bits are grouped into frames, and specifies frame formats. Responsible for error correction, flow control, hardware addressing (such as MAC addresses), and how devices such as hubs, bridges, repeaters, and Layer 2 switches operate. The Project 802 specifications divide this layer into two sublayers, the logical link control (LLC) layer and the media access control (MAC) layer.
1	Physical layer	Defines network transmission media, signaling methods, bit synchronization, architecture (such as Ethernet or Token Ring), and cabling topologies. Defines how network interface cards (NICs) interact with the media (cabling). You can think of each layer as being logically connected to the same layer on a different computer on the network. For example, the application layer on one machine communicates with the application layer on another machine. But this communication is logical only; physical communication occurs when packets of data are sent down from the application layer of the transmitting computer, encapsulated with header information by each lower layer, and then put on the wire at the physical layer of the transmitting computer. After traveling along the wire, the packets are picked up by the physical layer of the receiving computer, passed up the seven layers while each layer strips off its associated header information, and then passed to the application layer of the receiving computer, where the receiving application can process the data.

2.3 TRANSPORT PROTOCOL (INTRODUCTION TO TCP/IP)

TCP/IP, an abbreviation for Transmission Control Protocol/Internet Protocol, is an industry-standard protocol suite for wide area networks (WANs) developed in the 1970s and 1980s by the U.S. Department of Defense (DoD). TCP/IP is a routable protocol that is suitable for connecting dissimilar systems (such as Microsoft Windows and UNIX) in heterogeneous networks, and it is the protocol of the worldwide network known as the Internet.

The Internet began as a project funded by the United States Department of Defence in the 1970s to interconnect educational institutions and government installations. At that time it was called ARPAnet (Advanced Research Projects Agency Network). Over time it has evolved into the huge, worldwide network known as the Internet. The protocols that make up the Internet protocol suite, the best known being TCP (Transmission Control Protocol) and IP (Internet Protocol), have become de-facto standards because of the success of the Internet. The entire protocol suite is sometimes referred to as TCP/IP

☞ The Internet protocol suite is unique in that it is made up of nonproprietary protocols. This means that they do not belong to any one company and that the technology is available to anyone who wishes to use it. As a result, the Internet protocol suite is supported by the widest variety of vendors.

The Internet suite was developed about ten years before the OSI model was defined and can therefore be only roughly mapped to it. The Internet protocol suite was defined according to its own model, known as the Internet or DOD model. Figure 2.13 illustrates the relationship between the Internet protocol suite and the OS reference model.

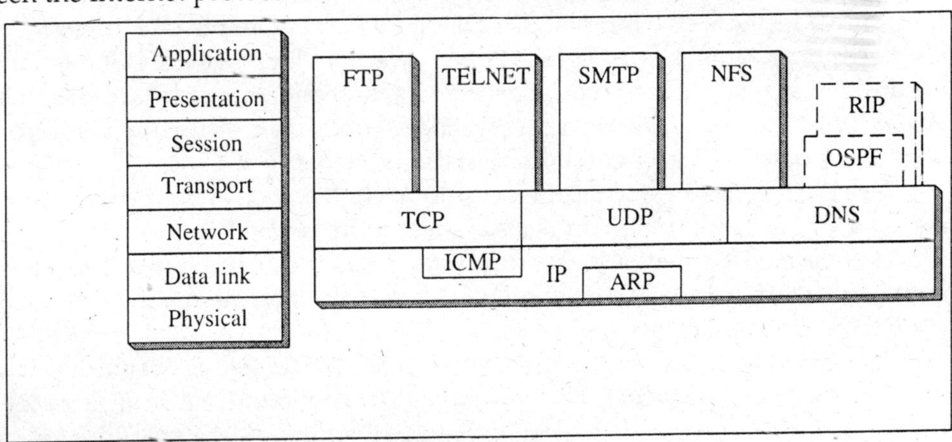

Figure 2.13 The relationship between the Internet protocol suite and the OSI model

The four DOD model layers (shown in Figure 2.13) and the OSI model layers they correspond to are as follows:

1. The network access layer corresponds to the physical and data link layers of the OSI model.

2. The Internet layer corresponds to the OSI network layer. Protocols at this layer are concerned with transporting packets through the internetwork. The main Internet layer protocol is IP (Internet Protocol).
3. The host-to-host layer corresponds roughly to the OSI transport layer. Protocols at this layer communicate with peer processes in other hosts or networked devices. An example of a host-to-host protocol is TCP.
4. The Process/application layer corresponds to the OSI session, presentation, and application layers. Protocols at this layer provide applications services on the network. Examples of protocols at this layer are Telnet (a terminal emulator) and FTP (a file transfer protocol).

Figure 2.14 The Internet (DOD) model mapped to the OSI model

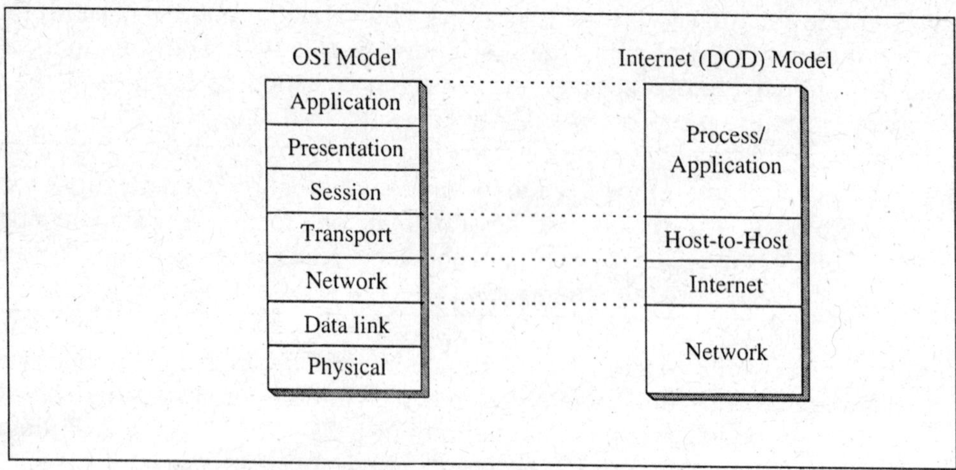

Figure 2.14 shows the Internet (DOD) model mapped to the OSI model.

The Internet protocols do not cover the lower two layers of the OSI model. This is because the designers of TCP/IP used existing physical and data link standards, such as Ethernet and Token Ring, to make TCP/IP hardware independent. As a result, the protocols of the Internet suite are widely used to connect *heterogeneous* systems.

Since the Internet protocol suite does not include lower-layer protocols, we will begin our discussion of the individual protocols at the middle layers.

The OSI model's network and transport layers are concerned with transporting packets across the internetwork. TCP/IP and other internet protocols use three types of addresses for network addressing. These are as follows:

(a) Hardware or physical addresses are used by the data link and physical layers. Physical addresses are usually hardcoded into the network cards at each device.
(b) IP addresses provide logical node IDs. IP addresses are unique addresses assigned by an administrator according to certain guidelines. They are expressed in four-part dotted-decimal notation. For example, 123.144.131.12
(c) Logical node names, which an administrator can also assign, are easier to remember than an IP address. For example, BANIYA.COM

Each layer of the TCP/IP protocol suite has its associated component protocols, the most important of which are listed as follows:

(a) Application layer protocols: Responsible for application-level access to TCP/IP networking services. These include Dynamic Host Configuration Protocol (DHCP), Domain Name System (DNS), Hypertext Transfer Protocol (HTTP), File Transfer Protocol (FTP), Telnet, Simple Mail Transfer Protocol (SMTP), and Simple Network Management Protocol (SNMP). In the Microsoft implementation of TCP/IP, application layer protocols interact with transport layer protocols by using either Windows Sockets or NetBIOS over TCP/IP (NetBT).

(b) Transport layer protocols: Establish communication through connection-oriented sessions and connectionless broadcasts. Protocols at this layer include Transmission Control Protocol (TCP) and User Datagram Protocol (UDP).

(c) Internet layer protocols: Responsible for routing and encapsulation into IP packets. Protocols at this layer include Internet Protocol (IP), Address Resolution Protocol (ARP), Internet Control Message Protocol (ICMP), and Internet Group Management Protocol (IGMP).

(d) Network layer protocols: Place frames on the network. These protocols include the various local area network (LAN) architectures (such as Ethernet and Token Ring) and WAN telecommunication service technologies-such as Plain Old Telephone Service (POTS), Integrated Services Digital Network (ISDN), and Asynchronous Transfer Mode (ATM).

☞ TCP/IP is a constantly evolving protocol suite whose development is steered by such bodies as the Internet Society (ISOC), the Internet Architecture Board (IAB), and the Internet Engineering Task Force (IETF). The current version of TCP/IP is called IPv4 (Internet Protocol version 4); a new version called IPv6 is under development.

2.3.1 Internet Protocol (IP)

IP works at the network layer. The functions it handles and methods it uses are as follows:

(a) For addressing, IP uses the logical network address.

(b) For switching purposes, it uses the packet-switching method.

(c) For route selection, it uses the dynamic method.

(d) For connection services, IP provides error control.

IP is a connectionless, datagram protocol. (IP packets are also referred to as IP datagrams.) IP uses packet switching and performs route selection by using dynamic routing tables that are referenced at each hop. The packets making up a message could be routed differently through the internetwork depending on the state of the network at each hop. For example, if a link were to go down or become congested, packets be sent through a different route.

Appended to each packet is an IP header, which includes source and destination information. IP uses sequence numbering if it is necessary to fragment a packet into smaller parts and reassemble it at its destination or at an intermediate point. IP performs error checking on the header information by way of a checksum.

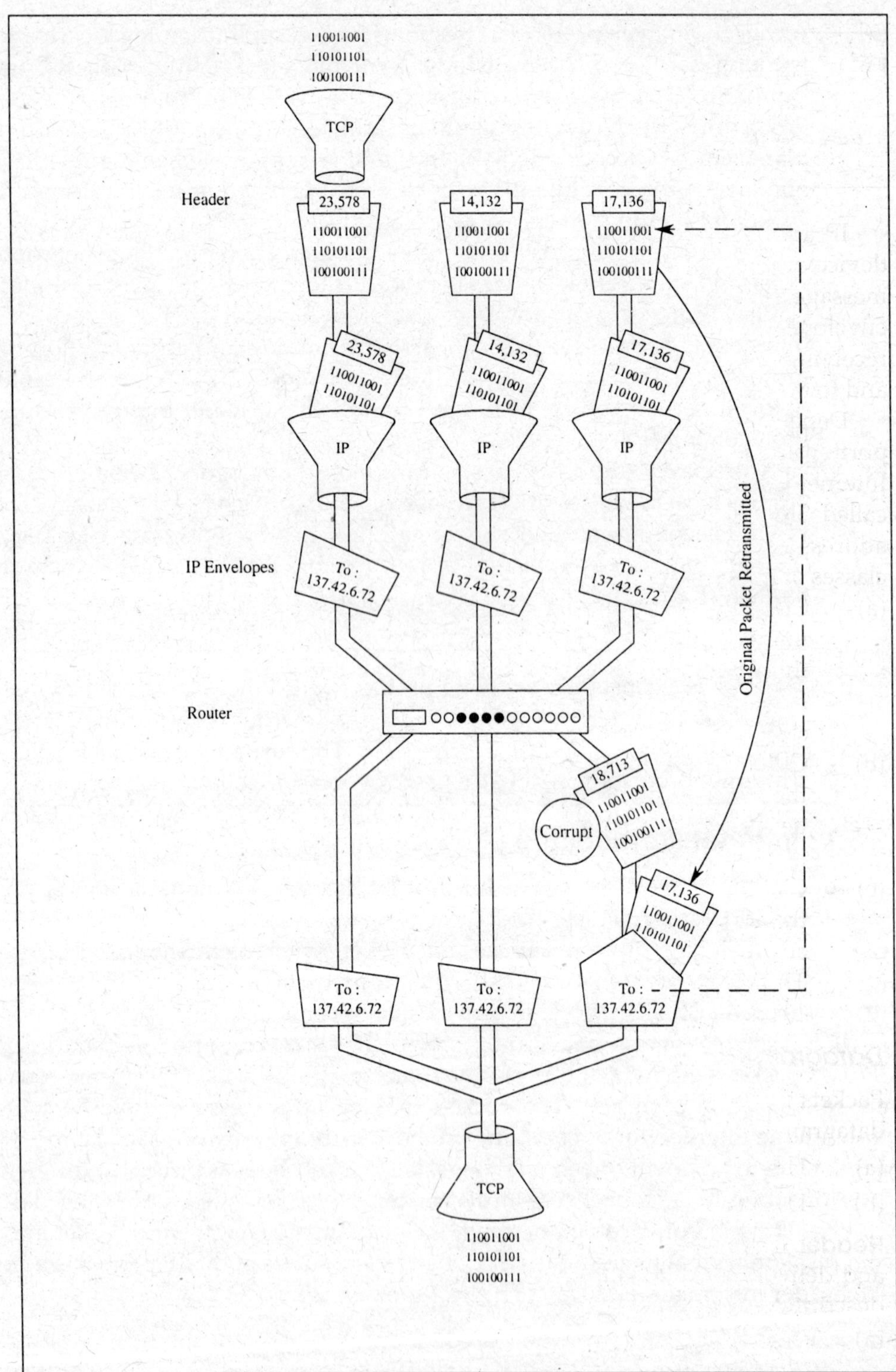

Figure 2.15 Working of TCP/IP Protocol

☞ A checksum is an error-checking method in which the data is submitted to an algorithm and the result is appended to the packet. When the packet arrives at its destination, the same calculation is performed on the data to see whether it matches the checksum value.

IP addresses are unique, 4 byte addresses that must be assigned to every addressable device or node on the internetwork. (See Figure 2.15) In this figure you will notice that a big message is divided into smaller packets by the TCP. These are given a header and then enveloped by the IP to be sent to the addresses by various routes using the router. At the receiving end, each envelop is placed in order and the message is reassembled by the TCP and forwarded to the addressee.

Depending on the class of IP address, a certain number of bytes specifies the network portion and a certain number of bytes specifies the host or node portion. If a connection to the Internet is desired, a unique IP network address must be requested from a governing body called SRI Network Information Center. This ensures that the new network will have an address different from any other on the Internet. IP addresses are assigned according to three classes of networks:

(a) Class A addresses: Used for systems with a small number of networks and a large number of hosts. These addresses use the first byte to specify the network and the last three bytes to specify the host. The first byte of a Class A address can be in the range from 0-127 e.g., 80.23.102.3. The available IP addresses for this class have already been assigned.

(b) Class B addresses: Provide for an equal number of networks and hosts by assigning the first two bytes to the network and the last two bytes to the host. The range of values for the first byte of a Class B address is 128-191. Namely as 132.45.67.28. This class is most often assigned to universities and commercial organizations.

(c) Class C addresses: Use the first three bytes of the address to specify the network and the last byte to specify the host. Because there is only one byte available for host addresses, a Class C network will only support a small number of hosts (or nodes). The range of values for the first byte of a Class C address if 192-223. For example, 194.123.45.7.

Datagram

Packets in the IP layer are called datagrams. Figure 2.16 shows the *IP datagram* format. A datagram is a variable-length packet (up to 65,536 bytes) consisting of two parts:

(a) Header

(b) Data

Header The header can be from 20 to 60 bytes and contains information essential to routing and delivery. It is customary in TCP/IP to show the header in four byte sections. A brief description of each field in the header is as follows:

(a) *Version* - The first field defines the version number of the IP. The current version is 4 (*IPv4*), with a binary value of 0100. The newer version 6 (IPv6) is under development.

Figure 2.16
IP diagram format

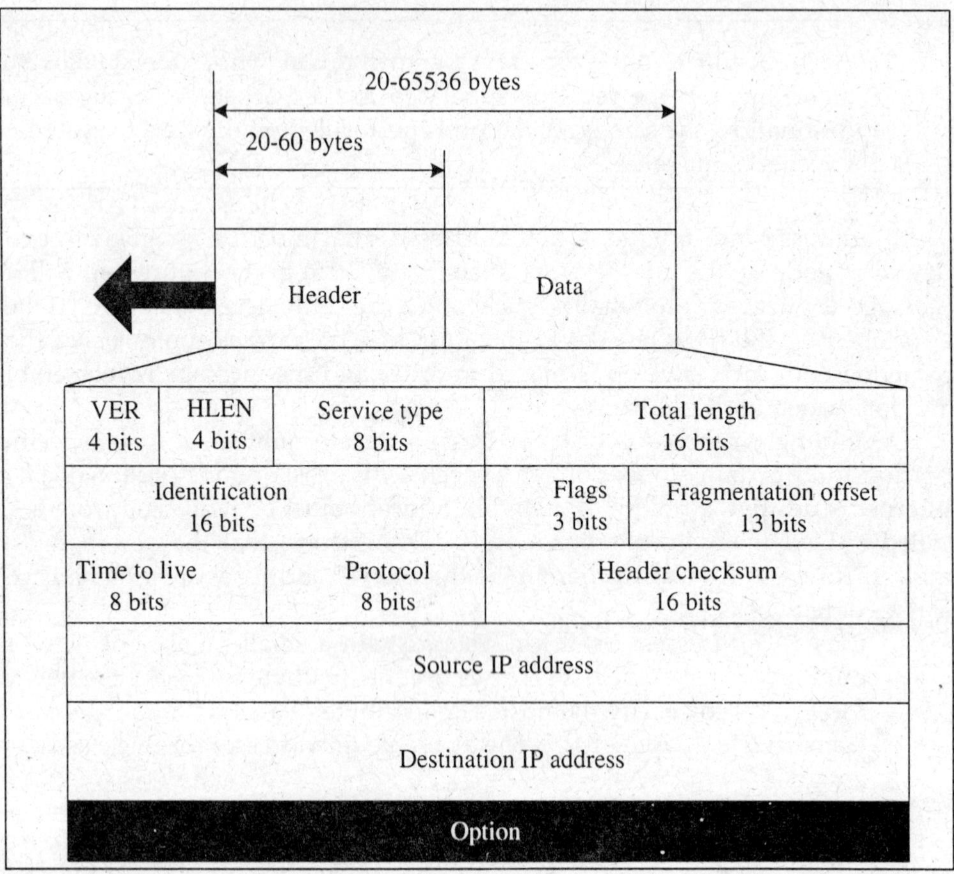

(b) *Header length (HLEN)* - The HLEN field defines the length of the header in multiples of four bytes. The four bits can represent a number between 0 and 15, which, when multiplied by 4, gives a maximum of 60 bytes.

(c) *Service type* - The service type field defines how the datagram should be handled. It includes bits that define the priority of the datagram. It also contains bits that specify the type of service the sender desires such as the level of throughput, reliability, and delay.

(d) *Total length* - The total length field defines the total length of the IP datagram. It is a two-byte field (16 bits) and can define up to 65,535 bytes.

(e) *Identification* - The identification field is used in *fragmentation*. A datagram, when passing through different networks, may be divided into fragments to match the network frame size. When this appears, each fragment is identified with a sequence number in this field.

(f) *Flags* - The bits in the flags field deal with fragmentation.

(g) *Fragmentation offset* - The fragmentation offset is a pointer that shows the offset of the data in the original datagram (if it is fragmented).

(h) *Time to live* - The time-to-live field defines the number of hops a datagram can travel before it is discarded. The source host, when it creates the datagram, sets this field to an initial value. Then, as the datagram travels through the Internet, router by router, each router reduces this value by 1. If this value becomes 0 before the datagram reaches its final destination, the datagram is discarded.

(i) *Protocol* - The protocol field defines which upper-layer protocol namely, TCP, UDP, ICMP, etc. are encapsulated in the datagram.

(j) *Header checksum* - This is a 16-bit field used to check the integrity of the header, not the rest of the packet.

(k) *Source address* - The source address field is a four-byte (32-bit) Internet address. It identifies the original source of the datagram.

(l) *Destination address* - The destination address field is a four-byte (32-bit) Internet address. It identifies the final destination of the datagram.

(m) *Options* - The options field gives more functionality to the IP datagram. It can carry fields that control routing, timing, management and alignment.

Addressing

In addition to the physical addresses contained on network interface cards (NICs) that identify individual devices, the Internet requires an additional addressing convention. This address identifies the connection of a host to its network.

Each *Internet address* consists of four bytes (32 bits), defining three fields:

(a) class type
(b) netid
(c) hostid

These parts are of varying lengths, depending on the class of the address (See Figure 2.17).

Figure 2.17 Internet address

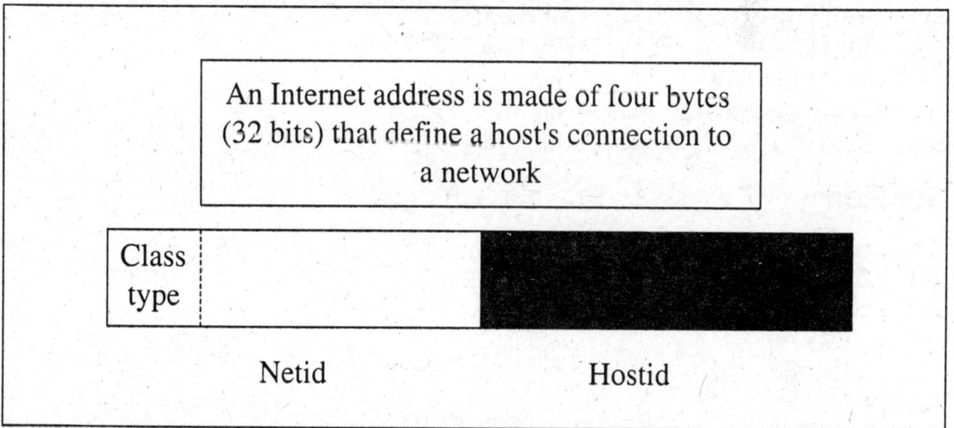

Classes There are five different field-length patterns in use, each defining a *class of address*. All such classes are designed to cover the needs of different types of organizations. For example, class A addresses are numerically the lowest. They use only one byte to identify class type and netid, and leave three bytes available for hostid numbers. This division means that class A networks can accommodate far more hosts than can class B or class C networks, which provides two- and one-byte hostid fields, respectively.

☞ Currently both class A and class B are full. Addresses are available in class C only.

Class D is reserved for *multicast addresses. Multicasting* allows copies of a datagram to be passed to a select group of hosts rather than to an individual host. Multicasting allows transmission to a selected subset. Class E addresses are reserved for future use. Figure 2.18 shows the structure of each *IP address class.*

Figure 2.18
IP address classes

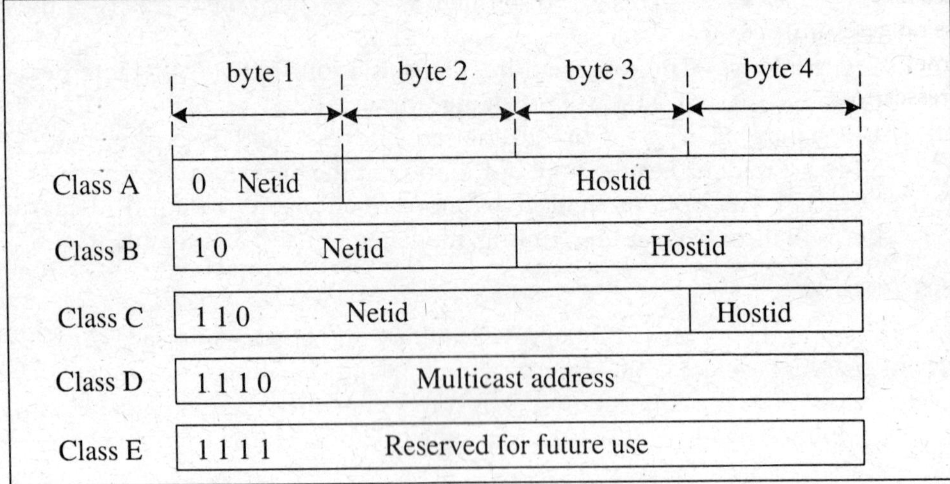

Example 2.1

What is the class of each of the following addresses?

(a) 11011101 10001111 11111100 11001111
(b) 10011101 10001111 11111100 11001111
(c) 01111011 10001111 11111100 11001111
(d) 11110101 10001111 11111100 11001111
(e) 11101011 10001111 11111100 11001111

Solution

The first bits define the class:

(a) Class C
(b) Class B
(c) Class A
(d) Class E
(e) Class D

Dotted-Decimal Notation

Internet addresses are usually written in decimal form with decimal points separating the bytes–*dotted-decimal notation*. This is done to make the 32-bit form shorter and easier to read. Figure 2.19 shows the bit pattern and decimal format of a possible address.

Looking at the first byte of an address in decimal form, we can determine at a glance to which class a particular address belongs (See Figure 2.20)

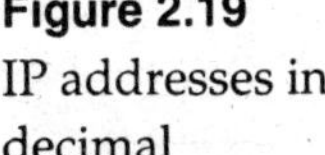

Figure 2.19
IP addresses in decimal notation

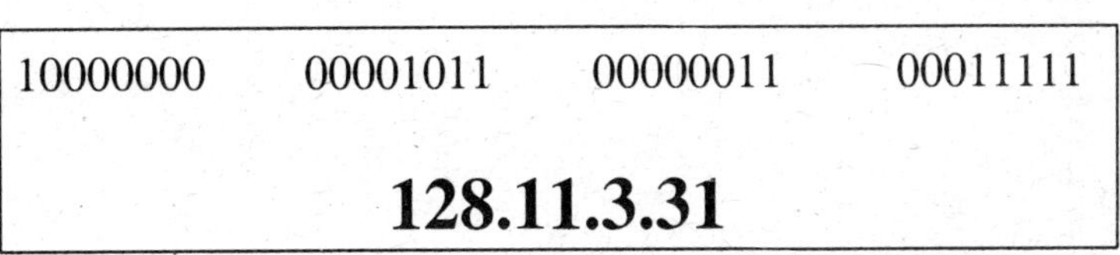

Figure 2.20
Class ranges of internet addresses

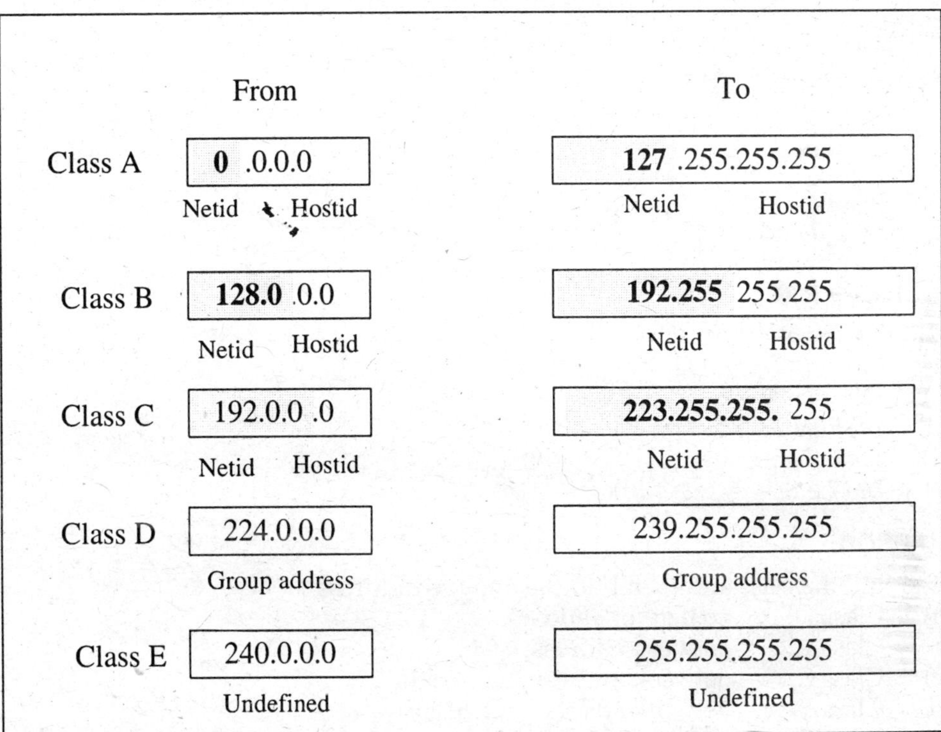

Example 2.2

Write each of following in dotted-decimal notation:

(a) 11011101 10001111 11111101 00001111
(b) 10011101 10001111 11111100 11001111
(c) 11111110 10000001 01111110 00000001
(d) 11111101 10001010 00001111 00111111
(e) 01011101 00011111 00000001 11110101

Solution

Each byte is converted to a decimal number between 0 and 255.

(a) 221.143.253.15
(b) 157.143.252.207
(c) 254.129.126.1
(d) 253.138.15.63
(e) 93.31.1.245

Example 2.3

Find the class of each address:
(a) 226.34.78.7
(b) 4.22.145.90
(c) 245.7.3.8
(d) 197.76.9.23
(e) 28.6.8.4

Solution

The first byte defines the class
(a) Class D
(b) Class A
(c) Class E
(d) Class C
(e) Class B

Example 2.4

Find the network for each address:
(a) 227.34.78.7
(b) 4.23.145.90
(c) 198.76.9.23
(d) 129.6.8.4
(e) 246.7.3.8

Solution

First find the class and then find the network address
(a) Class D, no network address
(b) Class A, network address: 4.0.0.0
(c) Class C, network address: 198.76.9.0
(d) Class B, network address: 129.6.0.0
(e) Class E, no network address

Example 2.5

Find the netid and hostid for each address:
(a) 227.34.78.7
(b) 4.23.145.90
(c) 198.76.9.23
(d) 129.6.8.4
(e) 246.7.3.8

Solution

First find the class and then find the netid and hostid

(a)	Class D,	no hostid or netid	
(b)	Class A,	netid: 4	hostid: 23.145.90
(c)	Class C,	netid: 198.76.9	hostid: 23
(d)	Class B,	netid: 129.6	hostid: 8.4
(e)	Class E,	no hostid or netid	

A Sample Internet An internet address specifies both the network to which a host belongs (*netid*) and the host itself (hostid). Figure 2.21 shows a portion of the Internet made up of LANs (three Ethernets and a Token Ring). Routers are indicated by circles containing the letter **R**. Gateways are indicated by boxes containing the letter **G**. Each has a separate address for each of its connected networks. The figure also shows the network addresses.

☞ A network address is the *netid* with the *hostid* part set to 0s. The network addresses in the figure are 128.8.0.0 (class B), 124.0.0.0 (class A), 134.18.0.0 (class B), and 220.3.6.0 (class C).

Figure 2.21 Network and host addresses

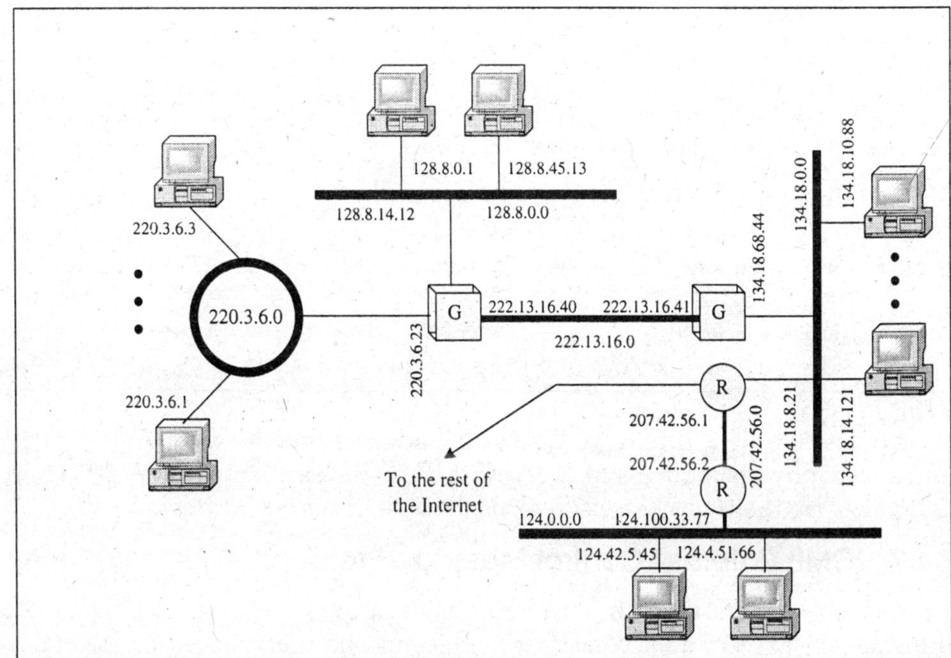

2.4 PROTOCOLS FORMING PART OF INTERNET PROTOCOL

2.4.1 ARP (Address Resolution Protocol)

ARP is a network layer protocol concerned with mapping node names to IP addresses. It equates logical and physical device addresses.

☞ The *address resolution protocol* (ARP) associates an IP address with the physical address.

On a typical physical network, such as a LAN, each device on a link is identified by a physical or station address usually imprinted on the network interface card (NIC). ARP maintains tables of name-to-address mappings and can send out packets for searching the address if a desired name or address is not currently in its table.

Physical addresses have local jurisdiction and can be changed easily. For example, if the NIC on a particular machine fails, the physical address changes. The IP addresses, on the other hand, have universal jurisdiction and cannot be changed. ARP is used to find the physical address to the node when its Internet address is known.

Any time a host, or a router, needs to find the physical address of another host on its network, it formats an ARP query packet that includes the IP address and broadcasts it over the network.

☞ Every host on the network receives and processes the ARP packet, but only the intended recipient recognizes its internet address and sends back its physical address.

The host holding the datagram adds the address of the target host both to its cache memory and to the datagram header, then sends the datagram on its way.

Reverse Address Resolution Protocol (RARP)

RARP (Reverse Address Resolution Protocol) performs the same function as ARP does but in reverse, that is given an IP address, it determines the corresponding node name.

☞ The *reverse address resolution protocol (RARP)* allows a host to discover its internet address when it knows only its physical address.

The host wishing to retrieve its internet address broadcasts an RARP query packet that contains its physical address to every host on its physical network. A server on the network recognizes the RARP packet and returns the host's internet address.

2.4.2 ICMP (Internet Control Message Protocol)

ICMP is a protocol used with IP to augment error-handling and control procedures. It works at the network layer and is concerned with connection services. ICMP provides error control and network layer flow control.

☞ ICMP detects error conditions such as internetwork congestion and downed links and notifies IP and upper-layer protocols so packets can be routed avoiding problem areas.

IP is essentially an unreliable and connectionless protocol. ICMP, however, allows IP to inform a sender if a datagram is undeliverable. A datagram travels from router to router until it reaches one that can deliver it to its final destination. If a router is unable to route or deliver the datagram because of unusual conditions (disabled links, or the device is on fire) or because of network congestion, ICMP allows it to inform the original source.

2.4.3 RIP (Routing Information Protocol)

RIP is a network layer protocol. It is a distance-vector routing protocol, which means it periodically broadcasts routing tables across the internetwork. Similar to NetWare RIP, Internet

RIP causes bottlenecks in WANs and is therefore being replaced by OSPF which is described below.

2.4.4 OSPF (Open Shortest Path First)

OSPF is another network layer protocol that addresses route discovery. It is a link-state routing protocol. It was developed to be more efficient and to create less overhead than RIP. It provides load balancing and routing based on class of service.

2.4.5 TCP (Transmission Control Protocol)

TCP is the Internet protocol suite's main transport layer protocol. It also provides addressing (with service addresses) services at the network layer.

☞ TCP provides reliable, full-duplex, connection-oriented transport service to upper-layer protocols.

TCP works in conjunction with IP to move packets through the internetwork. TCP assigns a connection ID (port) to each virtual circuit. It also provides message fragmentation and reassemble using sequence numbering. Error checking is enhanced through the use of TCP acknowledgements.

2.4.6 UDP (User Datagram Protocol)

UDP is a connectionless protocol that works at the transport layer. UDP transports datagrams but does not acknowledge their receipt. UDP also uses a port address to achieve datagram delivery, but this port address is simply a pointer to a process, not a connection identifier, as it is with TCP. The lack of overhead makes UDP faster than TCP.

2.4.7 DNS (Domain Name System)

DNS is a distributed database system that works at the transport layer to provide name-to-address mapping for client applications. DNS servers maintain databases that consist of hierarchical name structures of the various domains in order to use logical names for device identification. This type of address/name resolution is called service-provider initiated. The largest use of DNS is in the Internet.

In the Internet, the domain name space (tree) is divided into the three different sections:

(a) Generic domains
(b) Country domains
(c) Inverse domains

Generic Domains

The *generic domains* define registered hosts according to their generic behavior. Each node in the tree defines a domain, which is an index to the domain name space database. The first level in the generic domain section allows seven possible three-character labels. These labels describe the organization types as listed in Table 2.1.

Table 2.1 Generic domain names

Label	Description
com	Commercial organization
edu	Educational institutions
gov	Government institutions
int	International organizations
mil	Military groups
net	Network support centers
org	Nonprofit organizations

Recently a few more first-level labels have been proposed: these are shown in Table 2.2.

Table 2.2 Additional first labels proposed

Label	Description
art	Cultural organizations
firm	Business or firms
info	Information service providers
nom	Personal nomenclatures
rec	Recreation/entertainment organization
store	Business offering goods to purchase
web	Web-related organizations

Country Domains

The *country domain* section follows the same format as the generic domains but uses two-character country abbreviations (e.g., "us" for United States) in place of the three-character organizational abbreviations at the first level. Second-level labels can be organizational, or they can be more specific, national destinations. The United States, for example, uses state abbreviations as a subdivision of "us" (e.g., ca.us.).

Inverse Domain

The *inverse domain* is used to map an address to a name. This may happen, for example, when a server has received a request from a client to do a task. Whereas the server has a file that contains a list of authorized clients, the server lists only the IP address of the client (extracted from the received IP packet). To determine if the client is on the authorized list, it can send a query to the DNS server and ask for a mapping of address to name.

2.5 INTERNET UPPER-LAYER PROTOCOLS

The upper layer Internet protocols generally provide applications or services for use on the Internet, such as file transfer and electronic mail.

2.5.1 FTP (File Transfer Protocol)

FTP is used for file transfer between internetwork nodes. In addition, it allows users to initiate processes on the remote host. FTP enables users to log in to remote hosts. It functions at the top three layers of the OSI model, as follows:

(a) At the session layer, FTP provides session administration, handling connection establishment, file transfer, and connection release.

(b) At the presentation layer, FTP is concerned with translation, using a machine-independent file syntax.
(c) At the application layer, this protocol supplies network services, namely file services and collaborative service use.

☞ *File transfer protocol (FTP)* is the standard mechanism provided by TCP/IP for copying a file from one host to another. Transferring files from one computer to another is one of the most common tasks expected from a networking or internetworking environment.

☞ FTP is a peer-to-peer protocol. FTP supports the ability to transfer files between dissimilar hosts because it uses a generic file structure that is operating system independent.

FTP differs from other client–server applications in that it establishes two connections between the hosts. One connections is used for *data transfer*, the other for control information (commands and responses). Separation of commands and data transfer makes FTP more efficient. The control connection uses very simple rules of communication. We need to transfer only a line of command or a line of response at a time. The data connection, on the other hand, needs more complex rules due to the variety of data types transferred.

2.5.2 TELNET

The main task of the Internet and its TCP/IP protocol suite is to provide services for users. For example, users want to be able to run different application programs at a remote site and create results that can be transferred to their local site. One way to satisfy these demands is to create different client-server application programs for each desired device. Programs such as file transfer programs (FTP and TFTP), e-mail (SMTP), and so on are already available. But it would be impossible to write a specific client-server program for each demand.

The better solution is a general-purpose client-server program that lets a user access any application program on a remote computer; in other words, allow the user to log on to a remote computer. After logging on, a user can use the services available on the remote computer and transfer the results back to the local computer.

Telnet is used for remote terminal emulation. It enables user to access host-based applications by emulating one of the host's terminals. Telnet provides connectivity between dissimilar operating systems.

Telnet functions at the top three layers of the OSI model, as follows:

(a) At the session layer, it provides dialog control, using the half-duplex method. It also provides session administration, handling connection establishment, file transfer, and releasing the connection.
(b) At the presentation layer, Telnet is concerned with translation, using the byte order and character codes.
(d) At the application layer, this protocol supplies the service use functions for remote operation.

☞ TELNET is a general-purpose client-server application program.

Local Login

When a user logs a local time-sharing system, it is called *local login*. As a user types at a terminal or at a workstation running a terminal emulator, the keystrokes are accepted by the terminal driver. The terminal driver passes the characters to the operating system. The operating system, in turn, interprets the combination of characters and invokes the desired application program or utility.

Remote login

When a user wants to access an application program or utility located on a remote machine, he or she performs *remote login*. Here the TELNET client and server programs come into use. The user sends the keystrokes to the terminal driver where the local operating system accepts the characters but does not interpret them. The characters are sent to the TELNET client, which transforms the characters to a universal character set called *network virtual terminal characters* and delivers them to the local TCP/IP stack

The commands or text, in NVT form, travel through the Internet and arrive at the TCP/IP stack at the remote machine. Here the characters are delivered to the operating system and passed to the TELNET server, which changes the characters to the corresponding characters understandable by the remote computer. However, the characters cannot be passed directly to the operating system because the remote operating system is not designed to receive characters from a TELNET server; it is designed to receive characters from a terminal driver. The solution is to add a piece of software called a *pseudoterminal driver*, which pertends that the characters are coming from a terminal. The operating system then passes the characters to the appropriate application program.

2.6 COMPARISON OF DIFFERENT MODELS (TCP/IP VS. OSI MODEL)

TCP/IP is a communications protocol that is designed to interconnect a wide variety of different computer equipment. TCP/IP was originally developed by the Department of Defense's Advanced Research Projects Agency (ARPA) and later adapted for the Ethernet Local area network. It is used with many Digital Vax computers running on UNIX and is supported by a large number of hardware vendors, especially in the scientific and technical environments. One of the important features of TCP/IP is its TELNET virtual terminal service, which allows users to log onto and interact with different types of host computers in the network.

Transmission Control Protocol (TCP) was developed before the OSI model. Therefore, the layers in the TCP/IP protocol do not match exactly with those in the OSI model. The TCP/IP protocol is made of five layers: physical, data link, network, transport, and application. The application layer in TCP/IP can be equated with the combination of session, presentation, and application layers of the OSI model.

Figure 2.22 shows the encapsulation of data units at different layers of the TCP/IP protocol suite. The data unit created at the application layer is called *message*. TCP or UDP creates a data unit that is called either a *segment* of a *user datagram*. The IP layer in turn will create a data unit called a *datagram*. The movement of the datagram across the Internet is the responsibility of the TCP/IP protocol. However, to be able to move physically from one network to another, the datagram must be encapsulated in a frame in the data link layer of the underlaying network and finally transmitted as signals along the transmission media.

Figure 2.22
TCP/IP OSI model

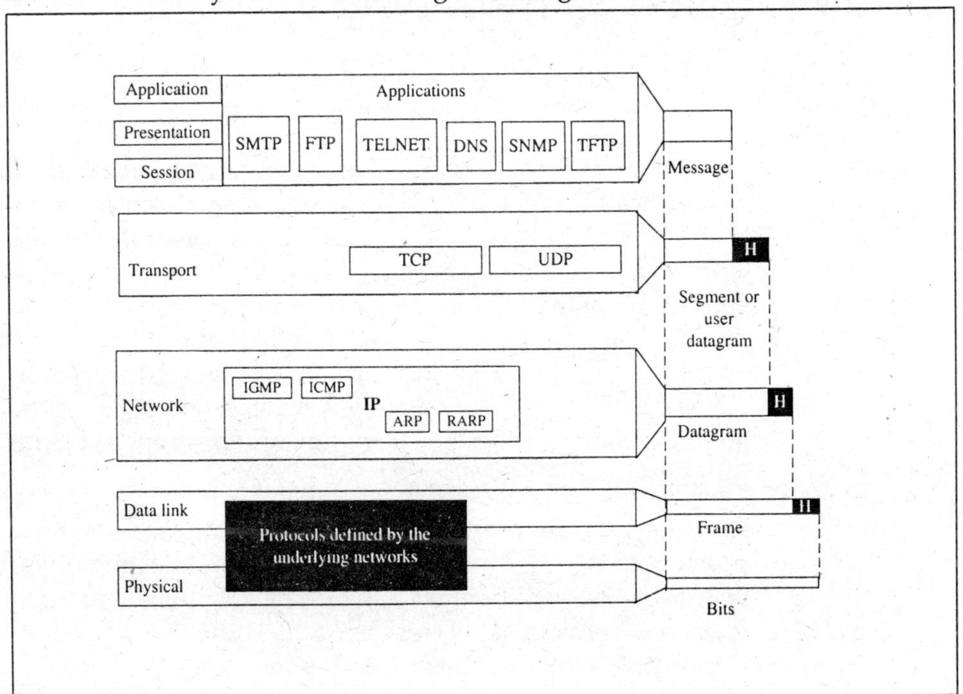

The Open Systems Interconnection (OSI) reference model was intended as a basis for developing universally accepted networking protocols. This initiative of developing OSI reference model failed for the following reasons:

(a) The standards process was relatively closed compared with the open standards process used by the Internet Engineering Task Force (IETF) to develop the TCP/IP protocol suite.

(b) The model was overly complex. Some functions (such as connectionless communication) were neglected, while others (such as error correction and flow control) were repeated at several layers.

(c) The growth of the Internet and TCP/IP-a simpler, real-world protocol model-pushed the OSI reference model out.

(d) The OSI reference model is best seen as an idealized model of the logical connections that must occur in order for network communication to take place. Most protocol suites used in the real world, such as TCP/IP, DECnet, and Systems Network Architecture (SNA), map somewhat loosely to the OSI reference model. The OSI model is a good starting point for understanding how various protocols within a protocol suite function and interact.

REVIEW QUESTIONS WITH ANSWERS

Question Number 1 Show the various layers in the ISO-OSI model and explain the functions of each layer. What are the enhancements to the OSI model?

Answer In the year 1978, the International Standards Organization (IS0) released a set of specifications that described a network architecture for connecting dissimilar devices. In 1984, the ISO released a revision of this model and called it the Open Systems Interconnection (OSI) reference model. This revision has become an international standard and serves as a guide for networking model. This revised OSI model provides the description of how network hardware and software work together in a layered fashion to make communications possible. It also helps with troubleshooting by providing a frame of reference that describes how components are supposed to function.

The OSI model is an architecture that divides network communication into seven layers. Each layer covers different network activities, equipment or protocols. Figure 2.2 represent the layered architecture of the OSI model. Each OSI layer has well defined networking functions and the functions of each layer communicate and work with the functions of the layers immediately above and below it namely, the Session layer must communicate and work with the Presentation and Transport layer.

The lowest layers —1 and 2 — define the network's physical media and related tasks, such as putting data bits onto the network adapter cards and cable. The highest layers define how applications access communication services. The higher the layer, the more complex its task is. Each layer provides some service to action that prepares the data for delivery over the network to another computer. The layers are separated from each other by boundaries called ***interfaces***. All requests are passed from one layer, through the interface to the next layer. Each layer builds upon the standards and activities of the layer below it.

The layers are setup in such a way that ea h layer acts as if it is communicating with its associated layer on the other computer. This is a logical or virtual communication between peer layers as shown in Figure 2.2. In reality, actual communication takes place between adjacent layers on one computer. At each layer there is software that implements certain network functions according to a set of protocols.

Before data is passed from one layer to another it is broken into packets. A packet is a unit of information transmitted as a whole from one device to another on a network. At each layer the software adds some additional formatting or addressing to the packet, which it needs to be successfully transmitted across the network.

At the receiving end, the packet passes through the layers in the reverse order. A software utility at each layer reads the information on the packet, strips it away and passes the packet up to the next layer. When the packet finally gets passed up to the Application layer, the addressing information has been stripped away and the packet is its original form which is readable by the receiver. (See Figure 2.3).

Except for the lowest layer in the networking model, no layer can pass information directly to its counterpart on another computer.

Application Layer

Layer 7, the topmost layer of the OSI model, is the Application layer. It serves as the window for application processes to access network services. This layer represents the services that directly support user applications, such as software for the file transfers, for database access, and for e-mail.

Presentation Layer

Layer 6, the Presentation layer, determines the format used to exchange data among networked computers. It can be called the network's translator.

(a) At the sending computer, this layer translates data from a format sent down from the Application layer into a commonly recognized, intermediary format.

(b) At the receiving computer, this layer translates the intermediary format into a format useful to that computer's Application layer.

(c) This layer is responsible for protocol conversion, translating the data, encrypting the data, changing or converting the character set, and expanding graphics commands.

(d) This layer also manages data compression to reduce the number of bits that need to be transmitted.

A utility known as the **redirector** operates at this layer. The purpose of the redirector is to redirect input/output operations to resources on a server.

Session Layer

Layer 5, the Session layer, allows tow application on different computers to establish, use, and end a connection called a session. This layer performs the following functions:

(a) Name recognition

(b) Security needed to allow two applications to communicate over the network.

(c) It provides the synchronization between user tasks by placing checkpoints in the data stream. This way, if the network fails, only the data after the last checkpoint has to be retransmitted.

(d) It implements dialog control between communicating processes, regulating which side transmits, when, for how long, and so on.

Transport Layer

Layer 4, the Transport layer, provides an additional connection level beneath the Session layer. The Transport layer ensures that:

(a) Packets are delivered error free, in sequence and with no losses or duplications.

(b) Repackages messages, dividing long messages into several packets and collecting small packets together in one package. In this way, the packets are transmitted efficiently over the network.

(c) At the receiving end, it unpacks the messages, reassembles the original messages and typically sends an acknowledgement of receipt.

(d) It provides flow control, error handling and is involved in solving problems concerned with the transmission and reception of packets.

Network Layer

Layer 3, the Network layer, is responsible for:

(a) Addressing messages and translating logical address and names into physical addresses.

(b) Determines the route from the source to the destination computer.

(c) Determines which path the data should take based on network conditions, priority of service and other factors.

(d) Manages traffic problems on the network such as packet switching routing and controlling the congestion of data.

If the network adapter on the router cannot transmit a data chunk as large as the source computer sends, the Network a layer on the router compensates by breaking the data into smaller units. On the destination end, the Network layer reassembles the data.

Data Link Layer

Layer 2, the Data Link layer, sends data frames from the Network layer to the Physical layer. On the receiving end, it packages raw bits from the Physical layer into data frames. A data frame is an organized, logical structure in which data can be placed. (See Figure below)

In this figure, destination address represents the address of the computer to which the information is being sent. The control information is used for frame type, routing and segmentation information. The user data is the information itself. The cyclical redundancy check (CRC) represents error correction and verification information to ensure that the data frame is received properly.

The Data Link layer is responsible for providing the error-free transfer of these frames from one computer to another through the Physical layer. This allows the network layer to assume virtually error-free transmission over the network connection.

Structure of a Data Packet

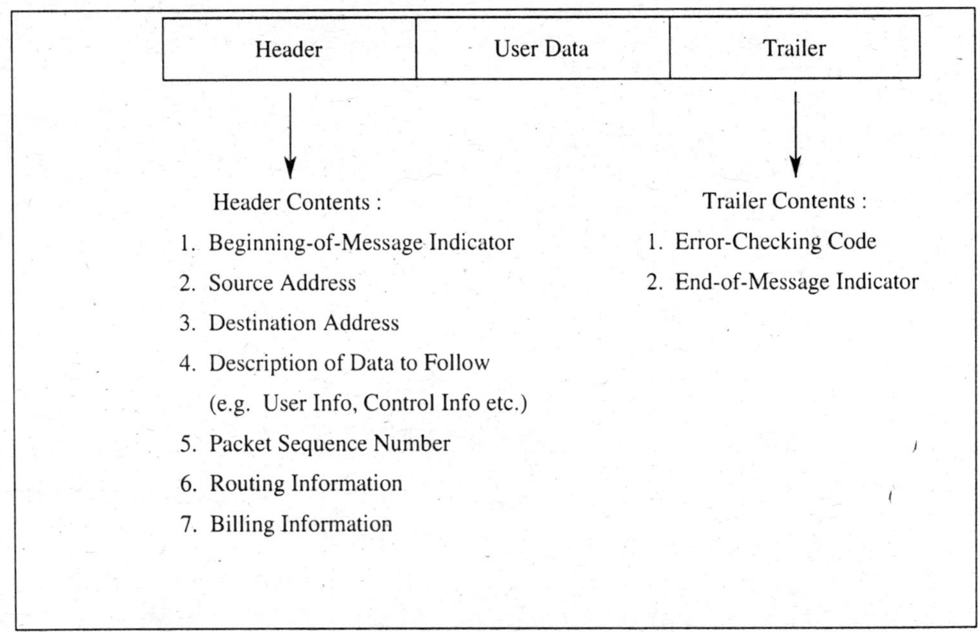

When the Data Link layer sends a frame, it waits for an acknowledgement from the recipient. The recipient Data Link layer detects any problems with the frame that may have occurred during the transmission. Frames that were not acknowledged, or frames that were damaged during transmission, are resent.

Physical Layer

Layer 1, the bottom most layer of the OSI model, is the Physical layer. This layer transmits the unstructured raw bit stream over a physical medium (such as the network cable). The Physical a layer relates the electrical, optical, mechanical and functional interfaces to the cable. The Physical layer also carries the signals that transmit data generated by all of the higher layers.

Physical layer also defines how the cable is attached to the network adapter card. This layer is also responsible for transmitting bits (zero and ones) from one computer to another. This layer defines data encoding and bit synchronization, ensuring that when a transmitting host sends a 1 hit, it is received as a 1 bit, not a 0 bit. This layer also defines how long each bit lasts and how each bit is translated into the appropriate electrical or optical impulse for the network cable.

Enhancements to the OSI Model

The bottom two OSI layers, the Physical layer and the Data Link layer, define how multiple computers can simultaneously use the network without interfering with each other.

The 802 standards committee decided that more detail was needed at the Data Link layer. They divided the Data Link layer into two sublayers:

- Logical Link Control (LLC)—error and flow control
- Media Access Control (MAC)—access control

Division of Datalink layer

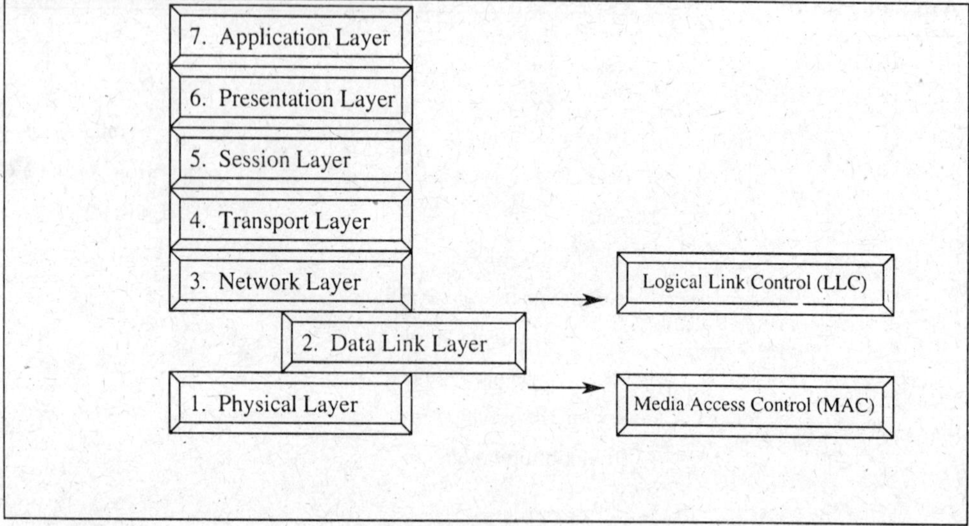

Logical Link Control Sublayer

The LLC manages data-link commination and defines the use of logical interface points, called service access points (SAPs). Other computers can refer to and use SAPs to transfer information from the LLC sublayer to the upper OSI layer. These standards are defined by 802.2.

LOGICAL LINK CONTROL (LLC)	**802.1 OSI Model and network Management** **802.2 Logical Link Control**

Media Access Control Sublayer

The Figure given below indicate the Media Access Control sublayer is the lower of the two sublayers, providing shared access for the computer's network adapter cards to the Physical layer. The Media Access Control layer communicates directly with the network adapter card and is responsible for delivering error-free data between two computers on the network.

Categories 802.3, 802.4, 802.5 and 802.12 define standards for both this sublayer and OSI layer 1, the Physical Layer.

MEDIA ACCESS CONTROL	**802.3 CSMA/CD** **802.4 TOKEN BUS** **802.5 TOKEN RING** **802.12 DEMAND PRIORITY**

Question Number 2 Explain using a table, the various protocols used in different layers of the OSI Model and the functionality of each layer.

Answer

LAYER	FUNCTIONALITY	PROTOCOLS
1. PHYSICAL [Lowest layer of the OSI Model]	It explained about mechanical, electrical and procedural interfaces and physical transmission medium between stations. It deals with electrical and physical requirement of a system. Puts the information on to the physical network and receives packets (or frames) from the network.	1. RS 232C- It addresses the physical layer within the ISO model. 2. IEEE 802 3. CCITT X.25
2. DATA LINK LAYER [the lowest protocol layer]	It deals with forming of the information sent on the wire. It is responsible for gaining access to the network and transmitting the physical block of data from one device to other. It defines the rules for node to node data transfer. Data format, sequence, acknowledgement process, bit-error detection used by the network to handle row digital data, etc. are explained in this layer.	1.BISYNC 2.HDLC/SDLC 3.IEEE 802
3. NETWORK LAYER	It keeps track which MAC [media access control the unique number that each network card has] address to send to i.e, decides which system receives the information. It makes routing of data through network from source to destination. Virtual circuits are established in this layer. Packets are formalised into frames to include virtual circuit routing and other pertinent data. It translates logical network address into physical machine address. It determines the Quality of service (namely, priority of the manage). It breaks large packets into smaller chunks so that these will be accepted by frame of data link layer. Flow control of packetised information and congestion avoidance is main concern of this protocol.	Protocols are responsible for the delivery of frames in some sequence they were sent. 1. Ethernet or DECNET 2. X.25 link connection for optimizing the network Class3: It combines the better feature of class 1 and 2 Class4: It is the highest level of error recovery. Besides the basic error recovery there are requirements for checking damaged data and out of sequence packets, or even lost packets.

(Contd....)

LAYER	FUNCTIONALITY	PROTOCOLS
4. TRANSPORT LAYER	Puts the information into a "language" that the other system understands. It converts or manages messages into the structures required for transmission over the network. Interfacing between the application software and the available hardware. The mapping of transport address on to the network Error detection and recovery to minimize data loss and time lost due to retransmission of bad-frames. Segmentation or fragmentation of message to maximize transmission efficiency. Flow control between layers below the transport layer (specifically the network layer) and the session layer.	Five classes of transport layer protocols They differ in the degree of error recovery and were designed to allow the most flexibility to the network system designer. Class 0- Lowest class It includes minimized error recovery and is used primarily for straight text transmission Class-1–Increases the amount of error recovery ability, expanding is to networks that is X.25 packet switch at the network level. Class-2–Increases error recovery to the point that the network becomes very reliable, requiring very few retransmission to handle errors. Multiplexing of data connections into a single data.
5. SESSION LAYER	This layers allows an application on separate computers to share an actual connection between systems called a session. It permits multiple application to share a virtual circuit. Its main function is related to file management and overhead functions. It takes care of connection and disconnection from the network and authentication of users access. It provides access availability and system time allocation, the binding of processes names to network address. It maintains the order of data packets and bidirectional (two way) communication.	1. NETBIOS [Network Basic Input Output Services Interface] Working: 1. Name management 2. Connection oriented data transfer 3. Connectionless data transfer 4. Session management

(Contd....)

	LAYER	*FUNCTIONALITY*	*PROTOCOLS*
		It provides lookup and security to allow the programs to find each other and establish the communication link. It provides data synchronization and check pointing so that in the event of network failure, only the data sent after the point of failure need to be resent. It controls dialogue between the processes or the application program to determine who can transmit data and who can receive data at what point during the communication. It provides for correcting and maintaining a logical connection between the hosts. It also keep tracks the resource currently in use.	
6.	PRESENTATION LAYER	This layer deals with the different systems representing data namely, what will happen when it tries to display UNIX-style data on an MS-DOS screen. This layer creates SMB (Server Message Block) in NT's case that tells the other system what is requested or contains the response to the requested. It provides several functionality on data used in this layer, These are (a) data compression (b) data (type) conversion between the format when the communication hosts are different. (c) data encryption (d) character set conversion (e) format and systems resolution (f) data transformation It provides interpretation of graphics commands	Devices are treated as virtual circuit in this layer. Three basic forms of protocols are:- 1. Virtual Terminal protocol– It is used to allow different types of terminals to support different application. 2. Virtual File Protocol– It handles code conversion within files, file communication and file formatting. 3. Job transfer and Manipulating Protocol– It controls the structure of jobs and records.

(Contd...)

	LAYER	FUNCTIONALITY	PROTOCOLS
7.	APPLICATION LAYER (Top most level/human interfaced level) provides 1. email, 2. query languages 3. FTP software 4. Telnet software	It defines user interface to lower level layers and various application processes. It provides for the connection of application programs on separate machine. It generates the requests and processes the requests that it receives. It deals with handling large amount of data, data-base access, bulk data transfer, remote Job entry and actual user requirement for the network. It is highest level of security since it deals with the user entry point into the system. Some typical uses are credit checks, Inventory and point of sales terminals.	Deals with identification, authentication and determination of availability of combined end user Protocols 1. NETWARE 2. DECNET (digital equipment corporations networking).

Question Number 3 Explain the layered architecture of TCP/IP suite. Mention the different protocols working in each layer.

Answer *[Refer to Section 2.3]*

Question Number 4 Write a short note on the following:

(a) Transport Control Protocol

(b) Internet Protocol

(c) File Transfer Protocol

(d) Telnet

Answer (a) Transport Control Protocol (TCP) is a reliable connection-oriented protocol that allows a byte stream originating on one machine to be delivered without error on any other machine in the Internet. It fragments the incoming byte stream into discrete messages and passes each one onto the internet layer. At the destination machine, the receiving TCP process reassembles the received messages into the output stream. TCP also handles flow control to make sure a fast sender cannot swamp a slow receiver with more messages than it can handle.

Answer (b) IP works at the network layer. The functions it handles and methods it uses are as follows:

(a) For addressing, IP uses the logical network address.

(b) For switching purposes, it uses the packet-switching method.

(c) For route selection, it uses the dynamic method.

(d) For connection services, IP provides error control.

IP is a connectionless, datagram protocol. (IP packets are also referred to as IP datagrams.) IP uses packet switching and performs route selection by using dynamic routing tables that are referenced at each hop. The packets making up a message could be routed differently through the internetwork depending on the state of the network at each hop. For example, if a link were to go down or become congested, packets be sent through a different route.

Appended to each packet is an IP header, which includes source and destination information. IP uses sequence numbering if it is necessary to fragment a packet into smaller parts and reassemble it at its destination or at an intermediate point. IP performs error checking on the header information by way of a checksum.

IP addresses are unique, 4 byte addresses that must be assigned to every addressable device or node on the internetwork. (See Figure 2.15) In this figure you will notice that a big message is divided into smaller packets by the TCP. These are given a header and then enveloped by the IP to be sent to the addresses by various routes using the router. At the receiving end, each envelop is placed in order and the message is reassembled by the TCP and forwarded to the addressee.

Answer (c) *[Refer to Section 2.5.1]*

Answer (d) *[Refer to Section 2.5.2]*

Question Number 5 With the help of diagrams explain how a large print job must be sent from a computer to a print server.

Answer

1. First the sending computer establishes a connection with the print server. (See the following figure)
2. As shown below, the computer then breaks the large print job into packets with each packet containing the destination address, the source address, the data, ad control information.
3. The network adapter card in each computer examines the receiver's address on all frames sent on its segment of the network. However, because each network adapter card has its own specific address, the card does not interrupt the computer until it detects a frame addressed specifically to it.
4. At the destination computer, in this example it is the print server, the packets enter through the cable into the network adapter card.
5. The network software processes the frame stored in the network adapter card's receive buffer. Sufficient processing power to receive and examine each incoming frame is built into the network adapter card. This means that no computer resources are used until the adapter card identifies a frame addressed to the specific computer.
6. The network operating system in the receiving computer reassembles the packets back into the original text file and moves the file into the computers memory. From there it is sent to the printer.

Establishing a connection with a print server

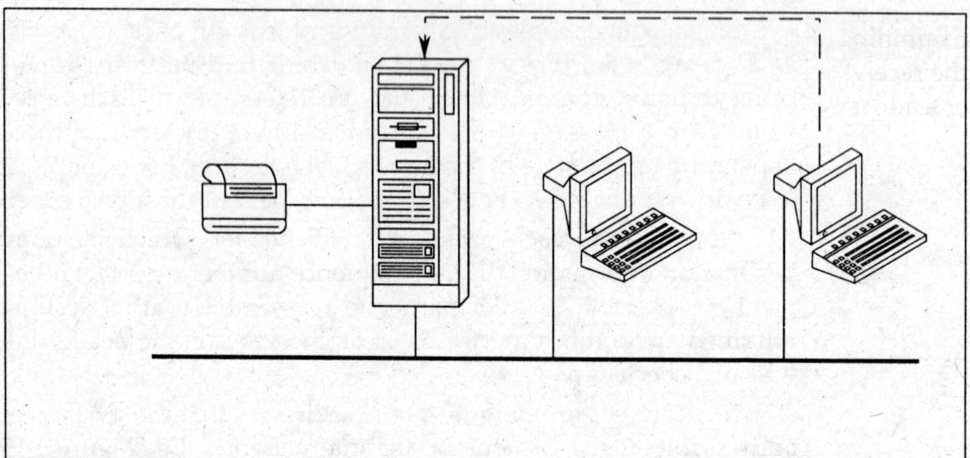

Creating packets

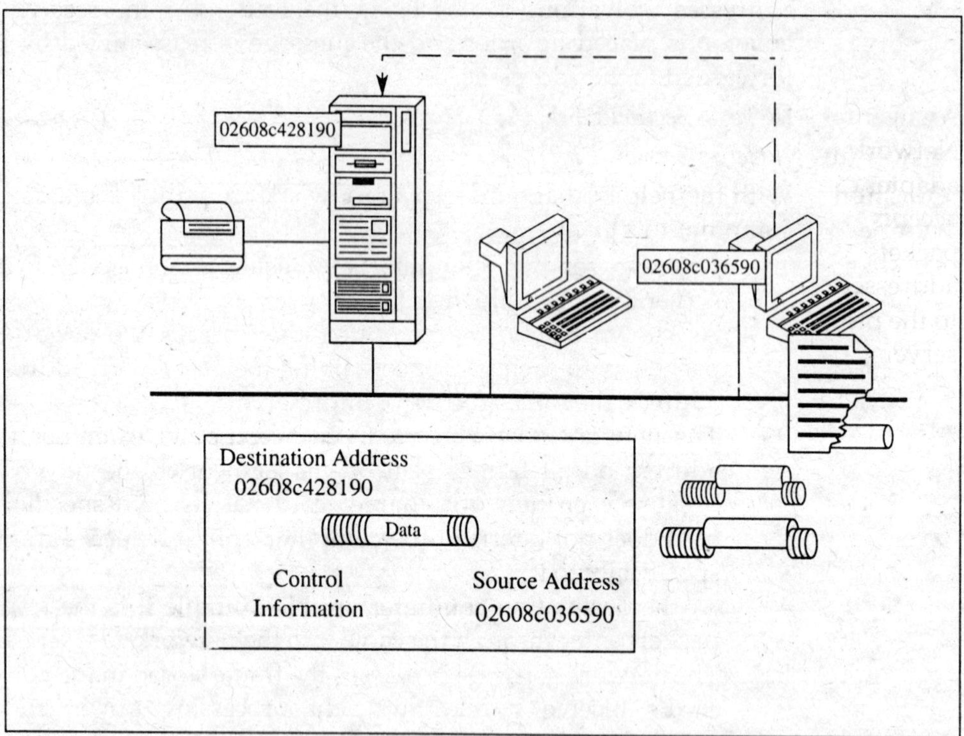

Examining the receiver's address

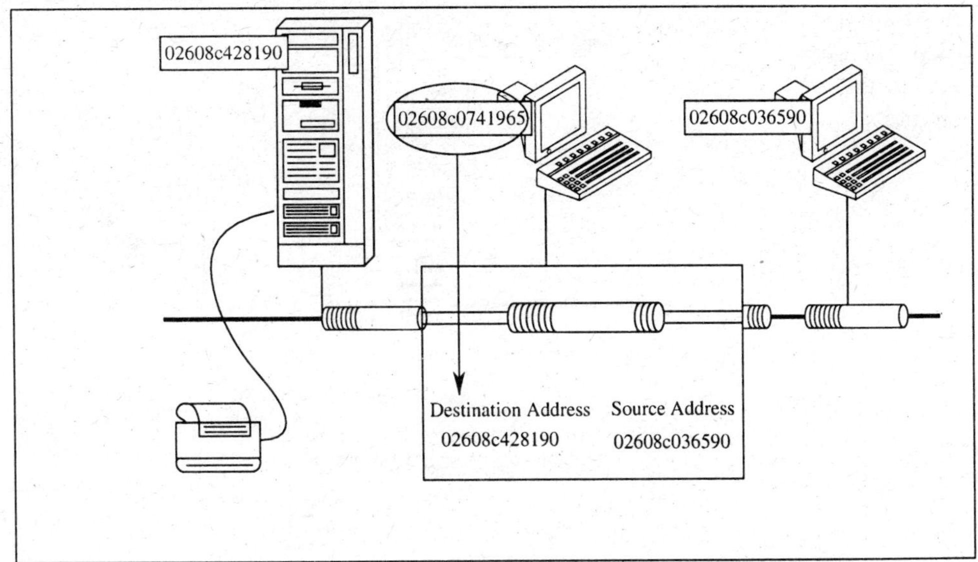

Network adapter card accepts packets addressed to the print server

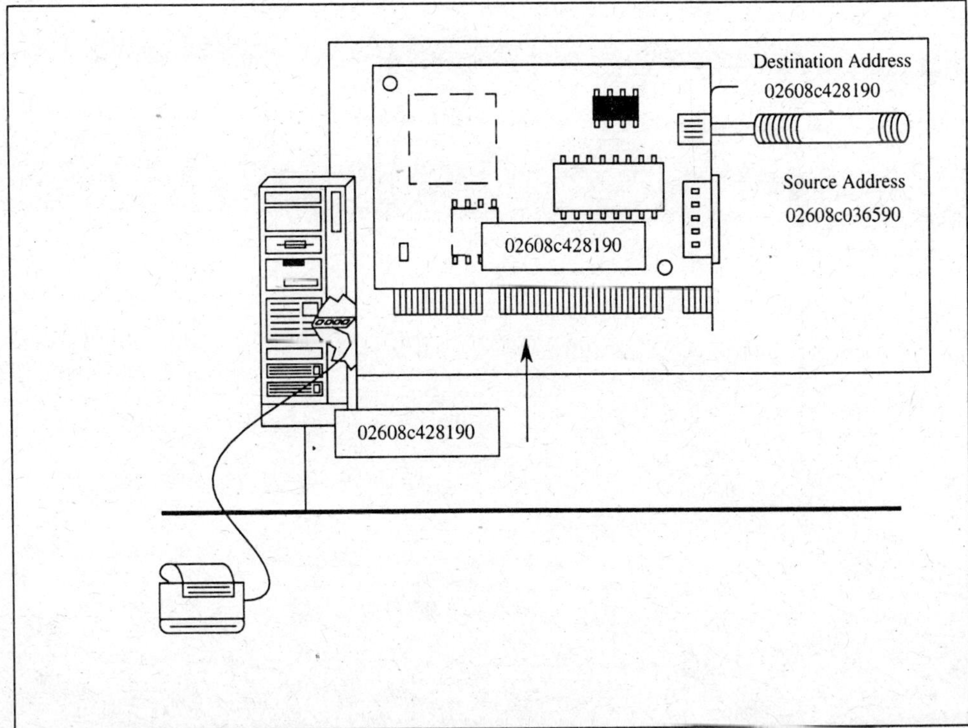

Reassembled packets sent to the printer

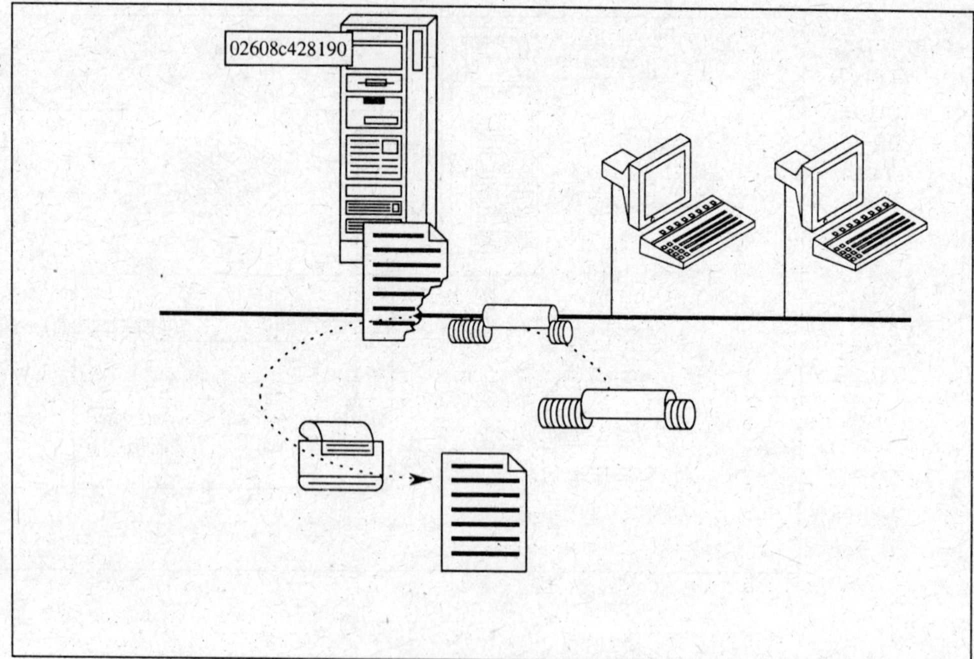

TEST PAPER

Time: 2 Hrs. Marks: 50

Note: Answer all questions.

1. Which of the OSI layers handles each of the following?
   (a) Breaking the transmitted packets into frames.
   (b) Determining which route through the network to use?
   (c) Providing synchronization.
2. Explain TCP/IP Model in detail with its critique analysis.
   [*GNDU, BIT Part–III, Paper–I, 2002 examination*]
3. Work done in the presentation layer of OSI model is performed in the application layer of TCP/IP model. Discuss.
4. Compare and contrast the OSI 7-layer model with TCP/IP model.
5. Write short notes on:
   (a) IP classes
   (b) IP datagram

CHAPTER 3

Digital Transmission Interfaces and Modems

3.1 INTRODUCTION

Since the time there had been a fall in the prices of PCs, computers have started playing an important role in the communication field. The main reason for this is that computers can send data extremely fast. They can even pass pictures, sound in a very secured manner. Further, PCs can send information on the existing telephone line. So, users do not have to spend any extra money except for the purchase of a PC machine and its connection to the telephone line using an instrument called *modem*.

3.2 TYPES OF DATA

3.2.1 Digital Data

You would have noticed on the hockey playground that the referee blows a whistle and all the players in the field understand the message instantaneously. The whistle is blown in short bursts of high pitched sound like PEE, PE, PE, PE or it may have a long burst PEEEEEEE. Both of these whistle calls convey different meaning to the players. The first one is an indication to the players to start the game. The second long whistle is to stop the match immediately. The message conveyed by the burst of these sound energy in short pulses is very clear

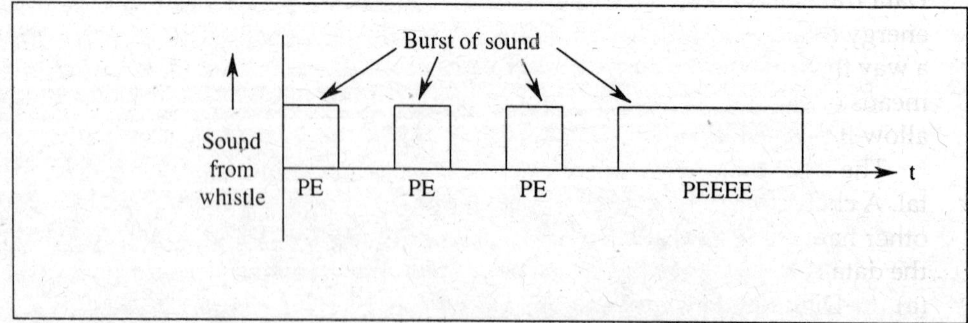

Figure 3.1 A sample of digital pulses of sound blown using a whistle

to all the players. There is no chance of any confusion even if the player is far away from the referee. This is an example of *Digital* data. Short burst of sound energy is sent by the sender to the receiver and the receiver is able to understand it clearly. This type of digital data are shown pictorially in Figure 3.1.

3.2.2 Analog Data

Let us take another situation. You are sitting in a concert hall where many musical instruments are being played by different players. Say one musician is playing *Sitar* and the other is playing *Tabla*. Both Sitar and Tabla are sending sound waves in the same sequence and there is a rhythm and harmony between the two. The harmony of sound coming out from these two instruments gives you the pleasure of listening. If there is any mismatch between the timing of the tune of Sitar and the Tabla, you get the unpleasantness and thus consider it a noise rather than music. This is an example of analog data. So long as the harmony is there, you enjoy listening to music. The moment there is some disturbance, say noise in the mike system, you feel disturbed.

A pictorial representation of analog signal or data is shown in Figure 3.2.

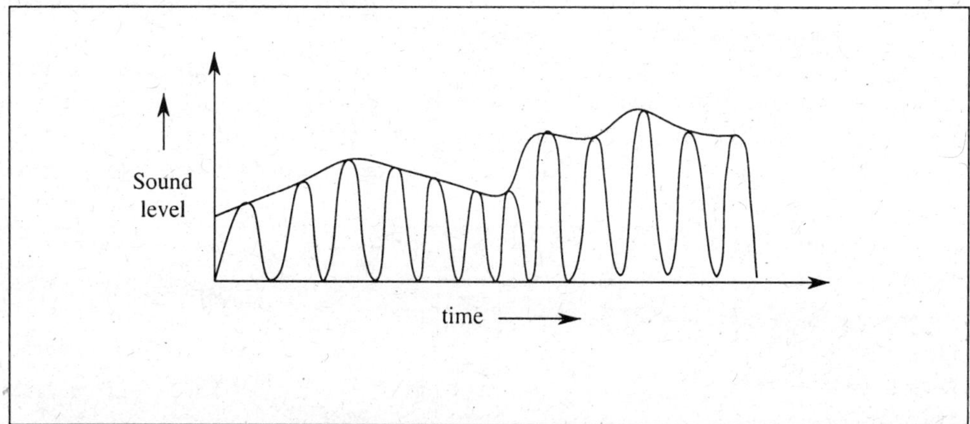

Figure 3.2
A sample of analog data

All music systems presently convey the songs in the analog form. Casettes are recorded using analog recording system and playing the music gives you the analog sound waves. However, Compact Disks are available these days that have recording in digital form.

3.3 DATA TRANSMISSION

Data transmission or signaling is the way data are sent across the medium. It uses electrical energy to communicate. Somehow, the data or the bits and bytes must be represented in such a way that the sender can create a message and the receiver can understand it. This is done by means of encoding (also called modulation). The original signal is altered in a certain way to allow it to represent data.

The information to be communicated can exist in either of the two forms: analog or digital. A characteristic of analog information is that it changes continuously. Digital data, on the other hand, consists of discrete states: On or Off, 1 or 0, and so on. The two methods to send the data correspond to the two types of methods namely:

(a) Digital data transmission
(b) Analog data transmission

Before we learn in details, the two different types of data transmissions, let us understand the differences between them.

3.3.1 Difference between Digital Data and Analog Data Transmission

In general, digital data transmission provides the following advantages over analog data transmission:

(a) Fewer errors from noise and interference
(b) Uses less expensive equipment

On the other hand, one disadvantage is that digital signals suffer from greater attenuation than analog signals over the same distance for the same transmission media because it needs larger bandwidth for transmission. In general, analog data transmission provides the following advantages:

(a) Less attenuation than digital signals over the same distance.
(b) Can be multiplexed to use bandwidth.

One disadvantage is that analog signals is that analog signals are more prone to errors from noise and interference.

Figure 3.3 shows pictorially the different kinds of digital and analog data transmission. The digital data transmission is known as baseband transmission because it needs the whole bandwidth of the channel to ensure proper flow of digital pulses through the medium. However, the same bandwidth can be utilised by three or more analog data channels using multiplexing techniques.

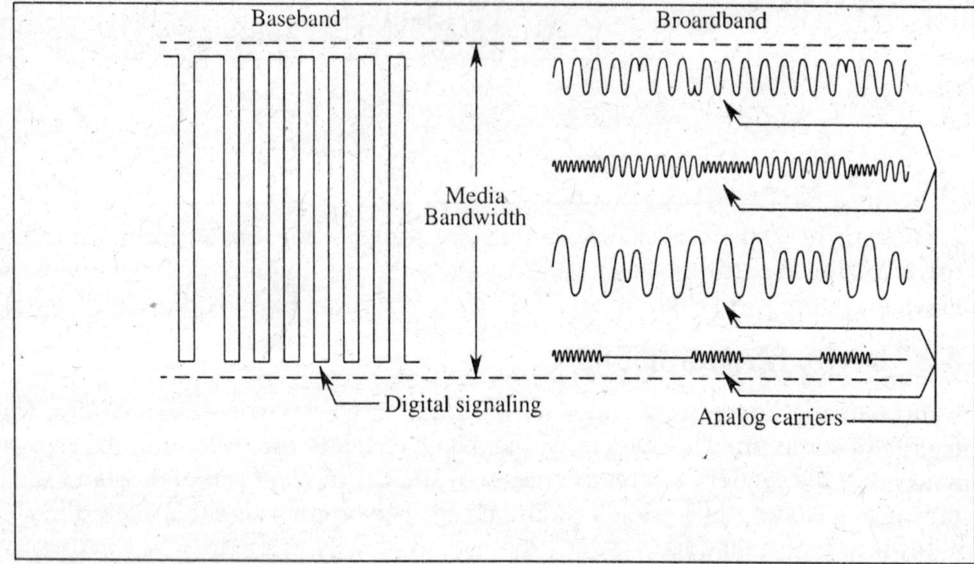

Figure 3.3 Digital and analog data transmission. Digital data transmission using baseband and analog data transmission using broadband

3.3.2 Digital Data Transmission

Because computers are inherently digital, most computer network use digital data transmission. There are different coding schemes for encoding data for transmission. Broadly we can classify them into two main encoding techniques namely:

(a) Current-state encoding
(b) State-transition encoding

Current-State Encoding

In this coding method, data are encoded by the presence or absence of a signal characteristic or state. For example, a voltage of +5 might represent a binary 0, while a voltage of -5 could represent a binary 1. The signal is monitored periodically by network devices in order to determine its current state. That state then indicates the data value encoded within it. The encoding schemes that use current-state encoding are:

(a) Unipolar signal
(b) Polar signal

Unipolar signal

When all the signal elements have the same algebraic sign, i.e. all positive or negative, then signal is unipolar.

Polar signal

In polar signaling, one logic state is represented by a positive voltage level and the other by a negative voltage level.

State-Transition Encoding

State transition encoding methods differ from current-state encoding in that they use transitions in the signal to represent data, as opposed to encoding data by means of a particular voltage level or state. For example, a transition occurring from high to low voltage could represent a 1 while a transition from low to high voltage could represent a 0.
Most common methods of State transition coding are further explained.

(a) Non Return to Zero (NRZ)
(b) Non Return to Zero-Level (NRZL)
(c) Non Return to Zero-Invert (NRZI)

Non Return to Zero (NRZ)

The most common, and easiest way to transmit digital signal is to use two different voltage levels for the two binary digits. Codes that follow this strategy share the property that the voltage level is constant during a bit interval; there is no transition (no return to a zero level).

Non Return to Zero-Level (NRZL)

In this method, 0 is represented by positive voltage (high level) whereas, 1 is represented by negative voltage (low level). This code is generally used to generate or interpret digital data by terminals and other devices. The maximum bit rate is twice the bandwidth.

Non Return to Zero-Invert (NRZI)

A variation of NRZ is known as NRZI. As with NRZ-L, NRZI maintains a constant voltage pulse for the duration of a bit time. The data themselves are encoded as the presence or absence of a signal transition at the beginning of the bit time. A transition (low-to-high or high-to-low) at the beginning of a bit time denotes a binary 1 for that bit time. If there is no transition, it is an indication of 0. In brief, Here, 0 is represented by no transition at the beginning of interval. 1 is represented by transition at beginning of the interval. NRZI is an example of differential encoding. In differential encoding, the signal is decoded by comparing the polarity of adjacent signal elements rather than determining the absolute value of a signal element. Because of their simplicity and relatively low frequency response characteristics, NRZ codes are commonly used for digital magnetic recording. But their limitation of DC components make these codes not useful for signal transmission applications. (See Figure 3.4)

Advantage and limitation of NRZ technique

The NRZ codes are the easiest to engineer and in addition, make an efficient use of bandwidth. The main limitations of NRZ signals are the presence of a DC component and the lack of synchronization capability. To picture the problem, consider a long string of 1s or 0s for NRZ-L, or a long string of 0s for NRZI. The output is a constant voltage over a long period of time. Under these circumstances, an drift between the timing of transmitter and receiver will result in a loss of synchronization between the two.

☞ The main benefit of differential encoding is that it may be possible to detect a transition in the presence of noise than to compare a value to a threshold.

Figure 3.4
Digital Signal encoding formats

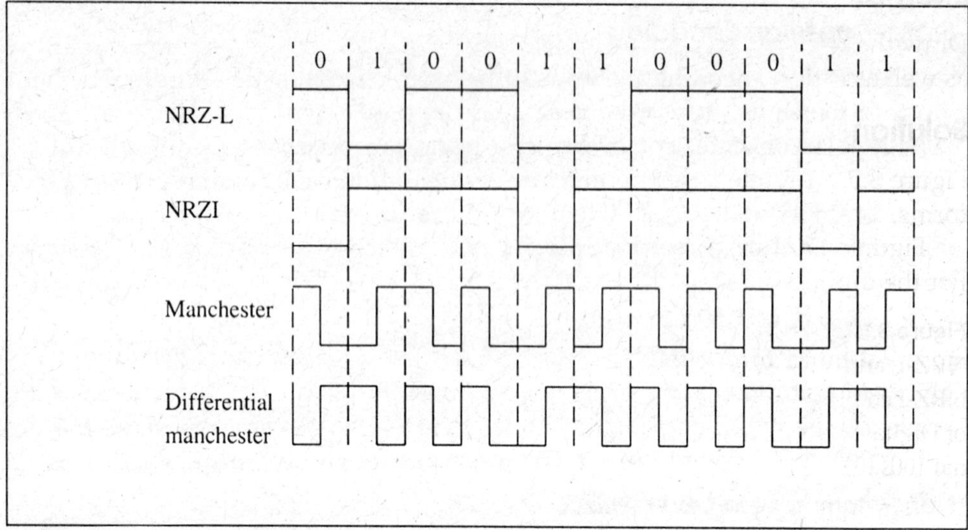

Biphase coding

Under this coding techniques, the two types are:

(a) Manchester Code
(b) Differential Manchester Code

Manchester Code

In the Manchester code, there is a transition at the middle of each bit period. The mid-bit transition serves as a clocking mechanism and also as data. A low-to-high transition represents a 1, and high-to-low transition represents a 0. The Manchester coding require at least one transition per bit time and may have as many as two transitions. Thus, the maximum modulation rate is twice that for NRZ. This means that the bandwidth required is correspondingly greater. The main advantages of Manchester coding are:

(a) **Synchronization:** Because there is a predictable transition during each bit time, the receiver can synchronize on that transition. Hence, it is also known as self-clocking code.

(b) **No DC Component:** This type of coding does not have DC component.

(c) **Error Detection:** The absence of an expected change in the voltage i.e. transition can be made use of to detect an error. Noise on the line would have to invert both the signal before and after the expected transition to cause an undetected error.

Differential Manchester Code

In differential Manchester, the mid-bit transition is used only to provide clocking. The encoding of a 0 is represented by the presence of a transition at the beginning of a bit period, and a 1 is represented by the absence of a transition at the beginning of a bit period. Differential Manchester has the added advantage of employing differential encoding. (See Figure 3.4).

Example 3.1

Draw the representation of digital signal 1001101 for NRZ-L, NRZ-I, and Manchester coding as well as for Differential Manchester coding waveforms.

Solution

Figure 3.5 (a) gives the representation of the digital signal 1001101 in the NRZ-L and NRZ-I forms.

Figure 3.5(b) gives the representation of Manchester and Differential Manchester coding. For the digital signal 1001101.

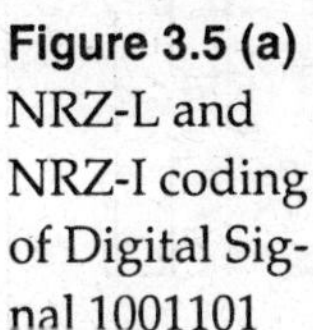

Figure 3.5 (a) NRZ-L and NRZ-I coding of Digital Signal 1001101

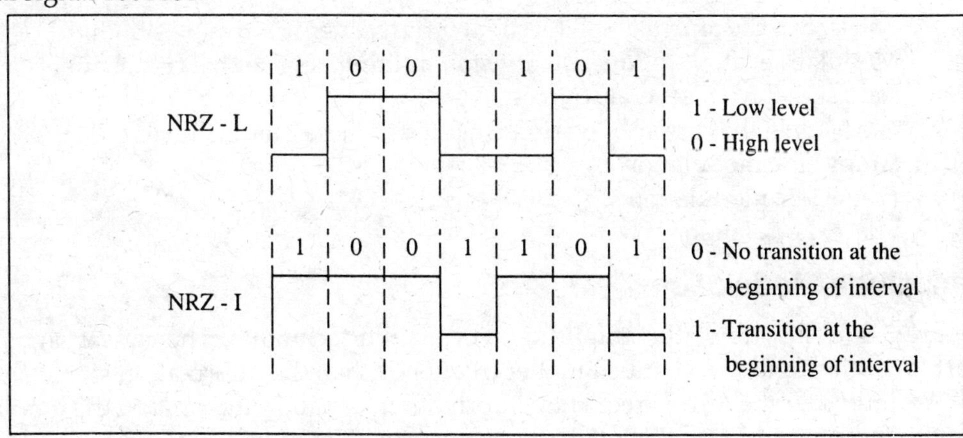

3.3.3 Analog Data Transmission

In order to understand Analog data transmission, we need to first learn about the three methods of modulation. 'To Modulate' is to mix a data signal onto a carrier and modify its characteristics for transmission in a communications network. A carrier is a electromagnetic wave that vibrates at a fixed frequency.

Figure 3.5 (b) Manchester and Differential Manchester coding of Digital Signal 1001101

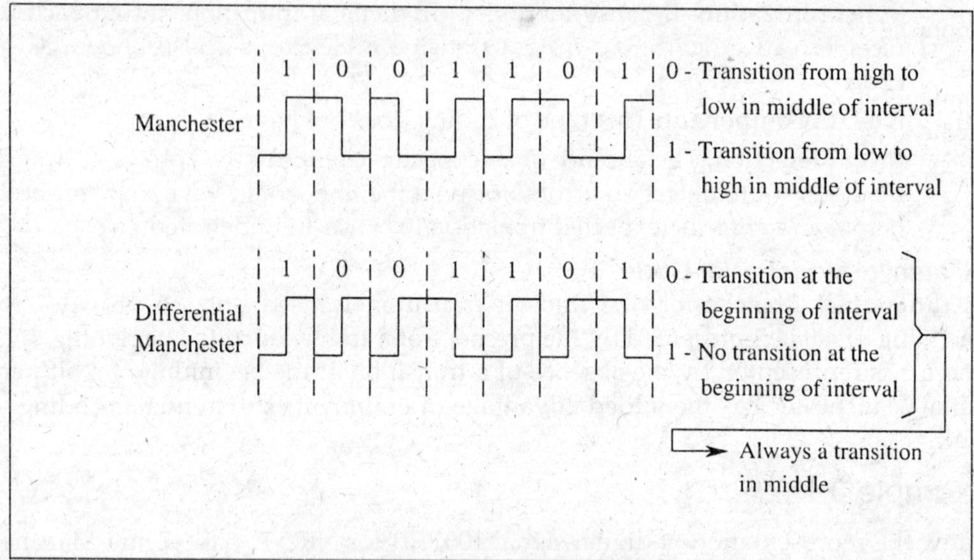

Why to Modulate

When only analog transmission facilities are available, modulation is required to convert the digital data to along form. If the data is already in the analog form then the reason for modulating the voice signal is :

(a) A high frequency wave used as a carrier will be able to carry larger energy and will cause effective transmission.

(b) The size of the antenna will be small if the carrier frequency is high.

(c) Modulation allows frequency division multiplexing so that one channel can be used to send signal from several sources.

Data modulate the carrier by various methods. These methods are:

(a) Amplitude modulation

(b) Frequency modulation

(c) Phase modulation

Amplitude Modulation

Figure 3.6 (a) illustrates the amplitude modulation technique. The carrier signal as seen in part (a) of this figure has a much higher frequency than the information signal shown in part (b). By imposing the lower frequency information signal on the carrier, the amplitude of the resulting compound signal is made to vary in the form of information signal. Part (c) of the figure shows the resulting modulated signal. Songs transmitted via Akashvani on medium wave and shortwave in India are examples of amplitude modulation.

Advantages

(a) Amplitude modulation is easy to implement.

(b) It can be used both for analog and digital signal.

Figure 3.6 (a) Generation of amplitude modulated signal

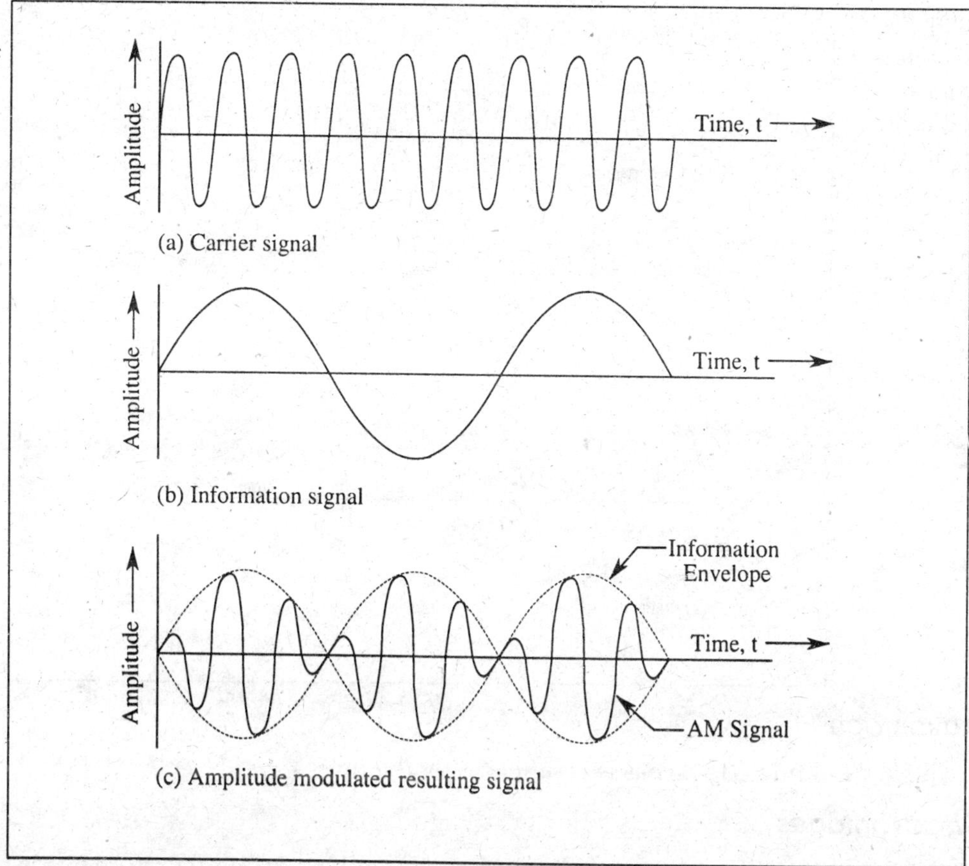

Disadvantages

(a) It is affected by the noise signal that may add up with the information signal. Electrical noise causes this problem.

(b) As the strength of the signal decreases in a channel with distance traveled, it reaches a minimum level unacceptable for adequate communications. Before signal strength goes down to this extent, it must be amplified. But amplifiers add noise and adversely affect the characteristics of the information signal.

Frequency Modulation

Figure 3.6 (b) illustrates the principle of Frequency Modulation. An FM signal has a constant amplitude but varies in frequency over time to convey information. Part (a) and (b) of this figure show that the carrier has a frequency much higher than the information signal it has to transport. After imposing the lower frequency information signal of the carrier, the frequency of the resulting compound signal varies to match the form of the information signal. Part (c) of this figure shows the resulting modulated signal.

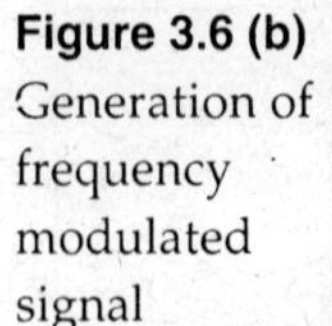

Figure 3.6 (b) Generation of frequency modulated signal

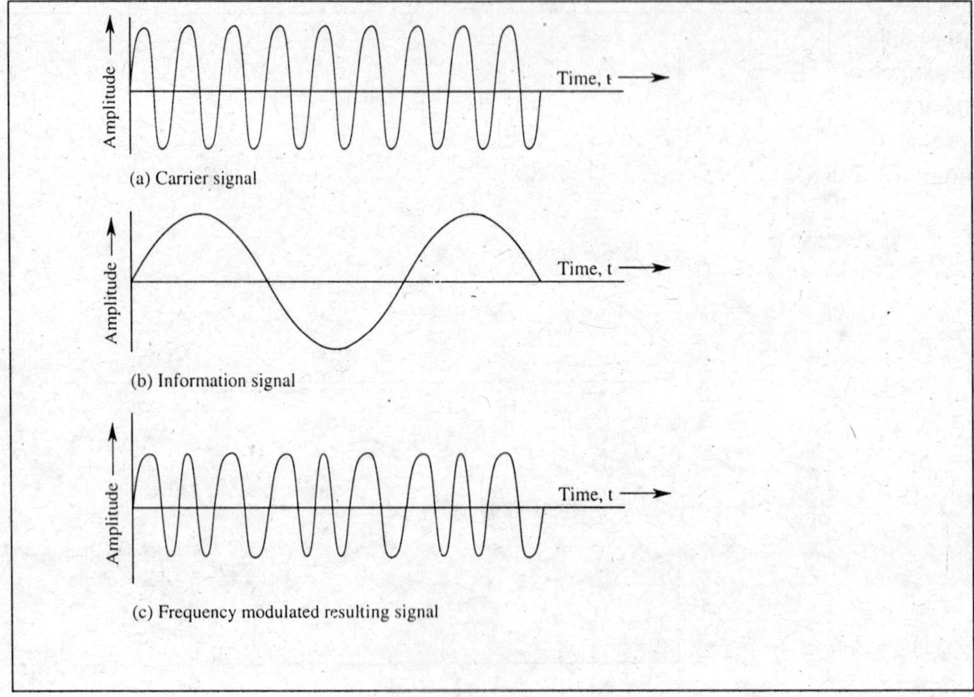

Advantage

Frequency modulated wave is least affected by the noise due to electrical disturbance.

Disadvantages

(a) Frequency signal has a wide spectrum of frequencies and therefore needs much higher bandwidth than amplitude modulation.

(b) The number of FM signals one can transmit over a channel with a fixed total bandwidth is smaller than the number of AM signals one can transmit through the same medium.

Phase Modulation

Phase modulation uses at least two analog signals. The first signal is a carrier, and the other signals modify the carrier signal to convey information. In Phase modulation, the shape of the carrier's signal curve is made to change at given points in time. Figure 3.7 shows the process of phase modulation. Both signals are sine waves that have the same fixed frequency and amplitude. They are however offset from each other. The two cross the amplitude reference line at different times. Therefore, they have different phase.

The difference in phase between the two sine waves is a phase angle. As seen in the above figure, the two signals are offset by one-half cycle or 180 degrees out of phase. The resulting compound phase modulated signal is shown in Figure 3.8.

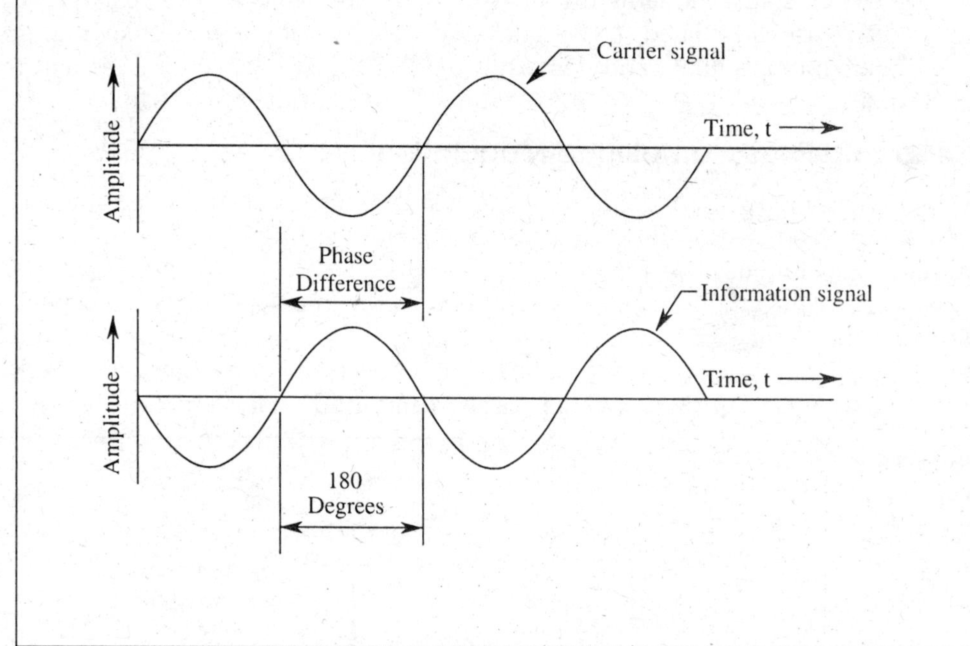

Figure 3.7 Carrier and information signals 180 degrees different in phase

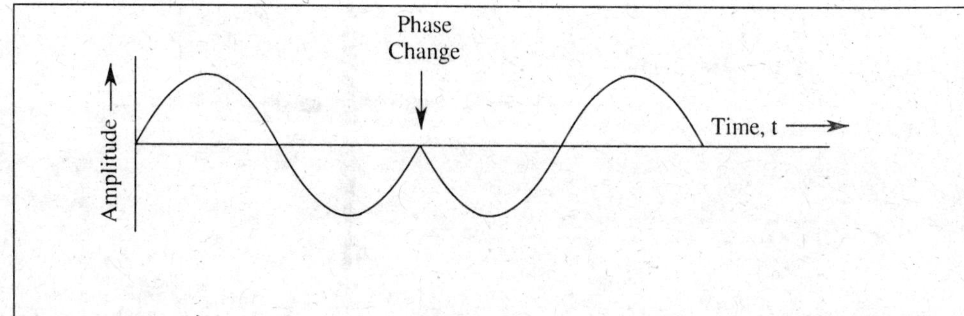

Figure 3.8 Phase modulated signal

Advantages

Phase modulation provides the signal modulation that allows computers to communicate at higher data rates through telephone system.

Disadvantages

Phase modulation requires two signals with a phase difference between them. A reference pattern and a signal pattern are both required.

Uses

(a) This technique is used to convey colour information in colour television broadcasts.

(b) Medium speed modems use Phase Modulation techniques to convert digital signals into phase modulated (PM) signals. This process of phase shift keying (PSK) allows a modem to modulate and demodulate a PM signal between phases that represent the digital signals it receives from or transmit to a computer or terminal.

Combining Phase-amplitude Modulation

By combining modulation techniques, you can develop greater throughput in a given channel than its band width allows for a single technique. The most popular combination of modulation techniques is AM and PM.

By altering the amplitude of a carrier and creating a phase difference between the carrier and the information signal, we can get the quadrature amplitude modulation (QAM). With this technology, higher data rates can be obtained using computers on telephone system. Figure 3.9 shows the QAM signal that has two amplitude states and four phase shift.

Figure 3.9 Quadrature amplitude modulated (QAM) Signal

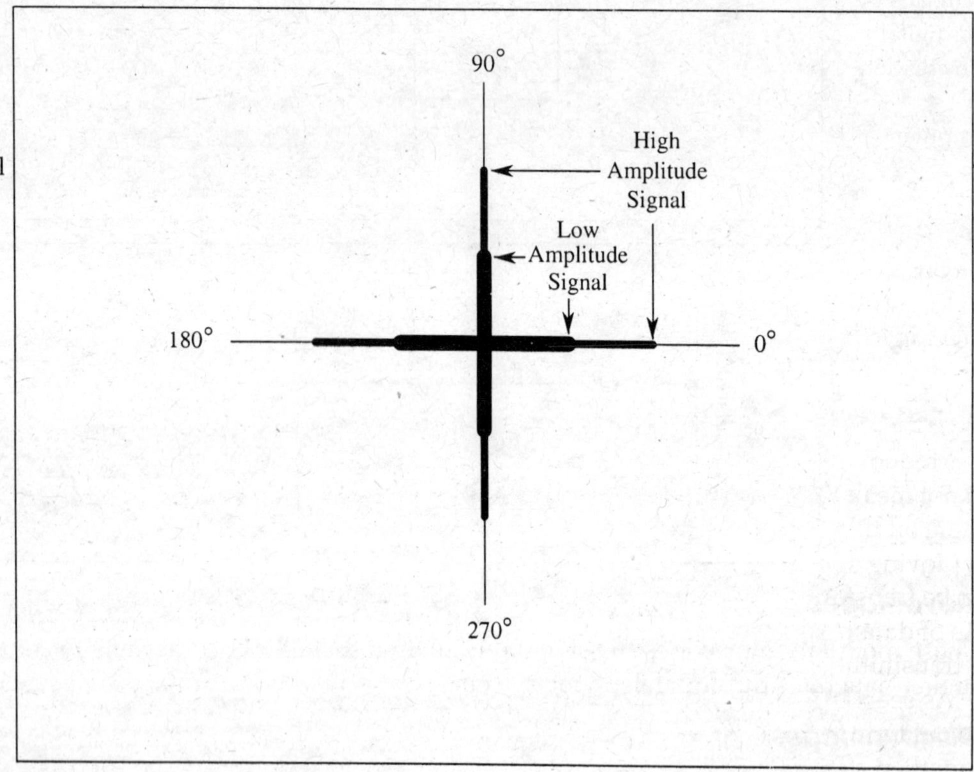

Advantages

This method provides high data rates.

3.4 DIGITAL TO ANALOG CONVERSION

If we want to send digital data over the telephone lines then we need to convert the pulses to an analog form so that they can be carried by the telephone lines efficiently. Modem is a device which performs the modulation/demodulation of digital data to analog form and vice versa. Modems convert communications signals from a form the computer can understand to a form the phone system can convey and vice versa. Modulation is the process of converting a digital signal from a computer into an analog signal the telephone system will accept. When you pick up the phone while your computer modem is communicating, or while you are sending a fax from you fax machine, you hear the sound of digital information that has been converted to analog signals. At the other end of the connections, whether it be across town or across the world, another modem interprets those analog signals the telephone system has conveyed and converts them back into digital form so the receiving computer can understand them. A modem can be installed internally, in the computer, in which case it is called an internal modem, or it can be an external device that is connected to the computer with a serial cable. Figure 3.10 shows the example of computers communicating via modems.

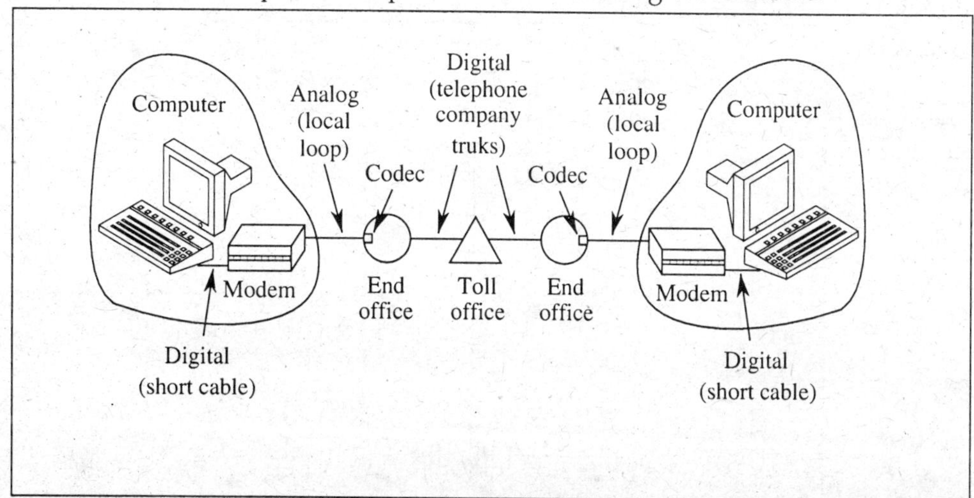

Figure 3.10 Using analog and digital transmission for a computer call

Modems speed is often discussed in baud rates or Bps, which are similar terms, but they do not mean exactly the same. Baud rate refers to the oscillations of a sound wave on which a single bit of data is carried. Bits per second is the amount of data transferred in a second. By employing special techniques that manipulate analog signals so that more than 1 bit of data can be transferred in a single cycle of the signal, a modem can encode data and achieve higher rate of data transfer. A modem that is modulating its sound waves at 9600 baud may actually be transmitting 28,800 Bits per second.

As seen in Figure 3.10, when a computer wishes to send digital data over a dial-up line, the data must first be converted to analog form by a modem for transmission over the local loop, then converted to digital form for transmission over the long-haul trunks, then back to analog over the local loop at the receiving end, and finally back to digital form by another modem for storage in the destination computer.

The digital data can also be modulated to one of the following types:

(a) Analog Modulation
(b) Frequency Modulation
(c) Phase Modulation

As seen in Figure 3.11, the digital pulses are converted to amplitude modulation in Part (b) of this figure. Where the pulse is 1, the analog signal is present and when the pulse is 0, the analog signal is absent. In Part (c) of this figure, when the pulse is 1, the frquency of the analog signal is high and when the pulse is 0, the frequency of analog signal is low. This is the modulation of digital pulse into frquency modulation. As the frquency is changing, the technique is also called frquency shift keying (FSK)

In Part (d) of this figure, the phase modulation of digital data is shown. Here the phase is changing proportional to the level of the pulses and the way the variation of the pulse amplitude is changing. As the phase is changing, the method is also known as Phase shift keying (PSK) If we combine the phase with the amplitude, then the method is called QAM (quadrature amplitude modulation).

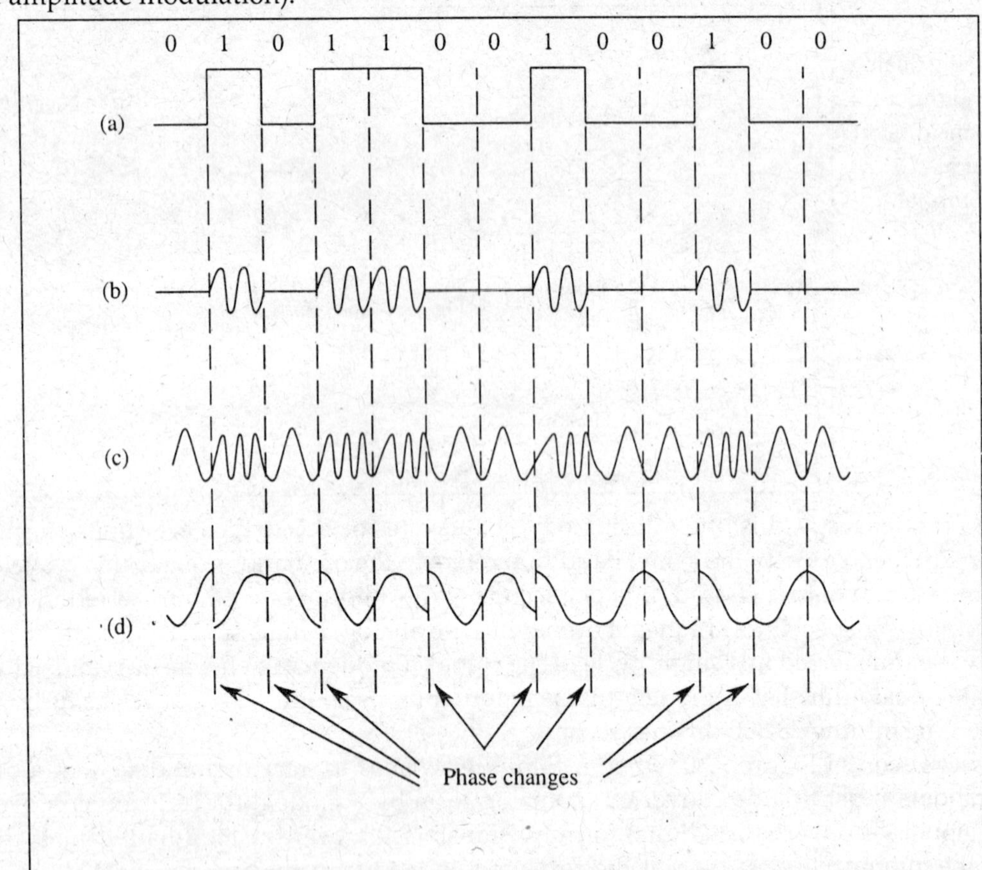

Figure 3.11 Different modulation techniques (a) Digital data (b) AM (c) FM (d) PM

Comparison of FSK, PSK and QAM

As seen in Figure 3.12, QAM can convey eight times more information during a given period than a signal that just used FSK (Frequency shift Keying) and PSK (Phase Shift Keying) techniques. The part (a) of this figure shows changes in the signal frequency at the data bits vary

Figure 3.12 Comparision of FSK, PSK and QAM signals

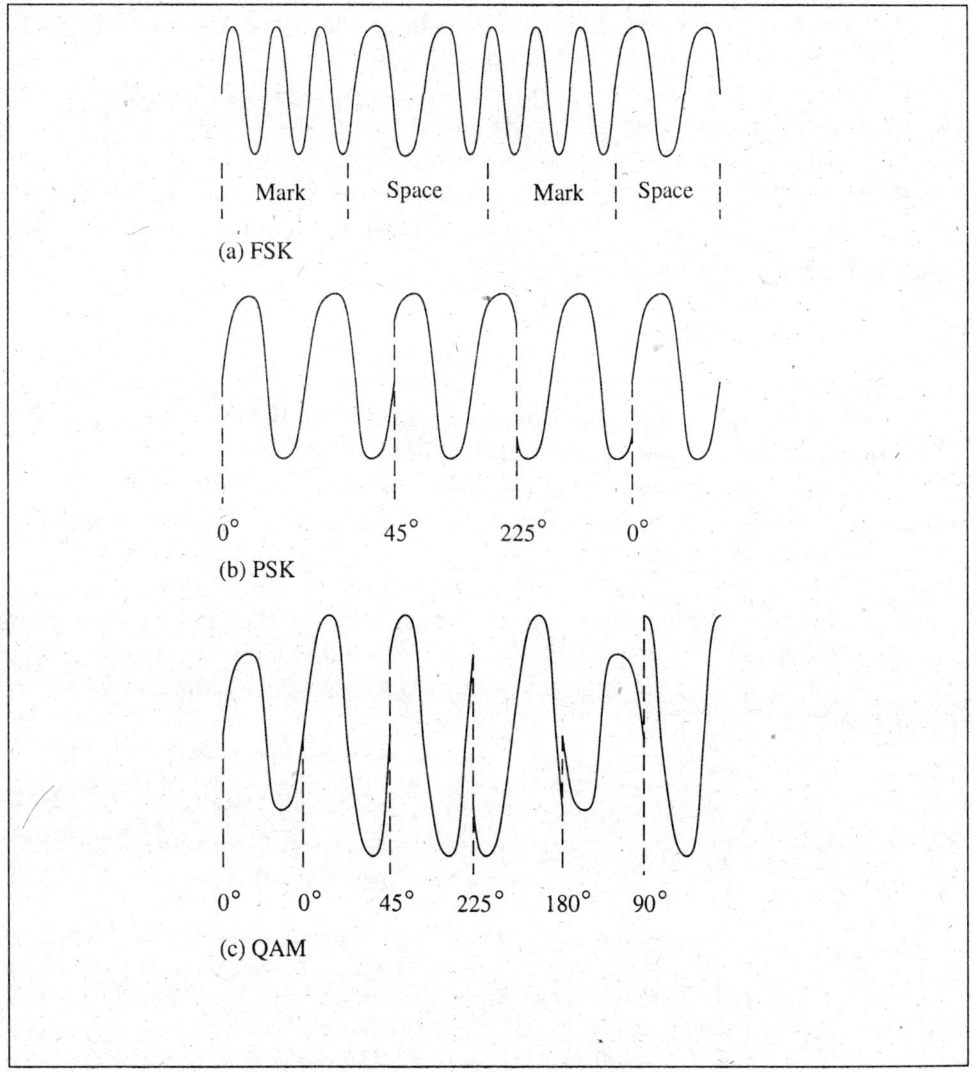

between mark and space states. Phase shift keying (PSK) signal in Part (b) of this figure shows variation in phase caused by the modulating symbol information. In part (c) QAM signal shows changes in both phase and amplitude. In this diagram, the changes are shown to the minimum values to avoid confusion.

Digital Signal Modulation Vs. Analog Signal Modulation

An analog signal varies through a range of energy values with time, a digital signal makes step changes between two or more discrete energy states.

☞ Analog signal modulation depends upon a carrier signal and an information signal that modulates the carrier signal. Digital modulation does not require the presence of an analog carrier.

The digital signal remains at a given voltage for a specified period to signal a binary or digital value. The signal modulates from one discrete value to another only when the information changes value. However, you may use a digital carrier signal with a digital information signal to increase the amplitude of the information. By modulating a strong digital signal to match the bit pattern of a weaker information signal, the resulting high-amplitude digital signal has enough strength to go for a longer distance than the original information signal. In this way, the information signal can travel farther, even if the channel is noisy.

3.5 INTERFACES AND MODEMS

3.5.1 DTC-DCE Interface

A standard or mechanism for transferring data from one device to another is called an interface. An interface specifies the nature of the boundary between two devices and determines the procedures and protocols that make it possible for the devices to exchange data.

The two main types of networking and communication interfaces are:

(a) *Serial interfaces,* which transfer data one bit at a time. The most common serial interface is the RS-232 interface.

(a) *Parallel interfaces,* which transfer data several bits at a time, usually one or more bytes at a time. The most common parallel interface is the one used for connecting printers to computers, which uses a female DB-25 or 36-pin Centronics connector.

Table 3.1 Serial Interfaces for Networking

Serial Interface	Description
RS-232	A common interface for communication over unbalanced lines. Uses DB-9 or DB-25 connectors.
RS-422/485	For communication over balanced lines. More suitable than RS-232 for environments with significant electromagnetic interference (EMI) or with DB-9 or DB-37 connectors.
V.35	A high-speed serial interface for data transmission at 48 Kbps. Combines balanced lines with unbalanced lines and is used in Integrated Services Digital Network (ISDN) and frame relay connections. Uses a 24-pin block connector.
X.21	A high-speed serial interface that uses the International Telecommunication Union (ITU) standard for connecting DCE and DTE for synchronous communication. Uses a DB-15 connector.

Table 3.1 shows some common examples of serial interfaces used in networking. Serial interfaces are commonly used for connecting data terminal equipment (DTE), such as computers or routers, to data communications equipment (DCE), such as modems or CSU/DSUs (Channel Service Unit/Data Service Units).

☞ The type of interface a device uses is related to the kind of connector or cable used to connect to the device, but not in a one-to-one fashion. For example, you could say that a device has an RS-232 serial interface, but it is incorrect to say that you use an RS-232 connector or an RS-232 cable to connect to that device. RS-232 specifies the interface, but several cabling options can support it, such as a cable terminated with a DB-9 or a DB-25 male connector.

RS232-C/EIA 232-D INTERFACE

In an attempt to ensure that one serial device will talk to another, the Electronics Industries Association (EIA) created a standard to define the electrical signaling and cable connection characteristics of a serial port. In 1969, the EIA established Recommended Standard (RS) number 232 in Version C, or RS-232C, the most common type of communications circuit in use today.

☞ The ASCII character set defines what numbers to use for each character, and the RS-232C standard defines a way to move the data over a communications link. RS-232C can also be used to transmit EBCDIC data.

The RS-232C defines two classes of serial connections. These are:

(a) For terminals or DTE (Data Terminal Equipment)

(b) For communication equipment or DCE (Data Communications Equipment)

A DTE device usually connects to a DCE device. For example, a personal computer (DTE) can connect to a modem (DCE). The serial port on most personal computers is configured as a DTE port.

An RS-232C connection normally uses a 25-pin D-shell connector with a male plug on the DTE end and a female plug on the DCE end. Figure 3.14 shows a typical RS 232C female connector.

An RS-232C serial connection consists of several independent circuits sharing the same cable and connector. There are two data circuits (send and receive), and there are several control circuits, called handshaking lines, which control the flow of data between the terminal and the host.

Figure 3.15 shows the circuits of the RS-232C. The electrical specification for RS-232C is that a voltage more negative than -3 volts is a binary 1 and a voltage more positive than +4 volts is a binary 0. Data rates up to 20 kbps are permitted, as are cables up to 15 meters.

The functional specification tells which circuits are connected to each of the 25 pins, and what they mean. Figure 3.15 shows 9 pins that are nearly always implemented. The remaining ones are frequently omitted.

The most important part of the RS-232C interface is the data path. There are two circuits in the data path: one from the DTE (Data Terminal Equipment) to the DCE (Data Communications Equipment) and another from the DCE back to the DTE. In the above figure, the terminal sends data to the host computer on pin 2 of the cable and receives data from the host on pin 3. Pin 7 serves as the ground connection for both circuits.

☞ If two computers must be connected using RS-232C, then there is an interface problem. This problem is solved by connecting them with a device called a null modem. The null modem connects the transmit line of one machine to the receive line of the other. It also crosses some of the other lines in a similar way.

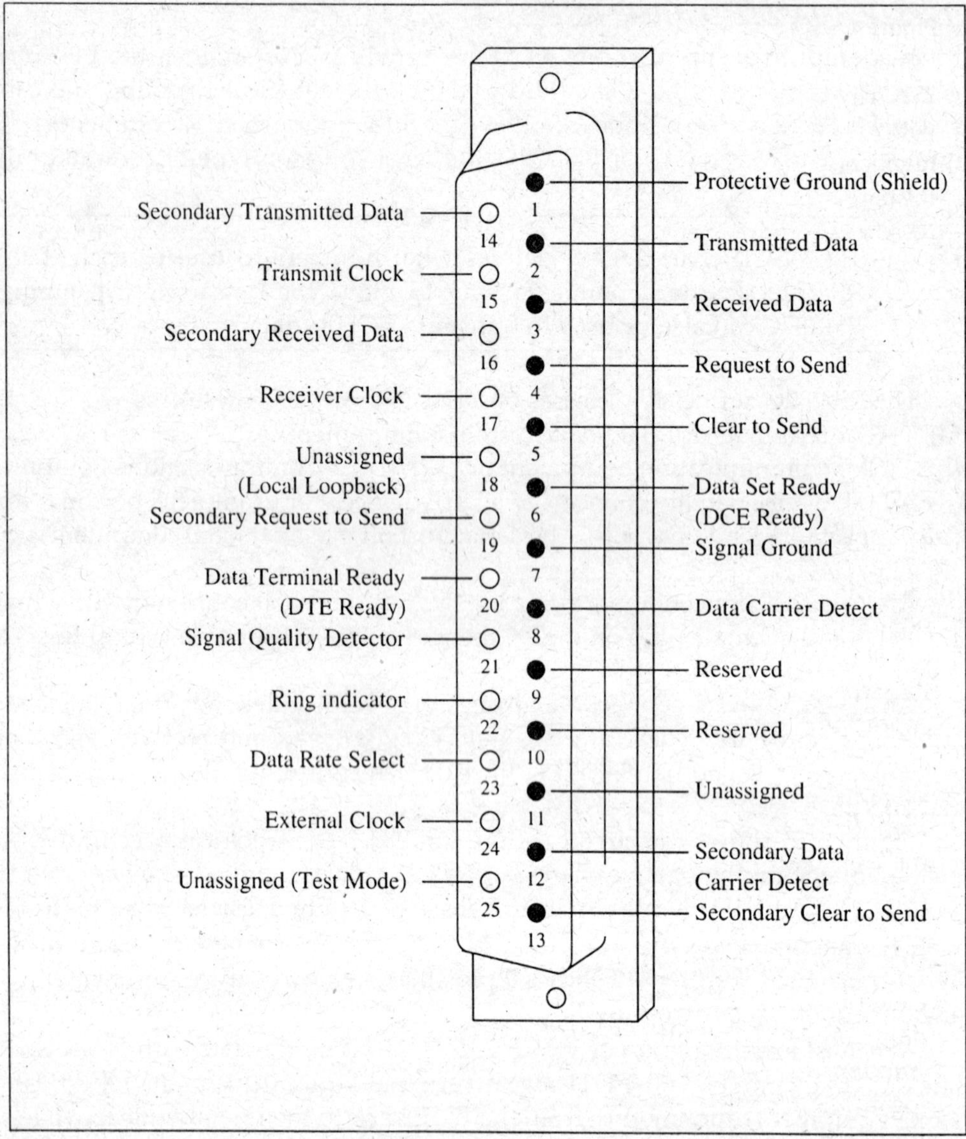

Figure 3.14 A typical RS 232 D additio n/changes to RS 232C indi- cated in parentheses

RS-232C has been in use for the past few years. Gradually, the limitations of the data rate to not more than 20 kbps and the 15-meter maximum cable length have caused lot of dissatisfaction among users. The new standard, called RS 449 is actually three standards in one. The mechanical, functional and procedural interfaces are given in RS 449. However, the electrical interface is given by two different standards. The first of these, RS-423-A, is similar to RS-232C in that all its circuits share a common ground. This technique is called unbalanced transmission, in which each of the main circuits requires two wires, with no common ground. As a result, RS-423-A can be used at speeds up to 2 Mbps over 60 meter cables.

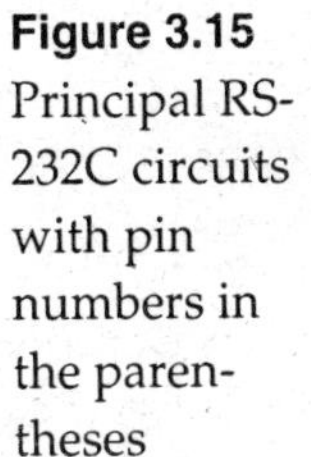

Figure 3.15 Principal RS-232C circuits with pin numbers in the parentheses

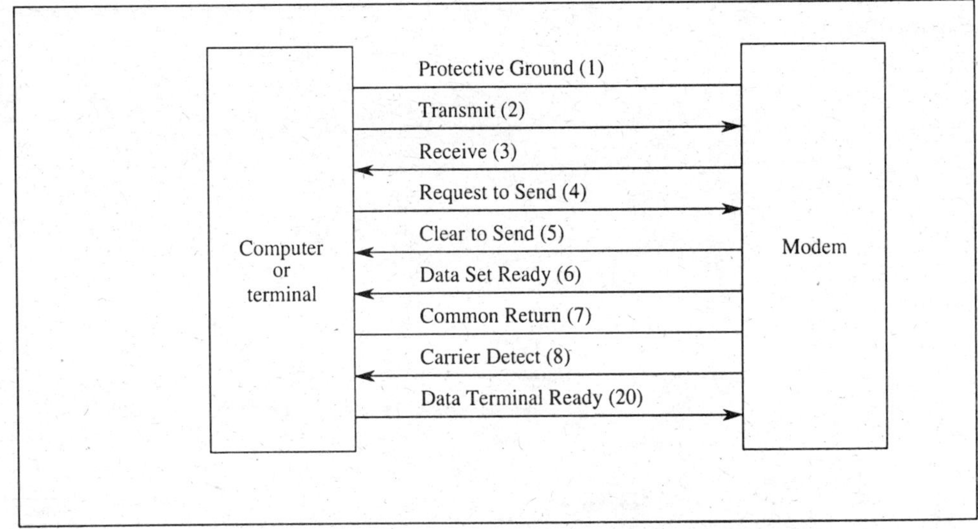

Although the RS-232 standard defines the procedures for automatic answering by the modem and for reversing the transmission direction in half-duplex communications, it does not define automatic dialing. This is covered in EIA Standard RS-366.

The basic units of a low-speed data communications system are illustrated in Figure 3.16. Regardless of the original source of information, it is eventually presented to the communications network as a parallel binary word usually of either 8 bits (byte), 16 bits (referred to as a half-word or 32 bits (or word) depending on the system used. The deciding factor on the size of the parallel data are the size of the data bus employed by the Data Terminal Equipment (DTE) that delivers the data. The functional block which receives the parallel data from the computer terminal that is to be sent eventually to the secondary station is the Universal Asynchronous Receiver Transmitter (UART.)

3.6 MODEMS

Generally, Modem is any type of data communications equipment (DCE) that enables digital data transmission over the analog Public Switched Telephone Network (PSTN). The term "modem" (which actually stands for "modulator/demodulator") is usually reserved for analog modems, which interface, through a serial transmission connection such as the RS-232 interface, with data terminal equipment (DTE) such as computers. The modem converts the digital signal coming from the computer into an analog signal that can be carried over a Plain Old Telephone Service (POTS) line. The term "digital modem" is sometimes used for ISDN terminal adapters, but this is something of a misnomer because no signal modulation actually takes place. Modems were developed in the 1960s by Bell Labs, which developed a series of standards called the Bell Standards. These standards defined modem technologies of up to a 9600-bps transmission speed. The Bell Standards have been superseded by the V series standards from the International Telecommunication Union (ITU), which defines standards of up to V.90 (which supports 56-Kbps downloads and 33.6-Kbps uploads). Modems generally have two interfaces:

Figure 3.16 Low speed data communication system

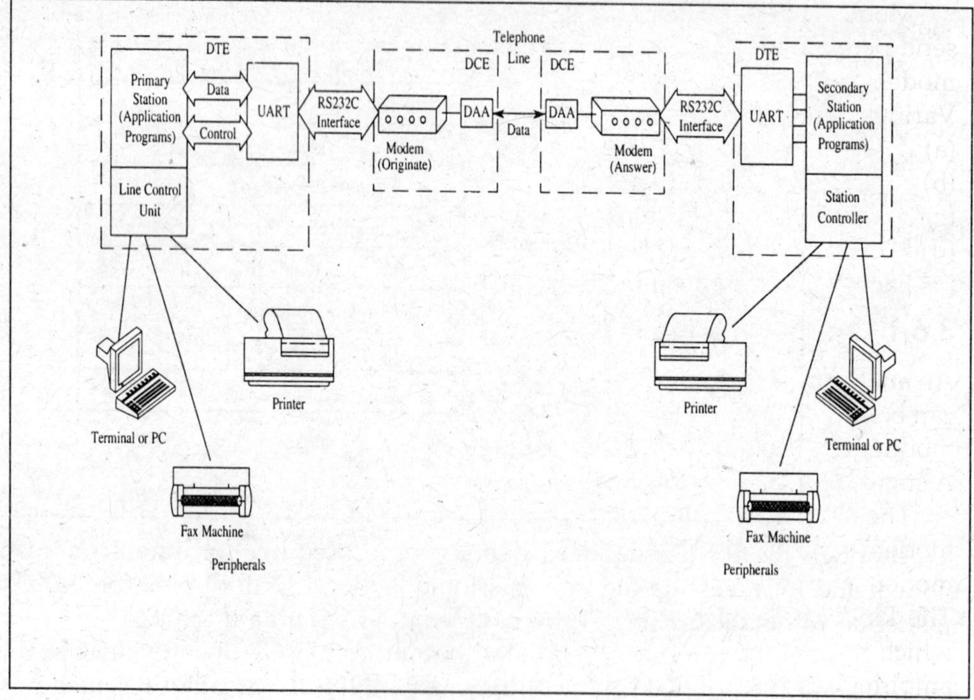

(a) An RS-232 serial transmission interface for connecting to the DTE, usually the computer.

(b) An RJ-11 telephone interface for connecting to the 4-wire PSTN telephone outlet in the local loop connection.

Modem are of the following types :

(a) ***Internal modems,*** which are installed as interface cards inside the computer and might use some of the machine's CPU processing power for functions such as encoding and data compression.

(b) ***External modems,*** which are generally more expensive and connect to the serial port on the computer using a DB9 or DB25 connector. External modems are useful when several users need to share a modem.

(c) ***PCMCIA modems,*** which are credit-card-sized modems for laptop computers used by mobile workers.

(d) ***Voice/data/fax modems,*** which can be used for file transfer, sending and receiving faxes, and voice mail using associated software.

☞ Modem are the devices that enables computers, FAX machines, and other equipment to communicate with each other across telephone lines or over cable television network cables. In the strictest sense, a modem is a device that converts between analog signals, such as sound waves, and digital signals, which are used by computers. However, the term has also come to include devices that permit the transmission of entirely digital signals.

Modems transmit data at different speeds, measured by the number of bits of data they send per second (bps). A 28.8 Kbps modem sends data at 28,800 bits per second. A 56 Kbps modem is twice as fast, sending and receiving data at a rate of 56,000 bits per second.
Various types of modes are:
(a) Analog Modem
(b) Digital Modem
(c) Asynchronous
(d) Synchronous

Each of them are further described below.

3.6.1 Analog Modem

An analog modem converts the digital signals of the sending computer to analog signals that can be transmitted through telephone lines. When the signal reaches its destination, another modem reconstructs the original digital signal, which is processed by the receiving computer. A standard analog modem has a maximum speed of 33.6 Kbps.

The word modem is an acronym formed from the two basic functions of an analog modem: modulation and demodulation. To convert a digital signal to an analog one, the modem generates a carrier wave and modulates, or adjusts, it according to the digital signal. The kind of modulation used depends on the application and the speed of operation for which the modem is designed. For example, many high-speed modems use a combination of amplitude modulation, in which the amplitude (see Wave Motion) of the carrier wave is changed to encode the digital information, and phase modulation, in which the phase of the carrier wave is changed to encode the digital information. The process of receiving the analog signal and converting it back to a digital signal is called demodulation.

3.6.2 Digital Modem

Any type of modem used for synchronous transmission of data over circuit-switched digital lines. One example of a digital modem is an ISDN terminal adapter. Digital modems are not used for changing analog signals into digital signals because they operate on end-to-end digital services. Instead, they use advanced digital modulation techniques for changing data frames from a network into a format suitable for transmission over a digital line such as an Integrated Services Digital Network (ISDN) line. They are basically data framing devices, rather than signal modulators.

☞ ISDN requires a special phone line from the MTNL in INDIA. This phone line is not an analog phone line. It is a digital connection to the telephone company or telephone exchange in the case of MTNL . This line can carry more information than the regular telephone line, any where between 56- or 64 Kbps for single-channel. Digital modems can communicate only on ISDN lines or on digital lines.

3.6.3 Asynchronous Modems

Asynchronous modems were developed specifically for use with telephone lines, and they are the most common type of modem. Almost any modem you purchase in a computer store will be an asynchronous modem.

Asynchronous Data Transfer

When your computer sends data to another computer using an asynchronous modem connection, the data are first divided into bytes. The bytes are sent 1 bit at a time (serially), and the byte is preceded by a start bit and followed by a stop bit.

The computers do not coordinate in terms of when data will be sent. The receiving computer uses the start and stop bits to recognized when it has an entire byte of data. The start and stop bits and other coordinates mechanisms in asynchronous communications can take up as much as 25 percent of data traffic. See Figure 3.17 for an example of data being sent asynchronously.

Start	10101010	Stop	Start	10101010	Stop	Start	10101010	Stop

Figure 3.17 Data bytes sent asynchronously are framed by start and stop bits

Asynchronous Modem Standards

Standards are especially important in computer communications equipment because it is the standards that make it possible for devices (such as modems) from different manufacturers to talk to each other. You have already been introduced to the MNP and V.42 error-correction standards and the V.35 bis compression standard. There are several more standards you should know about to make an informed decision on which type of modem to use in your network.

Hayes Microcomputer products in the early 1980s introduced a modem that could dial the phone as well as sent data; the person using the modem did not have to use a telephone to dial the number. A Hayes modem had many special commands to configure the modem and manage the phone line. Many other modem manufacturers adopted the Hayes set of commands, and the Hayes compatible command set has become an industry standard. Any communications software you have is likely to use the Hayes-compatible setting as its default configuration.

The International Telecommunication Union (ITU) has developed a number of standards for modems. These standards usually start with a *V*, and many contain the word *bits*, which means *second* in French. If the standard includes the word terbo, it means third, not fast. Table 3.2 contains several of the ITU standard for modems.

Table 3.2 Various tyes of modes and thier speeds

STANDARD	BPS
V.22 bits	2400
V.32	9600
V.32 bits	14,400
V.32 terbo	19,200
V.FastClass (V.FC)	28,800
V.34	28,800
V.42	57,600

Microcom, in addition to specifying error-control protocols, created a data compression specification called MNP class 5. The ITU also specified the V.42 bits compression protocol. As mentioned earlier in this chapter, fast modem can be combined with compression to provide even faster data transfer rates. For instance, a very good modem might have V.32 bits signaling, V.42 error control, and V.42 bits compression.

Synchronous Modems

As you learned in the previous section, an asynchronous modem can spend up to 25 percent of its time negotiating the transmission and reception of data. This process is called *handshaking*. Synchronous communications can more effectively use the available bits per second and give you a faster connection than asynchronous communication can.

Synchronous Data Transfer

Synchronous modems can transmit more data than asynchronous modems (at the same number of bits per second) because they use careful timing and coordination between to send large blocks of data, without start and stop bits. These large blocks, called frames, have multiple bytes within them. Special characters are used to facilitate sychronization.

Synchronous communication requires that some kind of clocking mechanism be put into place to keep the clocks of the sender and receiver synchronized. (See Figure 3.18)

Comparison between Asynchronous and Synchronous Transmission

Synchronous communications tend to be more expensive than asynchronous as the hardware involved is more costly due to integral clocking mechanism that have to be used as well as more sophisticated engineering efforts. Yet, synchronous communication can eliminate up to 20% of associated overheads inherent in asynchronous communications. This allows greater throughout of data and better error detection.

Synchronous transmission is well suited to remote communication between a computer and such devices as buffered card readers and printers. It is also used for computer to computer communications.

The primary advantage of synchronous transmission is its efficiency. Not only does it eliminate the need for individual start-stop bits on each character, but much higher data rates can be used than with asynchronous transmission. The period between blocks is kept small and the block itself is sent at nearly the maximum line speed. This ensures efficient utilization of the transmission line. The main disadvantage is the need for local buffer storage at the two ends of the line to assemble blocks and also the need for accurately synchronized clocks at both ends. Therefore synchronous equipment usually cost more.

Asynchronous transmission is well suited to many keyboard type terminals. The advantage of this method is that it does not require any local storage at the terminal or the computer as transmission takes place character by character. Hence it is cheaper to implement. The main disadvantage of asynchronous transmission is that the transmission line is idle during the time intervals between transmitting characters. If there are short, this is not bad because line cost would be low and idle time not expensive. Even though less efficient than synchronous transmission, it is also used with devices such as card readers and printers to reduce cost.

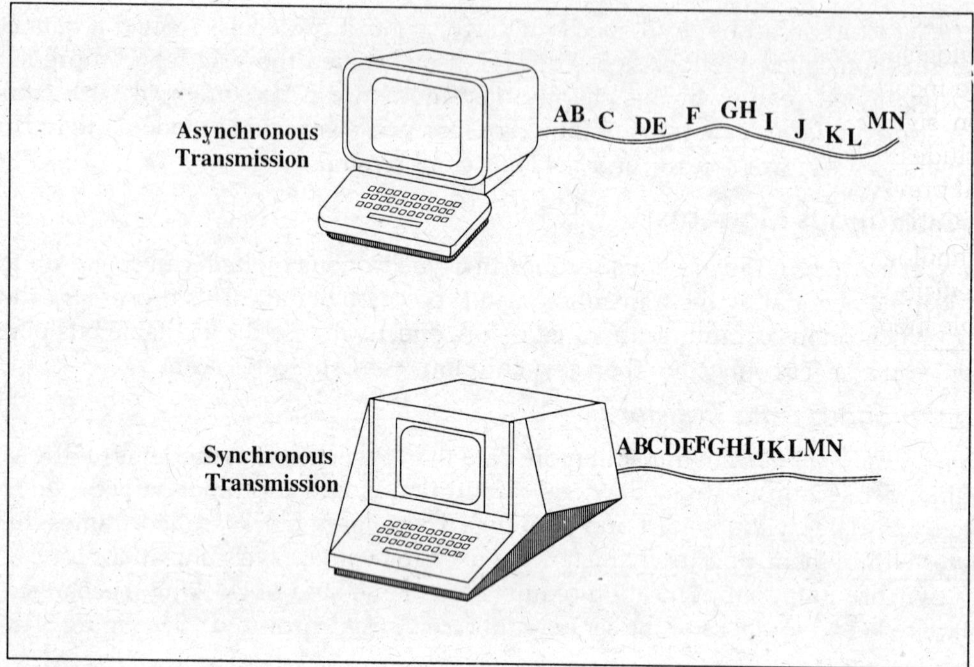

Figure 3.18 Asynchronous and synchronous transmissions

Synchronous Modem Standards

The three primary protocols in synchronous communications are Synchronous Data Link Control (SDLC), High-level Data Link Control (HDLC) and Binary synchronous Communications Protocol (bisync).

Uses of Synchronous Modems

Synchronous modems are used most often to make dedicated connections to remote computers using telephone lines leased from the telephone company.

 Synchronous modems provides a better data transfer rate and better error control than do asynchronous modems. However, synchronous modems cost more than asynchronous modems.

3.6.4 Cable Modem

Cable Modem is a modem that operates over the coaxial cable that is used by cable TV providers. Because the coaxial cable provides greater bandwidth than telephone lines, a cable modem offers much faster access than an analog modem.

Cable modems permit the transmission of data over community antenna television (CATV) networks-that is, the network of cables used to distribute cable television. A cable modem transmits data from the network at about 3 Mbps and transmits data to the network at between 500 Kbps and 2.5 Mbps.

Like a standard analog modem, a cable modem converts between a digital signal and an analog signal. Cable modems are much more complex than standard analog modems. They also incorporate a tuner that separates the digital data from the rest of the broadcast television signal. Because users in multiple locations share the same cable, the modem also includes hardware that permits multiple connections and an encryption/decryption device that prevents data from being intercepted by another user or being sent to the wrong place.

Cable modems send data back and forth over a cable television network using broadband technology, in which multiple signals, or channels, are sent over a single coaxial cable. Cable television companies allocate one of their cable television channels for sending data to their cable modem users. A second channel is used to send information back.

☞ Cable modem technology can send data from the Internet out to its customers at speeds as high as 30 mbps. However, that bandwidth is shared by all the cable modem users in a particular neighborhood, which may range from 500 to 2,000 subscribers. The actual bandwidth that most cable modem users experience when they retrieve, or download, information from the Internet is generally in the range of 200 to 400 kpbs.

REVIEW QUESTIONS WITH ANSWERS

Question Number 1 What do you understand by the term channel bandwidth. How is it effected by the signal to noise ratio.

Answer **Channel Bandwidth**

The term channel bandwidth refers to the range of frequencies that is available for the transmission of data. This is the term used to describe the data handling capacity of the communication system. The more the bandwidth of the channel, the more data it can transmit.

For a channel, with the Band width of H hertz, and signal to noise ration as S/N dB, the channel capacity is limited by the formula $H\log_2(1 + (S/N))$.

Question Number 2 The bit pattern 0101100100100 is to be transmitted using the following techniques:

(a) ASK
(b) FSK and
(c) PSK

Sketch the transmitted waveforms separately for each keying technique.

Answer Bit pattern 101100100100 is to be transmitted using the following techniques:

(a) ASK (b) FSK (c) PSK

ASK (Amplitude Shift Keying

In the ASK, the two binary values are represented by 2 different amplitudes of the carrier frequency. One digit is represented by the presence and one digit is represented by the absence of the carrier frequency. (See Figure 3.19 (b))

FSK (Frequency Shift Keying)

In FSK, the two binary numbers are represented by two different frequencies near the carrier frequency. FSK is less susceptible to error than ASK. Figure 3.19 (c) shows the pattern of FSK when the signal is sent.

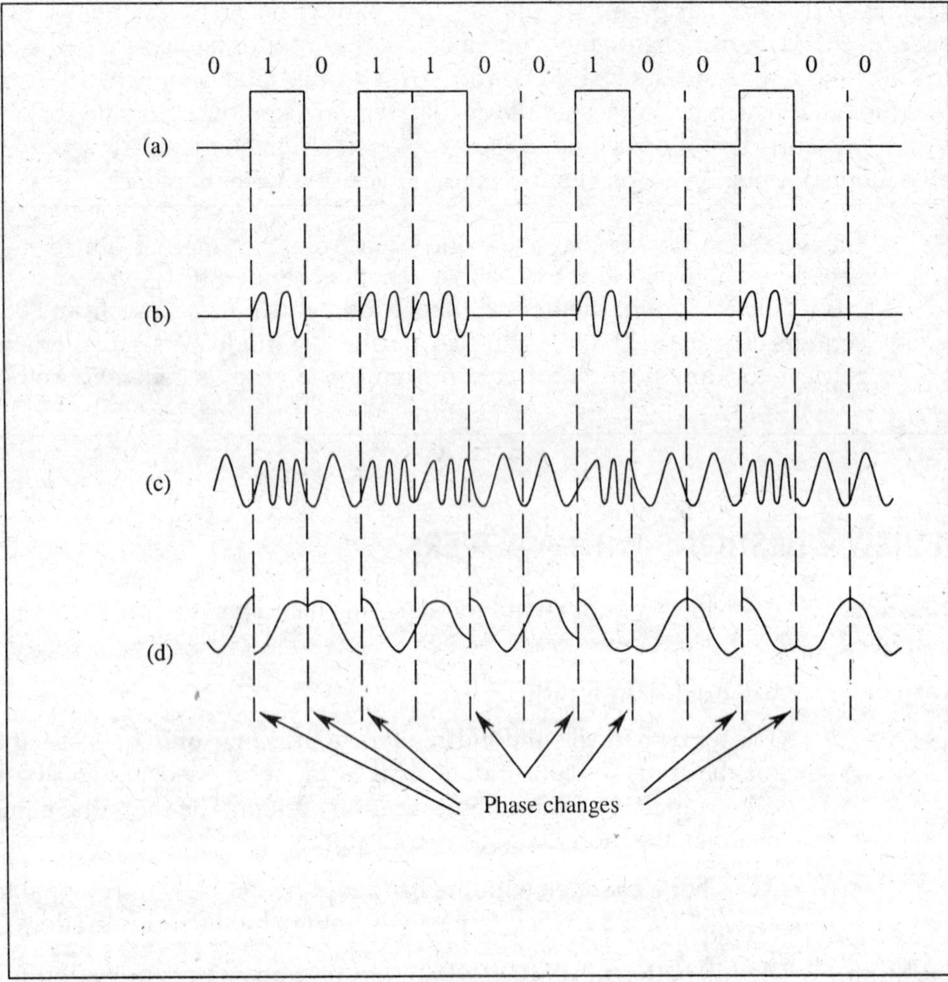

Figure 3.19 Different modulation techniques (a) Binary data (b) AM (c) FM (d) PM

PSK (Phase Shift Keying)

In PSK, phase of the signal is shifted to represent data. In Figure 3.19 (d), a binary 0 is represented by sending a signal burst of the same phase as the previous one and binary one is represented by sending signal burst of opposite phase to the preceding one. This is the form of Differential Phase shift keying.

Question Number 3 Illustrate with appropriate diagrams the followings:

(a) Amplitude modulation
(b) Frequency modulation
(c) Phase modulation

Answer Following are the figures that illustrates the different modulation techniques.

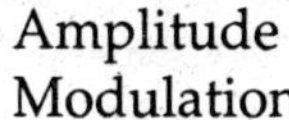

Amplitude Modulation

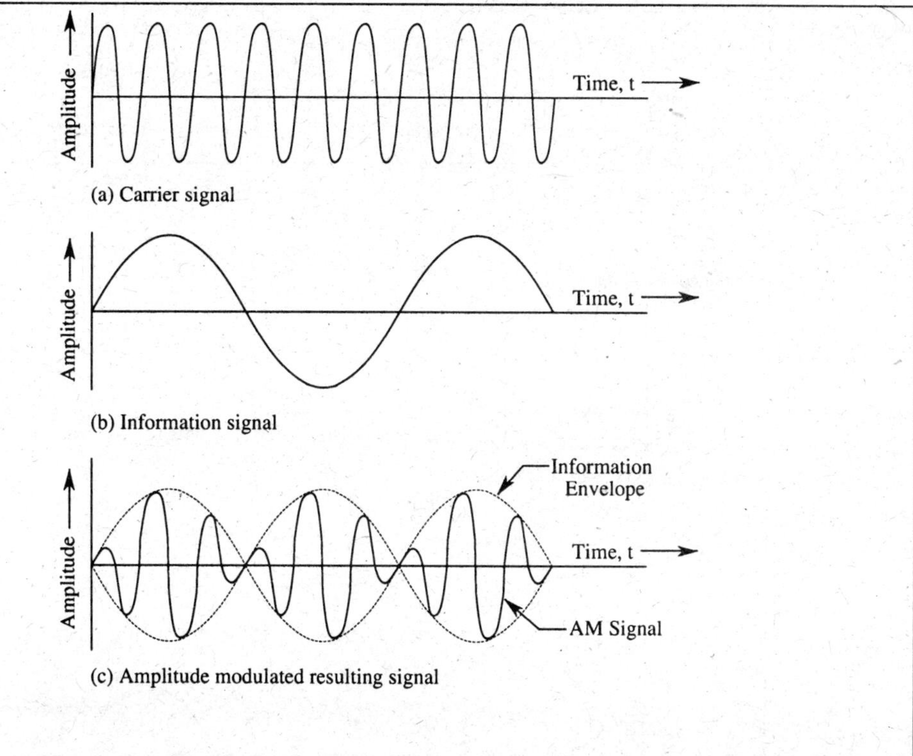

(a) Carrier signal

(b) Information signal

(c) Amplitude modulated resulting signal

Frequency modulaion

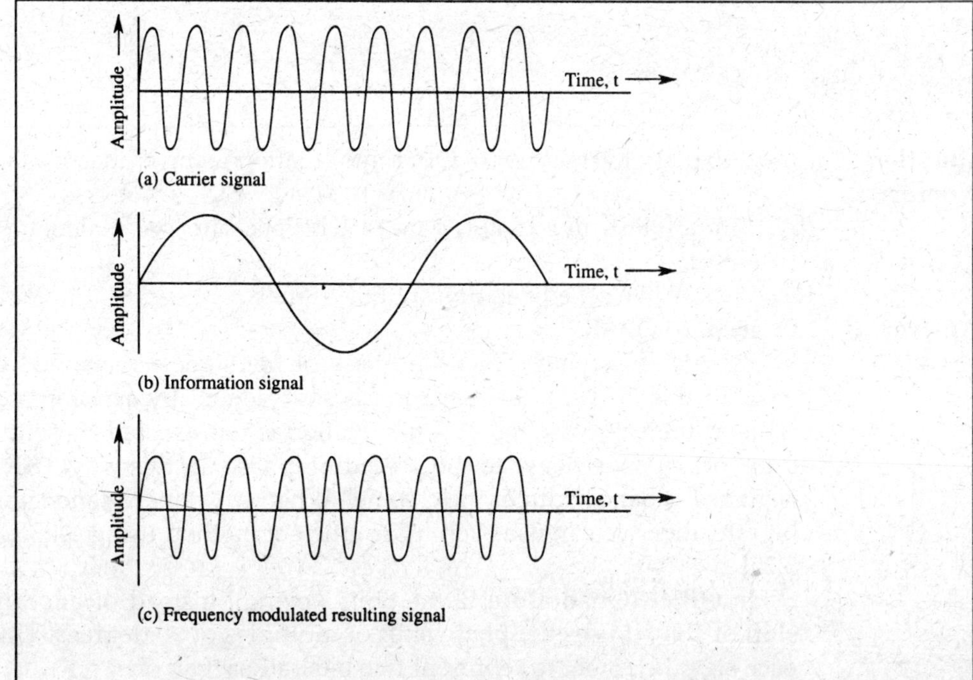

(a) Carrier signal

(b) Information signal

(c) Frequency modulated resulting signal

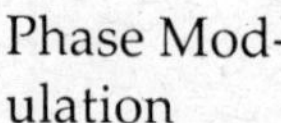

Phase Modulation

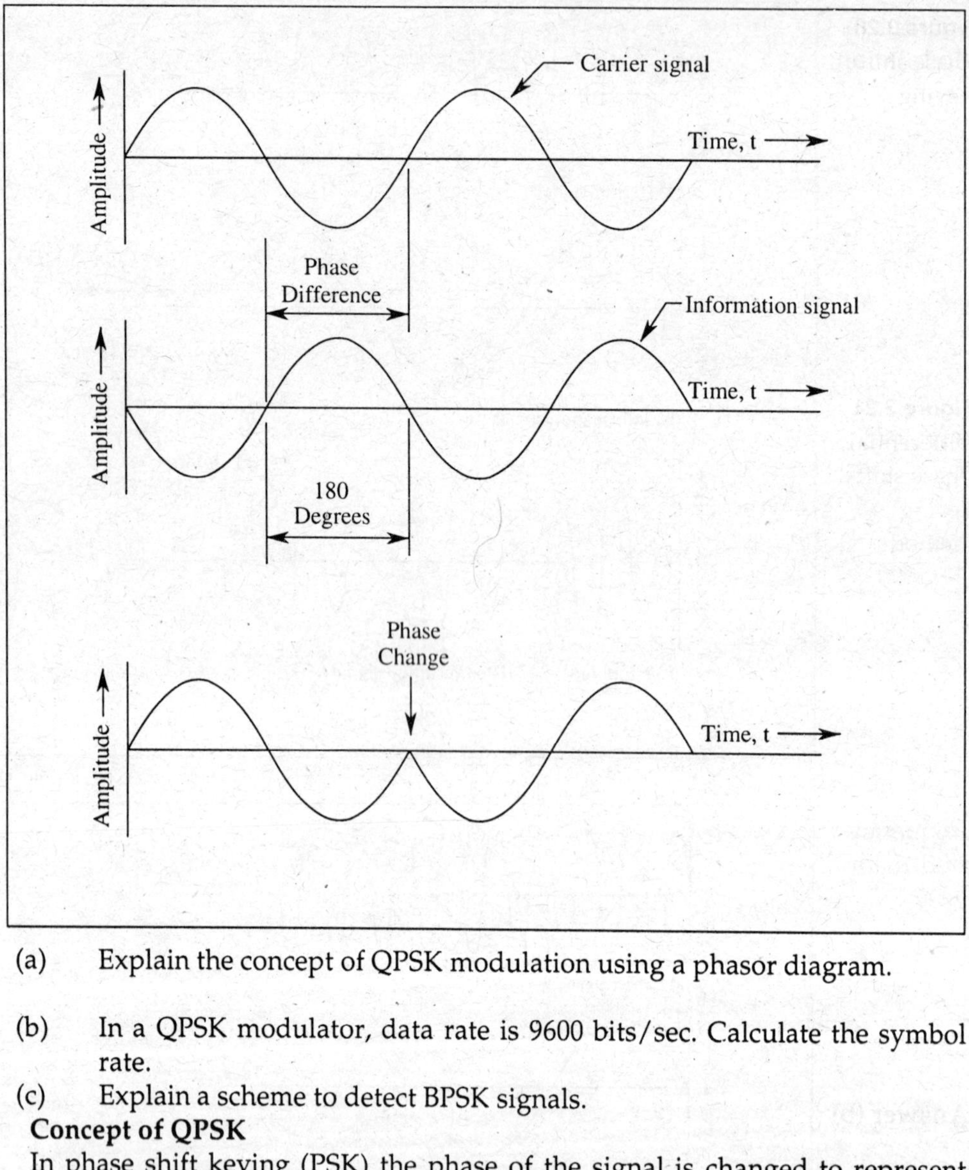

Question Number 4

(a) Explain the concept of QPSK modulation using a phasor diagram.

(b) In a QPSK modulator, data rate is 9600 bits/sec. Calculate the symbol rate.

(c) Explain a scheme to detect BPSK signals.

Answer (a) **Concept of QPSK**

In phase shift keying (PSK) the phase of the signal is changed to represent data. In this system, 'off' situation is represented by sending a signal burst same as the previous one. A 'on' situation is represented by sending a signal burst of opposite phase to the preceding phase. In this way, PSK makes efficient use of bandwidth of the channel. When we want to send signal at higher bit rate, then we can use even more efficient method using QPSK. [See Figure 3.20]

In QPSK (Quadrature Phase Shift Keying), instead of allocating a phase shift of 180^0, it uses the phase shift of multiples of 90 degrees. This will cause each signal element to represent two bits rather than one.

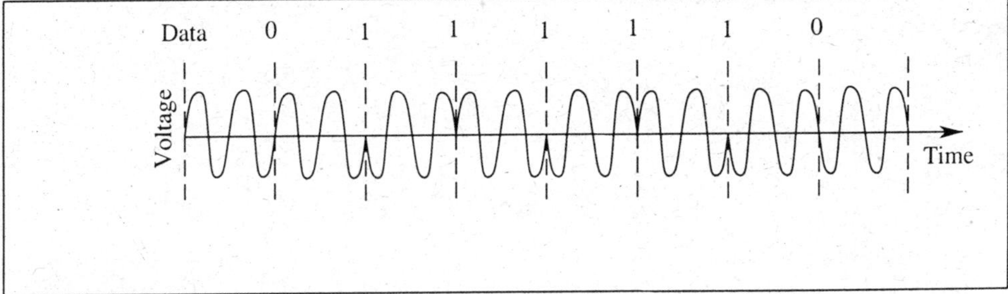

Figure 3.20 Phase shift Keying

Figure 3.21 shows the QPSK method of phase shift keying. Figure 3.22 shows the QPSK modulator. Figure 3.23 shows the phasor diagram of QPSK.

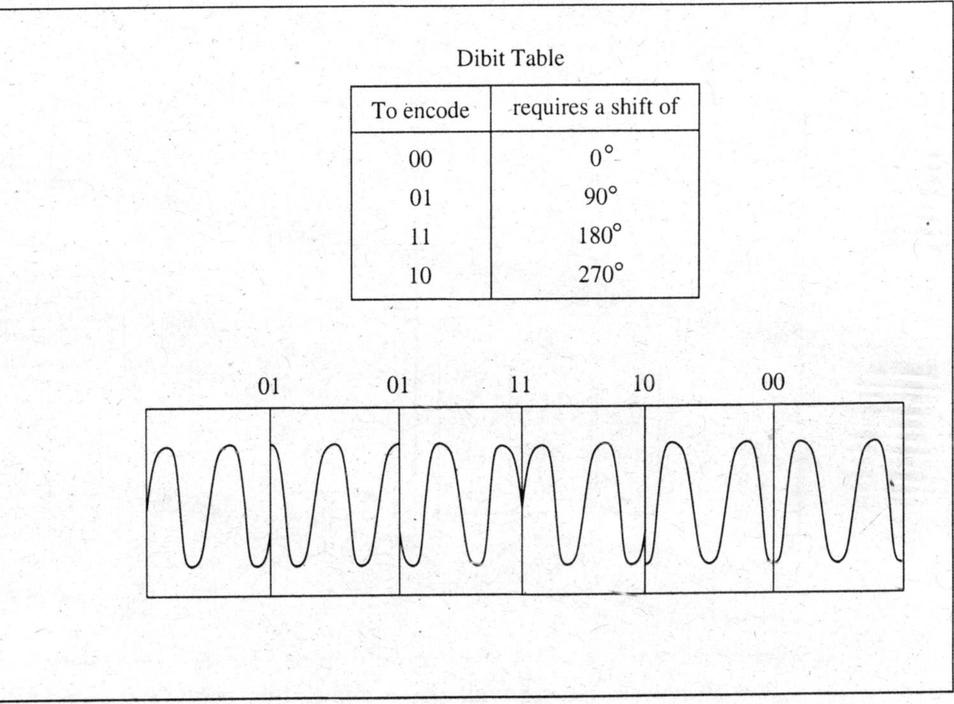
Dibit Table

To encode	requires a shift of
00	0°
01	90°
11	180°
10	270°

Figure 3.21 Differential Phase shift keying method

Answer (b) **The number of symbols possible for QPSK = 4 or 2^2.**

Hence symbol rate = bit rate/(number of bits per symbol)
or symbol rate = 9600/2 = 4800

Answer (c) **Scheme to detect BPSK**

Figure 3.24 shows the PSK detector. This diagram differs from the modulator diagram shown in Figure 3.22. The only change being the replacement of the transformer found in the modulator by capacitor and resistor which form the peak detector circuit.
Following steps indicate the operation of the detector:

1. Clock is fed into the balanced modulator and 90 degree phase shifter.

Figure 3.22
DPSK Modulator

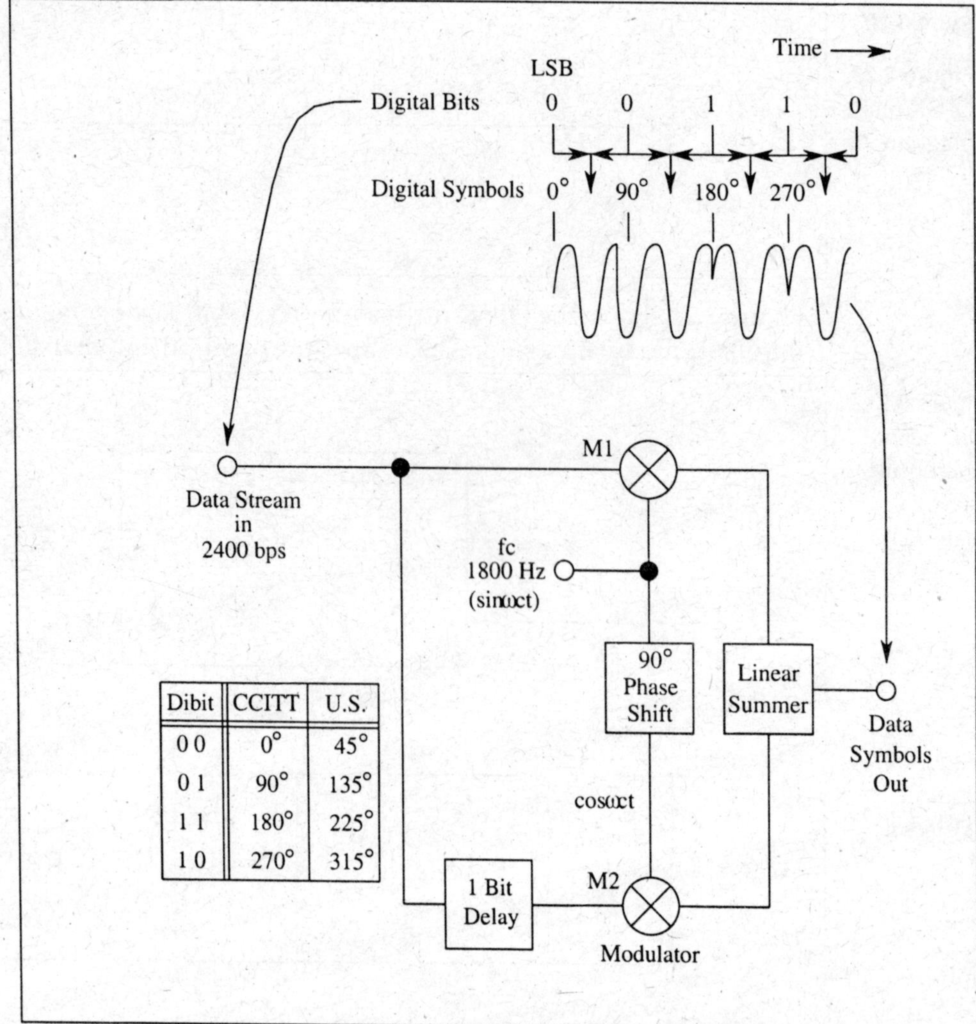

2. The shifted signal is presented to the second balanced modulator as fc.
3. The incoming data stream is the other input to the balanced modulator along with the signal.
4. The output is altered to perform the function of the phase detector.
5. The capacitors and the resistors charge to the peak value of the sine waves and the filter out the AC components.
6. Signal fc is applied to inputs. The positive alternation of fc switches on D1 and D4 while the negative half switches on D2 and D3.
7. The effect is to pass the incoming signals f(in) to the RL circuit. The amount the capacitors will charge depending on the phase relationship between (fin) and fc.

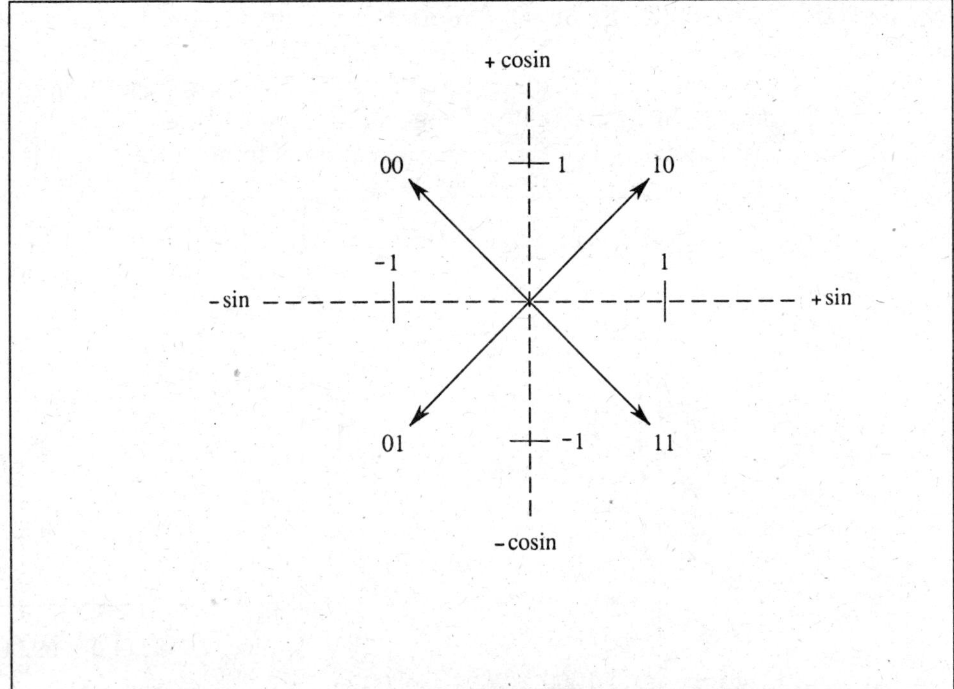

Figure 3.23 QPSK phasor diagram

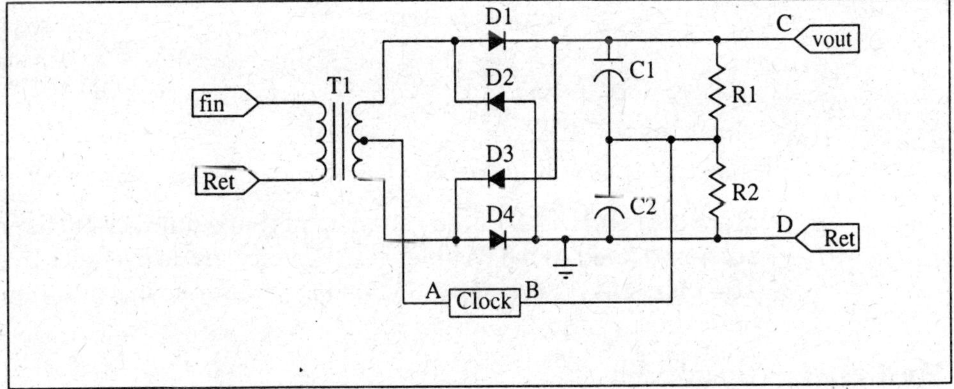

Figure 3.24 PSK Phase Detector

In effect the carrier may split in four waves, each with the frequency of the original but starting at a different phase of the original cycle. Four phases can represent all the possible combination of 2 bits. The modem chooses the appropriate phase shift for the dibit to be encoded.

Question Number 5.

(a) With the help of a diagram, show the use of FDM technique for voice grade channels.

(b) Explain the term guard band.

(c) Differentiate between broadband and baseband transmission.

Answer (a) **Three voice grade telephone channels multiplexed using FDM Techniques**

FDM is a method for sharing a transmission line by dividing the bandwidth into paralleled paths defined and separated by guard band frequencies. All signals are carried simultaneously for saving the cost of the channel. Figure 3.25 shows the pictorial representation of three voice channels.

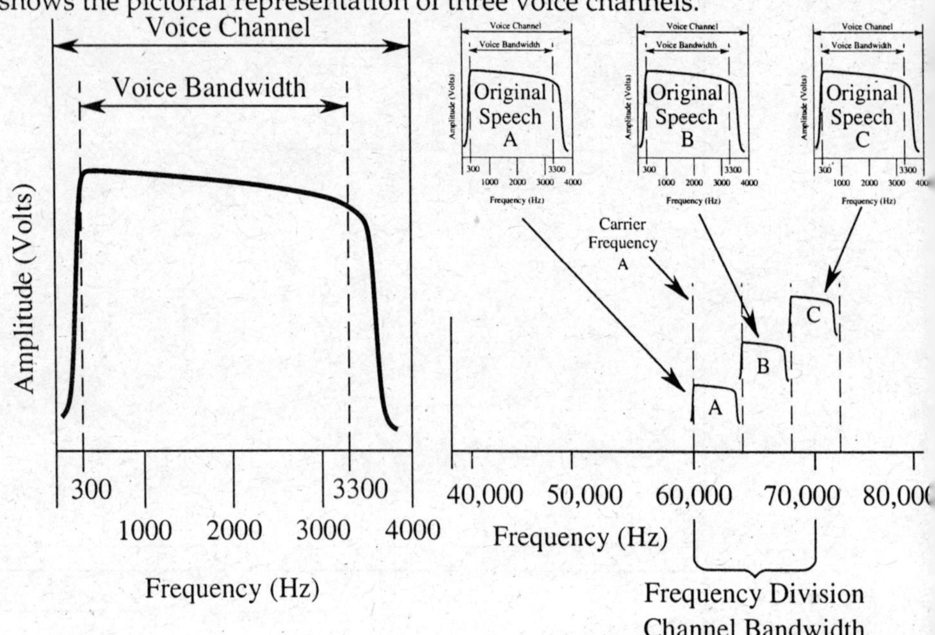

Figure 3.25 Using the voice band for accomodating voice channels

More the bandwidth of the channel, more the number of channels that can be accommodated in the channel. All the voice grade channels need a bandwidth of 4 kHz. Mixers are used to create the multiplexing of different voice channels.

Answer (b) **Guard band**

Guard band is the frequency range between the two multiplexed channels used to clearly identify the channels. There is no signal on the guard band and thus causes a waste of the band width of the channel.

Answer (c) **Differentiate between broadband and baseband transmission.**

Baseband systems use digital signaling over a single frequency. Signals flow in the from of discrete pulses of electricity or light. With baseband transmission, the entire communication channel capacity is used to transmit a single data signal. The digital signal uses the complete bandwidth of the cable, which constitutes a single channel. A cable's total bandwidth is the difference between the highest and the lowest frequencies that are carried over that cable. Figure 3.3 shows the broadband and baseband transmissions.

Broadband systems use analog signaling and a range of frequencies. With analog transmission, the signals are continuous and nondiscrete. Signals flow across the physical medium in the form of electromagnetic or optical waves. With broadband transmission, signal flow is unidirectional. If sufficient total bandwidth is available, multiple analog transmission systems such as cable television and network transmissions can be supported simultaneously on the same cable. Each transmission system is allocated a part of the total bandwidth. All devices associated with a given transmission system, such as all computers using a LAN cable, must then be tuned so that they use only the frequencies that are within the allocated range. While baseband systems use repeater, broadband systems use amplifiers to regenerate analog signals at their original strength. Since broadband transmission signal flow is unidirectional, there must be two paths for data flow in order for a signal to reach all devices.

TEST PAPER

Time: 2 Hrs. Marks: 50

Note: Answer all questions.

1. Write a brief note on following:
   (i) Analog vs Digital Transmission
   (ii) Pulse Code Modulation
   (iii) Multiplexing

[*GNDU, BIT Part–III, Paper–I, 2002 examination*]

2. Mention atleast two differences between analog modulation and digital modulation.
3. Compare asynchronous and synchronous data transmission.
4. Discuss DTC-DCE Interface standard.
5. Draw the representation of digital signal 011101010110 for NRZ-L, NRZ-I, Manchester coding and differential Manchester coding waveforms.

CHAPTER 4

Transmission Media

4.1 INTRODUCTION

Media is the general term used to describe the data path that forms the physical channel between sender and the receiver. Media can be twisted-pair wire such as that used for telephone installations, coaxial cable of various sizes and electrical characteristics, fiber optic cables and wireless supporting either light waves or radio waves. Wire or fiber-optic media are referred to as *bounded* media. Wireless media are sometimes referred to as unbounded media.

Media differ in the capability to support high data rates and long distance transmission. The reasons for this are:

(a) Noise absorption
(b) Radiation
(c) Attenuation
(d) Band width

4.1.1 Noise absorption

Noise absorption is the susceptibility of the media to external electrical noise that can cause distortion of the data signal and thus data errors.

4.1.2 Radiation

Radiation is the leakage of signal from the media caused by undesirable electrical characteristics of the media.

4.1.3 Attenuation

Attenuation is the decline of magnitude of signal with distance due to absorption of energy by the media. Radiation and the physical characteristics of the media contribute to attenuation, or the reduction in signal strength as the signal travels down the wire or through free space. Attenuation limits the usable distance that data can travel on the media.

4.1.4 Bandwidth

Bandwidth is similar to the concept of frequency response in a stereo amplifier—the greater the frequency response, the higher the bandwidth. According to a fundamental principle of information theory, higher bandwidth communications channels support higher data rates.

4.2 GUIDED AND UNGUIDED MEDIA

The media of transmission of energy can be either guided or unguided.

4.2.1 Guided Media

The guided media refers to the method of transmission of data over which signals can travel in a network. Examples of guided media include the following:

(a) Twisted-pair wire

(b) Coaxial cabling

(c) Fiber-optic cabling

Twisted-pair wire

A twisted pair consists of two insulated copper wires, typically about 1 mm thick. The wires are twisted together in a helical shape. The purpose of twisting the wires is to reduce electrical interference from similar pairs that are close by.

Figure 4.1 (a) A twisted pair of wires

Twisted pair wires (Figure 4.1 (a)) are commonly used in local telephone communication, and for digital data transmission over short distances up to 1 km. When many twisted pairs (Figure 4.1 (b)) run in parallel for a substantial distance, such as all the wires coming from a multistory apartment building to the telephone exchange, they are bundled together and placed in a protective sheath. The pairs in these bundles would interfere with one another if they are not twisted.

Figure 4.1 (b) Unshielded twisted-pair (UTP) cable

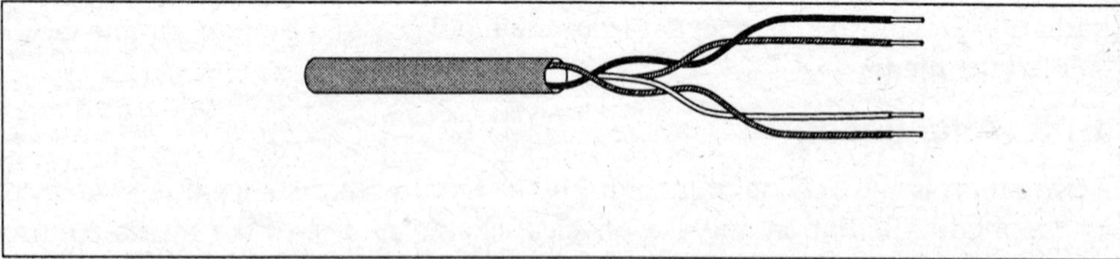

Wire pairs are normally used to connect terminals to the main computer up to short distances from the main computer. Data transmission speeds of up to 9600 bits per second can be achieved if the distance is not more than 100 meters.

Advantages of Twisted-pair Wires

(a) Being the oldest method of data transmission, trained manpower to repair and service this media of communications is easily available.

(b) In telephone system, signal can travel several kilometers without amplification when twisted-pair wires are used.
(c) This media can be used for both analog and digital data transmission. The band width depends on the thickness of the wire and the distance travelled, but several megabits per second can be achieved for a few tens of meters in many cases.
(d) It is the least expensive media of transmission for short distances.
(e) If portion of a twisted-pair cable is damaged, the entire network is not shut down, while it may be the case with coaxial cable.

Disadvantages of Twisted-pair Wires

(a) Easily pickup noise signals which results in higher error rates when the line length exceeds 100 meters.
(b) Being thin in size, they are likely to break easily.
(c) It can support 19,200 bps up to 50 feet on RS-232 port. On a 10BASE-T, it supports 10Mbps up to a distance of 100 meters.

Shielded wire

Shielded wire (Figure 4.1 (c)) is used in an electrically noisy environment to limit the effects of noise absorption. Unshielded twisted pair, commonly referred to as UTP is by far the more common of the two configurations. Twisted-pair wiring is more commonly used for LAN media. The twisted pair version of Ethernet is designated as 10BASE-T, in which 10 refers to the Ethernet clock rate of 10 Mbps.

Figure 4.1 (c)
Shielded four pair cable

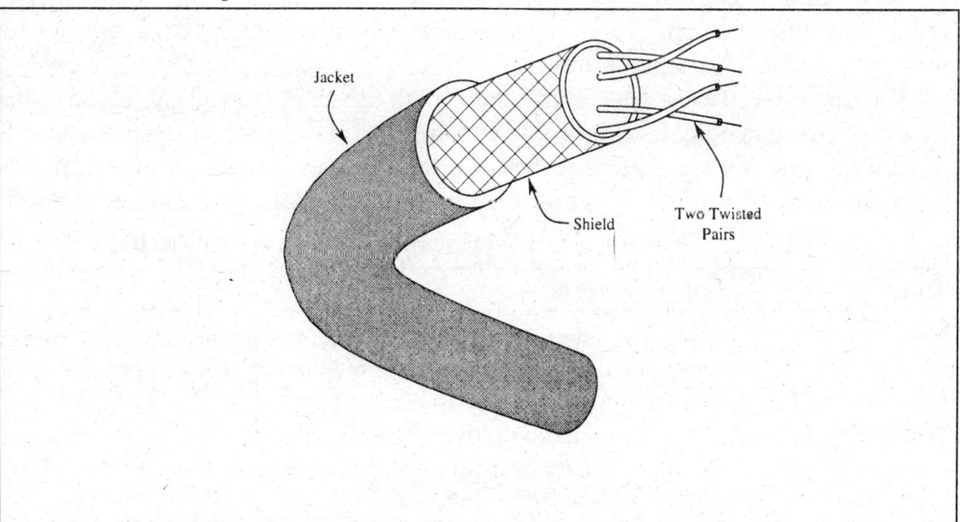

Twisted pair cabling comes in several varieties. In computer networks, two of these are important. Category 3 twisted pairs cable consists of two insulated wires gently twisted together. Four such pairs are typically grouped together in a plastic sheath for protection and to keep the eight wires together. Another more advanced category, 5 twisted pairs were introduced. They are similar to category 3 pairs, but with more twist per centimeter and Teflon insulation, which results in less crosstalk and better quality signal over longer distances, making them more suitable for high-speed computer communication.

Coaxial cabling

A coaxial cable consist of a stiff copper wire as the core, surrounded by an insulating material. The insulator is encased by a cylindrical conductor, often as a closely woven braided mesh. The outer conductor is covered in a protective plastic sheath. A cutaway view of a coaxial cable is shown in Figure 4.2. The signal is transmitted by the inner copper wire and it is electrically shielded by the outer metal sleeve.

Figure 4.2
Coaxial cable

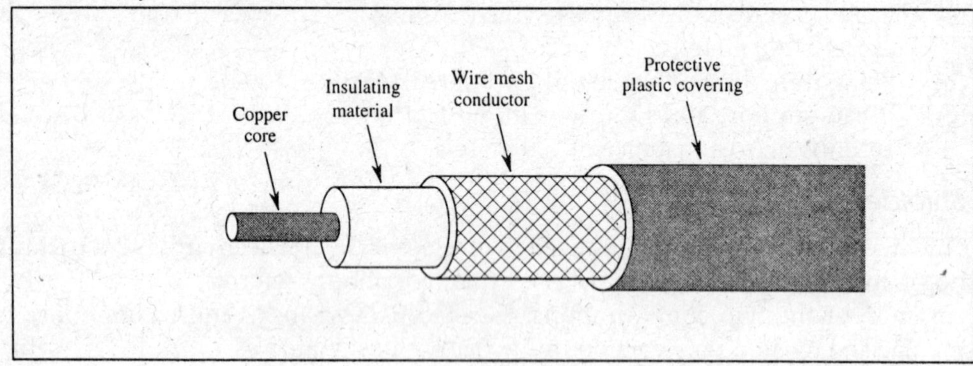

Two kinds of coaxial cable are widely used. One kind, 50-ohm cable, is commonly used for digital transmission. The other kind, 75-ohm cables, is commonly used for analog transmission in cable TV transmission.

IEEE uses the 10Base5 designation for thick Ethernet coaxial cable and 10Base2 for the thin Ethernet coaxial cable. Coaxial cable can support data rates of up to several tens of Mbps at distances up to several thousand feet. Certain types of signaling enable high data rates over distances of several miles. Various terms used in coaxial cabling are explained in Table 4.1.

Table 4.1 Different terms of Coaxial Cable Implementation

Terms	Implementation
10Base2	An implementation of the 802.3 Ethernet standard on thin Ethernet (RG-58) coaxial cable. It has a data-transfer rate of 10 megabits per second and a maximum cable segment length of 185 meters.
10Base5	An implementation of the 802.3 Ethernet standard on thick Ethernet coaxial cable. It has a data-transfer rate of 10 megabits per second and a maximum cable segment length of 500 meters over a bus topology.
10BaseF	Emerging 802.3 standards that define the use of on Ethernet over fiber-optic cable.
10BaseT	An implementation of the 802.3 Ethernet standard over unshielded twisted-pair (UTP) wiring. It is similar to wiring used with modern telephone systems using RJ-45 connectors. The standard is based on a star topology, with each node connected to a central wiring center and a maximum cable-segment length of 100 meters.

(Contd...)

Thick Ethernet	Connecting coaxial cable used on an Ethernet network. The cable is 1 centimeter (0.4 inch) thick, and can be used to connect network nodes up to a distance of approximately 1006 meters.
Thin Ethernet	Connecting coaxial cable used on an Ethernet network. The cable is 5 millimeters (0.2 inch) thick, and can be used to connect network nodes up to a distance of approximately 165 meters. Used for office installations.

Coaxial cable is difficult to connect to network devices and generally requires more planning than twisted-pair system. Many coaxial systems require the connectors on the main cable to be attached directly to the adapter on the PCs. This reduces flexibility in locating workstations and servers.

☞ Baseband networks are the networks where the entire bandwidth of the cable is utilized for a single channel. Broadband is basically a frequency division multiplexed situation, where the coaxial cable's bandwidth is separated into subchannels of either equal or varying frequency ranges that can be treated as separate communication media.

Advantages of Coaxial Cable

(a) It has better shielding than twisted pairs, so it can span longer distances at higher data bits per second.

(b) It can be used for both analog data transmission as well as digital data transmission. For analog, 75 ohm, broad band coaxial is used and for digital data transmission, 50 ohm baseband cable is used.

(c) Coaxial cable has higher bandwidth and excellent noise immunity. RG-58 cable (10Base2) is a thin coaxial cable (50-ohm) in widespread use for LAN connections. RG-11 (10Base5) cable is a coaxial cable that is much thicker and sturdier and can withstand more rugged surroundings and can be used with much longer segment lengths. RG-59, a 75-ohm coaxial cable and RG-62 (93-ohm) cable are used in ARCnet Local Area networks or the IBM 3270 applications.

(d) It is relatively inexpensive as compared to fiber optic cables and they are easy to handle.

(e) Coaxial cable has a bandwidth in the range of 300-400 MHz.

☞ Coaxial cable are capable of carrying over 50 standard 6 MHz colour TV channels or thousands of channels of voice-grade and/or low-speed data over a single cable. CD-quality audio (1.4 Mbps), or a digital bit stream at 3 Mbps can be mixed on coaxial cable for transmitting video signal. Broadband cable is inferior to baseband cable for sending digital data but has the advantage that a huge amount of it is already available in the Cable TV and systems. Therefore, cable TV systems may begin operating as Metropolitan Area Network's and offer telephone and Internet services at low cost.

Optical Fiber

Optic fiber is the newest form of bounded media. This media is superior in data handling and security characteristics. The fiber optic cable transmits light signals rather than electrical signals. It is far more efficient than the other network transmission media. Each fiber has an inner core of glass or plastic that conducts light. There are two types of light sources for which fiber cables are available. These sources of light are:

(a) Light Emitting Diodes (LEDs)

(b) Light Amplification by Stimulated Emission Radiation (Lasers)

Figure 4.3 Transmission through optical fibers

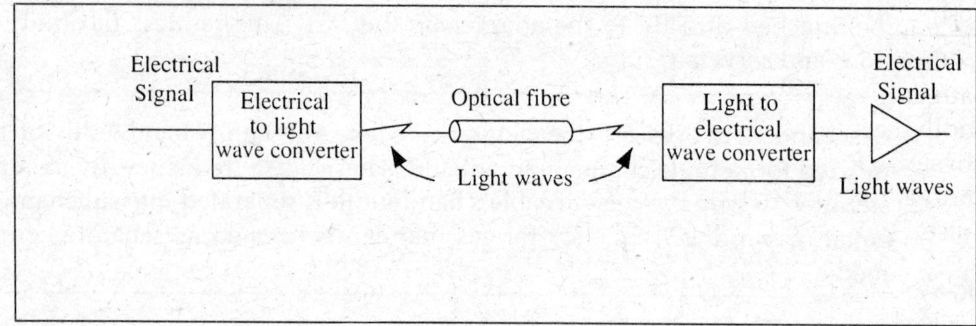

Figure 4.3 shows the principle of operation of the fiber optic system. The system basically consists of fiber optic cables that are made of tiny threads of glass or plastics. In a single-mode fiber the core is 8 to 10 microns (about the size of hair). In multimode fibers, the core is 50 microns in diameter.

Towards its source side is a converter that converts electrical signals into light waves. These light waves are transmitted over the fiber. Another converter placed near the sink converts the light waves back to electrical signals by photoelectric diodes. These electrical signals are amplified and sent to the receiver.

Each fiber has an inner core of glass or plastic that conducts light. The inner core is surrounded by cladding, a layer of glass that reflects the light back into the core. Each fiber is surrounded by a plastic sheath. The sheath can be either tight or loose. (See Figure 4.4)

Figure 4.4 Fiber-optic cables with cladding and sheath

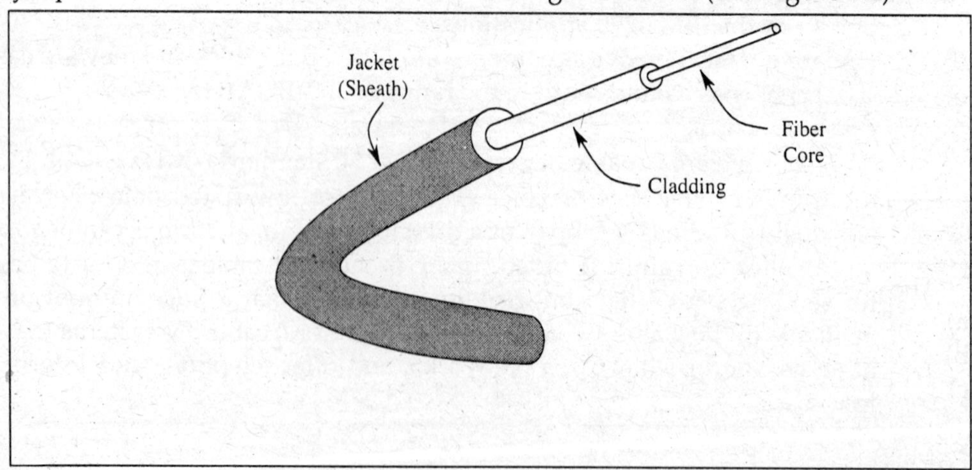

A comparison of semiconductor laser diodes and LEDs is given in Table 4.2.

Table 4.2 Comparison of Semiconductor diode lasers and LEDs as light source

Item	Light Emitting Diode (LED)	Semiconductor Laser
Data rate	Low	High
Mode	Multimode	Multimode or single mode
Distance	3 km.	30 km.
Lifetime	Long life	Short life
Temperature Sensitivity	Minor	Substantial
Cost	Low	Substantial

Optical fibers may be multimode or single mode. Single mode fibers allow a single light path and are typically used with laser signalling. Single mode fiber can allow greater bandwidth than multimode but is more expensive. Multimode fibers use multiple light paths. The physical characteristics of the multimode fiber make all parts of the signal (those from the various paths) arrive at the same time, appearing to the receiver as though they were one pulse. Figure 4.5 shows the single mode and multimode optical fibers.

Figure 4.5 Single-mode and multi-mode optical fibers

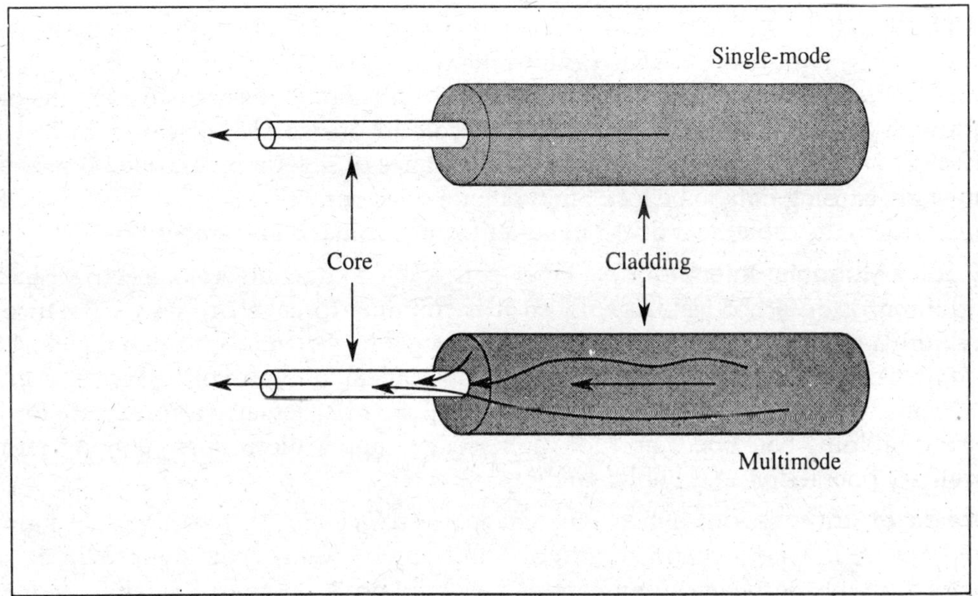

☞ Optical fibers are differentiated by core/cladding size and mode of operation.

The common types of fiber-optic cable:

(a) 8.3-micron core/12.5-micron cladding, single-mode,

(b) 62.5-micron core/125-micron cladding, multimode

(c) 50-micron core/125-micron cladding, multimode, and 100-micron core/140-micron cladding, multimode.

Micron is one millionth of a meter = 1/25,000 inch (approximately).

Characteristics of Fiber-optic Cable

Fiber-optic cable has the following characteristics.

Cost: Fiber-optic cable is more expensive than copper cable. However, the costs are falling. Associated equipment costs can be much higher than for copper cable, making fiber-optic networks much more expensive. Single mode fiber devices are more expensive and more difficult to install than multimode devices.

Installation: Fiber optic cable is more difficult to install than copper cable. Every fiber connection must be carefully made to avoid obstructing the light path. Also the cables have a maximum bend radius, which makes cabling more difficult.

Bandwidth capacity: Because it uses light, which has higher frequency than electricity, fiber optic cabling provides data rates from 100 Mbps to 2 Gbps per second. The data rate depends on the fiber composition, the mode, and the wavelength (frequency) of the transmitter light. A common multimode installation can support 100 Mbps over several kilometers.

Node Capacity: In the case of Ethernet network fiber optic cables have the useful upper limit is around 75 nodes on a single collision domain.

Attenuation: Fiber optic cable has much lower attenuation than copper wires, mainly because the light is not radiated out in the way electricity is radiated from copper cables. It has a different problem namely, chromatic dispersion. Different wavelengths of light travel through glass at different velocity, and the colours of a single pulse of light will spread apart slightly as they travel down a cable. At a distance of several miles, one bit may shift into the next bit, causing data to be lost. Single-mode fiber-optic cable conveys only one frequency of light down the cable, so it does not suffer from chromatic dispersion.

Electro Magnetic Interference: Fiber-optic cable is not subject to electrical interference. In addition, it does not leak signals, so it is immune to eavesdropping. Because it does not require a ground, fiber-optic cable is not affected by potential shifts in the electrical ground, nor does it produce sparks. This type of cable is ideal for high-voltage areas or in installations where eavesdropping could be a problem. Fiber is particularly appropriate for campus and multi-building backbones and for high security applications such as financial transactions, military operations, and public safety.

Mode of Transmission: Fiber optic channels are *half-duplex*, meaning that light signals can only move in one direction at a time. A full-duplex circuit would cause light wave interference without special electronics and is generally not economically viable. Moreover, a bend radius that is too tight causes distortion and attenuation of the light signal due to changes in the electrical and physical characteristics of the inner core.

Uses of Optical Fiber

Fiber-optic media can support high bandwidth applications including video conference to the desktop, digital voice/image/graphics networking in the local area network environment. Fiber-optic media are the basis for several high bandwidth networking standards such as Fiber Distributed Data Interface (FDDI) and Synchronous Optical Network (SONET)

Fiber optics can be used for LANs as well as for long transmission although tapping onto it is more complex than connecting to an Ethernet. One way around the problem is to realize that a ring network is really just a collection of a point-to-point links as shown in Figure 4.6.

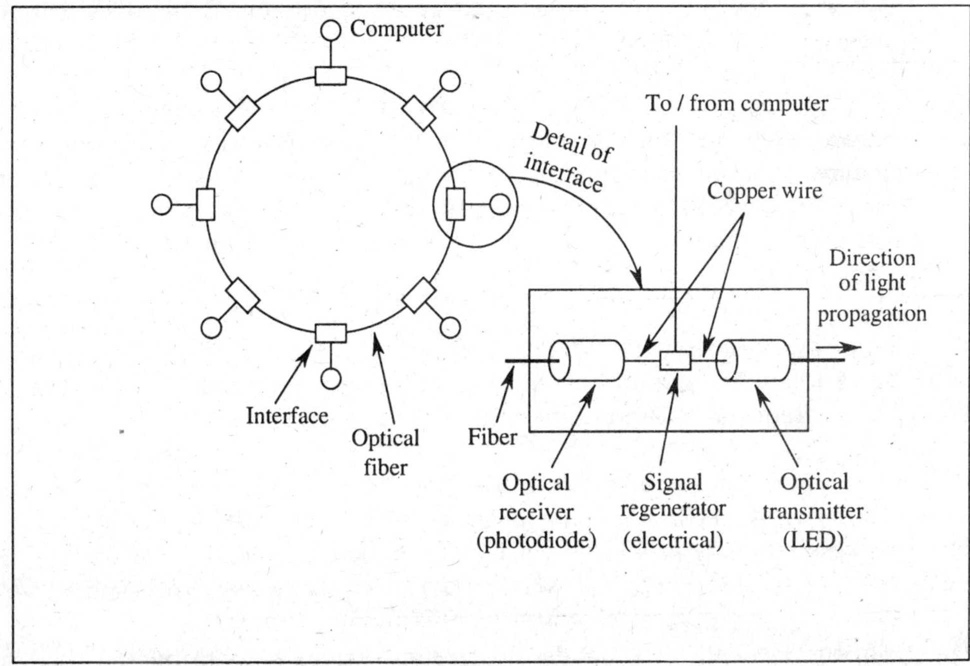

Figure 4.6 A fiber optic ring with active repeaters

The interface at each computer passes the light pulse stream through to the next link and also serves as a T junction to allow the computer to send and accept messages. The figure shows the active repeater. The incoming light is converted to an electrical signal regenerated to full strength if it has been weakened, and re-transmitted as light. The interface with the computer is an ordinary copper wire that comes into the signal regenerator. Purely optical repeaters are now being used too.

4.2.2 Unguided Media

Air is the media through which electromagnetic energy can flow easily. Therefore, there are several methods which are in use to send electromagnetic energy through air. These methods are:

(a) Radio Wave communication including VHF and Microwave Links

(b) Satellite Links

(c) VSATs (Very Small Aperture Terminals)

(c) Infrared and Millimeter Waves

Radio Transmission

Some of the characteristics of radio waves are as follows:

(a) Radio waves are easy to generate.

(b) They can travel long distances.

(c) They can penetrate buildings easily so they are widely used for communications both indoors and outdoors.
(d) Radio waves are omnidirectional, meaning that they travel in all directions from the source, so that the transmitter and receiver do not have to be carefully aligned physically.

☞ The properties of radio waves are frequency dependent. At low frequencies, radio waves pass through obstacles well, but the power falls off sharply with distance from the source, roughly, as $1/r^3$ in air. At high frequencies, radio waves tend to travel in straight lines and bounce off obstacles. They are absorbed by rain. At all frequencies, radio waves are subject to interference from motors and other electrical equipment.

In Very Low Frequency (VLF), Low Frequency (LF) and Medium Frequency (MF) bands, radio waves follow the ground. Amplitude modulated radio broadcasting uses the MF band. This band of frequencies can not be used for data transfer because they offer relatively *low bandwidth.*

The amount of information that an electromagnetic wave can carry is related to its bandwidth. With current technology, it is possible to encode a few bits per Hertz at low frequencies, but often as many as 48 bits per Hertz can be coded under certain conditions at high frequencies. So a cable with a 500 MHz bandwidth can carry several gigabits/sec.

☞ In the HF and VHF bands, the ground waves tend to be absorbed by the earth. However, the waves that reach the ionosphere, a layer of charged particles circling the earth at a height of 100 to 500 km, are reflected by it and sent back to earth.

Microwave Transmission

Above 100 MHz, the waves travel in straight lines and can therefore be narrowly focused. Concentrating all the energy into a small beam using a parabolic antenna (like the satellite TV dish) gives a much higher signal to noise ratio, but the transmitting and receiving antennas must be accurately aligned with each other. Before the advent of fiber optics, these microwaves formed the heart of the long distance telephone transmission system.

In order to overcome the problems of line-of-sight and power amplification of weak signals, microwave systems use repeaters at intervals of about 25 to 30 km in between the transmitting and receiving stations (Figure 4.7). The first repeater is placed in line-of-sight of the transmitting station and the last repeater is placed in line-of-sight of the receiving station. Two consecutive repeaters are also placed in line-of-sight of each other. The data signals are received, amplified, and re-transmitted by each of these stations.

Since microwaves travel in a straight line, if the towers are too far apart, the earth will get in the way. Consequently, repeaters are needed periodically. The higher the towers are, the further apart they can be. The distance between repeaters goes up very roughly with the square root of the tower height. For 100 meter high towers, repeaters can be spaced 80 km apart.

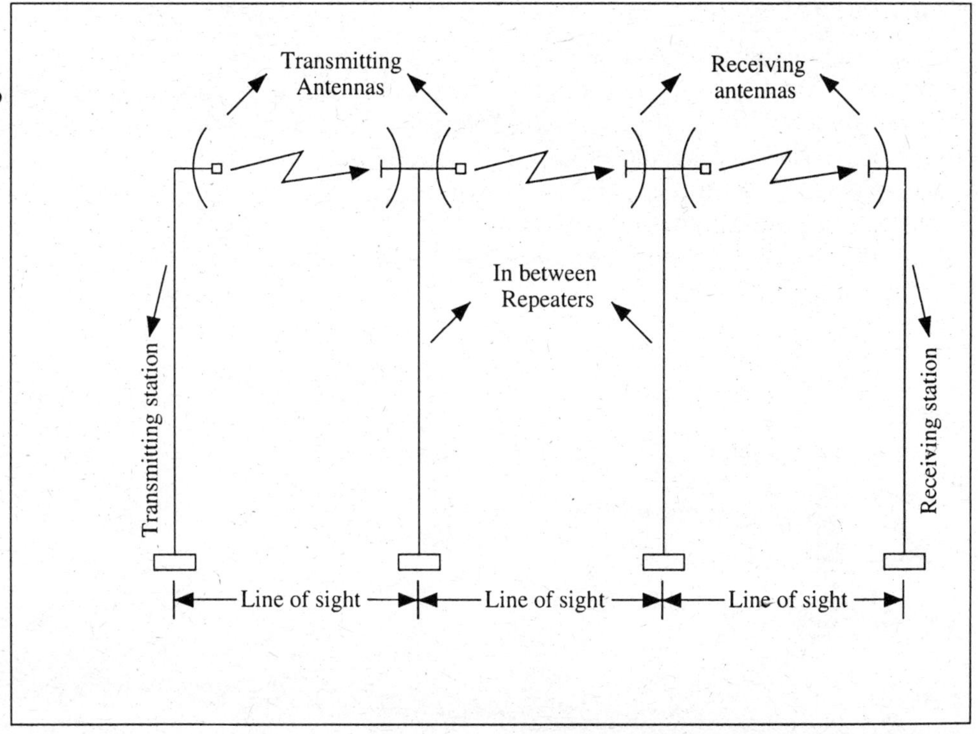

Figure 4.7 Illustrating microwave communication from one point to another

☞ Unlike radio waves, at lower frequencies, microwaves do not pass through buildings well. In addition, even though the beam may be well focused at the transmitter, there is still some divergence in space. Some waves may be reflected off low-lying atmospheric layers and may take slightly longer to arrive than direct waves. The delayed waves may arrive out of phase with the direct wave and thus cancel the signal. This effect is called *Multipath Fading*. It is often a serious problem in Microwave communication systems.

Characteristics of Microwave Communication

Microwave transmission is weather and frequency dependent. The frequency band of 10 GHz is in the routine use. Microwave communication is widely used for long-distance telephone communication, cellular telephones, television distribution, etc. The following are the characteristics of Microwave communications:

(a) Microwave is relatively inexpensive as compared to fiber optics system. For example, putting up two simple towers and antennas on each ends may be cheaper than burying 50 km of fiber through a congested area.

(b) Microwave systems permit data transmission rates of about 16 Giga (1 giga = 10^9) bits per second. At such high frequencies, microwave systems can carry 250,000 voice channels at the same time. They are mostly used to link big metropolitan cities which have heavy telephone traffic between them.

Satellite Links

Satellite Microwave systems transmit signals between directional parabolic antennas as shown in Figure 4.8. Like terrestrial microwave systems, they use low giga hertz frequencies and must be in line-of-sight. The main difference with satellite systems is that one antenna is on the satellite in geo-synchronous orbit about 36,000 kilometers (22,300 miles) above the equator. Because of this, satellite microwave systems can reach the most remote places on earth and communicate with mobile devices.

Figure 4.8 Satellite communication from one point to another

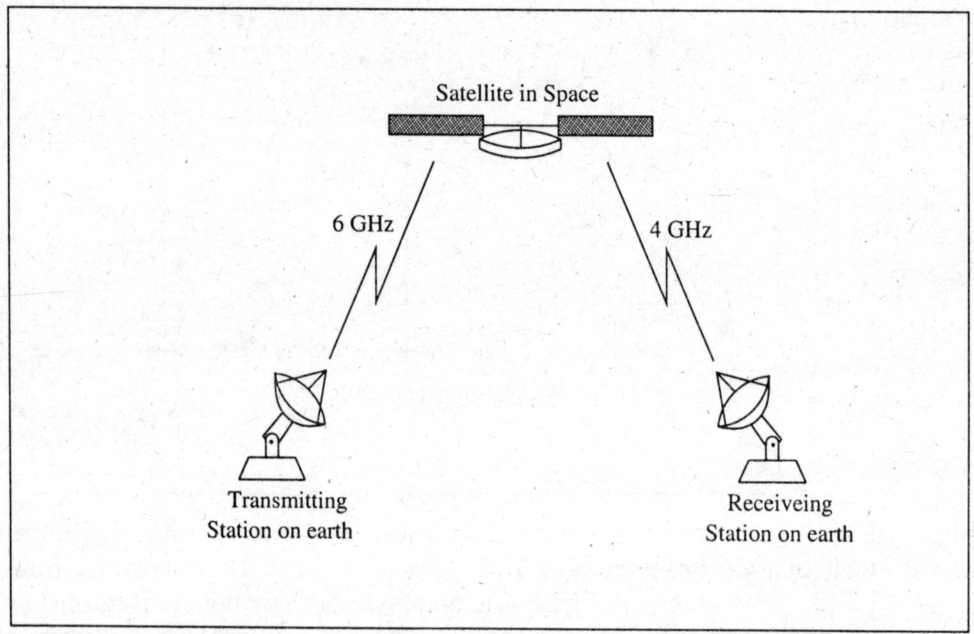

☞ A communication satellite is basically a microwave relay station placed precisely at 36,000 km above the equator where its orbit speed exactly matches the earth's rotation speed. Since a satellite is positioned in a *geo-synchronous* orbit, (i.e. the orbit where the speed of the satellite matches the earth's rotation speed), it appears to be stationary relative to earth and always stays over the same point with respect to earth. This allows a ground station to aim its antenna at a fixed point in the sky.

In satellite communication, microwave signals at 6 GHz (read as giga hertz = 10^9 Hz) are transmitted from a transmitter on earth to a satellite positioned in space. By the time this signal reaches the satellite it becomes weak as it travels a distance of 36,000 km. The transponder in a satellite amplifies the weak signals and sends them back to the earth at a frequency of 4 GHz. These signal are received at a receiving station on the earth. It may be noted that the transmitting frequency is different from the receiving frequency of the satellite. This is done to avoid interference of the powerful re-transmitted signal with the weak incoming signal.

Satellite microwave systems have the following characteristics:

Frequency range: Satellite links operate in the low giga hertz range typically, 4-6 GHz and 11-14 GHz.

Cost: The cost of building and launching a satellite is very expensive. Many companies such as AT &T, Hughes, etc. lease services, making them affordable for larger number of organizations. Although satellite communications are expensive, the cost of cable to cover the same distance may be even more expensive.

Installation: Satellite microwave installation for orbiting satellites is highly technical and difficult. In addition, the earth stations too need very high accuracy for moving antennas directed to the satellite.

Bandwidth Capacity: Capacity depends on the frequency used. Typical data rates are 1 to 10Mbps.

Attenuation: Attenuation depends on frequency, power, antenna size, and atmospheric conditions. Higher-frequency microwaves are more affected by rain and fog.

Advantages and Limitations of Satellite Communication

The main advantage of satellite communication is that it is a single microwave relay station visible from any point of a very large area on the earth. For example, satellites used for national transmission are visible from all parts of the country. Thus, transmission and reception can be between any two randomly chosen places in that area. Moreover, transmission and reception costs are independent of the distance between the two points. In addition to this, a transmitting station can receive back its own transmission and check whether the satellite has transmitted the information correctly. If an error is detected, the data would be retransmitted.

☞ A major drawback of satellite communications has been the high cost of placing the satellite into its orbit. Moreover, a signal sent to a satellite is broadcast to all receivers within the satellite's range. Hence necessary security measures need to be taken to prevent unauthorized tampering of information.

Table 4.3 lists the major commercial bands. The C band was the first to be designated for commercial traffic. This band is already overcrowded because it is also used by the common carriers for terrestrial microwave links. The next higher bands available to commercial telecommunication carriers are the Ku and Ka bands. These bands are not congested. However, at these frequencies rain water is an excellent absorber of short microwaves. In the earliest satellites, the division of the transponders into channels was static by splitting the bandwidth up into fixed frequency bands (FDM). Nowadays, time division multiplexing is also used due to its greater flexibility.

Table 4.3 Principal Satellite Bands of Frequencies

Uplink (GHz)	Frequencies (GHz)	Downlink(GHz)	Uplink(GHz)	Problems
C	4/6	3.7 - 4.2	5.925-6.425	Terrestrial interference
Ku	11/14	11.7-12.2	14.0-14.5	Rain
Ka	20/30	17.7-21.7	27.5-30.5	Rain; equipment cost

VSATs (Very Small Aperture Terminals)

These tiny terminals have 1-meter antennas and can put out about 1 watt of power. The uplink is generally good for 19.2 Kbps, but the downlink is more, often 512 kbps. In many VSAT systems, the micro-stations do not have enough power to communicate directly with one another. Instead, a special ground station, the hub, with a large high gain antenna is needed to relay traffic between VSATs as shown in Figure 4.9.

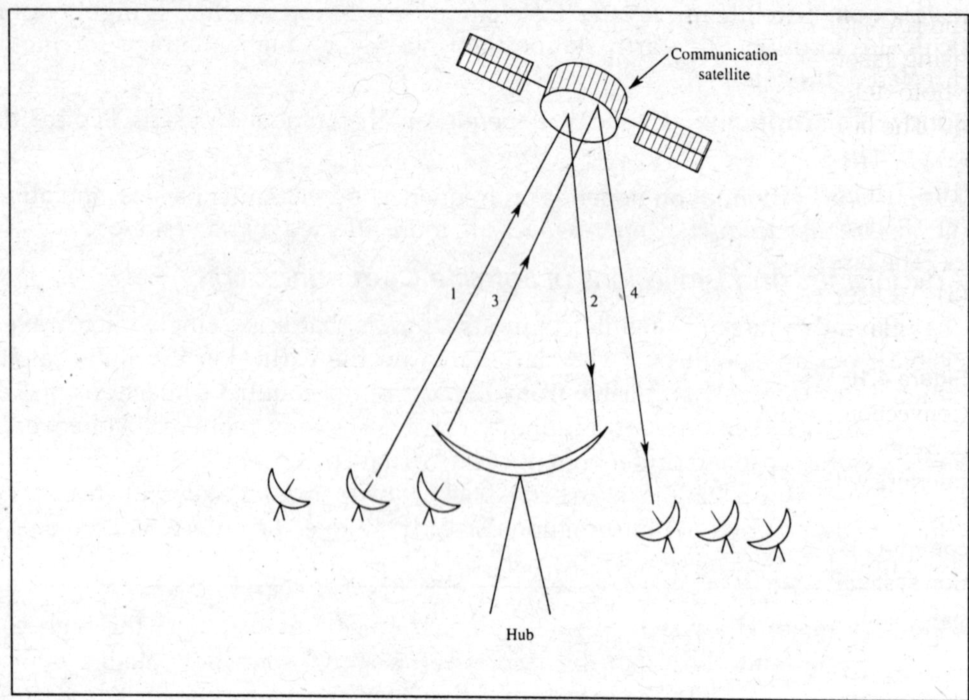

Figure 4.9 VSATs using a hub

In this mode of operation, either the sender or the receiver has a large antenna and a powerful amplifier. The trade-off is a longer delay in return for having cheaper end-user stations. The delay time or end-to-end transit time is between 250 to 300 msec (540 msec for a VSAT system with a hub)

Infrared and Millimeter Waves

Unguided infrared and millimeter waves are widely used for short-range communication. The remote controls used on television, VCRs, and stereos all use infrared communication. They are relatively directional, cheap and easy to build but do not pass through solid objects. An infrared system in one room of a building will not interfere with a similar system in adjacent rooms. Further, security of infrared systems against evesdropping is better than that of radio systems. Precisely for this reason, no government licence is needed to operate an infrared system in contrast to radio systems which must be licensed.

Infrared is used for indoor wireless LANs. For example, the computers and offices in a building can be equipped with relatively unfocussed infrared transmitters and receivers. In this way, portable computers with infrared capability can be on the local LAN without having to physically connect to it. When several people show up for a meeting with their portables, they can just sit down in the conference room and be fully connected without having to plug in.

Light Wave Transmission

Unguided optical signalling has been in use for long time. A modern application is to connect the LANs in two buildings via lasers mounted on their roof tops. Coherent optical signaling using lasers is inherently unidirectional, so each building needs its own laser and its own photo detector.

The laser beam transmission method has the following advantages:

(a) The band width is very high at very low cost.
(b) It is relatively easy to install.
(c) It does not require any licence.

The laser beam transmission method has the following disadvantages:

(a) Laser beams cannot penetrate rain or thick fog, but they normally work well on sunny days.

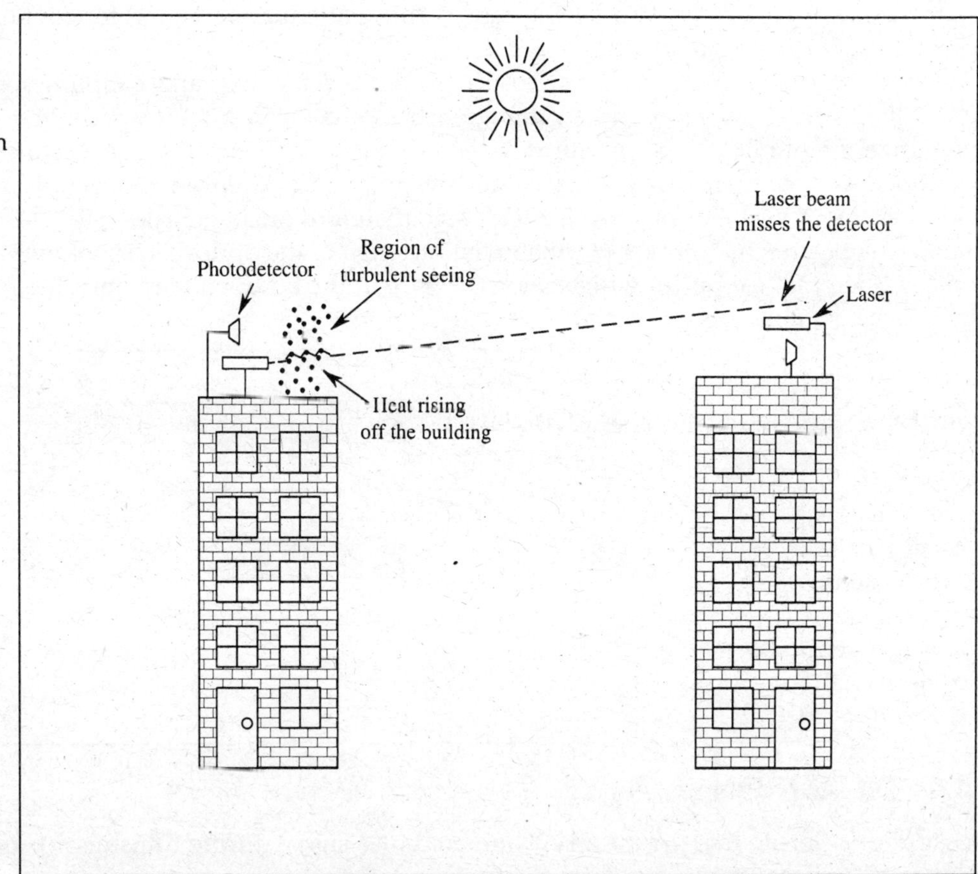

Figure 4.10 Convection currents interfere with laser communication systems

(b) Heat from the sun during the daytime causes convection current to rise up from the roof of the building as shown in Figure 4.10. This turbulent air diverts the beam and makes it dance around the detector.

4.3 ATTENUATION

Attenuation is the loss of signal strength with long distances when signals travel along cabling. Attenuation values for actual cables are measured in units of decibels (dB), standard measurement value used in communication for expressing the ratio of two values of voltage, power, or some other signal-related quantity. For example, a drop of 3 dB corresponds to a decrease in signal strength of 50 percent or 2:1.

☞ Attenuation values for cabling media are expressed in units of decibels per 1000 feet, which express the amount of attenuation in decibels for a standard 1000-foot length of cabling composed of that media.

Copper cabling has much greater attenuation than fiber-optic cabling; therefore, copper is suitable only for relatively short cable runs. Typical attenuation values for copper category 5 cabling vary with frequency.

Attenuation is caused by signal absorption, connector loss, and coupling loss. To minimize attenuation, use high-grade cabling such as enhanced category 5 cabling. Also try to minimize the number of connector devices or couplers, ensuring that these are high-grade components as well. When a signal attenuates to a large extent, the receiving device might not be able to detect it or might misinterpret it, therefore causing errors.

As can be seen in Figure 4.11, due to the message of the optical energy flowing through a optical fiber, the two pulses which are very sharp at the input end are quite attenuated when they leave the fiber cable.

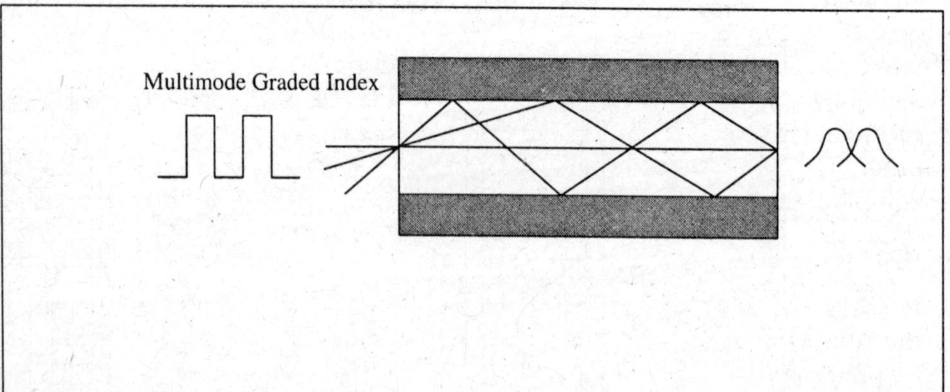

Figure 4.11 Attenuation in a fiber cable where shape of the pulse at the input and out put are quite different due to attenuation

4.4 DISTORTION

Distortion refers to the corruption encountered by a signal during transmission or processing that mutilates the signal waveform.

Distortion can be classified into the following types:

(a) Linear distortion
(b) Non-linear distortion
(c) Distortion due to Time-variant Multipath Channels

4.4.1 Linear distortion

Filtering of signal through an electronic filter causes the linear distortion. An ideal filter or distortionless filter is one that has a band of frequency equal to or exceeds the bandwidth of the input signal. If that is not the case, the input waveforms and the output waveforms will differ. This can only be avoided by employing a filter of better quality having larger bandwidth than that of the waveform which it is going to filter.

4.4.2 Non-linear distortion

Non linear distortion is caused due to the high amplitude of the input signal. All the frequencies are not amplified equally due to non-linear characteristic of the amplifier for frequencies and therefore, the output of the amplified signal is not the replica of the input signal with higher amplification. This type of distortion can be observed when you increase the volume of the TV audio circuit or the HI-FI music system. The sound of the drum and the sound of flute do not have the same level of loudness as it is in the original signal.

4.4.3 Distortion due to Time-Variant Multipath Channels

Radio waves from a transmitting antenna often reach the receiving antenna through many different paths. Examples include different reflecting layers in the ionosphere, numerous scattering points in the troposphere, reflections from the Earth's surface and the direct line-of-sight path. Each of these paths will contribute a different attenuation and the time delay. Because these variations in channel characteristics are generally unpredictable, the received signal at the receiving antenna is distorted and when amplified by the receiver amplifier, the distortion becomes significant. You can observe this effect during the night time on Short wave radio stations. The phenomenon is called fading. In this type of distortion, the signal is sometimes high when the reflected signal and directly received signals are in phase at the receiving antenna. And at another time, if two signals are opposite in phase, they cancel each other. This type of distortion is more prominent in amplitude modulated radio signals as compared to frequency modulated signals.

4.5 NOISE

Noise is the random electrical interference on network cabling that is generated by networking components such as network interface cards (NICs). It is also the one induced in cabling by proximity to the electrical equipment that generates electromagnetic interference (EMI).

☞ Noise is generated by all electrical and electronic device, including motors, fluorescent lamps, power lines and office equipment.

The better the signal-to-noise ratio of an electrical transmission system, the greater the efficiency of the system.

One source of performance degradation, which cannot be easily overcome, is due to noise. The source of noise, it seems to come from the airwaves, or in other words the signal that arrives at the receiving antenna. In addition, some of the noise is created internally by the electronic circuits also. This internally generated noise is called the thermal noise. This noise is mostly dependent on the temperature of the source and it is independent of frequency of the source. In digital circuits, it is called the error rather than the word noise. The noise in the semiconductor devices is called the shot noise. It is similar to thermal noise except that it is independent of temperature. In low frequency applications, below a few kilohertz, some transistors exhibit burst noise and flicker noise, which tend to fall off quickly with increasing frequency.

You can generally reduce noise by using higher-quality components, lowering the temperature of components, or using shielded cabling. You should locate sensitive networking components and cabling away from heavy machinery, generators, motors and other equipment that can generate a lot of interference.

4.6 THROUGHPUT

Throughput is the total amount of useful processing carried out by a computer system within a given time period. It is a measure of the efficiency of a computer system. Throughput is a measure of the average rate of processing a problem or batch of problems.

For calculating the throughput in data transmission, let us define the following parameters:

R = data rate of the channel
d = maximum distance between any two stations
V = velocity or signal propagation
L = average of fixed frame length

The throughput is just the number of bits transmitted per unit time. A frame contains L bits, and the amount of time devoted to that frame is the actual transmission time (L/R) plus the propagation delay (d/V). Thus,

$$\text{Throughput} = \frac{L}{d/V + L/R} \tag{4.1}$$

4.7 PROPAGATION SPEED AND TIME

The Effect of Propagation Delay and Transmission Rate is of important consideration when sending data through a media. We shall first define a parameter a as follows:

$$a = \frac{\text{Propagation time}}{\text{Transmission time}}$$

This parameter is also important in the context of LANs and MANs, and, in fact, determines an upper bound on utilisation. Consider a perfectly efficient access mechanism that allows only one transmission at a time. As soon as one transmission is over, another station begins transmitting. Furthermore, the transmission is pure data; there are no overhead bits. What is the maximum possible utilisations of the network? It can be expressed as the ratio of total throughput of the network to its capacity:

$$U = \frac{\text{Throughput}}{\text{Capacity}} \tag{4.2}$$

Using equations (4.1) we can rewrite a as:

$$a = \frac{d/V}{L/R} = \frac{Rd}{LV} \tag{4.3}$$

Using equations 4.2 and 4.3 we can derive easily the following relation:

$$U = \frac{1}{1+a} \tag{4.4}$$

So, utilisation varies with a.

4.8 RADIO COMMUNICATION WAVELENGTHS

Radio waves have frequencies between 10 kilohertz (KHz) and 1 giga hertz (GHz). Radio waves include the following types:

(a) Short-wave
(b) Very-high-frequency (VHF) television and FM radio.
(c) Ultra-high-frequency (UHF) radio and television

The range of frequency and type of medium used for their transfer is shown in Figure 4.12. Radio waves can be broadcast omnidirectionally or directionally. Various kinds of antennas can be used to broadcast radio signals. The power of the radio frequency (RF) signal is determined by the antenna and trans-receiver (a device that TRANSmits and reCEIVEs a signal over a medium such as copper, radio waves, or fiber-optic cables).

In vacuum, all electromagnetic waves travel at the same speed, no matter what their frequency is. This speed, usually called the speed of light, c, and it is approximately 3×10^8 meters per second or about 1 foot per nanosecond. In copper or fiber the speed slows to about 2/3 of this value and becomes slightly frequency dependent. The fundamental relation between frequency, (f), wave length λ, and c (in vacuum) is

$$\lambda f = c \tag{4.5}$$

For example, 1 MHz waves are about 300 meters long and 1 cm waves have a frequency of 30 GHz.

4.9 SHANNON CAPACITY

The maximum data rate of a noisy channel whose band width is H Hz, and whose signal-to-noise ratio is S/N, is given by:

Maximum number of bits/sec = $H \times [\log_2 (1 + S/N)]$

This equation is known as Shanon's formula, for Channel's capacity.

For example, a channel of 3000 Hz band width, and a signal to thermal noise ratio of 30 dB (typical parameters of the analog part of the telephone system) can never transmit much more than 18,000 bps, no matter how many or few signal levels are used and no matter how often or how infrequent samples are taken. These results are derived based on Shannon's formula and is called the Shannon's limit. A bit rate of 9600 bps on a voice grade telephone line is considered excellent.

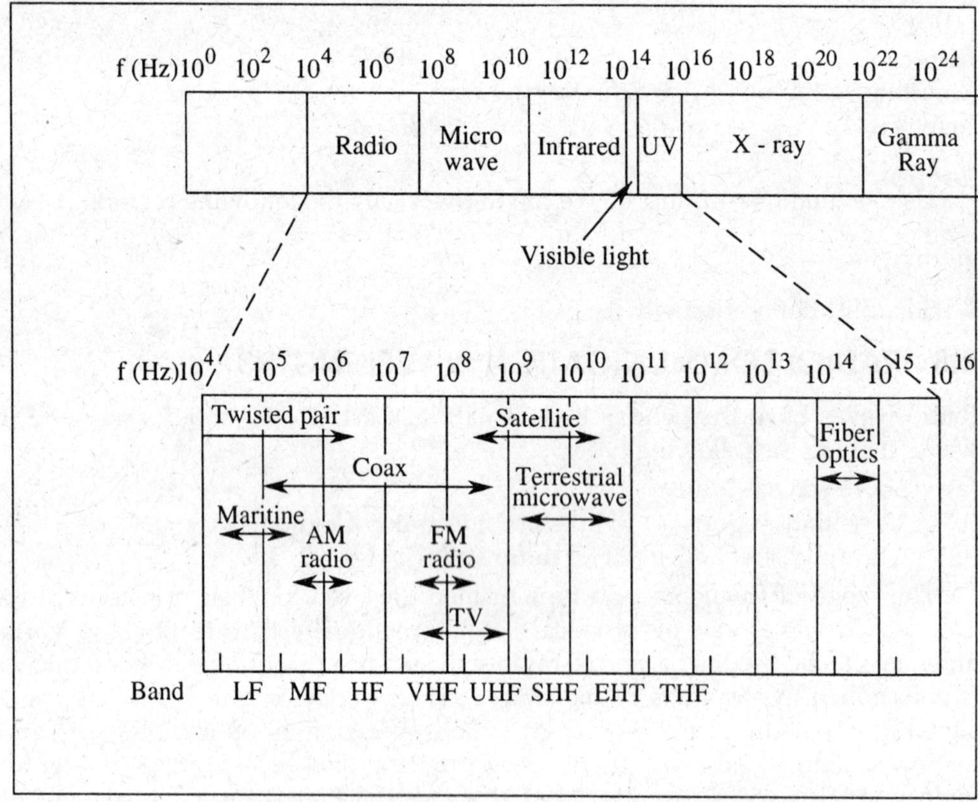

Figure 4.12 Radio frequency range and type of transmission media

4.10 COMPARISON OF MEDIA

4.10.1 Trade-off between Coaxial Cable and Twisted-pair Wiring

Following factors give the comparison between the coaxial cable and twisted pair wiring as transmission media.

Cost

In general, coaxial cable is more expensive by a factor of two or three than twisted pair, and more expensive by a smaller factor than shielded twisted pair.

Data Rate

The difference between coaxial and twisted pair is more apparent in the data rate that they support. For comparable distances to be spanned, twisted pair will typically be suitable for data rates at least an order of magnitude less. If the data rate of choice is 1-Mbps, then either coax or twisted pair will suffice at distances out to several hundred meters. At 10 Mbps, only coaxial will serve.

Security

Cables that employ copper conductors can easily be breached by listening equipment. If the main consideration is security, then fiber cable is the only choice to avoid espionage. However, it is to be remembered that no system can ever be perfectly secure. Even fiber-optic lines can be tapped without detection.

Electromagnetic compatibility

Coaxial cable emits less radiation which may cause interference with the communication equipment as compared to twisted wires.

4.10.2 Comparison of Fiber Optics and Copper Wire

Advantages

Fiber has many advantages over copper wire as a transmission medium. These are:

(a) It can handle much higher band widths than copper. Due to the low attenuation, repeaters are needed only about every 30 km on long lines, versus about every 5 km for copper.

(b) Fiber is not affected by power surges, electromagnetic interference, or power failures. Nor it is affected by corrosive chemicals in the air, making it ideal for harsh factory environments.

(c) Fiber is lighter than copper. One thousand twisted pair copper cables of 1 km long weigh 8000 kg. But fibers have more capacity and weigh only 100 kg.

(d) Fibers do not leak light and are quite difficult to tap. This gives them excellent security against potential wiretappers.

Disadvantages

Fibers have the following disadvantages over copper wires:

(a) Fiber is an unfamiliar technology requiring skills most engineers do not have.

(b) Since optical transmission is inherently unidirectional, two-way communication requires either two fibers or two frequency bands on one fiber.

(c) Fiber interfaces cost more than electrical interfaces.

Characteristics of Bounded and Unbounded Media

Table 4.4 gives the comparative study of the Bounded media.

Table 4.4 Characteristics of Bounded Media

Factor	(UTP)	(STP)	Coaxial Cable	Fiber optic
Cost	Lowest	Moderate	Moderate	Highest
Installation	Easy	Fairly easy	Fairly easy	Difficult
Bandwidth Capacity	1 to 155 Mbps (typically 10 Mbps)	1 to 155 Mbps (typically 16 Mbps)	typically 10 Mbps	2 Gbps (typically 100 Mbps)

(Contd...)

Factor	(UTP)	(STP)	Coaxial Cable	Fiber optic
Attenuation	High (Range few hundred meters)	High (Range few hundred meters)	Lower (range of a few kilometers)	Lowest (range of tens of kilometers)
Electromagnetic Interference (EMI)	Most vulnerable to EMI and eaves-dropping	Less vulnerable than UTP but still vulnerable to EMI and eves-dropping	Less vulnerable than UTP but still vulnerable to EMI and eves-dropping	Not affected by EMI or evesdropping

Table 4.5 gives the comparative study of the Unbounded media.

Table 4.5 Comparison of Unbounded media

Characteristics	Terrestrial Microwave Link	Satellite Microwave Link
Construction	Consists of directional parabolic antennas. Both antennas are on the ground.	Uses directional antennas, with one antenna on the ground and other is on a satellite. The satellite is in geo-synchronous orbit (36,000 km.) above the equator.
Range of operation	Relay towers are used to extend the range.	Range is quite high. A transponder is used in the satellite which transforms the received weak signal from the earth station into high power signal at a different down link frequency to reach the receiving earth station.
Frequency range	4 to 6 GHz and 21 to 23 GHz.	4 to 6 GHz and 11 to 14 GHz.
Cost	Compared to satellite communication, the cost is low.	Very high.
Band width and capacity	Data rates are from 1 to 10 Mbps.	1 to 10 Mbps.
Range of operation	With in line-of-sight. Repeaters are needed for higher range of communication.	Communication can be established around the earth because the range of satellites is very high.

Table 4.6 gives the comparison of STP and coaxial cable.

Table 4.6 Comparison of STP and Coaxial Cable

Characteristics	STP	Coaxial Cable
Construction	They are available in different varieties. Category 3 twisted pairs consist of two insulated wires gently twisted together. Four such	Coaxial cable consist of a stiff copper wire as the core surrounded by insulating material. The signal is transmitted by the inner copper

(Contd...)

Characteristics	STP	Coaxial Cable
	pairs are typically grouped together in a plastic sheath for protection and to keep the eight wires together	wire and electrically shielded by the outer sleeve.
Effect of noise due to EMI	Comparatively low because of shielding.	Very low.
Breakable	Being thin in size, the wires are likely to break.	Comparatively, more robust.
Band width and range	can support 19,200 bps up to 50 feet on RS-232C port. On a 10BASE-T, it can support 10 Mbps up to 100 meters.	Can support up to tens of Mbps at a distance of several thousand feet.
Ease of maintenance of equipment	Easy to join and connect the STP cables.	Difficult to network devices and needs more planning compared to STP.
Electromagnetic compatibility	STP emits large amount of electro-magnetic radiation	Emit very low radiation and causes less interference with the communication equipment.
Cost	Low	High

REVIEW QUESTIONS WITH ANSWERS

Q. No. 1 Compare the following:

(a) Twisted pair and optical fiber.

(b) Terrestrial microwave link and satellite microwave

(c) STP and coaxial cable

Answer 1(a) Twisted pair and optical fiber.

Characteristics	Twisted Pair	Optical Fiber
Construction	Two insulated copper wire, twisted together in a helical shape. The copper conductors are of typically of the size of about 1 mm thick.	Made up of tiny threads of glass or plastics. The core is about the size of hair i.e. 8-10 microns in single mode fiber and 50 microns diameter in multimode fibers.
Principle of Transmission	Transmission of electro- magnetic energy along the wires.	Transmission of optical energy along the fiber.
Cost	Least expensive	It is very expensive.
Band width	Low. Depends on the thickness of the wire and the length of the cable. Several mega	Very high. Data rates of the order of 100 Mps to 2 Gbps is available. A

(Contd...)

Characteristics	Twisted Pair	Optical Fiber
	bits/sec can be achieved for a few km.	common multimode installation can support 100 Mbps over several km. length.
Attenuation	Attenuation is high because of the electromagnetic radiation of energy.	Attenuation is very low because there is light beam travelling in the fiber.
Chromatic dispersion	It is not there.	Fiber is effected by chromatic dispersion and causes error in the signal by shifting a bit value in multimode type of fibers.
Mode of data transmission	Full-duplex	Half-duplex
Effect of the damage in the cable	Only a part of the network will be effected.	The whole system containing many channels will suffer total damage.
Availability of trained manpower	Being the oldest method of data communication, ample trained manpower is available to maintain the twisted pair cables.	It is a new technology, therefore only few trained mechanics are available.
Uses	Can be used for both analog and digital data.	Used mainly for digital data.

Answer 1(b) Terrestrial and microwave link.

Characteristics	Terrestrial Microwave Link	Satellite Microwave Link
Construction	Consists of directional parabolic antennas. Both antennas are on the ground.	Uses directional antennas, with one antenna on the ground and other is on a satellite. The satellite is in geo-synchronous orbit (36,000 km.) above the equator.
Range of operation	Relay towers are used to extend the range.	Range is quite high. A transponder is used in the satellite which transforms

(*Contd...*)

Characteristics	Terrestrial Microwave Link	Satellite Microwave Link
		the received weak signal from the earth station into high power signal at a different down link frequency to reach the receiving earth station.
Frequency range of operation	4 to 6 GHz and 21 to 23 GHz.	4 to 6 GHz and 11 to 14 GHz.
Cost	Compared to satellite communication, the cost is low.	Very high.
Band width and capacity	Data rates are from 1 to 10 Mbps.	1 to 10 Mbps.
Range of operation	With in line of sight. Repeaters are needed for higher range of communication.	Communication can be established around the earth because the range of satellites is very high.

Answer 1 (c) STP and coaxial cable.

Characteristics	STP	Coaxial Cable
Construction	They are available in different varieties. Category 3 twisted pairs consist of two insulated wires gently twisted together. Four such pairs are typically grouped together in a plastic sheath for protection and to keep the eight wires together.	Coaxial cable consist of a stiff copper wire as the core surrounded by insulating material. The signal is transmitted by the inner copper wire and electrically shielded by the outer sleeve.
Effect of noise due to EMI	Comparatively low because of shielding.	Very low.
Breakable	Being thin in size, the wires are likely to break.	Comparatively, more robust.
Band width and range	Can support 19,200 bps up to 50 feet on RS-232C port.	Can support up to tens of Mbps at a distance of several thousand feet.
Ease of maintenance of equipment	On a 10BASE-T, it can support 10 Mbps up to 100 meters. Easy to join and connect the STP cables.	Difficult to network devices and needs more planning compared to STP.

(Contd...)

Characteristics	STP	Coaxial Cable
Electromagnetic compatibility	STP emits large amount of electromagnetic radiation	Emits very low radiation and causes less interference with the communication equipment.
Cost	Low	High

Q. No. 2 A fiber optic system requires 5 micro watts (μW) of power for proper functioning at the receiver. The cable is 10 km long and has an attenuation loss of 2 dB/km. There is a loss of 2 dB at both the source and the receiver. Calculate the required level of optical power at the optical source.

Answer

We know that the loss in the cable = dB loss per km × number of km length of the cable
= $2 \times 10 = 20$ dB.

Loss at the source = 2 dB (given)

Loss at the receiver = 2 dB (given)

Therefore total loss = $20 + 2 + 2 = 24$ dB

If X is the transmitted power then, the received power = 24 dB down

We know that at every 3 dB loss, the power becomes half the value.

Therefore, if X watts is the transmitted power, then the received power

$= 3 + 3 + 3 + 3 + 3 + 3 + 3 + 3 = 24$ dB. (Down)

$$= \frac{1}{2} \times \frac{1}{2} \times \frac{1}{2} \times \frac{1}{2} \times \frac{1}{2} \times \frac{1}{2} \times \frac{1}{2} \times \frac{1}{2}$$

$$= \left[\frac{X}{(2^8)}\right]$$

It is given to us that for proper working of the receiver, the received energy at the receiver should be $= 5 \times 10^{-6}$ watts.

As indicated above, if X is the transmitted power, then the total received power after losses = $[X/(2^8)]$ watts $= 5 \times 10^{-6}$ watts

Therefore $X = 5 \times 10^{-6} \times 2^8 = 10 \times 2^7 \times 10^{-6} = 1280$ (μW) micro watts.

Q. No. 3 Answer the following:

(a) Why do you connect the wire mesh conductor of a coaxial cable to the ground?

(b) Why the digital communication systems are more resistant to channel noise than analog systems.

Answer 3(a) We connect the outer conductor of a coaxial cable to the ground, in order to avoid the interference caused by the electromagnetic noise. The voltage induced by electromagnetic interference is sent to earth by grounding the outer conductor of a coaxial cable.

Answer 3(b) Digital communication systems are more resistant to channel noise because of the following reason:

The detector in the digital system needs to find the presence and the absence of a pulse and therefore even if there is noise, the detection is not very difficult. Moreover, noise is not a static quantity. Sometimes, noise signal is large and some times small but the pulses are of constant magnitude. Hence, their detection becomes easier. It is similar to the case of the sound of the whistle blown by a referee in a play ground can be easily discriminated even when there is noise in the field.

Q. No. 4

(a) Illustrate with the help of a schematic diagram the different components of a typical fiber optic link. Mention the various components of signal loss.

(b) State the advantages of semiconductor laser diode over light-emitting diodes (LED) for fiber transmission?

(c) State the mechanism by which an optical pulse travelling along a optical fiber suffers from dispersion.

(d) With a diagram show the structure of an optical fiber cable.

(e) What are the advantages and disadvantages of single mode optical fiber over multimode optical fiber.

Answer 4(a) Illustrate with the help of a schematic diagram the different components of a typical fiber optic link. Mention the various components of signal loss.

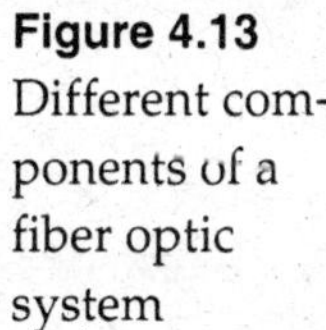

Figure 4.13 Different components of a fiber optic system

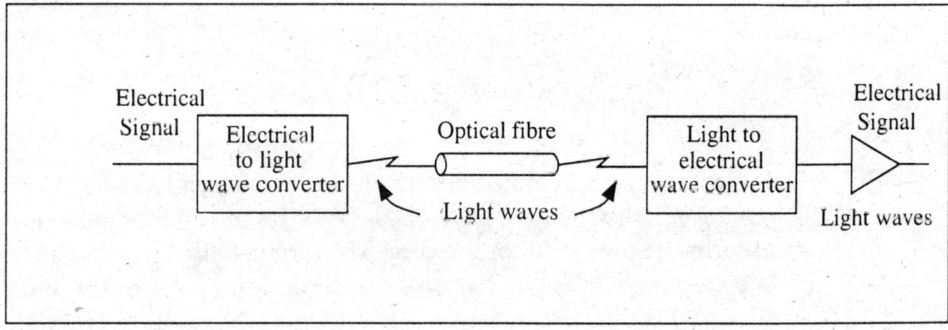

Figure 4.13 shows the different components of a fiber optic system.

Losses are due to the following reasons:

(a) Absorption and attenuation of the cable because the cladding is not completely opaque. So some of the light energy is absorbed into the cladding.

(b) Large losses result from the physical connections that bring light sources and detectors into alignment with the fiber cable.

(c) Misalignment of the light source to cable cause loss of light energy. The misalignments are reduced by precise fittings coupling and splices and by careful following the connecting processes given by the manufacturer.

(d) Loss of light also occurs because of bands in laying the cable.

Answer 4(b)

Advantages of semiconductor laser diode over light-emitting diodes (LED) for fiber transmission are:

(a) Data rate is high.
(b) Light can be transmitted in single mode as well as in multimode.
(c) The distance over which light pulses can be transmitted is about 30 km without any amplifier.

Answer 4(c) As shown in the Figure 4.14, light that enters the core at the center line travels in an unimpeded straight line through the core (as long as the core itself is straight).

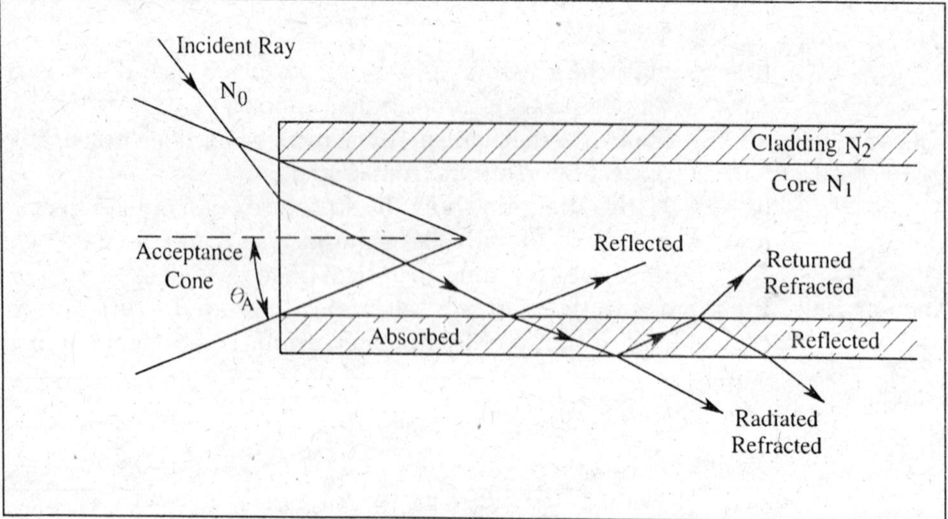

Figure 4.14 Light travelling through the core of a fiber optic system

Light entering at any other angle will eventually hit the cladding and be "bounced" down the cable. These rays travel greater distances than the ray entering at the center of the core. The larger the angle of incidence, the further the rays have to travel before exiting the core. As a result, the rays emerge at different times, resulting in a phenomenon called pulse spreading (dispersion) which causes the replicated electrical information to be distorted by the varying arrival times of the light rays through the cable. The distortion is not great, but it present a limiting factor to the length of the fiber cable and the data rates that are propagated through it. If the length is too long, then the spreading can cause the loss of digital bits and create data errors.

Answer 4(d) Each fiber has an inner core of glass or plastic that conduct light. This inner core of glass or plastic that conduct light. The inner core is surrounded by cladding, a layer of glass that reflects the light back into the core. Each fiber is surrounded by a plastic sheath. The sheath can be either tight or loose. (See Figure 4.11. Optical fibers are differentiated by core/cladding size and mode of operation. The following are the common types of fiber optic cable:

(a) 8.3-micron core/12.5-micron cladding, single-mode

(b) 62.5-micron core/125-micron cladding, multimode
(c) 50-micron core/125-micron cladding, multimode

Answer 4(e) Advantages of Single mode optical fiber over multimode optical fiber are:
(a) Greater band width
(b) Smaller size of core and cladding namely 8.3 micron core and 12.5 micron cladding
(c) Distortion and attenuation is very low

Disadvantages of Single mode optical fiber over multimode optical fiber are:
Multimode allows more light energy to enter the cable because wider acceptance angle as compared to single mode.

Q. No. 5. Define the following terms:
(a) Cladding
(b) Pulse spreading
(c) Refractive index

Answer 5(a) **Cladding:** It is the material that surrounds a fiber optic core which has a refractive index that causes light rays to be reflected back into the core.

Answer 5(b) **Pulse Spreading:** It is the signal distortion caused by different propagation times for each light ray travelling through a cable.

Answer 5(c) **Refractive Index:** It is the value that determines the amount of a light ray will be reflected or refracted by comparing the values of the indexes of two surfaces.

Q. No. 6. (a) How does an optical detector indicate the difference between a logic 1 (high-intensity light) and logic 0 (low-intensity light)?
(b) Describe what bends do to the losses in a fiber cable.
(c) What is the resulting effect of the light signal due to scattering?

Answer 6(a) The electron-hole generation of a photo detector varies directly with the amount of light it senses.

Answer 6(b) Bends in the fiber causes reflected and refracted rays to change directions. This can increase the absorption loss and distort the light pattern at the receiving end.

Answer 6(c) The effect of scattering is to attenuate the light energy as the ray travels through the core.

Q. No. 7. Describe in your own words, the nature of attenuation of an optical signal through a glass fiber and how does it vary with the wavelength of the optical signal. State the principal causes of attenuation in a fiber.

Answer 7 Fiber optic cables have very low attenuation as compared to copper wires. Chief reason being the transmission media is light. But fiber optic cables have another disadvantage and that is 'Chromatic dispersion'

The problem with fiber cable is that due to chromatic dispersion. Different wavelengths of light travel through glass differently, and the colours of a single pulse of light will spread apart slightly as they travel down a cable. At a distance of several miles, one bit may shift into the next bit, causing data to be lost.

Single mode fiber optic cable conveys only one frequency of light down the cable, so it does not suffer from chromatic dispersion. Hence, a semiconductor laser can convey data rate of 100 Mbps to 2 Gbps over a distance of 30 Km. This problem is very much present in the multimode fiber in which it transmits many beams simultaneously.

Some reasons for the losses in the data are the following:

(a) Absorption and attenuation of signal because of the cladding is not completely opaque.

(b) Large losses result from the physical connections between two wires that bring light sources and detectors into alignment. If alignment is not made properly, the losses increase.

(c) Losses also occur between the splices between the connectors.

(d) Bends in the fiber cables cause losses.

Q. No. 8. Illustrate with appropriate diagrams the light transmission in:

(a) single mode fiber

(b) step index multimode fiber

(c) graded index multimode fiber

Answer 8(a) Light transmission in single mode optical fiber

Systems using laser diodes as the light-emitting sources employ single mode optical fiber. The single mode concentrates the passage of light to the center of the fiber core. Where the center is very narrow about 6 to 12 micro meters in diameter, the ray concentrates at the centre moves the quickest through the cable with the least distortion and attenuation. (See Figure 4.15 (a))

Answer 8(b) Light transmission in step index multimode fiber

While the single mode fiber accepts only one light ray at a time, in a narrow diameter, the multimode fiber allows more than one ray of the light at a moment. With each ray at a slightly different angle from the other in a wider core. (See Figure 4.15 (b))

The first kind of multimode fiber is the step index. In the step index core, the incident ray enters the core, is refracted slightly and travels through the core as it is reflected from one side of the cladding to the other. The main disadvantage of this is that every time the ray strikes the cladding, the cladding absorbs some of its energy, resulting in a little of attenuation.

Answer 8(c) Light transmission in graded index fiber

The disadvantage of the step index core is removed by the graded index core. The incident ray enters the cable in the same way as in the case of the step index. However, instead of being reflected straight from the cladding, it is refracted in small increments as it travels through the core. The refraction bends the ray away from the cladding back towards the core. Thus, there is on loss due to the absorption of light by the cladding.

Figure 4.15
(a) Single mode optical fiber
(b) Step index fiber

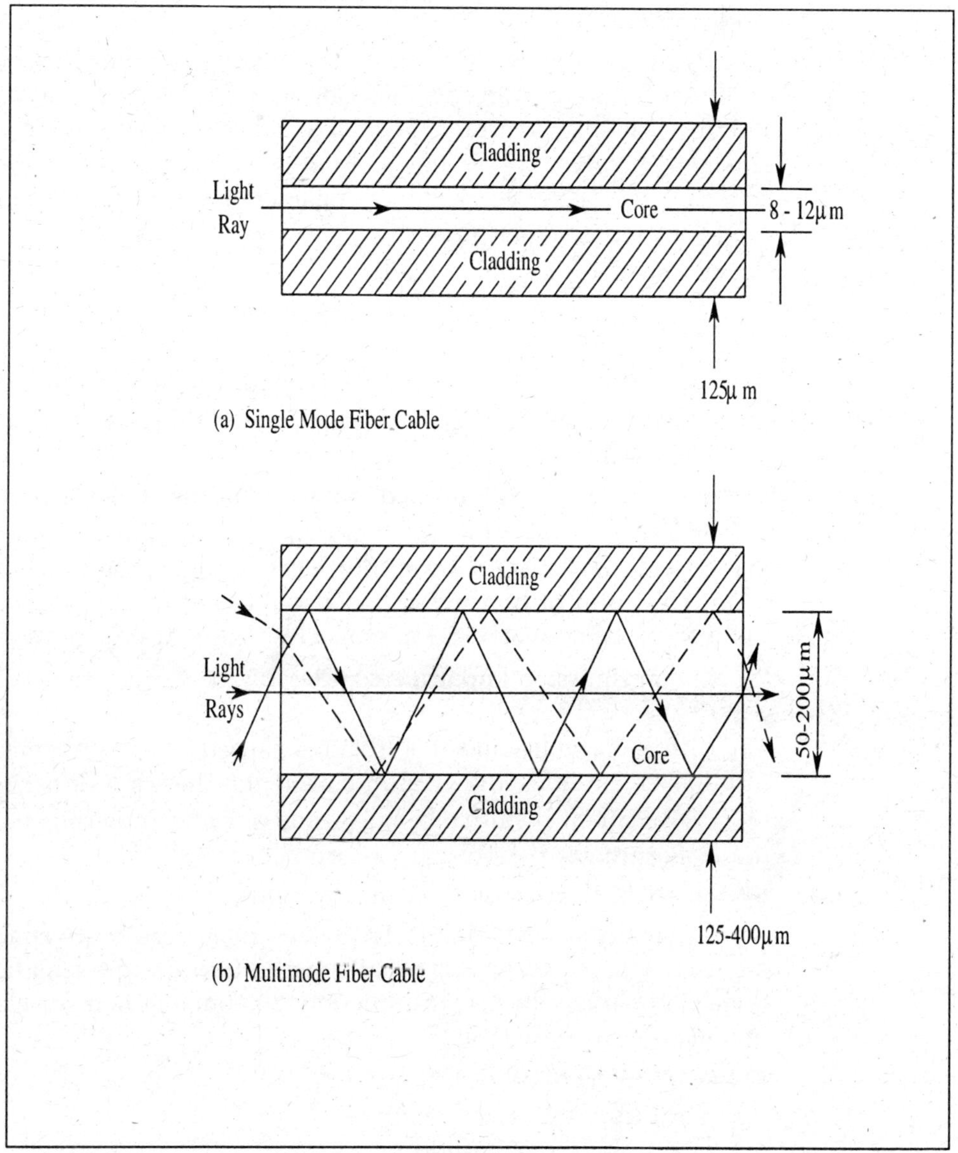

Q. No. 9. What do you understand by the term transmission media. Classify the different transmission media.

Answer Transmission media is the physical path between transmitter and receiver in a data transmission system.

Classification of transmission media

(a) Magnetic media
(b) Guided media or bounded media
(c) Unguided media or unbounded media

Magnetic media

Magnetic media is one of the most common ways to transport data from one computer to another. In this method, we write data on the magnetic media and physically transport the media like floppy disk, etc. to the other machine. The main disadvantage of this method is that it does not support the on-line data transfer. Moreover, there is considerable delay in the transfer of data from one place to other place.

Guided media or bounded media

With guided medium, the waves are guided along the a transmission medium such as:

(a) Twisted pair wires which are used for telephonic system.
(b) Coaxial cable of various sizes and electrical characteristics.
(c) Optical fiber.

Unguided media or unbounded media including wireless transmission

The atmosphere and the outer space are the examples of unguided medias, that provide a means of transmitting electromagnetic signals but do not guide them. This form of transmission is also referred to as wireless transmission. Cellular phone networks use microwaves to broadcast signals.

Q. No. 10. What is transmission impairments. Classify the various types of transmission disturbances.

Answer The distortion, noise and disturbances caused in the transmission of signal through a medium is known as impairments. These are classified as:

(a) Systematic disturbance/distortion or static impairments
(b) Fortuitous disturbance/distortion or transient impairments

Systematic distortion or static impairments

It occurs every time we transmit a given signal over a given channel. Knowing the channel, we can predict what is going to occur. Systematic distortion is, then, something which might possibly be compensated for electronically so that its effects are eliminated.

Types of static impairments

(a) Loss of energy
(b) Attenuation distortion
(c) Delay distortion
(d) Harmonic distortion
(e) Frequency offset

Fortuitous disturbance/distortion or transient impairments

It occurs at random so it is not predictable except in terms of probability. It refers to transient impairments rather than continuing conditions on the line. This type of disturbance is more difficult to compensate for except that steps can be taken to minimize its effects and repair the damage it does.

Types of transient impairments

(a) White noise/thermal noise

(b) Impulse noise

(c) Cross talk

(d) Intermodulation noise

(e) Radio fading

(f) Phase jitter

TEST PAPER

Time: 2 Hrs. Marks: 100

Note: Answer all questions.

1. Discuss the different guided and unguided media you have studied. Which media would you prefer for TV transmission and reception?
2. Write short notes on:
   (a) Transmission media
   (b) Transmission impairment
   (c) Bandwidth
3. What is the difference between serial and parallel transmission? Why do most communication systems use serial transmission?
4. What is the purpose of placing twists in a pair of wires used in a twisted pair as transmission medium? Why do we earth the shield of a co-axial cable.
5. What are the characteristics of terrestrial microwave and satellite microwave? Compare and contrast fiber optical communication with satellite communication. Which one would you prefer for higher bandwidth and why?

CHAPTER 5

Introduction to Signals

5.1 INTRODUCTION

Two basic types of signals are used with transmission media:
(a) analog
(b) digital

Analog signal technology is an old one and most of the electronic equipment designed are still working on the analog principles. But with the progress of digital communications and their benefits over analog signals, the digital signals are taking a lead over analog signals.

5.2 ANALOG AND DIGITAL SIGNALS

5.2.1 Analog Signals

Analog signals (See Figure 5.1) constantly vary in one or more values, and these changes in values can be used to represent data. Analog waveforms frequently take the form of sine waves.

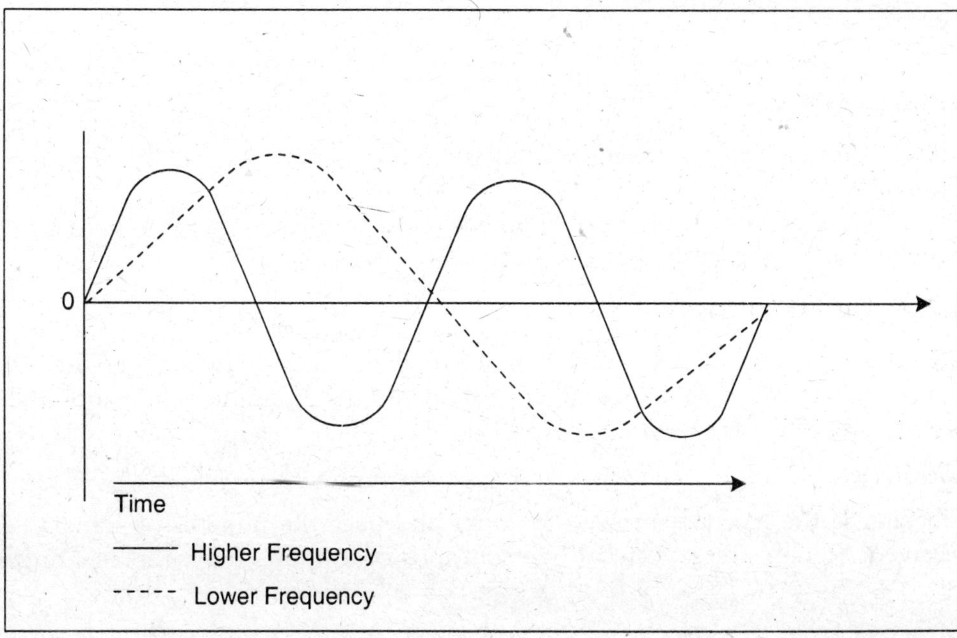

Figure 5.1 An example of analog signal or continuous signal

The two characteristics that define an analog waveform are as follows:

(a) Fréquency

(b) Amplitude

Frequency

Frequency indicates the rate at which the waveform changes. Frequency is associated with the wavelength of the waveform, which is a measure of the distance between two similar peaks on adjacent waves. Frequency generally is measured in Hertz (Hz), which indicates the frequency in cycles per second. The concept of frequency is illustrated in Figure 5.2.

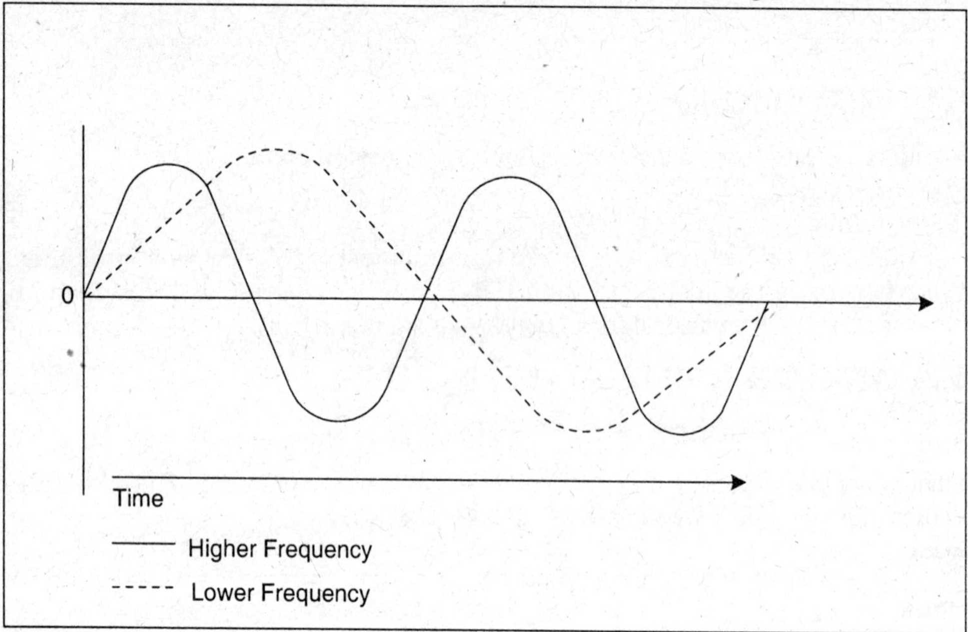

Figure 5.2 The two analog waveforms differing in frequency

Amplitude

Amplitude measures the strength of the waveform. The concept of amplitude is illustrated in Figure 5.3.

Each of these characteristics—frequency and amplitude—can be used to encode data to transmit and receive through a communication media.

5.2.2 Digital Signals

Digital signals are different than analog signals in that digital signals have two distinct or discrete states. These states are either "off" or "on". An example of how a digital signal is represented is seen in Figure 5.4.

Clocking

Clocking is the mechanism used to count and pace the number of signals being sent and received. Signals are expected to be sent in a continuous flow, representing the start and

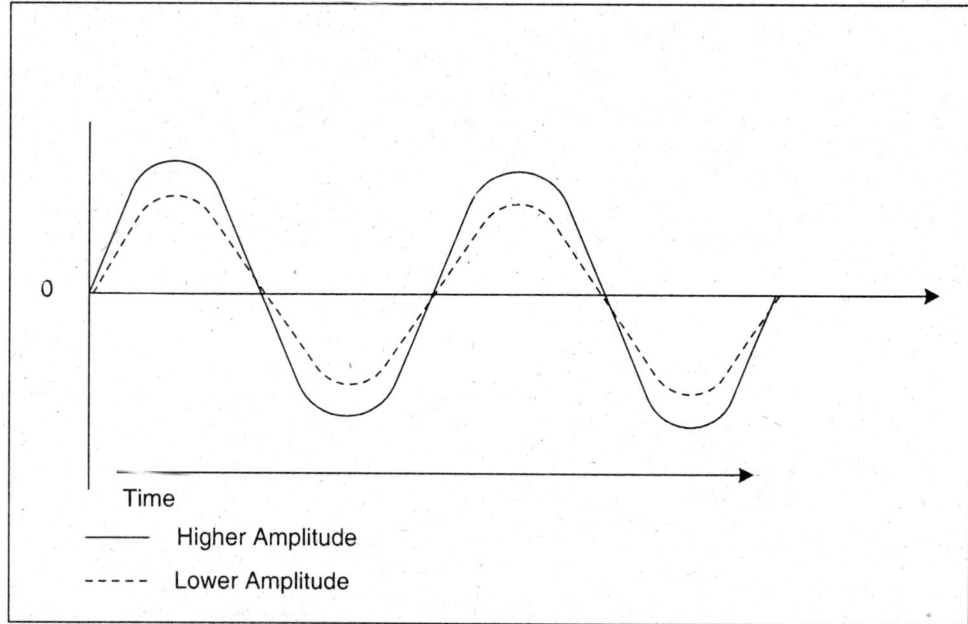

Figure 5.3 The two analog waveforms differing in amplitude

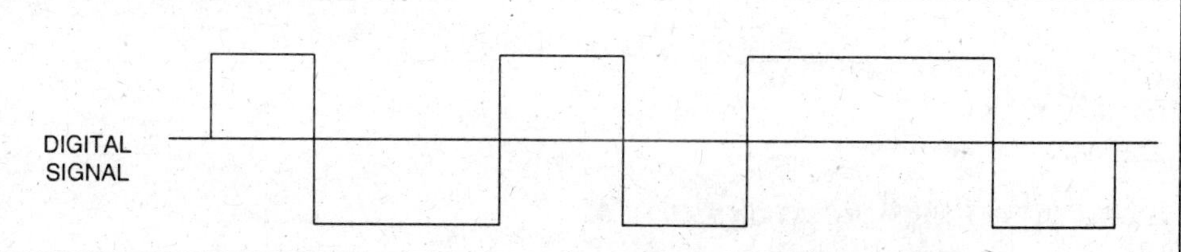

Figure 5.4 An example of digital signal or discrete signal

ending of data. Clocking is the mechanism used by the network adapter card to determine how much data has been sent. For example, if a network card is designed to transmit data at 20 millions cycles a second, then the other card receiving this data will also read data at 20 millions cycles a second.

☞ Clocking is a mechanism used by all network adapter cards to measure how much data has been sent or received. A good example of clocking is when a person taps his feet to keep the time to music. The person doing the tapping expects a set number of music beats each moment. Similarly, computer network cards also expect fixed number of signals each second.

Measurement of Digital Signals

Digital signals use one of two common measurement mechanisms:

(a) Current state

(b) State transition

The manufacturer of network cards builds these measurement capabilities into a network adapter card.

Current State Current state is a mechanism that uses the clock count to analyse the current state of the signal during that count. Thus, the signal is either "on" or "off" during the clock count. Figure 5.5 shows the idea of current state measurement. As seen in this Figure, during each count, the state of the digital signal is either "on" or "off".

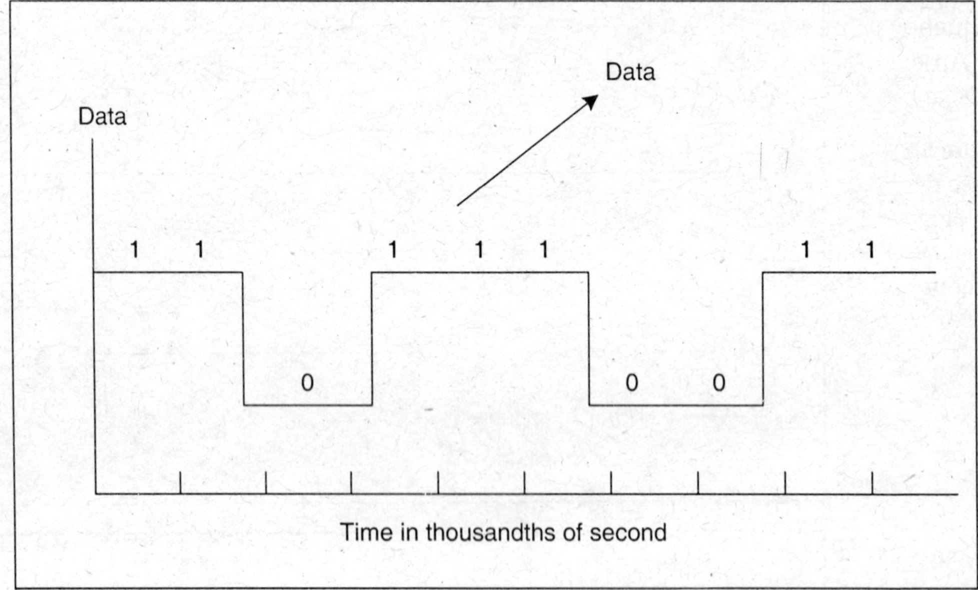

Figure 5.5 Measurement of current state

State transition Changes in the voltages happen during a state transition that measures the changes in the count of pulses.

Measurement of Analog Signals

Analog signals, much like digital, also follow a similar mechanism of measurement of signals. The main difference between digital and analog signals is that digital signals have two discrete states—"on" and "off"—and analog signals change frequencies.

Current State Two mechanisms using current state measurement technologies for analog signals are the frequency shift keying (FSK) and amplitude shift keying (ASK).

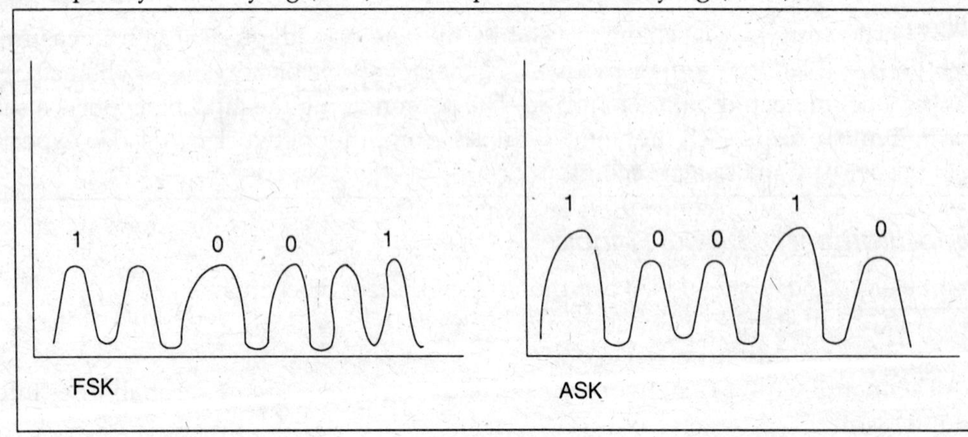

Figure 5.6 Signal using FSK and ASK signaling

FSK uses a change in frequency to indicate 1 or 0. An example of FSK and ASK is shown in Figure 5.6. In ASK, the amplitude change indicates a change in 1 or 0.

State Transition: State transition of a frequency is the measurement of a frequency's phase during a clock count. A *phase* is a difference in transition of a frequency. The *transition* of a frequency is the change between two frequencies. Figure 5.7 illustrate this.

An example of phase measurement is that a 1 may be represented by a 90 degree phase shift, and a 0 by no phase shift.

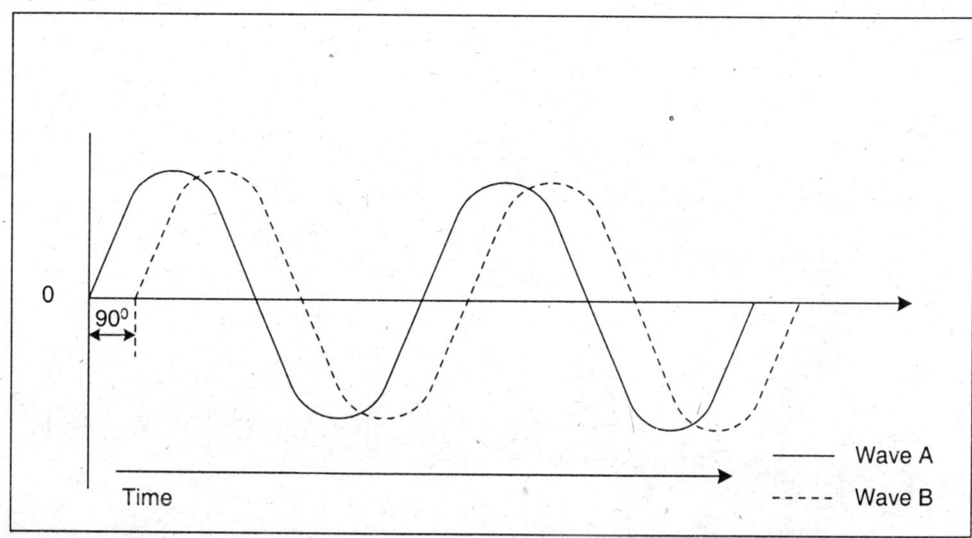

Figure 5.7 These two analog signals differ in phase

5.3 PERIODIC AND APERIODIC SIGNALS

Viewed as a function of time, an electromagnetic signal can be either continuous or discrete. A continuous signal is one in which the signal intensity varies in a smooth fashion over time. In other words, there are no breaks or discontinuities in the signal. A discrete signal is one in which the signal intensity maintains a constant level for some period of time and then changes to another constant level.

Figure 5.1 shows an examples of continuous or analog signal and Figure 5.4 shows a signal of discrete type or digital signal. The continuous signal might represent speech, and the discrete signal might represent binary 1s and 0s, just like the ringing of the bell in a church.

☞ The simplest sort of signal is *periodic signal*, in which the same signal pattern repeats over time. Figure 5.8 (part a) shows an example of periodic analog signal (sine wave) and Figure 5.8 (part b) shows the aperiodic or digital (discrete) signal (square wave).

Figure 5.8
Example of periodic signal
(a) analog
(b) digital

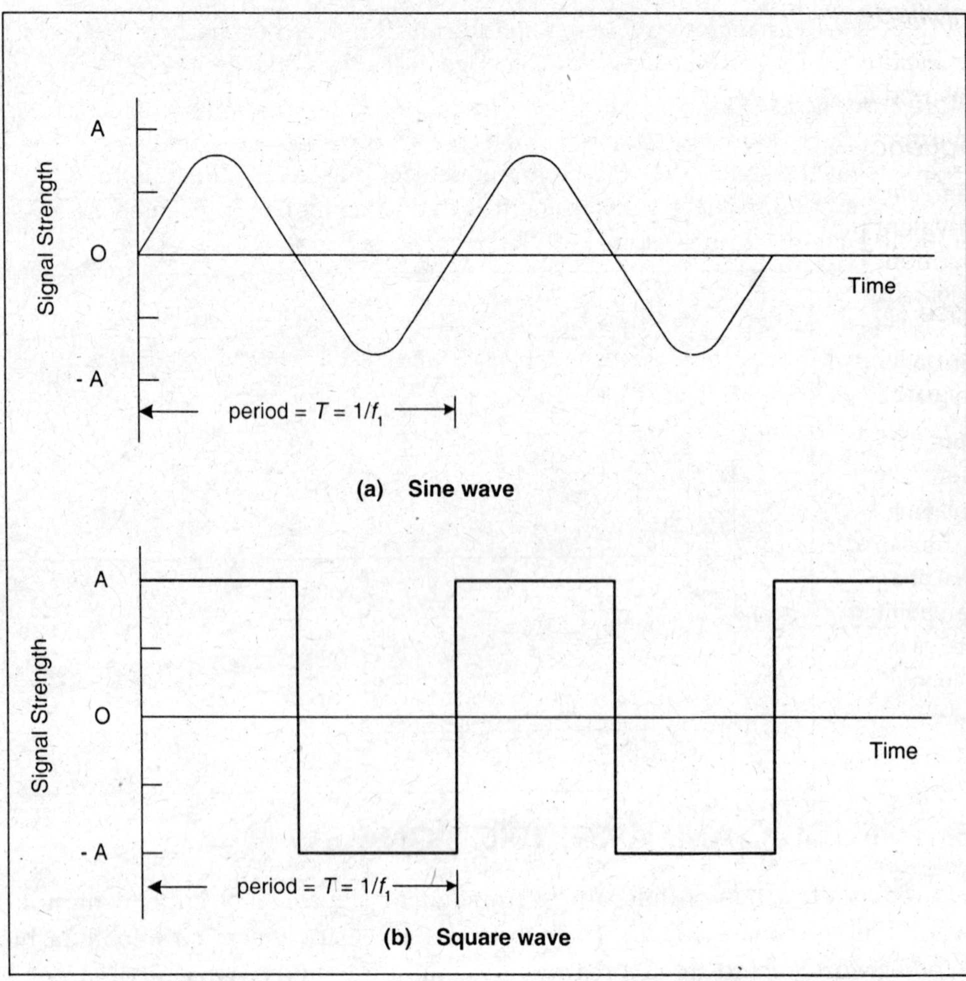

5.4 TIME AND FREQUENCY DOMAINS

5.4.1 Time Domain Concepts

Mathematically, a signal $s(t)$ is defined to be periodic if and only if

$$s(t+T) = s(t) \qquad -\infty < t < +\infty$$

where the constant T is the period of the signal. (T is the smallest value that satisfies the equation). Otherwise, a signal is not periodic or it is aperiodic.

The sine wave is the fundamental continuous signal. A general sine wave can be represented by three parameters:

(a) amplitude
(b) frequency
(c) phase

Amplitude (A)

The *amplitude* is the peak value or strength of the signal over time; typically, this value is measured in volts or watts.

Frequency (f)

The *frequency* is the rate (in cycles per second) or Hertz (Hz) at which the signal repeats. An equivalent parameter is the *period* (T) of a signal, which is the amount of time it takes for one repetition. Therefore, $T = 1/f$.

Phase (φ)

Phase is a measure of the relative position in time within a single period of a signal, as shown in Figure 5.9.

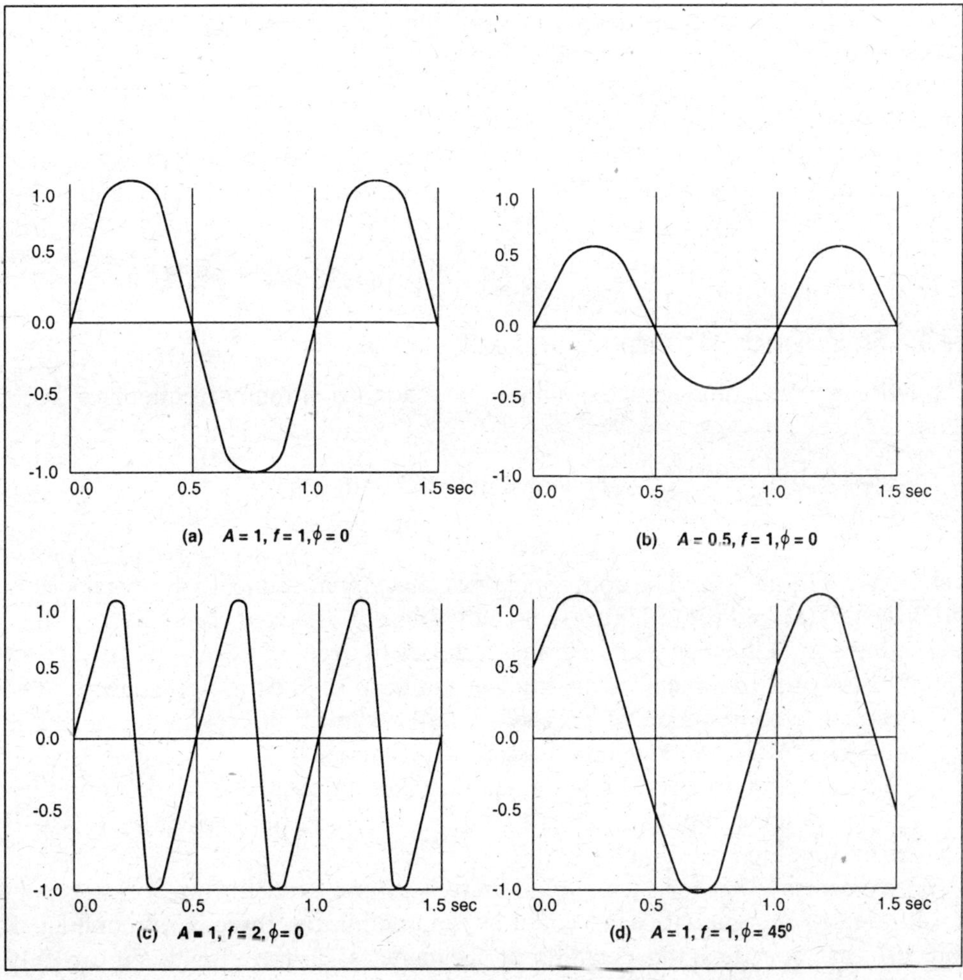

Figure 5.9 Graph displaying the value of a signal at a given point in space as a function of time

The general sine wave can be written as:

$$s(t) = A\sin(2\pi ft + \phi)$$

Figure 5.9 also shows the effect of varying each of the three parameters. In part (a) of the figure, the frequency is 1 Hz; thus, the period is $T = 1$ second. In part (b) it has the same frequency and phase but an amplitude of 1/2. In part (c), we have $f = 2$, which is equivalent to $T = 1/2$. Finally, part (d) shows the effect of a phase shift of $\pi/4$ radians, which is 45 degrees (2 π radians = 360^0 = 1 period).

In Figure 5.9, the horizontal axis is time; the graphs display the value of a signal at a given point in space as a function of time. These same graphs, with change of scale, can apply with horizontal axes in space. In this case, the graphs display the value of a signal at a given point in time as a function of a distance. For example, for a sinusoidal transmission (say an electromagnetic radio waves some distance from a radio antenna, or sound some distance from a loudspeaker), at a particular instant of time, the intensity of the signal varies in a sinusoidal way as a function of distance from the source.

There are two simple relationships between the two sine waves, one in time and one in space. Define the *wavelength*, λ, of a signal as the distance occupied by a single cycle, or, put another way, as the distance between two points of corresponding phase of two consecutive cycles. Assume that the signal is travelling with a velocity v. Then, the wavelength is related to the period as follows:

$$\lambda = vT$$

Equivalently, $\lambda f = v$.

5.4.2 Frequency Domain Concept

In practice, an electromagnetic signal will be made up of many frequencies. For example, the signal

$$s(t) = \sin(2\pi f_1 t) + \frac{1}{3}\sin(2\pi(3f_1)t)$$

is shown in Figure 5.10. The components of this signal are just sine waves of frequencies f_1 and $3f_1$. Parts (a) and (b) of Figure 5.10 show these individual components. There are several interesting points that can be made out from this figure:

(a) The second frequency is an integer multiple of the first frequency. When all of the frequency components of a signal are integer multiples of one frequency, the latter frequency is referred to as the fundamental frequency.

(b) The period of the total signal is equal to the period of the fundamental frequency. The period of the component sin $(2\pi f_1 t)$ is $T = 1/f_1$, and the period of $s(t)$ is also T, as can be seen from Figure 5.10 (c).

So we can say that for each signal, there is a time-domain function $s(t)$ that specifies the amplitude of the signal at each instant in time. Similarly, there is a frequency-domain function $s(f)$ that specifies the constituent frequencies of the signal. Figure 5.11 shows the frequency-domain function for the signal in Figure 5.10 (c).

Figure 5.10 Addition of frequency components

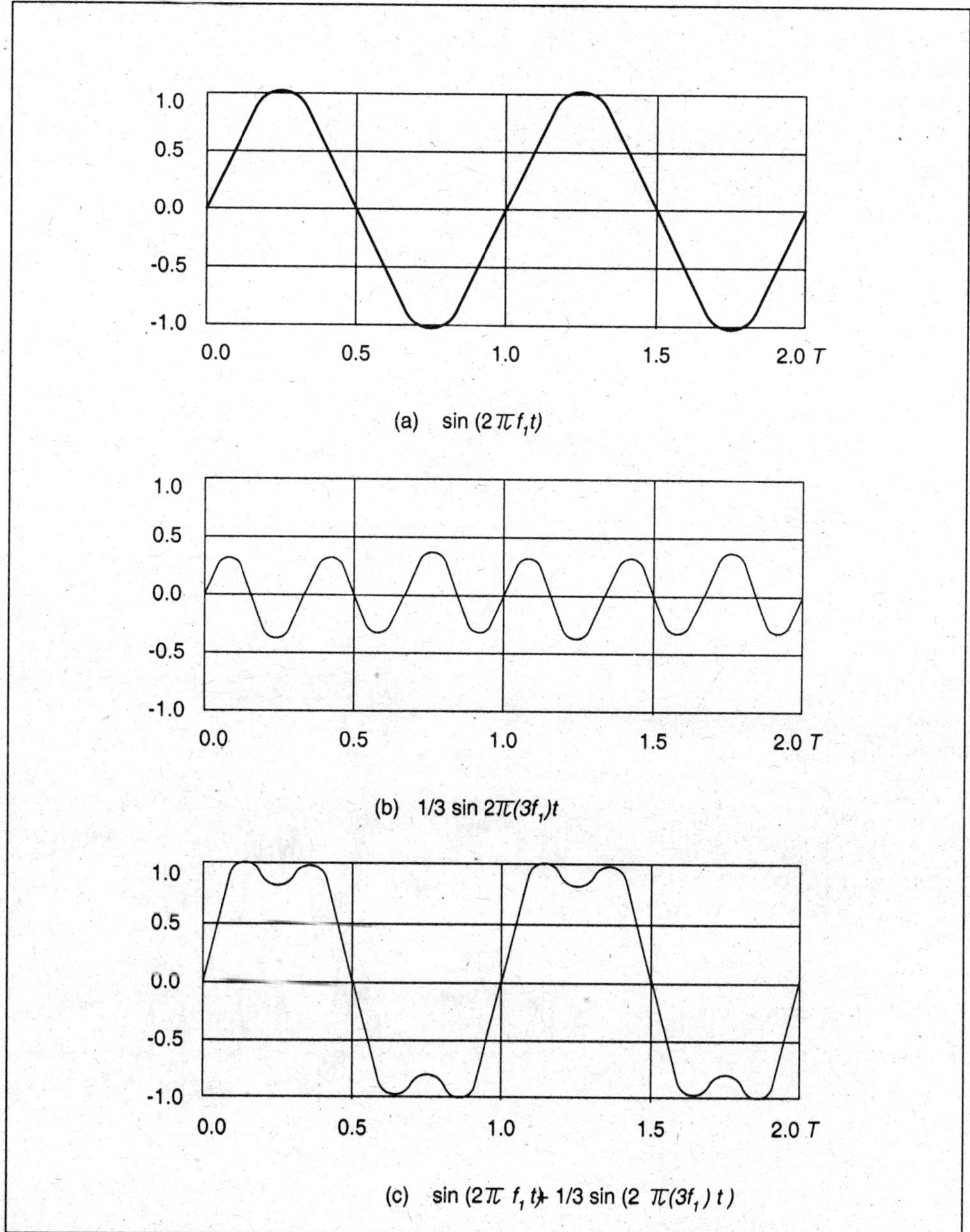

5.5 COMPOSITE SIGNALS

Composite signal may be due to Noise (an analog signal) superimposed on the discrete signal. Noise is normally found to be analog signal and it is always present whether data is sent as digital data or analog data.

Figure 5.11
Frequency domain representation of the signal in Figure 5.10 (c)

1.4
1.2
1.0
0.8
0.6
0.4
0.2
0.0
S (f)
1
2
3
4f1
(a) sin (2π f1 t) + 1/3 sin (2π (3f1) t)

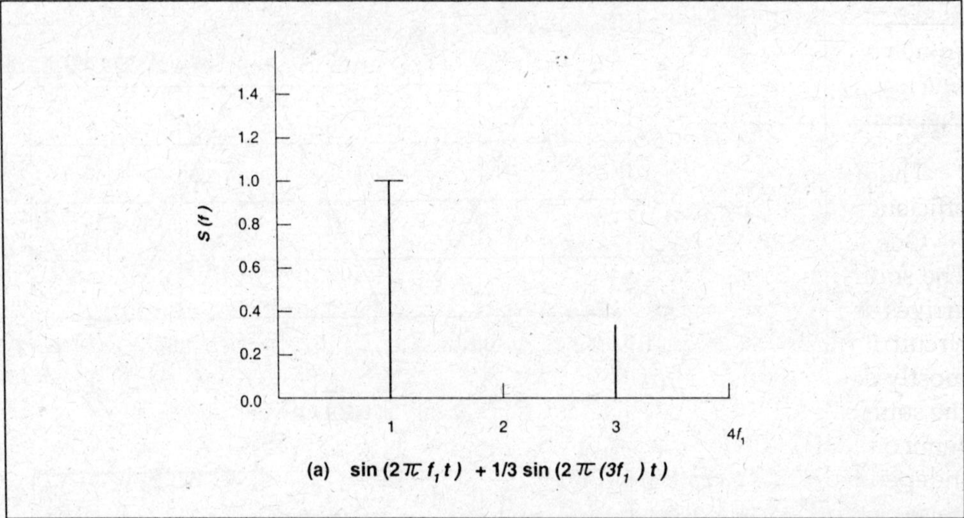

Figure 5.12
A Composite signal containing digital data transmitted and noise

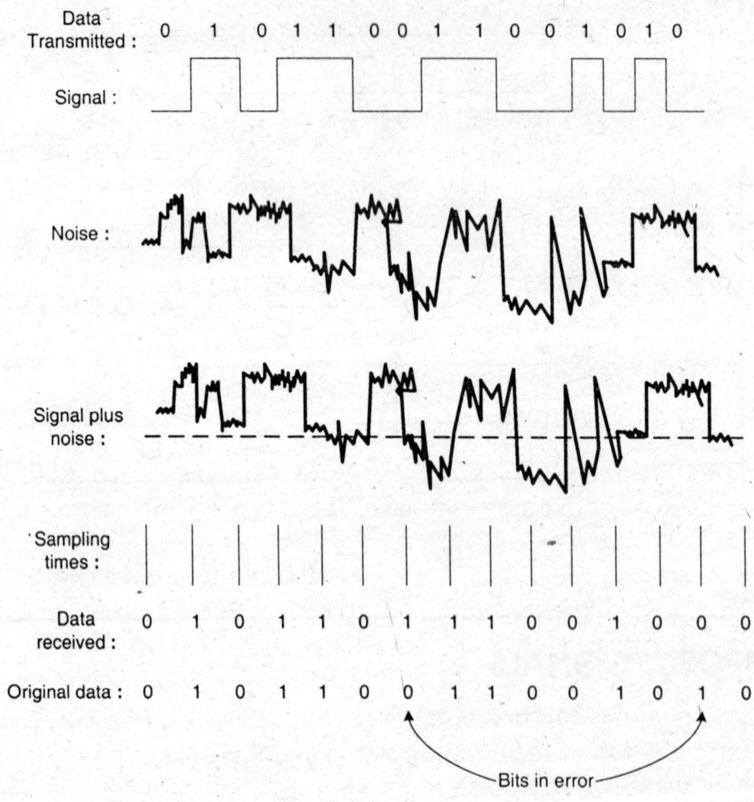

Data Transmitted : 0 1 0 1 1 0 0 1 1 0 0 1 0 1 0
Signal :
Noise :
Signal plus noise :
Sampling times :
Data received : 0 1 0 1 1 0 1 1 1 0 0 1 0 0 0
Original data : 0 1 0 1 1 0 0 1 1 0 0 1 0 1 0
Bits in error

☞ Noise is generated by all electrical and electronic devices, including motors, fluorescent lamps, power lines and office equipment.

The better the signal-to-noise ratio of an electrical transmission system, the greater the efficiency of the system.

One source of performance degradation, which cannot be easily overcome, is due to noise. The source of noise, it seems to come from the airwaves, or in other words the signal that arrives at the receiving antenna and part of it seems to be created internally by the electronic circuit itself. This internally generated noise is called the thermal noise. These noises are mostly dependent on the temperature of the source and they are independent of frequency of the source. In digital circuits, it is called the error rather than the word noise. The noise in the semiconductors devices is called the shot noise. It is similar to thermal noise except that it is independent of temperature. Figure 5.12 shows the composite signal and the effect that the noise causes on the digital data.

REVIEW QUESTIONS WITH ANSWERS

Question Number 1. What do you mean by periodic and aperiodic signals? Mention the formulae used to determine whether a signal is periodic or not.

Answer *[Refer to Section 5.3]*

A signal s(t) is said to be periodic if and only if

$s(t + T) = s(t)$ where $t > -\infty$ and $t < \infty$ and T is the period of the signal. Otherwise the signal is not periodic or aperiodic.

Question Number 2.
(a) A sine wave has a frequency of 6 Hz. What is its period?
(b) A sine wave completes one cycle in 25 μs. What is its frequency?

Answer (a) Period = 1/frequency = 1/6 second = 0.17 second.

Answer (b) Frequency = 1/Period = $1 / 25 \times 10^{-6}$ Hz = 40000 Hz = 40 kHz.

Question Number 3. Describe the three characteristics of a sine wave.

Answer *[Refer to Section 5.4.1]*

Question Number 4. What is do you mean by the term bandwidth of a signal? If a periodic signal is decomposed into five sine waves with frequencies of 100, 300, 500, 700 and 900, what is the bandwidth?

Answer The bandwidth of a signal is the range of frequencies the signal occupies. Bandwidth is determined by finding the difference between the highest and lowest frequency components.

The lowest frequency = 100 and highest frequency = 900.

∴ Bandwidth, B = 800 Hz

Question Number 5. What is a composite signal? Draw a composite signal containing digital data and transmitted noise.

Answer *[Refer to Section 5.5]*

TEST PAPER

Time: 3 Hrs. Marks: 100

Note: Answer all questions.

1. What do you mean by spectrum of a signal? How is the bandwidth of a signal related to its spectrum?
2. What is the difference between information and signals? Give two examples of analog information and two examples of digital information.
3. Contrast an analog signal with a digital signal.
4. What is the difference between analog data and digital data?
5. What is bit rate and what is its counterpart in analog signal?

CHAPTER 6

Encoding and Modulation

6.1 INTRODUCTION

The waveform of binary signals normally used in computers and terminals is called unipolar. The voltage representing the bits varies between 0 V and +5 V. This representation works well inside machines where the transmission paths are short and well shielded, but it is unsuitable for long paths because of the presence of residual DC levels and the potential absence of enough signal transitions to allow reliable recovery of a clocking signal. Signal conditioning devices are used to convert the unipolar waveform which would be created if a series of 1s or 0s are to be sent as data bits. The conditioning devices will change such a DC voltage into a pattern of changing bit pattern.

6.2 DIGITAL TO DIGITAL CONVERSION

There are several methods to convert the digital code into digital signal for transmission. Each one has some advantage and disadvantage over the other.

6.2.1 Nonreturn to Zero (NRZ) Code

The most common and easiest, way to send digital signals is to use two different voltage levels for the two binary digits. Codes that follow this method share the property that the voltage level is constant during a bit interval. There is no transition (i.e. no return to a zero voltage level). For example, the absence of voltage can be used to represent binary 0, with a constant positive voltage used to represent binary 1. In this method, a negative voltage is used to represent one binary value and a positive voltage is used to represent the other. This latter code is known as Nonreturn-to-zero-Level (NRZ-L) as shown in Figure 6.1.

This code is generally used to generate or interpret digital data by terminals and other devices. The maximum bit rate is twice the bandwidth.

6.2.2 Nonreturn to Zero, Invert on Ones (NRZI) (Differential Encoding)

A variation of NRZ is known as NRZI. As with NRZ-L, NRZI maintains a constant voltage pulse for the duration of a bit time. The data themselves are encoded as the presence or absence of a signal transition at the beginning of the bit time. A transition (low-to-high or high-to-low) at the beginning of a bit time denotes a binary 1 for that bit time. If there is no transition, it is an indication of 0.

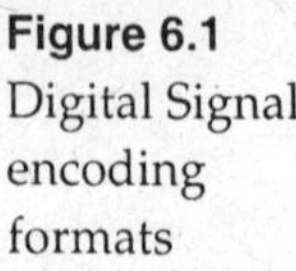

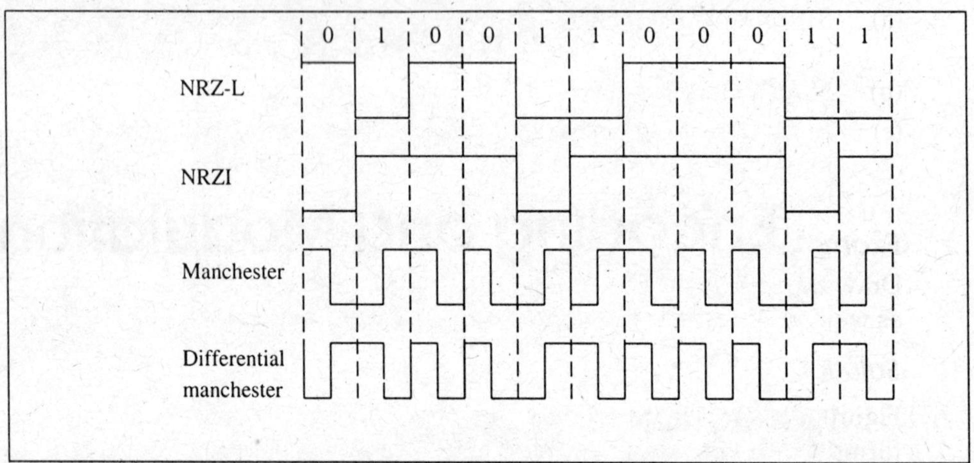

Figure 6.1 Digital Signal encoding formats

NRZI is an example of differential encoding. In differential encoding, the signal is decoded by comparing the polarity of adjacent signal elements rather than determining the absolute value of a signal element. The main benefit of differential encoding is that it may be possible to detect a transition in the presence of noise than to compare a value to a threshold.

☞ The NRZ codes are the easiest to engineer and in addition make efficient use of bandwidth. The main limitations of NRZ signals are the presence of a dc component and the lack of synchronization capability.

As an example, with a long string of 1s or 0s for NRZI, the output is a constant voltage over a long period of time. Under these circumstances, any drift between the timing of transmitter and receiver will result in a loss of synchronization between the two. (See Figure 6.1)

Because of their simplicity and relatively low frequency response characteristics, NRZ codes are commonly used for digital magnetic recording. But their limitation of DC components make these codes not useful for signal transmission applications.

6.2.3 Manchester Code

In the Manchester code, there is a transition at the middle of each bit period. The mid-bit transition serves as a clocking mechanism and also as data. A low-to-high transition represents a 1, and high-to-low transition represents a 0. In differential Manchester, the mid-bit transition is used only to provide clocking. The encoding of a 0 is represented by the presence of a transition at the beginning of a bit period, and a 1 is represented by the absence of a transition at the beginning of a bit period. Differential Manchester has the added advantage of employing differential encoding. (See Figure 6.1)

The Manchester coding requires at least one transition per bit time and may have as many as two transitions. Thus, the maximum modulation rate is twice that for NRZ. This means that the bandwidth required is correspondingly greater. The main advantages of Manchester coding are:

(a) **Synchronization:** Because there is a predictable transition during each bit time, the receiver can synchronize on that transition. Hence it is also known as self-clocking code.

(b) **No DC Component:** This type of coding does not have dc component.

(c) **Error Detection:** The absence of an expected change in the voltage i.e. transition can be made use of to detect an error. Noise on the line would have to invert both the signal before and after the expected transition to cause an undetected error.

Example 6.1

Draw the representation of digital signal 1001101 for NRZ-L, NRZ-I, and Manchester coding as well as for Differential Manchester coding waveforms.

Solution

Figure 6.2(a) gives the representation of the digital signal 1001101 in the NRZ-L and NRZ-I forms.

Figure 6.2(b) gives the representation of Manchester and Differential Manchester coding for the digital signal 1001101.

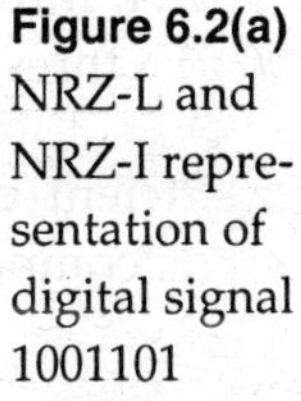

Figure 6.2(a) NRZ-L and NRZ-I representation of digital signal 1001101

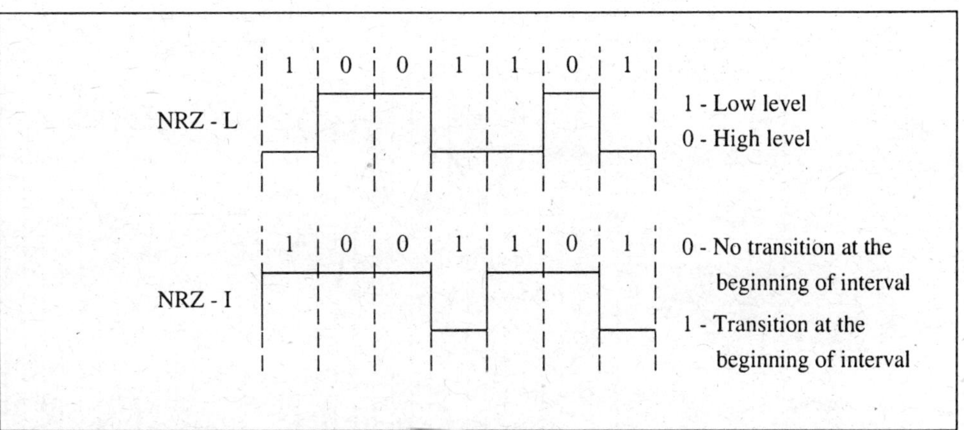

6.3 ANALOG TO DIGITAL CONVERSION

Pulse Code Modulation abbreviated as PCM is a digitizing process in which an analog or continuous signal is represented in digital or discrete form.

The varying sounds of human speech must first be transformed into discrete pulses to be sent by digital means. The device for making this transformation is called a *codec,* a name derived from its function of coding an analog signal into digital form at the sending end and then decoding it back to analog form at the receiving end. These are mainly used at exchanges for routing calls over main trunk lines. A codec accomplishes its tasks in three stages.

6.3.1 Stage 1

In the first stage, codec does the sampling of the amplitude of the analog signal at very short intervals. See Figure 6.3. The voltage of the signal is measured at discrete intervals.

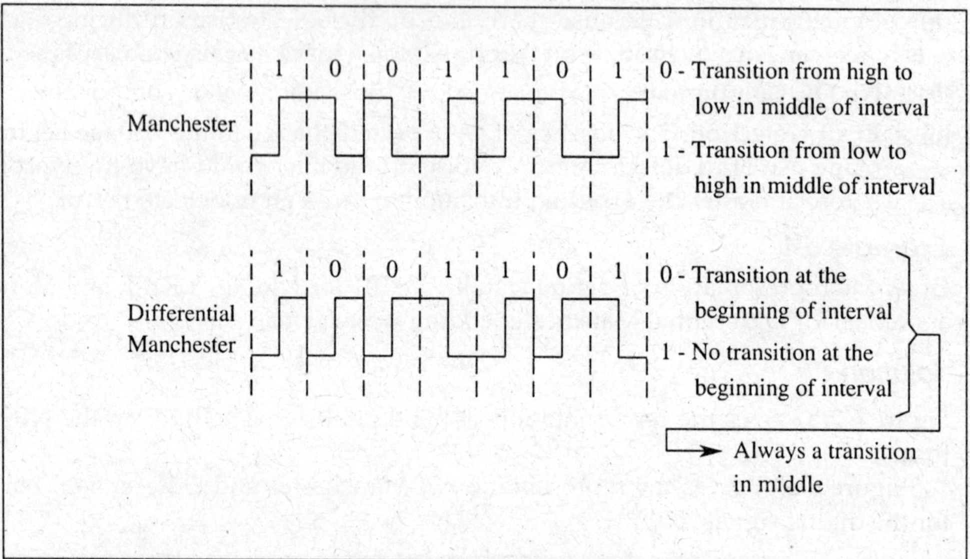

Figure 6.2(b) Manchester and Differential Manchester coding of the digital signal of 1001101

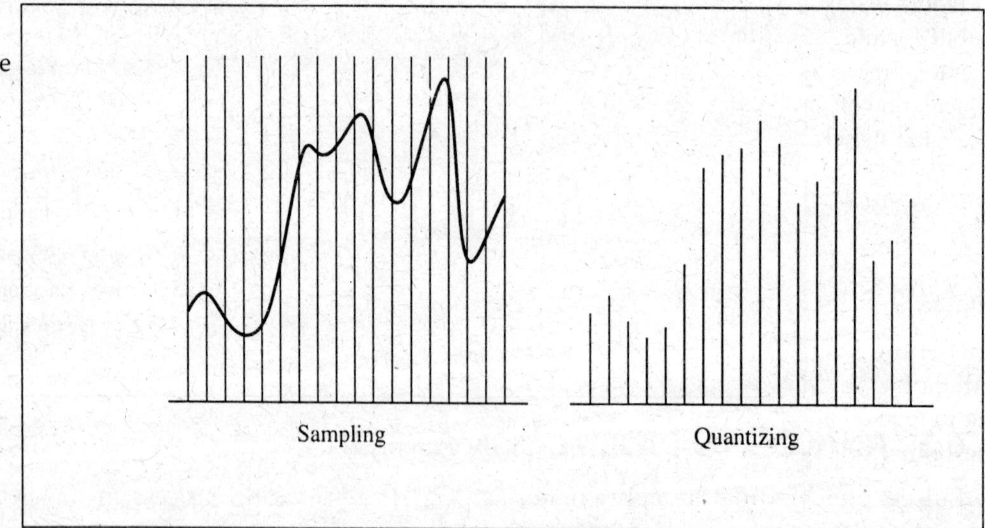

Figure 6.3 Digitizing the voice

Quantization

Quantization is the process of approximating sample levels into their closest fixed value. The values are preselected and since they are fixed, they are easy to encode. The new waveform called the quantized waveform has either quantum changes in amplitude or no change in amplitude.

Given a signal, fs, with peak voltage point of *Vh* and *Vl*, the size (S) of a quantum step is determined by the following relationship:

$$S = (Vh - Vl)/n$$

Here, *n* is the number of steps between *Vh* and *Vl*. Figure 6.4 shows the relationship between *fs* and a quantized example. The quantized levels are those fixed levels that are the nearest to *fs* at the point the sample is taken.

Figure 6.4 Quantized signal

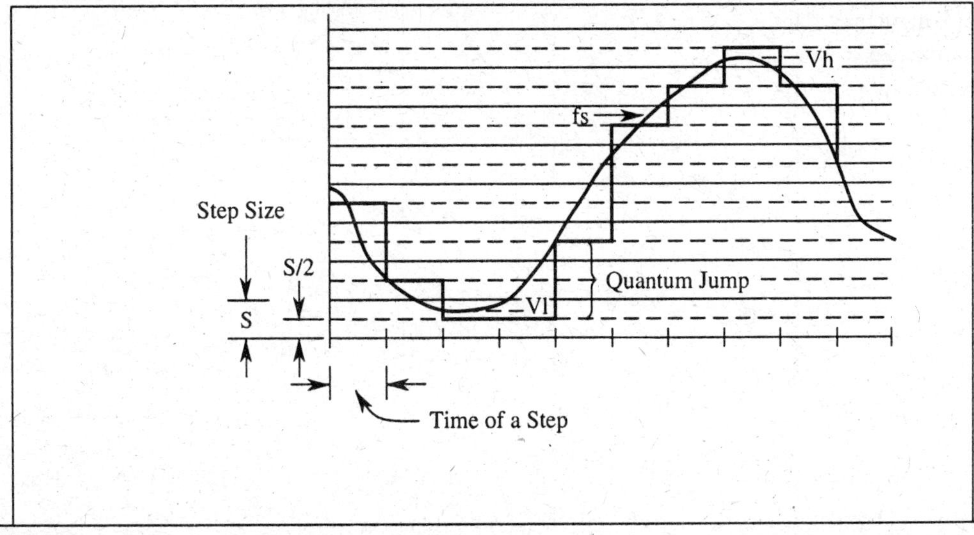

☞ The process of sampling and quantizing a signal is a form of pulse amplitude modulation (PAM) where the samples produce pulses of varying amplitudes. When these amplitudes are restricted to discrete quantized values and assigned specific binary codes which are to be transmitted, then a technique called pulse coded modulation is used.

Stage 2

This is the stage of quantizing or assigning decimal values to the amplitude samples. The value of each voltage sample is quantized, or assigned a specific measurement (bars of varying height in Figure 6.3, which is then converted to a digital number expressed in the 1s and 0s of binary code [See Figure 6.5]. The digital numbers can then be transmitted.

Stage 3

In this stage, the voltage values converted or coded, into binary numbers for digital transmission are sent through a communications link as a stream of digital bursts. Figure 6.3 shows the digital encoding of speech signal.

At the receiving end, the original analog-to-digital conversion is reversed. Voltage values are read and the sampled voltages recreated, producing a signal that exactly duplicates the quantized one as shown in Figure 6.5. A simple filter converts the samples into a continuous wave and finally, the telephone receiver converts the recreated signal into sound waves. Because the recreated signal depends only on numbers, not on gradations in transmitted voltages, it produces sound virtually identical to the original, even over extremely long distances. (See Figure 6.6)

Figure 6.5
Digitizing the voice channel using 8 bit binary encoding

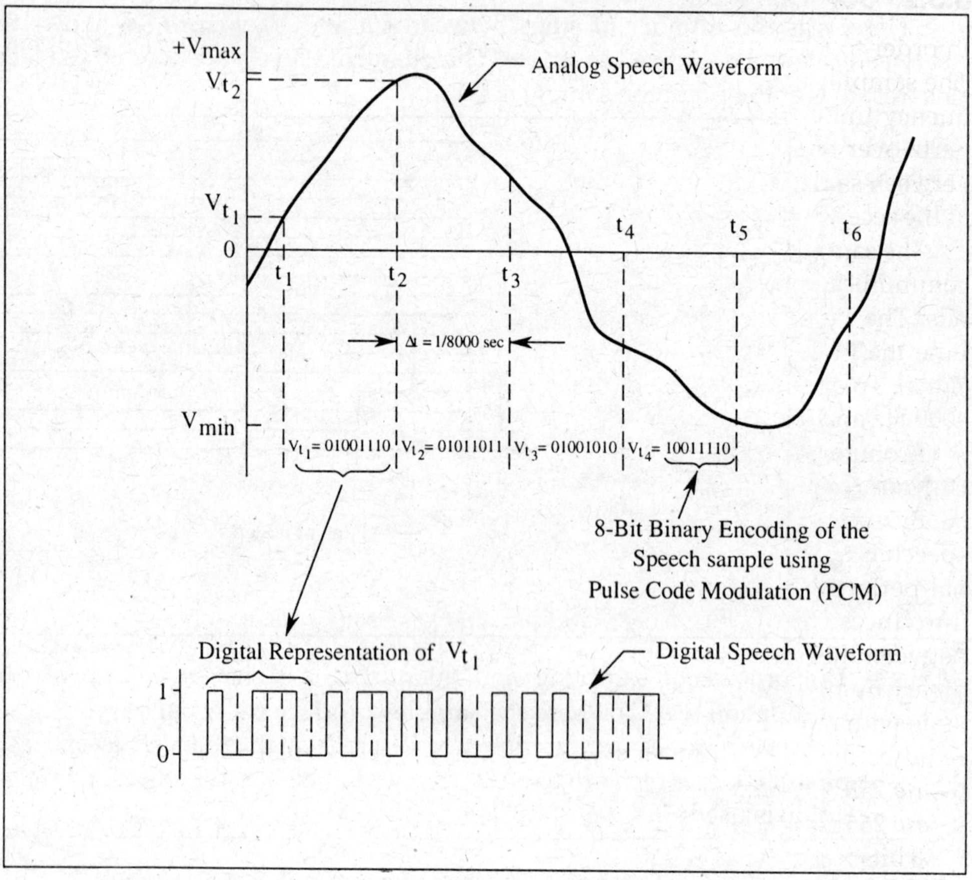

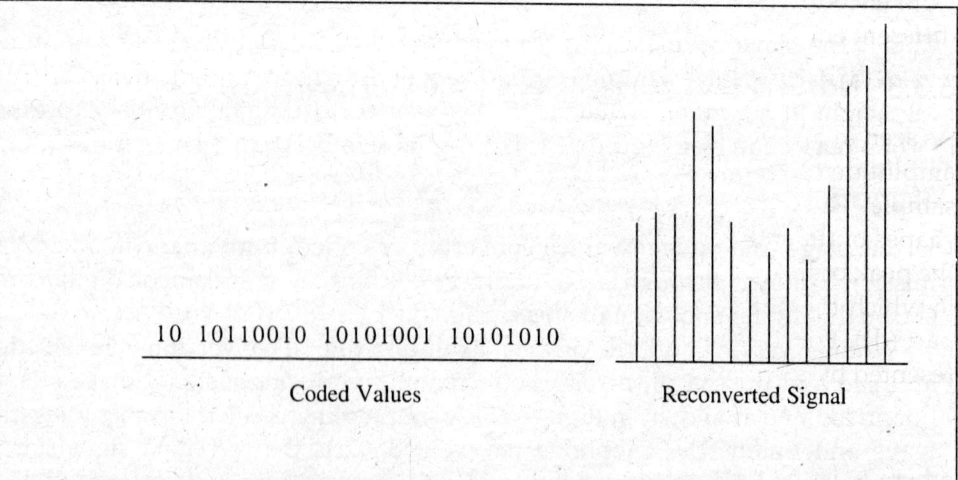

Figure 6.6
Reconverting the analog signal

6.3.2 Sampling Rate

In order to make sure that speech remains intelligible, a great many samples must be taken. The sampling rate as per Nyquist theorem, must be twice that of the highest significant frequency to be transmitted. Thus, for a voice signal, with an upper frequency limit of 4,000 hertz over the phone system, the codec must take 8,000 samples per second. The speech lost between samples, known as the Nyquist interval, is unnoticeable when the signal is decoded at the receiving end.

The sampling rate and the number of quantizing levels determine the bit rate of the digital communications channel. To convey 256 discrete volume levels requires eight binary data bits. The Pulse Code Modulation (PCM) component must generate all eight data bits each time the Pulse Amplitude Modulation (PAM) component performs a sample of the analog signal. To operate the system, you need to sample at a rate of 8,000 samples per second i.e. 2 × 4000 Hz and generate eight data bits each time. This produces 8 × 8,000 = 64,000 bps.

Economies of scale for long-distance communications require vendors to combine several 64-Kbps channels into one channel of larger capacity.

By sampling a signal of limited bandwidth at twice its highest frequency, which for speech is taken as 4000 Hz (8000 times per second), it is possible to reproduce the speech signal perfectly. However, the process of assigning a discrete binary number to each sample introduces an error known as the quantization error. This unavoidable error is the difference between the actual value of the analog sample and the nearest value encoded by one of the binary numbers. The average quantization error is a measure of the trade-off between using a scale with more bits per sample (which yields smaller steps) versus using a coarser scale that requires fewer bits. The standard scale used in USA is an 8-bit nonlinear scale known as *μ-law 255*. The required bit rate or digital bandwidth for a PCM encoded speech signal using *μ-law 255* is then

8 bits × 8000 samples/second = 64,000 bits/second.

PCM encoding according to μ-255 is standard throughout the USA. European countries use a different encoding algorithm known as A-law.

6.3.3 Natural Sampling

As seen in Figure 6.7 samples are created by generating a short pulse at the specific time. The amplitude of the pulse is determined equal to the amplitude of the signal at the time of the sample. The width of the pulse is designated *tp* and the time period pulses (*1/Sr*) is *Tr*. The shapes of the pulses themselves come in two forms. One is called *Natural Sampling*, in which the peak of the pulse follows the signal's actual shape. The second pulse form is *Flattop* shape in which the peak amplitude is held flat by the sample and the hold circuit. (See Figure 6.7 part (d)). For the flattop sampling, the reconstructed signal (*So*) for a given signal *f*(*s*) is represented by the relationship:

$$So = \frac{tp}{Tr}\sin(2\pi f(s)) \tag{6.1}$$

where *tp* is the time period for the sampling pulse and *Tr* is the reciprocal of sampling rate (*Sr*). Since *tp*/*Tr* is the duty cycle of the sampling signal, the relationship of *So* to sin(2π*f*(*s*)) is directly proportional to the duty cycle.

Figure 6.7 Sampling types

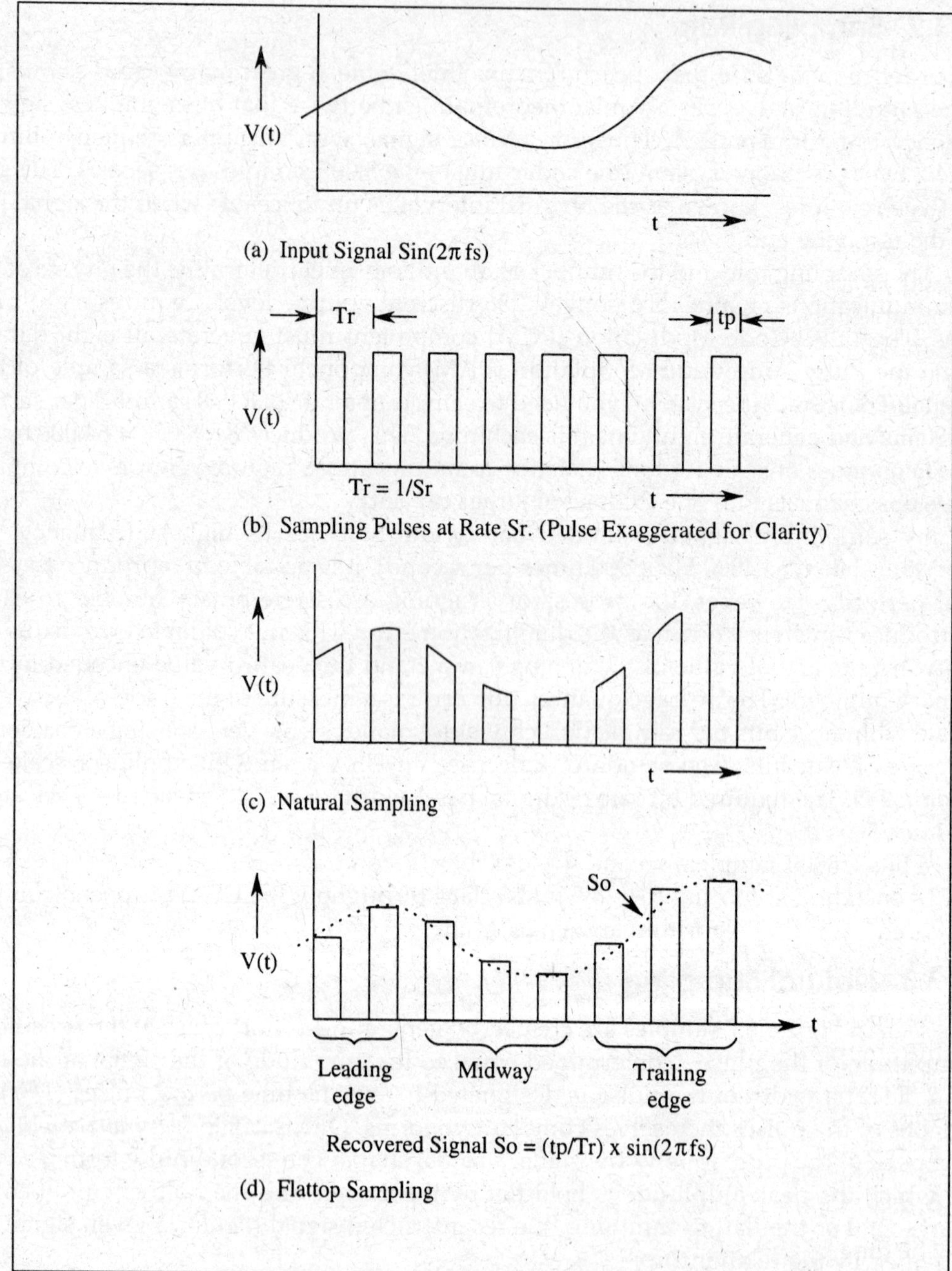

Example 6.2

A 3.6 cos(*f*) signal is naturally sampled at the rate of 56 kHz using 1.25 microsecond sampling pulses. What is the value of the reconstructed output signal?

Substituting the values in Equation 6.1 we have
$tp = 1.25 \times 10^{-6}$, $Tr = 1/56 \times 10^{3}$
Therefore $So = (1.25 \times 10^{-6} \times 3.6 \cos(f)/(1/56 \times 10^{3})$
Calculating we get

$So = 0.252 \cos(f)$

6.3.4 Sample and Hold

In order to reproduce the waveform accurately, we use what is called the method of Sample and Hold. In this, sample pulse's amplitude is detected and that value retained until the occurrence of the next sample pulse (See Figure 6.8). For this method to be effective, the hold time between samples is relatively small compared with he time period of the original signal.

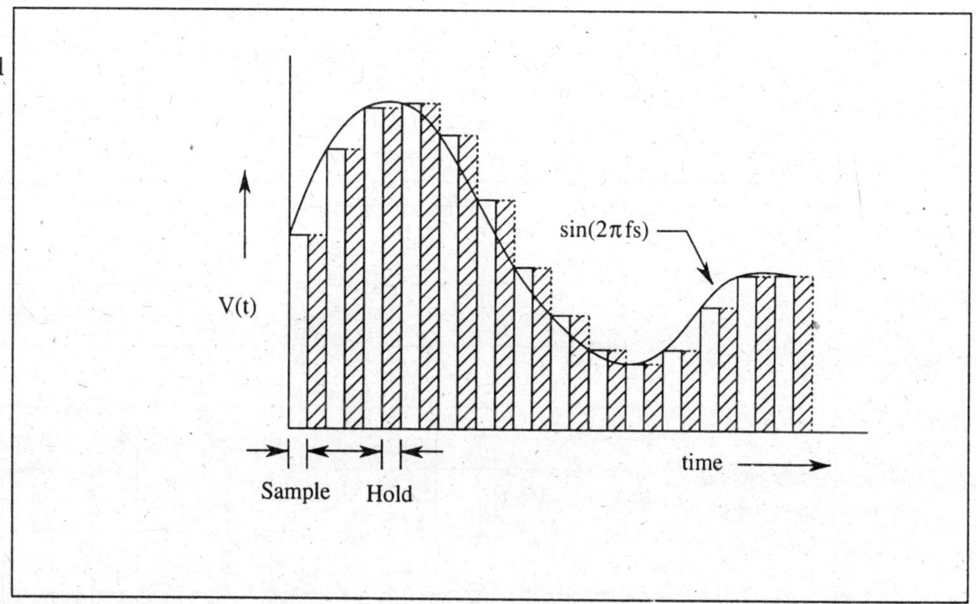

Figure 6.8 Sampling and Hold waveform

The most common method used for sample and hold circuits is to employ a capacitance at the output of the buffer amplifier. The capacitor is charged to the sample pulse value. When the amplitude falls to zero between pulses, the capacitor remains charged to the pulse value. The next sample pulse causes the capacitor to charge or discharge to that value. Again the value is held until the next pulse arrives. Figure 6.9 shows the circuit diagram for sample and hold waveform creation for accurate reproduction of the waveform.

6.3.5 Coding a Quantized Signal

The range of voltages for signal as illustrated in Figure 6.10 is divided into discrete quantized steps (S). The signal is sampled at each step, with the resulting amplitude of the samples coded into binary values. The binary equivalents are actually associated with analog values midway between step amplitudes to minimize errors. These binary codes are shown at the bottom of the figure. The original waveform is transmitted as a serial stream of binary bits representing the quantized levels of each of the samples. At the receiving station the binary bits are decoded into the quantized samples and the original signal is reproduced from the resulting samples.

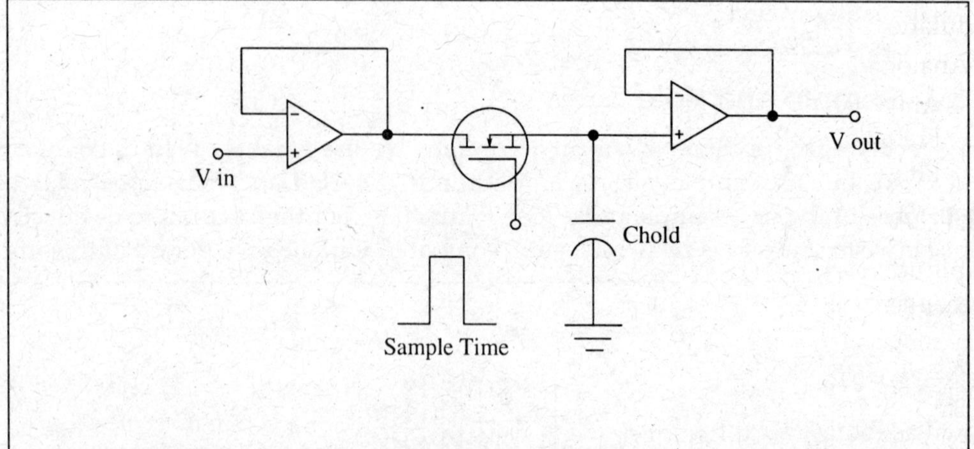

Figure 6.9
Sampling and Hold Circuit

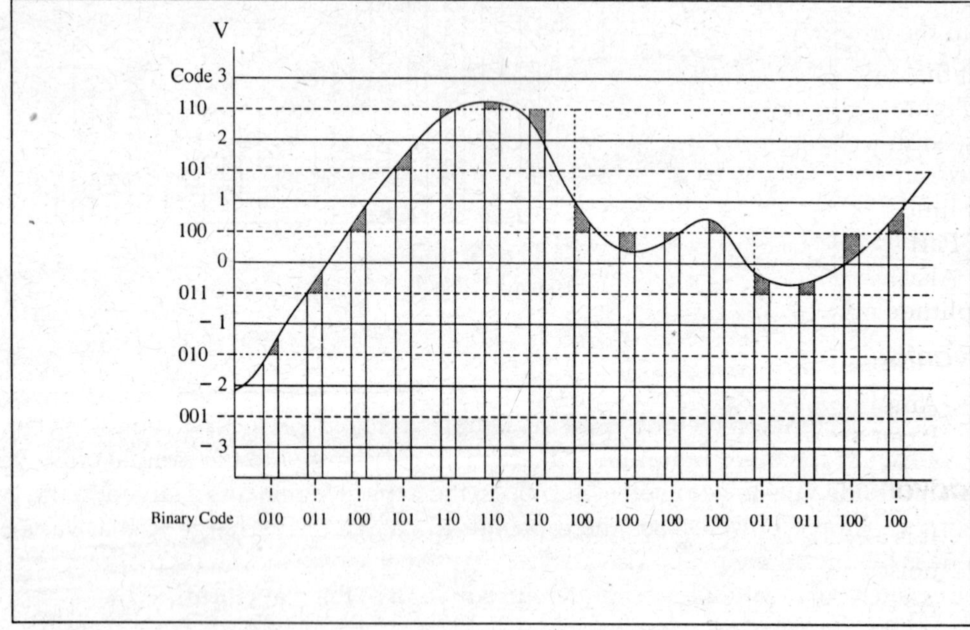

Figure 6.10
Codification of a Signal

6.4 ANALOG TO ANALOG CONVERSION

In order to send analog data over the transmission media, we use a carrier wave which is modulated to take the intelligence along with it.

☞ To modulate means to mix data signal onto a carrier and modify the characteristics of the carrier for transmission in a communication network. A carrier is an electromagnetic wave that vibrates at a fixed frequency.

Thus, if the input signal is *m(t)* and a carrier at frequency f_c to propagate a signal *s(t)* whose band width is centered on f_c. Then *m(t)* will modify the characteristics of f_c and the resultant signal *s(t)* will be passed on the transmission medium. This change is known as modulation. When the input signal is analog, then we call it as analog modulation.

Analog data modulate the carrier by any one of the following methods:

(a) Amplitude modulation (AM)
(b) Frequency modulation (FM)
(c) Phase modulation (PM)

6.4.1 Amplitude Modulation

Amplitude modulation is the simplest form of modulation and is shown in Figure 6.11. Mathematically, the process is expressed as follows:

$$s(t) = [1 + n_a x(t)] \cos 2\pi f_c t \tag{6.2}$$

Where $\cos(2\pi f_c t)$ is the carrier and *x(t)* is the input signal carrying data. The parameter n_a, is known as the modulation index. Modulation index is the ratio of the amplitude of the input signal to the amplitude of the carrier signal. Thus the input signal $m(t) = n_a x(t)$.

In the signal $s(t) = [1 + n_a x(t)] \cos(2\pi f_c t)$, the component 1 is the DC (direct current) component that prevents the loss of information.

Figure 6.11 elaborates the concept of amplitude modulation technique. The carrier signal as seen in part (a) of this figure has a much higher frequency than the information signal shown in part (b). By imposing the lower frequency information signal on the carrier, the amplitude of the resulting compound signal is made to vary in the form of information signal. Part (c) of the figure shows the resulting modulated signal. Radio programs transmitted via Akashvani on medium wave and shortwave frequencies in India are examples of amplitude modulation.

Advantages

(a) Amplitude modulation is easy to implement.
(b) It can be used both for analog and digital signal.

Disadvantages

(a) It is affected by the noise signal that may add up with the information signal. Electrical noise causes this problem.
(b) As the strength of the signal decreases in a channel with distance traveled, it reaches a minimum level unacceptable for adequate communications. Before signal strength goes down to this extent, it must be amplified. But amplifiers add noise and adversely effect the characteristics of the information signal.

Example 6.3

Derive an expression for *s(t)* when the modulating signal is represented by *x(t)* and is given by $\cos(2\pi f_c t)$.

Figure 6.11 Generation of amplitude modulated signal

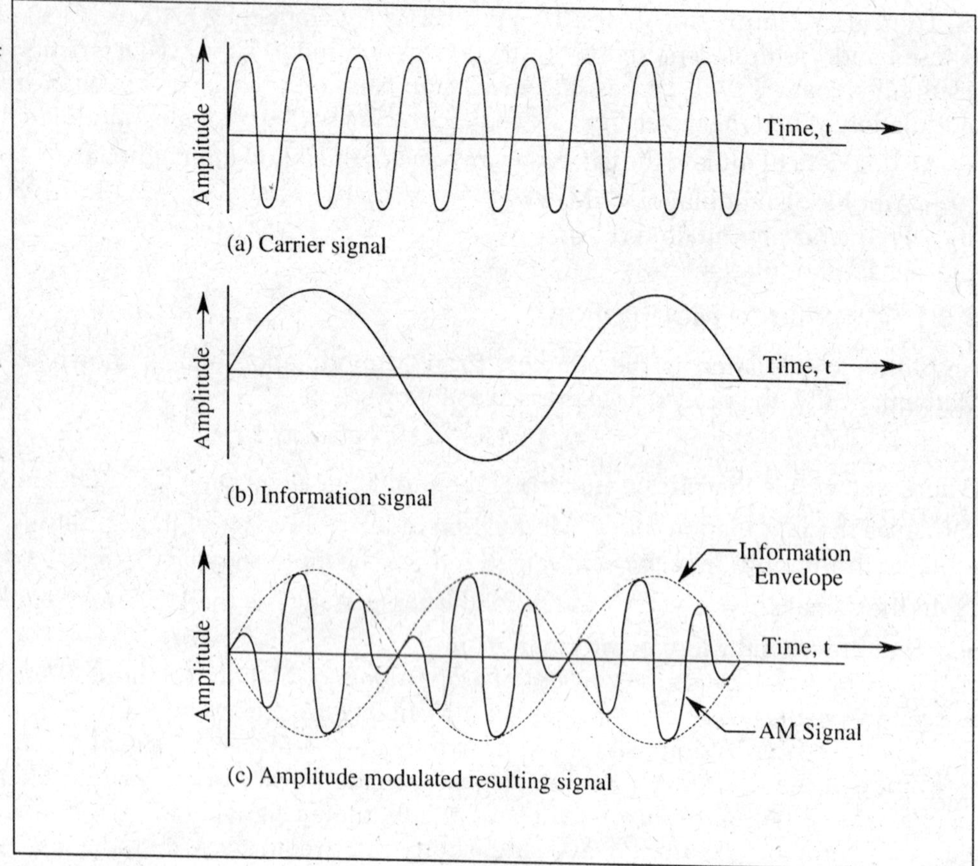

Solution

The resulting $s(t)$ i.e. output amplitude modulated signal when carrier (f_c) is being modulated by the input analog signal $x(t)$ is given by:

$$s(t) = [1 + n_a \cos 2\pi f_m t] \cos(2\pi f_c t) \tag{6.3}$$

Using the trigonometric identity, this is further simplified as:

$$s(t) = \cos 2\pi f_c t + \frac{n_a}{2} \cos 2\pi (f_c - f_m)t + \frac{n_a}{2} \cos 2\pi (f_c + f_m)t$$

Here the modulated signal contains the frequencies $(f_c + f_m)$ and $(f_c - f_m)$. It means, the band width for the modulated signal will be from $(f_c - f_m)$ to $(f_c + f_m)$.

☞ $(f_c - f_m)$ is called the lower side band and $(f_c + f_m)$ is called the upper side band.

Suppose the voice frequency is in the range of 300 Hz and 3000 Hz and it modulates a carrier of 60 kHz. The resulting signal contains the upper side band of 60.3 to 63 kHz and a lower side band of 57 to 59.7 kHz.

Power Transmission

The relationship for the power transmission is given by the following:

$$P_t = P_c\left(1 + \frac{n_a^2}{2}\right) \tag{6.4}$$

Where P_t is the total transmitted power in modulated signal *s(t)* and P_c is the transmitted power in the carrier. Also n_a is the modulation index and from equation [6.4], it is natural that n_a should be large enough for getting optimum value of P_t, which carries the information. However, n_a should be less than 1.

In Single Side Band (SSB), only one of the band frequencies is used for transmitting the signal. The other band as well as the carrier is filtered out. Therefore, less power is required because no power is used to transmit the carrier on the other side band.

6.4.2 Frequency Modulation

In frequency modulation, the modulated signal *s(t)* is represented as the following:

$$s(t) = A_c \cos[2\pi f_c t + \phi'(t)]$$

where $\phi'(t) = n_f m(t)$ and n_f is the frequency modulation index.

Figure 6.12 illustrates the principle of Frequency Modulation.

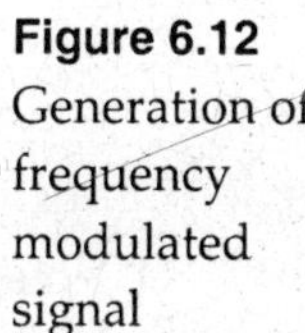

Figure 6.12 Generation of frequency modulated signal

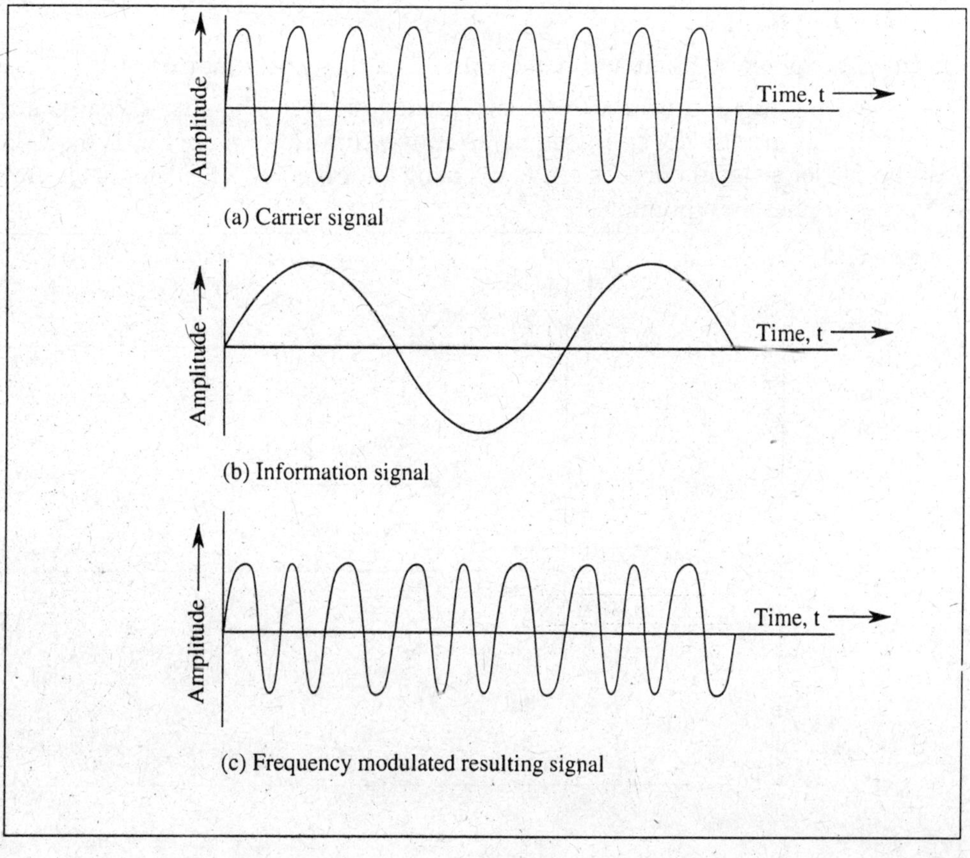

Amplitude → Time, t →

(a) Carrier signal

Amplitude → Time, t →

(b) Information signal

Amplitude → Time, t →

(c) Frequency modulated resulting signal

An FM signal has a constant amplitude but varies in frequency over time to convey information. Part (a) and (b) of this figure show that the carrier has a frequency much higher than the information signal it has to transport. After imposing the lower frequency information signal of the carrier, the frequency of the resulting compound signal varies to match the form of the information signal. Part (c) of this figure shows the resulting modulated signal.

Advantage

Frequency modulated wave is least effected by the noise due to electrical disturbance.

Disadvantages

(a) Frequency signal has a wide spectrum of frequencies and therefore needs much higher band width than amplitude modulation.

(b) The number of FM signals one can transmit over a channel with a fixed total band width is smaller than the number of AM signals one can transmit through the same medium.

6.4.3 Phase Modulation

In phase modulation, the modulated signal is expressed in the following form:

$$s(t) = A_c \cos[2\pi f_c t + \phi(t)] \tag{6.5}$$

where $\phi(t) = n_p m(t)$.

Here n_p is the phase modulation index and A_c is the carrier index.

Phase modulation uses at least two analog signals. The first signal is a carrier, and the other signals modify the carrier signal to convey information. In Phase modulation, the shape of the carrier's signal curve is made to change at given points in time. Figure 6.13 shows the process of phase modulation.

Figure 6.13 Carrier and information signals 180 degrees different in phase

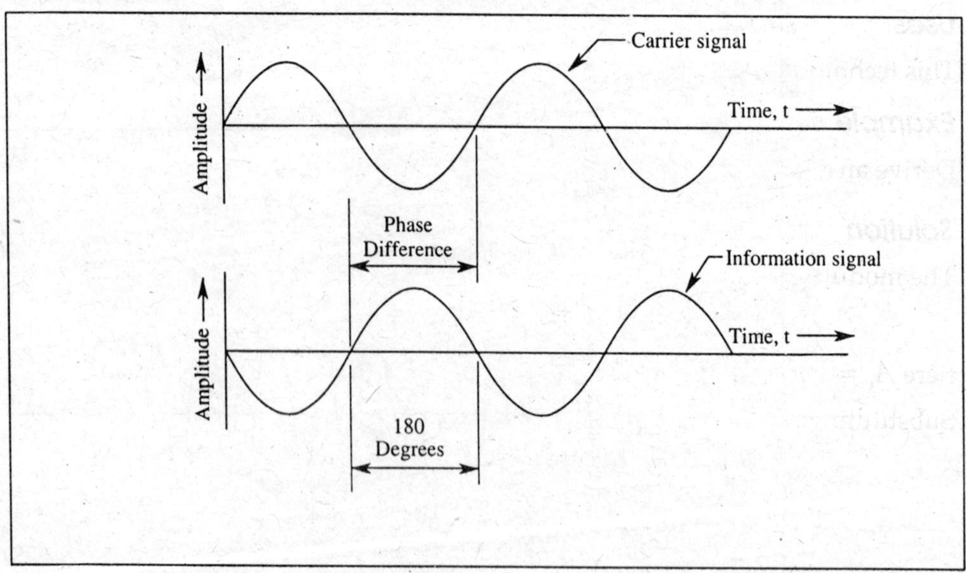

Both signals are sine waves that have the same fixed frequency and amplitude. They are however offset from each other. The two cross the amplitude reference line at different times and hence have different phase. The difference in phase between the two sine waves is the phase angle. As seen in the above figure, the two signals are offset by one-half cycle or 180 degrees out of phase. The resulting compound phase modulated signal is shown in Figure 6.14.

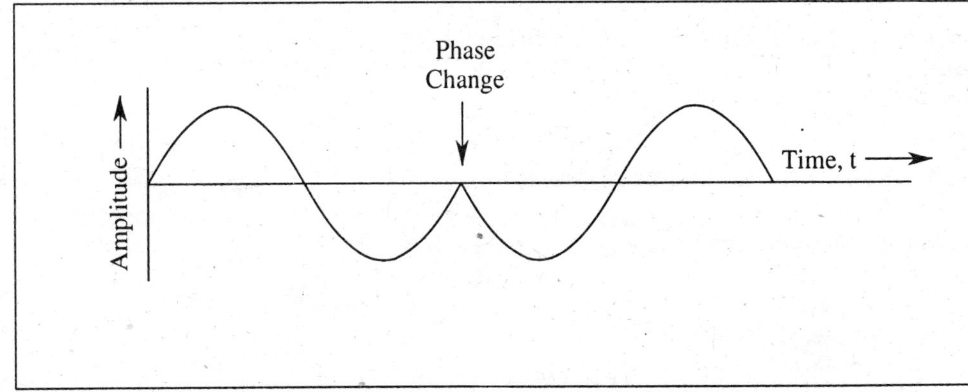

Figure 6.14 Phase modulated signal

Advantages

Phase modulation provides the signal modulation that allows computers to communicate at higher data rates through telephone system.

Disadvantages

Phase modulation requires two signals with a phase difference between them. A reference pattern and a signal pattern are both required.

Uses

This technique is used to convey colour information in colour television broadcasts.

Example 6.4

Derive an expression for *s(t)* if φ(t) is the phase modulating signal $n_p \cos 2\pi f_m t$. Assume A_c as 1.

Solution

The modulated signal is given as follows:

$$s(t) = A_c \cos[2\pi f_c t + \phi(t)]$$

here $A_c = 1$ and $\phi(t) = n_p \,\text{Cos}\, 2\pi f_m t$

Substituting these values we get the expression s(t) as:

$$s(t) = \cos[2\pi f_c t + n_p \cos 2\pi f_m t]$$

REVIEW QUESTIONS WITH ANSWERS

Question Number 1. Explain the term modulation. How does it help in data communication.

Answer Modulation is the method of mixing intelligent signal on to the carrier signal so that a weak intelligent signal can be transmitted over long distance over a transmission media such as copper conductor or coaxial cable.

Question Number 2. Describe Manchester coding with an example.

Answer [*Refer to Section 6.2.3*]

Question Number 3. The signal 3.6 cos(*f*) is naturally sampled at the rate of 56 kHz using 1.25 microsecond sampling pulses. What is the value of the reconstructed output signal?

Answer Substituting the values in the equation

$$So = \frac{tp}{Tr} \sin(2\pi fs)$$

we have

$tp = 1.25 \times 10^{-6}$, $Tr = 1/56 \times 10^{3}$

$\therefore So = (1.25 \times 10^{-6} \times 3.6 \cos(f))/(1/56 \times 10^{3})$

Calculating we get $So = 0.252 \cos(f)$.

Question Number 4. A communication system uses an 8-bit converter at exactly the Nyquist rate for signals with 30 kHz bandwidth. Calculate the bit-rate at the output.

Answer Assuming the maximum frequency of speech signal is 4 kHz. Then according to Nyquist sampling rate theorem, the sampling signal frequency should be 8 kHz. Each of this sample will use 8 bit for its amplitude. Therefore, the bit rate needed is equal to 8 × 8 kHz or 64 kHz.

Question Number 5. What is differential phase shift keying? How is it achieved? Explain the advantage of a differential phase-shift keying modulation over ordinary PSK.

Answer Differential phase shift keying is a concept in phase shift keying using which we can transmit more than one bit per symbol under the limited bandwidth of the transmission channel. Number of bits transmitted per symbol has $\mathbf{2^n}$ combinations, and we can transmit them by the phase angle of $\mathbf{(360°/2^n)}$. In 4 bit combination, signals are transmitted using same phase angle but of a different amplitude.

In DPSK, a combination of bit can be transmitted using different phase angles and at different amplitudes. In this way, we can transmit a number of bits but limited by the speed of modem. In Phase shift keying, we can transmit 2 bits by the phase shift of 180°.

Question Number 6. A system is designed to sample analog signals, convert them to digital form with a 3-bit converter, and transmit them, What bit rate is required if the analog signal contains frequencies between 300 Hz to 3400 Hz?

Answer The highest frequency of signal is 3400 Hz. The sampling rate required is twice this value. Therefore, the sampling rate is 2×3400 Hz. Since there are 3 bits used for each sample, that means there would be 2^3 or 8 levels for each of the samples taken. Hence the bit rate required = 2 × 3400 × 8 = 54.4 kHz.

Question Number 7. A system can support a data rate of 100 kbps. How many users can it multiplex if each user is a 3 kHz bandwidth signal, sampled at the Nyquist rate, and using 7 bit digitization coding?

Answer The sampling rate is 2 × 3 = 6 kHz.

Since 7 bits are used for digitization, therefore, no of bits used for one channel = 6 × 7 = 42 kbps.

Since, the communication system can support up to 100 kbps. Therefore, the number of channels = 100/42 = 2 (approx).

Question Number 8. With the help of a diagram, explain how an analog signal is converted to a digital signal?

Answer As shown in Figure 6.4, we use quantization technique. Quantization is the process of approximating sample levels into their closet fixed value. The values are preselected and since they are fixed, they are easy to encode. Given a signal fs, with peak voltage point of Vh and Vl, the size (S) of a quantum step is determined by the following relationship:

$$S = (Vh - Vl)/n$$

Here, n is the number of steps between Vh and Vl. The process of coding the sample is shown in Figure 6.10. The original waveform is transmitted as a serial stream of binary bits representing the quantized levels of each of the samples. At the receiving station, the binary bits are decoded into the quantized samples and the original signal is reproduced from the resulting samples.

Question Number 9.

(a) What do you understand by the term aliasing error? What is done to limit this error?

(b) Why has the PCM sampling time been set at 125 micro seconds?

Answer (a) **Aliasing Error**

If the sampling rate is less than twice the highest fundamental sine wave frequency, than a distortion known as aliasing error or fold over occurs.

To remove the aliasing error the sampling rate should be higher than or equal to twice the highest sine wave frequency i.e. if Sr is the rate of sampling and fs the frequency of the highest frequency, then Sr = 2 × sin(2πfs)

This is also known as Nyquist sampling rate theorem. In order to limit this error, the sampling rate of the signal is maintained at least twice the highest frequency. If still some aliasing error occurs, then digital filters are used for removing the error.

Answer (b) For a voice channel, such as a telephone line, maximum voice frequency is 4 KHz.

Using Nyquist sampling rate, we need to have 4000 × 2 = 8000 samples per second.

The time taken to take each sample = 1/8000 = 125×10^{-6} or 125 micro seconds.

Question Number 10. A system is designed to sample analog signals, convert them to digital form with a 4 bit converter and transmit them. What bit rate is required if the analog signal consist of frequencies between 400 Hz to 3400 Hz?

Answer Highest frequency of signal = 3400 Hz

By Nyquist sampling rate theorem, sampling rate required = 2 times the highest signal frequency. Hence, sampling rate required = $3400 \times 2 = 6800$ samples per second.

Since, it uses a 4-bit converter to convert analog signal to digital signal, therefore, 4 bits are used for each sample.

Therefore, total no of bits per second = 6800 samples × 4 bits per sample = 27200 bits per seconds or 27.2 kbps.

TEST PAPER

Time: 2 Hrs. Marks: 100

Note: Answer all questions.

1. A TDM system multiplexes 24 voice-channels; each channel is obtained by digitization of voice of 4 kHz. The voice samples are coded using 256 levels. The total frame uses 1 overhead bit. Calculate the digital data rate on the multiplexed line.
2. (a) Explain the concept of QPSK modulation using a phasor diagram.
   (b) In a QPSK modulation, data rate is 9600 bits per second. Calculate the symbol rate.
   (c) Explain a scheme to detect FSK signals.
3. (a) How are the radio waves propagated? Illustrate the above using diagrams.
   (b) Show the NRZI waveform for 1010011 bit pattern.
   (c) Show an amplitude modulated waveform and define modulation index for the above.
4. How is Manchester encoding realized using a digital logic? Illustrate.
5. (a) What is modulation? Describe the pulse code modulation technique.
   (b) Distinguish between frequency shift keying and phase shift keying techniques.

CHAPTER 7

Multiplexing

7.1 INTRODUCTION

If every message is required to move as a single file through every link in the global telecommunications network,—like bicyclists on a narrow path—then, communications would be hopelessly slow and very costly. But, if at some point the bicyclist can be loaded onto buses and sent down a multi-lane highway, traffic is enormously speeded. That, in effect, is what happens when many signals from telephones or computers reach a local exchange or central office on their way across a big city. This "multiplexing" allows multiple streams of electronic messages to be transmitted over the same channel in the time otherwise required for one message.

7.2 MANY TO ONE MULTIPLEXING

Multiplexing is the method of dividing a communication channel into many logical channels so that a number of independent signals may be simultaneously transmitted on it. This is, thus, a scheme that allows multiple logical signals to be transmitted simultaneously across a single physical channel. The electronic device that performs this task is known as a multiplexer.

☞ The multiplexer brings together several low speed communications lines, transforms them into one high speed channel and reverses the operation at the other end.

Programmable multiplexers are also available these days. There are many applications in which several terminals are connected to a computer. If each terminal is operating at 300 bits per second over a communications line (channel) that can operate at 9600 bits per second, then we see a very inefficient operation. It has been found that the capacity of a channel exceeds that required for a single signal. A channel is an expensive resource. Hence, for its optimal utilization, the channel can be shared in such a way so as to simultaneously transmit multiple signals over it.

☞ A multiplexer takes several data communication lines or signals and converts them into one data communication line or signal at the sending location.

Example 7.1

As seen in Figure 7.1, there are four terminals connected to a multiplexer. The multiplexer takes the signals from the 4 terminals and converts them into one signal which can be transmitted over 1 communication channel. Then, at the receiving location, a demultiplexer takes the 1 large signal and breaks it into the original 4 signals.

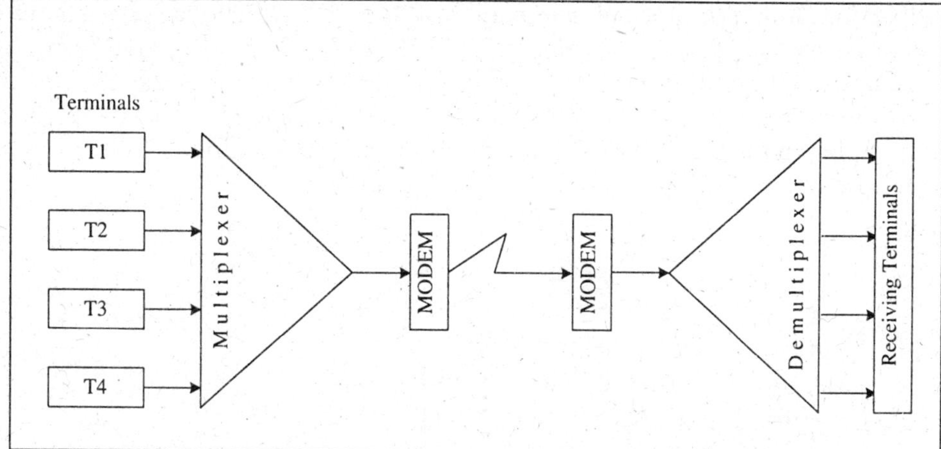

Figure 7.1
A multiplexed communication system

☞ With multiplexing it is possible for a single transmission medium to concurrently transmit data between several transmitters and receivers.

7.2.1 Where Multiplexing is most Suitable?

Multiplexing is most suited under the following situations:

(a) ***When media bandwidth is costly:*** For example, a high-speed leased line is expensive to lease. If the leased line has sufficient bandwidth, multiplexing can enable the same line to carry Mainframe, LAN, voice, video conferencing and various other types of data.

(b) ***When bandwidth is idle:*** Many organizations have installed fiber-optic cable that is used to only partial capacity. With the proper equipment, a single fiber can support hundreds of megabits or even a gigabit or more of data per second.

(c) ***When Large amounts of data must be transmitted through low capacity channels:*** Multiplexing techniques can divide the original data stream into several lower-bandwidth channels, each of which can be transmitted through a lower-capacity medium. The signals then can be recombined at the receiving end.

There are three basic methods of multiplexing channels. They are:

(a) Frequency division multiplexing
(b) Time division multiplexing
(c) Wave Length Division Multiplexing

Each method of multiplexing is explained in detail in the subsequent sections.

7.3 FREQUENCY DIVISION MULTIPLEXING (FDM)

The band width or range of a medium such as coaxial cable exceeds that of any one, given signal like single telephone subscriber frequency. This fact is utilized for frequency division multiplexing. In FDM, the available band width of a physical medium is split up (divided) into several smaller, disjoint logical band widths. Each of the component band widths is used as a separate communications line (channel). Figure 7.2 illustrates the concept of FDM. Here, signals 1 to 5 on the left get multiplexed through a modulator. The combined frequency of the signal can move through single media. At the receiving end, this combined frequency signal is separated out and flows to the receiver as signals 1 to 5.

Figure 7.2 Frequency division multiplexing

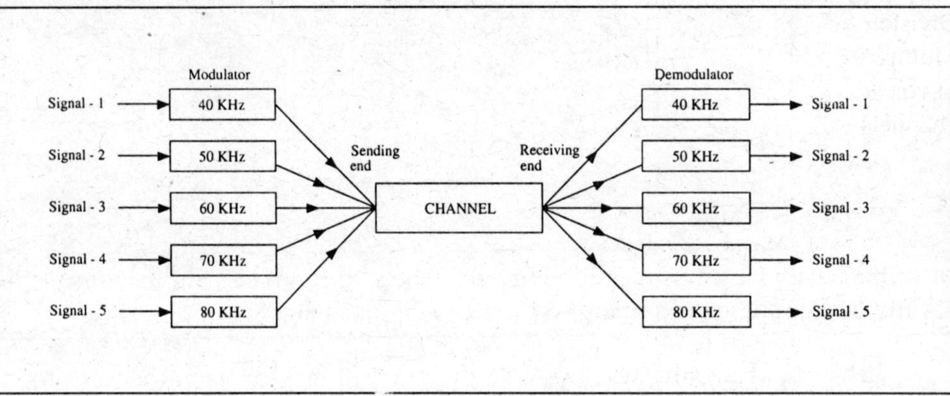

The best example of FDM is the way we receive various stations in a radio. Each radio station is assigned a frequency range within a band width of radio frequencies. Several radio stations may be transmitting electromagnetic signals simultaneously over the physical channel which is "ether" in this case. A radio receiver's antenna receives signals transmitted by all the stations. Finally, the tuning dial in the radio is used to isolate the specific signal of the station tuned.

☞ In FDM, the signals to be transmitted must be analog signals. Thus, digital signals must be converted to analog form if they are to use FDM.

In Frequency Division Multiplexing (FDM) we share a transmission channel by dividing the band width into several parallel paths, defined and separated by guard bands of different frequencies. All signals are carried simultaneously.

7.3.1 How FDM is done?

The analog signal is impressed on another analog signal of different frequency—a carrier—altering the carrier's shape so that it bears the pattern of the message. The carrier frequency generally remains constant. Only its amplitude varies, at the rate corresponding to that of the message signal.

Since each carrier has a different frequency, carriers can be stacked on top the other and sent together over a cable or microwave radio link capable of carrying a broad range of frequencies. The carriers are then separated at the other end. The greater the medium's band width, the more carriers it can transmit, and more messages it can handle simultaneously.

Figure 7.3 shows the process of frequency division multiplexing (FDM) of three voice channels. The telephone exchange takes each voice channel and modulates the signal to a higher frequency as shown.

Figure 7.3 Frequency Division Multiplexing of voice channels

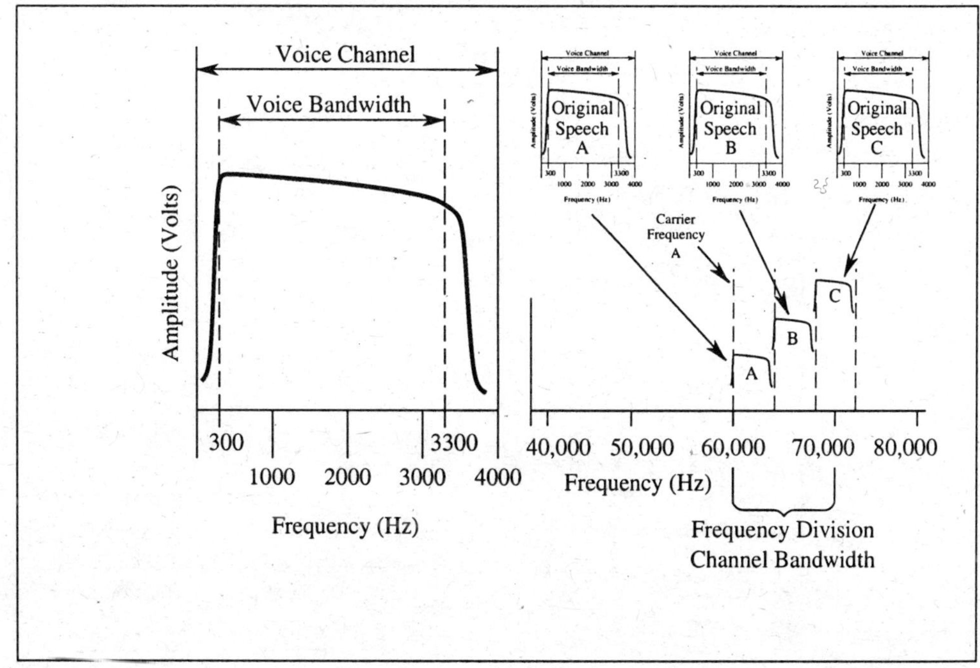

A mathematical representation of an FDM system is shown in Figure 7.4. A number of analog signals [*mi(t), i = 1, N*] are to be multiplexed for sending onto the same transmission medium, such as coaxial cable. Each signal $m_i(t)$ is modulated onto a carrier f_{sci}. Each of these carriers are known as sub-carriers. The resulting modulated analog signals are then summed to produce a composite signal $m_c(t)$. The lower part of this Figure shows the result. The spectrum of signal $m_i(t)$ is shifted to be centered on f_{sci}.

☞ The carrier frequency f_{sci} must be so selected that the bandwidths of the various signals do not overlap. Otherwise, it will be impossible to recover the original signals.

At the receiving end, the composite signal is passed through *N* bandpass filters, each filter centered on f_{sci} [See Figure 7.4 subpart (c)]. In this way, the signal is again split into its component parts. Each component is then demodulated to recover the original signal.

Figure 7.4 Mathematical representation of Frequency Division Multiplexing (a) Transmitter (b) Composite signal (c) Received signal

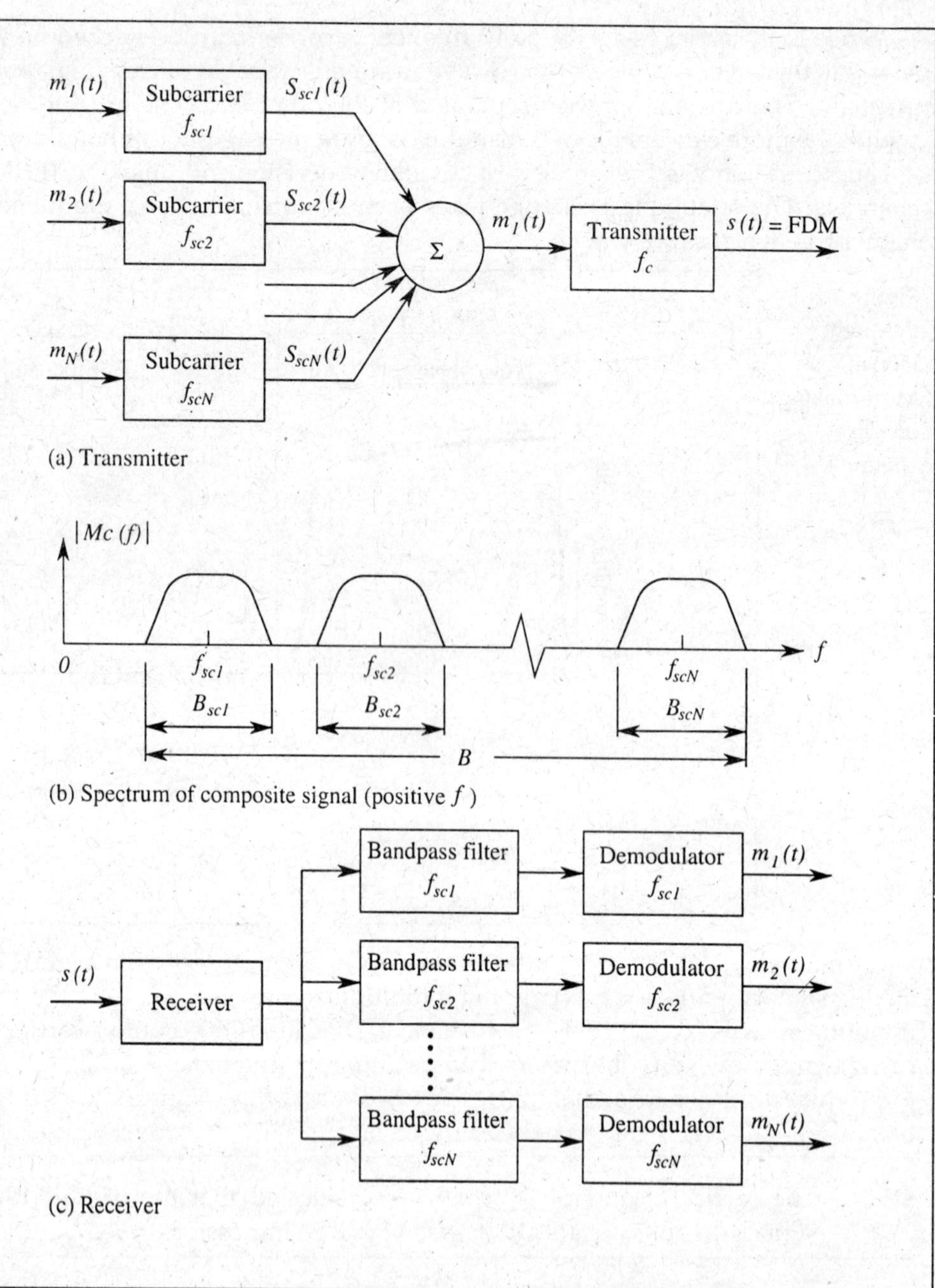

Each voice signal starts out in the 300 to 3,300 Hz range. The telephone exchange modulates the signal to a new frequency range with a clear space called a guard band between each signal. (See Figure 7.3) The first signal might have a range of 60,000 to 63,000. The second signal then starts at 64,000 and ends at 67,000, thus providing a 1,000 Hz guard band between the two signals. The third signal starts at 68,000.

Figure 7.5
Frequency Division Multiplexing with guard band

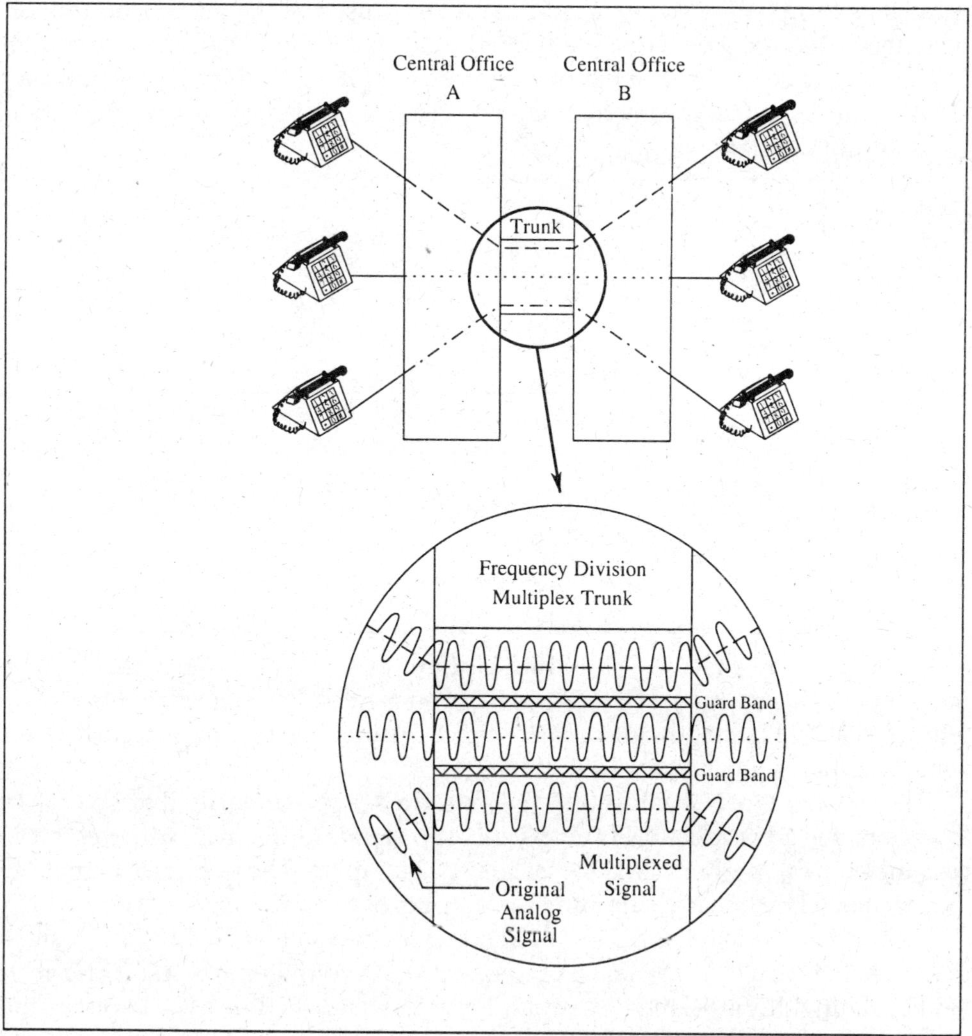

☞ The FDM technique of multiplexing requires guard bands to keep signals from contaminating each other. If the signals are modulated to new frequency ranges and without sufficient separation, then the extraneous signals would create noise called *cross talk*. Thus, as seen in Figure 7.5, adequate guard band allows several telephone connections to take place through the same trunk circuits using coaxial cable or microwave communication links.

7.3.2 FDM Groups

All voice-grade channels have a bandwidth of 0 to 4 kHz. In order to be transmitted as part of a broadband signal, the voice channel is mixed with a carrier frequency. A Mixer is a nonlinear circuit that produces the original signal and the sum and difference frequencies of two input wave forms. When a balanced modulator is used as the mixer's output, all frequencies above the difference frequency are filtered out, so that the mixer/filter circuit only produces the difference frequency. [See Figure 7.6] Here the filtered output from low pass filter has the signal $\sin[2\pi(f_c - f_s)]$ that means the frequency is equal to $(f_c - f_s)$ or the difference of carrier frequency f_c and the signal frequency f_s.

Figure 7.6
Mixer

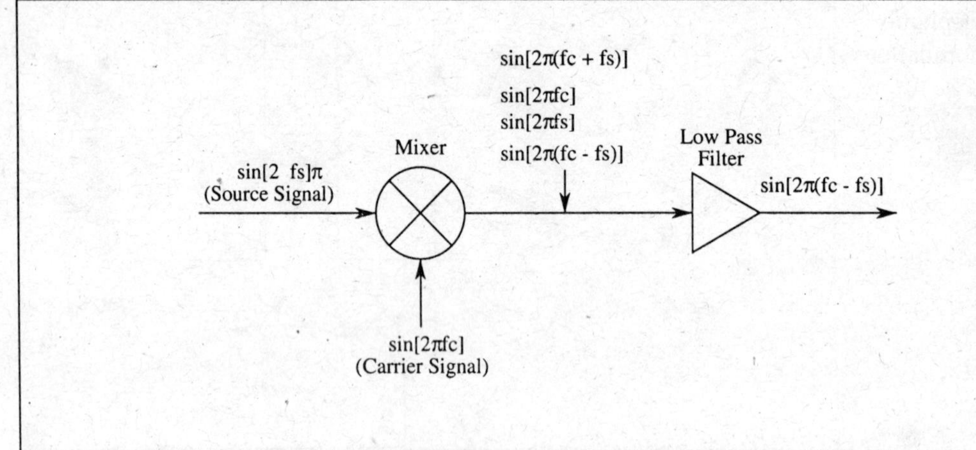

Figure 7.7 shows the basic building block of groups of channels used on the analog telephone lines. These *Channel Groups* use FDM to convey 12 voice channels through one trunk with a 48,000 Hz bandwidth. Each voice channel can convey voice signals or data communication signals.

The telephone communication system has a set of standards that specify the frequency allocations for a broadband FDM system. The standard begins with twelve voice channels, each mixed with carrier signals that are 4 kHz apart. These carrier signals form a single Group channel by linearly summing the outputs of several mixers as shown in Figure 7.8.

Each mixes a voice channel (0 to 4 kHz) with a carrier signal. The carrier signals are 4 kHz apart, placing each channel adjacent to the next group ranging from 60 kHz to 108 kHz. This 48 kHz bandwidth is verified by multiplying 12 channels times 4 kHz per channel, resulting in a 48 kHz. Notice that the 60-to-108 kHz bandwidth is well above the telephone system's 300 Hz to 3 kHz bandwidth. This group channel is meant to be sent by medias other than voice grade telephone lines. It could be sent on a fiber optic cable that has a larger bandwidth or using a radio microwave or a satellite transmission, since both these methods have very large bandwidths compared with 48 kHz. As such, larger groupings are created in similar manner to take full advantage of these large bandwidths.

Example 7.2

Consider the communication of three voice channels sent over a medium The bandwidth of a voice signal is taken as 4 kHz, with the effective spectrum of 300 to 3.4 kHz. (See Figure 7.9). When these voice channels modulate the three different carriers using the amplitude modulation, the spectrum of frequencies is represented in part (b) of Figure 7.9. The modulated

Figure 7.7 Group structure for analog telephone modulation

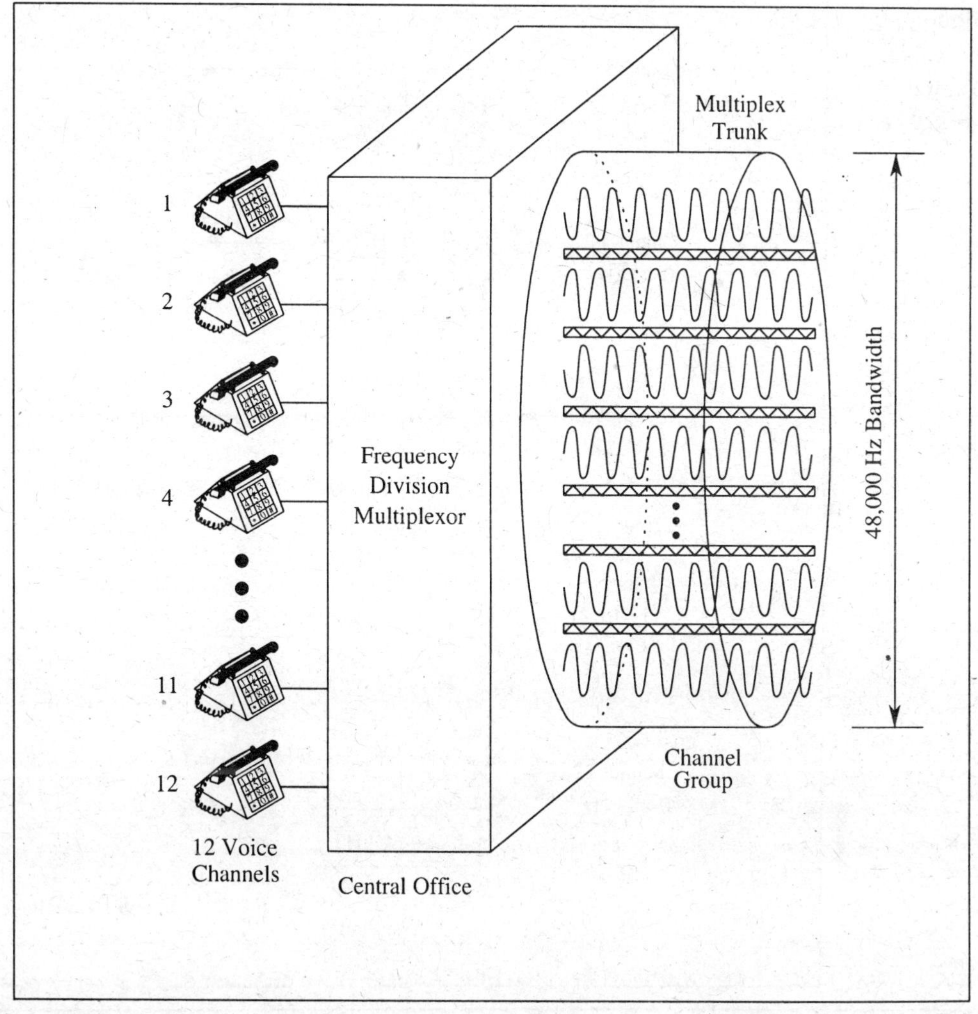

signal has a bandwidth of 8 kHz., Extending from 60 to 68 kHz. If we use the Single Side Band method of transmission using lower side band, then the three voice signals modulate carriers at 64, 68, and 72 kHz. The resulting spectrum of frequencies is shown in part (c) of Figure 7.9.

7.4 TIME DIVISION MULTIPLEXING (TDM)

FDM suffers from the problem that channels are permanently assigned. Although TDM is more efficient than FDM, in that it does not require guard bands and it operates directly in digital form but both are left behind by the advantages of Statistical Time Division Multiplexing (STATDM) which takes advantage of the statistics of data transfer in several sophisticated ways. This permits the efficiency of channel use to increase by ten-fold and in some cases even more.

Figure 7.8 A twelve-channel group

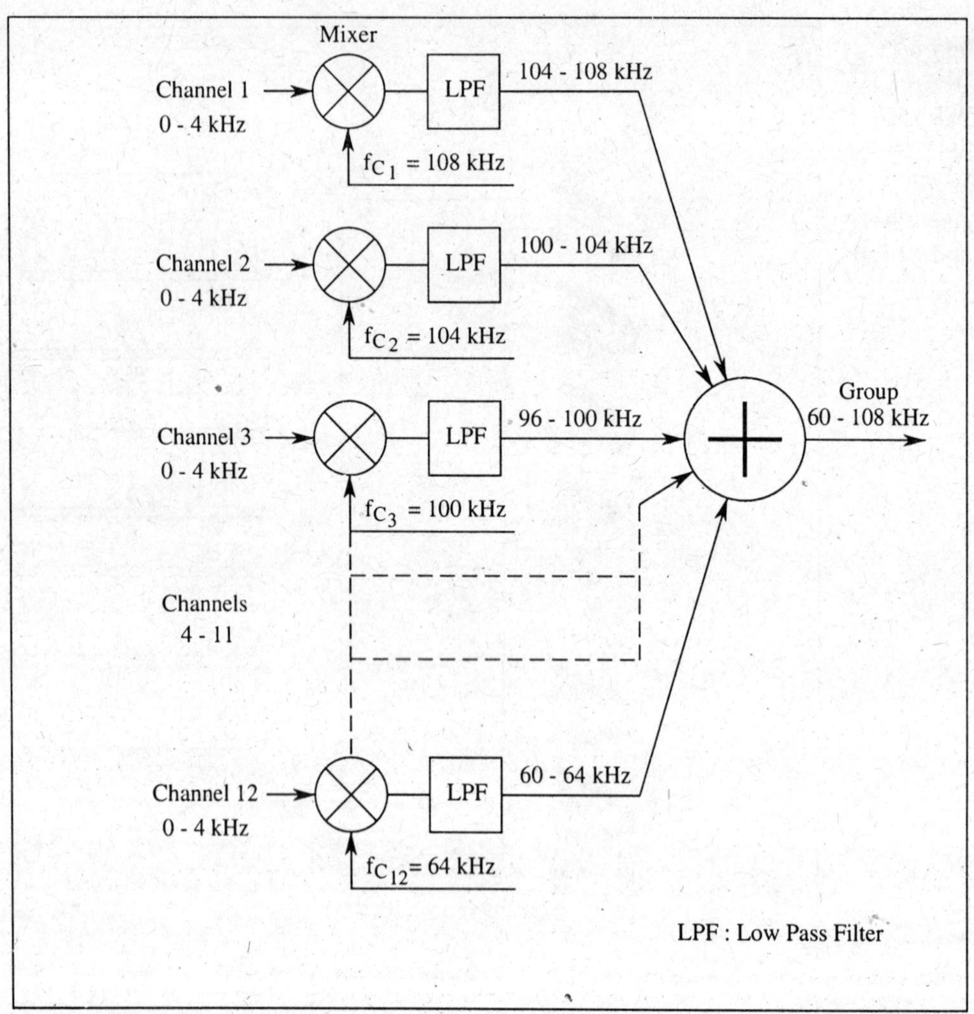

☞ TDM is a method of sharing a communication channel in which the total time available in the channel is divided between several users and each user of the channel is allotted a time slice during which he may transmit a message. The channel capacity is fully utilized by interleaving a number of data streams belonging to different users into one data stream.

Advantages of TDM

TDM is fast because it does not do error checking. Data are transparent to it. It just provides the slots for the data. TDM works well enough for applications that need continuous slots on the channel, such as voice and video.

Consider sending of three messages of varying lengths as shown in Figure 7.10. The main drawback is that message C must wait until messages A and B are sent before it can be transmitted.

Figure 7.9 FDM multiplexer with lower side band

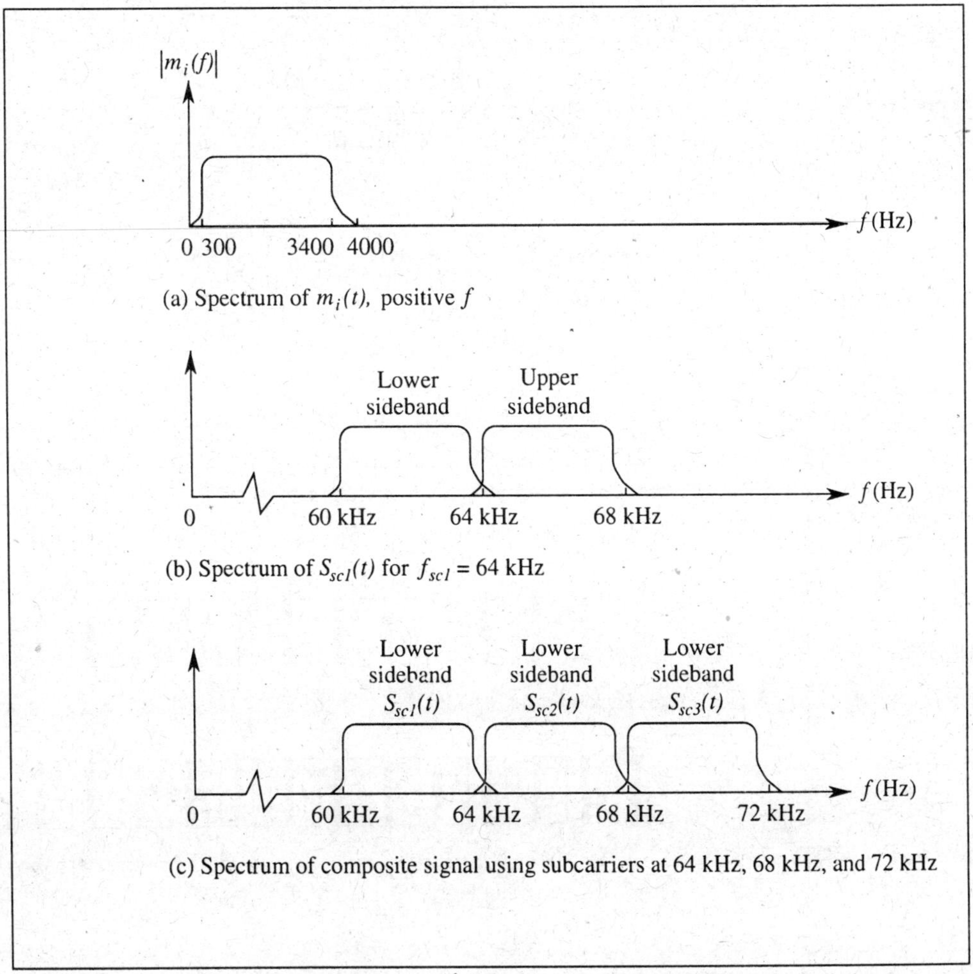

$|m_i(f)|$
f (Hz)
0 300
3400 4000
(a) Spectrum of $m_i(t)$, positive f
Lower sideband
Upper sideband
f (Hz)
0
60 kHz
64 kHz
68 kHz
(b) Spectrum of $S_{sc1}(t)$ for f_{sc1} = 64 kHz
Lower sideband $S_{sc1}(t)$
Lower sideband $S_{sc2}(t)$
Lower sideband $S_{sc3}(t)$
f (Hz)
0
60 kHz
64 kHz
68 kHz
72 kHz
(c) Spectrum of composite signal using subcarriers at 64 kHz, 68 kHz, and 72 kHz

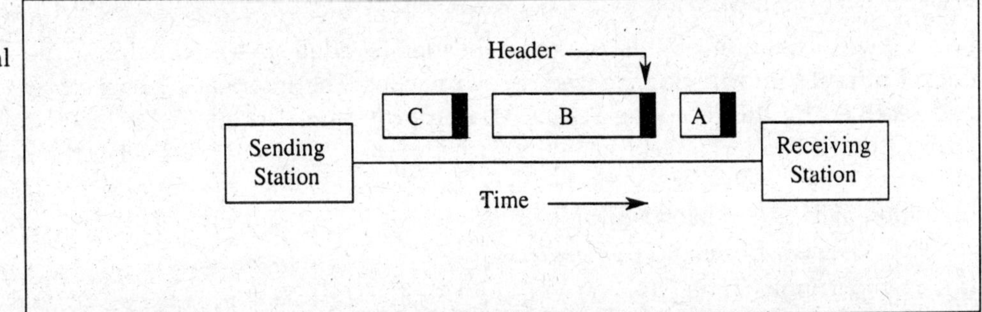

Figure 7.10 Conventional multipoint communication

Header
C
B
A
Sending Station
Receiving Station
Time

In Figure 7.11, the three messages are to be sent to three different places. The three stations should receive the messages just at the same time. To solve such a problem, all the three messages need to be reformed into smaller parts called packets. These packets are of equal length, as seen in Figure 7.12.

Figure 7.11 Conventional transmission

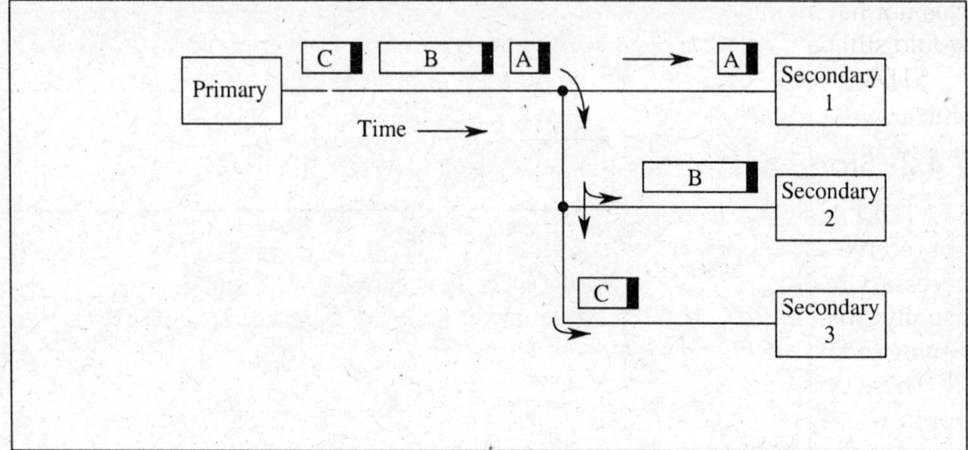

Figure 7.12 Packeted forms of TDM transmission

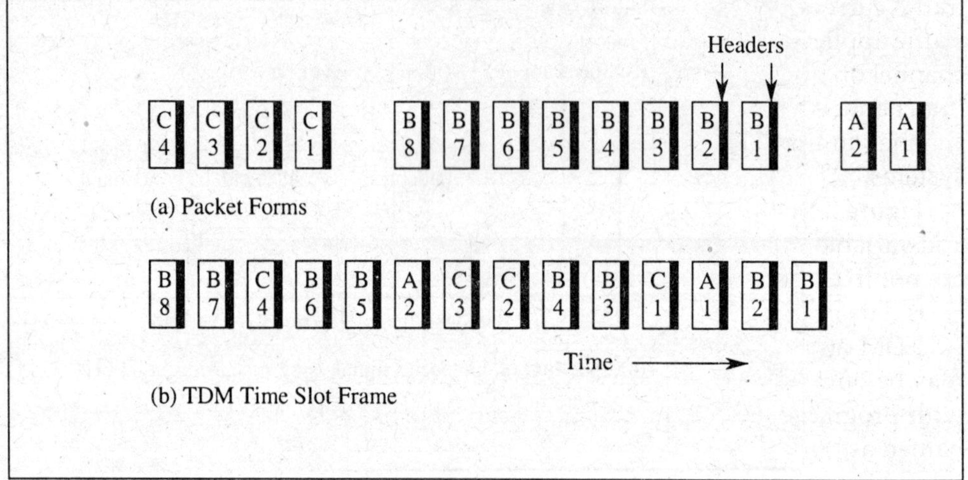

The packets forming messages A, B and C are interleaved and assigned time slots as seen in the lower diagram of this figure. A header (shaded area), containing the address and packet number information, precedes each packet. The interleaved packets are transmitted and received by the receiving station. The appropriate packets (determined by destination address in the header) are extracted by each station as they are received and reassembled (by packet number, included in the header) into their original message form. This is the full operation of Time Division Multiplexing.

The two basic forms of TDM are:

(a) Synchronous Time Division Multiplexing (STDM)

(b) Asynchronous Time Division Multiplexing (ASTDM) or Statistical TDM (STATDM)

7.4.1 Synchronous Time Division Multiplexing (STDM)

Synchronous TDM assigns time slots of equal length to all packets regardless whether or not anything is to be sent by each station with an assigned time slot. For example, if the message

A is not having any message to send, then its allotted time would still be allocated. Thus, A would still be allotted time but time slots for message A would not contain information.

STDM systems are comparatively easy to implement once the software allocates the time slots.

7.4.2 Statistical Time Division Multiplexing (STATDM)

STATDM does not make a fixed assignment of time slots so that any port which is idle does not receive a (full) slot. In order to identify which slot corresponds to which data stream, it is necessary to append address and control symbols to each slot that is used. This "overhead" is usually small and is more than compensated for by the increased efficiency derived from not having to take up channel space with idle bits.

These systems are more complex but allow for a means of reassigning time slots that are not in use. STATDM networks assign time slots only when they are to be used and delete them when they are idle. The total time used for a STATDM frame varies with the amount of traffic currently being handled. STATDM systems are most suitable for high-density, high-traffic applications. The continuous messages are assigned time slots and interleaved as each channel on the send side becomes active and requires communications with another channel. If a channel does not have any traffic, its time slots are deleted and reassigned to an active channel. In this way the interconnecting media achieves a higher efficiency that with STDM systems.

Figure 7.13 illustrates the comparison of FDM, TDM and Statistical TDM with fixed frame and variable frame methods. In thc variable-frame method, the size of the slots and the frame are not fixed but depend on the data itself. Statistical TDM are also built either for asynchronous data or synchronous data or both.

TDM and STATDM require a modem in order to interface with the voice line, but this may be built in. All modern STATDMs have at least one and usually many microprocessors with programmed and programmable functions of great diversity available. They are thus named as "Smart" or "Intelligent MUXs or multiplexers."

7.4.3 Multichannel TDM

Many channels of communication on a single line are managed by a Broadband system. In this method, each channel occupies a portion of that bandwidth. This would require the bandwidth of the system to be larger so as to contain all the channels. Multichannel use of a TDM system relies on sharing transmission time periods rather than a system's bandwidth. (See Figure 7.14)

7.5 WAVE LENGTH DIVISION MULTIPLEXING (WDM)

WDM is thc technology for achieving extremely high data rates over fiber-optic cabling. Also known as dense wave division multiplexing (DWDM), wavelength division multiplexing (WDM) will likely replace time-division multiplexing (TDM) as the standard transmission method for high-speed fiber-optic backbones in the next few years.

Figure 7.13 Different types of data multiplexing

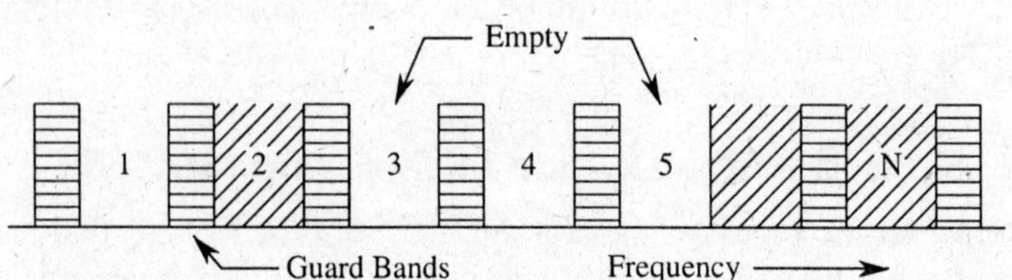

(a) Frequency division multiplexing; all frequency channels are permanently assigned to corresponding input ports.

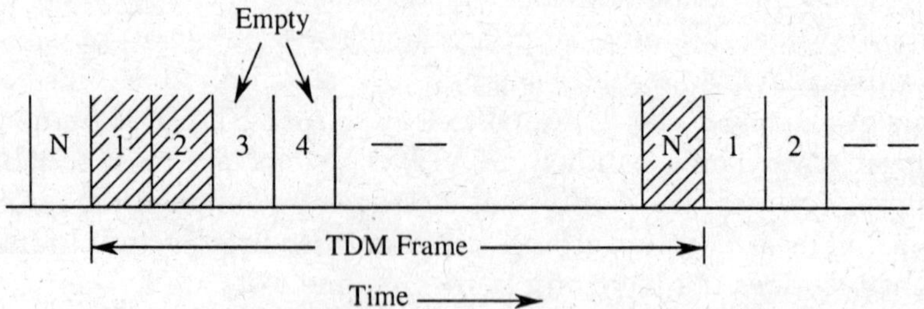

(b) Time - division multiplexing; all time slots are permanently assigned to corresponding input ports.

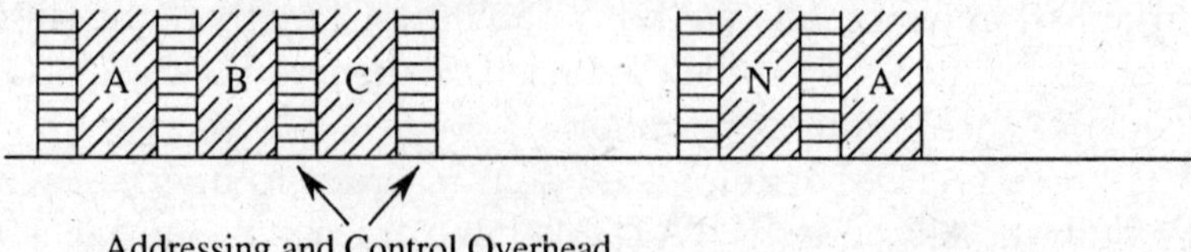

(c) Statistical time - division multiplexing (fixed frame); time slots are only assigned to active ports.

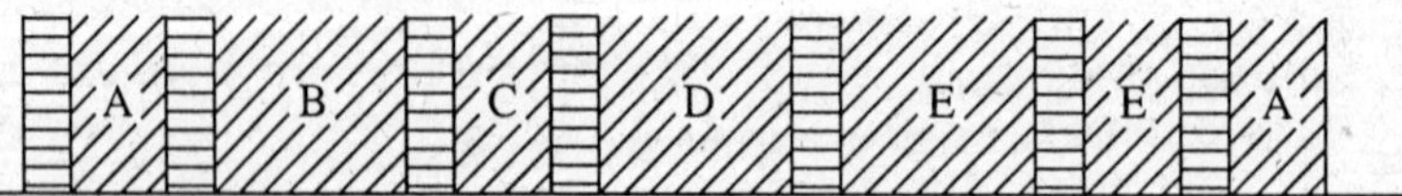

(d) Statistical time - division multiplexing (variable frame); the variable time slots are only assigned to active ports.

7.5.1 How WDM Works?

WDM modulates multiple data channels into optical signals that have different frequencies and then multiplexes these signals into a single stream of light that is sent over a fiber-optic

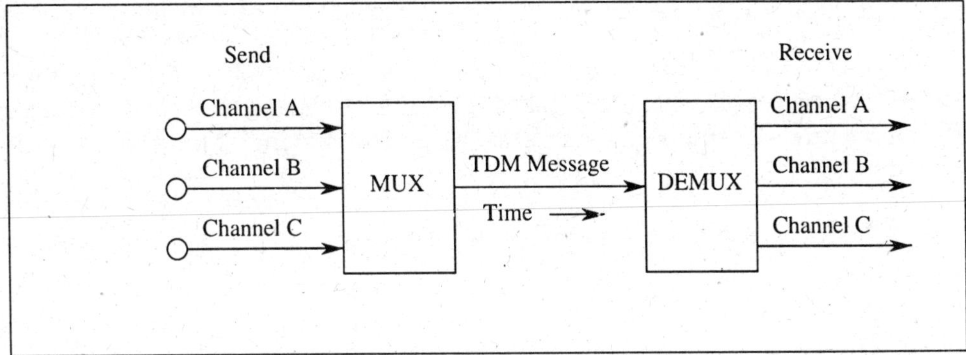

Figure 7.14 Multichannel TDM System

cable. Each optical signal has its own frequency, so up to 80 data streams can be transmitted simultaneously over the fiber using only eight different light wavelengths. In addition, each data stream can employ its own transmission format or protocol. This means that, using WDM, you can combine Synchronous Optical Network (SONET), Asynchronous Transfer Mode (ATM), TCP/IP, and other transmissions and send them simultaneously over a single fiber. At the other end, a multiplexer demultiplexes the signals and distributes them to their various data channels.

☞ Devices that support WDM are more costly because they use laser light sources for generating signals over fiber which must be highly stable.

7.5.2 SONET (Synchronous Optical Network)

SONET offers a method of interconnecting various types of fiber optic transmission systems. A SONET system consists of switches, multiplexers, and repeaters, all connected by fiber. A path from a source to destination with one intermediate multiplexer and one intermediate repeater is shown in Figure 7.15.

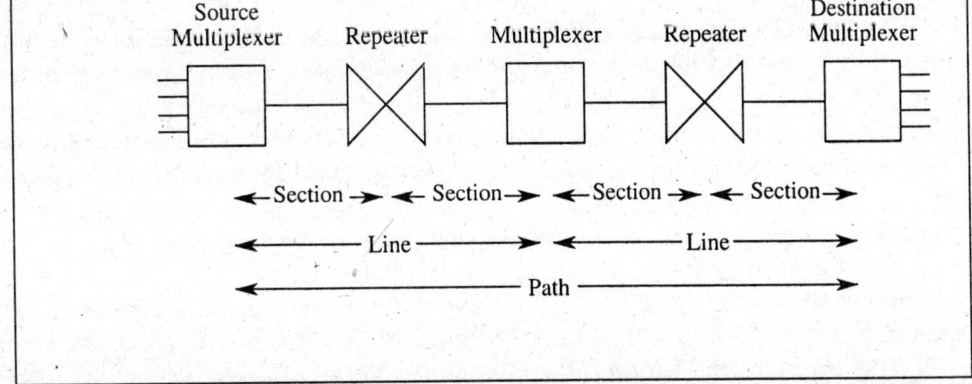

Figure 7.15 A SONET Path

In SONET terminology, a fiber going directly from any device to any other device, with nothing in between, is called a **section**. A run between two multiplexers is called a line. Finally, the connection between the source and destination is called a path. A SONET topology is often a dual ring.

The multiplexing of multiple data streams called **tributaries** plays an important role in SONET. Multiplexing is shown in Figure 7.16. On the left, we start with various low-speed input streams, which are converted to the basic STS-1 SONET rate. Next three STS-1 tributaries are multiplexed onto one 155.52 Mbps STS-3 output stream. This stream in turn is multiplexed with three others onto a final output stream having 12 times the capacity of the STS-1 stream.

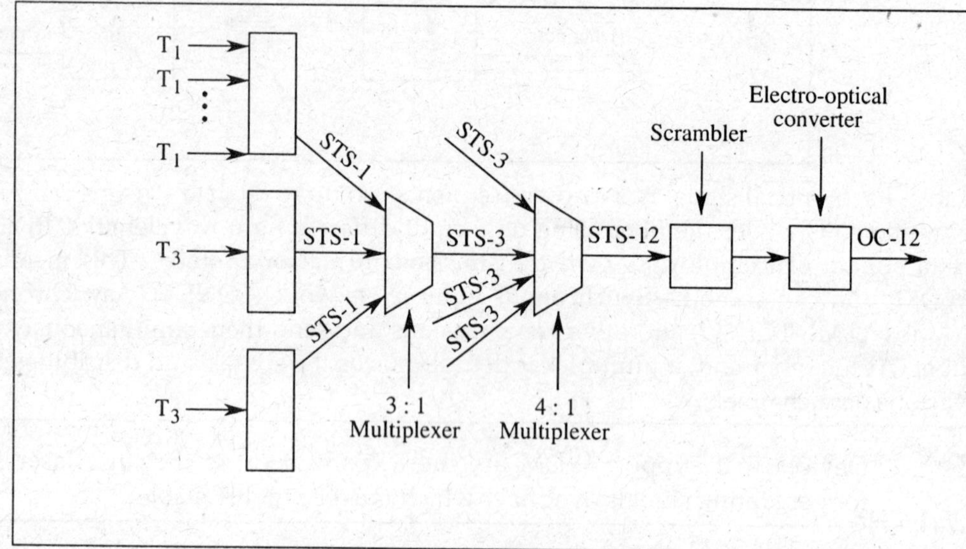

Figure 7.16 Multiplexing in SONET Path

7.6 ONE TO MANY MULTIPLEXING (DEMULTIPLEXING)

Demultiplexing is the process of separating of multiple input streams that were multiplexed into a common physical signal back into multiple output streams as can be seen in Figure 7.1.

7.7 TELEPHONE SYSTEM

Public telephone system provided by MTNL in big cities has analog connections that come out to our house or business centers. Analog telephone systems provide either two or four wire that convey a DC (direct current) signal between your telephone handset and a local telephone company CO (central office). Most public telephone vendors provide direct dial service to households through two-wire systems. Vendors set up four-wire system for high speed data communications or to convey several voice signals through the same channel. The signals that move through these lines have analog frequencies in the range of 350 Hz for dial tone and in the range of 400 Hz to 3.4 K Hz for voice signal.

Figure 7.17 shows a simplified diagram of a two-wire telephone connection between two telephones connected to the same central office. The telephone company or the telephone exchange provides the telephone wires with batteries. The voltage at the local CO (Central office) is about 48 volts DC. The power source is available at all times, even when you lose mains electric supply at your home. The company connects your telephone using twisted pair wires so that the interference is minimum on the telephone lines.

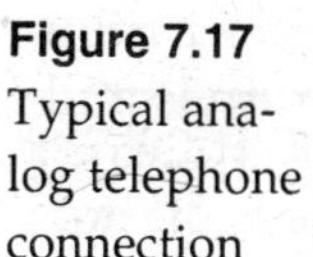
Figure 7.17
Typical analog telephone connection

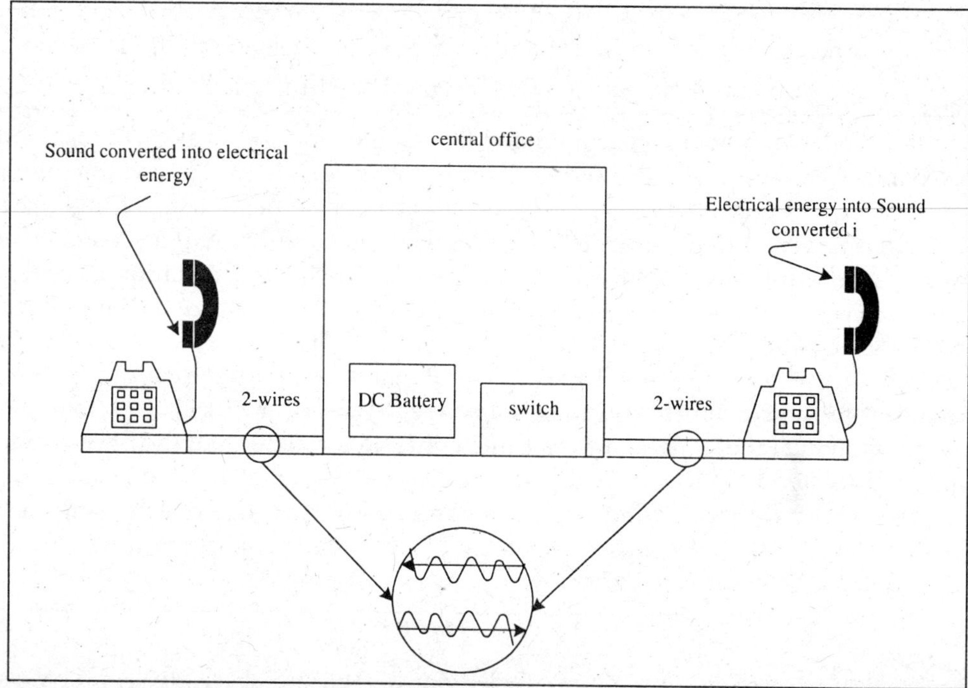

7.7.1 How Telephone dialing is done?

Telephone calls are initiated by subscribers (users) by going *Off Hook* that is by lifting the handset of the telephone off its cradle or hook. Physically, to go off hook is the act of lifting the handset from its cradle, causing a switch to close. The switch completes a direct current path (Local Loop) between the telephone set and the local switch office (CO). The Local telephone exchange detects the off-hook condition by sensing a drop in voltage from a 48 V battery source to less than 10 V on the subscriber's line caused by the change from an unloaded line (switch open) to a loaded line (switch closing the current loop).

The exchange then returns a dial tone, which is a mixture of two sine wave signals, one a 350 Hz and the other 440 Hz. Upon hearing the dial tone, the user can begin to dial the desired number. One way of doing this is by using a rotary dial. These rotary dials are found on the old model telephone instruments. A number is selected and the dial rotated to the stop position. Upon release, the dial returns to a rest condition. As the dial is returning to this position, a switch connected to the dial is opened and closed as each finger hole in the dial passes the stop position. This opening and closing of the switch causes a current path to be made and broken, generating current pulses at the rate of ten pulses per second (pps). The number of pulses generated is determined by the number selected by the user. The rate at which the dial returns, and hence the pulse rate, is physically fixed. There is an inter-digit period between each digit dialed.

Finally, after the last number is dialed, the line is active and the switch station begins to connect the call. The caller hears the ringing tone, and the called subscriber hears his or her telephone ring. These do not occur at the same time.

☞ A newer Touch Tone dialers use a more complicated system for dialing the number. The principle is named as DTMF (Dual Tone Multiple Frequency).

If the call is local one, it is completed by being connected to another local loop at the local exchange. The switch station senses whether the called party is in use (the phone is off hook) or is free. Upon detecting an off-hook condition a busy tone, which is a mixture of 480 Hz and 620 Hz is returned to the originating caller. It is sent altering half a second *on* and half a second *silence*. If the line is free, a ring signal is sent to the called station. It consists of a 20 Hz sine wave at a voltage between 90 and 120 V. This voltage is needed to operate the electro-mechanical ringing relay that strikes the bell in the telephone set. The ring is *on* for 2 seconds and *off* for 4 seconds. The ring signal that is heard by the calling party is not the same one sent to the ringer of the called subscriber. Instead, it is a 480 Hz tone returned by the switch station at the same *on* and *off* time to inform the caller that the phone should be ringing at the distant end.

Bear in mind that the ring signal you hear is not the same one causing the telephone set ringer to operate. This is why sometimes it seems that the party you were calling picked up the phone before you detect that it was supposed to ring.

Figure 7.18 Local loop calls through a Central Office (Telephone exchange)

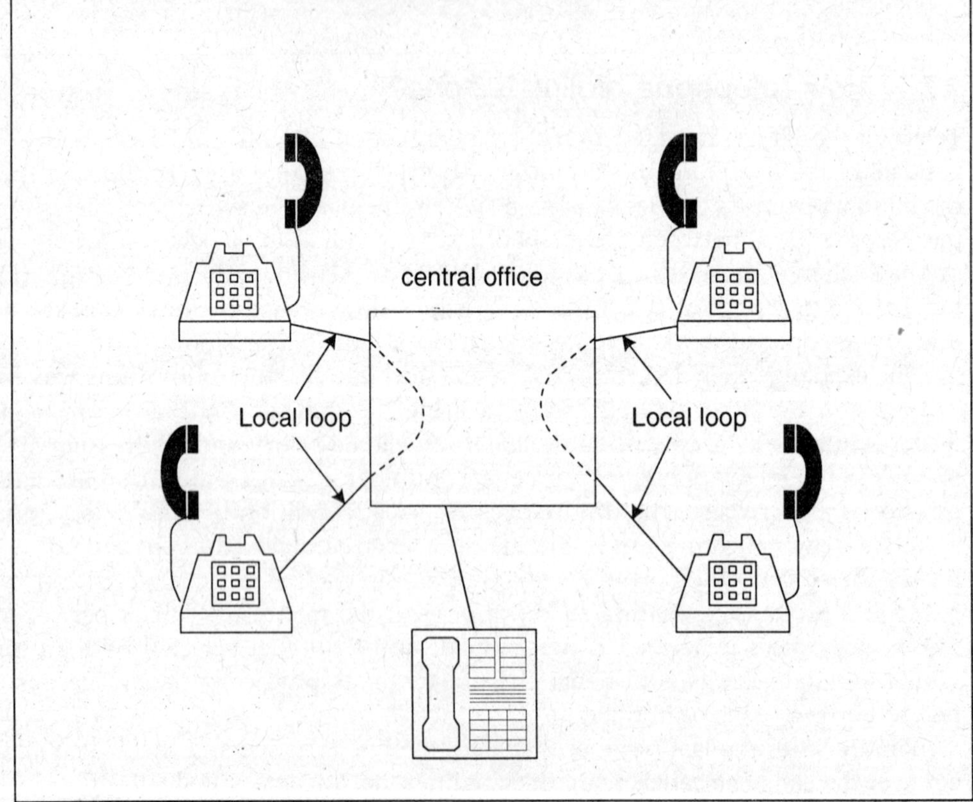

7.7.2 Types of Analog Telephone Connections

Telephone lines that go through a central office switch can make two types of connections with other telephones. First, you can direct dial another telephone connected with the same central office (CO).

Second, you can dial a telephone connected to another CO. In either case, the call requires the closure of electrical switches to make the connection. This is why, it is given the name circuit-switched connection.

Local calls between two telephones connected to the same CO make the simplest type of analog telephone circuit. This type of call goes through a local loop, as shown in Figure 7.18. After you dial the number you want, the CO makes the connection by closing the appropriate switches that create a continuous loop from your telephone to the other. If you make a call from one modem to another and the two modems connect to the same CO, the CO completes the same type of switched circuit for you.

Telephone calls between COs are more complex than local-loop calls. These calls go through trunk lines as shown in Figure 7.19.

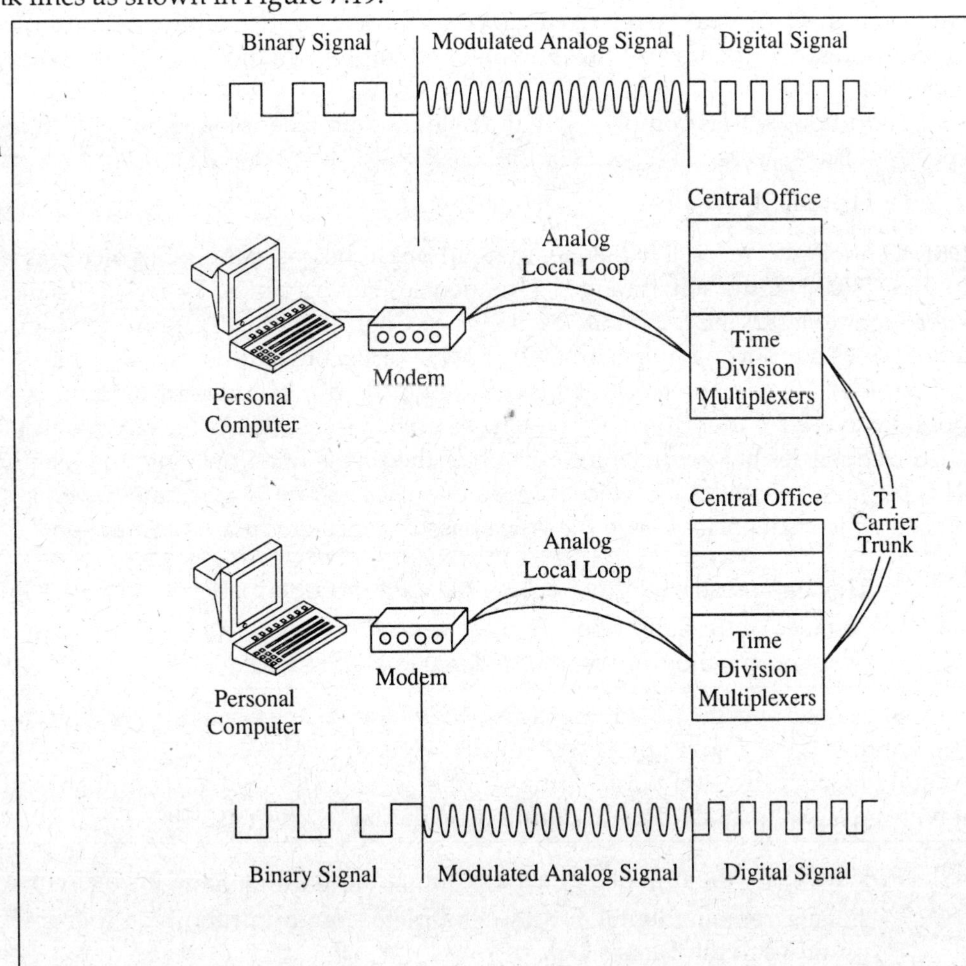

Figure 7.19 Trunk telephone line used between two computers connected using modems

How to Connect many Telephone Subscribers with few Telephone Lines?

The process of combining several signals and conveying them through the same channel simultaneously is multiplexing and has been explained earlier. The technique enables the telephone company to set up many telephone connections between telephones or computers through a few physical channels. This reduction in overhead enables the telephone provider to operate efficiently and keep operating cost down. As seen in Figure 7.5, through two trunk channels, many computers are connected using frequency division multiplexing.

7.8 DIGITAL SUBSCRIBER LINE (DSL)

DSL is a telecommunications technology for providing high-speed transmission to subscribers over the existing copper wire twisted-pair local loop between the customer premises and the Telco's central office (CO).

The Digital Subscriber Line (DSL) technology was designed to provide high-speed data and video-on-demand services to subscribers at speeds much faster than Integrated Services Digital Network (ISDN). The essential advantage of using DSL is that it allows much faster data transmission rates over existing copper local loop telephone lines than traditional modems. DSL standards are still evolving, and implementation is not yet widespread in most locations.

In addition, DSL is competing with cable modem technologies to replace ISDN for high-speed Internet access.

7.8.1 How DSL Works?

DSL technologies recognize the fact that although the passband of a voice channel is approximately 3000 Hz, the actual range of frequencies supportable on a twisted-pair circuit from a subscriber to a serving telephone exchange or Central Office (CO) is much higher, with some access lines supporting approximately 1 MHz of usable bandwidth. Because the voice channel passband is constructed at the CO through the use of filters or loading coils, it becomes possible to use a wider range of frequencies on the access line to move data and to remove the used frequencies before the voice portion of the access line flows into the telephone network. This technique, enables the voice portion of an access line to continue to be used to transport voice, while frequencies above the voice passband are modulated to transport data.

☞ The major restrictions governing the data rate obtainable on an access line include the distance of the subscriber from the central office, the gauge of the wire and its condition, and the modulation method used by DSL modems.

DSL is not a specific digital line technology but rather a form of digital modem technology that defines the signaling processes for high-speed, end-to-end digital transmission over the existing copper twisted-pair wiring of the local loop. DSL accomplishes this by using advanced signal processing and digital modulation techniques.

☞ With DSL, the digital signals are not converted to analog or vice versa; instead, the signals remain digital for the complete communication path from the customer premises to the Telco's CO.

Usually, a DSL modem and a signal splitter are installed at the customer premises to separate voice and data signals. DSL modems can use a variety of modulation methods, including carrierless amplitude and phase modulation (CAP) or discrete multitone (DMT) technology modulation, depending on the vendor's implementation. At the Telco's CO, a Digital Subscriber Line Access Multiplexer (DSLAM) connects subscribers to a high-speed Asynchronous Transfer Mode (ATM) backbone. DSL actually represents a family of related services commonly referred to as "xDSL," which includes the following:

(a) *Asymmetric Digital Subscriber Line (ADSL),* which allocates line bandwidth asymmetrically with downstream (CO to customer premises) data rates of up to 9 Mbps and upstream rates of up to 640 Kbps, depending on the implementation. ADSL allocates bandwidth asymmetrically in the frequency spectrum. This enables a greater data rate to be obtained downstream towards the user than on the return upstream channel.
For Internet access, ADSL is preferred because the data flow coming into the network operates much faster than the data routing out of the network. This is not as useful for WANs as it is for Internet access, where data coming into the network is more important than data going out.

(b) *High-bit-rate Digital Subscriber Line (HDSL),* which supports high-speed, full-duplex communication up to T1 or E2 speeds over multiple twisted-pair lines. HDSL allocates the bandwidth asymmetrically in both directions and functions as a replacement for T1 and E1 four-wire metallic circuits. Because HDSL permits subscribers to be located further from a central office but does not require repeaters, telephone companies often employ it as a substitute for more expensive repeated local loops.
HDSL transmits data at symmetrical speeds at T1 data rate which is 1.544 megabits per second over distances of 12,000 feet or less. Telephone companies have used HDSL lines to provision T1 lines for long time because HDSL can be installed much faster than regular T1 or T3 wiring.

(c) *Symmetric Digital Subscriber Line (SDSL),* supports standard telephone communication and T1 or E1 data communication over a single twisted-pair line. SDSL allocates bandwidth symmetrically, much like HDSL does. However, unlike HDSL (which operates on a four-pair circuit), SDSL is a single-pair implementation of DSL technology.

(d) *Very High-rate Digital Subscriber Line (VDSL),* which supports downstream speeds of up to 52 Mbps over short distances. Depending on the type of xDSL technology used, signal modulation by the DSL modem might use CAP, DMT, or some other modulation process. (CAP is currently the most popular implementation.)

7.9 CODE DIVISION MULTIPLE ACCESS (CDMA)

CDMA is a digital cellular phone technology that uses spread spectrum wireless networking technologies. Code Division Multiple Access (CDMA) can be used to refer both to a type of digital cellular phone system and to the specific media access method used by this kind of cellular system.

CDMA was developed by Qualcomm in 1993, and it was adopted and ratified by the Telecommunications Industry Association (TIA) as part of their Interim Standard 95.

7.9.1 How CDMA Works?

CDMA uses the spread spectrum wireless networking technology, first developed for military communication systems in the 1940s because it spreads its transmission over a large bandwidth, making it difficult to jam. Instead of dividing the available radio spectrum into a series of discrete channels using the older Time Division Multiple Access (TDMA) media access method, a CDMA channel occupies the entire available frequency band.

The disadvantage is that CDMA is more complex to implement than TDMA digital cellular technologies. The spread spectrum approach assigns a special digital code sequence to each user, and all users share the same broad portion of the radio frequency spectrum. Users thus share time and frequency resources on the available bandwidth, and their individual communications are channeled using these codes. The code tag then identifies the conversation to the transmission station. All users in a cell that are transmitting at the same time are thus employing the same frequency band for their transmission.

☞ CDMA combines voice and data into a single digital transmission at 9.6 Kbps, although speeds up to 19.2 Kbps per channel are possible by using error detection and correction techniques.

Advantages

(a) Without knowledge of a conversation's code tag, eavesdropping on CDMA conversations is difficult, making CDMA a more secure cellular phone technology.
(b) CDMA also has a much higher call capacity. Its call capacity is comparable to the Global System for Mobile Communications (GSM) standard for cellular communication used in Europe.

7.9.2 IS95 Type of CDMA Technique

In CDMA, signals are sent at the same time in the same frequency band. Signals are either selected or rejected at the receiver by recognition of a user-specific signature waveform, which is constructed from an assigned spreading code. The IS95 cellular system employs the CDMA technique. In IS95, an analog speech signal that is to be sent to a cell site is first quantized and then organized into one of a number of digital frame structures. In one frame structure, a frame of 20 milliseconds' duration consists of 192 bits. Of these 192 bits, 172 represent the speech signal itself, 12 form a cyclic redundancy check that can be used for error detection, and 8 form an encoder "tail" that allows the decoder to work properly. These bits are formed into an encoded data stream.

After interleaving of the encoded data stream, bits are organized into groups of six. Each group of six bits indicates which of 64 possible waveforms to transmit. Each of the waveforms to be transmitted has a particular pattern of alternating polarities and occupies a certain portion of the radio-frequency spectrum. Before one of the waveforms is transmitted, however, it is multiplied by a code sequence of polarities that alternate at a rate of 1.2288 megahertz, spreading the bandwidth occupied by the signal and causing it to occupy (after filtering at the transmitter) about 1.23 megahertz of the radio-frequency spectrum.

At the cell site one user can be selected from multiple users of the same 1.23-megahertz bandwidth by its assigned code sequence.

☞ CDMA is sometimes referred to as spread-spectrum multiple access (SSMA), because the process of multiplying the signal by the code sequence causes the power of the transmitted signal to be spread over a larger bandwidth.

Frequency management is eliminated in CDMA. When another user wishes to use the communications channel, it is assigned a code and immediately transmits instead of being stored until a frequency slot opens.

7.10 FREQUENCY DIVISION MULTIPLE ACCESS (FDMA)

FDMA is the signal multiplexing technology used in the Advanced Mobile Phone Service (AMPS) analog version of cellular phone technology. Frequency Division Multiple Access (FDMA) is one of three methods used for allocating channels to users over the shared wireless communications medium in cellular phone communication; the others are Time Division Multiple Access (TDMA) and Code Division Multiple Access (CDMA).

7.10.1 How FDMA Works?

FDMA is implemented at the media access control (MAC) layer of the data-link layer in the Open Systems Interconnection (OSI) reference model for networking protocol stacks. FDMA is based on the frequency-division multiplexing (FDM) technique used in wireless networking.

In FDMA, the user is assigned a specific frequency band in the electromagnetic spectrum, and during a call that user is the only one who has the right to access the specific band. In the AMPS cellular phone system, these frequency bands are allocated from the electromagnetic spectrum as given below.

(a) Transmission by mobile station: 824 MHz to 849 MHz
(b) Transmission by base station: 869 MHz to 894 MHz

Two different frequency bands are used to allow full-duplex communication between base and mobile stations. Both of these bands are then divided into discrete channels that are 30 kHz wide in bandwidth.

☞ One way to understand FDMA is to imagine different people in the same room communicating in voices with different pitches, some high and some low; they would all be able to talk simultaneously and (more or less) understand one another. FDMA works on a similar way. FDMA is used by traditional AM and FM radio bands to allow broadcast by individual stations.

In FDMA the goal is to divide the frequency spectrum into slots and then to separate the signals of different users by placing them in separate frequency slots. The difficulty is that the frequency spectrum is limited and that there are typically many more potential communicators than the available frequency slots. In order to make efficient use of the communications channel, a system must be devised for managing the available slots.

REVIEW QUESTIONS WITH ANSWERS

Question Number 1 What additional equipment do you need to transmit computer data over a telephone line? With the help of a diagram, draw its functional blocks and their interconnection?

Answer We would need additional equipment to transmit computer data over a telephone line. As seen in the figure below, this equipment is known as *modem*.

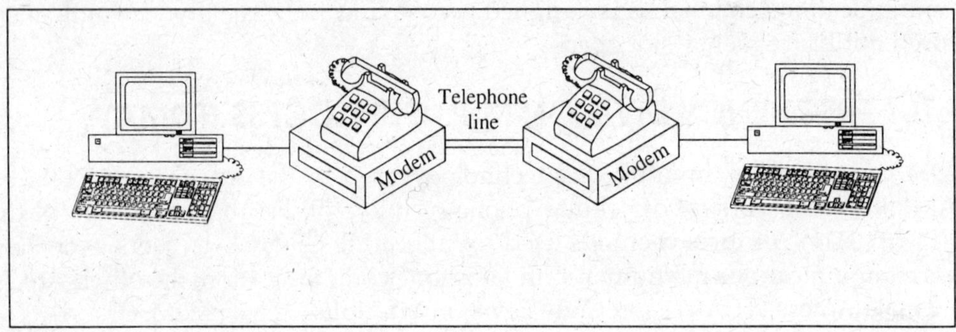

Modem stands for modulator/demodulator. Modem converts the digital data of the computer into analog form to be transmitted on telephone lines and vice versa. Telephone lines can take analog signal well but not the digital signal. But computers produce digital signal. Therefore, we need to convert the digital signal to analog signal before it can be sent on telephone lines. Similarly, when analog signal comes on the other side of the line, this is to be converted back to digital form using another modem. Figure above shows the connection of the modems on the two sides of the computer systems.

Question Number 2 What are the types of multiplexing used in telephone trunk circuits to transmit a large number of voice channels by the same transmitter? Explain with the help of a diagram, any one such a scheme.

Answer The types of multiplexing used in telephone trunk circuits are:

(a) Frequency Division Multiplexing (FDM)

(b) Time Division Multiplexing (TDM)

FDM

In Frequency Division Multiplexing (FDM), the available band width of a physical medium is divided into several smaller disjoint logical band widths. Each of the component band width is used as a separate communication channel. The best example is the way we receive various stations in Akashvani (All India Radio).

For telephonic communication, a voice channel ranges from 0 - 4 kHz. It is first mixed with the carrier frequency using a mixer (See Figure 7.8). Then the group of channels usually 12 are grouped and as the number of channels increases, their groups and subgroups are formed. Thus each channel is transmitted at separate frequency with a guard band so that one message can not be interfered by another message on the same media.

TDM

TDM is a form of multiplexing—combining separate signals into a single high-speed transmission—in which transmission time is broken into segments, each of which carries one element of one signal. In time division multiplexing, the separate signals are sampled in order at regular intervals—whether or not they have data to send—and the samples are then "loaded" onto a single channel. The effect is somewhat like orderly groups of pedestrians stepping singly, in turn, onto a moving walkway.

For example, in Figure 7.12, the messages A, B and C are broken into smaller packets. These are interleaved and assigned time slots as seen in the lower diagram in this figure. A header containing the address and packet number information, precedes each packet. The interleaved packet are transmitted and received by the receiving station. The appropriate packets (determined by destination address in the header) are extracted by each station as they are received and reassembled (by packet number, included in the header) into their original message. This is the full operation of TDM.

Question Number 3. What are the two types of TDM? How do they differ from each other?

Answer [*Refer to Sections 7.41 and 7.4.2*]

Question Number 4. How does TDM signal differ from FDM signal. What are the advantages and disadvantages of TDM over FDM.

Answer [*Refer to Sections 7.3 and 7.4*]

Question Number 5. Describe the analog hierarchy in which groups of signals are successively multiplexed onto higher bandwidth lines.

Answer [*Refer Section 7.3.1*]

TEST PAPER

Time: 3 Hrs. Marks: 100

Note: Answer all questions.

1. Compare time division and frequency division multiplexing schemes.
2. What is multiplexing? List different types of multiplexing techniques possible for signals. Describe any one of them. Which multiplexing technique is not possible for baseband LANs? Why?
3. What are the different types of multiplexing possible for analog signals? Explain each with example.
4. Write short notes on the followings:
   (a) Digital Subscriber Line (DSL)
   (b) Code Division Multiple Access (CDMA)
   (c) Frequency Division Multiple Access (FDMA)
5. What is a Telephone System? How telephone dialing is done? With the help of a diagram, describe the local loop calls between two telephones connected to the same Central Office.

CHAPTER 8

Datalink Control Protocols

8.1 INTRODUCTION

In sending data from one place to other place, communication requires at least two devices working together, one to send and one to receive. Such a basic arrangement requires coordination for an intelligible exchange to occur. For example, in half-duplex transmission, it is essential that only one device transmits at a time. If both devices at the two ends of the link put signals on the line simultaneously, they collide. The coordination of half-duplex transmission is part of a procedure called *line discipline.* This line discipline is one of the functions included in the data link layer of OSI model.

Besides line discipline, the another important functions in the data link layer are *flow control* and *error control* (See Figure 8.1). These three functions together are known as data link control.

Figure 8.1
Data link layer

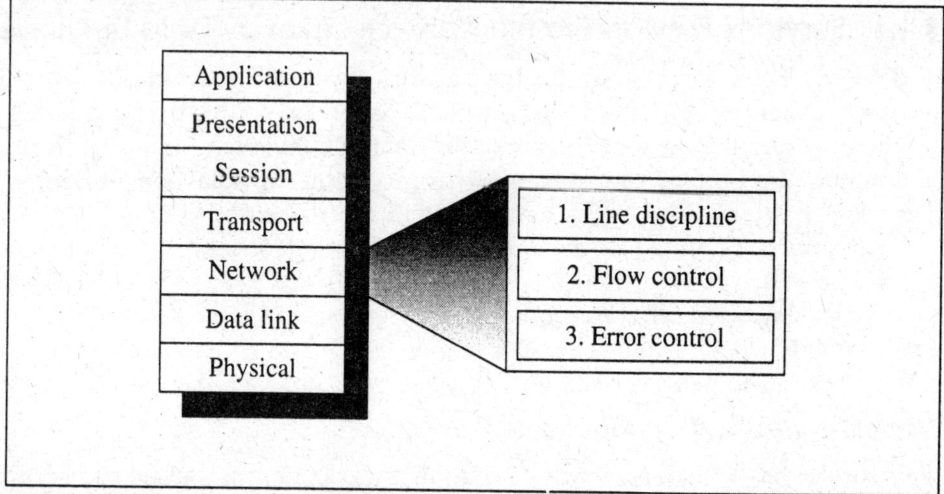

The data link control provides the following three functions:

(a) Line discipline i.e. it coordinates the link systems and determines which device can send data.

(b) Flow control i.e. coordinates the amount of data that can be sent before receiving acknowledgment. Flow control also provides the receiver's acknowledgment of frames received intact, and thus linked to error control.

(c) Error control i.e. provides error detection and correction. Error control allows the receiver to inform the sender of any frames lost or damaged in transmission. Error control also coordinates the retransmission of those frames by the sender. These functions are shown in Figure 8.2.

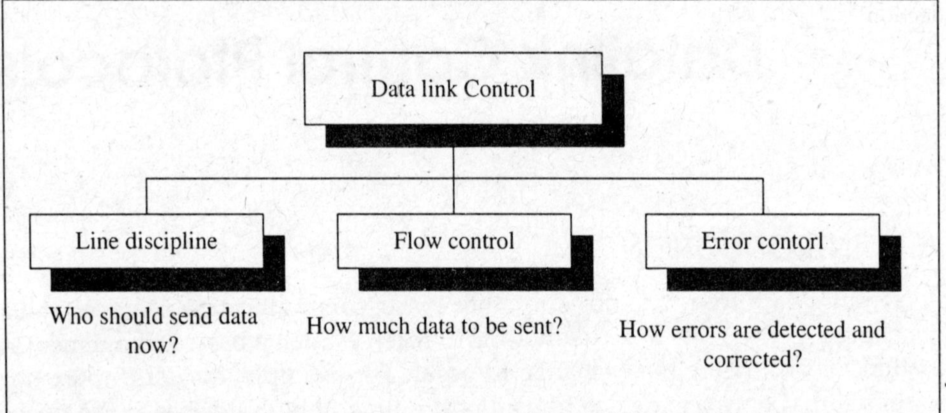

Figure 8.2
Data link layer functions

Data Link Control (DLC) is related to an international standard protocol called IEEE 802.2. Many token ring organisations use DLC to allow their PC workstations to talk to Mainframe gateways. Another common use of this protocol is to use it to communicate with network printers.

The data link layer also provides a well-defined service interface to the network layer, determining how the bits of the physical layer are grouped into frames.

8.1.1 Services Provided to the Network Layer by Data Link Layer

A data link layer can provide to the network layer, the connection oriented service. This means, transferring data from the network layer on the source machine to the network layer on the destination machine. The job of the data link layer is to transmit the bits to the destination machine, so they can be handed over to the network layer as shown in Figure 8.3 (a). The actual path followed by the data is seen in part (b) of this figure.

The services provided by the data link layer to network layer can be in one of the following forms:

(a) Unacknowledged connectionless service
(b) Acknowledged connectionless service
(c) Acknowledged connection-oriented service

Unacknowledged Connectionless Service

This service has the source machine sending independent frames to the destination machine without having the destination machine to acknowledge them (the frames). If a frame is lost due to noise on the line, no attempt is made to recover it in the data link layer. This class of service is good enough when the error rate is very low and also for real-time traffic, such as speech.

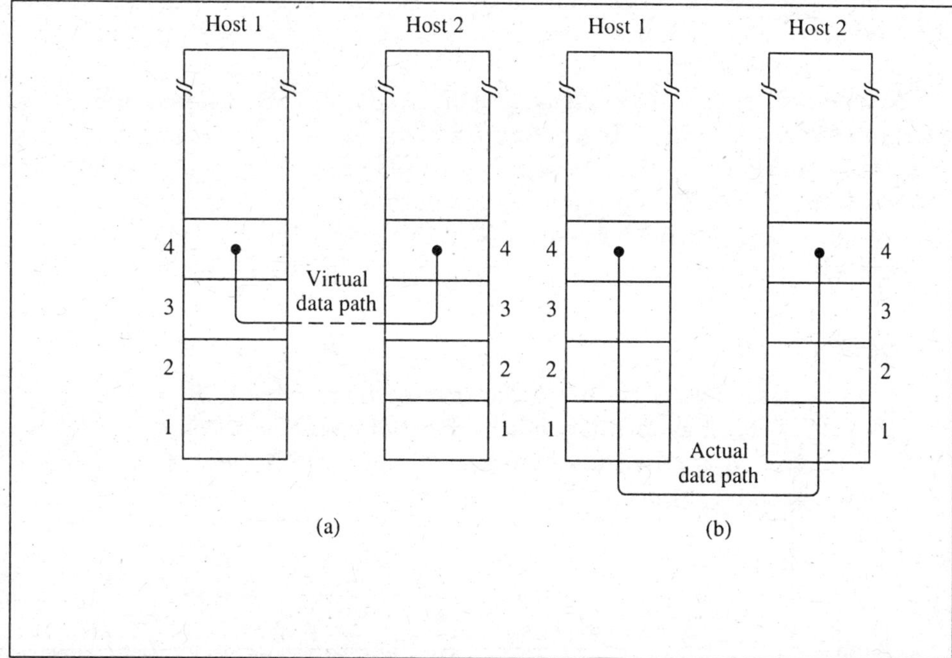

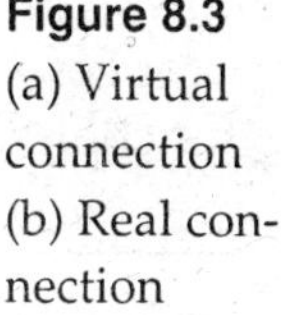

Figure 8.3 (a) Virtual connection (b) Real connection

Acknowledged Connectionless Service

This service is more reliable than unacknowledged connectionless service. When this service is offered, there are still no connections used, but each frame sent is individually acknowledged. In this way, the sender knows whether or not a frame has arrived safely. If it has not arrived within a specified time interval, it can be sent again. This service is useful over unreliable channels such as wireless systems.

Acknowledged Connection-oriented Service

This is the most sophisticated service that the data link layer can provide to the network layer. With this service, the source and destination machines establish a connection before any data are transferred. Each frame sent over the connection is numbered, and the data link layer guarantees that each frame sent is indeed received. It guarantees that each frame is received exactly once and that all frames are received in the right order.

There are three distinct phases in this service. In the *first* phase the connection is established by having both sides initialize variables and counters needed to keep track of which frames have been received and which ones have not. In the *second* phase, data frames are actually transmitted. In the third and *final* phase, the connection is terminated, freeing up the variables, buffers and other resources used to maintain the connection.

8.1.2 Services Provided by the Physical Layer to Data Link Layer

The data link layer must use the service provided to it by the physical layer to provide service to network layer. The physical layer accepts a raw bit stream and attempts to deliver it to the destination. The received bit stream may be less than, equal to or greater than the number of bits transmitted and they may have wrong values. It is for the data link layer *to detect* and if necessary *correct this error.*

The data link layer usually breaks the bit stream up into discrete frames and compute the checksum for each frame. When a frame arrives at the destination, the checksum is recomputed. If the newly computed checksum is different from the one contained in the frame, the data link layer knows that an error has occurred and takes steps to deal with it. This may be done by discarding the bad frames and sending back an error report.

There are four methods of designing frames. These are described in the following subsections.

Character Count

This method uses a field in the header to specify the number of characters in the frame. When the data link layer at the destination sees the character count, it knows how many characters follow and hence where the end of the frame is. Figure 8.4 shows four frames with and without error of character counts.

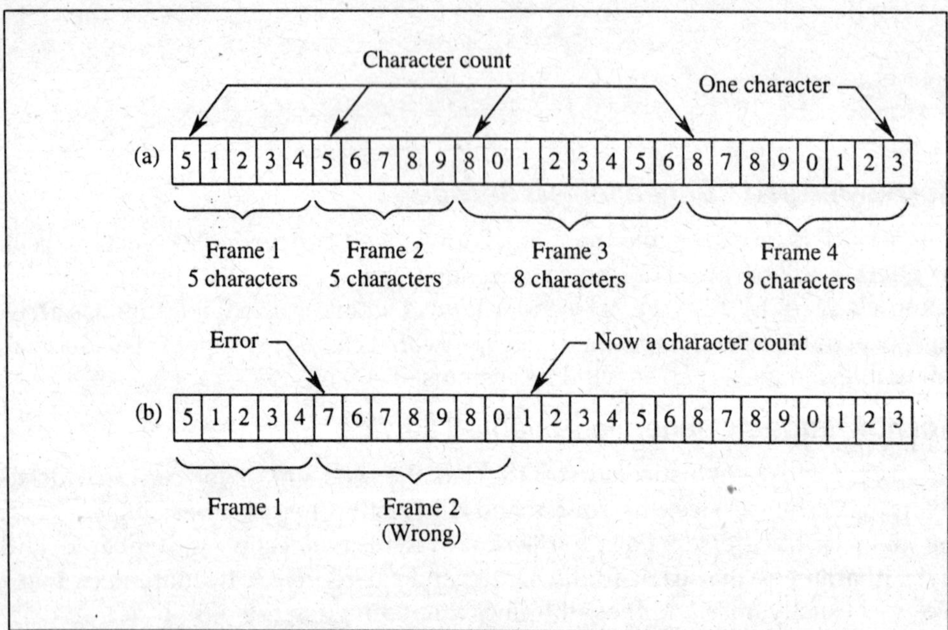

Figure 8.4 A character stream (a) With out errors (b) With one error

Starting and Ending characters, with Character Stuffing

In this method the problem of resynchronization, after an error, is overcome by having each frame start with the ASCII character sequence DLE STX and end with the sequence DLE ETX. In this technique, the frame can be checked where it is positioned. If the destination ever loses track of the frame boundaries, all it has to do is look for DLE STX or DLE ETX characters to find out where it is. The acronym DLE stands for **D**ata **L**ink **E**scape and STX for **S**tart of **T**e**X**t. Similarly, acronym ETX stands for **E**nd of **T**e**X**t.

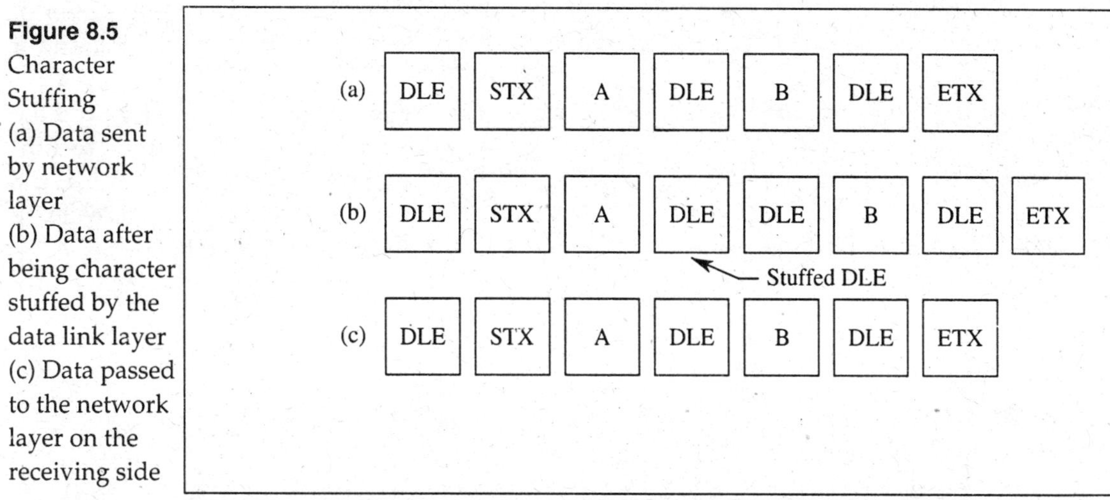

Figure 8.5 Character Stuffing (a) Data sent by network layer (b) Data after being character stuffed by the data link layer (c) Data passed to the network layer on the receiving side

Figure 8.5 illustrates the process of character stuffing technique. A major disadvantage of using this framing method is that it is closely tied to the ASCII code. As networks developed, the disadvantages of embedding the character code in the framing mechanism became more and more obvious so a new technique had to be developed to allow arbitrary sized characters.

Starting and Ending characters, with Bit Stuffing

The new technique allows data frames to contain an arbitrary number of bits and allows character codes with an arbitrary number of bits per character. Each frame begins and ends with a special bit pattern, 01111110, called a ***flag*** byte. Whenever, sender's data link layer encounters five consecutive ones in the data, it automatically stuffs a 0 bit into the outgoing bit stream. This bit stuffing is analogous to character stuffing, in which a DLE is stuffed into the outgoing character stream before DLE in the data. Figure 8.6 illustrates this concept. When the receiver sees five consecutive incoming 1 bits, followed by a 0 bit, it removes the 0 bit. Bit stuffing is completely transparent to the computer network layer in both computers.

If the user data contain the flag pattern, 01111110, this flag is transmitted as 011111010 but stored in the receiver's memory as 01111110.

☞ With the help of bit stuffing, the boundary between two frames can be recognized with out any error because of the flag pattern.

Thus if the receiver loses track of where it is, all it has to do is scan the input for flag sequences, since they can only occur at frame boundaries and never within the data as can be seen in part (b) of Figure 8.6.

The different parts of this figure show the following:

(a) The original data i.e. data sent by network layer

(b) The data as they appear on the line i.e. data after being bit stuffed by the data link layer

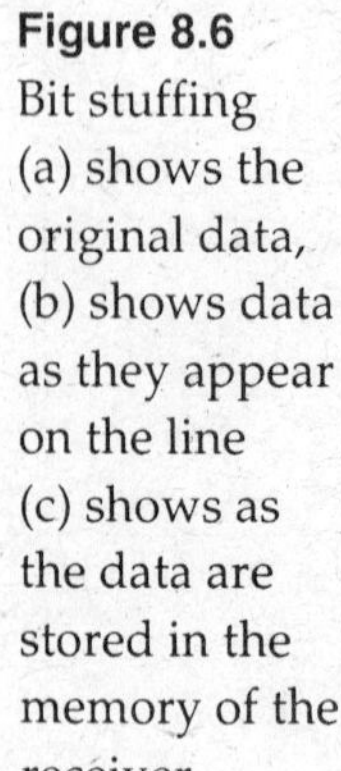

(a) 0 1 1 0 1 1 1 1 1 1 1 1 1 1 1 1 1 1 1 1 0 0 1 0

(b) 0 1 1 0 1 1 1 1 1 0 1 1 1 1 1 0 1 1 1 1 1 0 1 0 0 1 0

Stuffed bits

(c) 0 1 1 0 1 1 1 1 1 1 1 1 1 1 1 1 1 1 1 1 0 0 1 0

Figure 8.6
Bit stuffing
(a) shows the original data, (b) shows data as they appear on the line (c) shows as the data are stored in the memory of the receiver

(c) The data as they are stored in the receiver's memory after bit stuffing, i.e. data passed to the network layer on the receiving side.

☞ In framing techniques, many data link protocols use a combination of a character count with one of the other methods for extra safety. When a frame arrives, the count field is used to locate the end of the frame. Only, if the appropriate delimiter is present at that position, the checksum is correct, the frame accepted is valid. Otherwise, the input stream is scanned for the next delimiter.

8.2 LINE DISCIPLINE

Line discipline coordinates the link system and determines which devices can send data. This can be done in two ways, namely
(a) Enquiry/acknowledgment (ENQ/ACK)
(b) Poll/select

8.2.1 Enquiry/Acknowledgment (ENQ/ACK) Method

ENQ/ACK is used where there is no question of the wrong receiver getting the transmission. In other words, this is used when there is a dedicated link between two devices and there is one device capable of receiving the transmission.

As seen in Figure 8.7, ENQ/ACK coordinates which device may start a transmission and whether or not the intended recipient is ready and enabled.

☞ Using ENQ/ACK, a session can be initiated by either station on a link as long as both are of equal rank. For example, a printer cannot initiate communication with a CPU.

Working of ENQ/ACK

The initiator first transmits a frame called an enquiry (ENQ) asking if the receiver is available

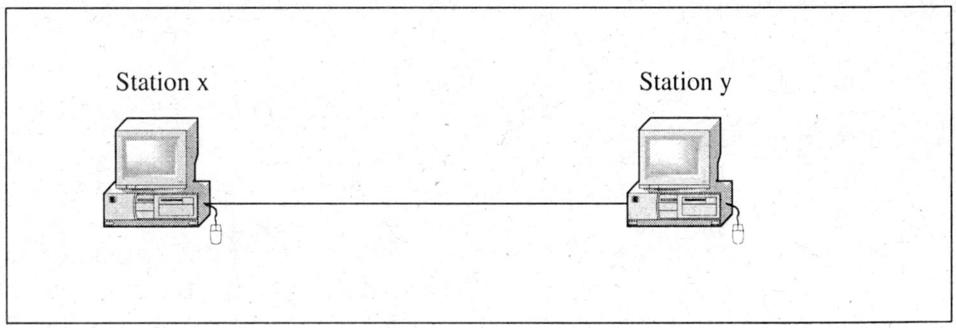

Figure 8.7
ENQ/ACK type of line discipline

to receive data. The receiver must answer either with an *acknowledgement (ACK)* frame if it is ready to receive or with a negative *acknowledgement (NAK)* frame if it is not. If neither an ACK nor a NAK is received within a specified time limit, the initiator assumes that the ENQ frame was lost in transit, disconnects, and sends a replacement. The initiating system usually makes three such attempts to establish a link before giving up.

☞ If the response to the ENQ is negative for all three attempts, the initiator disconnects and begins the process again at another time.

When the response is positive, the initiator is free to send its data. Once all of its data have been transmitted, the sending system finishes with an *end of transmission (EOT)* frame. This process is shown in Figure 8.8.

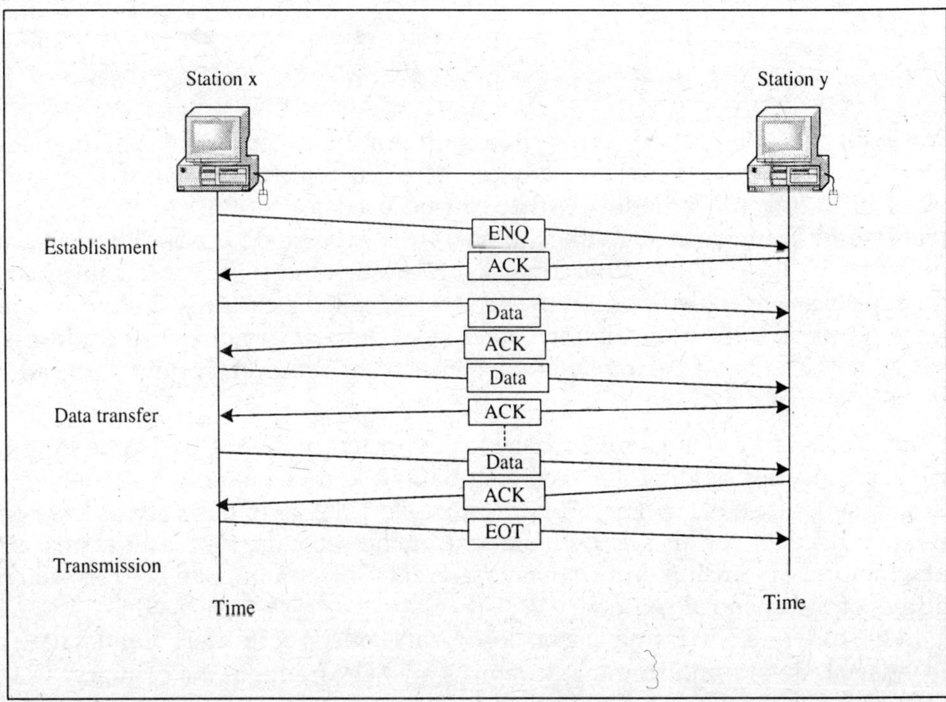

Figure 8.8
ENQ/ACK connection

8.2.2 Poll/Select

In *poll/select* method of line discipline, one device is designated as a *primary station* and the other devices are described as *secondary stations*.

Working of Poll/Select Method

In a multipoint link, i.e. a primary device and multiple secondary devices using a single transmission line, all transfers must be made through the primary device even when the ultimate destination is a secondary device. (See Figure 8.9). The primary device controls the link. The secondary devices follow its instructions whereas the primary device is always initiator of a session. If the primary wants to receive data, it asks the secondaries if they have anything to send. This function is called *polling*. If the primary wants to send data, it tells the target secondary to get ready to receive. This function is called *selecting*.

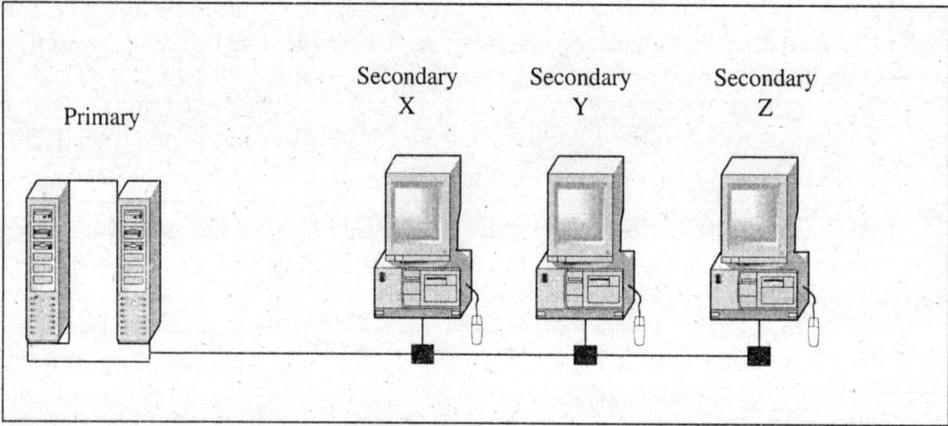

Figure 8.9 Poll/select line discipline method

Addresses For the primary device in a multipoint topology to be able to identify and communicate with specific secondary device, there must be an addressing method. Hence, every device on a link has an address that can be used for identification. Poll/select protocols identify each frame as being either to or from a specific device on the link. Each secondary device has an address that differentiates it from the others. In any transmission, that address will appear in a specified portion of each frame, called an address field or header depending on the protocol. If the transmission comes from the primary device, the address indicates the recipient of the data. If the transmission comes from a secondary device, the address indicates the originator of the data.

Select The *select* mode is used whenever the primary device has something to send. If the primary is neither sending nor receiving data, it knows the link is available. If it has something to send, it sends it. The primary must alert the secondary about the upcoming transmission and wait for an acknowledgment of the secondary's ready status. Before sending data, the primary creates and transmits a select (SEL) frame, one field of which includes the address of the intended secondary.

In the case of a SEL frame, the enclosed data consist of an alert that data are coming. If the secondary is awake and running, it returns an ACK frame to the primary. The primary then sends one or more data frames, each addressed to the intended secondary. Figure 8.10 shows this procedure.

Figure 8.10 Select procedure

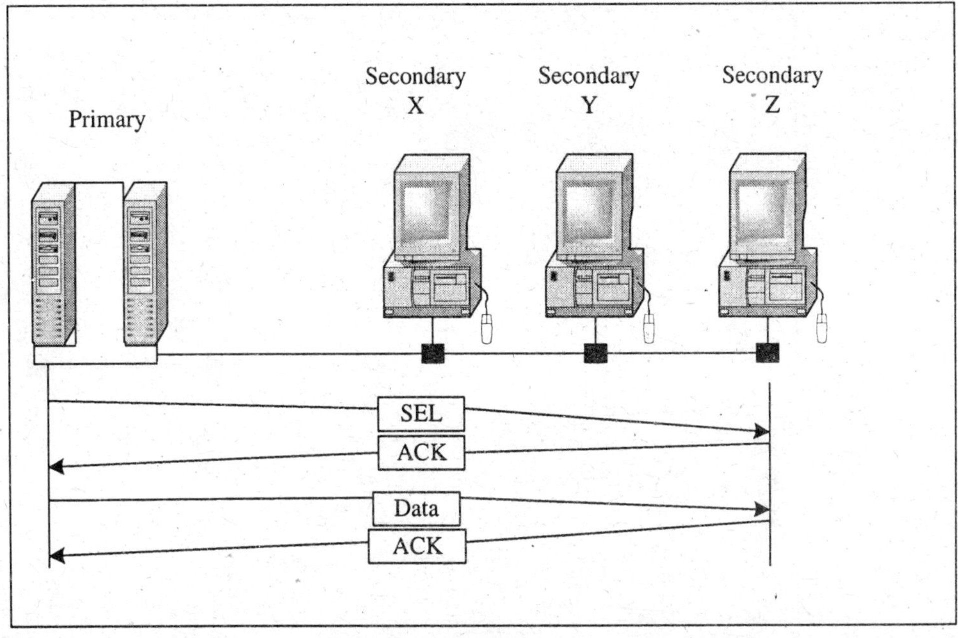

☞ Multipoint topologies use a single link for several devices, which means that any frame on the link is available to every device. As a frame makes its way down the link, each of the secondary devices checks the address field. Only when a device recognizes its own address does it open the frame and read the data.

Polling The polling function is used by the primary device to establish transmissions among the secondary devices. By keeping all control with the primary, the multipoint system guarantees that only one transmission can occur at a time, when the primary is ready to receive data, it must ask (*poll*) each device in turn if it has anything to send. When the first secondary is approached, it responds either with a NAK frame if it has nothing to send or with data (in the form of a data frame) if it does. When the response is negative (a NAK frame), the primary then polls the next secondary in the same way until it finds one with data to send. When the response is positive (a data frame), the primary reads the frame and returns an acknowledgment (ACK frame) verifying its receipt. The secondary may send several data frames one after the other, or it may be required to wait for an ACK before sending each one, depending on the protocol being used.

There are two possibilities for terminating the exchange

(a) The primary sends all its data, finishing with an end of transmission (EOT) frame.

(b) The primary says, "Time's up."

Which of these occurs depends on the protocol and the length of the messages. Once a secondary has finished transmitting, the primary can poll the remaining devices. (See Figure 8.11).

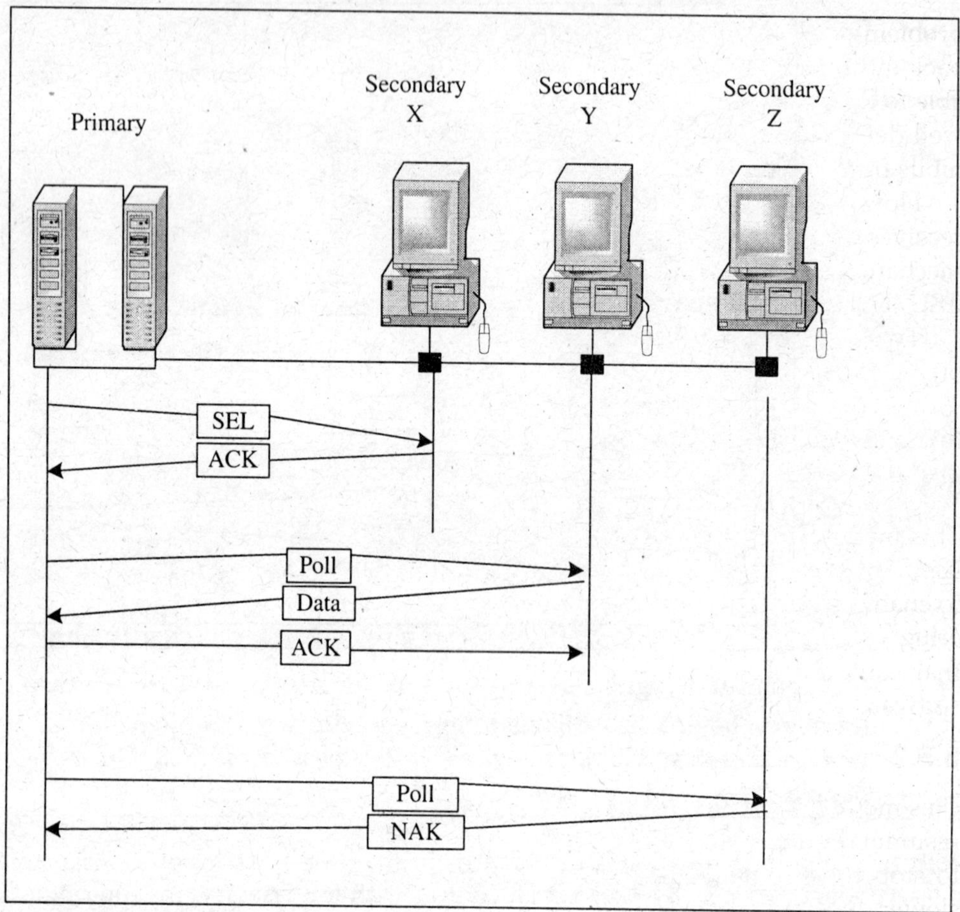

Figure 8.11 Polling procedure

8.3 FLOW CONTROL

Flow control is a set of procedures that tells the sender how much data it can transmit before it must wait for an acknowledgment from the receiver. The receiving device must be able to inform the sending device before those limits are reached and request the transmitting device to send fewer frames or stop temporarily.

☞ Incoming data must be checked and processed before they can be used. The rate of such processing is often slower than the rate of transmission. For this reason, each receiving device has a block or memory, called a *buffer*, reserved for storing incoming data until they are processed.

One of the problems that comes in the data link layer is what to do with a sender that systematically wants to transmit frames faster than the receiver can accept them. This situation occurs when the sender is running on a fast computer and the receiver is running on a slow machine. Even if the transmission is error free, at a certain point the receiver will simply not be able to handle the frames as they arrive and will start to lose some. The solution to this problem is to introduce ***flow control***. In this technique, called *throttling*, some kind of feedback mechanism is used, so the sender can be made aware of whether or not the receiver is able to keep up with the flow of data. The scheme may have the basic principle, which is the well defined rule about when a sender may transmit the next frame. Such a rule often prohibits frames from being sent until the receiver has granted permission.

Flow control is also the mechanism by which a modem controls the rate at which it receives data from another modem. You can also use flow control to describe data rate control mechanisms between other devices, such as computers and attached printers, or between CSU/DSUs (Channel Service Unit/Data Service Units) and routers.

Two basic types of flow control are:

(a) ***Hardware flow control:*** Also known as RTS/CTS (Request To Send/Clear To Send) control.

(b) ***Software flow control:*** Also known as XON/XOFF control.

8.3.1 Hardware flow control

This method uses special dedicated pinning on cables to leave flow control to the modem itself. In other words, a separate hard-wired signal link (wire) that does not carry data is used to enable one modem to send stop and start messages to the other modem by raising or lowering voltage levels on this wire. Hardware flow control is used with high-speed modems that can compress data and is usually the default setting for Microsoft Windows-based software, such as Hyperterminal, that uses modems.

8.3.2 Software Flow Control

This method uses special data characters (usually Ctrl+S to stop transmission, and Ctrl+Q to resume) sent within the data stream itself to enable a local modem to signal a remote modem to stop transmitting data so that the local modem can catch up. Software flow control is slower and less reliable than hardware flow control because a user, program, or line noise might inadvertently generate a stop signal for the remote modem. In addition, software flow control is used only when transmitting ASCII text information, not when transmitting binary data files, because the binary data might contain the Ctrl+S stop character and cause the remote modem to stop transmitting data.

8.4 FLOW CONTROL PROTOCOLS

Two protocols have been developed to control the flow of data across communications links. These are

(a) Stop-and-wait

(b) Sliding window

8.4.1 Simplex Stop-and-Wait Protocol

This is a half-duplex protocol and it is also referred to as a stop and wait protocol. This is so because transmission in one direction must stop before transmission in the opposite direction occurs. In this protocol, the sender sends one frame and then waits for an acknowledgement before proceeding .

After having passed a packet to its network layer, the receiver sends a little dummy frame back to the sender which, in effect, gives the sender permission to transmit the next frame. After having sent a frame, the sender is required by the protocol to hold its time until the little dummy (i.e. acknowledgement) frame arrives.

☞ The sender starts out by fetching a packet from the network layer, using it to construct a frame and sending it on its way. Only now, the sender must wait until an acknowledgement frame arrives before looping back and reaching the next packet from the network layer. The sending data link layer need not even inspect the incoming frame.

The only difference between one receiver i.e. receiver1 and the other receiver i.e. receiver2 is that after delivering a packet to the network layer, the receiver2 sends an acknowledgement frame back to the sender before entering the wait loop again. Because only the arrival of the frame back at the sender is important, not its contents, the receiver need not put any particular information in it.

Noisy Channel Simplex Protocol

If the channel is noisy, then the frames may be either damaged or lost completely due to attenuation or the noise in the channel. If the frame is damaged, then the receiver hardware will be able to detect this using the checksum error. If the frame is damaged in such a way that the checksum is never correct, then the protocol may totally fail. But such a situation is very less likely to occur.

PAR (Positive Acknowledgement with Retransmission) or ARQ (Automatic Repeat Request)

The protocol in which the sender waits for a positive acknowledgement before advancing to the next data item is called PAR or ARQ. This type of protocol also transmits data in one direction. This requires that the timeout interval should be long enough to prevent premature timeouts. If the sender times out too early, while the acknowledgement is still on the way, it will send a duplicate.

Many procedures require a device to respond or reply to an inquiry within a certain period of time; if the device does not respond, a timeout condition occurs, thus preventing the procedure from hanging up the computer. Timeouts are also used in communications to detect retransmission failures.

When the previous acknowledgement finally does arrive, the sender will mistakenly think that the just-sent frame is the one being acknowledged and will not realize that there is potentially another acknowledgement frame somewhere "in the pipe." If the next frame sent is lost completely but the extra acknowledgement arrives correctly, the sender will not attempt to retransmit the lost frame, and the protocol will fail.

Thus, after transmitting a frame, the sender starts the timer running. If it was already running, it will be reset to allow another full timer interval. The time interval must be chosen to allow enough time for the frame to get to the receiver, for the receiver to process it in the worst case, and for the acknowledgement frame to propagate back to the sender. Only when that time interval has elapsed, it is safe to assume that either the transmitted frame or its acknowledgement has been lost, and then try to send a duplicate.

After transmitting a frame and starting the timer, the sender can expect any one of the three happenings:

(a) an acknowledgement frame arrives undamaged or,

(b) a damaged acknowledgement frame staggers in, or

(c) the timer goes off.

If a valid acknowledgement comes in, the sender fetches the next packet from its network layer and puts it in the buffer, overwriting the previous packet. It also advances the sequence number.

If a damaged frame arrives or no frame at all arrives, neither the buffer nor the sequence number are changed, so that a duplicate can be sent.

At the receiver, when a valid frame arrives its sequence number is checked to see if it is a duplicate. If not, it is accepted, passed to the network layer, and an acknowledgement generated. Damaged and duplicate frames are not passed to the network layer.

8.4.2 Sliding Window Protocol

In this method, each outbound frame contains a sequence number, ranging from 0 up to some maximum. For an n-bit sliding window, the range of sequence numbers is 0 to 2^n-1 and frames are numbered module 2^n i.e. after sequence number 2^n-1, the next sequence number is 0.

Let us consider a 3-bit sliding window, the sequence number can range from 0 to 7. Accordingly frames are numbered modulo 8, i.e. 0, 1, 2, 3, 4, 5, 6, 7, 0, 1, 2, 3,...0, 1, 2,....

At any instant of time, the sender maintains a set of sequence numbers corresponding to frames it is allowed to send. These frames are said to fall within the *sending window*. Similarly, the receiver also maintains a *receiving window*, corresponding to the set of frames, it is allowed to accept.

At the beginning of the communication, the sender begins sending the frame with the first sequence number 0 and keeps on transmitting till sequence number 2^n-1 is reached for an *n-bit* sliding window.

The receiver also opens up a window with the same sequence number to receive the frames in the order in which they are sent. Any frame falling outside the receiver's window is discarded. In this way, all frames are received. Consider a 3 bit sliding window in Figure 8.12.

The shaded rectangle in the above figure indicates that the sender may transmit 7 frames, beginning with frame 6. Each time a frame is sent, the shaded window shrinks, each time an acknowledgement is received, the shaded window grows.

The mechanism described provides a form of flow control in which the receiver must only be able to accommodate 2^n-1 frames beyond the one it has last acknowledged. To supplement this, most protocols also allow a station to completely cut off the flow of frames from the other side by sending a Receiver-Not Ready (RNR) message, which acknowledges former frames but forbids transfer of future frames. At some subsequent point, the station must send a normal acknowledgement to reopen the window. All the above said discussion is for transmission in one direction only.

Figure 8.12 Sliding Window Depiction

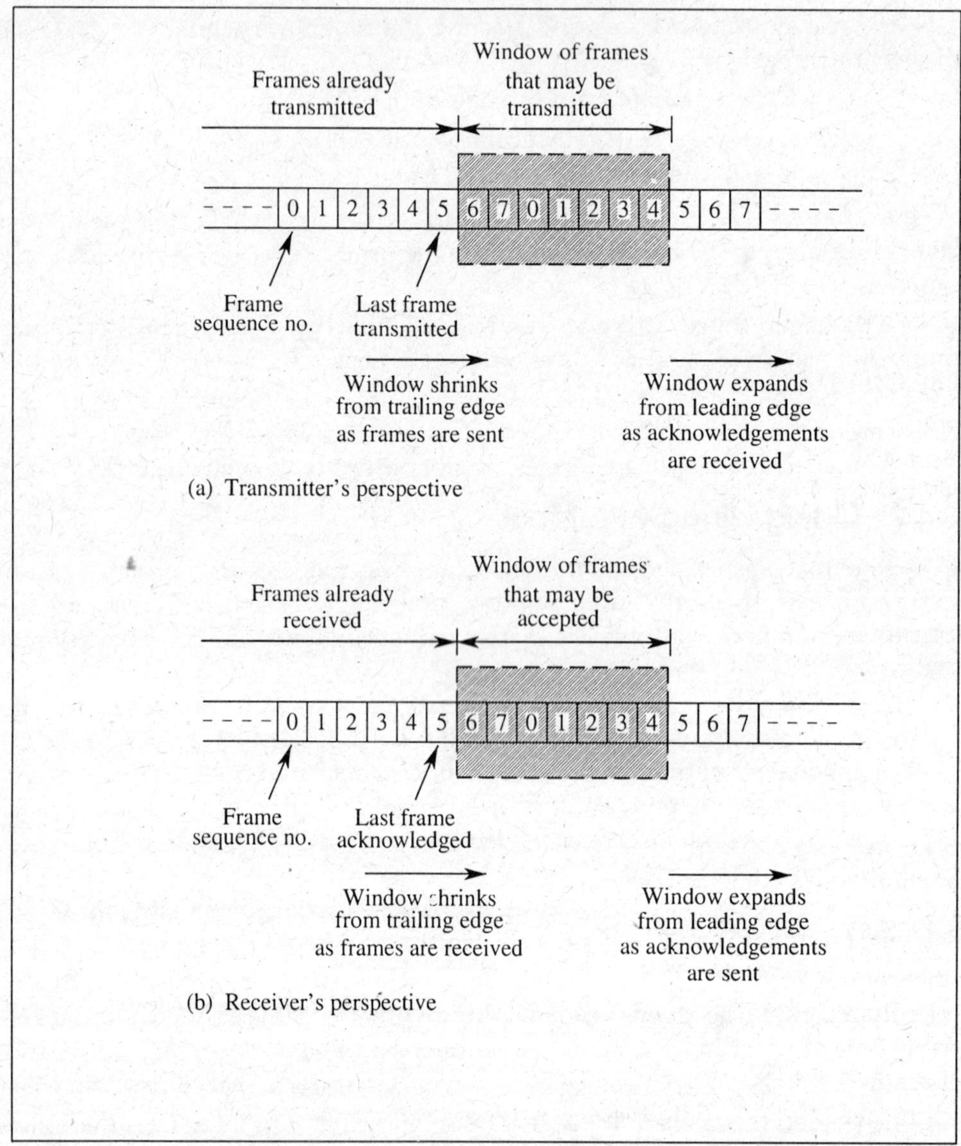

If two stations exchange data simultaneously, each needs to maintain two windows, one for transmit and one for receive, and each side needs to send the data and acknowledgements to the other. To provide efficient support for this requirement, a technique called *piggybacking* is used.

8.4.3 Piggybacking

In this technique each data frame includes a field that holds the sequence number of that frame plus a field that holds the sequence number used for acknowledgment. Three cases are in order:

(a) If a station has data to send and an acknowledgement to send, it sends both together in one frame, thereby saving communication capacity.

(b) If a station has an acknowledgement but no data to send, it sends a separate acknowledgement frame.

(c) If a station has data to send but no new acknowledgement to send, it must repeat the last acknowledgement that it sent because the data frame includes a field for the acknowledgement number and some value must be put into that field. When a station receives a duplicate acknowledgement, it simply ignores it.

☞ Combining data to be sent with control information is called piggybacking. Thus, piggybacking means combining data to be sent and acknowledgment of the frame received in one single frame.

8.4.4 Comparison of Sliding Window with Stop-and-Wait Flow Control

Sliding window flow control is potentially much more efficient than Stop-and-Wait flow control. This is because with sliding window flow control, the transmission link is treated as a pipeline that maybe filled with frames in transit. In contrast, with stop and wait flow control only one frame may be in the pipe at a time.

8.5 ERROR CONTROL

Error control provides error detection and correction. There are two basic strategies for dealing with errors. These are:

(a) To include only enough redundancy to allow the receiver to confirm that an error occurred, but not aware of which error and therefore request it for re-transmission.

(b) Second method is to include enough unwanted data along with each block of data sent to enable the receiver to extract what the transmitted character must have been.

The strategy stated in sub para (a) is error-detection and that in sub para (b) is the error-correction.

8.5.1 Asynchronous Data Error Detection (Parity Bit)

Asynchronous communication means the communication between two units operating independently. In this form of data transmission, information is sent one character at a time, with variable time intervals between characters.

Because asynchronous transmission does not rely on a shared timer that would enable the sending and receiving units to separate characters by specific time periods, each transmitted character consists of a number of data bits (the character itself) preceded by a "begin character" signal, called the start bit and ending in an optional parity bit followed by a stop bit.

Parity has been used for detecting errors in asynchronous data streams where burst-type problems either do not exist or are extremely rare. Both the Telex and Teletype networks employ this method.

☞ Parity bit is an added error-detection bit included with each character of the asynchronous data stream. Thus, it adds an additional bit to be transmitted with each character, reducing the efficiency of the data transfer because it takes more time to transmit a data character with a parity bit than to send one without a parity bit.

To correct errors detected using parity, the receiving station can only request that the message containing the error be re-transmitted. A system that is set to request re-transmission automatically in response to detecting an error includes *Automatic Repeat Request (ARQ)* processing within its communications software.

Not all systems using parity have ARQ. Some systems cause a parity error flag to be set in a status register, which, when read using applicable software, causes a message to be sent to a terminal to inform the user that a data error has occurred. It is then up to the user to request a message to be re-sent or not. The advantage of doing this is that some errors are less crucial. A user can easily figure what the correct character should have been. For example, if the word "today" has an error in the last character, so that the word read as "todaz", it can be readily understood and corrected without the need to re-transmit the message containing the word as it is obvious that the word is "today".

Data Correction Using Parity

An error-correction process used with asynchronous data stream called Longitudinal Redundancy Check (LRC), makes use of the parity process. A method to detect the parity error is to create the LRC character. This character is formed by summing the character bits and discarding the framing. Carries produced by the additions are ignored.

For example, suppose we have sent the word **Help!** For this we use the addition of the bits ignoring the last bit and the carry overs as seen below:

```
0001001  H
1010011  e
0011011  l
0000111  p
1000010  !
----------
0000100  LRC
```

The LRC error character is framed with start and stop bits and a parity bit is generated for it. It is then appended to the end of the message and sent to the receiver as (00000100111). The last two bits are as stop bits. The other bit is for parity.

The receiver shifts each character and checking for parity errors, detects the error in the middle character. The receiver then computes the LRC for the received message and compares the two characters. The bit position that does not compare is the one that is incorrect in the bad character. For example, if the said message is received as follows:

```
0001001  H
1010011  e
0001011  h
0000111  p
1000010  !
----------
0010100  Receiver generated LRC
0000100  received LRC with message
----------
0010000  comparison results because a 1 indicates the bad bit position.
```

The detection of a bad parity bit in the "*l*" character designated the location of an error in that character. As a result of the comparison of the LRC, bit 3 of that character is detected as incorrect and would be inverted to yield the corrected character.

Another method to show the detection of the bad bit is by using a matrix as shown in Figure 8.13. This is the matrix for the example word Help!. The character codes are arranged so that they are stacked vertically. Each individual parity bit is shown to the right of each character. These are not used as these are the redundancy bits. Longitudinal redundancy bits are shown at the bottom of the matrix. Note that the longitudinal parity bits form the LCR character, which includes its own parity (VCR) bit. In part (b) of this Figure, the matrix is shown with the error. The comparison of the LCR bits from the transmitter and receiver is accomplished by adding the LRC character received to the entire message (including transmitted LRC). This works because adding binary numbers and comparing them is the same process of using exclusive ORs. Note that the circled parity (VRC) and LRC bits point to the bad bit.

These methods of error-correction are known as Forward Error Correction (FEC) because errors are corrected as the message is received.

☞ A burst type of interference destroying several bits and cannot be corrected by any of these methods.

8.5.2 Error Detection for Synchronous Transmission

Synchronous transmission is the data transfer in which information is transmitted in blocks (frames) of bits separated by equal time intervals. Synchronous data does not contain start and stop framing bits and parity bits are omitted from the data stream. Most errors in high-speed transmissions occur in bursts. This means that some external interference or other effect on the line causes several bits to be corrupted at once. Single-bit errors occur less frequently. Hence, the error-detection methods have evolved to detect single or multiple errors within a data stream.

Cyclic Redundancy Check (CRC) or Block Check Characters

CRC is a procedure used in checking for errors in data transmission. CRC error checking uses a complex calculation to generate a number based on the data transmitted. The sending device performs the calculation before transmission and sends its result to the receiving device. The receiving device repeats the same calculation after transmission. If both devices obtain the same result, it is assumed that the transmission was error free. The procedure is known as a redundancy check because each transmission includes not only data but extra (redundant) error-checking values. Communication protocol such as XMODEM uses cyclic redundancy checking.

Cyclic Redundancy Check (CRC), developed by IBM is one of the most common and widely used error-detection methods for synchronous data transmission . IBM uses CRC-16 as the specific application of the CRC method. This process uses a constant "divisor" which is in binary form as:

1000 1000 0001 0000 1

The steps are as follows:

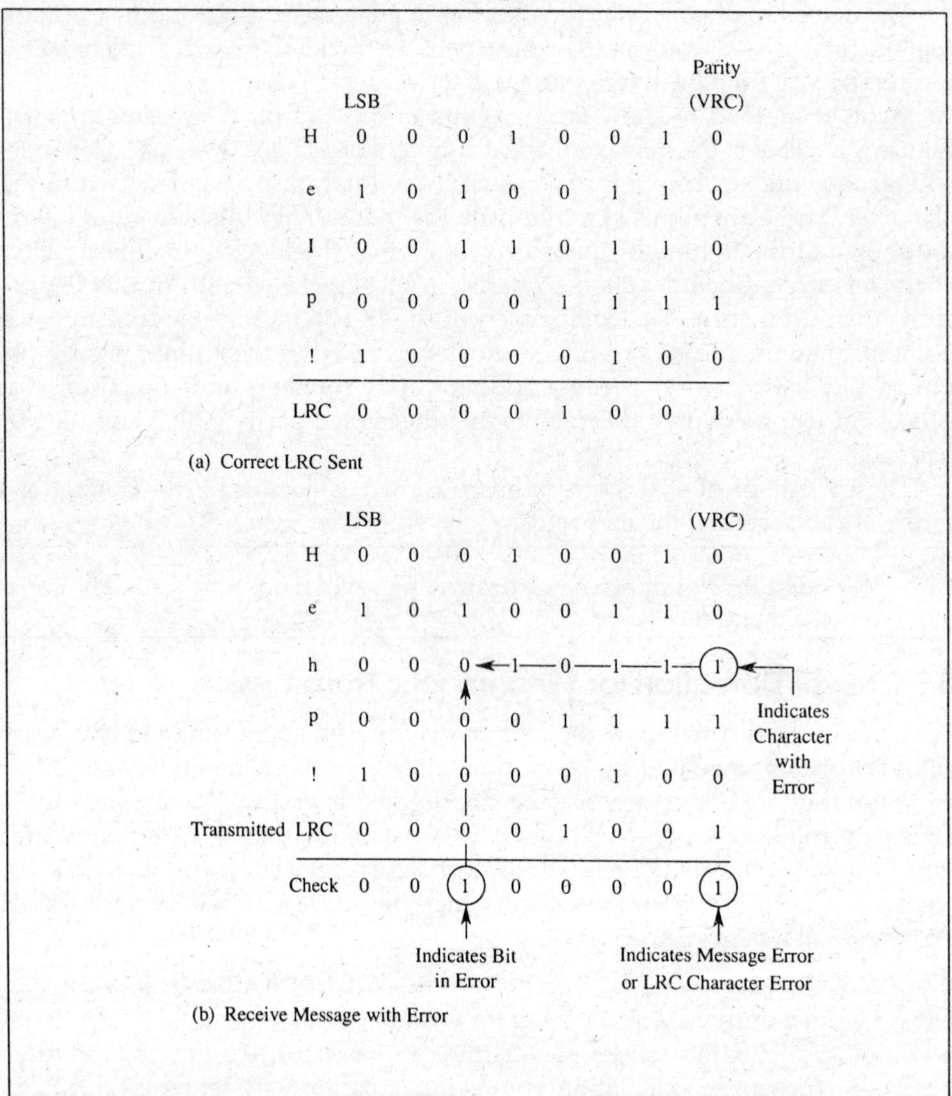

Figure 8.13 LRC Matrix Part (a) shows the correct LRC sent and part (b) shows received message with error

(a) Add 16 zeros (1 bit less than the number of bits in the "divisor") after the Least Significant Bit of the message to be sent. The message is then written down as it would be transmitted, with the extra bits sent first (i.e. most significant bits).

(b) The divisor is exclusive ORed with the 16 most significant bits of the message. Enough bits from the message are appended to the result of this to form another 16 bits of data headed by a 1.

(c) The exclusive ORing is repeated along with the rest of the process until all bits in the message are exhausted.

(d) The final exclusive OR result in the CRC characters. Enough leading zeros are appended to the CRC character to form a total of 16 bits.

We shall understand the CRC character calculation using the following CRC-4 method with the modified divisor constant of 10011:

Let the message be 1100 0110 1011 01 (The LSB is on the right)

There is one zero less than the total number of bits in the divisor which is 10011. To use the shortened CRC-4 divisor, four zeros are first appended to the message. The extended message becomes

110001101011010000

Now we set up the problem:

10011)110001101011010000

Exclusive OR the first five bits with the "divisor" we have:

```
10011)110001101011010000
      10011
      ----------
       1011
```

By bringing down the next bit from the message and repeat the process until all the bits in the appended message are used. We do this as follows:

```
10011)110001101011010000
      10011
      ----------
       10111
       10011
       ----------
          10010
          10011
          ----------
              11011
              10011
              --------
                10000
                10011
                ---------
                    11100
                    10011
                    ---------
                     11110
                     10011
                     ----------
                       11010
                       10011
                       -----------
                        1001 = CRC
```

The original message followed by the CRC-16 bits is sent to a receiving station. At the receiving station the data are shifted in and a CRC is computed using the entire message plus the CRC bits. If the same constant "divisor" is used, the result of the receiver's CRC computation is all zeros when there are no errors.

To detect and correct communications errors, a sender must provide a receiver with information that enables the receiver to verify proper receipt of information or data. The sender could simply send an entire set of information twice and let the receiver compare the two sets of information for error detection, but because of the time and computer resources it takes to perform this type of comparison, it is more popular to detect the error based on mathematical calculations, that hardware or software execute at high speed.

The sender must use a mathematical technique to calculate error-checking data. The sender generates this redundant data from the bit stream of information data it sends and then appends the redundant data to the end of the bit stream. The receiver must generate its own redundant data from the information data it receives and compare the results with the redundant data it receives from the sender. A favourable comparison indicates the absence of errors. An unfavourable comparison indicates the presence of errors. Figure 8.14 illustrates this process.

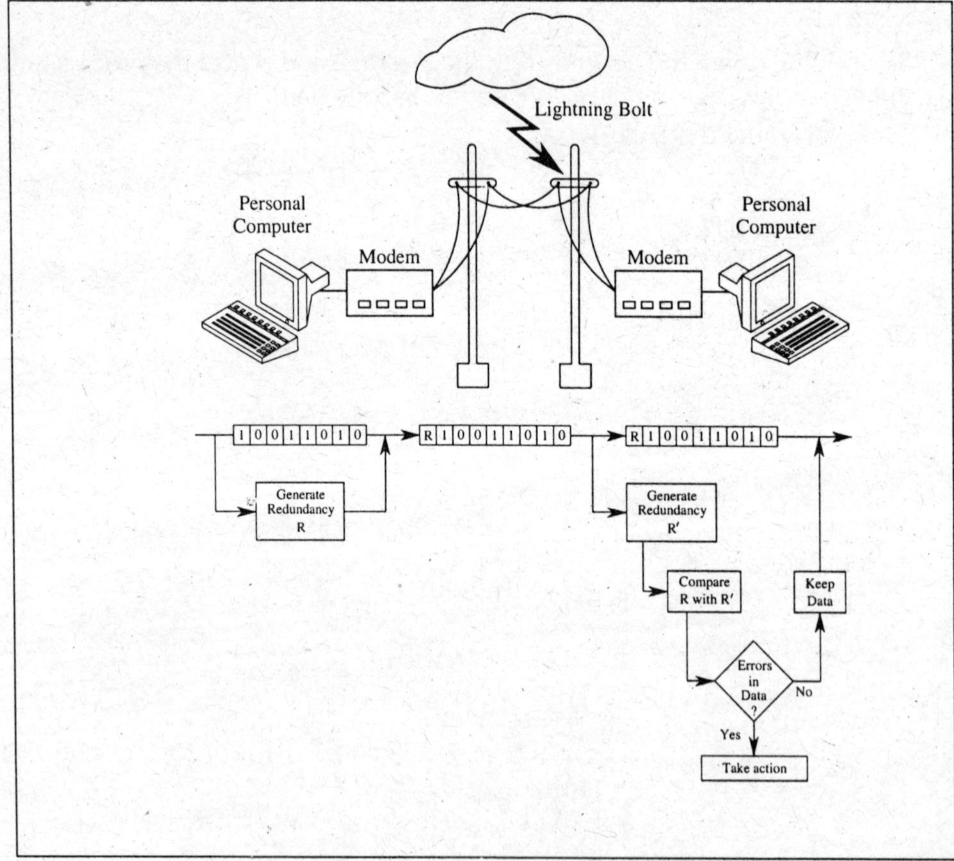

Figure 8.14 Creating and checking redundancy error detection data

Asynchronous communications can use any one of the methods whereas the synchronous communications always use the continuous error-detection method. Asynchronous communications can execute error detection at the data byte level by examining the bit pattern in each byte of data or at the data packet level by examining the bit pattern of groups of bytes. Synchronous communications execute error detection at the packet level only.

Example 8.1

Figure 8.15 shows the message frame 1101011011 for which the divisor is 10011. Calculate the CRC.

The frame after adding 4 zero bits becomes 11010110000. After the successive division, the remainder is 1110. Hence the CRC is 1110 and the transmitted frame is 11010110111110.

Figure 8.15 Solution to Example 8.1 for calculation of CRC

Frame : 1 1 0 1 0 1 1 0 1 1

Generator : 1 0 0 1 1

Message after appending 4 zero bits : 1 1 0 1 0 1 1 0 0 0 0

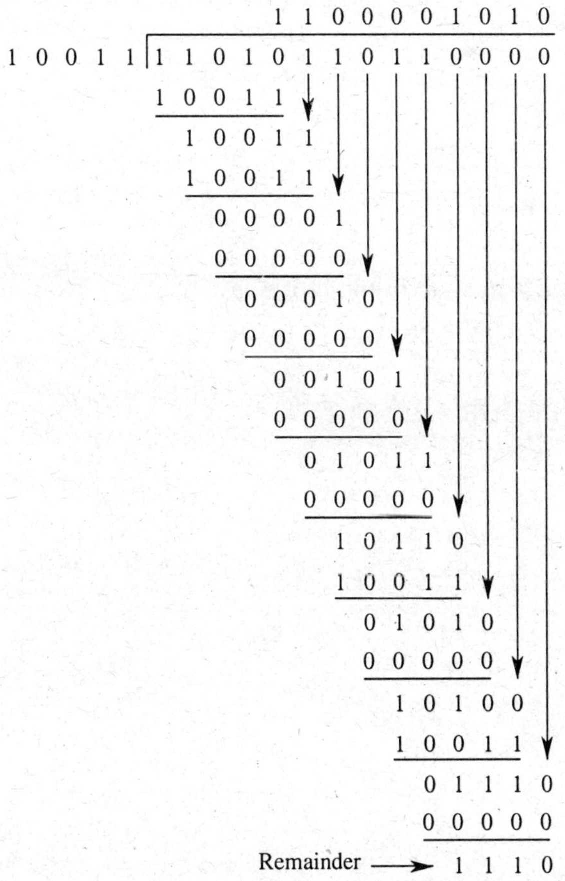

```
                1 1 0 0 0 0 1 0 1 0
          ______________________________
1 0 0 1 1 | 1 1 0 1 0 1 1 0 1 1 0 0 0 0
            1 0 0 1 1
              1 0 0 1 1
              1 0 0 1 1
                0 0 0 0 1
                0 0 0 0 0
                  0 0 0 1 0
                  0 0 0 0 0
                    0 0 1 0 1
                    0 0 0 0 0
                      0 1 0 1 1
                      0 0 0 0 0
                        1 0 1 1 0
                        1 0 0 1 1
                          0 1 0 1 0
                          0 0 0 0 0
                            1 0 1 0 0
                            1 0 0 1 1
                              0 1 1 1 0
                              0 0 0 0 0
            Remainder ------>   1 1 1 0
```

Transmitted frame : 1 1 0 1 0 1 1 0 1 1 1 1 1 0

☞ The CRC or the check character is calculated by dividing the entire numeric binary value of the block of data by a constant, called a generator polynomial. The quotient is discarded, and the remainder is appended to the block and transmitted along with the data.

Representing Divisor and Message in Polynomial Form

The divisor P expressed with the dummy variable x is $P(x)$.
When P = 11001, it is expressed with dummy variable x as

$P(x) = x^4 + x^3 + 1.$

and if $P(x) = x^5 + x^4 + x^2 + 1$ then P = 110101
Similarly, when message M is expressed with dummy variable x i.e. $M(x)$ and if:
$M(x) = x^5 + x^4 + x + 1$ then M = 110011 and if
$M(x) = x^9 + x^7 + x^3 + x^2 + 1$ then M = 1010001101

Example 8.2

Calculate the BCC (Block check character) for the message 1101011011, using generator polynomial $x^4 + x^2 + 1$. What will be the transmitted message?

Solution

The divisor in the polynomial form is $x^4 + x^2 + 1$ which means that the divisor is 10101.

So we set up the problem as follows:

```
10101)11010110110000
      10101
      ----------
       11111
       10101
       ----------
         10101
         10101
         ----------
           11000
           10101
           --------
            11010
            10101
            ---------
              1111 = CRC
```

The transmitted message = 11010110111111

☞ A sender and receiver must use identical techniques of generating redundant information. The parity error correction techniques are good for detecting single-bit errors in a single byte of data. The LRC is good for detecting single-bit and multiple-bit errors in individual bytes of data. The CRC-16 detects all single-and double-bit errors, all errors in bit streams with an odd number of bits in error, all error bursts shorter than 16 bits, and 99.9% of error bursts longer than 16 bits. The CRC-32 detects essentially all errors, which is the primary reason for IEEE selecting this technique for all LAN standards.

8.5.3 Checksum Error Detection

Checksum is a calculated value that is used to test data integrity. Errors can occur when data is transmitted or when it is written to disk. One means of detecting such errors is use of a checksum. Checksum is a value calculated for a given chunk of data by sequentially combining all the bytes of data with a series of arithmetic or logical operations. After the data is transmitted or stored, a new checksum can be calculated (using the possibly faulty transmitted or stored data) and compared with the original one. If the checksums do not match, an error occurred, and the data should be transmitted or stored again. If they do match, the transmission or storage was probably error-free. Checksums are simple validation mechanism. They cannot detect all errors and they cannot be used to correct errors.

The parity and LRC methods are not very reliable, when more than one error occurs within a character or message. One major advantage of the CRC method is its ability to detect multiple errors within any length of message.

Another major advantage of checksum is that it is simple to implement. In this method, each character being transmitted is exclusive ORed with an accumulated total of all previous characters. The final accumulated total is the checksum character sent with the message. Once again, at the receiver exclusive ORing all the characters and the transmitted checksum should produce a result of zero. Any other result indicates that an error has occurred.

In comparison with CRC, checksum is more likely to experience similar values for different messages. While the odds that enough errors would cause a duplicate checksum to the one originally sent are reasonably high, that possibility is still far more likely than a similar occurrence using the CRC method.

8.5.4 Hamming Coding Technique for Error Correction

Hamming is a code used to detect and correct errors in individual bits of transmitted data. Most land-based communications are satisfied by relying on checksum or CRC methods to detect errors. CRC correction requires re-transmission of faulty messages. But let us take the case of a satellite transmitting visual data as binary streams of information around another planet say Jupiter. The time it takes those messages to arrive at an Earth station from the satellite is measured in hours. During this time the satellite has adjusted its orbit and is going across new territory and sending additional data. Correcting errors in these messages cannot be done by re-transmission. A request for that re-transmission takes as long to get to the satellite as the original message took to get to Earth. Then consider the time it would take to resent the message. First satellite would have to be found. During the time it took to send the original message and get the request to resent it, the satellite has gathered billions of additional data. The memory needed to hold data long enough to assure that were sent properly is staggering. Instead, an error-correction method such as the *Hamming code* is used so that errors can be corrected as they are detected.

Hamming codes provide a method for error correction. Error bits called Hamming bits, are inserted into the message at random locations. It is believed that the randomness of their locations reduces the odds that these Hamming bits themselves would be in error. This is based on a mathematical assumption that because there are so many more message bits compared with Hamming bits, there is a greater chance for a message bit to be in error than for a Hamming bit to be wrong. Determining the placement and binary value of the Hamming bits can be implemented using hardware, but it is often more practical to implement them using software. The number of bits in a message (M) are counted and used to solve the following equation to determine the number of Hamming bits (H) to be used:

$$2^{H} \geq H + M + 1$$

Once the number of Hamming bits is determined, the actual placement of bits into the message is performed. It is important to note that despite the random nature of the Hamming bit placements, the exact placements must be known and used by both the transmitter and receiver. This is necessary so that the receiver can remove the Hamming bits from the message and compare them with a similar set of bits generated at the receiver. Once the Hamming bits are inserted into their positions, the numerical values of the bit positions of the logic 1 bits in the original message are listed. The equivalent binary numbers of these values are added and the sum produced is used as the sets of the Hamming bits in the message. The numerical difference between the Hamming values transmitted and that produced at the receiver indicates the bit position that contains a bad bit which is then inverted to correct it.

We shall see the following example for sending the message Help!

When sending the message Help! using synchronous data, start and stop bits as well as parity are not used. Each ASCII character contains 7 bits, for a total of 35 bits.. The number of Hamming bits is computed using equation

$$2^{H} \geq H + M + 1$$

H = 6 is the smallest value that satisfies the equation:

$$64 > 35 + 6 + 1 > 42$$

For simplicity we will insert the Hamming bits, less randomly, at every other bit position, starting with the least significant bit:

H e I P !

1001000110010111011001110000001H0H0H0H0H1H

To begin the process of determining the states of each of the Hamming bits, list the numerical value of each bit position whose state is a 1. Start with the least significant bit as 1 and increase the count by 1 for each succeeding bit position. H bits must be included in the counting (but not the listing) process. In our example, the first bit position with a 1 in it is position 2. The following are all the bit positions containing a 1 that is the positions 2, 12, 18, 19, 20, 23, 24, 26, 27, 28, 30, 33, 34, 38, and 41.

2	0	0	0	0	1	0
12	0	0	1	1	0	0
18	0	1	0	0	1	0
19	0	1	0	0	1	1
20	0	1	0	1	0	0
23	0	1	0	1	1	1
24	0	1	1	0	0	0
26	0	1	1	0	1	0
27	0	1	1	0	1	1
28	0	1	1	1	0	0
30	0	1	1	1	1	0
33	1	0	0	0	0	1
34	1	0	0	0	1	0
38	1	0	0	1	1	0
41	1	0	1	0	0	1
H =	0	1	1	0	1	1

The next step is to list the numbers vertically along with the binary equivalent of each one. The value of the Hamming bits (H) is created by adding each binary bit column in the list, ignoring any carry condition.

These H values are substituted for the "H" bits in the message in the order shown. The receiver repeats the process, again ignoring the Hamming bit positions in the list. If everything is all right, a comparison of the H values sent and those generated by the receiver produces zero. When the receiver does the Hamming process, number 23 is omitted from the list. This causes the Hamming bits to have a value of 0 0 1 1 0 0 instead of 0 1 1 0 1 1. When the H bits computed at the receiver are compared with the transmitted H bits the result is as follows:

H sent:	0	1	1	0	1	1	as shown above
H computed at receiver:	0	0	1	1	0	0	*
comparison results:	0	1	0	1	1	1	= 23 decimal

* because 23rd 1 will be changed to zero so the sum!

To correct the message the receiver would invert bit 23.

The reason why the Hamming code works is as follows:

The originally transmitted codes are formulated by adding binary bits together, ignoring carries. The process of this addition is nothing more than exclusive ORing these bits together. A similar process occurs at the receiver. If a bit has changed state between being sent and received, it either will not be included in the process or, in the case of changing from a 0 to a 1, will be added to the process. By exclusive ORing the two Hamming codes, the process is reversed. The errant bit appears as the difference between the transmitted and received Hamming bit values.

8.6 SYNCHRONOUS AND ASYNCHRONOUS PROTOCOLS

Data link protocols can also be divided into two subgroups. These are:

(a) Asynchronous Protocol
(b) Synchronous Protocol

8.6.1 Asynchronous Protocol

The asynchronous protocol treats each character in a bit stream independently. Today, these protocols are employed mainly in modems. A variety of asynchronous protocols developed are:

(a) XMODEM
(b) YMODEM
(c) ZMODEM
(d) BLAST (Blocked asynchronous transmission)

XMODEM Protocol

XMODEM protocol has an error checking technique that can be used between microcomputers. It requires that one terminal or computer be set up as the sender and other be set up as the receiver. After the protocol is started, the transmitter waits for the receiver to send a Negative Acknowledge (NAK) character. The receiver meanwhile is set to send NAKs every 10 seconds. When the transmitter detects the first NAK, it begins sending messages as blocks of 128 data characters, surrounded by some protocol control characters. The beginning of each block is signaled by a Start Of Header (SOH) character. This is followed by a block number character in ASCII, followed by the same block number with each bit inverted. The bit inversion, known as the 1's complement, results in the block number being followed by the same block number with each bit inverted. A 128-character piece of the file is sent, followed by a checksum that is the remainder of the sum of all the 128 bytes in the message divided by 255. Mathematically, the XMODEM checksum can be represented as:

$$\text{CHECKSUM} = R\left[\frac{\sum_{1}^{128} \text{ASCII Value of Character}}{255}\right]$$

in which R is the remainder of the division process.

Start of Header	Block Number	1's Complement of Block Number	128 Data Characters	Checksum

The receiver checks each part of the received block:

(a) Was the first character an Start Of Header (SOH) ?
(b) Was the block number exactly one more than the previous block received?
(c) Were exactly 128 characters of data received?
(d) Was the locally computed checksum identical to the last character received in the block?

If the receiver is satisfied, it sends an Acknowledge (ACK) back to the transmitter, and the transmitter sends the next blocks. If not, a NAK is sent, and the transmitter resents the block found in error. This process is continued, block by block, until the entire file is sent and verified. At the end of the data, the transmitter sends an End Of Text character. The receiver replies with an ACK, and the session is terminated.

Limitations of XMODEM Protocol

There are several points to be made about the XMODEM protocol.

(a) It is easy to implement with a small computer, but it does require a computer at each end.

(b) It requires manual setup for each file to be transferred.

(c) The error detection technique (ordinary sum of the data characters) is unsophisticated and unable to detect reliably the most common type of transmission error, which is a noise burst that can last on the order of 10 milliseconds (the duration of about 12 bits at 1200 bps).

(d) It is a half-duplex protocol; that is, information is sent, and then the sender waits for a reply before sending the next message.

Because operation of the XMODEM protocol generally assumes a full duplex line, it is inefficient in use of the transmission facility.

Support for XMODEM Protocol

In spite of the previously mentioned limitations, the XMODEM protocol and several derivatives are supported by most asynchronous communication programs designed for operation on PCs. The rationale for the widespread support of those protocols is related to the initial placement of the XMODEM protocol into the public domain.

Most of the asynchronous communications programs developed during the early 1980s eventually included XMODEM support. In the late 1980s, several derivatives of the XMODEM protocol gained acceptance due to the increased level of functionality they provided. Some new versions of the XMODEM protocol added CRC error checking. Other versions provided a full-duplex transmission capability with CRC error detection, thus increasing the efficiency of the protocol. Today, almost all communication programs designed for use on PCs support XMODEM and several of its derivatives.

YMODEM Protocol

YMODEM Protocol is a protocol similar to XMODEM, with the following differences.

(a) The data unit is 1024 bytes.

(b) Multiple files can be sent simultaneously.

(c) ITU-T CRC-16 is used for error checking.

ZMODEM Protocol

ZMODEM is a newer protocol combining features of both XMODEM and YMODEM.

BLAST (Blocked asynchronous transmission)

BLAST (Blocked asynchronous transmission) is more powerful than XMODEM. It is full-duplex with sliding window flow control. It allows the transfer of data and binary files.

8.6.2 Synchronous Protocol

Synchronous protocols take the whole bit stream and chop it into characters of equal size. Protocols governing synchronous transmission can be divided into two classes.

(a) Character oriented protocol

(b) Bit oriented protocols

Character Oriented Protocol

Character oriented protocols also called byte-oriented protocols interpret a transmission frame or packet as a succession of characters, each composed of one byte (eight bits). All control information is in the form of an existing character encoding system such as ASCII coding method.

Character oriented protocols are not as efficient as bit-oriented protocols and therefore are now seldom used.

Bit Oriented Protocols

Bit oriented protocols can pack more information into shorter frames and avoid the transparency problems of character-oriented protocols. SDLC and HDLC are the two bit oriented protocols. SDLC was developed by IBM. HDLC is one of the ISO designed and has become the basis for all bit-oriented protocols in use.

Synchronous Data Link Control (SDLC)

SDLC is a data-link layer protocol developed in the 1970s by IBM for its Systems Network Architecture (SNA) networking environment. It is primarily used in wide area networks (WANs) that use leased lines to connect Mainframe SNA hosts and remote terminals.

In a serial SDLC link, data is sent as a synchronous bit stream divided into frames that contain addressing and control information in addition to the payload of data.

SDLC uses a master/slave architecture in which one station is designated as primary (master) and the remaining stations are secondary (slaves). The primary station establishes and tears down SDLC connections, manages these connections, and polls each secondary station in a specific order to determine whether any secondary station wants to transmit data.

SDLC can be used in a variety of connection topologies, including direct point-to-point connections between a primary and a secondary station and multipoint connections between a primary and a group of secondary stations. Ring topologies are also possible in which a primary controls a ring of secondary stations and is itself part of the ring.

High Level Data Link Control Procedures (HDLC)

This is a protocol to prevent aliasing error. It determines where a true message block begins and ends and what part of the message is to be included in the CRC.

Because the data being transmitted is examined bit by bit to screen out possible errors, this protocol is referred to as bit-oriented protocol or BOP. It uses bit stuffing for data transparency.

In HDLC, all information is carried by frames that can be of the following types:

(a) Information Frames (I-frames)

(b) Supervisory control sequences (S-frames), or unnumbered command/responses (U-frames).

Figure 8.16 (a) shows one information frame as a rectangular block divided into six fields. These fields are:

1. A beginning Flag(F1) field.

2. An address (A) field. It is used to identify one of the terminals. It is of 8 bits.
3. A control (C) field. It is used for sequence numbers, acknowledgements. It is of 8 bits.
4. An information field (I) field or data fields contains information.
5. A frame check sequence (FCS) field. It is similar to CRC.
6. A final flag (F2) field.

S-frames and U-frames have the same fields except that the I field is left out.

Figure 8.16(a)
HDLC format

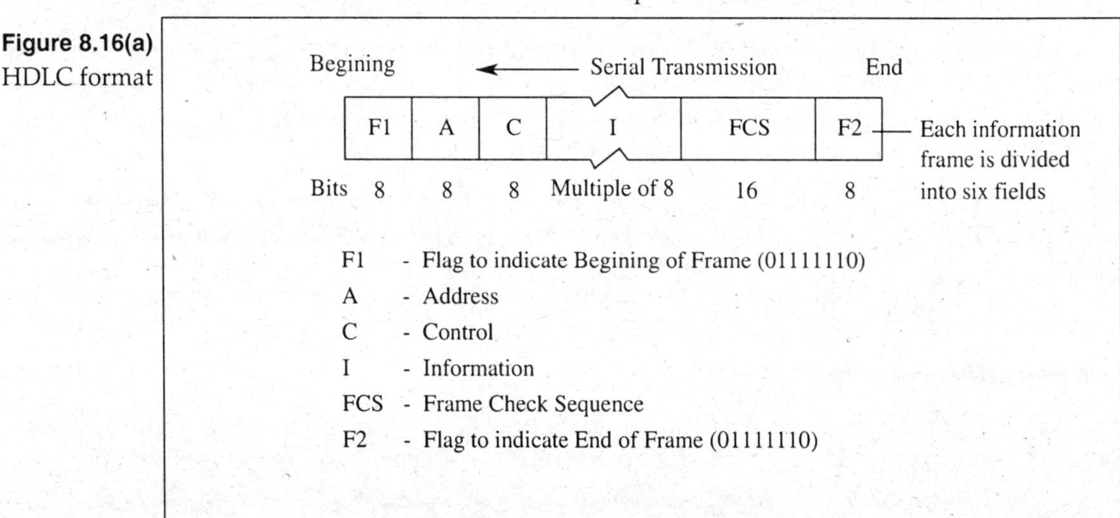

There are three kinds of controls.. Control field for Information (I-Frame), Control field for Supervisory (S-Frame) and control field for Unnumbered (U-frame). The contents are shown in Figure 8.17 (b)

Figure 8.17
(a) control field of an information frame
(b) a supervisory frame
(c) an unnum bered frame

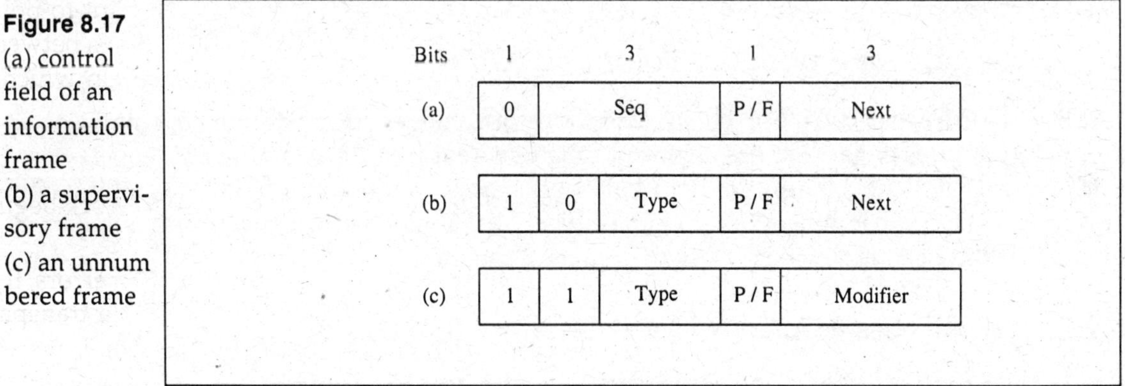

The P/F bits stand for Poll/Final. It is used when a computer is polling a group of terminals. When used as P, the computer is inviting the terminal to send data. All the frames sent by the terminal, except the final one, have the P/F bit set to P. The final one is set to F.

I-frames (Information frame)

It perform information transfer and independently carry message acknowledgments, and Poll of final bits.

S-frames (Supervisory frames)

They perform link supervisory control such as message acknowledgments, retransmit requests, and requests for temporary holds on I-frame transmissions. The various kinds of Supervisory frames are distinguished by the *Type* field. Type acknowledgement frame (called receive ready) is used to indicate the next frame expected. This frame is used when there is no reverse traffic to use for piggybacking.

Type 2 is Receive Not Ready. It acknowledges all frames up to but not including Next, just as Receive Ready. But it tells the sender to stop sending. Receive Not ready is intended to signal certain temporary problems with the receiver, such as a shortage of buffers, and not as an alternative to the sliding window flow control.

Type 3 is the Selective Reject. It calls for retransmission of only the frames specified. In this sense it is most useful when the sender's window size is half the sequence space size or less. Thus, if a receiver wishes to buffer out of sequence frames for potential future use, it can force the retransmission of any specific frame using Selective Reject.

U-frames (Unnumbered frames)

It provides a flexible format for additional link control data by omitting the frame sequence numbers and thus providing a place for an additional command and response functions.

8.7 LINK ACCESS PROCEDURES

Several protocols under the general category link access procedure (LAP) have been developed. Each of these is a subset of HDLC designed for a specific purpose. LAPB, LAPD and LAPM are the three most important of all these.

8.7.1 Link Access Procedure Balanced (LAPB)

LAPB is a simplified subset of HDLC used only for connecting a station to a network. It therefore provides only those basic control functions required for communication between a DTE and a DCE. LAPB is used only in balanced configurations of two devices, where both devices are of the combined type. Communications is always in asynchronous balanced mode. LAPB is used today in ISDN networks on B channels.

8.7.2 Link Access Procedure for D Channel (LAPD)

LAPD is another simplified subset of HDLC used in ISDN. It is used for control signaling. It uses asynchronous balanced mode.

8.7.3 Link Access Procedure for Modems (LAPM)

LAPM is a simplified subset of HDLC for modems. It is used to dc asynchronous -synchronous conversion, error detection and retransmission. It has been developed to apply HDLC features to modems.

REVIEW QUESTIONS WITH ANSWERS

Question Number 1. Mention the services provided by physical layer and network layer to the datalink layer.

Answer *[Refer to Sections 8.1.1 and 8.1.2]*

Question Number 2. Explain the Poll/Select method.

Answer *[Refer to Section 8.2.2]*

Question Number 3. Discuss the sliding window protocol with an example.

Answer *[Refer to Section 8.4.2]*

Question Number 4. What are the different methods by which the data link layer detects error in the transmitted data?

Answer *[Refer to Section 8.5]*

Question Number 5. Mention the different flow control protocols in the data link layer.

Answer *[Refer to Section 8.4]*

TEST PAPER

Time: 2 Hrs. Marks: 100

Note: Answer all questions.

1. Define the term protocol in terms of data communications.
2. Explain the major functions performed by the data link layer of an OSI reference model.
3. Explain the four methods of designing frames.
4. What do you mean by Poll/Select method and ENQ/ACK method.
5. Compare the hardware flow control and software flow control.

CHAPTER 9

LANS AND MANS

9.1 LOCAL AREA NETWORK (LAN)

Local area network (LAN) is a group of computers located in the same room, on the same floor, or in the same building that are connected to form a single network. Local area networks (LANs) allow users to share storage devices, printers, applications, data, and other network resources. They are limited to a specific geographical area, usually less than 2 kilometers in diameter.

Figure 9.1 illustrates the basic physical characteristics, information transfer and shared device concepts underlying LAN operation. The line printer and magnetic tape storage are "shared" resources, since any of the four set of users attached to the network can access these devices through PCs acting as the resource manager, or server, as it is commonly called in LAN terminology. In some networks, the users can directly exchange data or files from Mainframe or mini computers.

9.1.1 Advantages of LANs

(a) Local area networks allow sharing of expensive resources such as laser printers and high-capacity, high-speed mass storage devices among a number of users.

(b) Local area networks allow for high-speed exchange of essential information between key people in an organization. If properly managed, this sharing will promote greater efficiency and productivity and will lead to more sophisticated applications such as electronic mail.

(c) Local area networks provide the catalyst to increase the range of potential applications for the IBM PC.

(d) LANs are a productivity tool. A LAN installation should be studied closely in the context of its proposed contribution to the long-range interests of the organization. In the case of a business, a LAN should be a visible contributor to increased profitability.

9.1.2 Disadvantages of LANs

(a) The financial cost of local area networking is still high in comparison with many other alternatives. If one plans to use a network to share a laser printer, the user might find it cheaper to purchase another laser printer than to purchase today's networking hardware and software.

Figure 9.1 Typical LAN system in an organization with different departments namely financial, engineering, sales, operations, and publications each connected with shared storage devices and peripherals such as printers

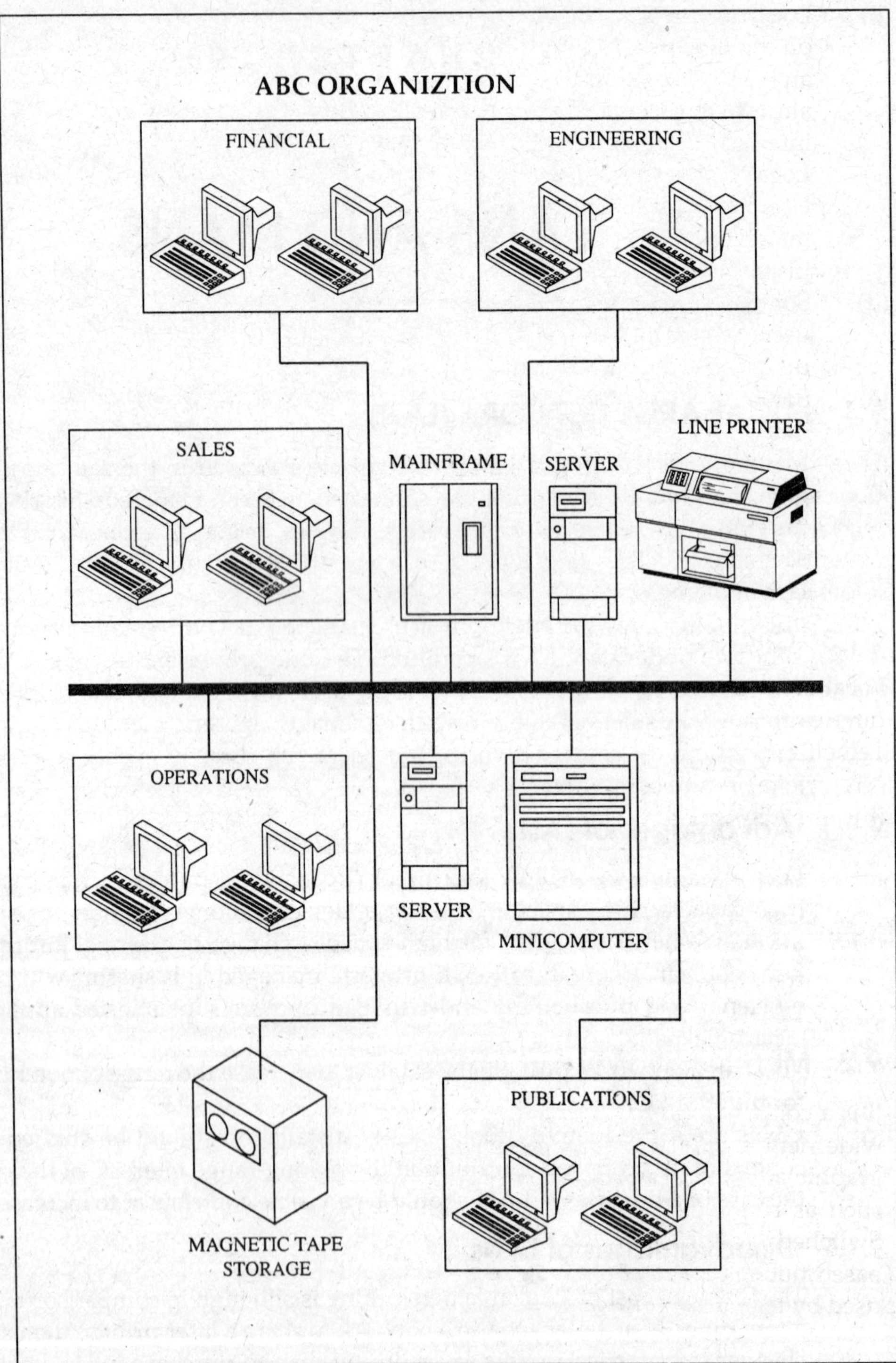

(b) Local area networking software requires memory space in each of the computers used on the network. For an IBM PC/AT computer, with 2 megabyte of main memory, in an IBM Token-Ring Network that has a printer or a disk space shared with other users, almost 20 per cent of the computer's memory will be needed to manage the network interface. This reduces the memory space available for the user's programs.

(c) Local area networking adds another level of complexity to the computer operation. Users may have difficulty in learning the network commands. The installation and management of a LAN requires far more technical and administrative skills than installing and managing several computers that are not networked.

(d) Some control on the part of the user is lost. You may have to share a printer with other users. You may face a situation like, for example, the entire network suddenly locking up because one user has made a mistake.

(e) Some type of security system must be implemented if it is important to protect private data.

(f) Many current application programs will not run in a network environment. The program may require too much memory or have other technical constraints. In other cases the program may run, but the execution leaves too little memory for data. Memory-intensive programs, such as spreadsheets and expert systems, are particularly vulnerable to networking.

9.1.3 Characteristics of LANs

Local area networks are a specialized form of communication systems, however, there are three primary characteristics of LANs that distinguish them from wide area networks such as Telnet, Tymnet, CompuServe and the public-switched telephone network (PSTN). These are:

(a) LANs are designed to work in a restricted geographical area.

(b) LANs operate at relatively high speeds when compared to the typical wide area networks currently in use. LAN data transfer speeds may be as high as 80 million bits per second (80 Mbps), or slightly less than 10 million characters per second (10 Mcps). Compare this to the maximum data transfer speed of 56 Kbps (7000 Cps) for high-grade telephone company digital trunk lines, or the 1200/2500 bps (120/250 Cps) transmission speed used by most personal computer communications systems.

(c) LANs are private networks, not subject to tariffs or other regulatory controls.

9.2 METROPOLITAN AREA NETWORK (MAN)

It is a collection of multiple networks that are connected within the same city to form a city-wide network for a specific government or industry. MAN generally spans a larger geographic area than a LAN. Such networks are being implemented by innovative techniques, such as running fiber cables through subway tunnels. A popular example of a MAN is Switched Multimegabit Data Service (SMDS). SMDS is an emerging high-speed datagram based public data network service developed by Bellcore in USA and expected to be widely used by telephone companies as the base for their data networks.

9.3 IEEE 802

IEEE 802 is an ongoing project of the Institute of Electrical and Electronics Engineers (IEEE) for defining local area network (LAN) and wide area network (WAN) standards and technologies. The 802 specifications define the operation of the physical network components-cabling, network adapters, and connectivity devices such as hubs and switches.

IEEE 802 has a number of subsections, described as follows:

IEEE 802.10

Standard for Interoperable LAN Security, also known as SILS. It was approved in 1992.

IEEE 802.12

This specifies the standard for 100 Mbps demand-priority access method, physical-layer and repeater specifications, also known as 100VG-AnyLAN. It was approved in 1995.

IEEE 802.2

This specifies the logical link control (LLC) layer of the Open Systems Interconnection (OSI) reference model data-link layer.

IEEE 802.3

Standard for LAN-based Carrier Sense Multiple Access with Collision Detection (CSMA/CD) access methods and physical layers, as well as the basis of ISO/IEC 8802-3. This is sometimes referred to as the 'Ethernet standard". It was revised in 1996.

IEEE 802.311

Standard for wireless LAN MAC and physical-layer specifications. Current drafts and focus is on the 2.4 GHz band.

IEEE 802.3b

Standard for broadband media attachment unit and specifications for 10Broad36. It was approved in 1985 and incorporated into ISO/IEC 8802-3.

IEEE 802.3c

Standard for 10 Mbps baseband repeaters. Approved in 1985 and incorporated into ISO/IEC 8802-3.

IEEE 802.3d

Standard for media attachment units and base-band media specifications over fiber-optic repeater links. It was approved in 1987 and incorporated into ISO/IEC 8802-3.

IEEE 802.3e

Standard for physical signaling, media attachment, and baseband media specifications, for a 1Mbit/sec network—that is, 1Base5. It was approved in 1987 and incorporated into ISO/IEC 8802-3.

IEEE 802.3h

Standard for layer management in Carrier Sense Multiple Access with Collision Detection (CSMA/CD) networks. It was approved in 1990 and incorporated into ISO/IEC 8802-3.

IEEE 802.3i

Standard covering two areas: Multisegment 10 Mbps baseband networks and twisted-pair media for 10Base-T networks. It was approved in 1990 and incorporated into ISO/IEC 8802-3. Also conformance statement for the 10Base-T media attachment unit protocol was approved in 1992 and incorporated into ISO/IEC 8802-3.

IEEE 802.3j

Standard for 10 Mbps active and passive star-based segments using fiber optics—that is, 10Base-F. It was approved in 1993 and incorporated into ISO/IEC 8802-3.

IEEE 802.3k

Standard for layer management for 10 Mbps baseband repeaters. Approved in 1992, it was incorporated into ISO/IEC 8802-3.

IEEE 802.3p

Standard for the 10 Mbps base-band media attachment units' layer management. It was approved in 1993 and incorporated into ISO/IEC 8802-3.

IEEE 802.3q

Guidelines for the development of managed objects. It was approved in 1993 and incorporated into ISO/IEC 8802-3.

IEEE 802.3r

The standard for the Carrier Sense Multiple Access with Collision Detection (CSMA/CD) access method and physical layer specifications using 10Base-5. It was updated in 1996.

IEEE 802.3t

Standard for supporting 120-ohm cables in 10Base-t simplex link segments. It was approved in 1995 and incorporated into ISO/IEC 8802-3.

IEEE 802.3u

Supplement to 802.3 covering MAC parameters, the Physical layer, and repeaters for 100 Mbps operation — that is, 100 Base-T, generally known as Fast Ethernet. It was approved in 1995.

IEEE 802.3v

Standard for supporting 150ohm cables in 10Base-T link segments. Approved in 1995 and incorporated into ISO/IEC 8802-3.

IEEE 802.3w

Proposed standard for enhanced MAC algorithms.

IEEE 802.3x

Proposed standard for 802.3 full-duplex operation.

IEEE 802.3y

Proposed physical-layer specification for 100 Mbps operation on two pair of Category 3 or better balanced twisted-pair-cable — that is, 100Base-T2.

IEEE 802.3z

Proposed standard for physical layer, repeater, and management parameters for 1,000 Mbps operation; often referred to as "Gigabit Ethernet".

IEEE 802.4

Standard for token-passing bus access methods and physical-layer specifications. It was approved in 1990.

IEEE 802.5

Standard for Token-Ring access methods and Physical-layer specifications—that is, common Token Ring architecture. It became the basis of ISO/IEC 8802-5. The current version was approved in 1995.

IEEE 802.6

The family of standards for a LAN's Distributed-Queue Dual-Bus (DQDB) subnetwork. It was approved in 1990.

IEEE 802.7:

Broadband technologies.

IEEE 802.8:

Fiber-optic technologies.

IEEE 802.9

Standard for Integrated Services LAN (ISLAN), designed to connect 802.x LANs to publicly and privately administered backbone networks such as FDDI or ISDN. It was approved in 1994 and is the basis of ISO/IEC 8802-9.

IEEE 802.10

Network security standards and technologies

IEEE 802.11

Wireless networking technologies and standards.

IEEE 802.12

Demand priority access technologies

IEEE 802.14

Cable Television access.

9.4 ETHERNET

Ethernet is the most popular network architecture for local area networks (LANs). Ethernet was originally developed by Xerox in the 1970s and was proposed as a standard by Xerox, Digital Equipment Corporation (DEC), and Intel in 1980. A separate standardization process for Ethernet technologies was established in 1985 in the Institute of Electrical and Electronics Engineers (IEEE) 802.3 standard known as Project 802. The IEEE standard was then adopted by the International Organization for Standardization (ISO), making it a worldwide standard for networking. Because of its simplicity and reliability, Ethernet is by far the most popular networking architecture used today. It is available in three different speeds:

(a) 10 Mbps, which is simply called Ethernet
(b) 100 Mbps, which is called Fast Ethernet
(c) 1000 Mbps or 1 Gbps, which is an emerging standard called Gigabit Ethernet

Ethernet specifications define the functions that occur at the physical layer and data-link layer of the Open Systems Interconnection (OSI) reference model, and package data into frames for transmission on the wire. Ethernet is a baseband networking technology that sends its signals serially one bit at a time. It operates in half-duplex mode, in which a station can either transmit or receive, but cannot do both simultaneously.

The Ethernet architecture is based in concept on the Aloha satellite communications network developed at the University of Hawaii. The Aloha system allows multiple distributed devices to communicate with each other over a single radio channel using a satellite as a transponder. One station communicates with another by waiting until the radio channel is idle (determined by carrier sensing) and then sending a packet of data with a destination address, a source address, and redundant check bits to detect transmission errors. All idle stations continuously monitor incoming data and accept those packets with their address and valid checksums. Whenever a station receives a new packet, the receiving station returns an acknowledgment to the source. If an originating station receives no acknowledgment within a specified time interval, it retransmits the packet under the assumption that the previous packet was interfered with by noise or by a transmission from another station at the same time. (The latter situation is referred to as a collision.) Ethernet employs the same basic system concept, originally using coaxial cable for distribution throughout a building or campus.

9.4.1 Physical Layer

The transmission media of Ethernet was originally restricted to the use of conventional "thick" coaxial cable using baseband transmission at 10 Mbps. Other media now used for Ethernet transmission include "thin" coaxial cable and different types of twisted-pair wire. Both types of coaxial cable media support the use of a bus technology, and the use of twisted pair wire requires the use of a star topology for an Ethernet LAN.

☞ Baseband transmission implies that data are transmitted without the use of a carrier and with only one channel defined in the system. In comparison, broadband signaling results in the bandwidth of the media subdivided by frequency into multiple channels that can support the concurrent transmission of different types of signals, such as voice, data, and video.

Figure 9.2 illustrates the operation of baseband and broadband signaling. Under the IEEE 802.3 set of LAN network standards, a broadband Ethernet referred to as 10BASE-36 was standardized.

Figure 9.2
Baseband versus broadband signaling

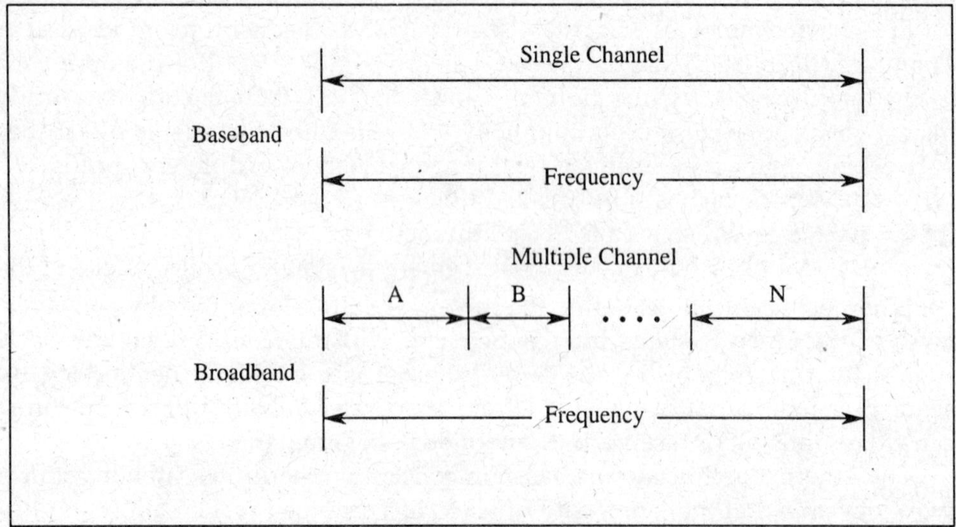

Figure 9.3
Manchester line code.

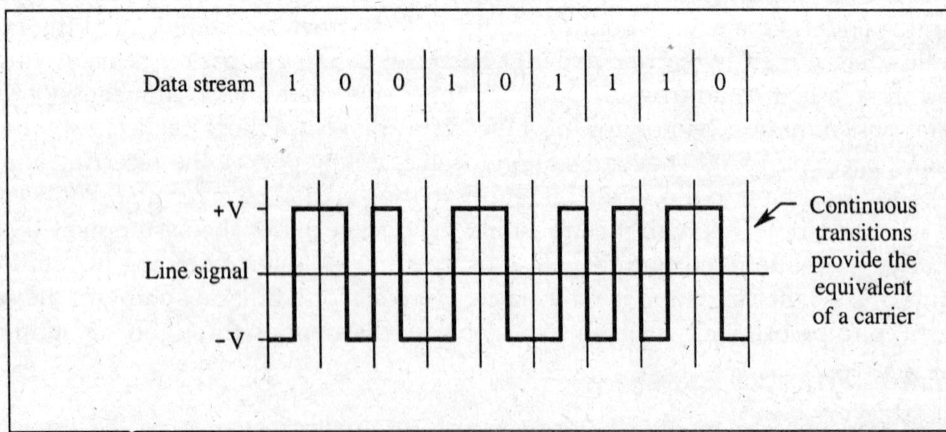

In a 10 Mbps Ethernet environment, when a station is transmitting, it uses the entire capacity of the system. Data are encoded using a Manchester code as shown in Figure 9.3. On 100 Mbps versions of Ethernet, different coding methods are used. The use of a Manchester code provides a strong timing component for clock recover because a timing transition always occurs in the middle of every bit. In this type of coding, each bit period is divided into two complementary halves. A negative-to-positive voltage transition in the middle of the bit period designates a binary 1, whereas a positive-to-negative transition represents a binary 0. The Manchester line code has the additional property of always maintaining equal amounts of positive and negative voltages. This method prevents the build-up of a DC component, which simplifies the implementation of decision thresholds in the data detectors.

Although the data are not transmitted with a carrier, the continuous transitions of the Manchester code provide the equivalent of a carrier, so the channel is easily monitored for activity (for example, by a carrier sense technique). Multiple access to a coaxial cable based network is provided by passive taps, thereby allowing station connections (called drops) to be added or removed without disrupting traffic in the system.

Another requirement of the transmission link and its associated access electronics is that while transmitting, a transceiver must be capable of detecting the existence of another active transmitter. This is referred to as collision detection. Thus, the three basic steps for accessing an Ethernet are denoted as CSMA/CD (Carrier Sense, Multiple Access with Coliision Detection).

☞ A transceiver must be able to detect any other active transmitters on the line while it is transmitting. This is called collision detection.

The capability to detect collisions allows colliding stations to release the channel after using it for only a short period. A conventional Aloha system (one without collision detection), on the other hand, transmits entire messages without knowing whether a collision has occurred. Because an Ethernet station checks for carrier presence before transmitting, collisions occur only if two stations begin transmitting within a time interval equal to the propagation delay between the stations. By restricting the maximum distance between transceivers on a bus-based coaxial cable LAN to 2500 meters, the collision window is limited to 23 microseconds (μs) including amplifier delays.

When a station begins transmitting, it can be sure that no collision will occur if none is detected within a round-trip propagation of 46.4 μs. Because one bit time is 0.1 μs at 10 Mbps, the collision-detection decision is made within 464 bit times. The maximum length of a frame is 12,144 bits; thus the collision-detection feature detects a collision very early in the frame to save significant transmission time that would be wasted if the entire frame were transmitted before detection.

Whenever a collision occurs, all colliding stations detect the condition and wait individually random amounts of time before retrying the transmission. Thus, the stations do not wait for acknowledgement timeouts to trigger a retransmission. (Acknowledgments are unnecessary at this level of the protocol but might be used at a higher level to ensure that the message was received at the final destination). The method of waiting for random amounts of time before transmitting reduces the probability of repeated collisions. In heavy traffic conditions, the average delay before retransmission begins to increase after 10 unsuccessful attempts. After 16 collisions, no further attempts are made to transmit that message, and the station is notified of the error by the transceiver.

☞ In preparation for transmitting a data frame, the physical layer must insert a 64-bit preamble so that all receivers on the network can synchronize with the data stream before the desired data frame begins. The preamble consists of alternating ones and zeros, ending in two ones to signify the start of a frame.

9.4.2 Physical Layer Interface

Standard Ethernet transceiver cable connectors are 15-pin D-shell connectors (MIL-C-24308 or equivalent). The transceiver has a male connector, and the station apparatus has a female connector. Thus, the interconnecting cable must have one connector of each type.

Figure 9.4 illustrates the relationship of the Ethernet hardware components required to connect a workstation to a bus-based coaxial cable. The interface board or adapter card is normally installed in a system expansion slot within the system unit of a personal computer. That board or card is also known as a controller and is often referred to as an Ethernet controller.

Figure 9.4 The relationship of Ethernet hardware components

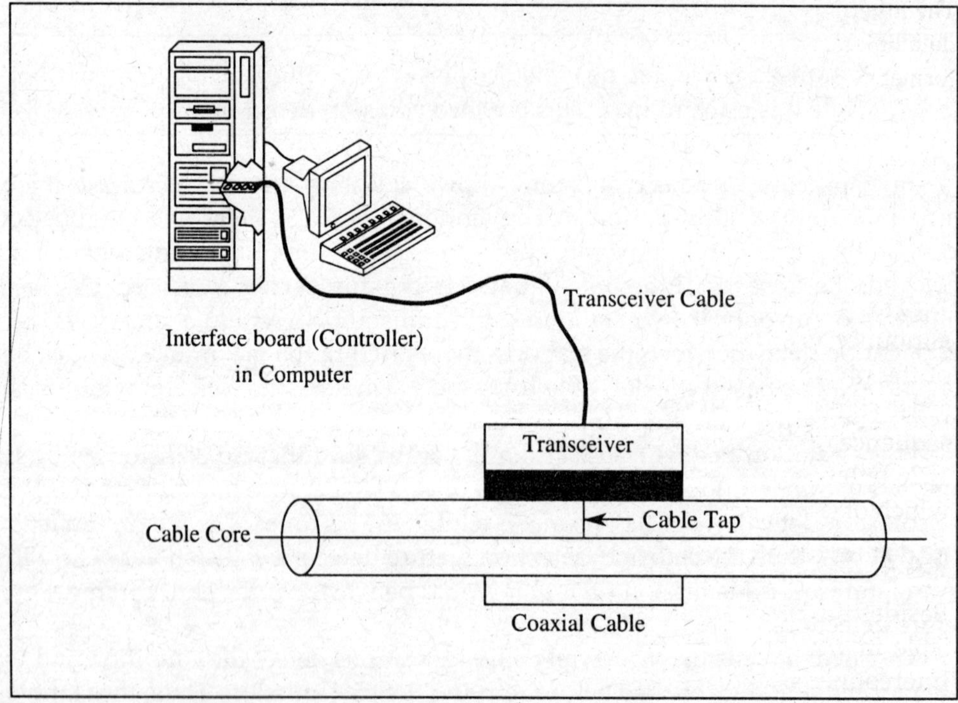

The Ethernet controller formats data from the computer into frames for transmission via the transceiver cable to the transceiver. The transceiver converts unipolar digital signals generated by the computer into Manchester encoded digital signals. In addition, the transceiver is responsible for detecting collisions by examining the voltage level on the cable. That is, when the voltage level rises beyond its normal nominal height, it indicates the occurrence of a collision.

9.4.3 Data Link Layer

The data link layer is primarily concerned with message packaging and link management. It is largely independent of the medium-dependent physical channel.

The message packaging function includes the following items:

(a) **Framing:** Identification of the beginning and end of a message.

(b) **Addressing:** Specified fields for source and destination addresses.

(c) **Error checking:** Redundant codes for detecting channel errors.

☞ The data link is concerned with message frame format, message addressing, and error checking, and as such, it is largely independent of the medium-dependent physical channel.

The format of an Ethernet frame is shown in Figure 9.5.

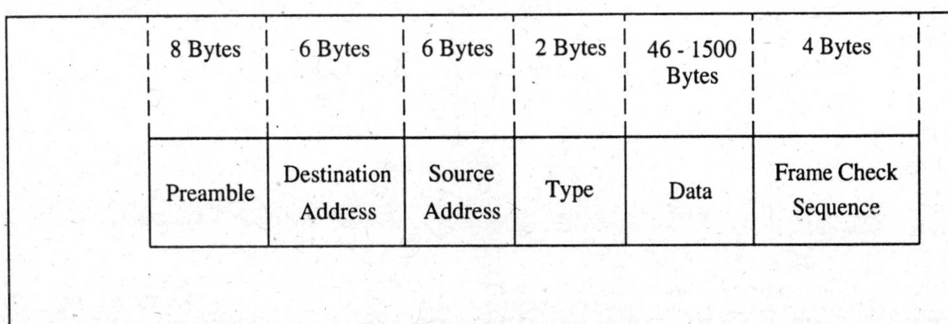

Figure 9.5 The Ethernet data link frame format

The preamble, which consists of the repeating sequence 101010... For 8 bytes or 64 bits, announces the occurrence of the frame. The preamble's generation and removal are functions of the physical layer. Similarly, the end of a frame is provided by the removal of the carrier sense signal detected by the absence of a bit transition following the last bit of the frame check sequence. Notice that frame sizes must be an integral number of bytes, ranging from 72 to 1526 bytes (at 8 bits per byte, that is 576 to 12,208 bits). The Type field is reserved to indicate which of several possible higher-level protocols might be in use.

9.4.4 System Configurations

Besides the single cable system indicated in Figure 9.4, other Ethernet configurations are possible in which several multidrop segments (possibly one in each of several buildings) are interconnected with point-to-point cables and repeaters.

Figure 9.6 shows a typical configuration of a multisegment system. The following specifications apply:

Maximum Lengths:

1500 meters of multidrop cable

1000 additional meters of point-to-point cable between cable segments

300 additional meters in six transceiver cables

50 meters in a single transceiver cable

Maximum Number of Stations: 1024

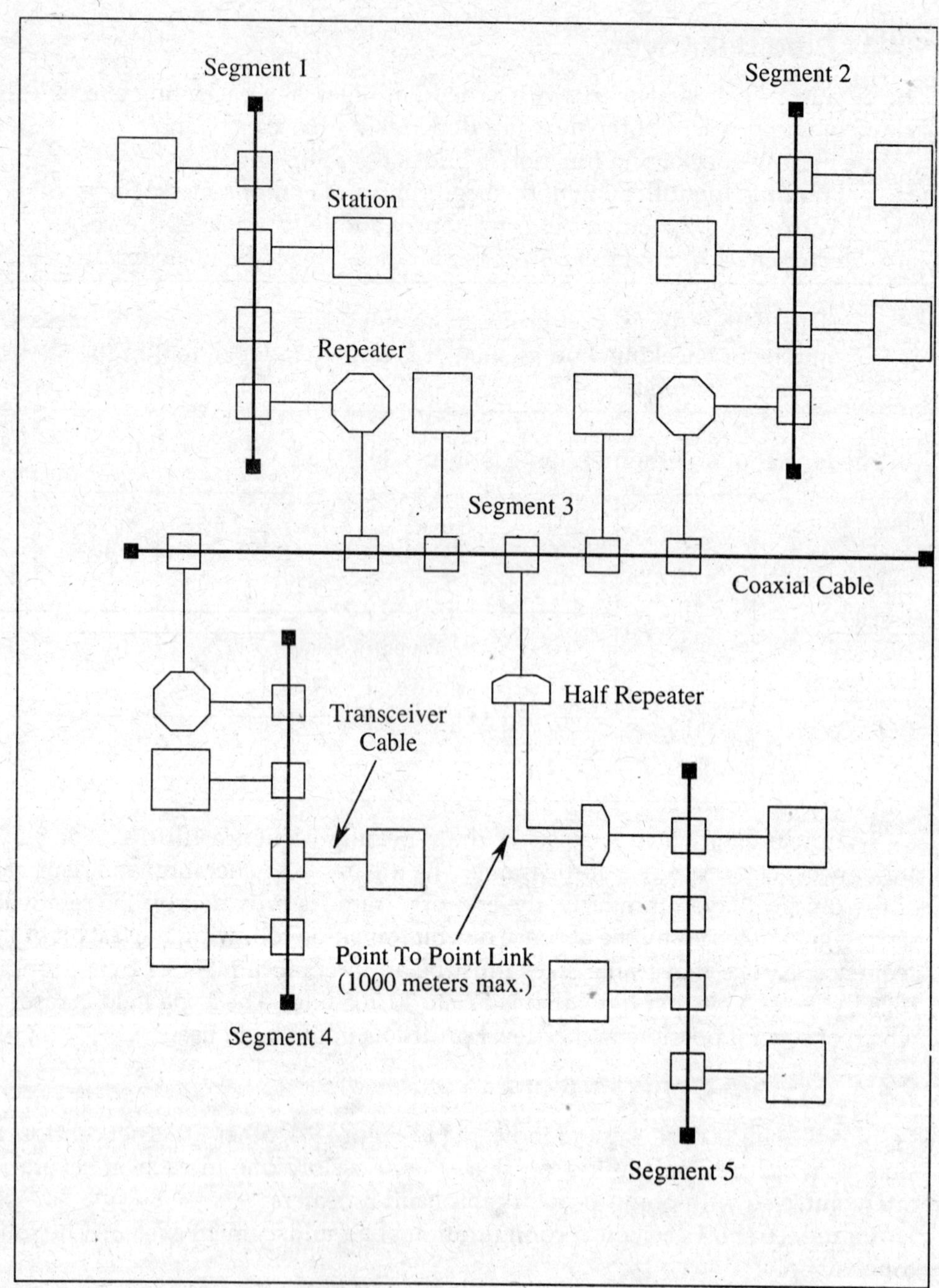

Figure 9.6 A typical large-scale Ethernet configuration

☞ By use of point-to-point cables and repeaters, several multidrop segments can be connected to add flexibility to Ethernet systems.

Other Ethernet Networks

In actuality, when referring to Ethernet, we reference a group of networks based on the CSMA/CD access protocol. The original Ethernet standard defined by Xerox, Digital Equipment, and Intel operated at 10 Mbps over a bus-based thick 50 ohm coaxial cable. When Ethernet was standardized by the IEEE 802.3 committee, five additional "Ethernet" standards were promulgated that provided support for operating rates up to 10 Mbps. Since then, several new high-speed "Ethernet" standards have been promulgated. The IEEE 802.3μ Fast Ethernet standard actually references a series of three 100 Mbps physical layer LAN specifications that use the CSMA/CD access protocol. Although some professionals refer to the IEEE 802.12 standard, known as 100VG-AnyLAN, as an Ethernet LAN, that standard actually represents a demand priority access scheme that can be used to support Ethernet or another type of local area network however, such support is restricted to one type of LAN.

☞ The IEEE 802.3 Committee defined five additional types of CSMA/CD networks.

Table 9.1 compares the operational characteristics of each low-speed IEEE.802.3 network standard with the characteristics of the original Ethernet standard.

Table 9.1 Ethernet and IEEE 802.3 network characteristic

Operational Characteristics	Ethernet	10BASE-5	10BASE-2	1BASE-5	10BASE-T	10BROAD-36
Operating rate Mbps	10	10	10	1	10	10
Access protocol	CSMA/CD	CSMA/CD	CSMA/CD	CSMA/CD	CSMA/CD	CSMA/CD
Type of signaling	baseband	baseband	baseband	baseband	baseband	broadband
Data encoding	Manchester	Manchester	Manchester	Manchester	Manchester	Manchester
Maximum segment length (meters)	500	500	185	250	100	1800
Stations/ segment	100	100	30	12/hub	12/hub	100
Media	50 ohm coaxial (thick)	50 ohm coaxial (thick)	50 ohm coaxial (thin)	unshielded twisted pair	unshielded twisted pair	75 ohm coaxial
Topology	bus	bus	bus	star	star	bus

The IEEE uses the general format *s type l* to develop the name of each CSMA/CD network. Here, *s* references to the speed in Mbps; type indicates the type of signaling, either BASE for baseband or BROAD for broadband; and *l* generally indicates the maximum segment length in hundreds of meters. For example, 10BASE-5 denotes the standard for a 10 Mbps baseband LAN that has a maximum segment length of 500 meters and uses the CSMA/CD access protocol. Note that *l* does not always indicate the maximum segment length or an accurate maximum segment length. For example, 10BASE-2 has a maximum segment length of 185 meters, and 10BASE-T, in which T indicates the use of twisted-pair wiring, has a maximum segment length of 100 meters.

Under the IEEE 802.3 standard, changes occurred to the Ethernet frame is illustrated in Figure 9.5. A few minor changes resulted in the incompatibility or equipment designed for computers based on the original Ethernet specification and the IEEE 802.3 frame format.

Figure 9.7 illustrates the IEEE 802.3 data link frame format. In comparing that format to the Ethernet data link frame format illustrated in Figure 9.5, note that the Preamble field was reduced to 7 bytes, and a Start of Frame Delimiter field was added under the IEEE 802.3 frame format. The Start of Frame Delimiter field is actually a continuation of the preamble, with the sequence 10101011. However, the ending two bits are 11 rather than the 10 contained in the Ethernet Preamble field.

IEEE 802.3

Preamble	Start of Frame Delimiter	Destination Address	Source Address	Length	Data	Frame Check Sequence
7 bytes	1 byte	2/6 bytes	2/6 bytes	2 bytes	46-1500 bytes	4 bytes

Figure 9.7 The IEEE 802.3 data link frame format

Another difference between the two frame formats is the replacement of the Type field by a Length field in the IEEE 802.3 frame. Here the length field specifies the number of bytes that follow that field as data.

9.4.5 10BASE-5

Although a 10BASE-5 network follows the same configuration rules as the original Ethernet network, certain changes in terminology cause some confusion to many persons. To minimise confusion, Figure 9.8 illustrates the changes in terminology between the original Ethernet 50 ohm coaxial cable bus-based network and the IEEE 802.3 10BASE-5 bus-based network.

As indicated in Figure 9.8, the controller under 10BASE-5 is now referred to as a NIC (pronounced "nick"), or network interface card. The transceiver cable is now known as an AUI, or Attachment Unit Interface, and the transceiver is called a MAU (pronounced to rhyme with "cow"), or Media Attachment Unit.

Most 10BASE-5 NICs include both a DB-15 and a BNC connector. The DB-15 provides a connection to the AUI, whereas the BNC permits the use of the NIC on a 10BASE-2 network. Thus, the dual connectors permit the use of the NIC on two types of 802.3 standards.

9.4.6 10BASE-2

A 10BASE-2 network is based on the use of thin coaxial cable that provides a degree of cabling flexibility not obtainable with the thick coaxial cable used with a 10BASE-5 network. In addition, the use of thin coaxial cable makes cabling more economical. A 10BASE-2 workstation is connected to the thin coaxial by BNC connectors, which are also referred to as barrel connectors.

Figure 9.8 Terminology changes between Ethernet and IEEE 10BASE-5

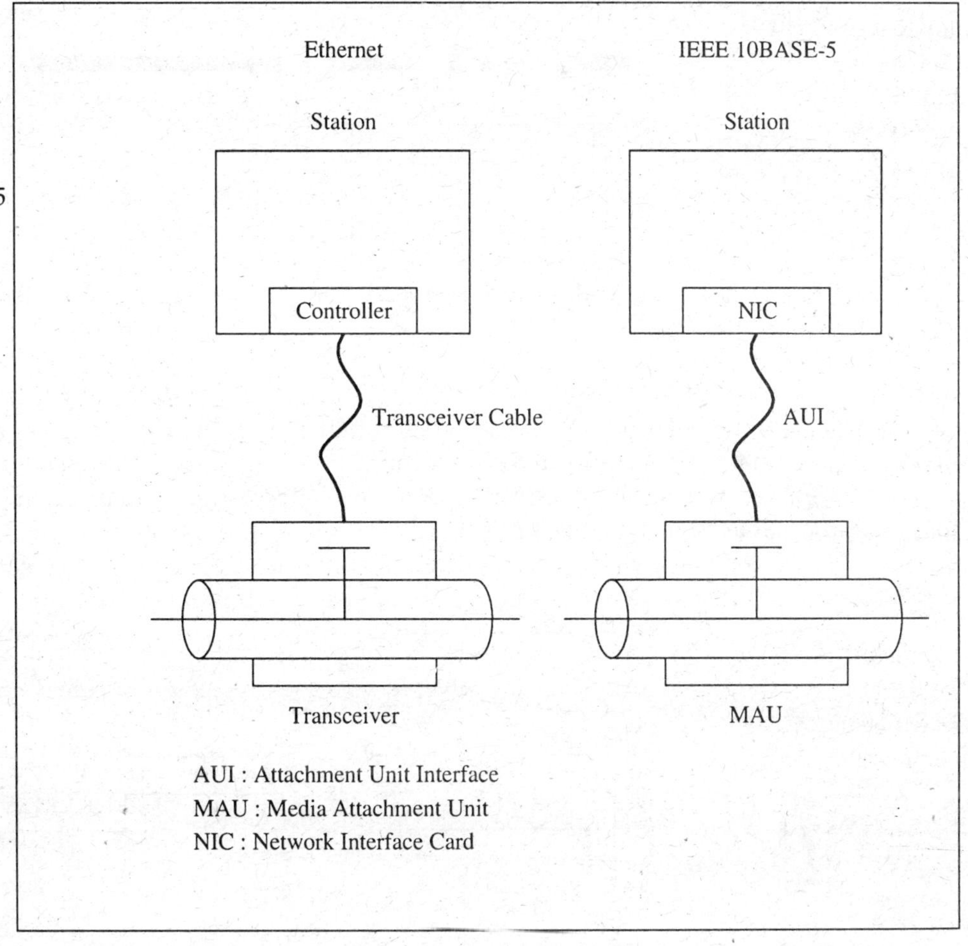

☞ A 10BASE-2 network is limited to 30 stations per segment and uses thin coaxial cable for the transmission media.

Figure 9.9 illustrates the cabling of stations to a 10BASE-2 network. This type of Ethernet network permits a maximum of 30 stations per cable segment. You can extend a 10BASE-2 network through the use of inter--repeater cable segments (IRCS), or you can combine 10BASE-2 and 10BASE-5 networks, although when doing so you must ensure that you do not violate any cabling rules.

9.4.7 10BASE-T

Another series of configurations is obtainable through the use of 10BASE-T, which is a more modern standard that allows the construction of 10 Mbps Ethernet LANS over unshielded twisted-pair wire. Under the 10BASE-T standard, which is also referred to as the IEEE 802.3i

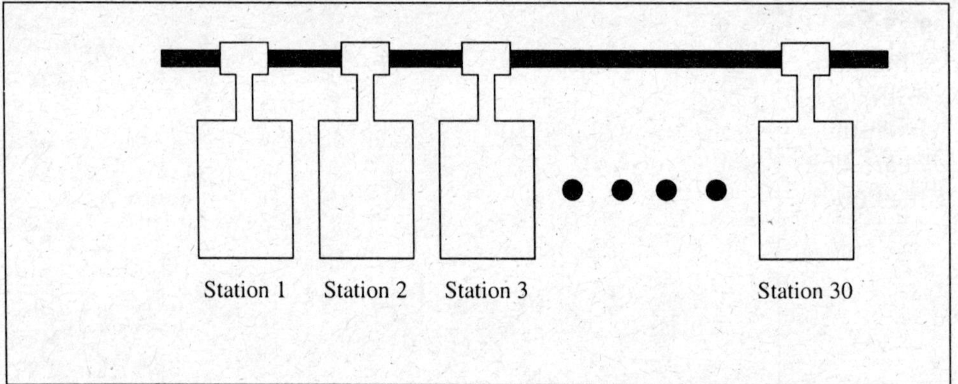

Figure 9.9 Cabling a 10BASE-2 network

standard, workstations are cabled using twisted-pair wire to medium access units (MAUs). Each MAU normally has a built-in attachment interface unit (AIU) that can be cabled to a coaxial transceiver attached to a coaxial cable. Thus, workstations can be configured in a star topology and cable to a bus structured backbone cable that serves to interconnect MAUs. Figure 9.10 illustrates a hybrid Ethernet media configuration in which personal computer workstations are cabled to MAUs via the use of twisted-pair wire.

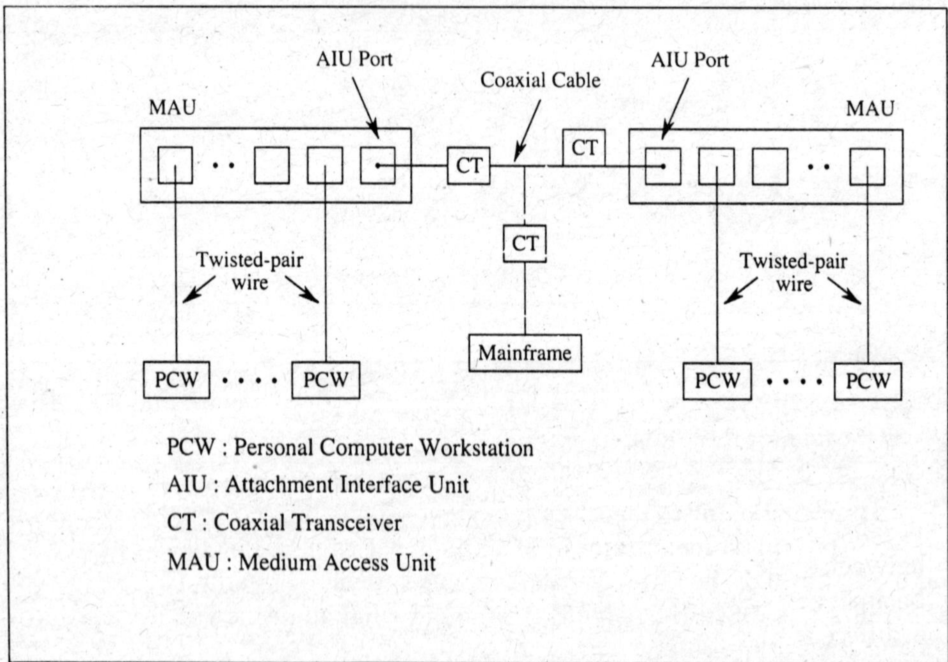

Figure 9.10 A hybrid Ethernet media configuration

The MAUs in turn are connected to a coaxial cable that not only links MAUs, but also provides access to a Mainframe computer.

9.4.8 Physical Networking Topology used for Ethernet

Ethernet can use virtually any physical networking topology and cabling system (medium). Although a star topology (stations wired in a star-like fashion to a central hub) is often used from the physical point of view, all Ethernet networks are logical bus topology networks at heart. One station places a signal on the bus, and that signal travels to every other station on the bus.

☞ The more stations on an Ethernet network, the higher the number of collisions, and the worse the performance of the network. Typical performance of a 10-Mbps Ethernet network with around 100 stations will support a bandwidth of only about 40 to 60 percent of the expected value of 10 Mbps. One way of solving the problem of collisions is to use Ethernet switches to segment your Ethernet network into smaller collision domains.

Ethernet is available in three different speeds and can be further differentiated by media and other considerations, as shown in the following table.

Table 9.2 Ethernet Speeds, Types, Standards, and Specs

Speed	Type of Ethernet	IEEE Standard	IEEE Specs
10 Mbps	Ethernet	10 Base2 10 Base5 10 BaseF 10 BaseT	802.3
100 Mbps	Fast Ethernet	100 BaseFX 100 BaseT 100 BaseT4 100 BaseTX	802.3u
1000 Mbps or 1 Gbps	Gigabit Ethernet	1000 BaseCX 1000 BaseLX 1000 BaseSX 1000 BaseT	802.3u

9.5 TOKEN-PASSING NETWORKS

Because access to a CSMA network involves a certain amount of contention (competition) between stations trying to send a message at the same time, the behavior of the network must be analyzed and controlled statistically. Token passing networks, on the other hand, provide a different access procedure. Access is determined by which station has the token; that is, only one station at a time, the one with the token, is given the opportunity to seize the channel. The token is passed from one idle station to another until a station with a pending message receives it. After the message is sent, the token is passed to the next station. In essence, a token passing network is a distributed polling network.

☞ Token passing networks provide access to the network by only one station at a time—the one with the token that is ready to send a message. Token topologies can be either a token-passing ring or a token-passing bus; each has its own strength and weakness.

Two basic topologies (configurations or arrangements) exist for token-passing networks: token-passing buses and token-passing rings.

9.5.1 Token-passing Bus

Token bus is the name given to a linear or tree shaped cable onto which the nodes are attached. But logically, the nodes are organised in a ring form (See Figure 9.11 (a)), with each node knowing the address of the nodes to its "left" and "right". When the logical ring is initialized, the highest numbered node can first send the data. After it is done, it passes over the *token* to its immediate neighbor. In this way the token propagates around the logical ring, with only the token holder being permitted to transmit data. Since only one node at a time holds the token, collisions do not occur.

Figure 9.11(a) A token-passing bus

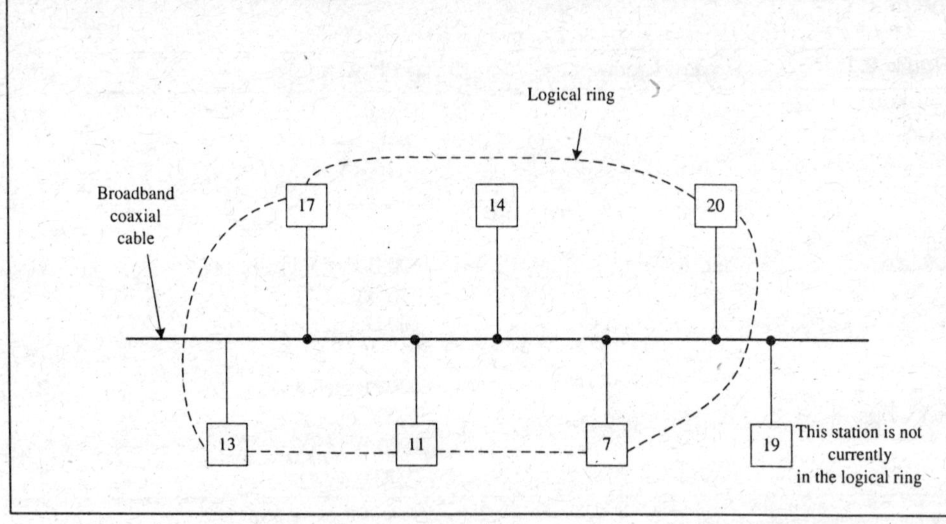

☞ Note that the physical order in which the nodes are located on the cable is not important. A node passes the token specifically addressed to its adjacent logical neighbor, no matter where the neighbor is physically located on the cable.

MAC protocol can add or delete nodes from the ring. For example, nodes 14 and 19 are not in the ring.

A token-passing bus, has more operational flexibility because the token-passing order is defined by tables in each node. If a node (for example, a printer) never originates communications, it will be a terminate-only node, and it need not be in the polling sequence. If a node needs a high priority, it can appear more than once in the polling sequence.

9.5.2 Token-Passing Ring

Ethernet CSMA/CD networks provide a relatively simple way of passing data. However, CSMA/CD breaks down under the pressure exerted by many computers on a network segment. In order to overcome this problem, IBM and the IEEE created another networking standard called 802.5. IEEE 802.5 is more commonly known as Token Ring, FDDI also uses the 802.5 method of operation.

Token Ring works very differently from Ethernet (See Figure 9.11 (b)). In Ethernet, any computer that has data can transmit until it senses a collision with another computer. In token Ring and FDDI networks, by contrast, a single special packet called *a token* is passed around the network. When a computer has data to transmit, it waits until the token is available, grabs hold of it, and transmits a data packet while simultaneously releasing the token to the next computer in line. Then the next computer grabs the token if it has data to transmit.

Figure 9.11(b) A token-passing ring

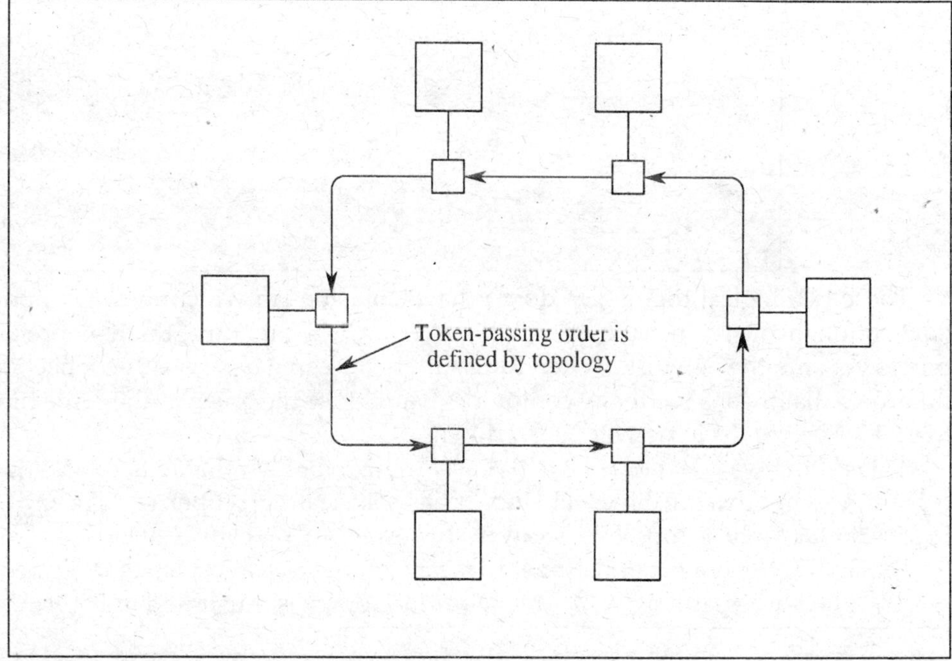

The wiring and physical arrangement is similar to that in a star network. Instead of having a concentrator at the center of a ring network, however, there is a device called a *Multistation Access Unit*, or *MAU* as seen in Figure 9.12. The MAU does the same thing a hub does but it works with Token Ring networks instead of Ethernet networks and handles communications between computers slightly differently.

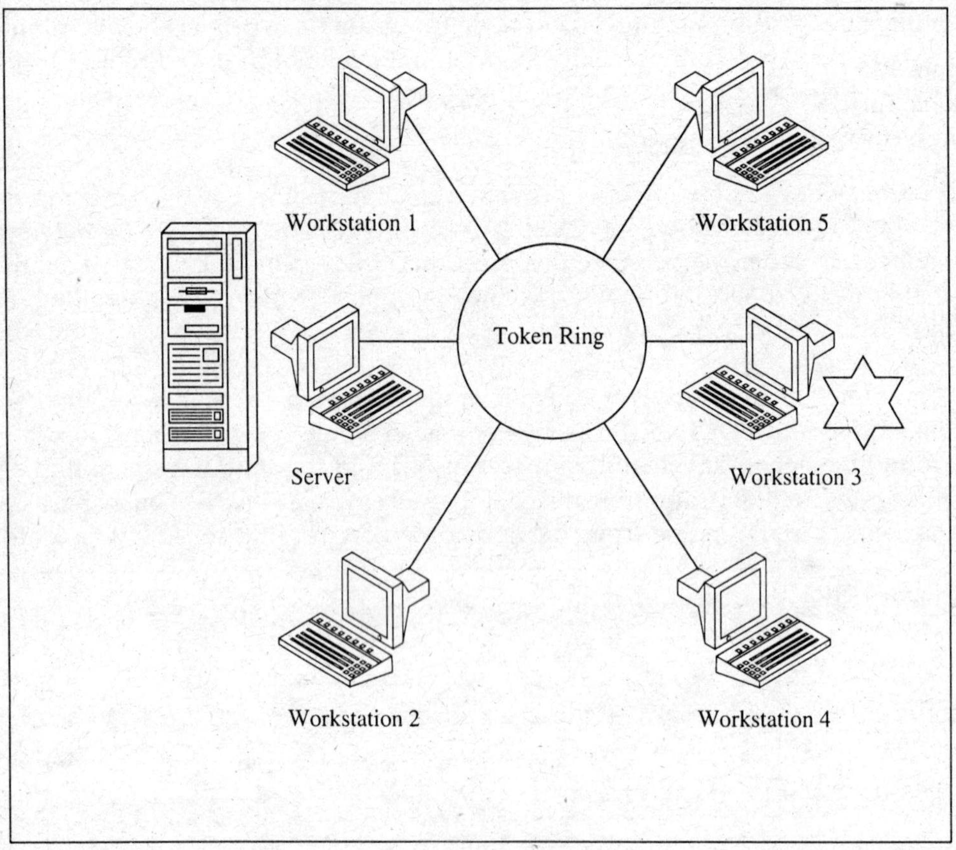

Figure 9.12
A Token ring topology: only one computer can transmit data at a time

These two logical topologies do not have collisions in which multiple nodes try to send data simultaneously. Instead, every computer waits for its turn. But as more and more computers get onto the network, Token Ring suffers the same bandwidth-connection problems as Ethernet. That means too many computers waiting for the token at the same time. Ultimately, this situation results in network slow downs.

Token Ring was developed by IBM as a robust, highly reliable network (See Figure 9.13). It is more complex than Ethernet since it has self-healing properties. Token Ring is an IEEE 802.5 standard whose topology is physically a star but logically a ring.

Workstations connect to the bus by means of individual cables that connect to an MSAU or controlled-access unit (CAU). This type of topology is illustrated in Figure 9.14.

☞ Select the appropriate topology for various token-ring and Ethernet networks.

Hubs (MAUs, MSAUs, and SMAUs)

Much of the functionality in a Token Ring network is in the hub. A Token Ring hub may also be referred to in the following ways:

(a) MAU (Multi Access Unit)
(b) MSAU (Multistation Access Unit)
(c) SMAU (Smart Multistation Access Unit)

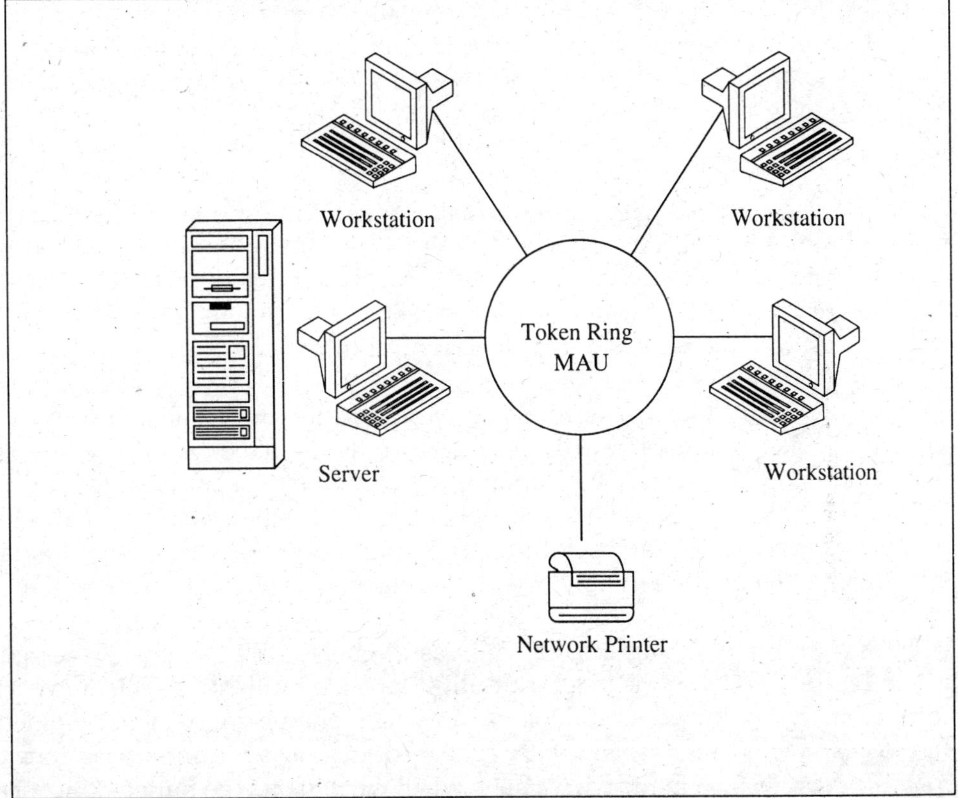

Figure 9.13
Simple Token Ring Network

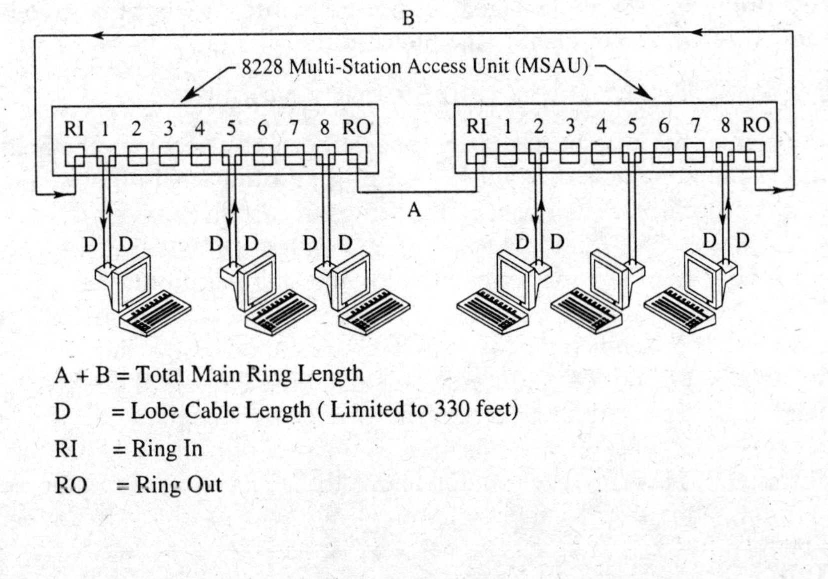

Figure 9.14
A Token Ring network in a physical star and a logical ring.

Token Ring adapter cables are used to connect a workstation's Token Ring LAN adapter to a MSAU. The cable has a 9-pin male connector on one end and an IBM Data Connector on the other end. You will find the 9-pin connector only on Token Ring LAN cards. All other equipment uses the IBM Data Connector.

How Token Ring Works?

The token ring passes a free token (a small frame with a special format) around the ring in one consistent direction. A node receives the token from its *Nearest Active Upstream Neighbour (NAUN)* and passes it to its *Nearest Active Downstream Neighbour (NADN)*. If a station receives a free token, it knows it can attach data and send it on down the ring. Each station is given an equal chance to have the token and take control in order to pass data. This is called media access.

Each station in the ring receives the data from the busy token with data attached and repeats the token and data, exactly as it received them, to the next active downstream neighbour on the ring. The addressed station (the station the data are intended for) keeps the data and passes it to its upper-layer protocols. It then switches two bits of the frame before it retransmits the information back to the ring to indicate that it received the data. The token and data are sent repeatedly until they reach the source workstation, and the process begins again.

Each station in the ring acts basically as a repeater. The data are received and retransmitted by each node on the network until it has gone full circle. This is something like the party game called Rumor or Telephone, in which one person whispers something into one player's ear, who in turn repeats it in next one's ear, and so on, until it has gone full circle. The only difference is that, in the party game, when the person who initiated the message receives it back, it has usually undergone substantial permutations. When the originating node on the network receives the message, it is normally intact except that two bits have been flipped to show the message made it to its intended destination.

9.5.3 Active Monitors and Standby Monitors

The station that has been up the longest normally becomes the active monitor. Token Ring allows only one active monitor on a ring at a time. All other stations on the ring becomes standby monitors. They wait in the wings in case the active monitor bites the dust, in which case a new active monitor is negotiated. Minor errors, such as the active monitor being turned off, are dealt with by the active monitor and standby monitors.

The active monitor does a sort of system check every seven seconds. In this check, the active monitor sends out a token to the next station on the ring. This token informs the station of the active monitor's address. This station also lists the active monitor as its upstream neighbour. The station then informs the station next in the ring of the active monitor's address. This process proceeds around the ring until the token returns to the active monitor. Through this process, each station learns three pieces of information: the address of the active monitor, who its upstream neighbour is, and who its downstream neighbour is.

9.5.4 Beaconing

If a station does not hear from its upstream neighbour in the seven seconds, it assumes something bad has happened and acts on its own. It sends a message down the ring announcing three basic pieces of information: who it is (its network address), its NAUN address (the station it has not heard from in the allotted time), and the type of beacon (the condition being indicated, such as no response from the node). This action is called *beaconing*. It occurs when the Nearest Active Upstream Neighbour Notification fails, as illustrated in Figure 9.15.

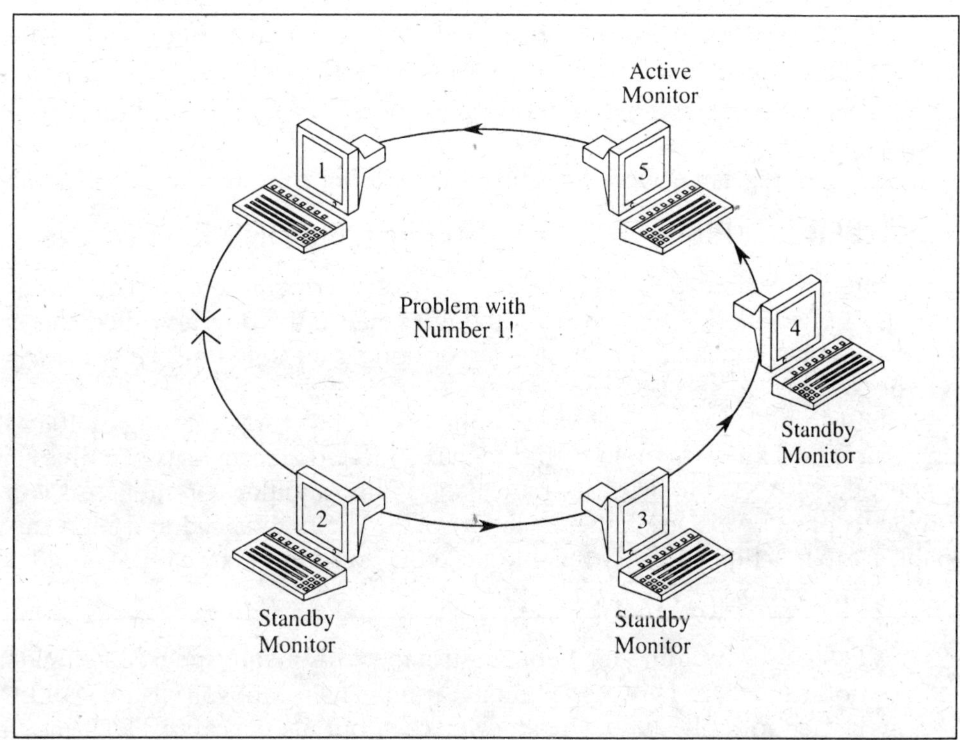

Figure 9.15 Beaconing points out breaks on a Token Ring networks

The beaconing process serves to identify any area on the ring where there is a problem. (A problem area on the ring is called the fault domain). Once the fault domain is located, the workstation that reported the problem–the downstream neighbour of the faulty workstation–has the job of removing the faulty station's packets from the network, ensuring that the network remains stable.

During the beaconing process, each Token Ring card takes itself out of the ring and does an internal diagnostic to determine whether it has a problem. If it can, it repairs itself without administrator intervention. The automatic corrective action process of the card is called auto-reconfiguration. If the card finds an error during auto-reconfiguration, it does not attempt to reenter the ring.

With the information obtained during auto-reconfiguration, the ring can repair itself without the network falling apart. This is sort of a built-in self-diagnostics and repair program. Like other network standards, Token Ring has unique features and its own list of advantages. Here are some of the advantages:

(a) Unlike Ethernet, Token Ring continues to operate reliably under heavy loads.
(b) Built-in diagnostic and recovery mechanisms, such as beaconing and auto-reconfiguration, make the protocol more reliable.
(c) Token Ring makes connecting a LAN to an IBM Mainframe easier since IBM created it and supports it.
(d) Fault-tolerance features are provided through ring reconfiguration, called *ring-wrap*.

Some of the disadvantages of Token Ring are as follows:

(a) Token Ring cards and equipment are more expensive than Ethernet or ARCnet systems.
(b) Token Ring can be very difficult to troubleshoot and requires considerable expertise.

9.6 FIBER DISTRIBUTED DATA INTERFACE (FDDI) FOR MANs

FDDI (Fiber Distributed Data Interface) is another ring-based network, and unlike Token Ring, is implemented without hubs, although you can use devices called concentrates to perform a similar function. FDDI uses fiber-optic cables to implement very fast, reliable networks.

FDDI is a high performance fiber optic token ring LAN running at 100 Mbps over distances up to 200 km with up to 1000 stations connected . It can be used in the same way as any of the other LANs, but with its high bandwidth, another common use is a backbone to connect copper LANs, as shown in Figure 9.16. The high speed and high capacity of FDDI enables it to function as a very reliable backbone to connect large number of LANS, as can be seen in Figure 9.16.

☞ FDDI uses multimode fibers because the additional expense of single mode fibers is not needed for networks running at only 1000 Mbps. It also uses LEDs rather than lasers, not only due to their lower cost, but also because FDDI may sometimes be used to connect directly to user workstations.

The FDDI cabling consists of two fiber rings, one transmitting clockwise and the other transmitting counterclockwise, as illustrated in Figure 9.16. If either one breaks, the other can be used as a backup. If both break at the same point, for example, due to a fire or other accident in the cable duct, the two rings can be joined into a single ring approximately twice as long, as shown in Figure 9.17. Each station contains relays that can be used to join the two rings or bypass the station in the event of station problems. Wire centers can also be used, as in 802.5.

How FDDI Works?

FDDI (like Token Ring) uses a token-passing schemes to control network access. Unlike Token Ring, several FDDI devices can transmit data simultaneously.

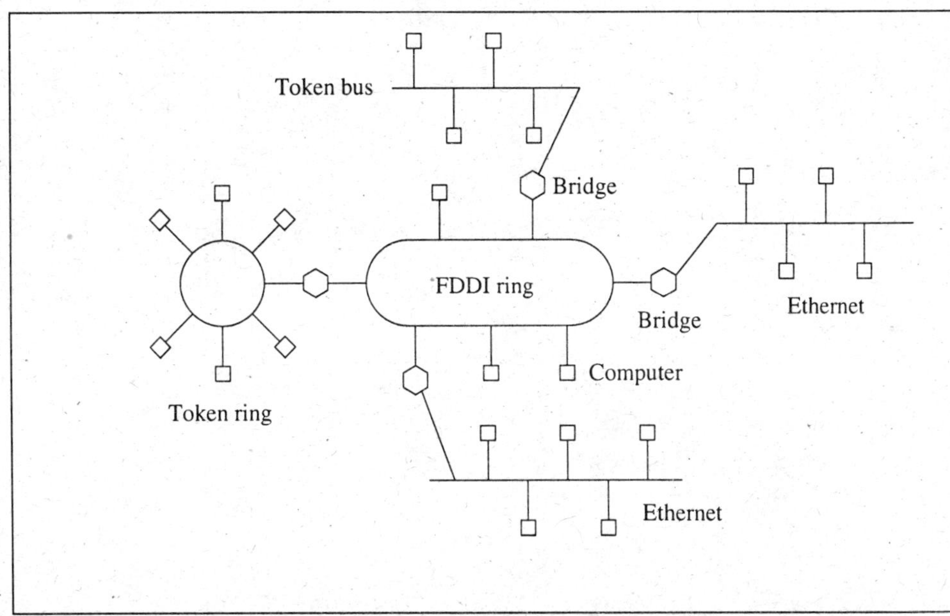

Figure 9.16
AN FDDI ring being used as a backbone to connect LANs and computers

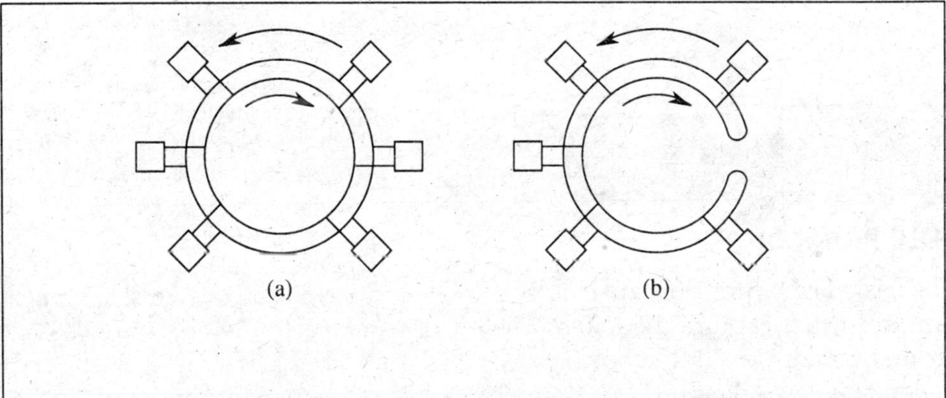

Figure 9.17
(a) FDDI consisting of two counter rotating rings (b) Two rings joined together

FDDI uses an even more sophisticated method of accessing the network than does Token Ring. Like Token Ring, a token is passed around the ring, and the possessor of the token is allowed to transmit FDDI frames. Unlike Token Ring, a FDDI network may have several frames simultaneously circulating on the network. This is possible because the possessor of the token may send multiple frames, without waiting for the first frame to circulate all the way around the ring before sending the next frame.

The possessor of the FDDI token is also allowed to release the token and send it to the next station in the ring as soon as it is through transmitting frames, rather than having to wait for the frames to make it all the way around the ring. This means that the next station may begin transmitting while the frames from the first station are still circulating, as can be seen in Figure 9.18.

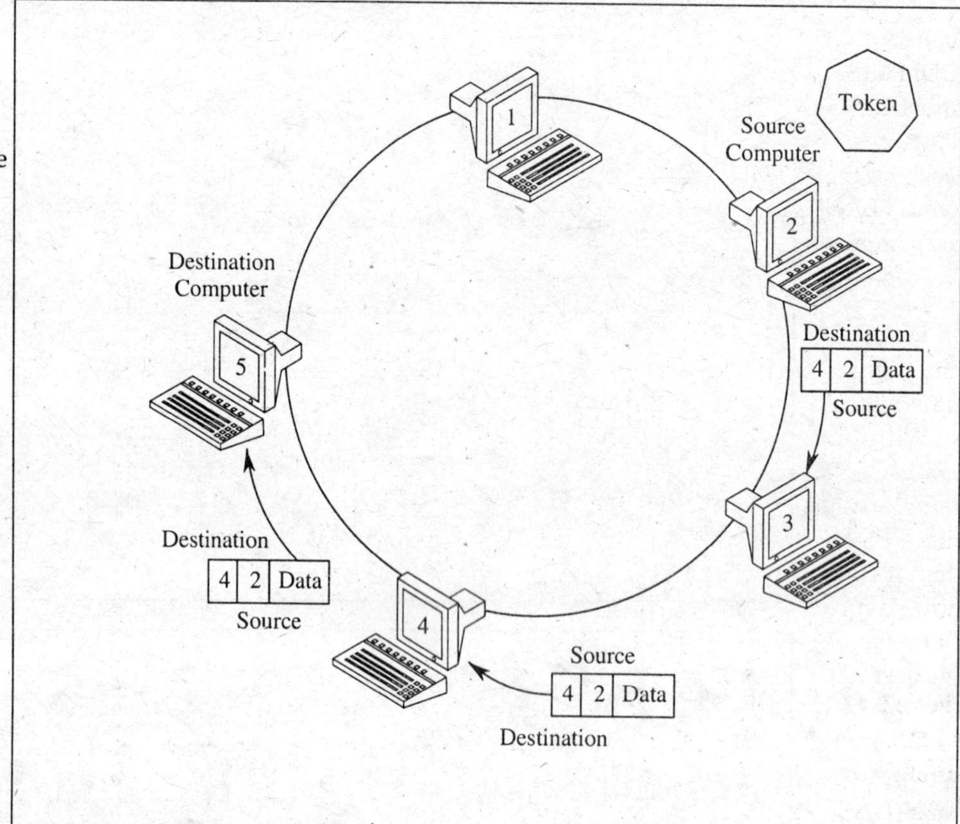

Figure 9.18 Dual counter-rotating rings allow FDDI to operate in spite of network faults

FDDI Protocol

The basic FDDI protocols are closely modeled in the 802.5 protocols. To transmit data, a station must first capture the token. Then it transmits a frame and removes it when it comes around again. One difference between FDDI and 802.5 is that in 802.5 a station may not generate a new token until its frame has gone all the way around and come back. In FDDI, with potentially 1000 stations and 200 km of fiber, the amount of time wasted waiting for the frame to circumnavigate the ring could be substantial. For this reason, it was designed to allow a station to put a new token back onto the ring as soon as it has finished transmitting its frames. In a large ring, several frames might be on the ring at the same time.

FDDI data frames are similar to 802.5 data frames. The FDDI format is shown in Figure 9.19. The *Start delimiter* and *End delimiter* fields mark the frame boundaries. The *Frame control* field tells what kind of frame this is (data, control, etc). The *Frame status* byte holds acknowledgement bits, similar to those of 802.5. The other fields are analogous to 802.5.

In addition to the regular (asynchronous) frames, FDDI also permits special synchronous frames for circuit-switched PCM or ISDN data. The synchronous frames are generated every 125 µsec by a master station to provide the 8000 sample/sec needed by PCM systems. Each of these frames has a header, 16 bytes of noncircuit-switched data, and up to 96 bytes of circuit-switched data (i.e., up to 96 PCM channels per frame).

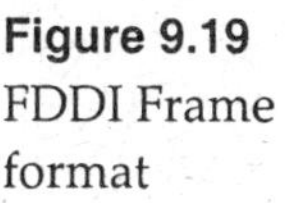

Figure 9.19
FDDI Frame format

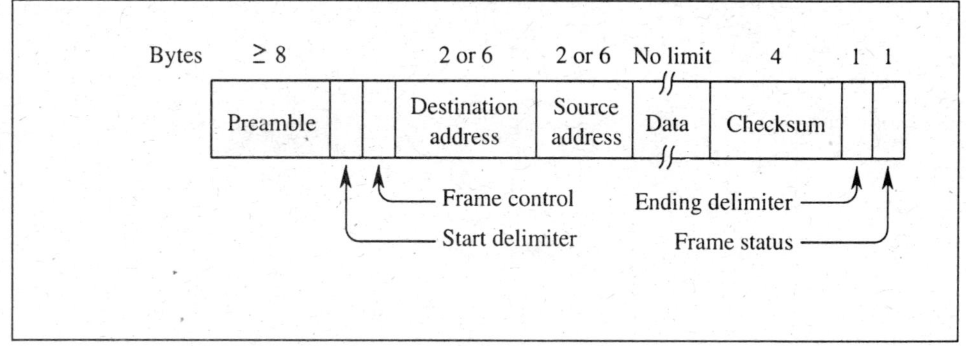

FDDI also has a priority algorithm similar to 802.4. It determines which priority classes may transmit on a given token pass. If the token is ahead of schedule, all priorities may transmit, but if it is behind schedule, only the highest ones may send.

With FDDI, a station must have a token before it can transmit frames. The size of FDDI frames can be between 17 and 4500 bytes. Stations on the network read the messages that travel around the ring from Network Interface Card (NIC) to NIC. When a station reads a frame that matches its address, it copies the frame and creates an acknowledgment frame. Then it transfers the token to the next attached network node. FDDI uses the primary ring to move data and a second ring to provide system fault tolerance and backup. The two rings rotate (send messages) in opposite directions, so they are called dual counter-rotating rings. The second ring is inactive until it is needed. Figure 9.20 shows the design of an FDDI topology.

Devices such as workstations, bridges, and routers can be attached to the rings. There are two types of stations: Class A and Class B. Class A stations are also called dual-attached stations (DASs) because they can be attached to both rings at the same time. Class B stations are called single-attached stations because they attach to only one ring. Class B workstations are not as fault-tolerant as Class A workstations because they cannot use *wrapping*. Wrapping is the system fault-tolerance feature that takes effect when a break occurs on one or both of the rings. When a break occurs in a ring, the first step is the identification of a failure domain (the area affected by the break that cannot carry data).

☞ Wrapping reroutes the packets around the two workstations bordering that failure domain.

A break in the ring on which a Class B station is attached will probably isolate a Class B workstation. Figure 9.21 shows how FDDI wrapping works.

Advantages and Disadvantages of FDDI

Advantages

(a) **High bandwidth:** It has bandwidth as high as 250 Gbps. High bandwidth allows for tremendous speed. FDDI implementation can handle data rates of 100 Mbps.
(b) **Security:** It is difficult to eavesdrop on fiber-optic cable transmission.
(c) **Physical durability:** Fiber optic cable does not break as easily as do other kind of cable.

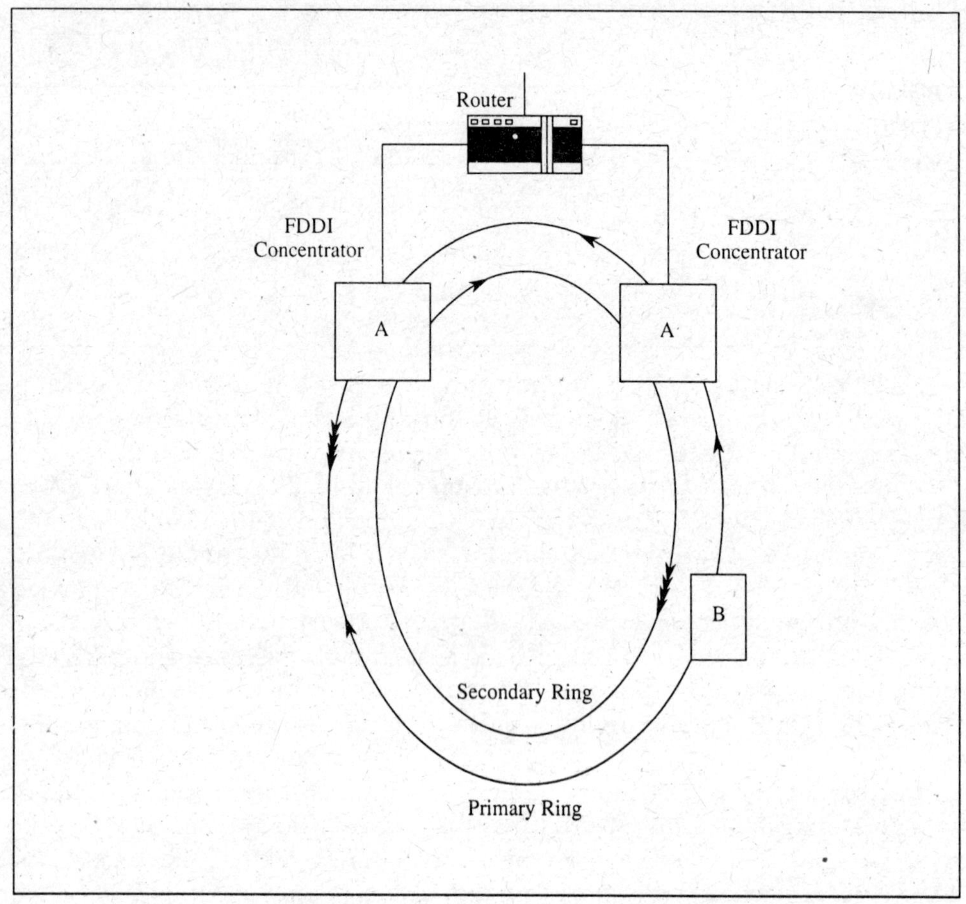

Figure 9.20 FDDI topology design

(d) **Resistance to EMI:** Fiber optic cables are not susceptible to electromagnetic interference.
(e) **Cable distance:** Fiber-optic cables transmit signals over 2 kilometers.
(f) **Weight:** Fiber optic cable weighs a lot less than copper wire with similar bandwidth.
(g) **Use of multiple tokens:** FDDI uses multiple tokens to improve network speed.
(h) **Ability to prioritize workstations:** FDDI can designate some work stations as low-priority workstations. This allows FDDI to bypass low-priority workstations when necessary, providing faster service to high priority station.
(i) **System fault tolerance:** FDDI can isolate faulty nodes with the use of wiring concentrators for instantaneous rerouting. Wiring concentrators function as centralized cabling connection devices for workstations. Wrapping is the other advantage.

Disadvantages

(a) FDDI is a complex technology. Installation and maintenance require a great deal of expertise.
(b) FDDI is costly. In addition to the fiber-optic cable cost, the adapters and concentrators are also very expensive.

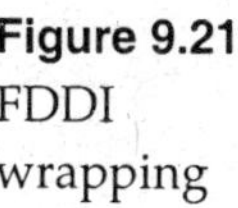

Figure 9.21 FDDI wrapping

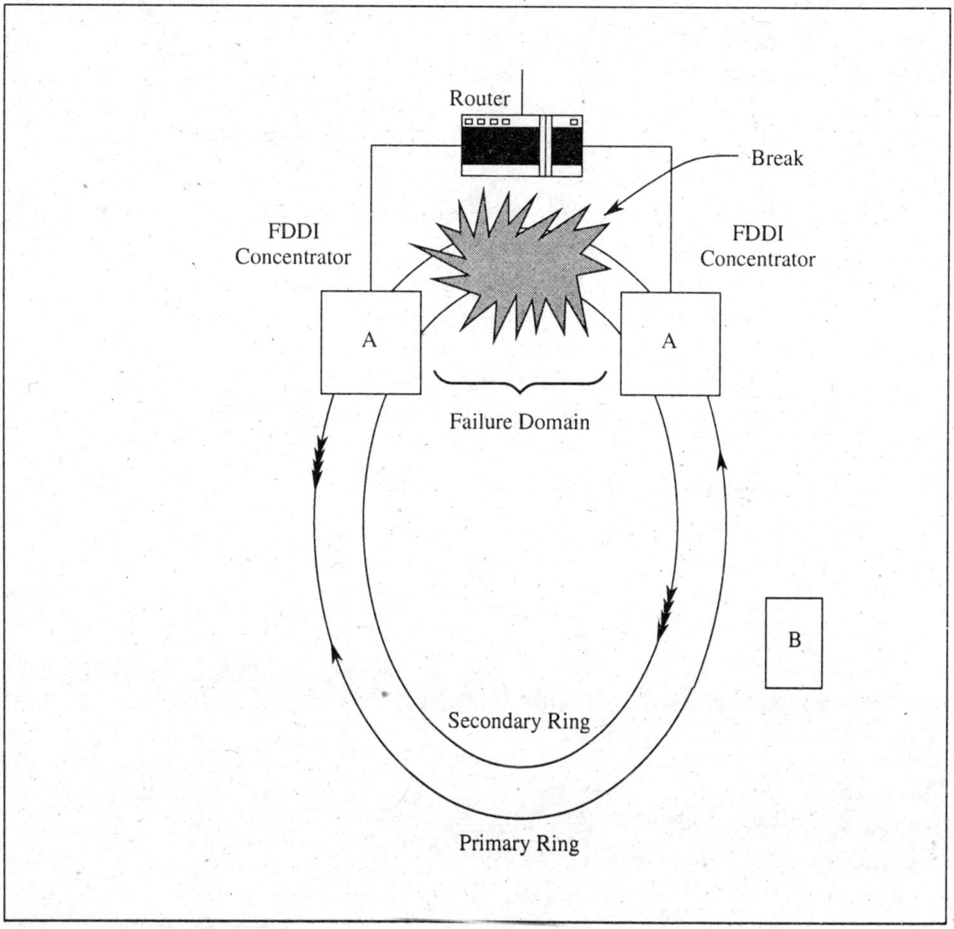

9.7 SWITCHED MULTIMEGABIT DATA SERVICES (SMDS)

Switched Multimegabit Data Services (SMDS) is a connectionless, packet-switched telecommunications service with speeds ranging from 56 Kbps to 34 Mbps. Switched Multimegabit Data Services (SMDS) was designed by Bellcore in the 1980s for high-speed wide area network (WAN) communication. It was the first high-speed broadband networking technology offered to subscribers and was a precursor to Asynchronous Transfer Mode (ATM) networking. Most carriers are now phasing out SMDS.

SMDS is based on a packet-switching technology. A subscriber's local area network (LAN) typically connects to the SMDS service through a router using a RS-449 interface and a Channel Service Unit/Data Service Unit (CSU/DSU) using a copper DS1 connection (1.544 Mbps) for low-speed access or a fiber DS3 connection (44.736 Mbps) to achieve the highest possible transmission speeds. This point of connection between the subscriber's LAN and the telco's central office (CO) is called the *Subscriber Network Interface* (SNI). The CO provides a gateway to the SMDS packet-switching network, which consists of high-speed switches joined by trunk lines connecting different Telco COs.

An SMDS packet consists of a header with the source address, destination address, and a payload of up to 9188 bytes. The SMDS payload is large so that SMDS can easily encapsulate Ethernet, Token Ring, and Fiber Distributed Data Interface (FDDI) frames for WAN transmission. The E.164 addressing scheme uses decimal numbers up to 15 digits long and includes a country code, area code, and subscriber ID number (similar to ordinary telephone numbers).

Different address classes support different data transfer speeds. The serial protocol used for communication between the customer premises equipment and SMDS equipment at the Telco's CO is called the SMDS Interface Protocol (SIP), which is based on the IEEE 802.6 standard for metropolitan area networks (MANs). The primary function of SIP is to provide encapsulation of the LAN protocol. (Internet Protocol, Internetwork Packet Exchange, AppleTalk, and just about anything else is supported.) Higher-layer protocols support processes such as address resolution and source address screening.

☞ SMDS supports ATM communication and is suitable for use in high-capacity mesh topology WANs. SMDS is offered by long-distance carriers such as AT&T and by some Regional Bell Operating Companies (RBOCs). SMDS is not as widely supported as frame relay even though it uses similar packet-switching technology.

SMDS is a switched service provided by common carriers; subscribers pay only for the time they use. Subscriber LANs link to an SMDS network through routers that are connected to switches using DQDB architecture. (See Figure 9.22)

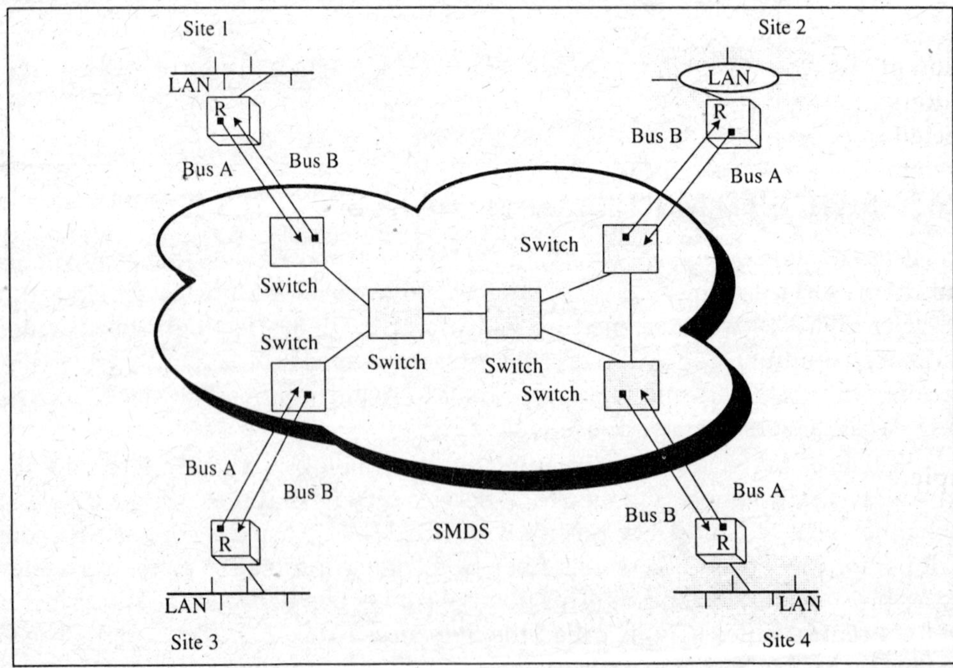

Figure 9.22 SMDS as a MAN: Subscriber LANs linked to SMDS through routers

REVIEW QUESTIONS WITH ANSWERS

Q. No. 1 What is a LAN? Discuss the advantages and disadvantages of LAN?

Answer **LAN**

LAN stands for Local Area Network. Due to the need of communicating data both written and oral the need to create LAN arose. Because the communication should be cost effective.

The term network means connecting communication devices of many types together. The devices may be dispersed geographically at vast distances. These devices so connected that they can exchange data of various types efficiently and accurately.

Networks can be small or big depending upon the need and the necessity of the organizations.

For advantages and disadvantages of LAN *refer to Sections 9.1.1 and 9.1.2.*

Q. No. 2 How does LAN differ form MAN, CAN and WAN? List and describe in brief different topology and transmission media used in LAN.

Answer Table 1 gives a comparison of the different kinds of networks.

Table 1 Comparison between LAN, CAN, MAN and WAN

Characteristics	LAN	CAN	MAN	WAN
Full form	LAN stands for Local Area Networks	CAN stands for Campus Area Networks	MAN stands for Metropolitan Area Networks	WAN stands for Wide Area Networks
Location of computers connected in the system	Computers are located within the same building.	Computers are confined within the limited physical area. The machines may be installed in two different buildings close by or within the campus of the industry or the institute.	Computers are located in the city are connected using modem or telephone lines so that they can be easily connected with each other.	Computers are distributed all over the country or the continent. The connection is made via satellite communication link or via Internet.
Example	Example of LAN can be an office whose different departments such	Example of CAN is a University whose different departments and	Example of MAN is a bank whose different branches in a city like Delhi	Example of WAN is the connection of various branches of a

(Contd...)

Characteristics	LAN	CAN	MAN	WAN
	as personnel, accounting etc. are located in the same building and connected via bus topology using Ethernet cards.	library etc. are located in the near surroundings and the systems are connected using fiber optic cables and FDDI ring topology.	are connected using public telephone exchange and the systems are connected with each other using LANs within each branch and the different branches are connected using Modems and bridges.	multinational corporation such as Proctor & Gamble. These branches are linked using Microwave satellite communication system or Internet connection. Each branch has its own LAN circuit but the different LANs in various branches are communicating with the Head Office using WAN link.

Q. No. 3 Mention with a brief description the different subsections of project 802 of IEEE.

Answer [*Refer to Section 9.3*]

Q. No. 4 Write short notes on the following:

(a) Token ring
(b) Token bus

Answer (a) Token Ring was developed by IBM as a robust, highly reliable network. In a token Ring a single special packet called *a token* is passed around the network. When a computer has data to transmit, it waits until the token is available, grabs hold of it, and transmits a data packet while simultaneously releasing the token to the next computer in line. Then the next computer grabs the token if it has data to transmit.

The wiring and physical arrangement is similar to that in a star network. Instead of having a concentrator at the center of a ring network, however, there is a device called a *Multi-station Access Unit*, or *MAU* as seen in Figure 9.12. The MAU does the same thing a hub does but it works with Token Ring networks instead of Ethernet networks.

Token ring topology do not have collisions in which multiple nodes try to send data simultaneously. Instead, every computer waits for its turn. But as more and more computers get onto the network, Token Ring suffers the same bandwidth-connection problems as Ethernet. That means too many computers waiting for the token at the same time. Ultimately, this situation results in network slow downs.

Answer (b) Token bus is the name given to a linear or tree shaped cable onto which the nodes are attached. But logically, the nodes are organised in a ring form (See Figure 9.11 (a)), with each node knowing the address of the nodes to its "left" and "right". When the logical ring is initialized, the highest numbered node can first send the data. After it is done, it passes over the *token* to its immediate neighbor. In this way the token propagates around the logical ring, with only the token holder being permitted to transmit data. Since only one node at a time holds the token, collisions do not occur.

Token bus topology also do not have collisions in which multiple nodes try to send data simultaneously. Instead, every computer waits for its turn.

MAC protocol can add or delete nodes from the ring. A token-passing bus, has more operational flexibility because the token-passing order is defined by tables in each node. If a node (for example, a printer) never originates communications, it will be a terminate-only node, and it need not be in the polling sequence. If a node needs a high priority, it can appear more than once in the polling sequence.

Q. No. 5 What do you mean by 10BASE-2, 10BASE-5 and 10BASE-T networks?

Answer [*Refer to Sections 9.4.5, 9.4.6 and 9.4.7*]

TEST PAPER

Time: 3 Hrs. Marks: 100

Note: Answer all questions.

1. Explain the working of a token ring.
2. Distinguish between LAN and MAN.

   [*GNDU, BIT Part–III, Paper–I, 2002 examination*]
3. What are the general issues to be taken care of while designing a bridge from 802.x to 802.y?
4. Explain how networks may be classified by the technique employed in transporting message between the nodes. Compare any two of them.
5. Write short notes on
   (a) FDDI
   (b) Ethernet

CHAPTER 10

Switching

10.1 INTRODUCTION

Human telephone conversations are characterized by irregular pauses, alternating with irregular bursts of speech. However, the transmission of voice signals is relatively constant. The traditional method of creating and maintaining a telephone connection has been circuit switching. But many computer communications in contrast, are characterized by relatively long pauses between short bursts of transmission. For example, during a credit check, a department store's PC terminal might transmit a customer's identification number to a central data bank, then wait several seconds to receive a quick spurt of credit information. Excluding other electronic traffic from the transmission line while the data bank processes the store's inquiry is costly and inefficient. A technique known as *packet switching* prevents such wastefulness by allowing multiple computer communications to travel over the same link in specially organized network.

10.1.1 What is Switched Network?

A switched network consists of a series of interlinked nodes, called *switches*. Switches are hardware and/or software devices capable of creating temporary connections between two or more devices linked to the switch but not to each other. In a switched network, some of these nodes are connected to the communicating devices. Other nodes are used only for the purpose of routing packets.

Figure 10.1 (a) shows a network that uses switches. The Nodes are labeled as A, B, C,..., L. The switches are also hardware/software combinations and are marked as I, II, ...VII. Each switch is connected to multiple links and is used to complete the connections between them, two at a time.

Three methods of switching are:

(a) Circuit switching
(b) Packet Switching
(c) Message Switching

10.2 CIRCUIT SWITCHING

Circuit switching is a method of networking in which communicating machines have exclusive use of the circuit linking them—even during pauses when the circuit is momentarily

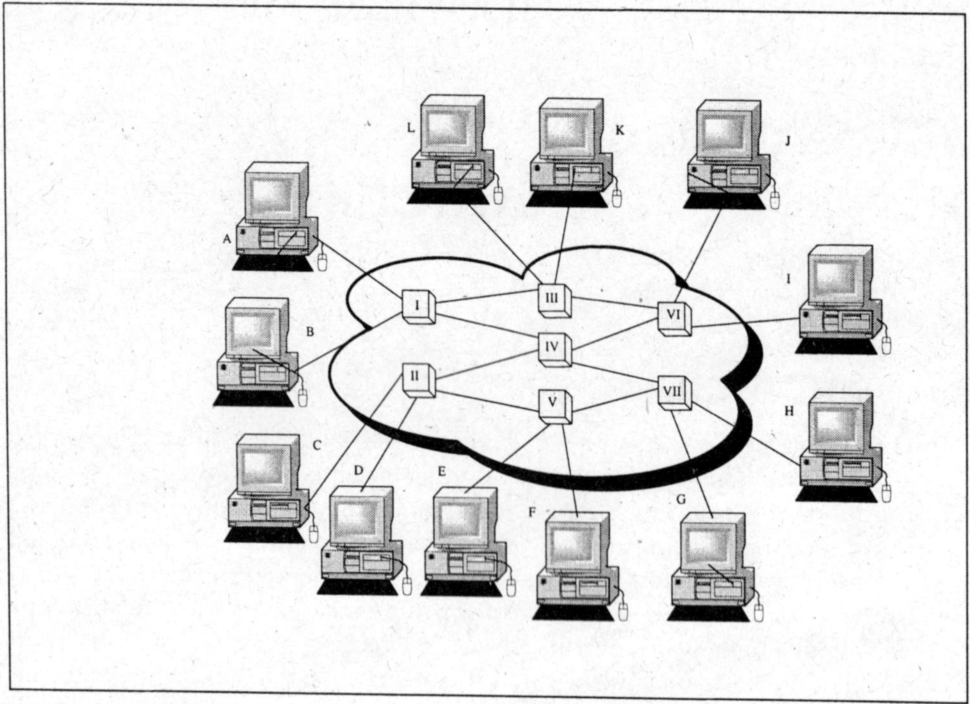

Figure 10.1(a) Point to point connection

idle—until the circuit is released. In the traditional method of telephone connection, this technique is used. In this method, transmission line is opened between two parties and held open until their communication is finished. Even during moments of silence, when the line between the two parties is temporarily idle, the circuit remains dedicated to their exclusive use. Although transmission time is essentially wasted during those idle moments, the loss is insignificant in relation to the overall rate of information flow.

☞ A circuit may be defined as "a route between certain limits or boundaries." In communications, circuit switching usually refers to the establishment of a connection in which the data path is fixed in time and space. Moreover, the path remains fixed until the circuit is disconnected.

To establish a circuit-switched connection, it is first necessary to find an available data path, seize it, and dedicate it to the exclusive use of the communicants. As a result of this circuit set-up overhead, circuit switching is most efficient for connections that carry a large amount of data relative to the data that must be exchanged during set-up. Once the connection is in place, little or no processing is required to maintain it. However, the bandwidth and other resources allocated to a circuit are "owned" by the communicants until the connection is terminated. The circuit thus represents an efficient use of resources only to the extent that the allocated bandwidth is utilized.

Circuit switching is suited to voice conversation, which tend to be long lived (over two minutes on the average) relative to the set-up time required (about 0.1 to 0.5 seconds). Further, data flow occurs during a relatively large percentage of the connection time in most voice conversations.

10.2.1 Difficulties in Circuit Switching

The main difficulty with a circuit switch occurs when two different stations attempt to establish a data link with the same station. One caller will be successful, while the other hears a busy tone, which is an indication of line contention i.e. the two callers contended for the connection to the third station. The successful caller's connection was made, while the unsuccessful caller, who receives the busy tone, has to wait until the line is free again before the call can be made and data can be sent. If more than one callers attempt to make the call at exactly the same instant, a condition called *collision* occurs. It means, the call requests collide with each other. The collision must be resolved before one of the calls can be connected. The solution usually requires both callers to disconnect the line for a random amount of time and try making the call again.

Figure 10.1 (b) shows the point-to-point connections which are adequate when the number of communicating elements are few. The direct link as shown above between two computers might also be used to connect a computer with a printer or other peripheral device.

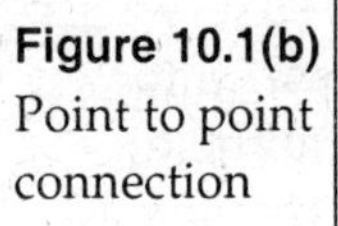

Figure 10.1(b)
Point to point connection

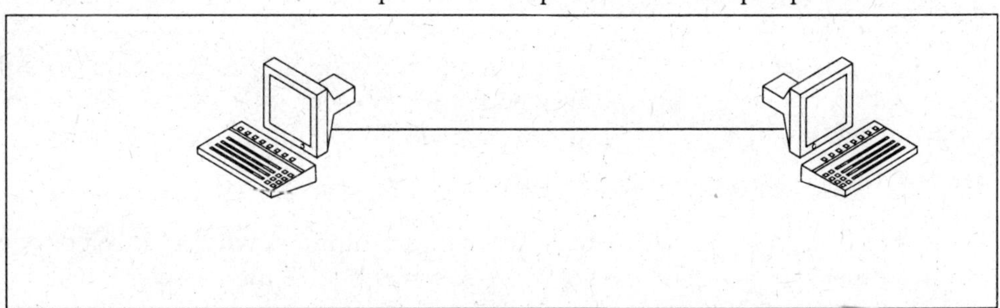

As seen in Figure 10.2, when the number of machines increases, point-to-point connection becomes less practical. In the system in this figure, each of the six machines requires ports, or plug-in-slots and 15 lines are needed to link the machines to one another.

The circuit switch method transfers data in real time but has problems either with the number of interconnecting lines or with line contention. Message switching is an alternative method designed to overcome these limitations.

Computer networks were developed to allow users in several locations to share computing facilities and resources, whether the users are on different floors of the same building or in the cities thousands of miles apart. The alternative to a network is a point-to-point system in which each computer is directly linked to every other computer terminal or peripheral with which it must communicate. Such a configuration quickly grows unwieldy. The number

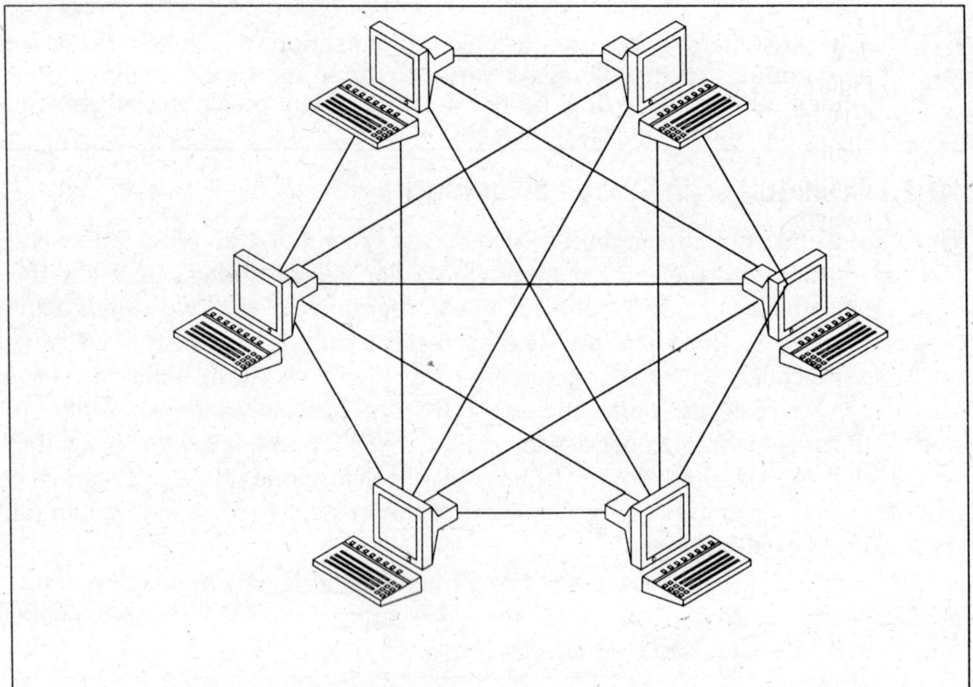

Figure 10.2 Network of connections

of direct links required can be found by the formula N(N-1)/2, where N is the number of communicating machines in the system. For example, enabling 10 computers to communicate with one another in a point-to-point system would require 45 separate lines.

10.2.2 Circuit Switching in Telephone Systems

When you place a telephone call, the switching equipment within the telephone system seeks out a physical path all the way from your telephone to the receiver's telephone. This technique is called circuit switching and is shown schematically in Figure 10.3.

Each of the six rectangles represents a carrier switching office. Each office has three incoming lines and three outgoing lines. When a call passes through a switching office, a physical connection is established between the line on which the call came in and one of the output lines as seen by the dotted lines. Once a call has been set up, a dedicated path between both ends exists and will continue to exist until the call is finished.

An important property of circuit switching is the need to set up an end-to-end path before any data can be sent. The elapsed time between the end of dialing and the start of ringing can be 10 seconds. It can be even more than this value if the calls are for long distance or international calls. Note that before data transmission can even begin, the call request signal must propagate all the way to the destination, and be acknowledged. For many computer applications, such as point-of-sale credit verification, long setup times are undesirable.

10.3 PACKET SWITCHING

Long messages are broken into smaller units called *packets*. Each packet contains a header, which includes destination and source identifiers or addresses and packet number. Packets

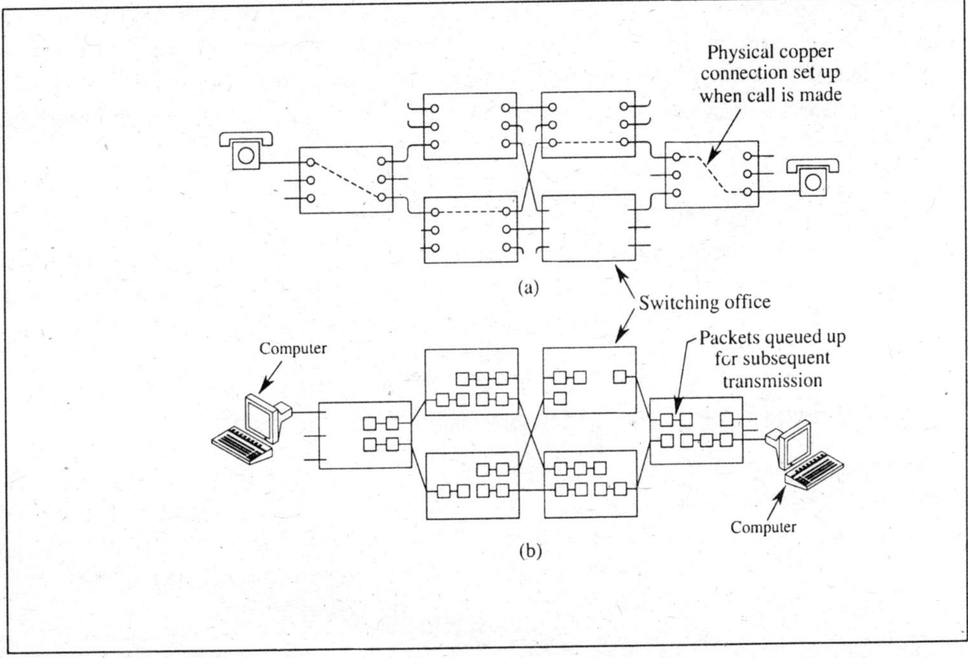

Figure 10.3 (a) Circuit switching (b) Packet switching

from several sources are routed to their destinations, where they are reassembled into their original messages (See Figure 10.4).

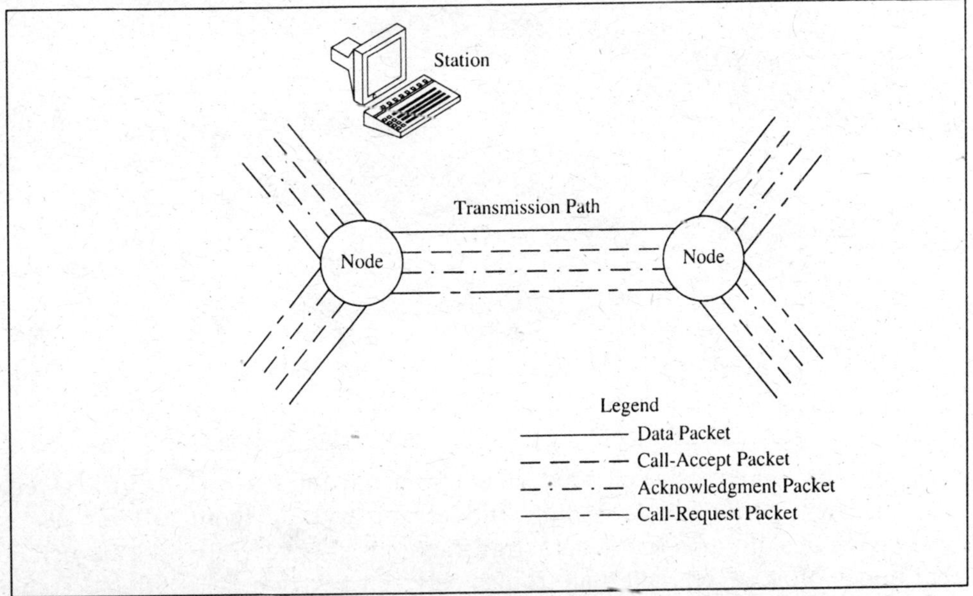

Figure 10.4 Packet Switching Network components

The packets are sent continually as long as there are messages to be sent. They are sent to various destination stations in a mixed sequence, which result in continually receiving data until all packets of the messages are received. The receiving stations then utilize the destination addresses to identify packets intended for that station. Next packet number in the headers is used by the receiving stations to assemble the messages into a complete and correct order. This form of network switching, called *Packet Switching*, is used with many different networks.

☞ Packet Switching derives its name from the way a message is split into many segments, or packets, each of which is handled as a separate communication. Not only many packets from many different messages be interleaved on a common transmission line, but packets from the same message may travel along several different lines.

10.3.1 Packet-switching Communication Network

Packet-switching communication network is made up of stations, nodes and transmission paths (See Figure 10.5). A station may be a terminal that provides access to the network's resource, or it may contain some part of those resources. For example, a host computer may act as a station to which data are sent from distant terminals for processing. Stations may also include peripherals such as printers.

Figure 10.5 Packet Switching Network

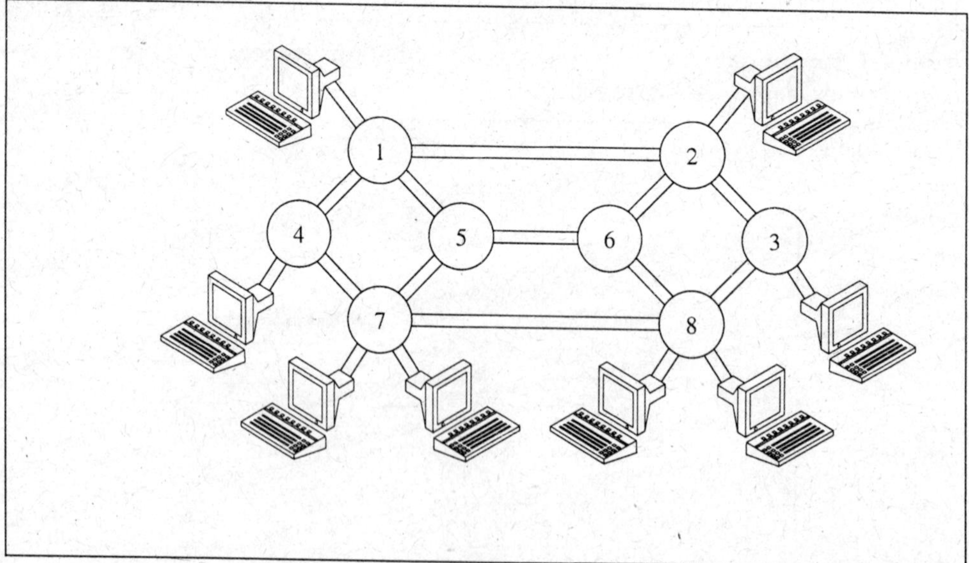

Nodes are usually special processors that act as the networks' traffic directors, receiving packets from stations or from other nodes and routing them to their destinations. Paths between nodes often handle several transmissions at once. Networks are usually arranged so that nodes offer several alternate routes between any two destinations. Transmission paths are the lines along which packets travel.

Packets come in two forms. These are:

(a) Data Packets
(b) Control Packets

Data Packets

Data packets contain message segment as well as sequence and routing information.

Control Packets

Control packets are brief messages—transmission requests and acceptances, acknowledgements of data-packet receipt—that keep traffic flowing smoothly. These control packets initiate and maintain communication.

As seen in Figure 10.5, a network that uses relay stations, or nodes, eliminates the dense tangle of direct connections. The scheme shown here represents a communications system dispersed over a wide geographical area.

10.3.2 Difference between Packet and Circuit Switching

Packet switching is an allocation technique that utilizes bandwidth only when there is data to be transmitted. The efficient use of bandwidth comes at the expense of an increased processing and data content overheads that is incurred with the transmission of each packet. As seen in Figure 10.6, packets are formed by adding information to the beginning and end of each group of user data.

Figure 10.6
Structure of a Data Packet

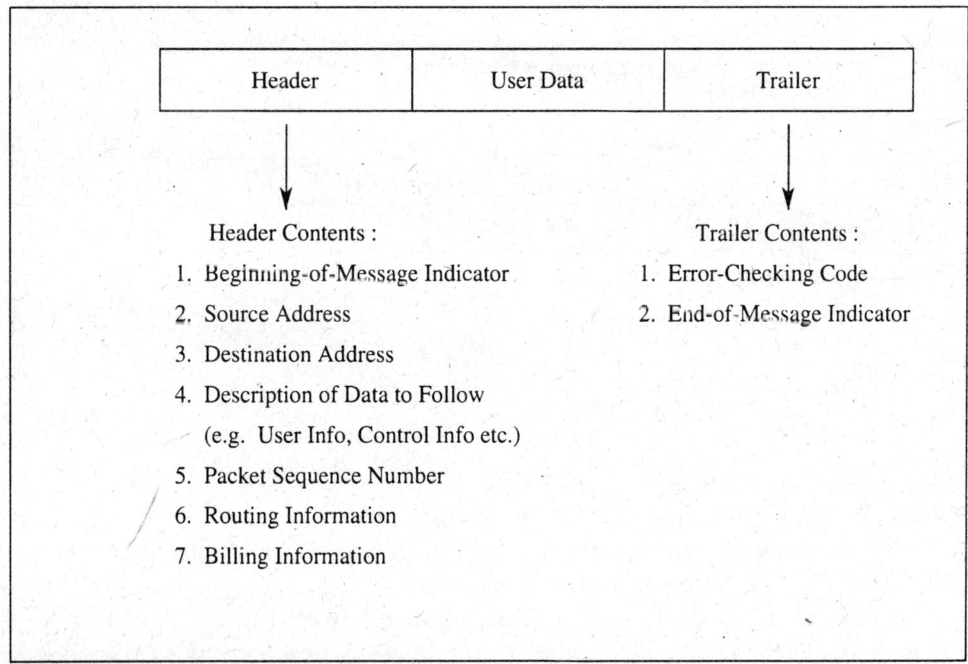

The packet header identifies the source of the data and its destination, and it can also identify the nature of the data, as well as providing billing and accounting information. The trailer contains error checking information, such as a CRC which is used to determine whether the packet has been corrupted in transmission. In packet switching, the length of each transmission is limited to the maximum packet size. Long messages are broken up into a number of packets, which are reassembled into the original messages on the receiving end.

☞ The circuit switching statically reserves the required bandwidth in advance, whereas packet switching acquires and releases it as it is needed. With circuit switching, any unused bandwidth on an allocated circuit is just wasted. With packet switching it may be utilized by other packets from unrelated sources going to unrelated destinations, because circuits are never dedicated.

Circuit switching is controlled by a centralized hierarchical control mechanism with global knowledge of the network's configuration. On the other hand, packet switching is associated with data traffic, and this lends itself to distributed control mechanisms in which most network nodes require very little information about the *network configuration* in order to get data from source to destination.

In contrast with circuit switching, when packet switching is used, it is straight forward for the routers to provide speed and code conversion. Also they can provide error correction to some extent.

Circuit switching is completely transparent. The sender and receiver can use any bit rate, format, or framing method they want to. The carrier does not know or care.

The difference between circuit switching and packet switching is summarized in Table 10.1.

Table 10.1 Difference between Circuit and Packet Switched Networks

Item	Circuit-switched	Packet-switched
Dedicated path	Yes	No
Bandwidth available	Fixed	Dynamic
Potentially wasted bandwidth	Yes	No
Store-and-forward transmission	No	Yes
Each packet follows the same route	Yes	No
Call setup	Required	Not needed
When can congestion occur	At setup time	On every packet
Charging	Per minute	Per packet

With packet switching, the carrier determines the basic parameters. A rough analogy between packet switching and circuit switching is road and railroad traffic respectively. In the former, the user determines the size, speed and the nature of the vehicle. But in the latter case, the railway authorities determine the size and the speed. It is this transparency that allows voice, data and fax to coexist within the phone system. As seen in lower part of Figure 10.3, packets are queued up for subsequent transmission.

With circuit switching, the charges are based on the distance and the time only and not on the amount of traffic. Whereas in the case of packet switching, the charges are made on the basis of the amount of data passed.

Packet switching is most efficient in transaction-oriented environments, in which occasional bursts of data are exchanged only during the small fraction of the time that processes are logically connected, or "in session" with one another. Circuit switching is most often associated with voice traffic.

An example of packet switching is an airline reservation system. Telephonic communication is an example of circuit switching.

10.3.3 Critical Job of a Network Node

Nodes in a data-communication network are comparable to the mechanical switches that shift railway trains from track to track. To find the destination of each data packet as it arrives, the node reads the control data located in a portion of the packet called the header. The node sends the packet out on the appropriate transmission path based on a calculation of the optimum route to that destination. The calculation may be carried out by each individual node or by a supervisory node that instructs subordinate node accordingly. Because nodes act as both senders and receivers, nodes are designed to perform several tasks to ensure the integrity of communications. For example, upon receiving a data packet, a node must inspect it for any electrical damage or distortion that may have occurred during transmission. If the packet has not arrived intact, the node requests the sending node or station to retransmit it. Conversely, before sending a packet to the node makes and stores a copy of it in case retransmission is necessary. To handle network traffic systematically, nodes hold data packets in temporary storage areas called buffers. Incoming packets queue up in a buffer while the node reads their headers and checks for damage; outgoing packets queue in a buffer along with other packets departing along the same path. Figure 10.7 illustrates the functioning of a node. It illustrates two way transmission paths which connect this node to two stations and to other nodes in the network. Each path is associated with two buffers, one for incoming and one for outgoing packets. Packets are held briefly in the buffers immediately upon arrival at the node and again before departure.

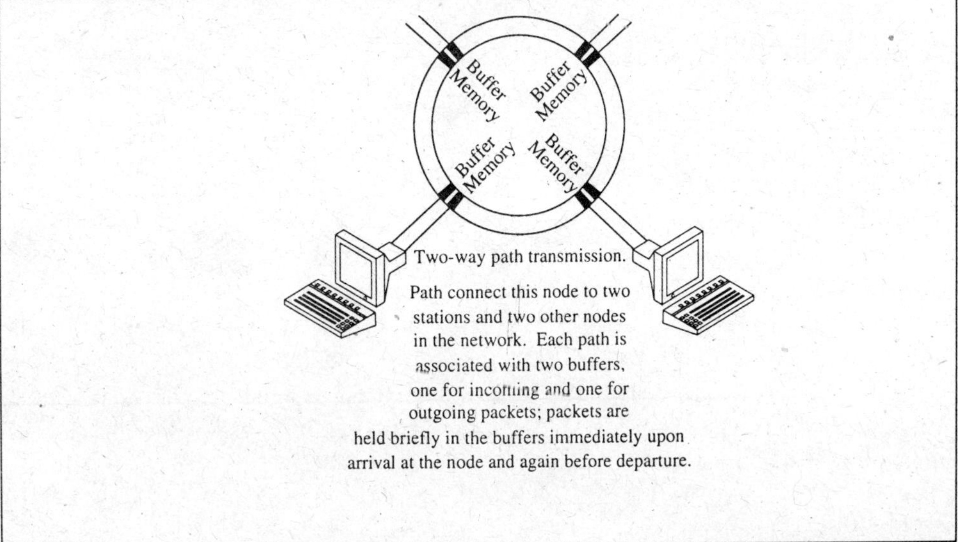

Figure 10.7 Function of a node in packet switching

10.3.4 Static Routing of Packets

Static routing is a packet switching technique which is more likely to malfunction and congestion but reduces a network's overhead by relieving the node of many computational responsibilities. Two types of static routing are available. These are *fixed routing* and *flooding*. These techniques are illustrated in Figures 10.8 and 10.9 respectively.

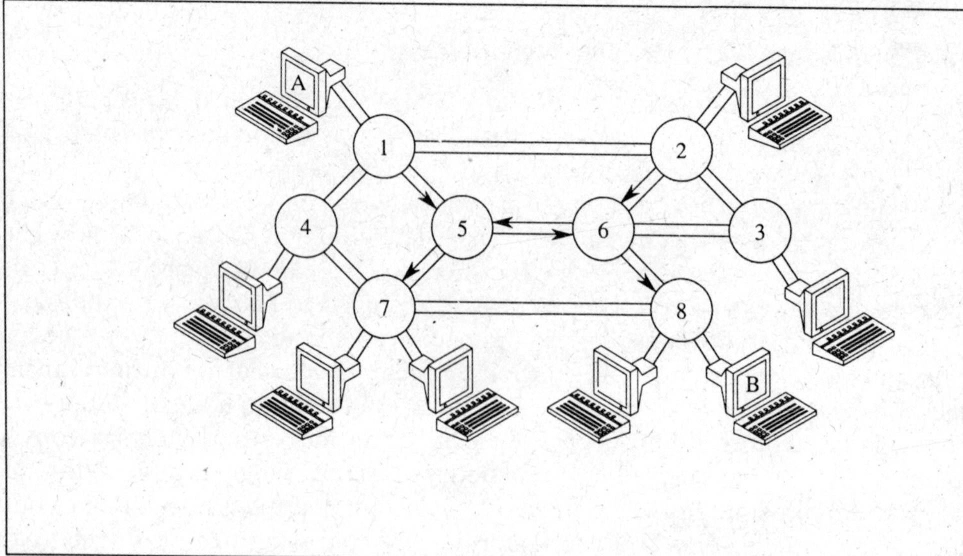

Figure 10.8
Fixed routing of data packet switching

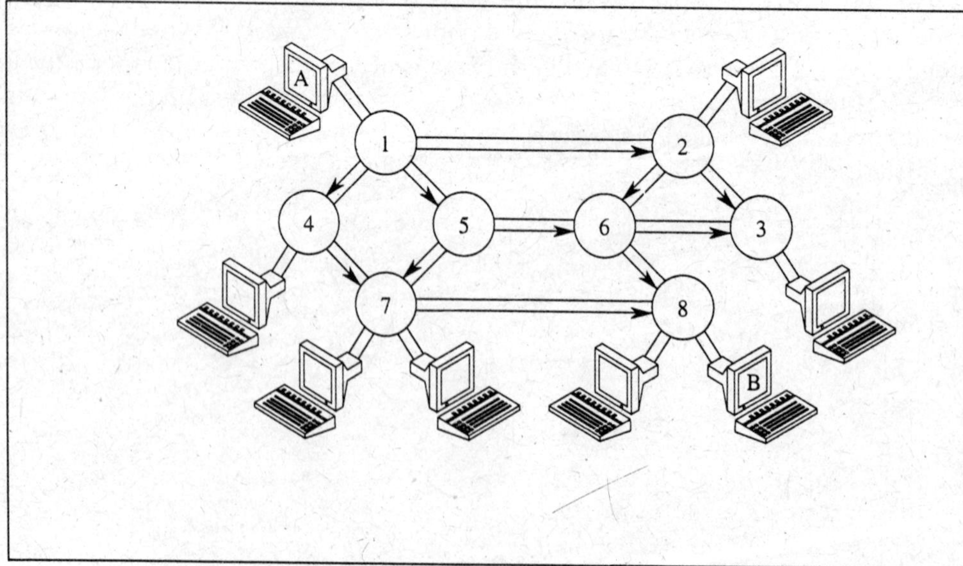

Figure 10.9
Flooding

Fixed Routing

With fixed routing, the network programmer establishes a directory of optimum routes to and from every point in the network. Each node simply reads a packet's header to learn its destination, then either looks up that destination in a stored directory or receives instructions from a supervisory node, as shown in the table in Figure 10.10.

Figure 10.10 Routing directory consulted by the supervisory node for routing packets from different nodes to destination

From Node \ To Node	1	2	3	4	5	6	7	8
1	-	2	2	4	5	5	5	5
2	1	-	3	1	6	6	6	6
3	2	2	-	2	6	6	6	6
4	1	1	1	-	7	7	7	7
5	1	6	6	7	-	6	7	6
6	5	2	3	5	5	-	5	8
7	5	5	5	4	6	5	-	8
8	6	6	6	7	6	6	7	-

Thus, every message and every packet of a message sent from Station A to Station B will follow the same route. For example, as seen in the Table in Figure 10.10, sending nodes are listed in the left most column and receiving nodes in the top row. If node 1 receives a packet destined for Node 8, the supervisory node consults the routing directory [Figure 10.10] and instructs Node 1 to send the packet to Node 5. Node 5 , in turn, is told to send the packet to Node 6 and so on. The supervisory node checks the directory for the route one node at a time.

Flooding

This technique is useful in cases where one message must go to all stations. Figure 10.9 illustrates the scheme. In a flooding scheme, each node obeys a sequence of instructions that might run as follows, for each packet it receives:

(a) Inspect the address in the packet's header.

(b) If this node is the packet's destination, forward it to the appropriate station.

(c) If this is not the destination, deduct 1 from the hop count. The value of the hop count is assigned in the header of every packet so that the packet can be routed only for a fixed number of times through the nodes.

(d) If the resulting value is greater than 0, make copies and send them along all routes except the one the packet arrived on.

(e) If the new value is zero, destroy the packet.

One obvious drawback to flooding is that the network can become clogged as the number of copies increases. One method for dealing with this problem is to program the destination node to accept only one copy of each packet, and to destroy duplicates as they arrive.

Transmission Delay

Transmission delay is the time required to send a message once transmission has started. For a message of a given length, transmission delay varies more or less directly with the distance between communicants and inversely with the bit rate. This applies to both packet and circuit switching.

Access Delay

Access delay is the time that a device, which is ready to send data, must wait before transmitting. In circuit switching, the bandwidth allocated to a connection is immediately and continuously available to the users following the initial circuit set-up delay. In packet switching, an access delay is incurred before the transmission of each packet of the system bandwidth is in use, or if other users waiting to send data have a higher access priority.

10.3.5 Virtual Circuit versus Circuit Switching

In a circuit-switching network, making a connection actually means a physical path is established from the source to the destination through the network. In a virtual circuit network, like the Asynchronous Transmission Mode (ATM), when a circuit is established, what really happens is that the route is chosen from source to destination, and all the switches (that is routers) along the way make table entries so they can route any packets on that virtual circuit. They also have the opportunity to reserve resources for the new circuit. (See Figure 10.11)

In this figure, single virtual circuit from the host PC H1 to Host PC H5 via switches (routers) A, E, C, D is established. The dotted line shows a virtual circuit. Such a circuit is defined by table entries inside the switches.

When a packet comes along, the switch inspects the packet's header to find out which virtual circuit it belongs to. Then it looks up that virtual circuit in its table to determine which communication line to send.

10.4 MESSAGE SWITCHING

In a message switch network, the central switch station accepts the traffic sent to it by the stations connected to the system. The messages are stored in the switch station's buffer memory and when a line is available, the data are forwarded to the appropriate station. Thus, message switching is referred to as a *store and forward method*. The benefit with message switching is that when the sending station has finished sending its traffic, it can go about its business, content that the message will eventually reach their destination. There is no waiting for an open line by the sending station.

Message switching is shown in part (b) of Figure 10.12. When this form of switching is used, no physical path is established in advance between sender and receiver. Instead, when the sender has a block of data to be sent, it is stored in the first switching office (i.e. router)

Figure 10.11
Establishing a virtual circuit

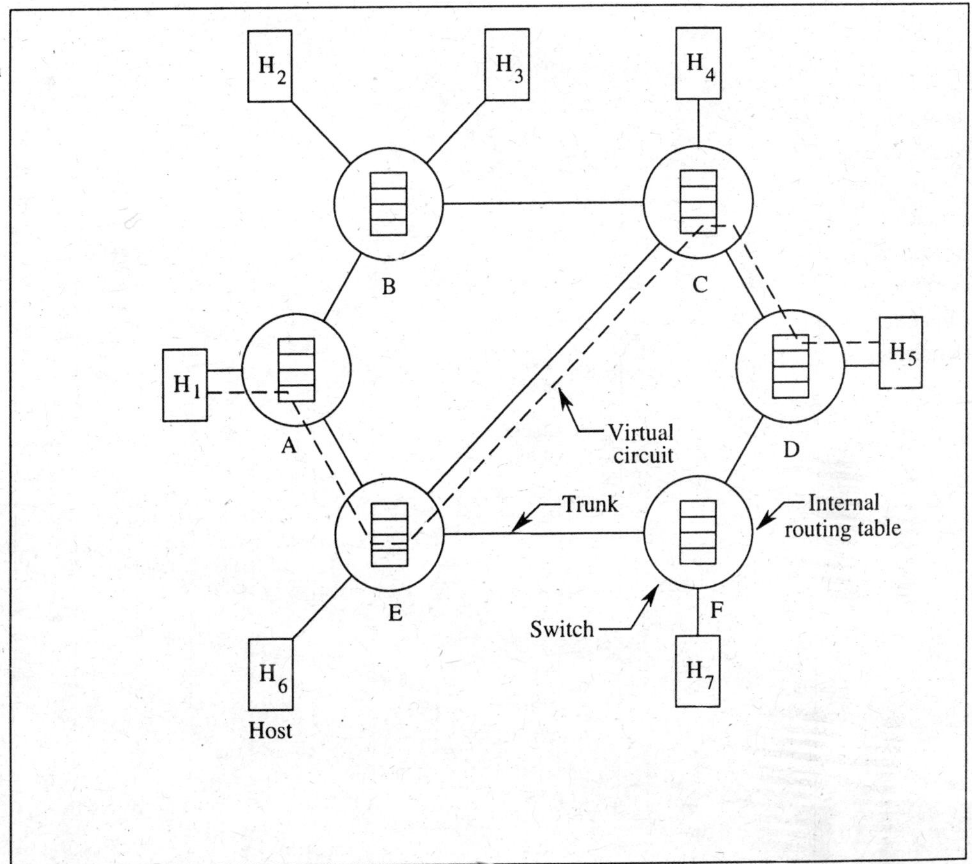

and then forwarded later, one hop at a time. Each block is received in its entirety, inspected for errors, and then retransmitted. A network using this technique is called a store-and-forward network. The first telecommunication systems used message switching for telegrams. The message was punched on paper tape off-line at the sending office, and then read in and transmitted over a communication line to the next office along the way, where it was punched out on paper tape. An operator there tore the tape off and read it in on one of the many tape readers, one per outgoing trunk. Such a switching office was called torn tape office.

With message switching, there is no limit of block size. A single block may tie up a router-router line for minutes, rendering message switching useless for interactive traffic. To get around these problems, packet switching was invented.

10.4.1 Shortcoming of Message Switching

The problems with message switching and the main difficulty with systems implementing it using message switching are the need to allocate a sufficiently large data buffer to hold incoming messages and the time it takes for a message to reach its destination. Fairly complicated software programs are required to manage the routing and storage of these

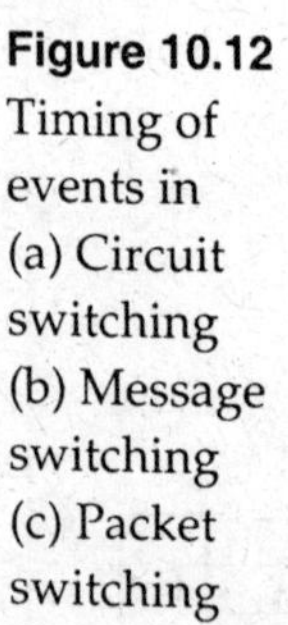

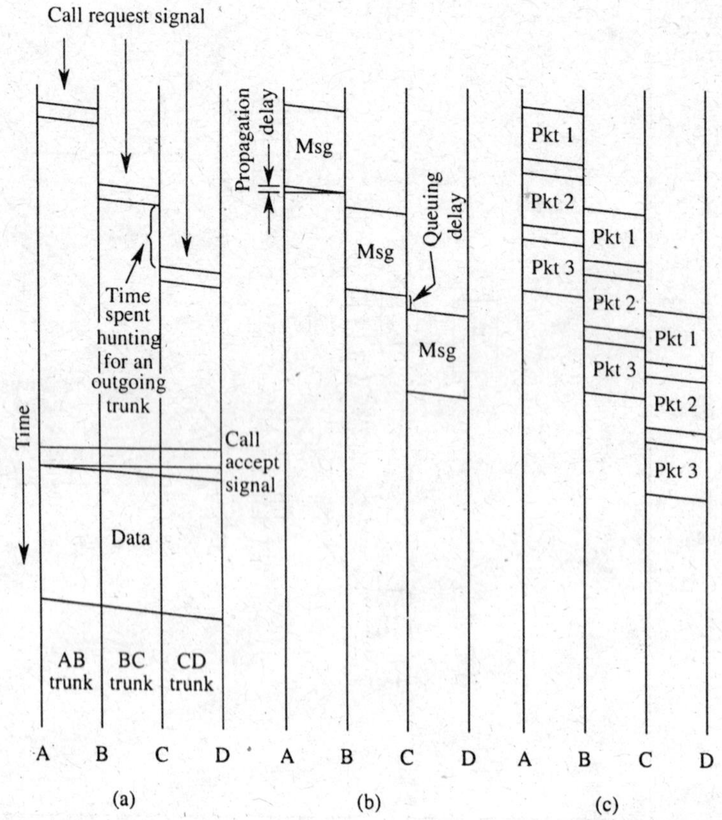

Figure 10.12 Timing of events in (a) Circuit switching (b) Message switching (c) Packet switching

messages. Moreover, if the system is very busy, a message could be delayed a long time before it finally is routed to its destination. Therefore, an alternate method is that allows shorter message "portions" to be sent to each station in a continuous sequence.

Packet switching networks place a tight upper limit on block size, allowing packets to be buffered in router main memory instead of on disk. By making sure that no user can monopolize any transmission line very long, packet-switching networks are well suited to handle interactive traffic. A further advantage of packet switching over message switching is illustrated in Figure 10.12 part (b) and part (c). The first packet of a multipacket message can be forwarded before the second one has fully arrived, reducing delay and improving throughput. For these reasons, computer networks are usually packet switched, occasionally circuit switched, but never message switched.

10.4.2 Hybrid Switching

In addition to the routine techniques of packet and circuit switching, there are other types called hybrid switching. These switching techniques are hybrid forms of circuit switching and packet switching.

In the circuit switching technique, the problem is a long connection time. This is because once a call has been set up, a dedicated physical path between communicating ends exists and continues to exist until the call is finished, even if the two parties are not communicating meanwhile. This drawback is overcome in a hybrid version of circuit switching called *fast connect circuit switching*. In this method, each line typed by a sender causes its microprocessor to "dial" the destination computer, send the typed line and then hang up. The same process is repeated for the second line and so on.

Similarly there exists a variation of packet switching also, called *time division switching*. In this method, as soon as the header of a packet is read, it is transmitted to its destination. Fixed sized packets and time synchronization is used for this purpose. This hybrid type of packet switching eliminates the need for buffer memory area used for storing incoming and outgoing packets.

REVIEW QUESTIONS WITH ANSWERS

Question Number 1 Explain the concept of circuit switching and message switching.

Answer

Circuit Switching

Circuit switching is a method of opening communication lines, as through the telephone system, by creating a physical link between the initiating and receiving parties. In circuit switching, the connection is made at a switching center, which physically connects the two parties and maintains an open line between them for as long as needed. Circuit switching is typically used in modern communications on the dial-up telephone networks, and it is also used on a smaller scale in privately maintained communications networks.

In other words, circuits switching is a method of networking in which communicating machines have exclusive use of the circuits linking them even during pauses when the circuit is momentarily idle until the circuit is released. To establish a circuit-switched connection, it is first necessary to find an available data path, site it, and dedicate it to the exclusive use of the connections. Circuit switching is most efficient for connections that carry a large amount of data relative to the data that must be exchanged during set-up.

Message Switching

Message switching is a technique used on some communication networks in which a message with appropriate address information, is routed through one or more intermediate switching stations before being sent to its destination. On a typical message-switching network, a central computer receives messages, stores them (usually briefly), determines their destination addresses, and then delivers them. Message switching enables a network both to regulate traffic and to use communications lines efficiently.

Question Number 2 Why circuit switching is preferred over packet switching in voice communication.

Answer Circuit switching is preferred over packet switching in voice communication because of the following reasons:

(i) The circuit switching statically reserves the required bandwidth in advance, whereas packet switching acquires and releases it as and when bandwidth is needed.

(ii) Circuit switching is controlled by a centralized hierarchical control mechanism with global knowledge of the network configuration.

(iii) Circuit switching is complex and completely compartmental. The sender and receiver can use any bit rate, format or framing method they want to use.

(iv) In circuit switching, the call charges are based on the distance and the time the call is made and not on the amount of data is transferred.

Hence, Circuit switching is normally confined to voice traffic.

Question Number 3 What are the difficulties faced in a circuit switched network?

Answer [*Refer to Section 10.2.1*]

Question Number 4 What are the two types of packets?

Answer [*Refer to Section 10.3.1*]

Question Number 5 Compare and contrast static and fixed routing of packets.

Answer [*Refer to Section 10.3.4*]

Question Number 6 Discuss the following

(a) Virtual Circuit Switching

(b) Message Switching and its drawbacks

Answer [*Refer to Sections 10.3.5 and 10.4*]

TEST PAPER

Time: 2 Hrs. Marks: 100

Note: Answer all questions.

1. What is meant by a switched network? Why do you prefer it over point-to-point network?
2. Explain following Switching techniques in brief:
   (i) Packet Switching
   (ii) Circuit Switching
   (iii) Message Switching
   (iv) Hybrid Switching

   [*GNDU, BIT Part–III, Paper–I, 2002 examination*]
3. What are the disadvantages of circuit switching? How does it compare with packet switching? Which switching technique is used in telephone networks?
4. Why packet switching is preferred over circuit switching in data communications? Explain using a diagram, the concept of fixed routing of data in packet switching.
5. Write short notes on the following:
   (a) Jobs performed by the network node.
   (b) Fixed routing of packets.

CHAPTER 11

Point to Point Protocols

11.1 INTRODUCTION

Point-to-Point Protocol (PPP) is an industry standard data-link layer protocol for wide area network (WAN) transmission that was developed in the early 1990s. PPP handles error detection, supports multiple protocols, allows IP addresses to be negotiated at connection time, permits authentication, etc.

PPP provides the following:

(a) A framing method that unambiguously indicates the end of one frame and the start of the next one. The frame format also does error detection.

(b) A link control protocol for bringing lines up, testing them, negotiating options, and bringing them down again gracefully when they are no longer needed. This protocol is called LCP (Link Control Protocol).

(c) A way to negotiate network-layer options that is independent of the network layer protocol to be used. The method chosen is to have a different Network Control Protocol (NCP) for each network layer supported.

☞ Point-to-Point Protocol (PPP) allows Remote Access Service (RAS) products and devices from different vendors to interoperate for WAN communication.

11.1.1 What is Remote Access?

Remote access is any networking technology that gives users access to essential network services from remote locations. Remote access to a company network can be either dial-up access through a modem or dedicated access through a leased line. Remote access typically gives remote users access to the following services on a company network:

(a) File and print services

(b) Client/server applications such as database applications

(c) Applications for remote network administration

Figure 11.1 shows the connection of a remote PC for accessing the remote server or printer for the data collection or printing.

There are two basic types of remote access:

(a) Remote control

(b) Remote node

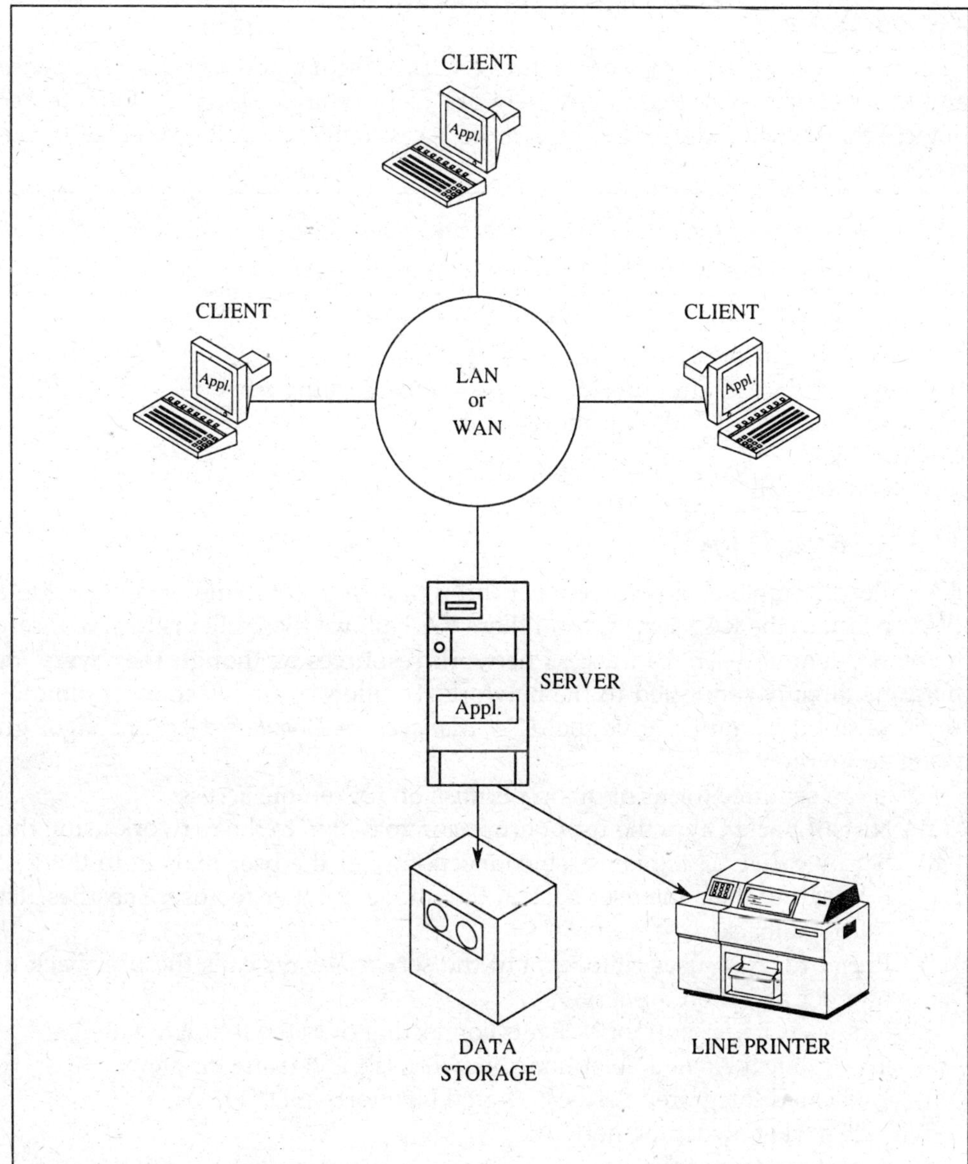

Figure 11.1 Remote access to a server / printer

Remote control

Remote control uses a program such as *pcAnywhere* to take control of the console of a computer remotely. Administrators generally use this method to troubleshoot server problems remotely. However, because the remote connection is often made through a relatively slow analog modem, the bandwidth restriction often makes remote control access slow and jerky. Remote control access provides high security, saves on hardware and licensing costs, and is simple to implement on a network.

Remote node

Remote node uses a remote access device to provide a gateway for users to access file, print, and other services on a company network from remote locations. Remote access gateway devices can be computers running remote access software and connected through multiport serial boards.

☞ A computer that makes remote access possible is generally called a *remote access server* (RAS), while a router that supports remote access is generally called an *access server*.

Remote node devices include following features:

(a) Network Address Translation (NAT)
(b) Dynamic Host Configuration Protocol (DHCP) support
(c) Password-based authentication
(d) Callback
(e) Basic firewall

11.1.2 What is RAS?

RAS allows remote clients to connect through a telephone line or other wide area network (WAN) link to the RAS server; from there RAS allows those clients to access resources on the network. Remote users can access network resources as though they were logged on to a machine directly connected to the network. To allow a user to connect remotely to the RAS server, use the administrative tool *User Manager for Domains*. User manager grants the user *dialin* permission.

You can set three forms of dialin permission for remote access:

(a) **No call back:** Gives the user permission to dial in to the network using the RAS server.
(b) **Set by caller:** Terminates the connection after the user dials in to the RAS server. The RAS server dials the user back at the phone number the user specifies. This function is called callback.
(c) **Preset to:** Also uses callback, but the server always calls the user back using a phone number preset on the server.

Windows NT RAS supports clients connecting over the following media:

(a) The Public Switched Telephone Network (PSTN) using modems.
(b) Dedicated Integrated Services Digital Network (ISDN) lines.
(c) X.25 packet-switching networks.
(d) A null modem cable.

11.2 TRANSMISSION STATES

The transmission states means how the transmission can be carried out. These can be of two types:

(a) Asynchronous Communications
(b) Synchronous Communications

11.2.1 Asynchronous Communications

Asynchronous mode refers to a series of events that take place which are not synchronized one after the other for example, the time interval between event A and B in Figure 11.2 is not the same as B and C.

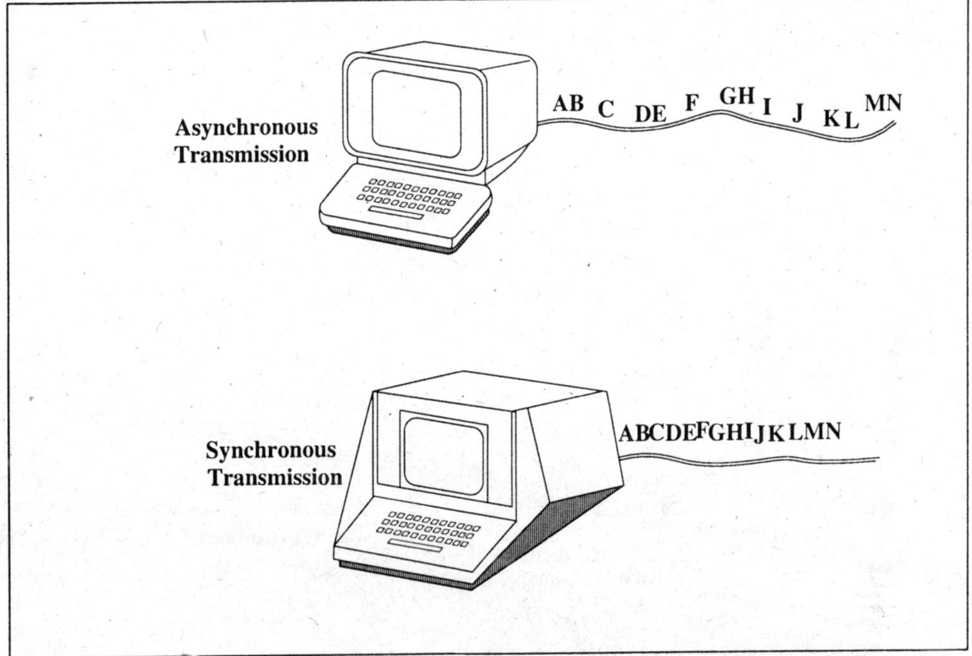

Figure 11.2 Asynchronous and synchronous transmissions

☞ Asynchronous transmission is often referred to as start-stop transmission because of the nature that the sender can send a character at any time convenient and the receiver will accept it.

Aysnchronous communication lines remain in an idle state until the hardware on the line is ready to transmit. Since the line is idle, a series of bits has to be sent to the receiving node to notify it that there are data coming. When data are finished, the node has to be notified that the transmission is complete and to go back to an idle state, hence the STOP bits are to be sent. This pattern continues for the duration of the time the link is operative. This is the characteristic of many terminals when on a terminal, the time spent between successive keystrokes would vary. Thus in an asynchronous transmission, data are transmitted character by character at irregular intervals.

11.2.2 Synchronous Communications

Synchronous devices usually do not use Start and Stop bits, so coordination between the two nodes i.e. the sender and the receiver is handled differently. In synchronous communications, there are two "channels"—one for data and another for link Synchronization. The channel for synchronization uses the integral clock in the hardware for link synchronization between the two nodes. When one of the nodes is ready to transmit data, a unique combination of bits called a *sync* character is sent to the receiver. Since the first character will probably get trashed, a second one usually follows to ensure that synchronization is complete.

Synchronous mode of data transmission involves blocking a group of characters in somewhat the same way records are blocked on magnetic tape. (See Figure 11.3)

Figure 11.3 Modes of Data Transmission

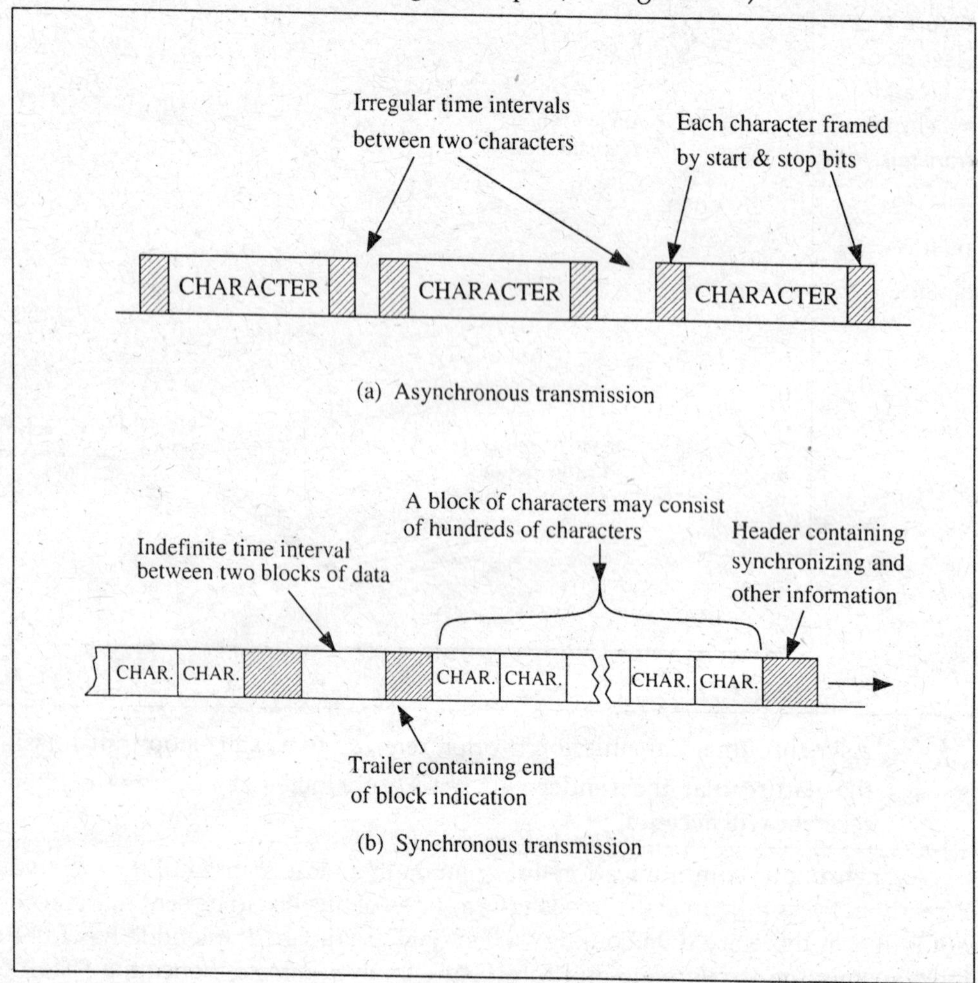

Each block is then framed by header and trailer information. The header consists of synchronizing information which is used by the receiving device to set its clock in synchronism with the sending end clock. The header also contains information to identify sender and receiver. Following the header is a block of characters that contains the actual message to be transmitted. The number of characters may vary and may consist of hundreds of characters. The message characters in the block are terminated by a trailer. The trailer contains an end of message character followed by a check character to aid detection of any transmission error. Thus, with synchronous transmission entire blocks of characters are framed and transmitted together.

11.2.3 Comparison between Asynchronous and Synchronous Transmission

Synchronous communications tend to be more expensive than asynchronous as the hardware involved is more costly due to integral clocking mechanism that have to be used as well as more sophisticated engineering efforts. Yet, synchronous communication can eliminate up to 20% of associated overheads inherent in asynchronous communications. This allows greater throughput of data and better error detection.

☞ Synchronous transmission is well suited to remote communication between a computer and such devices as buffered card readers and printers. It is also used for computer to computer communications.

Advantages and Disadvantages

The primary advantage of synchronous transmission is its efficiency. Not only does it eliminate the need for individual start-stop bits on each character, but much higher data rates can be used than with asynchronous transmission. The period between blocks is kept small and the block itself is sent at nearly the maximum line speed. This ensures efficient utilization of the transmission line.

The main disadvantage of synchronous transmission is the need for local buffer storage at the two ends of the line to assemble blocks and also the need for accurately synchronized clocks at both ends. Therefore synchronous equipment usually costs more.

Asynchronous transmission is well suited to many keyboard type terminals. The advantage of this method is that it does not require any local storage at the terminal or the computer as transmission takes place character by character. Hence it is cheaper to implement.

The main disadvantage of asynchronous transmission is that the transmission line is idle during the time intervals between transmitting characters. If they are short, this is not bad because line cost would be low and idle time not expensive. Even though less efficient than synchronous transmission, it is also used with devices such as card readers and printers to reduce cost.

11.2.4 Efficiency of Data Transmission in Synchronous and Asynchronous Modes

Asynchronous data incorporates the use of extra framing bits to establish the start and ending (stop) of a data character word. A receiver responds to the data stream when it detects a *start bit*. A data character is decoded and defined after the *stop bit* is received and confirmed. Asynchronous data are easier to detect and synchronize, but the efficiency of data transmission is reduced by the addition of framing bits as overhead (no message data) bits. A comparison of a single character using the two communication modes is as follows.

For comparison, the ASCII code of the letter E (100 0101) is used. The order of transmission is to send the Least Significant Bit (LSB) first. The number of framing bits used for asynchronous data varies depending on the stations in the communication link. For example, suppose we use 1 start and 2 stop bits. This adds 3 additional bits to the character word. Hence total 10 bits are required to send the letter **E** using asynchronous data. However, in the case of synchronous transmission, only 7 bits are required for transmission of the character **E**.

The efficiency to transmission is defined as the ratio of the number of message bits to the total number of transmitted bits.

or

$$\text{efficiency} = \frac{\text{data bits}}{\text{total bits}} \times 100\%$$

As seen in the above example, for the letter E, i.e. 1000101, in the synchronous mode, all bits carry message, so 100% efficiency is there.

However, in asynchronous mode, E is transmitted by using 7 bits as message and another three bits (one start bit and two stop bits) totalling 10 bits. So the efficiency is calculated as:

$$\text{efficiency} = \frac{\text{data bits i.e. 7}}{\text{total bits i.e. 10}} \times 100\% = 70\%$$

Example 1

On a transmission channel, 600-character message using ASCII 7 bit code is used. For synchronous data stream, there are two SYN characters and a single error-detection character is added.

In the case of asynchronous data transmission, there is one start bit and one stop bit and a single error-detection character is added.

Calculate the efficiency of transmission in the above two types of transmission modes.

Solution

For Synchronous Mode of Transmission

Total number of characters transmitted = 600 + 2(i.e. SYN. characters) + 1 (error detection character)

= 603 characters

= 603 × 7 or 4221 bits

But number of bits carrying actual message = 600 characters or 600 × 7 bits

$$\text{Hence efficiency} = \frac{4200}{4221} \times 100\% = 99.5\%$$

For Asynchronous Mode of Transmission

For every character in this mode, there is a start and a stop bit. So for each character, you need to send 9 bits [7 + 1 (i.e. start bit) + 1 (i.e. stop bit)].

Total number of characters to be sent = 600 + 1 (as error detection character)

or = 601 × 9 bits or 5409 bits.

Total number of message bits = 600 × 7 or 4200 bits.

$$\text{efficiency} = \frac{4200}{5409} \times 100\% = 77.65\%$$

11.3 POINT TO POINT PROTOCOL (PPP) LAYERS

PPP supports the transmission of network packets over a serial point-to-point link by specifying framing mechanisms for encapsulating network protocols, such as Internet Protocol

(IP), Internetwork Packet Exchange (IPX), or NetBEUI, into PPP frames. PPP encapsulation is based on the High-level Data Link Control (HDLC) derived from the Mainframe environment. These PPP frames can be transmitted over serial transmission lines such as Plain Old Telephone Service (POTS), Integrated Services Digital Network (ISDN), and packet-switched networks such as X.25.

☞ PPP includes an extensible Link Control Protocol (LCP) for establishing, tearing down, and testing data-link WAN connections, as well as a number of Network Control Protocols (NCPs) for establishing and configuring network communication using each network protocol.

PPP supports a number of authentication schemes, such as Password Authentication Protocol (PAP) and Challenge Handshake Authentication Protocol (CHAP).

A typical dial-up session using PPP is completely automated and requires no real-time user input. It has four stages:

(a) Link establishment
(b) User authentication
(c) Callback
(d) Configuration

Each one is given in the following Sections.

11.3.1 Link establishment

PPP uses LCP to establish and maintain a PPP link over a serial transmission line. LCP frames are sent over the data link to test its integrity and establish the link.

11.3.2 User authentication

PPP uses one of several authentication protocols, including PAP, CHAP, and Microsoft Challenge Handshake Authentication Protocol (MS-CHAP).

11.3.3 Callback

PPP Callback Control (Microsoft's implementation of PPP) uses Callback Control Protocol (CBCP) if it is configured.

11.3.4 Configuration

NCPs (Network Control Protocols) are used to establish network connections, perform compression and encryption, lease IP addresses using Dynamic Host Configuration Protocol (DHCP), and so on. NCP frames are sent over the link to establish a network connection between the PPP server and the remote PPP client.

☞ Point to Point Protocol is superior to the older Serial Line Internet Protocol (SLIP) in that it offers error correction and dynamic negotiation without user intervention. It supports multiple network protocols simultaneously, and is faster.

PPP is the basis for the Point-to-Point Tunneling Protocol (PPTP) and the Layer 2 Tunneling Protocol (L2TP), which can be used to create virtual private networks (VPNs). PPP is supported by Microsoft Windows 2000, Windows NT, Windows 95, and Windows 98 and is the default setting for Network and Dial-up Connections, Remote Access Service, and connectivity to the Internet.

11.3.5 What is Data Link Control (DLC)?

Data Link Control is related to an international standard protocol called IEEE 802.2. Many organisations employing token ring use DLC to allow their PC workstations to talk to Mainframe gateways. Another common use of this protocol is to use it to communicate with network printers.

The data link layer performs the following functions:

(a) To provide a well-defined service interface to the network layer, determining how the bits of the physical layer are grouped into frames.

(b) To deal with transmission errors and regulating the flow of frames so that slow receivers are not bogged down by fast senders.

11.4 LINK CONTROL PROTOCOL (LCP)

Link Control Protocol (LCP) operates at the data-link layer (layer 2) of the Open Systems Interconnection (OSI) reference model for networking and is considered a data-link layer protocol. During establishment of a PPP communication session, LCP establishes the link, configures PPP options, and tests the quality of the line connection between the PPP client and PPP server. LCP automatically handles encapsulation format options and varies packet sizes over PPP communication links. LCP also negotiates the type of authentication protocol used to establish the PPP session. Different authentication protocols are supported for satisfying the security needs of different environments. LCP can negotiate several authentication protocols.

11.5 AUTHENTICATION

Authentication is the process of validating users' credentials to allow them access to resources on a network. Different types of authentication protocols are explained in the following sub-sections.

11.5.1 Password Authentication Protocol (PAP)

PAP Transmits passwords in clear text using a two-way handshake. Password Authentication Protocol (PAP) is not a secure form of authentication because the user's credentials are passed over the link in *unencrypted* form. If the password of a remote client using PAP has been compromised, the authentication server can be attacked using replay attacks or remote client impersonation.

Working of PAP

PAP uses a two-way handshake to perform authentication. Once the PPP link is established using the Link Control Protocol (LCP), the PPP client sends a username and password to the PPP server. The server uses its own authentication scheme and user database to authenticate the user, and if the authentication is successful, the server sends an acknowledgment to the client. PAP is typically used only if the remote access server and the remote client cannot negotiate any higher form of authentication. The remote client initiates the PAP session when it attempts to connect to the PPP server or router. PAP merely identifies the client to the PPP server; the server then authenticates the client based on whatever authentication scheme and user database are implemented on the server.

11.5.2 Shiva PAP (SPAP)

This a vendor-specific implementation of PAP.

11.5.3 Challenge Handshake Authentication Protocol (CHAP)

Challenge Handshake Authentication Protocol (CHAP) is one of several authentication schemes used by the Point-to-Point Protocol (PPP). It is a serial transmission protocol for wide area network (WAN) connections. CHAP encrypts the transmitted password, while PAP does not.

 CHAP is an encrypted authentication scheme in which the unencrypted password is not transmitted over the network.

Working of CHAP

A typical CHAP session during the PPP authentication process works as follows:

(a) A client connects to a network access server (NAS) and requests authentication.
(b) The server challenges the client by sending a session ID and an arbitrary string.
(c) The client uses the MD5 one-way hashing algorithm and sends the server the user-name, along with an encrypted form of the server's challenge, session ID, and client password.
(d) A session is established between the client and the server. To guard against replay attacks, the challenge string is chosen arbitrarily for each authentication attempt. To protect against remote client impersonation, CHAP sends repeated, random interval challenges to the client to maintain the session.

11.5.4 Microsoft Challenge Handshake Authentication Protocol (MS-CHAP)

It is an encrypted authentication scheme used in wide area network (WAN) communication. Microsoft Challenge Handshake Authentication Protocol (MS-CHAP) is supported by the Point-to-Point Protocol (PPP) used by the Remote Access Service (RAS) of Microsoft Windows NT, and the Point-to-Point Tunneling Protocol (PPTP) used by the Routing and Remote Access Service (RRAS) of Windows NT Service Pack 4 and later and by Windows 2000 and Windows 98.

Working of Microsoft CHAP

MS-CHAP is similar to the Challenge Handshake Authentication Protocol (CHAP) that encrypts password information before transmitting it over a PPP link using the industry standard MD5 one-way encryption method. It differs from CHAP in the following ways:

(a) The MS-CHAP challenge response packet is in a format designed specifically for Windows platforms.
MS-CHAP does not require the use of plaintext or reversibly encrypted passwords the way CHAP does. Instead, the RAS server uses the MD4 hash of the password for validating the challenge response.

Both the client and the authenticating server generate independent initial keys for data encryption. For example, to establish a PPP session between a Windows NT RAS server and a Windows dial-up networking client, the client first requests authentication from the RAS server. The RAS server then sends the client, a challenge consisting of a session identifier and an arbitrary string of characters called the challenge string. The client returns a response to the server that consists of the username plus a one-way encryption of the password, session identifier, and challenge string. The RAS server examines the response and determines whether to authenticate the client.

11.6 NETWORK CONTROL PROTOCOL (NCP)

After the link has been established and authentication (if any) has been successful, the connection goes to the networking state. In this state, PPP uses another protocol called Network Control Protocol (NCP).

Network Control Protocol is a set of control protocols to allow the encapsulation of data coming from network layer protocols, such as IP, IPX and appleTalk in the PPP frame.

11.6.1 Internetwork Protocol Control Protocol (IPCP)

IPCP is the set of packets that establish and terminate a network layer connection for IP packets.

REVIEW QUESTIONS WITH ANSWERS

Question Number 1 List out the relative advantages and disadvantages of asynchronous and synchronous modes of data transmission.

Answer **Advantages of Synchronous Mode of data transmission**

(a) Efficiency of transmission of data is high because higher data rate can be used as compared to asynchronous transmission without the need of start and stop bits.

(b) The period between blocks of data is kept small and block itself is sent at the maximum line speed in synchronous transmission, hence efficient utilization of transmission lines.

Disadvantages of Synchronous Mode of data transmission

(a) There is a need for local buffer storage at the two ends of the line to assemble blocks of data.

(b) The need for accurately synchronized clocks at both ends.

(c) Because of accurate synchronization, the cost of the equipment using synchronous mode of transmission is high.

Question Number 2 What do you mean by Remote Control and Remote Node?

Answer [*Refer to Section 11.1.1*]

Question Number 3 Write a short note on the following.

(a) DLC (Data link control)

(b) LCP (Link Control Protocol)

(c) PAP (Password Authentication Protocol)

(d) CHAP (Challenge Handshake Authentication Protocol)

Answer (a) [*Refer to Section 11.3.5*]

Answer (b) [*Refer to Section 11.4*]

Answer (c) [*Refer to Section 11.5.3*]

Answer (d) [*Refer to Section 11.5.1*]

Question Number 3 Discuss the functions performed by Point to Point Protocol layers

Answer [*Refer to Section 11.3*]

Question Number 3 What do you mean by Data Link Control (DCL)? Write a note on Link Control Protocol.

Answer [*Refer to Section 11.3.5 and 11.4*]

TEST PAPER

Time: 3 Hrs. Marks: 100

Note: Answer all questions.

1. a) Which of the OSI layers handles each of the following?
   i) breaking the transmitted packets into frames
   ii) determining which route through the subnet to use
   iii) providing synchronization
2. What is the principal difference between connectionless communication and connection-oriented communication?
3. In asynchronous transmission how does a receiving device determine the presence of a start bit?
4. Compare and contrast the delivery of data units in the data link layer, network layer and transport layer.
5. Many of the duties of the transport layer (e.g., flow control and reliable delivery) are also handled by the data link layer. Is this a duplication of effort. Explain your answer.

CHAPTER 12

Integrated Services Digital Network (ISDN)

12.1 HISTORICAL OUTLINE

In 1984, anticipating considerable user demand for an end-to-end digital service (which at that time was part digital and part analog), the world's telephone companies got together under the backing of CCITT and agreed to build a new, fully digital, circuit-switched telephone system by the early part of the 21st Century. This new system, called ISDN, has its primary goal to integrate voice and non-voice services. It is already implemented in many parts of the world and is slowly growing.

☞ ISDN is a set of protocols that combine digital telephony and data transport services. The whole idea is to digitize the telephone network to permit the transmission of audio, video and text over existing telephone lines.

The goal of ISDN is to form a wide area network that provides universal end to end connectivity over digital media. This can be done by integrating all of the separate transmission services into one without adding new links or subscriber lines. The main concept behind ISDN is the digital bit pipe, a conceptual pipe between the customer and the carrier through which bits flow. The bits can flow from a digital telephone, or a digital computer or a digital FAX. All bits flow through the pipe in both directions. The ISDN bit pipe supports multiple communications interleaved by time division multiplexing. CCITT has standardized the following combinations.

(a) Basic access: 2 B + 1 D

(b) Primary access: 23 B + 1 D (in USA and Japan) or 30 B + 1 D (in Europe)

Here B consists of 64 kbps digital PCM channel for voice or data and D consists of 16 kbps digital channel for internal ISDN signaling.

In addition, 'A' channel consists of 4 kHz analog telephone channel and 'C' channel consists of 8 or 16 kbps digital channel. These two are shown in Figure 12.1.

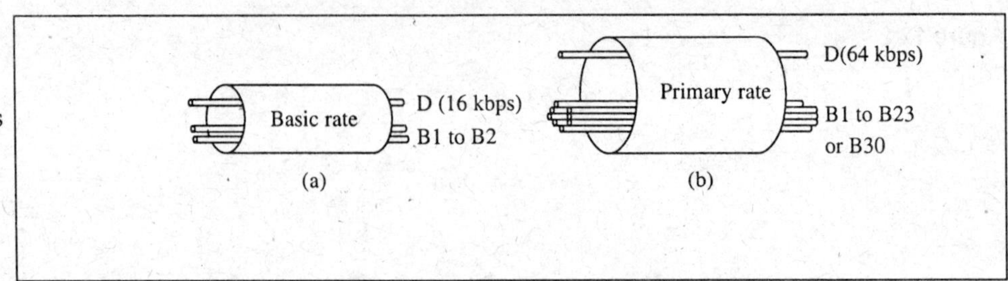

Figure 12.1
(a) Basic access digital pipe
(b) Primary access digital pipe

12.2 SERVICES

The features likely to be provided by ISDN system are:

(a) Telephones with multiple buttons for instant call setup to arbitrary telephones anywhere in the world will be available.
(b) Another feature is that telephones will display the caller's telephone number, name, and address on a display screen while ringing.
(c) Yet another feature is that it allows the telephone to be connected to a computer, so that the caller's database record is displayed on the screen as the call comes in. For example, a stockbroker could arrange to display the caller's portfolio on the screen.
(d) Other advanced voice services include call forwarding and conference calls worldwide.
(e) Advanced non-voice services are remote electricity meter reading, on-line medical, burglar and smoke alarms that automatically call the hospital, police, or fire department, respectively and give their address to speed up response.

12.2.1 Integrated Digital Services

The ISDN provides fully integrated digital services to users. These services fall into three categories. (See Figure 12.2).

(a) Bearer services
(b) Teleservices
(c) Supplementary services

Bearer Services

Bearer services provide the means to transfer information (voice, data and video) among the users without the network manipulating the content of that information. The network does not need to process the information and therefore does not change the content. Bearer services belong to the first three layers of the OSI model and are well defined in the ISDN standard. They can be provided using circuit-switched, packet-switched, or cell-switched network.

Teleservices

In teleservicing, the network may change or process the contents of the data. These services correspond to layers 4-7 of the OSI model. *Teleservices* rely on the facilities of the bearer services and are designed to accommodate complex user needs without the user having to be aware of the details of the process. Teleservices include telephony, teletex, telefax, videotex, telex and teleconferencing. These services are yet to become standards.

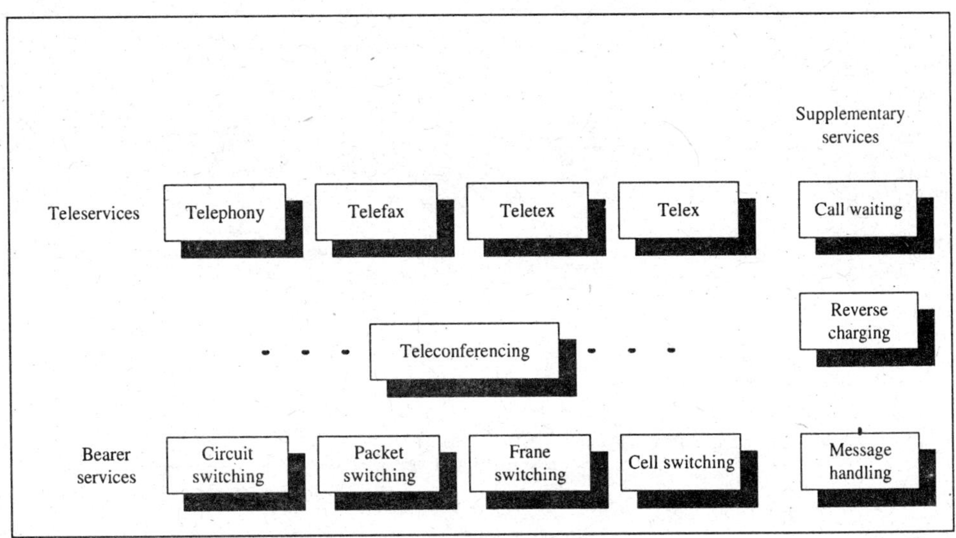

Figure 12.2 ISDN services

Supplementary Services

Supplementary Services are those services that provide additional functionality to the bearer services and teleservices. Examples of these services are reverse charging, call waiting and message handling.

12.3 SUBSCRIBER'S ACCESS

Two methods of access of ISDN have been defined—*Basic access and Primary access.* ISDN Basic access deals with the connection and operation of individual telephone instruments and terminals to the digital network. Primary access governs the methods by which many Basic access subscribers can be connected to the network over a common line facility.

Figure 12.3 part (a) shows the normal configuration for a home or small business. The carrier places a network terminating device, NT1, on the customer's premises and connects it to the ISDN exchange in the carrier's office, several meters away using the twisted pair that was previously used to connect to the telephone. The NT1 box has a connector on it into which a passive bus cable can be inserted. Up to eight ISDN telephones, terminals alarms, and other devices can be connected to the cable, similar to the way devices are connected to a LAN. From the customer's point of view, the network boundary is the connection on NT1.

Figure 12.4 illustrates the difference between the conventional telephone basic access and the ISDN access system.

☞ Under the Basic access format, up to three channels can be used to provide simultaneous data streams.

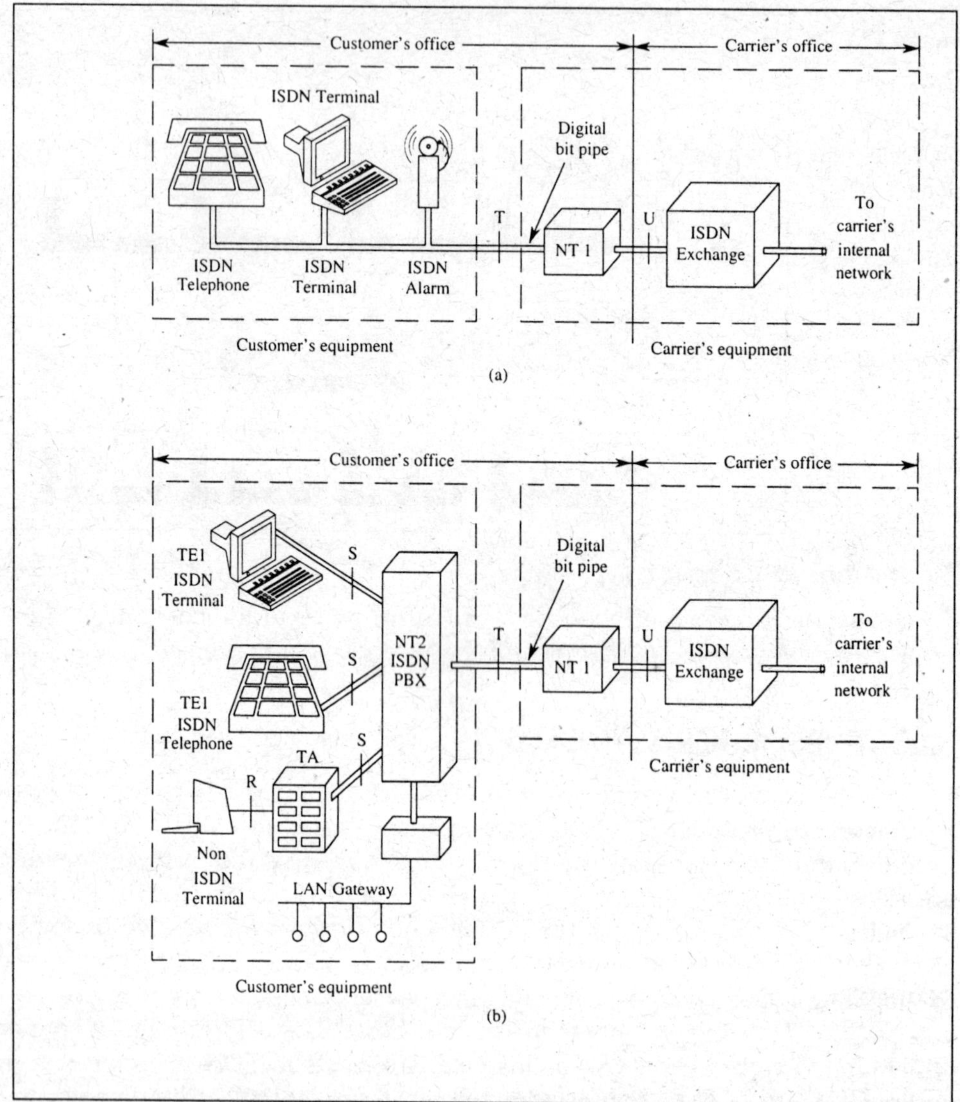

Figure 12.3 (a) ISDN system for home use (b) ISDN system with a PBX for use in a large business

12.3.1 Primary Access

Primary access is a multiplexing arrangement whereby a grouping of Basic access users share a common line facility. Primary access is designed to directly connect a PABX or high speed networking devices to the ISDN network.

Part (b) of Figure 12.4 illustrates ISDN system with a PBX for use in a large business. This access method eliminates the need to provide individual Basic access lines when a group of terminal devices shares a common PABX that could be connected directly to an ISDN network via a single high-speed line. Because of the different methods used to multiplex digitized voice conversations between telephone company offices in North America and Europe, two Primary access standards have been developed.

Figure 12.4
(a) Conventional telephone exchange
(b) Using ISDN basic access

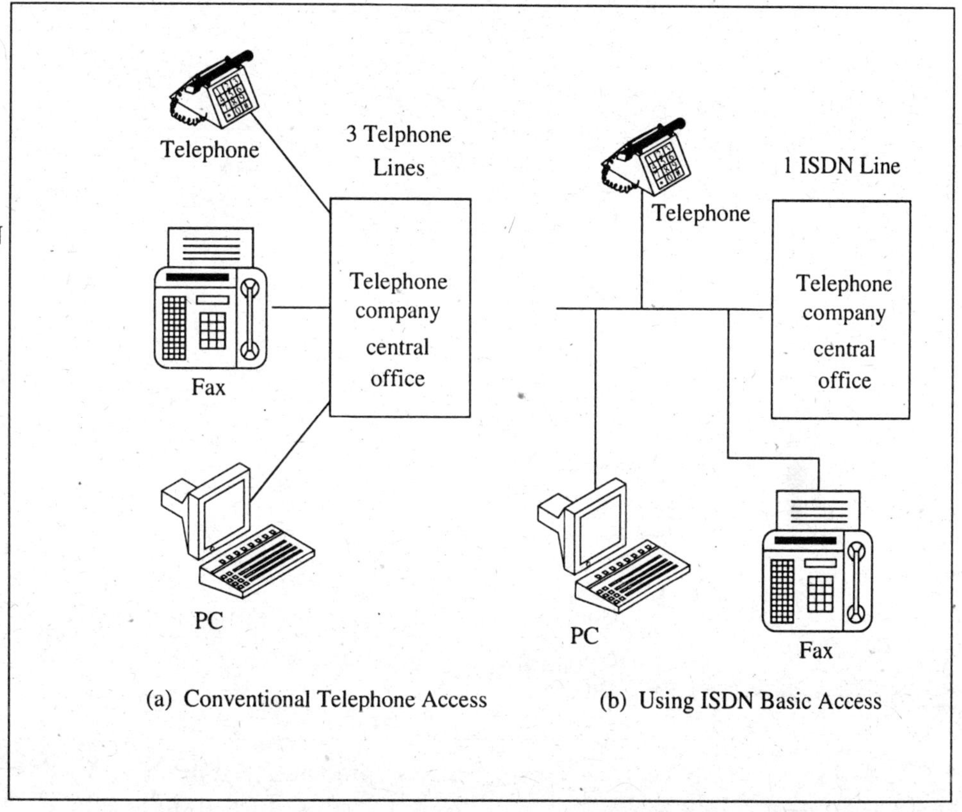

In North America, Primary access consists of a grouping of 23 B channels and one D channel to provide a 1.544 Mbps composite data rate. This data rate is more commonly known as the standard T1 carrier data rate. The D channel is for control and signaling, and each B channel, operates at 64 Kbps. Multiplexing 24 channels by 64 Kbps results in a data rate of 1.536 Mbps, which is precisely 8 Kbps fewer than the T1 carrier's 1.544 Mbps data rate.

A North American T1 carrier consists of 24 digitized voice channels. Each voice channel is sampled 8,000 times per second, and 8 bits are used to encode the digitized value of each sample. Thus, a 64 Kbps data rate is required to transmit a digitized voice conversation. To permit synchronization of the T1 signal, a single bit, known as a *framing bit*, is added to the data stream. The framing bit represents 24 channels, as illustrated in Figure 12.5. One sample of 24 channels of digitized voice is therefore represented by 193 bits. Because the sampling occurs 8,000 times per second, the data rate to a T1 carrier is 193 × 8,000, or 1.544 Mbps.

In Europe, the T1 carrier consists of 30 digitized voice channels and 2 separate signaling channels. Because each channel operates at 64 Kbps, the resulting T1 carrier data rate is 2.048 Mbps.

ISDN Standard

The ISDN standard defines three channel types, each with a different transmission rate: bearer channels, data channels, and hybrid channels (See Table 12.1).

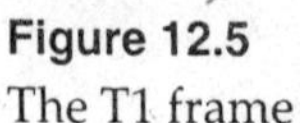

Figure 12.5
The T1 frame

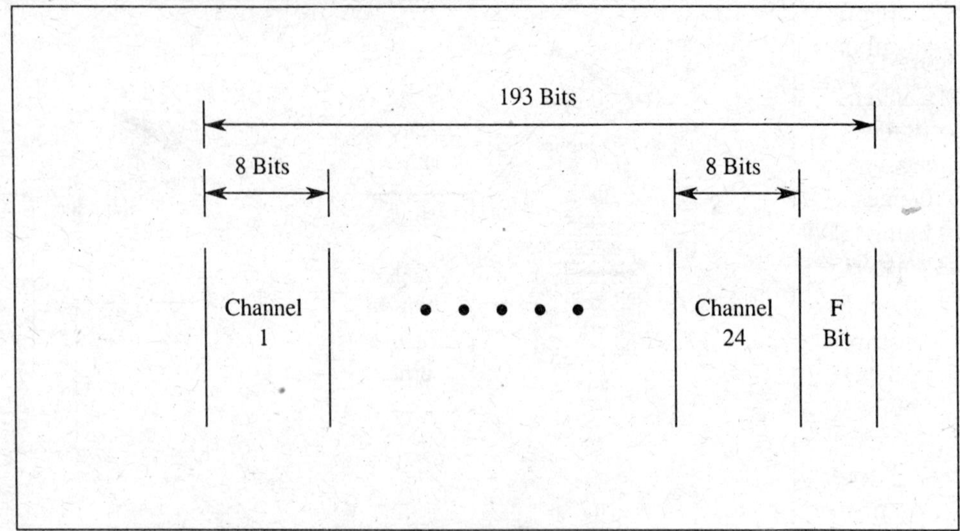

Table 12.1 Channel Rates

Channel	Data Rate (Kbps)
Bearer (B)	64
Data (D)	16, 64
Hybrid (H)	384, 1536, 1920

B Channels A *bearer channel* (*B channel*) is defined at a rate of 64 Kbps. It is the basic user channel and can carry any type of digital information in full-duplex mode as long as the required transmission rate does not exceed 64 Kbps. For example, a B channel can be used to carry digital data, digitized voice, or other low data-rate information. Several transmissions can be accommodated at once if the signals are multiplexed first. Multiplexed transmission of this sort, however, must be destined for a single recipient. The B channel carries transmission end-to-end. It is not designed to demultiplex a stream midway in order to separate and divert transmission to more than one recipient.

D Channels A *data channel* (*D channel*) can be either 16 or 64 Kbps, depending on the needs of the user. Although the name says *data*, the primary function of a D channel is to carry control signaling for the B channel.

All the transmission protocols we have examined so far, use in-channel (*in-band*) *signaling*. Control information (such as call establishment, ringing, call interrupt, or synchronization) is carried by the same channel that carriers the message data. The ISDN separates control signals onto a channel of their own, the D channel. Thus, the D channel carries the control signaling for all of the channels in a given path, using a method called common-channel (*out-of-band*) *signaling*.

In this mechanism, a subscriber uses the D channel to connect to the network and secure a B channel connection. The subscriber then uses the B channel to send actual data to another user. All the devices attached to a given subscriber loop use the same D channel for signaling, but each sends data over a B channel dedicated to a single exchange for the duration of the exchange. Using the D channel is similar to having a telephone operator place a call for you.

You pick up the phone and tell the operator what type of call you wish to place and the number you wish to contact. The operator finds an open line appropriate for your needs, rings your party, and connects you.

☞ The D channel acts like an operator between the user and the network at the network layer.

Use of ISDN for Video Conferencing

The growth in the use of video-conferencing, a substantial increase in the connectivity requirements for geographically separated LANs, and the literal explosion in the use of the Internet represent three key applications responsible for a significant increase in the use of ISDN.

Until the early 1990s, most video-conferencing systems were relatively expensive, requiring the use of 512 Kbps or greater bandwidth, and they were usually implemented on a point-to-point networking basis via the installation of T1 or fractional T1 leased lines. Although a company might use video-conferencing only an hour or two per day, it had to pay for the 24-hour-per-day use of the leased line. Recognizing this communications cost problem, as well as the requirement of many organizations to perform video-conferencing among many geographically separated locations, communication product manufacturers developed a product known as an *inverse multiplexer*, or a *bandwidth-on-demand multiplexer*.

The inverse multiplexer derives its name from the fact that it accepts high-speed input and subdivides the input into two or more output data streams. When the inverse multiplexer's output data streams are connected to an ISDN service, it becomes possible not only to perform video-conferencing on a dial-up basis, but also to adjust the band-width used for communications between two video-conferencing systems based on the bandwidth supported by each system and economics. For example, consider Figure 12.6 which illustrates the user of a video-conferencing system via an inverse multiplexer connected to an ISDN Primary Rate Interface (PRI) line operation.

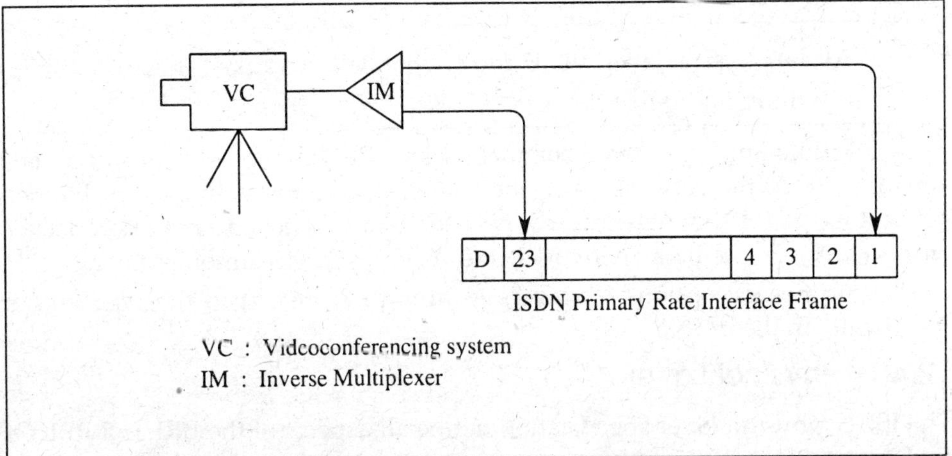

Figure 12.6 Video-conferencing via an inverse multiplexer and ISDN

Because an ISDN PRI line represents the multiplexing of 23 B channels and a D signaling channel, the inverse multiplexer could be used to support video-conferencing at data rates from 64 Kbps using one B channel to 1.472 Mbps using all 23 B channels. Due to advances in compression technology, most video-conferencing systems require the use of 4 to 6 B channels, in effect requiring four to six calls to be made via ISDN facilities from one video-conferencing location to another location. Although carriers typically bill each call on a per-minute basis, it is often far more economical to pay for several switched dial-up ISDN hours per day than to install a high-speed digital leased line between locations.

☞ Through the use of inverse or band-width-on-demand multiplexers, increments of bandwidth in multiples of 64 Kbps can be established via the use of ISDN to support video-conferencing.

Use of ISDN in Graphics Based World Wide Web

Another major application that has significantly increased the use of ISDN is represented by the explosive growth in the graphics-based World Wide Web. The integration of digital voice, video clips, graphics, and text on Web pages results in a requirement for Web servers to transmit hundreds of thousands to millions of bytes in response to a person clicking an icon on his browser's screen. Analog modems are limited under the best of connections to a data rate fo 33.6 Kbps, whereas ISDN access provides operating rates up to 128 Kbps. The use of ISDN can provide a mechanism for viewing web pages without irritating delays.

12.4 ISDN LAYERS

The ITU-T has devised an expanded model for the ISDN layers. Instead of a single seven-layer architecture like the OSI, the ISDN is defined in three separate planes: the *user plane*, the *control plane* and the *management plane* (See Figure 12.7).

These three planes are also divided into seven layers that correspond to the OSI model. Figure 12.8 shows a simplified version of the ISDN architecture for the user and control planes (B and D channels).

☞ At the physical layer, the B and D channels are alike. They use either the BRI or PRI interfaces and devices.

At the data link layer, the B channel uses LAPB (link access protocol broad band) or some version of it. At the network layer, the B channel has many options, B channels (and D channels acting like B channels) can connect to circuit-switched networks, packet-switched networks (X.25), Frame Relay networks, and ATM networks, among others.

The user-plane options for layers 4 through 7 are left to the user and are not defined specifically in the ISDN.

12.4.1 Physical Layer

The ISDN physical layer specification define all aspects of the BRI and PRI. Of these aspects, four are of primary importance.

(a) The mechanical and electrical specification of interfaces R, S, T and U.
(b) Encoding.
(c) Multiplexing channels to enable them to be carried by the BRI and PRI digital pipes.
(d) Power supply.

Physical Layer Specifications for BRI

A BRI consists of two B channels and one D channel. A subscriber connects to the BRI using the R, S and U interfaces (reference points). (See Figure 12.9)

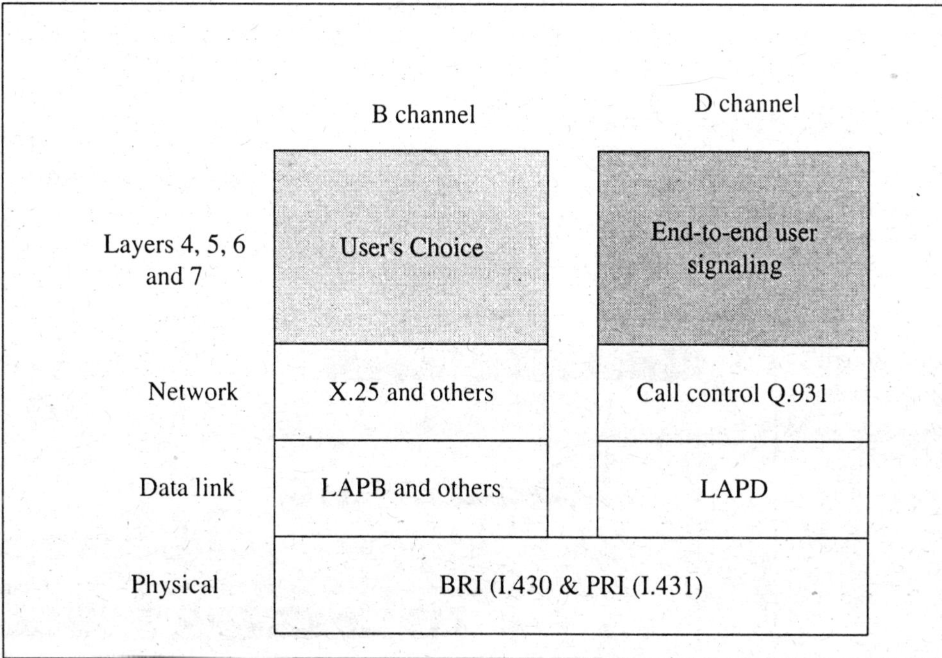

Figure 12.8 Simplified layers of ISDN

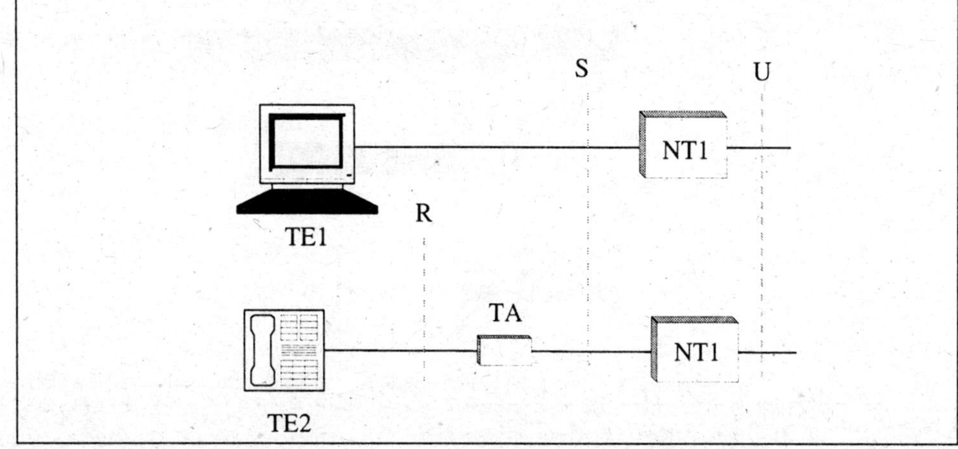

Figure 12.9 BRI interfaces

12.4.2 Data Link Layer

B and D channels use different data link protocols. B channels use LAPB protocol. The D channel uses link access procedures for D channels (LAPD). LAPD is similar to HDLC with a few modifications.

12.4.3 Network Layer

Once a connection has been established by the D channel, the B channel sends data using circuit switching, X.25, or other similar protocols.

The network layer packet is called a *message*. A message is encapsulated in the information field of an LAPD I-frame for transport across a link.

12.5 BROADBAND ISDN

When the ISDN was originally designed, data rates of 64 Kbps to 1.544 Mbps were sufficient to handle all existing transmission needs. As applications using the telecommunications networks advanced, these rates proved inadequate to support many applications.

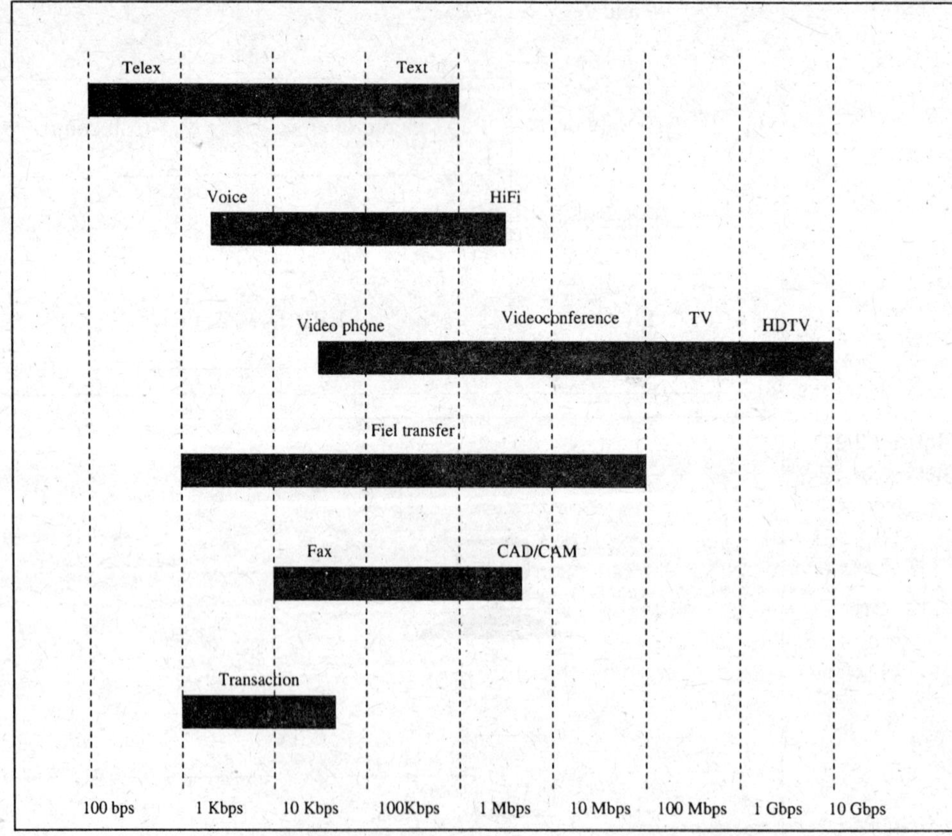

Figure 12.10 Data Bit Rates for different applications in electronics and computer engineering

Figure 12.10 shows the bit rates required by a variety of applications. As you can see, several are beyond the capacities of both the BRI and PRI.

☞ To provide for the needs of the next generation technology, an extension of ISDN, called *broadband ISDN* (*B-ISDN*), is under study. The original ISDN is now known as *narrowband ISDN (N-ISDN)*, B-ISDN provides subscribers to the network with data rates in the range of 600 Mbps, almost 400 times faster than the PRI rate. Technology exists to support higher rates but is not yet implemented or standardized.

12.5.1 Broadband ISDN Services

Broadband ISDN provides two types of services: (See Figure 12.11).

(a) Interactive
(b) Distributive

Figure 12.11 Broadband ISDN services

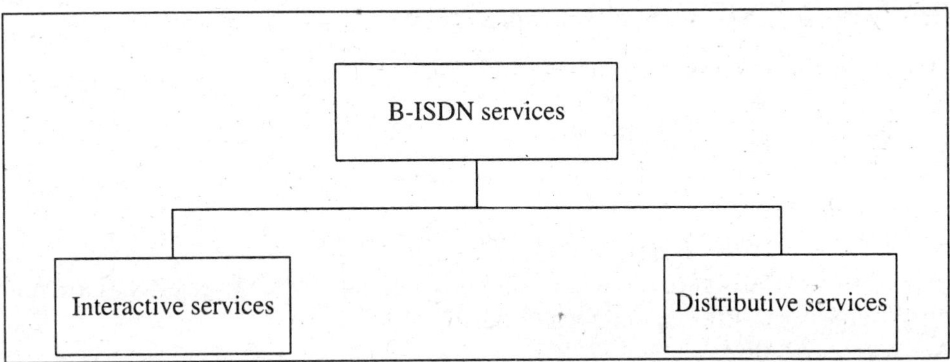

Interactive Services

Interactive services are those services which need two-way transfers between either two subscribers or between a subscriber and a service provider.

Distributive Services

Distributive services are of simplex communication form which are sent from a service provider to subscribers. The subscriber does not have to transmit a request each time a service is desired. These services can be without or with user control.

12.5.2 Physical Specifications of Broadband ISDN

The Broadband ISDN model is divided into layers which are closely tied to the design of Asynchronous Transmission Mode.

However, the physical aspects of B-ISDN that is not related to ATM include:

(a) Access methods
(b) Functional equipment groupings
(c) Reference points

Access Methods

Broadband ISDN has the following three access methods:

(a) Symmetrical (155.520 Mbps)
(b) Asymmetrical (155.520 Mbps/622.080 Mbps)

(c) Symmetrical (622.080 Mbps)

Functional Grouping

The functional groupings of equipment in the Broadband ISDN model are the same as those for Narrowband ISDN as seen in Figure 12.2. However, these equipments are called B-NT1, B-NT2, B-TE1, B-TE2 and B-TA.

Reference Points

Broadband ISDN also uses the reference points similar to Narrowband ISDN (R, S, T and U) as seen in Figure 12.2.

REVIEW QUESTIONS WITH ANSWERS

Question Number 1 Write short notes on Integrated Digital Services.

Answer [*Refer to Section 12.2.1*]

Question Number 2 What are the different applications of ISDN.

Answer [*Refer to Section 12.2*]

Question Number 3 What are the two methods of access of ISDN? Also what are the three channels defined by ISDN standard?

Answer [*Refer to Section 12.3*]

Question Number 4 Discuss briefly the evolution of ISDN.

Answer [*Refer to Section 12.1*]

Question Number 5 In Broadband ISDN, what is the difference between a distributive service and interactive service?

Answer [*Refer to Section 12.5.1*]

TEST PAPER

Time: 3 Hrs. Marks: 100

Note: Answer all questions.

1. What is the basic rate interface in ISDN? Explain.
2. Discuss the functions of the ISDN physical layer.
3. What are the datalink protocols used by ISDN.
4. Compare the three Broadband ISDN access methods.
5. What is the relation between the ISDN layers and the OSI model layers?

When you want something badly enough, never let a few rupees deprive you of it.

—RAI BAHADUR M. S. OBEROI

APPENDIX A

Designing Networks and Selecting Devices

A.1 INTRODUCTION

The economy of the whole world has made a rapid transition from an industrial economy to a knowledge based information economy. The force behind this change is the need for faster information storage, processing and rapid distribution. The computer and telephonic networks form the foundation of this new knowledge based economy.

Many newer applications of electronics communication and computer science such as dataware housing and mining, extranets, e-commerce, distance education, etc. are driving the networks to their design limits. For such applications, there is a vital need for network bandwidth, traffic management, security of circuits. New standards are being developed for accommodating these newer requirements with a radical change in the existing networks itself.

This appendix aims at providing the reader a structured and modular approach to network design philosophies. The new designs would satisfy the current requirements and should also be flexible to accommodate future requirements and technologies. This appendix thus focuses on identifying the customer's requirements and fulfillment at the cost effective manner.

A.2 DESIGN PHILOSOPHIES

There are two approaches to design a network. These are:

(a) Connecting the Black Boxes approach

(b) Modularizing the system approach

A.2.1 Connecting Black Boxes

In this method of designing the networks and their solution lays importance on the available technologies and products. The requirements of the customer are not given much importance. Here the emphasis is on the number of devices to be networked, their locations and distances and very small sight at the customer applications. For example, the vendor can suggest a high end switch as part of network implementation because it gives him better margins.

☞ The connecting black boxes approach does not fully address the issues of network management, security, IP addressing and subnetting and performance optimisation.

A.2.2 Modularizing System Approach

Modularizing system approach gives maximum importance to the customer's requirements. This method takes into account the physical as well as the application characteristics of a network. The factors such as network management, security, addressing, etc. are taken into consideration before the design is completed.

In this method, the design is broken down into multiple phases, with each phase focusing on specific design issues. This approach also allows the vendor to go back to earlier phases to correct an anomaly in the design or to incorporate new design parameters.

☞ The main idea in modular approach is the fact that the network should fit the customer's requirements and not vice versa.

Main Steps in Modular Design

Following are the main steps followed in the modular design of the networks.

(a) Indicate the customer's requirements
(b) Study the application packages—present and the future that would be run on the network. Also study their characteristics such as bandwidth requirements etc.
(c) Study the traffic patterns.
(d) Analyse the factors such as addressing, security, management and also draw the logical network map.
(e) Select the physical technologies and products like cabling, switches, routers which fit into the logical network map and satisfy all the requirements identified in the steps (a) to (d) above.
(f) Complete the physical network map.
(g) Plan out how the design will be implemented.
(h) Write down a document about the network after installation is complete and update this document from time to time.

Indication of Customer's Requirements

Customer's requirements can be classified into business and technical goals. The customer's requirements may be one or more of the following:

(a) Improvement of the communication facilities
(b) How to increase the productivity of the workers?
(c) Connect or extend the organization to supporting business houses which could be the suppliers or service providers.
(d) Improve the security or codification of critical data.
(e) Improvement of relationship with the customers

(f) To enable access to remote telecommunications

Business Goals Customers may have specific business goals. For this purpose, following are the key steps while planning networks design.

(i) Prepare a short statement which clearly states the goal of the network.

(ii) The document should contain the list of business goals to be achieved in the short term and the long term. This will help the network designer to phase out the network commissioning and incorporate scaleability in the network.

(iii) Define the criteria for success in objective terms.

☞ The success of the network project should not be limited to getting good network connectivity. However, the success criteria should also include the effect of the network on the business.

(iv) List down the constraints under which business could affect the network design and implementation. Such constraints may be purchasing policy, in house expertise, budget, etc.

(v) Establish the scope of the project. Determine whether the project involves setting up a new network or is it an expansion of an existing network.

Technical Goals Technical goals provide the network designer the expected operational characteristics of a network. Some such criteria to be kept in mind while planning network design could be as follows:

(i) *Scaleability:* It gives the information on the planned expansion of the network. This future expansion information helps in identifying technologies which are capable of handling future loads in terms of traffic and the number of networks and devices in a network.

(ii) *Availability:* Higher availability must translate into higher quality devices, reliable protocols and redundancy features in the network.

(iii) *Performance:* It means the throughput, utilization and efficiency of protocols.

(iv) *Security:* It will help us in setting criteria for physical security, file security, authentication of local and remote users of the servers and the encryption facilities.

(v) *Manageability:* This means the performance, fault tolerance, configuration and accounting management. This will help in identifying the network management framework and applications.

(vi) *Affordability.:* This means the performance vs. cost. It tells the network designer as to how much the customer is willing to pay for achieving a particular business or technical facilities. If the customer wants a cheap solution, he needs to accept the diluted performance.

A.2.3 Network Applications Identification

Here we need to find out what all the networks are going to be used and what application packages would be run. This knowledge is very vital for the proper design of the network solution. For example, some applications such as video and audio files need large bandwidth of the channel through which data would pass. For such networks, the media used should be capable of taking fast traffic.

All such form of applications required to improve the working of the organization can be put in the form of a table. Table A.1 gives the format for such purpose.

Table A.1 Desired Network Applications

Sl. No.	Name of the Application Software	Type of Application	Criticality of the Application

Study of the Traffic Pattern and its Classification as well as Bandwidth Requirements

Identifying the traffic flow in the network needs the study of the following parameters.

(a) Type of the traffic generated by the application and the amount of bandwidth required by the application.
(b) The type of server for loading the application.
(c) The location of the workgroup that will be allowed to use the specific application on the different servers.

The traffic can be categorized in any one of the following types:

(a) Terminal/Host
(b) Client/Server
(c) Pee to Peer

Terminal/Host Telnet is an example of Terminal/Host type of traffic. This traffic comprises the client sending a few characters to the server and the server responds with messages meeting the required query.

Client/Server This type of traffic comprises the client sending a short frame to the server and the server responding a sequence of large frame. File server is one such example.

Peer to Peer This type of traffic comprises the communicating equipment to contribute equally to the process.

Bandwidth Requirements

Bandwidth requirement will depend on the size of data transferred by the application packages and the overheads of the various network protocols.

Suppose we have a workgroup of 10 users which while accessing one application requires 100 Kbps bandwidth while for the other application requires only 30 Kbps. Therefore, the total bandwidth for this workgroup would be 130 Kbps because any one of the member of the group may access one application while the other member may access the other application at the same time.

Table A.2 Desired Network Bandwidth

Sl. No.	Name of the Workgroup	Location	Number of users	Name of the workgroup accessed	Requirement of the Bandwidth

Table A.2 gives the format for the calculation of the bandwidth of different workgroups.

After we have completed the information in Table A1 and Table A2, we can then complete Table A.3 and proceed to the logical design of the network map.

Table A.3 Desired Application and Bandwidth Requirements

Sl. No.	Name of the Application	Server on which the application is located	Name of the workgroup accessing the application	Requirement of the Band-width	Quality of Service Required

A.3 LOGICAL NETWORK DESIGNING

Logical network design requires the study of such factors as the topology, naming scheme and security management of the networks.

A.3.1 Study of the Customer's Needs

Table A.3 was tabulated based on the customer's requirement of the bandwidth and the quality of service required. While looking at the customer's requirements and the vendors solutions about the availability of the equipment matching such needs, the following point must be kept in mind.

(a) How the solution meets the security concerns of the customer.

(b) What addressing scheme would be suitable today and would also accommodate future network expansions?

The logical designing of the network needs to solve the following problems.

(a) Network topology to be used

(b) Addressing and Naming schemes

(c) Security and management needs

3.3.2 Network Topology To Be Used

The network topology is the key to a high performance, scaleable and robust network. Note that the star topology does not address the following issues:

(a) Redundancy of the network links

(b) Load balancing

(c) Hierarchy of the network components

☞ The network topology is the blueprint of the network. Like the blueprint of a town/city, it shows us the location of the various user workgroups, the servers, the links among them and the traffic flows. It also represents the hierarchy of the network.

The network topology can be planned in the following two ways.

(a) The flat network topology
(b) The hierarchical network topology

3.3.3 Flat Network Topology

This topology does not have any hierarchy as regards the functions carried out by the devices in the network. This topology is simple to operate but it is mainly used in Wide Area Networks (WANs).

The flat LAN topology is typically based on the hub. The LAN of this type suffers from performance bottlenecks. One solution is to use switches which divide the collision domain into smaller parts. Flat LANs could be made hierarchical using routers.

Characteristics of Flat Network Topology

(a) The flat topologies are simple to implement and maintain.
(b) The flat LAN topologies can be implemented at a lower cost.
(c) They are suitable for small networks which are not going to be extended heavily.
(d) Flat topologies do not provide adequate performance and availability guarantees.

3.3.4 Hierarchical Network Topology

In this method of designing the networks, the networks are divided into distinct areas of functionality. All the functional areas can be designed separately and then interconnected to form the complete network. The hierarchical networks are typically three tier networks as follows:

(a) The access layer
(b) Distribution layer
(c) Core layer

The Access Layer

The access layer is the bottom most layer. This layer is involved in providing connectivity to the end-devices like the machines, peripherals etc. The devices used here are hubs, workgroup switches etc.

The Distribution Layer

The distribution layer is the interface between the access and the core layer. This layer is used for implementing security policies. It controls the broadcast domains using Vertual Local Area Networks (VLAN) or physical networks defined by routers. This layer also implements traffic policy which controls the traffic moving into the core.

The Core Layer

The core layer is responsible for inter-connectivity of different distribution layer devices. The core layer is a very high throughput layer. The devices here are not overloaded with security policies. This layer is also responsible for connecting the network to the external world.

Advantages of Hierarchical Network Topology

(a) It offers a modularity in designing the networks.
(b) Broadcasts can be controlled by VLANs or Physical networks.
(c) Capacity planning can be done accurately.
(d) Scaleability is high.
(e) It is easier to identify the fault and also rectification of the fault.
(f) Changing the topology is easier because a topology change in one layer does not affect the other layers. Only the interface between layers has to be looked at again.

Redundancy in Hierarchical Network Topology

We need to consider various redundancy solutions which needs to be incorporated in the networks. The redundancy can be one of the following three types:

(a) Link redundancy
(b) Server redundancy
(c) Router redundancy

Link Redundancy Link redundancy provides alternative routes to a destination or a device in the event of failure of the primary network. Multiple segments can be connected between the LAN switches and configured as redundant links. If a particular link fails, the remaining keep functioning although at lower performance. These options should be thoroughly checked if devices from multiple vendors are to be integrated to the network.

Server Redundancy Server redundancy is essential for ensuring application up-time in the event of server failure. Server redundancy is different from data redundancy which is achieved through data backups. Server redundancy solutions can be on of the following types:

(a) Hot-standby backup server which involves some delay in bringing up the standby server.
(b) Two-node automatic fail over cluster which uses two active servers and shared storage.

These two types of server redundancy is cost effective for small networks.

Router Redundancy Router redundancy is critical if access to the Wide Area Network is essential. Router redundancy is implemented by vendor specific solutions.

☞ Redundancy is also needed for power supplies and many other areas where the availability of that equipment is vital for the proper functioning of the networks.

A.4 ADDRESSING AND NAMING

After selecting the network topology, and the redundancy, the next phase is the selection of the addressing and naming scheme for the network. The addressing schemes are dependent on the protocols which are used in the network. The following model may be used for the addressing schemes:

(a) Choose a structured addressing model. This method simplifies administration and address management.
(b) Leave room for the growth in the model. The structured model should not be violated in the event of the network expanding in the future.
(c) Use only meaningful numbers while assigning network addresses.
(d) Delegate authority of addressing to branch offices if appropriate.

A.4.1 IP Addressing Scheme

If we use IP as the network protocol, the main issues are the following:

(a) Which address to choose on the internal network?
(b) How to connect the IP network to the public network such as Internet.
(c) How to build extranets using the Internet as the medium?
(d) Should we use dynamic IP addressing on the client side?

Choosing private IP addresses on the internal network is useful. For example, the valid ranges are 10.0.0.0, 172.16.0.0 and 192.168.0.0. These addresses are never allocated to valid IP networks. The advantages of using Private IP addresses are:

(a) The use of private IP addresses provides a facility to hide them from the public networks like the Internet. This improves the security of the network.
(b) There is a flexibility in choosing the Internet Service Provider (ISP), since the internal IP addresses are governed by the ISPs.
(c) The size of the routing tables is reduced as only the valid IP address on the WAN side of the network is advertised on the public WAN.

Disadvantage of using Private IP addresses is that private addresses create some complexities for creating extranets. This should be considered if your organization is going to implement an extranet.

A.4.2 Factors to be kept in mind for using IP Addressing

(a) Use dynamic IP addresses on the client side with the help of DHCP. This greatly simplifies the address management tasks. You can also configure IP parameters like default gateway, DNS servers etc. using DHCP.
(b) Try to create a sub-netted network instead of using complete network addresses.
(c) Although Network Addressing and Naming provides address translation, the security offered by this scheme is not very high. Therefore, the proxy server and the specialized firewall is a better choice for the security.

A.4.3 Using Names for Addressing

Naming is also critical for a good and user-friendly network. Users prefer to use names instead of addresses for accessing resources. The naming scheme is therefore critical for simplifying resource access. Names are given to each resource on the network; routers, switches, servers, clients etc. Names are required by various protocols. For example, IP uses host names for domain names for naming. NetBIOS also requires names to be given to the Windows machines. It is necessary to understand this difference, because a machine can have different IP host name and NetBIOS name. It is critical that naming conventions are documented and strictly adhered to. Guidelines for naming schemes are as follows:

(a) Check whether the naming scheme can match the organizational structure. It helps the users in finding the necessary resources.
(b) Naming should be unique.
(c) Names should be short and meaningful. For example, the laser printer in the finance department with the name could be finlaser1.
(d) Use only case insensitive names.
(e) The security policy of the organization should be kept in mind while assigning names of the users.

A.4.4 Security Management

Guidelines for deciding on the security and management are the following:

(a) What level of security management is really required.
(b) What level of management should be deployed? Typically, performance and fault management is deployed. One can also deploy accounting, configuration and security management depending on the requirements.
(c) Physical security of the networks, devices etc., is also to be kept in mind.
(d) Security policy should be modified continuously depending on the threat perception from virus or external sources.
(e) One old truism in security is that the cost of protecting yourself against the threat should be less than the cost of recovering if the threat were to strike you. Cost in this context should include the losses expected expressed in real currency, reputation, trustworthiness, and other less obvious manner (as referred in RFC 2196)

Once we complete this analysis, we are ready with the logical network for the requirements. This helps to make the network design more robust and brings it closer to achieving the goals set by the client.

A.5 PHYSICAL NETWORK DESIGN

The physical network design consists of selecting the actual network technologies and products. The selected products and design of networks should be inline with the business and technical goals and the logical network topology.

A.5.1 Parts of Physical Network Design

Networks physical design consist of the following:

(a) Designing the cabling plan.
(b) Selection of devices in the access, distribution and core layer of the logical network.
(c) Selecting the appropriate access protocols for the links between work groups, data stores etc.

A.5.2 Factors affecting the Selection of Network Physical Topology

Various factors in selecting network physical topology that need to be considered are the following:

(a) Policies of the organization
(b) Technical expertise of In-house staff
(c) Budgeting and scheduling

Policies of the organization

The policies of the organization typically decide the type of LAN technology to be used. For example, the organization may decide to adopt Fast Ethernet as the technology of choice. It can also have a growth plan ready for its networks. In such a situation, as a designer, you do not have much choice in the selection of toplogy or the technology.

Technical expertise of In-house Staff

The in-house technical staff has to understand the statistics being gathered by the network management tools and prepare reports for taking the correct actions. The in-house staff needs to understand the technology in-depth to analyze any problems which might crop up every now and then.

Budgeting and Scheduling

Technologies such as ATM give a very good performance, in spite of the high price. Hence, the final technology selection has to be moderated by the budgetary consideration.

In addition, scheduling constraints are also important. For example, the time required for laying and commissioning a fiber-optic backbone may be prohibitive. The backbone would then have to depend on some other technology which gives satisfactory performance and can be implemented in the given time.

A.5.3 Technologies Available for Implementation

The key technologies used in LAN are:

(a) ATM
(b) FDDI
(c) Token Ring

FDDI and token ring are typically not used any more. Though they may have advanced feature. High growth bandwidth technologies in the Ethernet family have sidelined these two technologies. Ethernet is by far the most suitable technology for use in the networks at the access layers and in many case, the distribution layers.

ATM is a suitable technology for use in core layer of the network, where performance is paramount. Gigabit Ethernet is also suitable for core layers where budgetary constraints are present.

☞ There is a 10 GigaEtherent available these days. The competition between ATM and 10 GigaEtherent are going on. ATM is however unparalleled when it comes to networks which carry delay sensitive applications such as video traffic and voice traffic.

A.5.4 Factors for Selecting Network Technology

The following are some of the considerations to be kept in mind while selecting a network technology:

(a) Bandwidth requirement
(b) Delay requirements
(c) Quality of Service (QoS) required

Each application has different requirements for the network. QoS is one of the important considerations. One of the prominent solution for QoS is to use IEEE 802.1q or IEEE 802.1p implementations on the switches. This allows the administrator to create queues with different priorities to control the network traffic. IPv4 codes support some QoS levels through Type-Of-Service bits in the IP header. But support of QoS in IPv6 is in-built.

However, Ethernet provides low cost options for implementing networks. With the advent of structured cabling, the simplicity of design and implementation have increased tremendously. Also structured cabling greatly increases the reliability of the network. Ethernet is also scaleable from a meager 10 Mbps to 1000 Mbps.

A.5.5 Choice of Ethernet Technology

The choice of Ethernet technology would depend on the following considerations.

(a) Location and size of the workgroups
(b) Bandwidth and QoS requirements
(c) Logical network topology
(d) Location of the servers
(e) Traffic flow

Depending on the requirements of the organization, one can select between Ethernet, Fast Ethernet and Giga Ethernet. One can also use the full duplex option wherever possible. This would improve performance considerably. Whichever type of Ethernet technology is used, make sure that the following factors are observed:

(a) Follow the cabling norms strictly
(b) Follow the termination techniques strictly
(c) Where ever possible, use cable testers to check for the quality of the link.
(d) Type of cable used is critical. The cabling infrastructure is typically static. Also cabling incurs a lot of investment. Hence, the future expansion must also be kept in mind while selecting the type of cable used for Ethernet.

Some general consideration in selecting the devices and technology would also depend on:

(a) Ease of configuration, cost, mean time before failure (MTBF) and mean time before repair (MTBR).
(b) The availability of support and the quality of support for maintenance.
(c) The quality of documentation availability of independent test results.

The possible use of the types of Ethernet technology is given in Table A.4. The table suggest the possible uses but actual selection would vary from organization to organization.

Table A.4 Applicabilities of Technologies

Sl. No.	Technology	Where to use
1.	Ethernet	Low bandwidth applications. Low budget applications.
2.	Fast Ethernet	Server connectivity. Backbone connectivity. High bandwidth applications. Power workgroups.
3.	Giga Ethernet	Backbone connectivity. Traffic aggregation. Server connectivity.

A.5.6 Selecting the Devices

Usually for Ethernet network topology, one has to select from devices such as hubs, switches and routers for various applications. The choice has really become difficult because the vendors of these devices are creating products which blur the distinction between various products application. However the applicability of different products is given in Table A.5.

Table A.5 Applicabilities of Devices

Sl. No.	Device	Where to use
1.	Hubs	Small workgroups, small networks
2.	Switches	Used in access layer for high performance workgroups. Traffic management using Layer 4 switching techniques. Layer 3 functionality allows some security and broadcast control to be implemented.
3.	Routers	Switching routers are used in LANs while the normal routers are used in WANs.

Selecting Hubs

The following are the important parameters to be considered while selecting hubs:

Support for dual speed operation Many hubs have the ability to auto-switch their ports between Ethernet and Fast Ethernet.

Support for built-in segment switch If the hub supports dual speed operation, then the hub should also have a built-in switch for interconnecting the two segments. If the hub does not switch, then one has to purchase an external swatch for doing the same.

Segmentation features Many hubs support multiple segments in the hub and change the allocation of the ports on-the-fly based on the traffic levels on the various segments.

Selecting Switch

Important parameters to be taken into account while selecting switches are:

Backplane bandwidth This is the bandwidth of the switching fabric. The switch should work in a non-blocking mode of maximum performance.

Congestion control The switch should have enough buffers to take care of the traffic peaks. The switch can also support active congestion control.

A.6 DOCUMENTATION OF THE PROJECT

Documentation are the written document that are to compiled as soon as work starts on any project. If the project work is completed, but its maintenance and changes will become difficult to implement without thorough written documents. Hence document forms the backbone for any project implementation and prolonged execution. The documentation should be written with the following objectives:

(a) Set the requirements and the applications right away.

(b) Prepare the logical network topology. Indicate the workgroups, servers and thier inter connection on the network map. Also, decide on the addressing, naming, security and management policies. These will affect the selection of the devices in the next phase.

(c) Select the networking technologies and devices which are appropriate to your logical network and the business and technical goals.

(d) After you have got all the data, you can create your network design document. The design document should contain the following sections:

   (i) Goals of the network
   (ii) Scope of the network
   (iii) Design requirements
   (iv) Logical network
   (v) Physical network
   (vi) Implementation plan

If these are not properly made, then after the document is created, one can embark on another adventurous journey of implementing the network.

"TELL ME ONCE AND I WILL HEAR YOU
TELL ME TWICE AND I WILL LISTEN
LET ME DO IT AND I WILL UNDERSTAND"

APPENDIX B

Network Broadcasting

B.1 BROADCAST NETWORKS-NEED FOR A NEW CHANNEL ALLOCATION TECHNIQUE

This appendix is concerned with studies in shared media or broadcast type of networks based on satellite channels and packet radios. Because multiple uncoordinated users attempt to gain access to a single channel in a random manner and this results in contention, such networks are also known as multi access or random access or contention networks.

The central problem in shared media networks is how to allocate the channel, one at a time, to the large number of competing users who are uncoordinated and, possibly, geographically dispersed. None of the traditional techniques for sharing a channel, namely, FDM, TDM, Polling and concentration, works satisfactorily for shared channels like satellite, packet radio, coaxial cable, etc. The basic problem with FDM and TDM, both of which allocate a channel statically, is two-fold.

(a) The number of stations being large and time varying, channel allocation poses a big problem.

(b) The frequent non-utilization of their allocated frequencies or time slots by a large number of users gives rise to considerable wastage of channel capacity and causes increased delay.

Value of the mean delay actually increases N times if the bandwidth is reduced N times. So far as Polling is concerned, it is unsuitable because of the large polling overhead, especially for large propagation delay channels like satellites. The round trip delay for a satellite being around 270 msec, the minimum time to complete a polling cycle with 100 stations would be 54 seconds. Finally, concentration is simply not possible because, to allow possible simultaneous transmissions by several stations, it requires a dedicated or private port for each station. Thus, a new channel sharing technique is required for building shared media multiple access networks.

A novel and elegant technique for allocating a channel under the condition of multiple independent and random accesses was devised in 1971 by Norman Abramson of the University of Hawaii and his collagues while building a ground radio based computer network. The experiment was called ALOHA and the dynamic channel allocation technique it employed, popularly referred to as ALOHA technique, is the forerunner of a host of efficient multiple access techniques subsequently used in satellite based WANs and some LANs. The ALOHA protocol is described in the following section.

B.2 PURE ALOHA PROTOCOL

The ALOHA protocol recognizes the fact that even though the users are uncoordinated they can utilize the feedback property inherent in the broadcast channel to bring about, though in an isolated manner, and effective coordination between themselves. The basic ALOHA protocol is very simple, and it has two variation, namely, pure ALOHA or ALOHA in short, and SLOTTED ALOHA. In the pure ALOHA protocol, a station is allowed to send a frame (or packet) whenever it wants to but, obviously, this frame may "collide" (overlap in time) with one or more frames transmitted by other stations because the stations are uncoordinated. However, because of the feedback property of the broadcast channel, the sending station can discover by itself whether any collision took place by simply listening to the channel. If there has been a collision, the frame will obviously need to be retransmitted but only after waiting for a random period of time. The randomness of the waiting period is essential because, otherwise, the same set of frames (users) will collide over and over again. It should be noted that collision by two or more frames may be caused even by a partial overlap during as small as one bit period. For example, if the first bit of a frame even partially overlaps the last bit of a frame sent earlier, a checksum error will occur in both the frames.

Efficiency of the pure ALOHA protocol in terms of the throughput S was analyzed by Abramson under the following assumptions.

(a) The number of stations is infinitely large.

(b) The frames are of fixed length and, accordingly, the frame time, i.e., the time needed to transmit a frame, is also fixed, say τ sec.

(c) Transmission of frames (both new as well as old frames transmitted by all stations taken together) is a Poisson process with a mean of G frames/frame time.

Abramson argued that had there been no collision, S would have been equal to the offered traffic G itself. However, because of collisions, S is reduced (compared to G) by a factor p_s, i.e.,

$$S = p_s G \tag{B.1}$$

Here p_s is the probability that the transmission of any frame, taken at random, is successful or, equivalently, the transmitted frame does not offer a collision. It should be noted that although the throughput S is necessarily limited to unity (1 frame/frame time), G may exceed unity. However, a large value of G only increases the number of collisions and hence retransmissions but does not contribute to the throughput. The success factor p_s and hence the relation between S and G can be determined as follows.

Considering an arbitrary frame which is transmitted at time t_0, it occupies the channel during the period $[t_0, + t_0 + t]$. From Figure B.1 it may be observed that this frame will escape collision only if no other frame is transmitted within the 2τ sec period $[t_0 - \tau, t_0 + \tau]$ which may be termed as the collision zone.

Since the frame transmission process is Poisson with a mean of G frames/frame time, i.e., 2G frames/2τ seconds and the number of stations is infinite,

$$p_s = \text{Prob}\ \{\text{no frame is transmitted during} 2\tau\ \text{second}\}$$

$$= \frac{(2G)^0 e^{-(2G)}}{0!} = e^{-2G}$$

Hence $S_{PURE} = G \quad e^{-(2G)}$ (*B*.2)

The lower curve in Figure B.2 depicts the above relationship between the offered traffic G, i.e., the number of frames per frame time that is attempted to be transported across the broadcast subnet and the throughput S, i.e., the number of frames per frame time that is actually transported by the broadcast subnet.

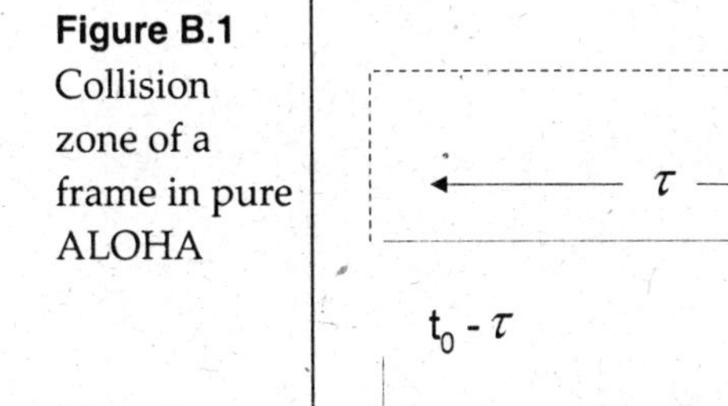

Figure B.1 Collision zone of a frame in pure ALOHA

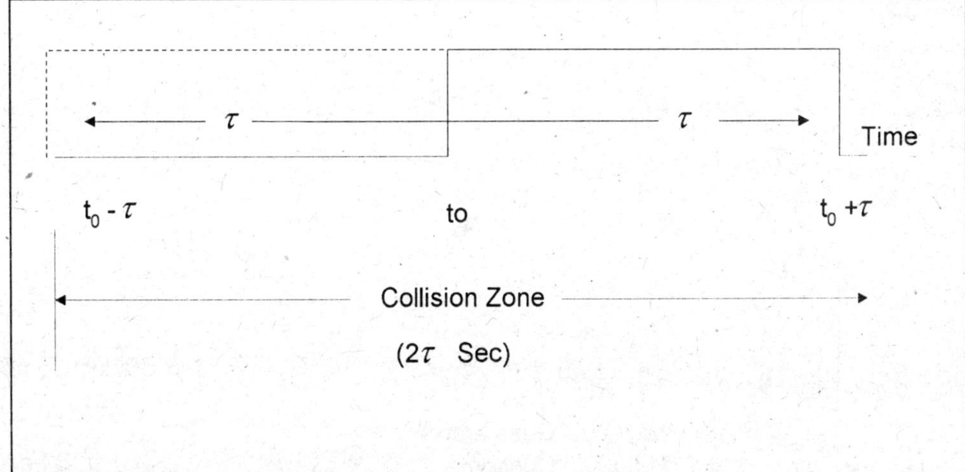

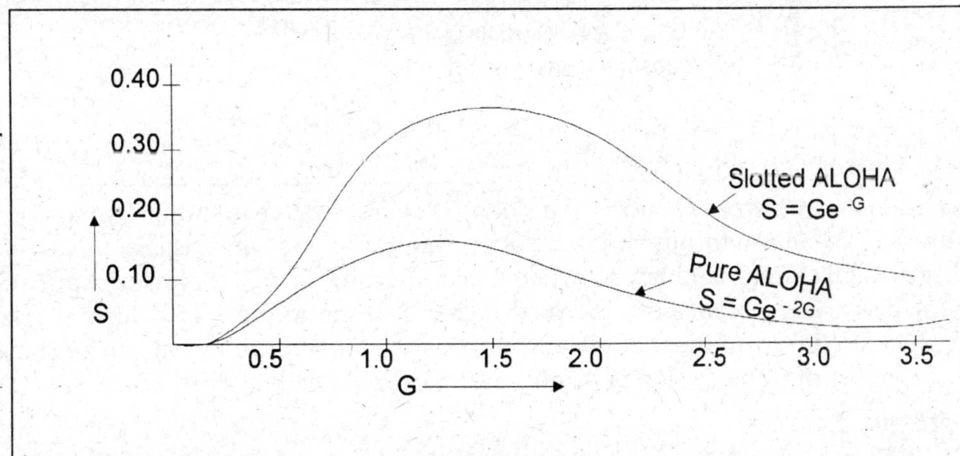

Figure B.2 Throughput Vs. offered load curve for pure and slotted ALOHA system.

The maximum throughput or, equivalently, the maximum efficiency or channel utilization of the pure ALOHA protocol is 1/(2e) (a little over 18%) and is obtained when G = 0.5 frames/frame time.

B.3 SLOTTED ALOHA PROTOCOL

In slotted ALOHA protocol which was proposed by L. Roberts in 1972, stations are not allowed to transmit whenever they want, i.e., asynchronously, but are constrained to transmit only in synchronism, with a system clock. Time is divided up into fixed size intervals or slots, each slot being equal to one frame time, and one of the stations emits a synchronization pulse at the beginning of each slot. This arrangement, shown in Figure B.3, which converts a continuous time ALOHA system (pure ALOHA) to a discrete time ALOHA system (slotted ALOHA) clearly reduce the collision zone to only τ seconds so that $p_s = e^{-G}$ and

$$S_{SLOTTED} = Ge^{-G} \quad (B.3)$$

Figure B.3 Functioning of a slotted ALOHA system.

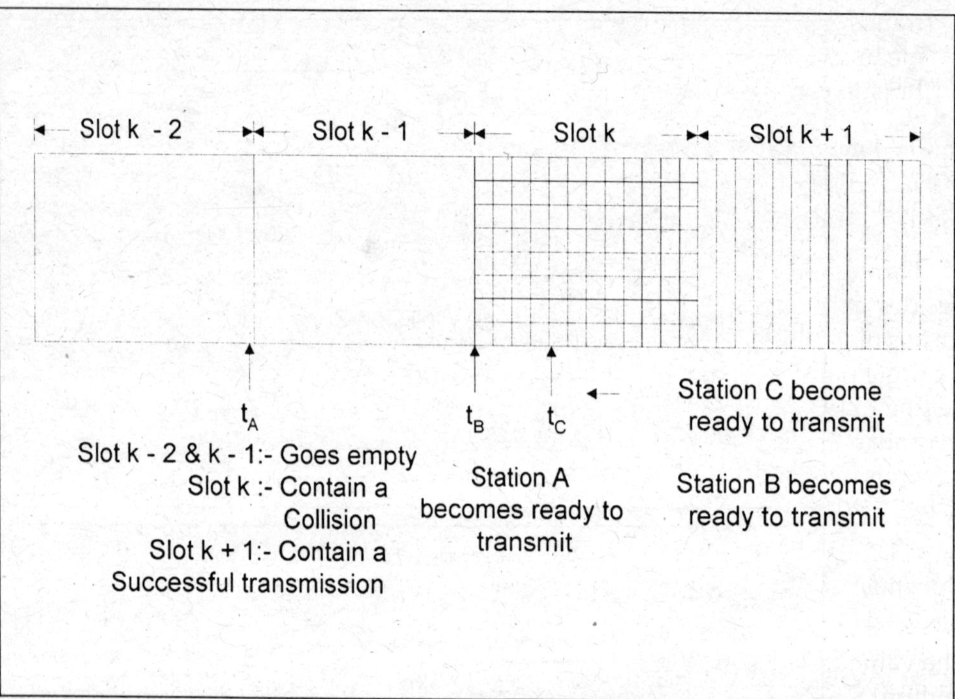

The relation between G and S for a slotted ALOHA system is shown by the upper curve in Figure B.2. Maximum throughput for slotted ALOHA is 1/e which is exactly double than that of pure ALOHA and is obtained when G = 1. Beyond G = 1, the throughput starts falling almost drastically because of a marked increase in the number of collisions resulting in a large increase in the number of retransmissions. As a matter of fact, it can be shown that the mean number of transmission per frame varies exponentially with G.

Example B.1

A slotted ALOHA system with a large population of users has a slot time of 10×10^{-3} sec. Packets (new and retransmission taken together) are generated in a Poisson manner at the mean rate of 100 packets/sec. and length of each packet is 100 K bits. Packets are transmitted at the rate of 5 Mbps. Determine

(a) the chance of success at the first attempt

(b) the chance of success at the third attempt

(c) the throughput of the system

Solution:

Time to send each packet $= \frac{100x10^3}{5x10^6}$ sec. = $20x10^{-3}$sec (i.e., 2 slot times).

Hence the collision zone extends over 3 slot times, i.e., 30 x 10^{-3} sec

(a) Considering a test packet sent at t_0 (beginning of a time slot) the packet will escape collision, i.e, will be successfully transmitted at the first attempt, if no other packet is transmitted during its collision zone. Since packet generation process is Poisson with a mean rate of 100 packets/sec,

Pr {success in the first attempt} = p_0 (3 slot times)

$$= \frac{(100 \times 30 \times 10^{-3})^0 e^{-100 \times 30 \times 10^{-3}}}{0!} = e^{-3}$$

(b) Success in the third attempt implies a success preceded by exactly two failures. Hence

Pr {success in the third attempt} = $(1\text{-}e^{-3})^2$ e^{-3}

(c) Throughput = 100 x e^{-3} packet/sec

Besides analyzing the performance of the pure ALOHA protocol with an infinite customer population, Abramnson also studied the performance of the slotted ALOHA protocol with a finite population of customers. Some results are given below.

Let the i-th user have a probability G_i of transmitting a frame (new or old) during any slot and a probability S_i of being successful. Then S_i, which equals the compound probability that user i sends a frame during a slot and none of the other users sends a frame in that slot, is given by

$$S_i = G\pi(1 - G_j) \qquad (B.4)$$

$$j \neq i$$

The value of $\{G_i\}$ are all known, then the values of $\{S_i\}$ can be determined and the system throughput S = ΣS_i can be found out. Abramson shown that throughput in a finite population slotted ALOHA system is so maximized at G = ΣG_i = 1.

Considering the special case of N identical users each having an individual throughput of S_i = S/N frames/slot and an individual mean transmission rate of G_i = G/N frames/slot, the following relation is obtained between the offered load and the throughput

$$S = G\left(1 - \frac{G}{N}\right)^{N-1} \qquad (B.5)$$

Example B.2

A slotted ALOHA system presently has 3 stations with a mean transmission rate (packets/slot) of G_1 = 0.1, G_2 = 0.2, G_3 = 0.3, respectively. A fourth station having a mean transmission rate of G_4 now joins the network and it is observed that the system throughout is now maximized. Determine (i) G_4 ; (ii) Individual throughputs and the system throughput.

Solution:

(i) Since the system throughput is maximized at

$$G = \sum_{i=1}^{4} G_i = 1, \qquad G_4 = 0.4;$$

(ii) Throughput of the first station is given by

$$S_1 = G_1 (1 - G_2) (1 - G_3) (1 - G_4) = 0.0336 \text{ packets/slot}$$

Similarly, $S_2 = 0.0756$; $S_3 = 0.1296$; $S_4 = 0.2016$;

Hence the system throughput $S = \sum_{i=1}^{4} S_i = 0.4404$

B.4 SATELLITE NETWORKS-EARLY APPROACH

Satellite networks have been assuming increased importance over the recent years because of their growing cost-effectiveness. A communication satellite has a number of transponders each of which has a beam focussing over some portion of the surface of the earth. Every transponder has a receiver to receive signals, sent from any earth station lying within its beam area, at a certain frequency called its uplink frequency. This received signal is error-checked, amplified and transmitted (broadcast) back to the earth at a different frequency called the downlink frequency so that all the earth stations within its beam area can hear it. Because of the different uplink and downlink frequencies, the channel is duplex and the upward and downward frames do not interface with each other. (See Figure B.4)

Figure B.4 Satellite link with different uplink and downlink frequencies

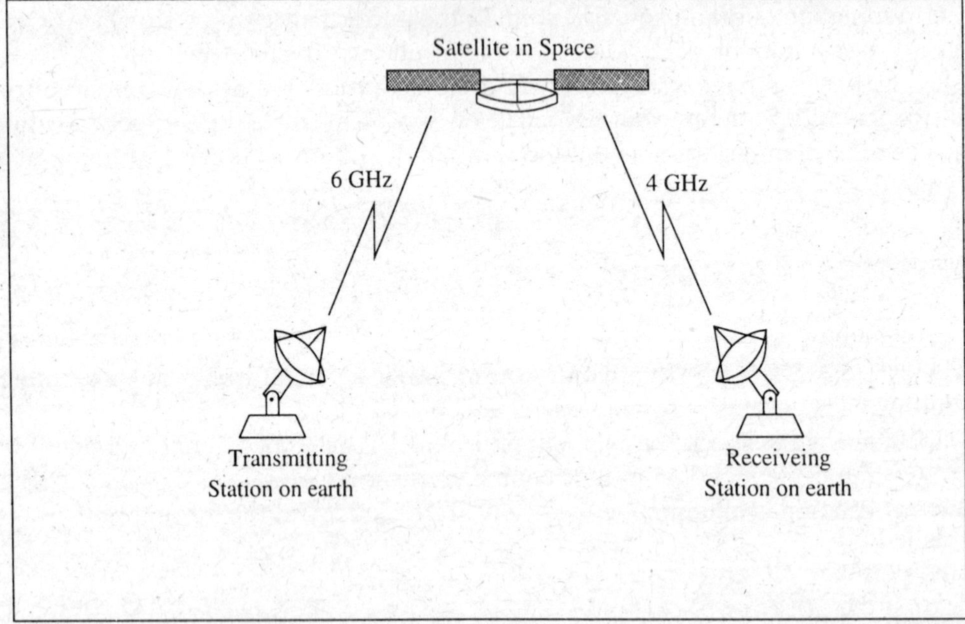

Early satellite networks were based on FDM or TDM. One example of such a system was the SPADE system used on some early Intelsat satellites. In the SPADE system, each transponder provides 794 simplex channels each having a 64 kbps data rate (suitable for accomodating one PCM channel) alongwith a single 128 kbps channel for çommon signalling. Each communication earth station uses a pair of simplex channels to achieve full duplex operation. TDM is used on the common signalling channel with continuously repeating frames of 50 msec duration having 50 slots each of 1 msec duration during which 128 bits can be transmitted. Each slot is dedicated to one ground station. Whenever a ground station has data to send, it randomly selects one of the currently unused channels and wires an allocation request message with this channel number in its own slot. When the feedback comes, the station can know whether his request was granted (i.e., whether no other station had sent, earlier to him, an allocation request against the same channel) or not. If granted, the station uses the channel for as long as it requires and then sends a deallocation request message again in his own slot. If the request is not granted, it makes a fresh request again.

As pointed out earlier in Section B.1, static allocation techniques like FDM and TDM are not much suitable for satellite so that the SPADE system is inherently inefficient. For building satellite networks with better performance ALOHA technique was next employed and many variations multiple uplinks and/or multiple downlinks, on-broad storage, etc. were employed to build efficient ALOHA networks. However, even the best ALOHA system could never achieve an efficiency above 1/e or 36.8% since a new approach as described in the following section was taken to achieve for satellite networks a much better performance than slotted ALOHA would provide.

B.5 RESERVATION ALOHA TYPE SATELLITE NETWORKS

It was observed that at high channel load while the performance of the ALOHA technique significantly deteriorates because of fast increase in the number of collisions, the performance of the TDM actually improves. Thus, various protocols have been put forward suggesting appropriate control techniques that basically make the channel behave like slotted ALOHA at low load and TDM at high load. Actually, all these schemes endeavour to strike, in a dynamic manner, a compromise between the complete absence and the total presence of the concept of reservation in the ALOHA and the TDM schemes, respectively. These techniques which have been categorized under the name Reservation ALOHA basically employ a varying degree of reservation and differ among themselves in the manner in which reservations are made and released. The present section will describe some of these reservation techniques.

A method by Binder starts out with TDM and changes back and forth between (slotted) ALOHA when the channel load is low and TDM when the channel load is high. Frames containing M equal slots are continuously repeated and each slot is permanently allocated to one of the stations. Whenever a slot goes idle, it become open for contention during the next frame. Any station can contend for an empty slot like this and whosoever succeeds becomes its temporary owner in the ALOHA mode and remains so till he either voluntarily releases his temporary ownership or is forced to release it by the permanent owner of the slot. When the permanent owner of a slot wants his slot back, he simply transmits a frame during his slot. If the slot is free, the transmission becomes successful and thereby the permanent owner retrieves his slot. Otherwise, his frame forces a collision with the frame transmitted by the temporary owner who then refrains from sending further in this slot and the slot is restored back to the permanent owner from the next frame onwards.

A serious problem with the Binder's method is that the number of users must be known in advance and must not vary with time. A possible solution, however, is that a slot may be permanently allotted to two or more stations who should then be assigned priority for resolving contention between themselves. An obvious inefficiency of Binder's method is that at least one slot must go idle to signal that the slot has become available for temporary ownership.

Roberts proposed a scheme based on transmissions only with prior reservation and this scheme was later extended by Greene and Edhremides. In accordance with this extended protocol named Distributed Reservation Control (DRC) Protocol each frame contains N data slots followed by a reservation slot containing N number of small subslots. When a station wants to send data, it first sends a short reservation request frame during one of the small τ-sec wide reservation subslots at the end of the current frame. If the transmission is successful then the station has been able to reserve a data slot in the next frame. However, the station must keep track of how many people have reserved before him (i.e., how long the queue is) so that it knows exactly in which data slot it must transmit. In the unusual case that there is no reservation during any frame, all the slots in the next frame are made reservation data slots (i.e., they contain only reservation subslots). It should be noted that since the reservation process is based on the slotted ALOHA algorithm, the success rate is limited to 1/e so that at most N data transmissions may occur during the next frame. Assuming that the reservation subslots are L times smaller than the data slots, the maximum efficiency of this DRC Protocol is

$$\frac{NL\tau}{NL\tau + Ne\tau} = \frac{L}{L+e}$$

Priority Oriented Demand Assignment (PODA) is the protocol proposed by Jacobs et Al which combines Robert's protocol and TDM. It employs a fixed number of slots/frame as in the other protocols but dynamically apportions them between data and reservation (in the form of subslots) depending on demand with the minimum allocated slots for reservation and data being 1 and 0, respectively. Thus, all slots contain reservation subslots when the channel is idle whereas no slots except the last one contains reservation subslots at the highest load. Figure B.5 illustrates the operation of the PODA as well as the DRC protocols. The reservation information includes several parameters like the frame size, priority, whether a single frame or a stream of frames (possibly corresponding to digitized speech signal) will be sent so that a complex channel scheduling is done rather than just first come first serve.

In addition to features like demand assignment, priority, integration of both voice and data, etc., the protocol also allows a station to make a reservation by setting some bits in a data frame to avoid waiting for the next reservation slot. Finally, the protocol has two variations, namely, Fixed PODA (FPODA) and Contention PODA (CPODA) depending on whether the reservation subslots are assigned to the users in a fixed (TDM) or contention (ALOHA) manner.

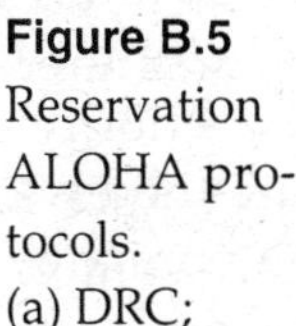

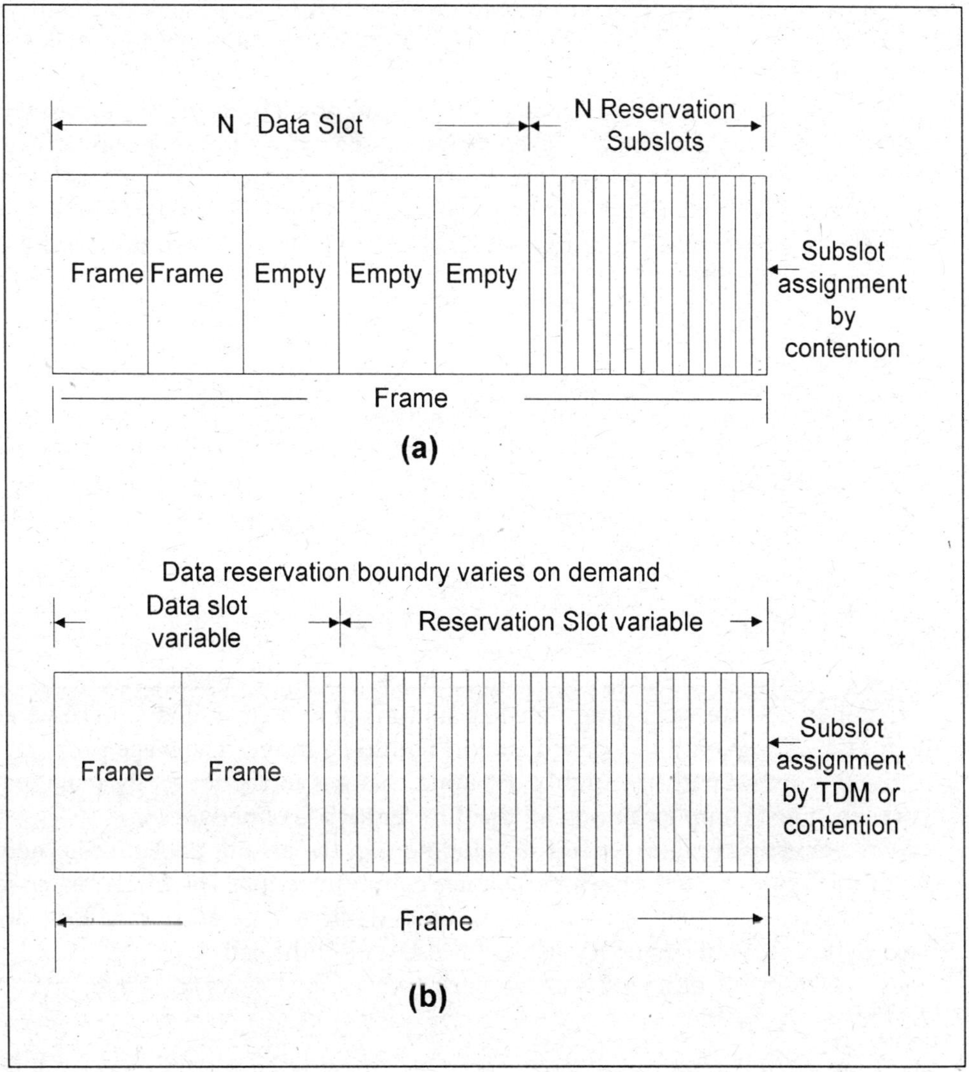

Figure B.5 Reservation ALOHA protocols. (a) DRC; (b) PODA.

B.6 PACKET RADIO NETWORKS

In a packet radio network, there are a large number of interconnected stations each equipped with a radio transmitter-receiver unit. The network is based neither entirely on point-to-point communication nor entirely on one broadcast channel; instead, it may be looked upon as a kind of "broadcast in parts" subnet. Each station can only hear a subset of the other stations and, correspondingly, it can be heard by all the stations in this subnet. Thus, any two stations transmitting simultaneously will collide at a station if they both belong to its subnet but will not collide otherwise. Thus, multiple nodes (stations) can transmit simultaneously without interference. Packet radio networks are attractive as relatively low cost networks (especially compared to satellites) where the stations are in poorly developed areas lacking telephone communication, the stations are mobile (e.g., a fleet of ship, cars and taxis in a metropolis, etc.) or the stations have a high peak-to-average traffic ratio making dedicated communication links wasteful.

The topology of a ratio network can be described by a graph, as shown in Figure B.6 although even for a moderate sized network the graph becomes unmanageably complex. Mobility of the stations dynamically changes the topology of a packet radio network. It should be noted that if a station's transmitting power is increased, it can be heard by a larger, set of stations and, in a similar manner, it can hear larger set of stations if the sensitivity of its receiver is increased.

Figure B.6 Graph representation of a packet radio network.

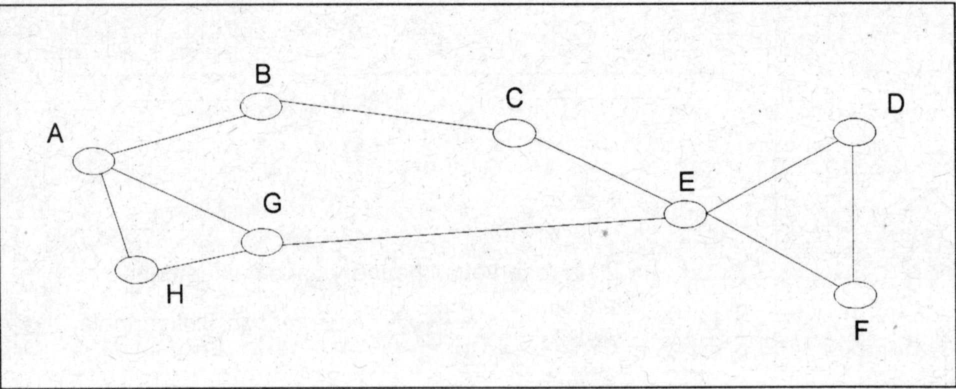

As an alternative measure, repeater stations may be installed to receive and rebroadcast the messages transmitted by each station within its range. The basic property of partial connectivity together with the highly dynamic changes in the topology make packet radio networks the most complex among all the different types of networks.

An interesting and important development in the area of packet radio network is the cellular radio which is used for mobile voice communication. The total area covered by the cellular radio network (e.g., a metroplis) is divided into a large number of local areas called cells. Each cell has a set of frequency bands for use within the cell.

Figure B.7 Partial graph of a cellular packet radio network.

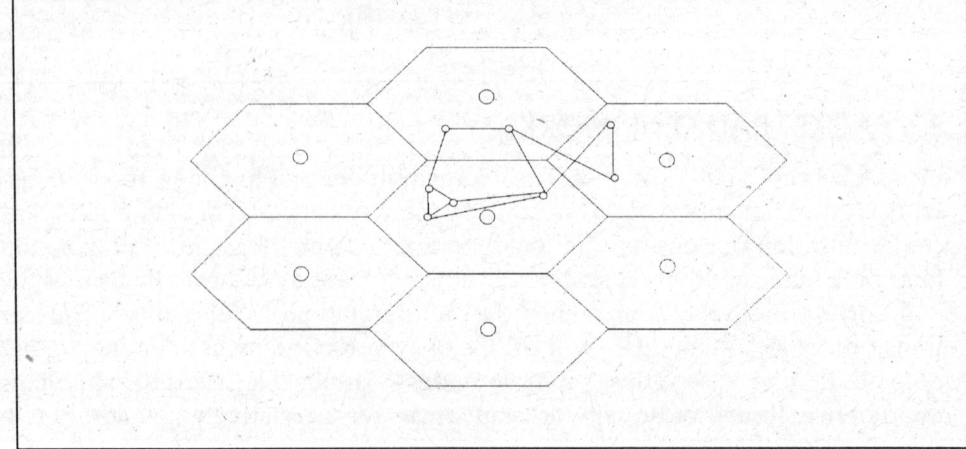

Theoretically, cell should have hexagonal shape so that the whole area is completely covered by cells in a mutually exclusive way (see Figure B.7). The cell size corresponds to the range of the mobile transmitters. This ensures that a station is heard by all stations within its own cell, some cell beyond that. Clearly, to avoid interference, neighbouring cell must have different frequencies. The problem of allocation of sets of frequencies to the cell under this condition is just the well known graph colouring problem. In addition to the large number of mobile stations in each cell, there is a centrally placed (at a high altitude) non-mobile "base" station which can communicate with all stations within its cell.

When a mobile station (for example, a cellular telephone in a car) is switched on, it first determines its base station by monitoring signals from all base stations and determining the strongest one among them. Immediately, it announces its telephone number to this base station which then tells it the cell number and the set of frequencies to be used. When the mobile telephone wants to make a call, it transmits a message to its base station which then allocates it a frequency, if available, and later deallocates this frequency at the end of the call. A station monitors all base station signals all the time. When it moves into a different cell, it discovers that the signal from some other base station has now become the strongest. It then informs its present base station about its new base station and the former then hands it over to the latter. Its new base station then instructs it to switch to the set of frequencies of the new base station. A central computer keeps track of the current location of every mobile station and all base stations have access to this central computer. Whenever a base station receives an incoming call to be forwarded to a particular station, it accesses the central computer to find out the destination station's whereabouts and then routes the incoming call via the proper base station.

Think big, always offer the best, and let it happen. The profits will automatically follow.

—RAI BAHADUR M. S. OBEROI

Glossary

32-bit In Windows, refers to the way memory is accessed. 32-bit applications access memory in 32-bit "chunks" (4 bytes). Large portions of Windows 95 and many of its new applications are 32-bit applications, and may run faster because it has become more efficient to access chunks of memory.

Abstract Syntax A machine-independent set of language constructs and rules used to describe objects, protocols, and other items.

Abstract Syntax Notation One (ASN.1) A machine-independent, abstract syntax developed as part of the OSI Reference Model. ASN.1 is used to describe data-structure and functions as a common syntax for sending data between two end systems that use different encoding systems.

Abuse of Privilege When a user performs an action that they should not have, according to organizational policy or law.

Access Control Lists Rules for packet filters (typically routers) that define which packets to pass and which to block.

Access Method A standardized procedure for locating desired records within a file. Access methods may be supported by a DATABASE MANAGEMENT SYSTEM or by an OPERATING SYSTEM.

Access operation Operations which access the state of a variable or object but do not modify it.

Access Router A router that connects your network to the external Internet. Typically, this is your first line of defense against attackers from the outside Internet. By enabling access control lists on this router, you'll be able to provide a level of protection for all of the hosts "behind" that router, effectively making that network a DMZ instead of an unprotected external LAN.

Account A form of access to a computer or network for a specific user name and password usually with a home directory, an E-mail in box, and a set of access privileges.

ACK Acknowledgement from a computer that a packet of data has been received and verified.

ACL access control list. List kept by a router to control access to or from the router for a number of services (for example, to prevent packets with a certain IP address from leaving a particular interface on the router).

Acoustic coupler A special type of modern (communications device) which allows an ordinary telephone to be used with a computer device for data transmission.

Action entry The lower right quadrant of a decision table; indicating the response to the question entered in the condition entry.

Active monitor Device responsible for monitoring a Token Ring. The active monitor ensures that tokens are not lost and that frames do not circulate indefinitely.

Adapters A network adapter is the hardware installed in computers that enable them to communicate on a network.

AFP Apple Talk Filing Protocol. Application- and presentation-layer protocol that allows users to share data files and application programs that reside on a file server.

Agent In network management, a process that resides in a managed device and reports the values of specified variables to management stations.

Anonymous FTP The most common use of FTP, the Internet file transfer protocol. FTP sites that allow anonymous FTP do not require a password or access–one only has to log in as anonymous and enter one's E-mail address as a password.

API An acronym for Application Program Interface. Foxpro's API allows your C and assembly language routines to interact with FoxPro.

APPC Advanced Program-to-Program Communication. IBM SNA system software that allows high-speed communication between programs on different computers in a distributed computing environment.

Application-Level Firewall A firewall system in which service is provided by processes that maintain complete TCP connection state and sequencing. Application level firewalls often re-address traffic so that outgoing traffic appears to have originated from the firewall, rather than the internal host.

Application layer Layer 7 of the OSI reference model. This layer provides services to application processes (such as electronic mail, file transfer, and terminal emulation) that are outside the OSI model. The application layer identifies and establishes the availability of intended communication partners (and the resources required to connect with them), synchronizes cooperating applications, and establishes agreement on procedures for error recovery and control of data integrity.

APPS In the network terminology, APPS is called the public directory on a server hard disk.

ARCNET Attached Resource Computer Network 2.5-Mbps token-bus LAN developed in the late 1970s and early 1980s by Datapoint Corporation.

ARP Address Resolution Protocol. Internet protocol used to map an IP address to a MAC address. Defined in RFC 826.

ASCII (American Standard Code for Information Interchange) A standard coding system for computers. ASCII-7 is a 7-bit code and its extended version ASCII-8 is an 8-bit code.

ASCII File It is a document file in the universally recognized text *format* called ASCII (American Standard Code for Information Interchange). An ASCII file contains characters, spaces, punctuation, carriage return, and sometimes tabs and an end-of-file marker, but it contains no formatting information.

Asynchronous communication Communication between units operating independently.

Asynchronous routing A function of a remote-access server that provides Layer-3 routing functionality to connect LANs via an asynchronous serial WAN link.

Asynchronous Transfer Mode (ATM) ATM is a switching and multiplexing technology that enables voice, data and video to be transmitted simultaneously over WAN's at high speed regardless of traffic, data is converted into fixed-length (53-byte) packet called cells, that are transported at high speeds through the network. These cells are then converted back to their respective traffic types at the destination.

ATM Switch A device that controls information traffic between PCs or workstation using high-speed link.

Attenuation Attenuation is decrease in the strength of transmitted signals.

Audit trail A feature of data processing systems that allows for the study of data as processed from step to step. In this, an auditor can trace all transactions that affect an account.

Authentication The process of determining the identity of a user who is attempting to access a system. Also in security, the verification of the identity of a person or process.

Authentication Token A portable device used for authenticating a user. Authentication tokens operate by challenge/response, time-based code sequences, or other techniques. This may include paper-based lists of one-time passwords.

Authorization The process of determining what types of activities are permitted. Usually, authorization is in the context of authentication: once you have authenticated a user, they may be authorized different types of access or activity.

Automatic Teller Machine (ATM) The ATM is a terminal of the bank's computer network and is operated by a customer himself through a VDU and a keyboard. The customer is given a plastic card at the time of opening his account. The name of the account holder and the account number are magnetically coded on the card. The customer is also given a PIN (Personal Identification Number) which is only known to him. When the customer inserts his card in the ATM, it checks the magnetically coded data and identifies the customer. He then types in his identification number and the amount to be withdrawn. The ATM checks the balance and gives out the currency along with a statement of the transaction. The amount gets debited from the account.

Bandwidth The range of frequencies available for data transmission. The wider the bandwidth of a communications system, the more data it can transmit in a given period of time. It is expressed in Kilobits per seconds. The bandwidth determines the rate at which information can be sent through a communication channel

Bandwidth domain In a LAN, the set of devices that share and compete for bandwidth. Bandwidth domains are bounded by switches, bridges, or routers. A hub or repeater does not bound a bandwidth domain. Also called a *collision domain* on Ethernet networks.

Bar Code A coding structure in which characters are represented by means of a series of parallel bars.

Baseband System A networking system in which the channel supports a single digital signal.

Baseline Characterization of the normal traffic flow and performance of a network, used as input to a new or enhanced design for the network.

BER Bit Error Rate. It is the ratio of received bits that contain errors to the total number of received bits.

BGP Border Gateway Protocol. Inter-domain routing protocol that exchanges reachability information with other BGP systems. BGP Versions 4 (BGP4) is the predominant inter-domain routing protocol used on the Internet.

Binaries newsgroup A Usenet newsgroup dedicated to the posting of uuen-coded binary files, often .gif or .jpg image files. Some sites will not carry binaries newsgroups because their uuen-coded binaries consume so much band width.

Binary transfer protocol When using a communications program to transmit binary files, it is very important to ensure that errors are not introduced into the data stream. Various binary transfer protocols check for matches between the data transmitted and the data received. The most common protocols are Xmodem, Ymodem, and Zmodem.

BISYNC Abbreviation for binary synchronous. A method of transmitting data—a half-duplex, character-oriented, synchronous data communications transmission method originated by IBM in 1964.

Bit Stands for binary digit. The values are 1 or 0 (zero).

BLOB Binary Large Object. Essentially, a long bit string used for complex data.

BOOTP Bootstrap Protocol. Protocol used by a network node to determine the IP address of its interfaces in order to achieve network booting.

Bridge A device that supports LAN-to-LAN communications. Bridges may be equipped to provide frame relay support to the LAN devices they serve. They also handles traffic between two similar or different LANs. As the name suggests, this device bridges two different network segments regardless of their wiring or topology. It memorizes all the network addresses on both sides of the segments, and manages the flow of traffic between the to LANs by reading the address of every packet of data that it receives. The address is contained in the header of each network packet being transmitted. It operates at the data link layer of the OSI model for computer-to-computer communications. Bridges can also be configured to segment off certain areas. In this sense, a bridge acts as a gatekeeper that keeps out unwanted packets. Bridges operate at the data-link layer (Layer 2) of the OSI reference model. A bridge filters, forwards, or floods an incoming frame based on the MAC destination address of the frame.

Broadband channel The fastest carriers which have data transfer rates of 1 million baud (bits/second) or more.

Broadband system A network system in which several analog signals share the same physical network channel.

Broadcast address Special address reserved for sending a message to all nodes. Generally, a broadcast address is a MAC destination address of all ones (FF:FF:FF:FF:FF:FF: in hexadecimal). Compare with *multicast address* and *unicast address*.

Broadcast domain The set of all devices that receives broadcast frames originating from any device within the set. Broadcast domains are bounded by routers (which do not forward broadcast frames). A switch or hub does not bound a broadcast domain.

Bus Circuits that provide a communication path between two or more devices of a digital computer system.

Bus Topology A network geometric arrangement in which a single connecting line is shared by a number of nodes.

Campus network A set of LAN segments and building networks in a geographical area that is a few miles in diameter.

Carrier Any device that is used to transmit data from one location to another.

Cell Basic data unit for ATM switching and multiplexing. Cells contain identifiers that specify the data stream to which they belong. Each cell consists of a 5-byte header and 48 bytes of payload.

CER Cell Error Ratio. In ATM, the ratio of transmitted cells that have errors to the total cells sent in a transmission for a specific period of time.

Challenge/Response An authentication technique whereby a server sends an unpredictable challenge to the user, who computes a response using some form of authentication token.

Channel (1) A path for carrying signals between a source and a destination. (2) A track on a magnetic tape or a band on a magnetic drum. (3) A pathway through which information can be transmitted. (4) It refers to the user access channel across which frame relay data travels.

CHAP Challenge Handshake Authentication Protocol. Security feature supported on links using PPP encapsulation that identifies the remote end of a PPP session using a handshake protocol and a variable challenge value that is unique and unpredictable. Compare with *PAP*.

CIP Channel Interface Processor. Channel attachment interface for Cisco 7000 series routers. The CIP is used to connect a host Mainframe to a control unit, eliminating the need for an FEP for channel attachment.

Circuit switching The simplest method of data communication in which a dedicated physical path is established between the sending and the receiving stations through the nodes of a network for the complete duration of information exchange.

Client Node or software program that requests services from a server.

Client/server Distributed-computing network systems in which transaction responsibilities are divided into two parts: client and server. Clients rely on servers for services such as file storage, printing, and processing power. Also a computing model in which the application processing load is distributed between a client and a server computer, which share information over a network. Typically, the client is a PC running front-end software that knows how to communicate with the server (usually database server). The client/server model improves performance, because the client and server share the processing load.

Client/Server architecture A configuration of computers on a network such that computing tasks are specialized—several computers (clients) interface to users while specialized operations are performed on another (typically smaller) group of one or more computers called servers. Structured Query Language (SQL) is typically used by clients to perform operations on data stored in servers.

Client/server networking As opposed to *peer-to-peer* networking, an arrangement in which central computers called *servers* supply data and peripherals for use by *client* computers (workstations). Typically, a server contains a large, hard disk that supplies not only data, but also programs. It even executes programs. A server might also supply printers and modems for clients to use on the network. In other words, client/server refers to an architecture for distributed processing wherein subtasks can be distributed between services, CPUs, or even networked computers for more efficient execution.

Collision Collisions are an error condition in Ethernet networks. A collision occurs when data packets are transmitted at the same time by two different network nodes. This is very common in large networks. There exist technologies like CSMA/CD which check for collisions in the network and recover. Also in Ethernet, the result of two nodes transmitting simultaneously.

Collision domain In Ethernet, the network area within which frames that have collided are propagated. Repeaters and hubs propagate collisions; LAN switches, bridges and routers do not. See also *bandwidth domain*.

Communications channel A medium through which data (in the form of electrical signals) is transferred from one location to another.

Communications processor A processing unit that coordinates networks and data communications. Within a computer network, it ensures that data flows to and from different computer systems correctly and efficiently.

Communications protocol A set of rules and procedures established to interconnect different computers and communicate between them.

Contention The method a network uses to determine access to a channel when two or more nodes wish to use it at the same time.

Copper Data Distribution Interface A network technology capable of carrying data at 100 Mbps over unshielded twisted pair (UTP) cable. CDDI is a trade name of Crescendo Communications (acquired by Cisco Systems in 1993) and commonly used instead of the general term Twisted Pair Physical Layer Medium (TP-PMD). TP-PMD is the general ANSI standard name for this FDDI-like service. CDDI cable lengths are limited to 100 meters.

Cryptographic Checksum A one-way function applied to a file to produce a unique "fingerprint" of the file for later reference. Checksum systems are a primary means of detecting filesystem tampering on Unix.

Cryptography A system of secret communications to improve the security of confidential computerized files.

CSMA/CD A contention method (Carrier sense, multiple access, collision detect) in which a transmitting node first tests the channel and, if the channel is clear, then transmits the desired message. If two stations transmit at the same time, the collision is detected and retransmission is forced. Also Carrier Sense Multiple Access with Collision Detection. Media-access mechanism wherein devices determine if another device is already transmitting before starting their own transmissions. If no transmission is sensed for a specific period of time, a device can transmit. If multiple devices transmit at once, a collision occurs and is detected by all colliding devices. This collision subsequently delays retransmission from those devices for some random length of time. CSMA/CD is used by Ethernet and IEEE 802.3.

CSU Channel Service Unit. Digital interface device that connects end-user equipment to the local digital telephone loop. Often referred to together with DSU, as CSU/DSU.

CTD Cell Transfer Delay. In ATM, the elapsed time between a cell-exit event at the source UNI and the corresponding cell-entry event at the destination UNI for a particular connection.

Cyberspace A term, popularised by author William Gibson, for the shared imaginary reality of computer networks. Some people use cyberspace as a synonym for the Internet. Others hold out for the more complete physical-seeming con-sensual reality of Gibson's novels.

Cycle time The time interval between the instant at which a read/write command is given to a memory and the instant when the next such instruction can be issued to the memory (also known as memory cycle time).

Data-link layer Layer 2 of the OSI reference model. This layer provides reliable transit of data across a physical link. The data-link layer is concerned with physical addressing, network topology, line discipline, error notification, ordered delivery of frames, and flow control. The IEEE has divided this layer into two sublayers: the MAC sublayer and the LLC sublayer.

Data communications system A system consisting of carriers and related devices used to transport data from one point to another.

DCE Data Communications Equipment or data circuit-terminating equipment Devices and connections of a communications network that comprise the network end of the user-to-network interface. Modems and interface cards are examples of DCE.

DDR Dial-on-Demand Routing. Technique whereby a router can automatically initiate and close a circuit-switched session as transmitting stations demand.

Dial-up Networking Dialing into a network from a remote site by using a modem.

Directory access protocol (DAP) An X-500 protocol governing communication between a directory user agent and a directory system agent.

Discontiguous subnet An IP subnet that is made up of two or more physical networks that are separated by routers.

Distance-vector routing algorithm Class of routing algorithms that call for each router to send its routing table in periodic update packets to its neighbors.

Distributed data processing (DDP) The decentralization of a computer system through the use of multiple computers interconnected by a communications network. It facilitates data processing capabilities at the location of the end-user.

Distribution layer Connects network services to the access layer in a hierarchical topology, and implements policies regarding security, traffic loading, and routing.

DNS Domain Name System. System used in the Internet for translating names of network nodes into addresses.

DNS spoofing Assuming the DNS name of another system by either corrupting the name service cache of a victim system, or by compromising a domain name server for a valid domain.

DTE Data Terminal Equipment. Device at the user end of a user-network interface that serves as a data source, destination, or both. DTE connects to a data network through a DCE device (for example, a modem) and typically uses clocking signals generated by the DCE. DTE includes such devices as computers, internetworking devices, and multiplexers.

Dual-Homed Gateway A dual-homed gateway is a system that has two or more network interfaces, each of which is connected to a different network. In firewall configurations, a dual-homed gateway usually acts to block or filter some or all of the traffic trying to pass between the networks.

Dumb terminal A terminal that has no local processing capability.

Duplex A data communication facility on which data can be transmitted in two directions. A facility where information travels both ways.

DVMRP Distance-Vector Multicast Routing Protocol. Multicast routing protocol, largely based on RIP. Packets are forwarded on all outgoing interfaces until pruning occurs. Defined in RFC 1075.

Dynamic SLIP A type of SLIP access to the Internet, in which the user is supplied with a new IP address, drawn from a pool of possibilities every time he/she connects. This enables the service provider to assign fewer IP addresses to its SLIP customers, with the trade-off being that the users can not function as a host without a consistent address.

EISA Bus Acronym for Extended Industry Standard Architecture, a bus standard introduced in 1988 by a consortium of nine computer-industry companies. This 32 bit bus was developed which was backward compatible with the existing expansion boards. It can accept ISA bus cards.

ELAN emulated LAN. ATM network in which an Ethernet or Token Ring LAN is emulated using a client/server model. ELANs are composed of an LEC, an LES, a BUS, and an LECS. ELANs are defined by the LANE specification.

Electronic Data Interchange (EDI) EDI is the transfer of electronic messages from one company to another using a network. Companies use EDI to facilitate business-to-business transactions like purchase orders, purchase confirmations, invoices, and payments. EDI messages can be exchanged using a WAN or the Internet.

Electronic funds transfer (EFT) A general term referring to a cashless approach used to pay for goods and services.

Electronic mail A general term to describe the transmission of messages by the use of computing systems and telecommunications facilities.

Electronic Mail/Message System (EMMS) A system that can store and deliver, by electronic means, text and messages that would otherwise be forwarded through the postal service or sent verbally over telephone lines.

Encapsulating bridging A bridging method for connecting LANs across a network of a different type, for example, connecting Ethernet LANs via an FDDI backbone. The entire frame from one network is placed inside the frame used by the data-link layer protocol of the other network.

Encryption Converting stored or transmitted data to a coded form in order to prevent it from being read by unauthorized persons. Also application of a specific algorithm to alter the appearance of data, making it incomprehensible to those who are not authorized to see the information.

Encryption Key A code used by an encryption algorithm to scramble and unscramble data.

End user Any individual who uses the information generated by a computer based system.

Enhanced Interior Gateway Routing Protocol Advanced version of IGRP developed by Cisco. Provides superior convergence properties and operating efficiency, and combines the advantages of link-state protocols with those of distance-vector protocols.

Enterprise network Large and diverse internetwork connecting most major points in an organization. An enterprise network typically consists of building and campus networks, remote-access services, and one or more WANs.

Ethernet LAN technology invented by Xerox Corporation and developed jointly by Xerox, Intel, and Digital Equipment Corporation. Ethernet networks use CSMA/CD and run over a variety of cable types at 10 Mbps. Ethernet is similar to IEEE 802.3. See also *Fast Ethernet.*

Ethernet Switch A network service that manages traffic between workstation, usually when there are many sources of information in a network.

Executive routine A master program in an operating system that controls the execution of other programs. It is also known as the executive, monitor, or supervisor.

Executive Workstation Expert System Special desktop computer-based units designed for busy people who do not like to type. They have special function keys, and may accept input through the use of a mouse or a touch screen. They have the ability to perform word/data processing, manage data bases, produce graphics, and support many other activities.

Extended ASCII Extended ASCII provides added capability by allowing for 128 additional characters, such as accented letters, graphics characters, and special symbols.

Extranet An extranet is the part of a corporate intranet that allows companies to communicate with the intranets of their customers and suppliers, facilitating electronic transactions.

Faceplate A connecting point in a cable system that permits a network cable from a movable computer to connect with a permanently installed cable system. This is generally a plate installed in the wall.

Facsimile (FAX) Transmission of pictures, texts, maps, graphs, etc., over transmission lines, phone lines, and other carriers between geographically separated points. An image is scanned at a transmitting point and duplicated at a receiving point.

Fast Ethernet An improved version of the Ethernet, Fast Ethernet provides customers with a flexible and affordable way to scale network performance and interoperate with a wide range of other networking technologies. It is unique tool for an enterprise to augment the throughput and performance of existing LANs, with a cost-effective high-speed connectivity option for linking work groups and servers. Also any of a number of 100-Mbps Ethernet specifications. Fast Ethernet offers a speed increase ten times that of the original IEEE 802.3 specification, while preserving such qualities as frame format, MAC mechanisms, and frame size.

FDDI A high-speed protocol standard for sending network data over fiber cabling. An FDDI network using multimode fiber-optic cable can include as many as five hundred stations up to 2 kilometers. With single mode fiber, run length increases up to 60 kilometers. LAN standard specifying a 100-Mbps token-passing network using fiber-optic cable and a dual-ring architecture to provide redundancy.

Fiber-optic cable Physical medium capable of conducting modulated light transmission. Fiber-optic cable is not susceptible to electromagnetic interference, and is capable of high data rates. Also a data transmission medium made of tiny threads of glass or plastic that can transmit huge amount of information at the speed of light.

File Server architecture A configuration of computers on a network that is similar to a client/server architecture, except that the server is mostly a repository of a data on which it cannot itself perform queries or processing. When a client needs to make a query, the server sends all data that could possibly be relevant over the network, which is not efficient. Hence this approach is replaced by client/server architecture.

File Transfer Protocol Permits files to be transferred from one computer to another using a TCP connection. A related but less common file transfer protocol. Trivial File Transfer Protocol (TFTP), uses UDP rather than TCP to transfer file data.

Firewall Router or remote-access server (or several routers or access servers) designated as a buffer between connected networks. A firewall uses access lists and other methods to ensure the security of a network. Also A system or combination of systems that enforces a boundary between two or more networks.

Flat network design A network design that has little or no hierarchy or modularity and is generally only appropriate for small shared or switched LANs.

Flooding Traffic-passing technique used by switches and bridges, in which traffic received on an interface is sent out all interfaces except the interface on which the information was received.

Forwarding Process of sending a frame toward its ultimate destination by way of an internetworking device.

Fragmentation Process of breaking a packet into smaller units when transmitting over a network medium that cannot support the original size of the packet.

Frame The basic package of information on a network channel. Also logical grouping of information sent as a data-link layer unit over a transmission medium. Often refers to the header and trailer, used for synchronization and error control, that surround the user data contained in the unit.

Frame Relay Industry-standard, switched data-link layer protocol that handles multiple virtual circuits between connected devices. Frame Relay is more efficient than X.25, the protocol for which it is generally considered a replacement.

Frame Relay Network A telecommunications network based on frame relay technology. In this technology, data is multiplexed.

Frequency division multiplexing A method used to concurrently transmit data between several transmitters and receivers over a single transmission medium. The available bandwidth of a physical medium is divided into smaller, disjointed logical bandwidths and each of the component bandwidths is used as a separate communications line (channel).

FTP File Transfer Protocol. It is an application protocol, Part of the TCP/IP protocol stack, used for transferring files between network nodes. FTP is defined in RFC 959.

Full duplex A method of using a communication channel in which signals can be transmitted between a source and a destination in both directions simultaneously. Also capability for simultaneous data transmission between a sending station and a receiving station.

Full mesh Term describing a network in which devices are organized in a mesh topology, with each network node having either a physical circuit or a virtual circuit connecting it to every other network node.

Gateway A device that is used to interface two otherwise incompatible network facilities. Also a term used in networking. It is a computer providing a connection between two networks, two E-mail handling systems, or a Usenet newsgroup and a mailing list. A gateway reformats the data so that it will be acceptable to the system it is passing into. A shared connection between a local-area network and a larger system, such as a Mainframe computer or a large packet-switching network, whose communications protocols are different. Usually slower then a bridge or router, a gateway is a combination of hardware and software with its own processor and memory used to perform protocol conversions.

Gigabit Ethernet 1000-Mbps LAN technologies specified in IEEE 802.3z. Gigabit Ethernet offers a speed increase 100 times that of the original IEEE 802.3 specification, while preserving such qualities as frame format, MAC mechanisms, and frame size.

Goodput Generally referring to the measurement of actual data successfully transmitted from the sender (s) to receiver (s). In an ATM network, this is often a more useful measurement than the number of ATM cells-per-second throughput of an ATM switch if that switch is experiencing cell loss that results in many incomplete, and therefore unusable, frames arriving at the recipient.

Gopher Gopher is an information gathering tool used for Internet that offers a smooth, menu-driven way to traverse international "gopherspace" —which these days literally means several hundred servers worldwide, offering text, computer programs, audio, still images, and even movie clips. It provides a seamless, "hidden programming" interface with which you can transfer files, browse databases, and telnet to sites around the globe, simply and easily.

Group Band A group consists of fields that appear together based on some criteria that you specify by choosing the Data Grouping...option on the Report menu.

H.320 Suite of international standard specifications for videoconferencing over circuit-switched media such as ISDN, fractional T1, or switched-56 lines.

Hacker A computer adept, some one who enjoys working with computers and testing the limits of systems, and enthusiastic or fast (or both) programmer. (Outside of the Internet, the word hacker has unsavory connotations, suggesting someone who breaks into computer network and steals or vandalizes information. On the Internet, such malevolent hackers are called crackers)

Half duplex Capability for data transmission in only one direction at a time between a sending station and a receiving station.

Handshake A trade term that refers to what takes place when two computers or a computer and a terminal device are interconnected in such a way that they can exchange information.

Handshaking Process whereby two protocol entities synchronize during connection establishment.

Hardware The physical components of a computer system such as electronic, magnetic, and mechanical devices.

Hierarchical network A communications network in which computers or processors are connected in a tree-like structure. In Usernet, the organisation of newsgroups into general areas, topics and subtopics, or the major groupings themselves.

Hierarchical network design A technique for designing scalable campus and enterprise network topologies using a layered, modular model.

Hierarchical routing A model for distributing knowledge of a network topology among internetwork routers. With hierarchical routing, no single router needs to understand the complete topology.

Hold down State into which a route is placed so routers will neither advertise the route nor accept advertisements about the route for a specific length of time (the holddown period). Holddown is used to flush bad information about a route from all routers in the network.

Hop Term describing the passage of a data packet between two network nodes (for example, between two routers).

Hop count Routing metric used to measure the distance between a source and a destination in number of routers or hops between the source and destination. Also in routing, the number of links that must be crossed to get from any given source node to any given destination node. The destination network cannot be more than 16 hops (servers or routers) from the source.

Host-based Security The technique of securing an individual system from attack. Host-based security is an -operating system and version dependent.

Host computer The main control computer in a network of distributed processors and terminals.

HSRP Hot Standby Router Protocol. Provides high network availability and transparent network topology changes. HSRP creates a Hot Standby router group with a lead router that services all packets sent to the Hot standby address. The lead router is monitored by other routers in the group, and if it fails, one of these standby routers inherits the lead position and the Hot Standby group address.

HTTP Hypertext transport protocol, the Internet protocol that defines how a Web server responds to requests for files, made via anchors and URLs.

Hub A network device where the information flow is accumulated and then distributed to various groups and users. It can be used between users on the same LAN and users on different LANs. One of the most essential components in a network. Hubs are devices that serve as the central point where cables from all nodes come together. Hubs are available in all shapes and sizes. There are dumb hubs which simply pass on the signals from one node to another. Smart hubs are also there that provide limited management capabilities. There are also intelligent hubs, which support multiple LANs and topologies, provide extensive management capabilities, and can ever house other module types, such as routers and bridges. Active and passive hubs are also there. Active hubs function as repeaters, and passive hubs simply pass on signals. In Ethernet and IEEE 802.3, an Ethernet multiport repeater, sometimes referred to as a *concentrator*.

Hub-and-spoke topology A topology that consists of one central network and a set of remote networks each with one connection to the central network and no direct connections to each other. Traffic between remote networks goes through the hub network.

Hypertext A metaphor for presenting information in which text, images, sounds, and actions become linked together in a complex, non-sequential web of associations that permit the user to browse through related topics, regardless of the presented order of the topics. These links are often established both by the author of a hypertext document and by the user, depending on the intent of the hypertext document.

Hypertext Markup Language (HTML) This is the format used for writing documents to be viewed with a World Wide Web browser. Items in the document can be text, image, sounds, and links to other HTML documents or sites, services and resources on the Internet.

ICMP Internet Control Message Protocol. Network-layer TCP/IP protocol that reports errors and provides other information relevant to IP packet processing. Documented in RFC 792.

IEEE 802 A quick reference to the ubiquitous IEEE 802 family of standards.

IEEE 802.10 Standard for Interoperable LAN Security, also known as SILS. It was approved in 1992.

IEEE 802.12 Standard for 100 Mbps demand-priority access method Physical-layer and repeater specifications, also known as 100VG-AnyLAN. It was approved in 1995.

IEEE 802.3 Standard for LAN - based Carrier Sense Multiple Access with Collision Detection (CSMA/CD) access methods and Physical layers, as well as the basis of ISO/IEC 8802-3. This is sometimes referred to as the 'Ethernet standard". It was revised in 1996.

IEEE 802.311 Standard for wireless LAN MAC and Physical-layer specifications. Current drafts and focus on the 2.4 GHz band.

IEEE 802.3b Standard for broadband media attachment unit and specifications for 10Broad36. It was approved in 1985 and incorporated into ISO/IEC 8802-3.

IEEE 802.3c Standard for 10 Mbps baseband repeaters. Approved in 1985 and incorporated into ISO/IEC 8802-3.

IEEE 802.3d Standard for media attachment units and base-band media specifications over fiber-optic repeater links. It was approved in 1987 and incorporated into ISO/IEC 8802-3.

IEEE 802.3e Standard for physical signaling, media attachment, and baseband media specifications, for a 1 Mbit/sec network-that is, 1Base5. It was approved in 1987 and incorporated into ISO/IEC 8802-3.

IEEE 802.3h Standard for layer management in Carrier Sense Multiple Access with Collision Detection (CSMA/CD) networks. It was approved in 1990 and incorporated into ISO/IEC 8802-3.

IEEE 802.3i Standard covering two areas: Multi-segment 10 Mbps baseband networks and twisted-pair media for 10Base-T networks. It was approved in 1990 and incorporated into ISO/IEC 8802-3. Also Conformance statement for the 10Base-T media attachment unit protocol. It was approved in 1992 and incorporated into ISO/IEC 8802-3.

IEEE 802.3j Standard for 10 Mbps active and passive star-based segments using fiber optics-that is, 10Base-F. It was approved in 1993 and incorporated into ISO/IEC 8802-3.

IEEE 802.3k Standard for layer management for 10 Mbps baseband repeaters. Approved in 1992, it was incorporated into ISO/IEC 8802-3.

IEEE 802.3p Standard for the 10 Mbps base-band media attachment units' layer management. It was approved in 1993 and incorporated into ISO/IEC 8802-3.

IEEE 802.3q Guidelines for the development of managed objects. It was approved in 1993 and incorporated into ISO/IEC 8802-3.

IEEE 802.3r The standard for the Carrier Sense Multiple Access with Collision Detection (CSMA/CD) access method and Physical lay specifications using 10Base-5. It was updated in 1996.

IEEE 802.3t Standard for supporting 120-ohm cables in 10Base-t simplex link segments. It was approved in 1995 and incorporated into ISO/IEC 8802-3.

IEEE 802.3u Supplement to 802.3 covering MAC parameters, the Physical layer, and repeaters for 100 Mbps operation — that is, 100 Base-T, generally known as Fast Ethernet. It was approved in 1995.

IEEE 802.3v Standard for supporting 150 ohm cables in 10Base-T link segments. Approved in 1995 and incorporated into ISO/IEC 8802-3.

IEEE 802.3w Proposed standard for enhanced MAC algorithms.

IEEE 802.3x Proposed standard for 802.3 full-duplex operation.

IEEE 802.3y Proposed Physical-layer specification for 100 Mbps operation on two pair of Category 3 or better balanced twisted-pair-cable — that is, 100Base-T2.

IEEE 802.3z Proposed standard for Physical layer, repeater, and management parameters for 1,000 Mbps operation; often referred to as "Gigabit Ethernet".

IEEE 802.4 Standard for token-passing bus access methods and Physical-layer specifications. It was approved in 1990.

IEEE 802.5 Standard for Token-Ring access methods and Physical-layer specifications—that is, common Token Ring architecture. It became the basis of ISO/IEC 8802-5. The current version was approved in 1995.

IGRP Interior Gateway Routing Protocol. An interior routing protocol developed by Cisco to address the problems associated with routing in large, heterogeneous networks.

Integrated Services Digital Network (ISDN) A special phone line that supports modem speeds up to 64 Kbps. However, these phone line can be quite expensive to acquire. Many ISDN adapters support two-channel access.

Intelligent terminal A terminal having local processing capability. It has a built-in CPU and can perform specific functions such as editing data, controlling other terminals, etc.

Inter process communication The topology provided by an operating system to allow concurrent processes to communicate with each other.

Interactive Mode Used to enter commands directly from the keyboard.

Interface The point at which independent systems or diverse groups interact. It consists of the devices, rules or conventions by which one component of a system communication with another. It is also the point of communication between a person and a computer.

Internet Protocol (IP) A low-level protocol that routes packets of data across separate networks tied together by routers to form the Internet or an intranet. Data travels in packets called IP datagrams.

Internet telephony Generic term used to describe various approaches to running voice traffic over IP networks, in particular, the Internet.

Internet work packet exchange (IPX) Novell's NetWare network layer protocol that specifies addressing, routing, and switching packets between a server and workstations and across interconnected LANs. Encapsulated IPX packets can be carried by Ethernet packets and token ring frames.

Internetworking General term used to refer to the industry and technologies devoted to connecting networks together. Also Collection of networks interconnected by routers.

Intrusion Detection Detection of break-ins or break-in attempts either manually or via software expert systems that operate on logs or other information available on the network.

IP Internet Protocol. Network-layer protocol in the TCP/IP stack offering a connectionless internetwork service. IP provides features for addressing, type-of-service specification, fragmentation and reassembly, and security. Defined in RFC 791.

IP address 32 bit address assigned to hosts using TCP/IP. An IP address belongs to one of five classes (A, B, C, D, or E) and is written as four octets separated by periods (dotted decimal format). Each address consists of a network number, an optional sub-network number, and a host number.

IP multicast Routing technique that allows IP traffic to be propagated from one source to a number of destinations. Rather than sending one packet to each destination, one packet is sent to a multicast group identified by a single IP destination group address.

IP Splicing or Hijacking An attack whereby an active, established, session is intercepted and co-opted by the attacker. IP Splicing attacks may occur after an authentication has been made, permitting the attacker to assume the role of an already authorized user. Primary protections against IP Splicing rely on encryption at the session or network layer.

IP Spoofing An attack whereby a system attempts to illicitly impersonate another system by using its IP network address.

ISA Bus Abbreviation for Industry Standard Architecture. It is an unofficial designation for the bus design of the IBM PC/XT, which allows various adapters to be added to the system by means of inserting plug-in-cards into expansion slots.

ISO International Organization for Standardization. International organization that is responsible for a wide range of standards, including those relevant to networking. ISO developed the OSI reference model, a popular networking reference model.

ISO 9000 Set of international quality-management standards defined by ISO. The standards, which are not specific to any country, industry, or product, allow companies to demonstrate that they have specific processes in place to maintain an effective quality system.

ISO protocol A communication protocol to interconnect geographically dispersed heterogeneous computers. This protocol has been standardized by the International Standards Organization (ISO).

ISP Internet service provider. Company that provides Internet access to other companies and individuals.

Jitter Communication line distortion caused by the variation of a signal from its reference timing positions.

Keepalive message Message sent by one network device to inform another network device that the virtual circuit between the two is still active.

Kerberos An authentication system that provides user-to-host security for application-layer protocols such as FTP and Telnet.

LAN Local Area Network. High-speed, low-error data network covering a relatively small geographic area (up to a few thousand meters). LANs connect workstations, peripherals, terminals, and other devices in a single building or other geographically limited.area. Also a digital communication system capable of interconnecting a large number of computers, terminals and other peripheral devices within a limited geographical area, typically within 1 km.

LANE (Local Area Network Emulation) LANE enables ATMLAN clients to access and use existing LAN application through a software layer added to the emulating devices. This software layer becomes an integral part of that device's ATM protocol Stack.

Latency 1. Delay between the time a device requests access to a network and the time it is granted permission to transmit. 2. Delay between the time a device receives a frame and the time that frame is forwarded out the destination port.

Latency time In case of disk storage, the time taken for the desired record to come under the read/write head positioned over that track. Maximum latency time equals the time taken by disk to rotate once.

Layer-3 switch Switch that filters and forwards packets based on MAC addresses and network addresses.

Leased line Transmission line reserved by a communications carrier for the private use of a customer.

Least Privilege Designing operational aspects of a system to operate with a minimum amount of system privilege. This reduces the authorization level at which various actions are performed and decreases the chance that a process or user with high privileges may be caused to perform unauthorized activity resulting in a security breach.

LLC (Logical Link Control) The LLC provides addressing and control of the data link. It specifies which mechanisms are to be used for addressing stations over the transmission medium and for controlling the data exchanged between the originator and recipient machines.

Link A communication path between two nodes or channel. Also Network communications channel consisting of a circuit or transmission path and all related equipment between a sender and a receiver.

Local acknowledgment Method whereby an intermediate network node, such as a router, responds to acknowledgments for a remote end host. Use of local acknowledgments reduces network overhead and, therefore, the risk of time-outs.

Logging The process of storing information about events that occured on the firewall or network.

Logical topology The geometric arrangement of the nodes and links of a network as they function to support information transfer in the network.

Long-haul Services Communication networks (such as the public telephone) that permit computer networking over extended geographic distances.

LSA Link-State Advertisement. Multicast packet used by link-state protocols that contains information about neighbors and path costs. LSAs are used by the receiving routers to maintain their routing tables.

MAC Media Access Control. Lower of the two sublayers of the data-link layer defined by the IEEE. The MAC sublayer handles access to shared media, such as whether token passing or contention will be used.

MAC (Media Access Control) Address A unique number assigned to each Network Interface adapter on a network. This layer works at the physical layer of the OSI reference model. NIC manufacturing companies have to get unique Mac addresses block from IEEE. Two network cards in the world can never have the same Mac address. Also standardized data-link layer address that is required for every port or device that connects to a LAN. Other devices in the netwrok use these addresses to locate specific ports in the network. MAC addresses are six bytes long and include a 3-byte vendor code that is controlled by the IEEE. Also referred to as a *hardware address, MAC-layer address, or physical address.*

MAN Metropolitan-Area Network. A network that spans a metropolitan area. Generally, a MAN spans a larger geographic area than a LAN, but a smaller geographic area than a WAN.

MBS Maximum Burst Size. Parameter defined by the ATM Forum for ATM traffic management. MCR is defined for VBR transmissions.

MCDV Maximum Cell Delay Variation. In an ATM network, the maximum two-point CDV objective across a link or node for the specified service category.

Mesh Network topology in which device are organized with many, often redundant, interconnections strategically placed between network nodes.

Message-oriented middleware (MOM) Middleware that uses messages and queues to exchange information. MOM allows application to continue processing before a remote-service call is complete. MOM is suitable for slower networks such as WANs and the Internet.

Message handling service (MHS) A popular E-mail protocol for storage, management and exchange, especially in corporate offices, licensed by Novell.

MTBF Mean Time Between Failure. The average time that elapses between network or system failures.

Multicast Message that is sent to a subset of nodes on a network.

Multimode fiber Optical fiber supporting propagation of multiple frequencies of light.

Multiplexing The method of dividing a physical channel into many logical channels so that a number of independent signals may be simultaneously transmitted on it. Also Scheme that allows multiple logical signals to be transmitted simultaneously across a single physical channel.

Multistation access unit (MAU) A hub in an IBM token-Ring Network. Each multistation access unit or MAU supports up to eight workstations, servers, or combinations. MAUs can be connected to create larger networks.

Nanosecond One-billionth (10^{-9}) of a second.

Narrowband channel Communication channels that handle low volumes of data, typically from 45 to 300 baud. They are used mainly for telegraph lines and low speed terminals.

NAT Network Address Translation. Mechanism for reducing the need for globally unique IP addresses. NAT allows an organization with addresses that are not globally unique to connect to the Internet by translating those addresses into globally-routable addresses.

NBMA NonBroadcast MultiAccess. Term describing a multiaccess network that does not inherently support broadcasting, for example, ATM.

NBP Name Binding Protocol. AppleTalk protocol that translates a character-string name into the network-layer address of the corresponding client.

NetBIOS Network Basic Input/Output System. API used by applications on a LAN to request services from lower-level network processes. These services include session establishment and termination, and information transfer. NetBIOS is used by network operating systems such as LAN Manager, LAN Server, Windows for Work-groups, and Windows NT.

NetFlow A Cisco Systems optimization technique that identifies traffic flows and speeds the forwarding of traffic for a flow. When a flow is identified, the switching, security, QoS, and traffic-measurement services required for the flow are used to build an entry in a NetFlow cache. Subsequent packets in the flow are handled via a single streamlined task that references the cache.

NetWare Popular distributed network-operating system developed by Novell. Provides transparent remote file access and numerous other distributed network services.

Network An inter-connection of computer systems and/or peripheral devices with carriers and data communications devices for the purpose of exchanging data and information.

Network-Level Firewall A firewall in which traffic is examined at the network protocol packet level.

Network address Network-layer address referring to a logical, rather than a physical, network device. Used by the network layer.

Network downtime It is the time duration during which the network is down or degraded.

Network file system (NFS) Network file system is an open operating system designed by Sun Microsystems that allows all network users to access shared files stored on computers of different types. NFS provides access to shared files through and interface called the Virtual File System (VFS) that runs on top of TCP/IP. Users can manipulate shared files as if they were stored locally on the user's own hard disk. With NFS, computers connected to a network operate as clients while accessing remote files, and as servers while providing remote users access to local shared files.

Network interface card A chip-based circuit board used to connect the PC to a network or server. The card is activated by loading software on the PC. Network Interface Card is a printed circuit board that is installed in a vacant slot in a computer I/O bus. The back of the card contains a physical interface for connectivity between a computer's internal resources and external resources connected to the network.

Network layer Layer 3 of the OSI reference model. This layer provides connectivity and path selection between two end systems. The network layer is the layer at which routing occurs.

Network monitor A relatively inexpensive computer device that is attached to a network segment and monitors all or a selected portion of networks traffic. It examines frame-level information in each packet and compiles statistics on network utilization, packet type, number of packet errors and other significant information.

Network topology The structure of interconnecting of nodes of a computer network.

NFS Network File System. A distributed file-system protocol suite developed by Sun Microsystems that allows remote file access across a network.

NHRP Next Hop Resolution Protocol. Protocol used by routers to dynamically discover the MAC address of other routers and hosts connected to an NBMA network. These systems can then directly communicate without requiring traffic to use an intermediate hop, thus increasing performance in ATM, Frame Relay, and SMDS environments.

NIC 1. Network Interface Card. Board that provides network-communication capabilities for a computer system. 2. Network Information Center. Organization that serves the Internet community by supplying addressing, naming, documentation, training, and other services.

NLM NetWare Loadable Module. Individual program that can be loaded into memory on a NetWare server and function as part of the NetWare network operating system.

NLSP NetWare Link Services Protocol. Link-state routing protocol based on IS-IS used in Novell networks.

NMS Network Management System. System responsible for managing a network. An NMS is generally a powerful and well-equipped computer such as an engineering workstation. NMSs communicate with agents to help keep track of network statistics and resources.

NNI Network-to-Network Interface. ATM Forum standard that defines the interface between two ATM switches that are both located in a private network, or are both located in a public network.

Node An end point of a branch in a network, or a common junction of two or more network branches.

OC Optical Carrier. Series of physical protocols (OC-1, OC-2, OC-3, and so on) defined for SONET optical signal transmissions. OC signal levels put STS frames onto fiber-optic lines at a variety of speeds. The base rate is 51.84 Mbps (OC-1); each signal level thereafter operates at a speed divisible by that number (thus, OC-3 runs at 155.52 Mbps).

OSI reference model Open System Interconnection reference model. Network architectural model that consists of seven layers, each of which specifies particular network functions such as addressing, flow control, error control encapsulation, and reliable message transfer. The OSI reference model is used universally as a method for teaching and understanding network functionality.

OSPF Open Shortest Path First. Link-state, hierarchical interior routing algorithm proposed as a successor to RIP in the Internet community. OSPF features include least-cost routing, multipath routing, and load balancing. Defined in RFC 2178.

Packet Logical grouping of information that includes a header containing control information and (usually) user data. Packets are most often used to refer to network-layer units of data.

Packet-switching Network A telecommunications network based on packet-switching technology, where in a transmission channel is occupied only for the duration of the transmission of the packet.

Packet Switching A method of communication between computers in a network in which blocks of messages to be transmitted are formed into packets and placed on the channel. Each packet contains source and destination addresses, synchronizing, error correction and control bits. The packets are routed using the source and destination addresses.

PAP Password Authentication Protocol. Authentication protocol that allows PPP peers to authenticate one another. Unlike CHAP, PAP passes the password and host name or username in clear text (unencrypted).

Parallel adder An adder in which all the bits of the two operands are added simultaneously.

Parallel operation A system changeover method whereby data is processed by both the old and the new system until the performance of the new system is verified satisfactorily.

Parity bit An extra bit added to a string of bits that enables the computer to detect internal errors in the transmission of binary data.

Partial mesh Term describing a network in which devices are organized in a mesh topology without requiring that every device have a direct connection to every other device.

Password A code by which a user gains access to a computer system. It is used for security purposes.

Permanent Virtual Circuit (PVC) A fixed communications circuit, created and maintained even when no data is being transmitted. The only difference between a PVC and a Switched Virtual Circuit (SVC) is that an SVC must be reestablished each time data is to be sent. Once the data has been sent, the SVC disappears. PVCs are more efficient for connections between hosts that communicate frequently. PVCs play a central role in Frame Relay networks. They're also supported in some other types of networks, such as X.25.

Phantom router In HSRP, two or more routers share the same virtual IP address and virtual MAC address thus creating a third, non-physical router, called the *phantom router*.

Phase modulation A form of modulation in which two binary values of digital data are represented by the shift in phase of the carrier signal. That is, a sine wave with phase = 00 represents a digital 1 and a sine wave with phase = 180° represents a digital 0.

Phased replacement A system changeover method in which the complete changeover to the new system takes place incrementally over a period of time. The new system is gradually implemented part by part and the old system is gradually phased out.

Physical layer Layer 1 of the OSI reference model. The physical layer defines the electrical, mechanical, procedural, and functional specifications for activating, maintaining, and deactivating the physical link between end systems.

Physical topology The geometric arrangement of the links and nodes of a network as they physically appear to an observer.

PIM Protocol Independent Multicast. Multicast routing architecture that allows the addition of IP multicast routing on existing IP networks. PIM does not require a specific unicast routing protocol, and can be operated in two modes: dense mode and sparse mode.

Ping 1. ICMP echo message and its reply. Used in IP networks to test the reachability of a network device. 2. Generic term for an echo mechanism in any protocol stack.

Pinging It is a technique to identify network problems, A LAN message is sent to a remote LAN node. The node, in turn, formulates an echo-reply and returns it to the original sender. Successful receipt of echo reply implies that the major components of transport systems are functioning.

Point-to-point protocol (PPP) A TCP/IP protocol, similar to SLIP, for transmitting IP datagrams over serial lines such as phone lines. With PPP, PC users can connect to the Internet and still function in their native environment (instead of having to deal with a character-based Unix environment). PPP was designed to work with several network-layer protocols, such as IP, IPv6, IPX, and AppleTalk.

Portability The capability of a program to run on different types of machines with minimum modification.

Post office protocol A protocol that specifies how a personal computer can connect to a mail server on the Internet and download E-mail.

PPS Packets Per Second. A measure of how quickly a switch or router can forward data.

Preprocessor A part of the compiler that manipulates the program text before any further compiling is done. Three important tasks of the preprocessor are (1) to replace each #include directive with the contents of the designated file, (2) to replace each escape sequence with the designated character, and (3) to process macro definitions and expand macro calls.

Presentation layer Layer 6 of the OSI reference model. This layer ensures that information sent by the application layer of one system is readable by the application layer of another.

PRI Primary Rate Interface. ISDN interface to primary-rate access. Primary-rate access consists of a single 64-Kbps data (D) channel for signaling, plus 23 (T1) or 30 (E1) bearer (B) channels for user data.

Protocol analyzer It is a specialized real-time computer software that connects to a network and analyzes the network traffic. A good protocol analyzer can record and display the data from data-link layer to application layer. It helps in detection, tracking-down and fixing the network problems. It has features of real-time traffic analysis, packet capturing, decoding and retransmission.

Protocol Data Unit (PDU) The technical term for a Datagram. PDUs are generated at all levels of the OSI Model, and are distinguished from one another by a prefix that indicates from which Layer (or sub layer) the PDU originates. For example, an SNMPv1 message consists of a message header and a PDU which contains specific commands and operands that indicate the object instances involved in the transaction.

Prototyping A working system to explore implementation or processing alternatives and evaluate results.

Proxy A software agent that acts on behalf of a user. Typical proxies accept a connection from a user, make a decision as to whether or not the user or client IP address is permitted to use the proxy, also does additional authentication, and then completes a connection on behalf of the user to a remote destination.

Remote-access server Communications server that connects remote nodes or LANs to an internetwork. Generally supports standard terminal services, such as Telnet, as well as remote-node, protocol-translation, and asynchronous-routing services.

Remote access Accessing a computer from a distant station using communication facilities.

Remote Access Server A Microsoft server component that allows remote users to dial in to the network. This is an alternative to expensive hardware like routers, and terminal servers if the traffic is not too high.

Remote job entry (RJE) A particular type of batch processing, where the input and output devices are located away from the central computer facility. The equipments for a RJE station can include terminals, card readers, card punching devices, printers, etc.

Ring network A computer network in which there is no host computer for controlling other computers and in which all stations are equal.

RMON-1 It defined by IETF RFC 1757 for Token-Ring. It specifies the method for an SNMP-based network management station to remotely gather, the network segment statistics at MAC layer to application layer. It extends the network

RMON-2 It is defined by RFC 2021. This is an extension of RMON-1. RMON-2 provides network statistics from MAC-layer to application layer. It extends the network segment view to end-to-end global view of the network.

Router A router interconnects two or more physically and logically separate network segments and operates at the Network Layer. Segments are joined together by a router, which maintains a separate logical identity. It constitutes an internetwork—a group of networks linked by routers. A router distinguishes data packets according to protocol types, such as TCP/IP, IPX/SPX, or Apple Talk. Routers forward traffic according to network level addresses. They can not access to a network, in some cases, depending on the type of application, thus providing a certain measure of security. This capability is used extensively in creating firewalls, which provide security when an organization is linked to Internet. Also a device that connects two or more different network segments, and allows information to flow between them only when necessary. The router, unlike a Bridge, examines the data contained in every packet it receives for detailed information. Based on this information, the router decides whether to block the packet from the rest of the network or transmit it. It also attempts to send the packet by the most efficient path through the network. Routers do this using various routing protocols (mentioned above), the most common among these being RIP, OSPF, and IGRP. Also network-layer device that uses one or more metrics to determine the optimal path along which network traffic should be forwarded.

Routing The process of choosing the best path throughout the LAN. Routing lets PCs which are not directly connected communicate by passing messages along to adjacent PCs.

Routing metrics Method by which a routing algorithm determines that one route is better than another. This information is stored in routing tables. Metrics include bandwidth, communication cost, delay, hop count, load, MTU, path cost, and reliability. Sometimes referred to simply as a *metric*.

RSVP Resource Reservation Protocol. A protocol that supports the reservation of resources across an IP network. Applications running on IP network. Applications running on IP end systems can use RSVP to indicate to other nodes the nature (bandwidth, jitter, maximum burst, and so on) of the packet streams they wish to receive. Defined in RFC 2205.

RTCP Real-Time Control Protocol. Protocol that monitors the QoS of an RTP connection and conveys information about the on-going session.

RTP Real Time Protocol. IETF protocol that provides end-to-end network-transport functions for applications transmitting real-time data, such as audio, video, or simulation data, over multicast or unicast network services. RTP provides services such as payload type identification, sequence numbering, time-stamping, and data delivery.

RTT Round-Trip Time. Time required for a network communication to travel from the source to the destination and back. RTT includes the time required for the destination to process the message from the source and generate a reply.

Screened Host A host on a network behind a screening router. The degree to which a screened host may be accessed depends on the screening rules in the router.

Screened Subnet A subnet behind a screening router. The degree to which the subnet may be accessed depends on the screening rules in the router.

Screening Router A router configured to permit or deny traffic based on a set of permission rules installed by the administrator.

Secure HyperText Transfer Protocol (S-HTTP) A secure version of HTTP which provides general transaction security over the web.

Secure Sockets Layer (SSL) A security layer sandwiched between the application and transport layers. SSL transparently protects application layer protocols (like HTTP, for which it was originally conceived) and data, with little effort on the part of the application developer. Also, public security protocol developed by Netscape. It can create a secure link between the Web server and the browser, thereby facilitating e-transactions.

Security The issues of protecting data from unauthorized use, tampering, or destruction are collectively referred to as security issues.

Segmentation A method of providing virtual memory. A multidimensional linear address space implementation differentiates this from paging.

Serial line Internet protocol (SLIPS) A TCP/IP protocol for transmitting IP datagrams over serial lines, such as phone lines. With SLIP, personal computer users can connect to the Internet and still function in their native environment (instead of having to deal with a character-based UNIX environment).

Server Node or software program that provides services to clients. Also the main high-capacity computer where all the information is stored. Also a system that shares resources with one or more workstations on a network.

Service programs Commonly used in all computer centers for providing better service to users. They include programs to prepare object programs for execution, to store programs on a magnetic disk, sort data stored on secondary storage devices, etc. They are a part of the operating system.

Session layer Layer 5 of the OSI reference model. This layer establishes, manages, and terminates sessions between applications and manages data exchange between presentation-layer entities.

Simple mail transfer protocol (SMTP) The TCP/IP protocol that specifies how computers exchange electronic mail. It works with post office protocol, and is one of the reasons that Internet E-mail functions so well.

Simple network management protocol (SNMP) A TCP/IP protocol that specifies how nodes are managed on a network, using agents to monitor network traffic and maintain a management information base.

Simplex Transmission of data in one direction.

Simulation To represent and analyze properties or behavior of a physical or hypothetical system by the behavior of a system model.

Single-mode fiber Fiber-optic cabling with a narrow core that allows light to enter only at a single angle. Such cabling has higher bandwidth than multimode fiber, but requires a light source with a narrow spectral width (for example, a laser).

SMTP Simple Mail Transfer Protocol. Internet protocol providing e-mail services.

SNA Systems Network Architecture. Large, complex, feature-rich network architecture developed in the 1970s by IBM for communication between terminals and mainframes.

SNAP (SUBNETWORK ACCESS PROTOCOL) A version of the IEEE local area network logical link control frame similar to the more traditional data link level transmission frame that lets you use non-standard higher level protocols.

SNMP Simple Network Management Protocol. Network management protocol for TCP/IP networks. SNMP provides a means to monitor and control network devices, and to manage configurations, statistics collection, performance, and security.

SOCKET A bi-directional pipe for incoming and outgoing data that enables an application program to access the TCP/IP protocols.

SONET Synchronous Optical Network. High-speed (up to 2.5 Gbps) synchronous network specification developed by Bellcore and designed to run on optical fiber. STS-1 is the basic building block of SONET. Approved as an international standard in 1988.

SOURCE ROUTE A route identifying the path a datagram must follow, determined by the source device.

Store-and-forward switching Frame-switching technique in which frames are completely processed before being forwarded out the appropriate port. This processing includes calculating the CRC and checking the destination address. In addition, frames must be temporarily stored until network resources (such as an unused link) are available to forward the frame.

STP Shielded Twisted-Pair. Two or four-pair wiring medium used in a variety of networks. STP cabling has a layer of shielded insulation to reduce noise and interference.

Stream A source from which input data can be obtained or a destination to which output data can be sent.

Subnet address Portion of an IP address that is specified as the subnetwork by the subnet mask.

Subnet mask 32-bit address mask used in IP to indicate the bits of an IP address that are being used for the subnet address.

Subnetwork In IP networks, a network sharing a particular subnet address. Subnetworks are networks that are arbitrarily segmented by a network administrator in order to provide a multilevel, hierarchical routing structure while shielding the subnetwork from the addressing complexity of attached networks.

Switched Virtual Circuit (SVC) A temporary virtual circuit that is set up and used only as long as data is being transmitted. Once the communication between the two hosts is complete, the SVC disappears. In contrast, a permanent virtual circuit (PVC) remains available at all times.

Switches Switches nowadays have become so popular that they have all but replaced bridges except for some small applications. Switches constantly monitor the traffic that comes across them, and reroute their internal connections automatically to provide the most efficient operation for the network. With the sophisticated Layer-3 switches rapidly getting accepted in the market, the router market is getting considerable displaced. Layer-3 switching has significant price/performance advantages over routers on account of their topological flexibility. A packet-by-packet Layer-3 switching facilities high-speed routing, and is interoperable with legacy routers. It also facilitates routing table construction and maintenance, and investigates packets to determine their destination before forwarding them. Layer-3 switching is rapidly emerging as a standard for 'certralised' networking. Also a network device that filters and forwards frames based on the destination address of each frame. It is and advanced form of a hub. Switches can provide dedicated bandwidth at each node. Due to this, the network traffic passing through one node does not affect another node. A switch is intelligent, and can turn on and off specific ports using software controls. Due to this, Switches automate network configuration, and hence increase network availability and capability. The *switch* operates at the data link layer of the OSI model.

Synchronous Optical Network A family of fibre-optic transmission rates from 51.84 Mbps to 13.22 Gbps, created to provide the flexibility needed to transport many digital signals with different capabilities, and to provide a design standard for manufacturers. It is an optical interface standard that allows internetworking of transmission products from multiple vendors.

TCP/IP A protocol stack, designed to connect different network on which the Internet is based. The suite includes protocols for remote login (Telnet), file transfer (FTP), E-mail (SMTP), etc. TCP/IP can work with any hardware or operating system.

TCP Transmission Control Protocol. Connection-oriented transport-layer protocol that provides reliable full-duplex data transmission. TCP is part of the TCP/IP protocol stack.

TDM 1. Time-division multiplexer. A device that implements time-division multiplexing. 2. Time-division multiplexing. Technique in which information from multiple channels can be allocated bandwidth on a single wire based on pre-assigned time slots.

Telecommunications Transmission of data between computer system and/or terminals at different locations through telephone facilities.

TELNET Remote terminal protocol that enables a terminal attached to one host to log in to other hosts, as if directly connected to the remote machine. Also Standard terminal emulation protocol in the TCP/IP protocol stack. Telnet is used for remote terminal connection, enabling users to log in to remote systems and use resources as if they were connected to a local system. Telnet is defined in RFC 854.

TFTP (Trivial File Transfer Protocol) A nofrills, unauthenticated protocol used to transfer files. TFTP depends on UDP and often is used to boot diskless workstations.

Time division multiplexing A method of sharing a communication channel in which the total time available in the channel is divided between several users and each user of the channel is allotted a time slice during which it may transmit a message. The channel capacity is fully utilized by interleaving a number of data streams belonging to different users into one data stream. TDM is fast because it does not do error checking. Data are transparent to it. It just provides the slots for the data. TDM works well enough for applications that need continuous slots on the channel, such as voice and video.

Token A channel access control method in which a token is passed between the nodes on the network; any station with the node at any particular time can then use the network channel. Also Frame that contains control information. Possession of the token allows a network device to transmit data onto the network.

Token passing Access method by which network devices access a physical medium in an orderly fashion based on possession of a small frame called a token.

Token Ring Token-passing LAN developed and supported by IBM. Token Ring runs at 4 or 16 Mbps over a ring topology. Token Ring was standardized in the IEEE 802.5 specification. A network system that uses a ring logical topology and a token channel access method. Examples include FDDI and Token Ring.

Top-down network design A network-design methodology that calls for analyzing business and technical requirements and developing a logical design, including a topology and protocols, before selecting products and devices to implement the physical design.

Topology Logical arrangement of network nodes and media within a networking structure.

Tracing routines Routines to aid the programmer in following the logic of a program during the execution of the program.

TRANSMISSION CONTROL PROTOCOL A connection-oriented transport protocol that provides reliable, full-duplex data transmission between two entities, often a client and a server application.

Transport layer Layer 4 of the OSI reference model. This layer is responsible for reliable network communication between end nodes. The transport layer provides mechanisms for the establishment, maintenance, and termination of virtual circuits; transport fault detection and recovery; and information flow control. Also On the Internet, the layer that implements TCP and UDP over the network layer.

TTL (TIME-TO-LIVE) The maximum number of router hops that a datagram of the network layer in TCP/IP protocol can experience on a network before it should be discarded. Used to prevent packets from looping endlessly.

Tunneling Router A router or system capable of routing traffic by encrypting it and encapsulating it for transmission across an untrusted network, for eventual de-encapsulation and decryption.

Twisted pair A commonly-used transmission medium consisting of 22 to 26 gauge insulated copper wire. Can be whether shielded (STP) or unshielded (UTP).

Twisted Pair Cable A type of networking channel cable in which a pair of insulated wires are twisted together. In the Type 1 standard used in the IBM token ring network, each cable supports two twisted pair channels (four wires).

Type or service 1. A byte in an IP header that indicates precedence and type of service. 2. Four-bit field within the type-of-service byte in an IP header that helps a router select a routing path when multiple paths are available. A source node can specify whether low delay, high throughput, high reliability, or low monetary cost is desired.

UDP User Datagram Protocol. Connectionless transport layer protocol in the TCP/IP protocol stack. UDP is a simple protocol that exchanges datagrams without acknowledgments or guaranteed delivery, requiring that error processing and retransmission be handled by other protocols. UDP is defined in RFC 768.

Universal naming convention (UNC) The standard format for paths that include a local area network file server that uses the following syntax:
\\server\share\path\filename

User Datagram Protocol A connectionless transport protocol. Delivery is not guaranteed, nor it is guaranteed that datagrams will be delivered in the proper order.

UTP Unshielded Twisted-Pair. Two or four-pair wire medium used in a variety of networks. Lacks shielding and is subject to electrical noise and interference. Compare with *STP*.

Video conferencing Conducting a conference between two or more participants at different sites by using networking devices and protocols to transmit digital audio and video data. Generally each participant has a video camera and microphone and equipment to transform analog signals into a digital bit stream for traversal across a LAN or WAN.

Virtual Network Perimeter A network that appeas to be a single protected network behind firewalls, which actually encompasses encrypted virtual links over untrusted networks.

VLSM Variable-length subnet mask. Ability to specify a different subnet mask for the same network number on different subnets. VLSM can help optimize available address space.

VoIP Voice over IP. Protocols and products that enable the transmission of telephone calls over IP networks.

VPN 1. Virtual Private Network. A network that implements virtual private networking. 2. Set of processes and protocols that enables an organization to securely interconnect sites that are part of a private network via a public network, such as a service-provider's network or the Internet.

VSATS Very Small Aperture Terminals (VSATS) can be described technically as an intelligent earth station connected to the geo-synchronous satellite suitable for supporting a variety of two-way telecommunication and information services such as voice, data and video.

W3C (THE WORLD WIDE WEB CONSORTIUM) An international standards body.

WAN Wide Area Network. Data communications network that serves users across a broad geographic area and often uses transmission devices provided by common carriers.

WAV files Named for the three-character extension WAV (for sound wave), a file containing a digitized sound. Depending on the sampling rate and resolution, the sound recorded in the WAV file seems realistic (provided you have the sound card and speakers to hear it). These files can be quite large, running into the multi-megabyte range for high-quality recordings.

WDM Wave Division Multiplexing. A type of multiplexing developed for use on fiber-optical cables. WDM modulates each of several data streams onto a different part of the light spectrum.

Web The most commonly used name for the World Wide Web, an interlinked collection of hypertext documents (Web pages) residing on Web servers and other documents, menus and database, available via URLs. Web documents are marked for formatting and linking with HTML, and Web servers use HTTP to deliver Web pages.

WEB-OF-TRUST A trust model used by PGP to validate public keys where trust is cumulative, not hierarchical, and depends on trust of "introducers".

Wide Area Network (WAN) A digital communication system which interconnects different sites, computer installations and user terminals, and may also enable LANs to communicate with each other. This type of network may be developed to operate nationwide or worldwide and the transmission medium used are normally public systems such as telephone lines, microwave and satellite links. It is used to interconnect LANs which may be at opposite sides of a country or located around the globe.

Workstation An access point in a local area network for services provided by the network. Also a desktop computer where network interface card is added with additional software to access the server. It usually has its own processing capability.

World Wide Web Also called the Web, www, and W3 an interlinked collection of hypertext documents (Web pages) residing on Web servers and other documents, menus, and databases, available via URLs (uniform resource locaters). Web documents are marked for formatting and linking with HTML (hypertext markup language), and Web servers use HTTP (hypertext transport protocol) to deliver Web pages. It is a non-proprietary, platform-independent, open document architecture based on ISO standard. It works equally well on stand alone computers, LANS, WANS, and the global Internet, on all major desktop computing platforms (UNIX, Mac, PC, OS/2).

WRAPPER A package that log requests for Internet services and provides an access control mechanism for Unix systems.

X.25 International standard that defines how a connection between a DTE and DCE is maintained for remote terminal access and computer communications in packet-switched networks.

X.509v.3 A certificate format used to prove identity and public key ownership that is based on a system of hierarchical trust. LAN

X Window System Distributed, network-transparent, device-independent, multi-tasking windowing and graphics system originally developed by MIT for communication between X terminals and UNIX workstations. Also A graphical windowing system developed at MIT that enables a user to run applications on other computers and view the output.

Xmodem An error-correction protocol used by the DOS application XMODEM and many other communications programs. Xmodem uses CRC (cyclical redundancy check), a means of detecting errors in transmissions between modems or across wired serial links.

Index

Q

R

S

T

U

V

"An Investment in Knowledge Pays the highest dividends"

–Ben Franklin

SAMPLE QUESTION PAPER – I

Computer Networks

Total Time : 3 Hours *Total Marks 100*

NOTE: *Attempt any five questions. All questions carry equal marks*

1. Distinguish among following:
   (i) LAN and MAN
   (ii) Interface and Services
   (iii) Connection oriented and Connection less services
   (iv) Protocol Hierarchy and Layers

2. Explain TCP/IP Model in detail with its critical analysis.

3. Explain following Switching techniques in brief:
   (i) Packet Switching
   (ii) Circuit Switching
   (iii) Message Switching
   (iv) Hybrid Switching

4. Write a brief note on following:
   (i) Analog vs Digital Transmission
   (ii) Pulse Code Modulation
   (iii) Multiplexing

5. What are the general assumptions made for sliding window protocols? Explain sliding window protocol with selective repeat in detail.

6. Explain following in context with 802.3:
   (i) Cabling
   (ii) MAC Sub-layer Protocol
   (iii) Manchestor Encoding

7. Write a short note on the following:
   (i) Internetwork routing
   (ii) IP Classes
   (iii) Network Security

8. Write a short note on the following:
   (i) Routers
   (ii) Bridges
   (iii) Repeaters

SAMPLE QUESTION PAPER – II

Computer Networks

Total Time : 3 Hours *Total Marks 100*

NOTE: *Attempt any five questions. All questions carry equal marks*

1. Briefly describe the 7 layer reference model of ISO-OSI. Compare it with TCP/IP.

2. Compare satellite communication with fiber optic communication. What are its advantages and disadvantages?

3. Write short notes on the following:
   (i) Digital telephony
   (ii) Channel bandwidth
   (iii) Step-index multimode fiber

4. Sketch the signal waveforms when the bit stream 1001101 is transmitted in the following signal codes:
   (i) NRZ-L
   (ii) Manchester
   (iii) Differential Manchester

5. What is the difference between synchronous and asynchronous communications? Which system is more efficient and why?

6. Compare time division and frequency division multiplexing schemes. How TDM compares with statistical TDM multiplexing?

7. Why bit stuffing is necessary in HDLC protocol? How is it done?

8. Why is circuit switching preferred over packet switching in voice communications? How circuit switching technique is used in local loop in telecommunications.

SAMPLE QUESTION PAPER – III

Computer Networks

Total Time : 3 Hours *Total Marks 100*

NOTE: *Attempt any five questions. All questions carry equal marks*

1. Write short notes on:
   (i) Transmission impairment
   (ii) Transmission media
   (iii) Bandwidth

2. What is modulation? Describe the pulse code modulation technique. Distinguish between frequency shift keying and phase shift keying techniques.

3. What is LAN? How does it differ from MANs and WANs? List and describe in brief different topologies and transmission media used in LAN.

4. Discuss any two layers of the OSI reference model. What are the principles used to arrive at the 7 layers of this model?

5. List major advantages and disadvantages of fiber optic communication over other types of communications. What are different modes used in fiber optic communications? Which is the cheapest and best mode of communication?

6. What is Nyquist frequency? What is the effect when an analog signal is sampled at less than the Nyquist frequency?

7. Write short notes on:
   (i) Internetwork layer of TCP/IP model
   (ii) ISDN
   (iii) Synchronous Vs Asynchronous Transmission

8. Explain how networks may be classified by the technique employed in transporting message between the nodes. Compare any two of them.

SAMPLE QUESTION PAPER – IV

Computer Networks

Total Time : 3 Hours

Total Marks 100

NOTE: *Attempt any five questions. All questions carry equal marks*

1. Compare and contrasts CSMA/CD and token-passing access methods.
2. Explain the concept of QPSK modulation using a phasor diagram.
3. What is the difference between simplex, half-duplex and full-duplex transmission?
4. How does a demodulator differ from an analog to digital converter? How does AM differ from ASK?
5. Consider a PCM system in which 24 signals are to be time-division-multiplexed. Each signal has a bandwidth from 400 Hz to 3.4 KHz. The sampling rate is 33.33% higher than the theoretical minimum, and 8 bits are used for each sample. Determine the output bit rate.
6. Write short notes on the following:

   (i) FDDI
   (ii) Satellite networks
   (iii) Project 802 of IEEE

7. Discuss the effect of cable break on star, bus and ring-based LANs.
8. Can a computer with 15 dumb terminals be called a computer network? Explain your answer.